Symbolism in Terrorism

Symbolism in Terrorism

Motivation, Communication, and Behavior

Jonathan Matusitz

ROWMAN & LITTLEFIELD
Lanham • Boulder • New York • London

Published by Rowman & Littlefield
A wholly owned subsidiary of The Rowman & Littlefield Publishing Group, Inc.
4501 Forbes Boulevard, Suite 200, Lanham, Maryland 20706
www.rowman.com

16 Carlisle Street, London W1D 3BT, United Kingdom

British Library Cataloguing in Publication Information Available

Library of Congress Cataloging-in-Publication Data

Matusitz, Jonathan Andre, 1976-
Symbolism in terrorism : motivation, communication, and behavior / Jonathan Matusitz.
pages cm. -- (Security and professional intelligence education series)
Includes bibliographical references and index.
ISBN 978-1-4422-3577-9 (cloth : alk. paper) -- ISBN 978-1-4422-3578-6 (pbk. : alk. paper) -- ISBN 978-1-4422-3579-3 (electronic)
1. Terrorism. 2. Symbolism. 3. Terrorism and mass media. I. Title.
HV6431.M3797 2014
363.325--dc23
2014019034

♾™ The paper used in this publication meets the minimum requirements of American National Standard for Information Sciences Permanence of Paper for Printed Library Materials, ANSI/NISO Z39.48-1992.

Printed in the United States of America

Contents

Introduction

OVERVIEW OF THE BOOK

Symbolism in Terrorism is a single-authored book that will serve as a core text. Overall, the book presents a conceptual look at terrorism from a highly symbolic perspective. In this comprehensive analysis, which incorporates descriptions, definitions, case studies, classic and recent data, theories, excerpts from terrorists' communiqués, and images, each chapter (1) isolates a specific dimension of symbolism in terrorism, (2) illustrates the contexts and processes that involve the main actors in terrorism, and (3) informs readers about the symbolism of both the purposes and targets of terrorism. In regard to the latter, it is the symbolic value of targets that differentiates terrorism from other forms of extreme violence; terrorism is designed to inflict deep psychological wounds on an enemy, rather than demolishing the enemy's material ability to fight.

This book does not attempt to make a political statement. Instead, it provides an understanding of an understudied area of counterterrorism, as well as an original and thought-provoking source of inspiration for teachers, students, and experts alike. Indeed, the often overlooked role of symbolism in terrorism increasingly dominates international affairs. For example, the September 11, 2001, terrorist attacks demonstrated its power: the World Trade Center was targeted by Al Qaeda because the Twin Towers epitomized Western civilization, U.S. imperialism, financial success, modernity, and freedom. Likewise, in chapter 14, one of the many visual motifs used in Islamism is the image of the dove. Whereas in Western culture the dove carries connotations of love and peace, this is not necessarily the case in Islamism, where the dove connotes a pure Muslim who has been chosen by Allah to wage or lead holy war.

Throughout all sixteen chapters, over forty areas of symbolism are covered. Examples are physical symbolism, nonphysical symbolism, linguistic symbolism, meaning making, anthroposemiosis, the social construction of reality, symbolic interactionism, organizational culture, symbolic convergence theory, the symbolic trinity, rituals, myths, positive cults versus negative cults, Conceptual Metaphor Theory, high context versus low context, performative violence, iconoclasm, imagery, visual motifs, brand management, logos, semiotics, new media, and the Global Village. So far, no book on terrorism has examined all major aspects of symbolism in one single work. Whereas some books on that topic deal mostly with the influence of society on the self, other texts tend to focus exclusively on imagery or visual motifs used in terrorist organizations. This is acceptable but not sufficient.

PREVIEW OF ALL CHAPTERS

Chapter 1 addresses the complex definition of symbolism as a specific method of communication. As such, symbolism has the objective to communicate a message by channeling information between a sender and a receiver. More precisely, a symbol is (1) a medium for conveying meaning, (2) something that stands for something else, (3) a categorization of reality, (4) a communication shortcut, and (5) communication beyond language.

In **chapter 2**, terrorism is defined in detail. As such, terrorism is the use of violence to create fear (i.e., terror, or psychic fear) for political, religious, or ideological reasons. This chapter is also an introduction to symbolism in terrorism. For example, the symbolic timing of a terrorist attack can be carefully selected by a terrorist group to coincide with the group's particular ideological, cultural, or religious requirements or to desecrate an enemy's sacred moments (e.g., religious holidays).

Chapter 3 looks at the symbolic targets of terrorism. The success of a terrorist act is not captured by the destruction of its target, but by the realization of a symbolic act that has far-reaching repercussions for audiences worldwide. For instance, blowback theory posits that the global hegemony of empires—at both the end of the twentieth century and the beginning of the twenty-first century—and the additional global military presence of the United States have prompted resistance in the form of terrorism and attacks on symbolic targets like the World Trade Center.

In **chapter 4**, the role of symbolic culture in terrorism is analyzed. A theory that can explain all this is symbolic interactionism. The theory postulates that human beings are able to communicate through shared meanings. The role of rituals is described in detail as well. A ritual is (1) a symbolic act, (2) communication, (3) a rite of purity, (4) tribalism, and (5) legitimizing cultural violence.

In **chapter 5**, the role of myth in symbolic terrorism is addressed. One method of looking at both myth and terrorism is symbolic convergence theory (SCT). SCT postulates that sharing group fantasies produces symbolic convergence. When humans have a good time together or have it rough together, they tend to increase group cohesion. Another three-part framework is the theory of symbolic trinity, which consists of symbolism, rhetoric, and myth.

Chapter 6 tackles the issue of symbolic place and territory in terrorism. Places and territories are often loaded with symbolism. Many ethnic groups have made claims to real or imaginary territories, a phenomenon called ethnonationalism. When terrorism is motivated by ethnonationalism, it is called separatist terrorism. In addition, terrorist groups (or their sympathizers) can express their attachment to land and ancestry through murals. Two striking cases studies in this chapter are murals in Northern Ireland and murals in the Palestinian territories.

Chapter 7 examines the symbolic relationship between terrorism and religion. When the use of religious terrorism is centered on an ideological and fanatical interpretation of selected religious scriptures, it is called junk terrorism (the hijacking of a religion). It was also found that religious terrorism regularly implies a battle between good and evil, and all-out struggle against enemies. Of equal relevance in this chapter is the fact that violent new religious movements (VNRMs) are religious-based terrorist groups that strongly believe in creating a radical transformation of society that they have been called to bring (i.e., by exterminating the world).

In **chapter 8**, four particular religions, with respect to symbolism in terrorism, are examined: Hinduism, Sikhism, Christianity, and Judaism. Hindu terrorism, also called saffron terror, thrives on the notion of Hindutva. Hindutva refers to "Hinduness" and reflects the idea that all Indians (of all backgrounds and walks of life) belong to the Hindu nation and need to be unified in a single community. The ultimate objective of Sikh terrorism is to establish

Khalistan: an autonomous, sovereign Sikh state. Religious terrorism has also been found in Christianity. For example, the Christian Identity Movement promotes the concept that white Christians are the real Israelites and need to wage war against the global Zionist conspiracy. Lastly, Jewish terrorist groups have committed symbolic attacks against Muslims. A tragic example was the 1994 Hebron massacre committed by Baruch Goldstein.

Chapter 9 focuses exclusively on Islamist terrorism. According to many recent surveys, Muslim support for terrorist violence worldwide is higher than in any other religious group. The renewed focus on violent warfare in Islamic fundamentalism is called jihadism. Another important phenomenon is Salafism, an Islamic movement that mandates a strict and ultraconservative approach to Islam. And the dream of Islamic global domination is captured in the concept of a "caliphate," a one-world Muslim government led by a supreme religious and political leader (the "caliph").

Chapter 10 deals with symbolism in suicide terrorism. Suicide terrorism is a weapon of mass persuasion, a method designed to influence the minds and behavior of a targeted population. A particular type of suicide terrorism is martyrdom. Martyrdom refers to heroic death, usually in battle, that is sanctified by a deity or Supreme Being. Regarded symbolically as an ultimate act of faith rather than a standard act of violence, martyrdom is to be viewed as a suicide terrorist's self-sacrificing conduct. Of equal relevance is the hunger strike, a form of pressure in which individuals fast as an act of political protest or to induce feelings of guilt in others, generally with the hope of achieving a particular goal. The 1981 Irish hunger strike turned IRA volunteers into martyrs deserving the highest rewards.

In **chapter 11**, the symbolism of terrorist weapons is discussed in detail. For example, the most popular terrorist weapon has been the AK-47. Likewise, improvised explosive devices (IEDs) and weapons of mass destruction (WMDs) are replete with symbolism as well. In Islamist culture, the sword is a premodern weapon that carries important meaning: it alludes to the violent reality of the jihadist fight. Last, a particular terrorist weapon is gender communal terrorism, or war rape.

Chapter 12 provides a thorough analysis of the symbolic role of female terrorism. Female terrorism symbolizes an opposition to homosocial reproduction (i.e., the traditional assignment of fixed roles to women in society). This is also referred to as "gender role reversal," "amazon feminism," and "girl militancy." In this chapter, female terrorism is also examined through six different themes that symbolize the attributes of the female terrorist: role model, emancipated woman, raped woman, infertile woman, pregnant woman, and divorcee.

In **chapter 13**, brand management in terrorism is examined as a symbolic form of public relations. A brand is a symbol that differentiates one product or service from another. Three traits can make a brand successful: differentiation, credibility, and authenticity. The case study of Hezbollah's brand sheds light on how a terrorist organization can grow rapidly and recruit new volunteers more easily through a massive "brand awareness" campaign. In line with these contentions, a dress code is also a type of brand management for a terrorist group. For example, the keffiyeh, an old-fashioned Arab headdress made from a square scarf (typically cotton), is a symbol of Palestinian resistance and a mark of their national identity.

Chapter 14 looks at visual motifs in Islamist terrorism through the lens of Conceptual Metaphor Theory (using the three categories of metaphors: structural, orientational, and ontological metaphors) and Edward T. Hall's distinction between low context and high context. For example, in one of the case studies, it was shown that waterfalls are used as metaphors to symbolize ideas of religious purity, the afterlife, and Allah's guaranteed generosity to devout Muslims.

Chapter 15 provides a semiotic analysis of terrorism. Semiotics is the study of signs, as well as their processes and systems. A sign is a thing that stands for something else. A particular semiotic model, Peirce's (1931) semiotic framework, consists of a three-part model of signification: (1) the representamen (i.e., the sign itself: what something is), (2) the object (i.e., the "referent": what the sign refers to or symbolizes), and (3) the interpretant (i.e., the audience's interpretation, or the effect in the mind of the interpreter). For example, in the case study of the 9/11 terrorist attacks, the representamen was the destruction of the Twin Towers by hijacked airliners. The object was what the sign represented: a deliberate act of terror. The interpretant was the resulting impact in the mind of the audience.

In **chapter 16**, the roles of the internet, new media, and the Global Village in symbolic terrorism are examined. For instance, the YouTube effect is the phenomenon whereby video clips can be rapidly diffused throughout the world. YouTube has become a new platform for propaganda diffusion and radicalization, with the luxury of little control or censorship. By extension, the "virtual caliphate" refers to the idea of a global Islamic state diffused through the internet. Two examples of this are the Al Qaeda magazines *Inspire* and *Jihad Cosmo*: the first one is an English-language online magazine aimed at British and U.S. readers, and the second one is a women's magazine written in Arabic.

Chapter One

What Is Symbolism?

SYMBOL: ORIGIN OF THE WORD

Symbols have characterized groups of people throughout history and are among humankind's oldest and most fundamental creations. **Symbols** communicate facts or ideas; they stand for something else. Some are physical, like flags and logos; others are nonphysical, like concepts or words. The word "symbol" comes from the Greek *symbolon*, meaning a token, mark, sign, emblem, or watchword. In ancient Greece, it was common to break a slate of burned clay into a few pieces and circulate them within a group. When the group was united again, the pieces were joined together. This was proof that the members belonged to the group or that broken relationships were now mended.[1] In business situations, the clay tablet was broken into two pieces; the halves were held by partners of a business transaction. To confirm that an agreement was reached, the two pieces had to be "thrown together."[2] The word *symbolon* was also discovered on an ancient Egyptian lead token, like those found in antiquity as a type of identification stamp composed of diverse materials. It served as a sign or pictorial reference.[3]

In terms of syntax, whereas *symbolon* is a Greek substantive or noun, the actual verb is *symballein*, a combination of *syn* ("together") and *bole* ("a throwing, a casting, the stroke of a missile, bolt, or beam").[4] The literal meaning of *symballein* is "to throw together," "to toss together," or "to join together." This relates to the idea of two elements that come together in one unit.[5] Indeed, when it is "thrown together" and fitted with the remaining half, the whole unit has significance because the symbol holds the pieces together.[6] In a similar vein, *symballein* was applied to styles of speech that indicated a gathering together, a hiding, or a veiling. As such, the aforementioned sign or pictorial reference, now a symbol, encoded or bent the obvious or outward meaning of an expression (or that which was represented). The unfamiliar observer could not comprehend—either in part or in whole—the statement so encoded. In other words, a symbol implies a different meaning or an "extra" meaning in addition to itself.[7]

SYMBOLISM: GENERAL DESCRIPTION

Symbolism is the language of symbols or the practice of representing things by symbols.[8] As a particular method of communication, symbolism has the objective to channel information between a sender and a receiver.[9] The notions of sender and receiver were first theorized by Shannon and Weaver (1949).[10] In their model, information (or content) is transmitted through some type of language (whether verbal or nonverbal) from an encoder (sender) to a decoder (receiver). The encoder is the human or electronic component transforming a message into a form that can be sent via a proper channel; the decoder reverses the encoding so that the message is received and understood clearly.[11] Later, this model was revised by David Berlo (1960)[12] and became the Sender-Message-Channel-Receiver (SMCR) model. As one can see, the main objective of symbolism is to convey information. **Information** is the most basic unit of communication; it can be a simple symbol or a complex message.[13] In Latin, *informare* initially meant "giving form to." Later, it evolved into "shaping an idea."[14]

Symbolism implies that symbols are created with five characteristics in mind. Taken as a whole, a symbol is (1) a medium for conveying meaning, (2) something that stands for something else, (3) a categorization of reality, (4) a communication shortcut, and (5) communication beyond language.

A Medium for Conveying Meaning

A symbol is a means by which meaning is conveyed. It is like an agent or intermediary that brokers between reality and other conceptions.[15] Morgan (1985)[16] remarks that a symbol provides "the medium through which we communicate and engage our realities" (p. 29). This notion of "medium for conveying meaning" can be captured in one word: **instrumentality**, or the useful and task-fulfilling property of a symbol (in addition to its symbolic value).[17] Through the medium of symbols, humans can communicate with others across space and time. A symbol, then, is referential. Its intent is communicative.[18] A chief purpose of symbolism is to communicate a message and influence people to a certain degree. However, it is also worth noting that a physical change in the position or appearance of a symbol can affect both its meaning and its context. Drawing on a symbol to convey meaning can lead to ambiguity.

Something That Stands for Something Else

A symbol can be a material object, a concept, an action, or an event that represents something other than itself. As such, a symbol is "something that stands for or suggests something else by reason of relationship, association, convention, or accidental resemblance" (Merriam Webster, 1976, p. 892).[19] For example, the crescent on most Islamic flags or logos represents Islam. Likewise, the Star of David symbolizes Judaism. Through symbolism, one can provide anything with a symbolic meaning or character. Symbolism offers unlimited ways for communicating meaning in cultures. Because a symbol stands for something else, it carries both denotative and connotative meanings. **Denotative meanings** refer to the direct or instrumental uses of a symbol. For example, a flag typically represents a nation or country, a government building, and so on. **Connotative meanings** are the expressive or particular uses of a symbol—the flag as standing for law and order, patriotism, chauvinism, national pride, and so on.[20] Similarly, from a denotative standpoint, a cat is a four-footed mammal that can be raised as a pet. From a connotative standpoint, that same animal symbolizes good luck in some places, bad luck in other places, and so on. Connotations vary across cultures. An important goal of symbolism is to establish a causal coherence, like a cause-and-effect relationship.

A Categorization of Reality

Symbolism is a method to create order by categorizing reality. For example, when generalizing Islam or classifying Muslim identity and politics, many people on the political right use symbolic concepts such as "the West," "sharia," "terrorist," "fundamentalist," "freedom," and "America." Or they will create visual symbols such as veiled women who are abused, jihadists standing in front of a black Islamic standard, or images of the collapsing Twin Towers. These categorizations serve to order Muslim collectives or their values.[21] This example reflects the fact that symbols help us interpret the world and situate people in an interactive environment. They play a significant role in constructing the situation to which a person becomes exposed on a daily basis.[22] Symbols help people create, encode, and decode their meaning systems. This is precisely how humans construct their world: through symbols to which they associate meaning with experiences. This is fundamental to human thought: people convert their daily experiences into symbols.[23] Through this **symbolic transformation of experience**, the mind categorizes reality by creating symbols to better process information. This information is stored in people's minds for later "recognition" of their constructed world.[24]

A symbol is a mental structure, some type of knowledge representation. By the same token, because symbols help us categorize reality, they make things more salient or less salient in each specific culture. For example, the symbol of the yellow hammer and sickle is salient (important) in communist countries but less so in the United States, Iceland, or Japan. As Stryker (1980)[25] explains it, "Symbols focus attention upon salient elements in an interactive situation, and permit preliminary organizations of behavior appropriate to it. Culture may be thought of, from this perspective, as a specification of what is important" (p. 56). This method of interpreting the world is passed on through history, culture, and socialization. Ultimately, new generations of social actors will rely on these symbols to communicate with others in their environment.

A synonym for categorization of reality is "schema." A **schema** (plural: schemata) is a mental structure of predetermined ideas, a framework that represents some characteristics of the world, or a prearranged pattern of thought or behavior. Schemata direct our attention; as a result, humans will pay more attention to elements that fit into their schema.[26] Through symbols, people can use schemata to organize the information they have about a material object, a concept, an action, or an event; they can also provide a framework for future understanding. Schemata color our entire view of the world. They are mental structures that shape our perception, memory, and action. People rely on schemata to interpret particular attributes, such as gender, when combined with other particular attributes. For example, people are inclined to look differently at the attribute of male or female when it is associated with an ethnic status, such as Caucasian, African American, Latino/a, or Native American.[27] What bestows schemata extra power is the fact that they are automatically aroused by cues in the world. This is precisely how symbolism works: the simple reference to a symbolic concept or the sight of a symbol will automatically bring to mind an entirely associated scenario in people's memories.[28] Symbolism, the communicative backdrop of terrorism, operates on the principle that one aspect of the world has to be emphasized over other aspects. Put simply, it is one way to categorize the world. Generally, a terrorist symbol provides no room for more than one interpretation. For example, the image of a burning Spanish flag next to an ETA terrorist (i.e., a Basque militant against the Spanish government) communicates just one powerful message: anti-Spanish sentiment or independence from Spain.

A Communication Shortcut

Symbols do not need to depend on language in order to convey meanings. The image of a fish communicates an important symbolic meaning across the Christian world.[29] As O'Shaughnessy (2004)[30] puts it, "Symbols are universally understood in ways that language can never be" (p. 65). Symbolism is condensed meaning; it is a communication shortcut. Why read a 10,000-word essay deploring Nazism when a drawing of a German officer with a rotten-dead Jewish prisoner reflected in his monocle does it so much more conspicuously and concisely? Symbols allow encoders to communicate with individuals for whom reading is seen as a chore.[31] They represent a tool for a quick understanding of oneself, others, daily experiences, and the universe at large.

Communication beyond Language

Symbolism is an extralinguistic communication system. This means that languages are only secondary to symbols. The latter can "penetrate the impenetrable, overwhelm the defensive, and convey complex messages without saying a single word" (Schirch, 2005, p. 4).[32] After World War II, the symbol of the Nazi swastika branded, by the French Resistance, on the cheeks of collaborators was the best way to portray those local villagers who betrayed their comrades in order to avoid Nazi search-and-destroy raids on their homes. Would a text or narrative be so deep and persuasive? This also means that the power of "communication beyond language" can be used for good or ill purposes. Symbolism possesses tremendous power. It is a method that allows for the creation of something—whether small or great—beyond the symbol's own restricted, literal meaning. In effect, any material object, concept, action, or event can acquire the status of a symbol and stand for something else. And it should not be astonishing that the world is replete with symbols and symbolism.[33]

ANTHROPOSEMIOSIS

Anthroposemiosis is the study of human communication. It uses all the sensory means of communication (i.e., visual, tactile, and so on) as well as purely verbal means. The latter are exceptional among species. The varieties of choices of transmission media, thanks to which human communication takes place, are also very flexible. Human beings communicate through three broad categories of media:[34]

- **Natural media**: voice (speech, language, and conversation), the face (expressions), and the body (gesture and posture).
- **Artifactual media**: visual symbols, pictures, paintings, sculptures, books, letters, and the like. An artifact is, literally, something fabricated with a particular cultural function in mind.
- **Mechanical media**: telephone, radio, television, computer, video, satellite, and so on.

What makes human communication unique among species, and probably not transferable to other species, is that it can occur or unfold through more than one means of transmission.

Communication

Anthroposemiosis consists of all communication processes in which humans are directly involved. **Communication** refers to an exchange or sharing of meanings represented by signs.[35] The notion of sharing is intrinsic to the word "communicate," which comes from the Latin *communicare*, "to make common." Communication is a process that makes something common; it is an outgrowth of the need to engage in shared or common action.[36] Caesar, in his Gallic commentaries, used *communicare* to relate the sharing of food, the exchange of money, the matching of a dowry, and the passing of information. Over time, this notion of sharing was narrowed down to "sharing meaning."[37]

Although animals can also exchange meaning to search for food, migrate, or reproduce, they have a limited range of signals to communicate. Conversely, humans have created complex means of communication that are used not only to improve their survival but also to express ideas and emotions, to tell stories, to remember the past, and to negotiate meanings with one another. These types of communicative functions cannot be found in other species, where communication has a rather straightforward purpose: to exchange information about the surroundings in order to survive and sustain reproduction.[38] Language is unique to anthroposemiosis. This allows humans not only to communicate or symbolize immediate reality, but also to create an unlimited number of possible worlds. The communicative power of humans is what Bonner (1980)[39] calls **true culture**.

Symbolic Culture

Human cultures emerge out of a pattern of evolution. In *The Selfish Gene*, Richard Dawkins (1976)[40] remarked that human cultures evolve in the same way that populations of organisms evolve. Various ideas get transferred from one generation to the next. Such ideas may either improve or worsen the survival of the people adopting those ideas. For instance, when a culture develops unique methods of tool building that are better than those of another culture (or that may not even exist in that culture), the former (with the superior methods) is likely to prosper over the latter. This produces a higher percentage of the overall population embracing the more effective methods as time passes. Each tool-building design functions similarly to a biological gene: it is present in some populations but not in others. At the same time, the tool's function has a direct impact on the use of the design in future generations. Symbolism, too, follows the same pattern: it is present in one particular species (i.e., the human species), but not in the other species. It is also transmitted from one human generation to the next.

Human cultural evolution is unique to the extent that it has developed a **symbolic culture**, a culture based on meaning or information shared through symbolic communication. It is another way to differentiate the cultural realm created and inhabited by *Homo sapiens* with the realm of ordinary culture, which the animal world possesses.[41] Symbolic culture assumes more than the capacity to learn and transmit artifacts, behaviors, or values from one generation to the next. It also necessitates the invention of an entirely new category of things—things that cannot be found in the "real" world without human creation, but that exist totally in the symbolic realm. Examples are moral absolutes like good and evil, social constructs like promises or gratitude, and mythical inventions like gods and angels.[42] The human power to enact symbolic communication gives details as to why the human race, unlike other primates, has evolved from interacting in small foraging groups to building huge communities that do not have to rely on face-to-face interaction.[43]

Anthroposemiosis versus Zoosemiosis

Human communication is a phenomenon of anthroposemiosis. **Zoosemiosis**, on the other hand, refers to animal communication. To ensure survival, animals do not require profound understanding, abstract thinking, the creation of symbols, or new methods of communication. Precisely, the difference between the human aspect of linguistic or symbolic communication and the animal aspect of communicative exchanges (i.e., vocal, visual, and gestural) is what makes anthroposemiosis very distinct from zoosemiosis.[44] The insect kingdom, for instance, allows bees to live in communities with relatively large populations thanks to a built-in system of chemical communication. This built-in system enables the bee colony to function as a collective unit. On the other hand, humans have to think harder or be more creative in order to accomplish amazing feats of coordination through methods such as those mentioned earlier (i.e., natural media, artifactual media, and mechanical media).[45]

In addition, as opposed to animals, humankind is made up of *both* zoosemiotic (physiological-genetic) and anthroposemiotic (human-using symbols) systems. Animals are only zoosemiotic. Human culture differs from orangutan culture in the sense that humans have speech communication. Human language is the symbolic key to human survival.[46] The constant invention and use of symbols throughout history have had truly incredible consequences on the evolution of humankind. For this reason, Ernst Cassirer (1946),[47] a twentieth-century philosopher, referred to the human being as a **symbolic animal**, capable of engaging in symbolic communication as well as human thought, affect, and action. Human beings, then, are unique creatures because of their symbolism.

MEANING MAKING

Meaning refers to a shared mental representation of a connection among things or events. Meaning connects things. It is fundamental to the aforementioned sender-receiver model. Meaning is a message that a sender creates and conveys to a receiver. In turn, meaning also includes what the receiver infers from that information in a specific context. Since meaning "connects things," it is intrinsically linked to the chief purpose of symbolism: to communicate a message and influence people to a certain degree.[48] Proulx and Heine (2006)[49] describe meaning as a mental representation of relationships between propositions or entities. For George Gerbner (1956),[50] meaning is anything that serves to create a message in a socially meaningful way. Meaning is a sign system—a collection of signs that attempt to fit each other in historically or culturally determined ways. The study of meaning is called **semantics**.

Symbolism is the creation of meaning through the use of symbols. It is a process of encoding and decoding that functions to organize experience. As symbolic animals, we underline such centrality of **meaning making**, a human activity that consists of assigning meaning to the experience of life.[51] Meaning making allows groups to assign meanings to the universe in which they live and to their own experiences. It also allows people to establish goals, plan activities, and order their behavior.[52]

In the same train of thought, meaning making is inherently associated with interpretation. Hence, symbolism depends on interpretation. A symbol cannot create its own meaning; it is dependent on what is perceived. **Interpretation** involves the construction of meaning out of contextual cues. In this respect, meaning making is a communicative activity. The perceiver is not a passive receiver of information but a conscious actor who infers information relevant to his or her experience and knowledge.[53] Because people use symbols and interpret them in socially meaningful ways, they do not usually make sense of them directly or automatically as they would when stopping at a traffic light when driving. Instead, they attribute meanings to things and then take actions based on these meanings. In other words, humans generally decide what to do or say on the basis of how they interpret the world around them; they react to symbols through the meanings they attribute to them. This is precisely a process of meaning making and interpretation.[54]

In this discussion of meaning making, a controversy that often emerges is that of **reductionism**, the practice of understanding an object or occurrence at one level of examination by reducing it to more fundamental processes (i.e., by reducing it to the simplest explanation possible).[55] In contrast, **hermeneutics** (from the Greek *hermeneuo*, "translate" or "interpret") denotes the science and art of trying to understand and interpret the meaning of universal or personal languages, texts, and symbols.[56] Because terrorism can be conceptualized as a form of symbolism, it is a meaning-making practice too. It gives terrorists a sense of meaning or purpose in life. This meaning making drives their actions or orients them toward a desired future state or objective.[57] Nevertheless, through a meticulous process of explanation and interpretation, it is the task of the author of this book to describe "symbolism in terrorism" in detail.

Symbolic Interpretivism

Meaning making refers to the ways that human groups interpret reality and, therefore, construct that reality (i.e., through symbols). A theoretical framework that illustrates this is symbolic interpretivism. **Symbolic interpretivism** is an approach based on the premise that meaning is a product of a culture's socially constructed reality. It emphasizes the importance of meaning making through social interaction. Meaning, then, is continuously upheld and changed through negotiation.[58] The reality does not emerge out of conditions in the physical world but out of interpersonal association and agreement. Anything has a meaning inasmuch as members regard them as existing and, hence, will behave accordingly. What this also means is that meaning can be created, changed, or abolished at any time.[59] Groups establish boundaries around their experiences and interpretations of the world, and they create meaning within these boundaries. **Meaning frameworks** are the social boundaries that surround those definitions.[60]

Cultures construct a reality around concepts, determining many aspects of their world through the meanings they assign to the construct. The fundamental notion of this **social construction of reality** is that humans interacting in society generate, as time passes, **concepts** (mental representations) of the universe in which they live.[61] The social construction of reality leads to the concept of consensus reality, the myriad of ways to answer the question "What is real?"[62] What is accepted as "real" by a group does not exist in a concrete sense but is the product of what Bakhtin (1965)[63] calls a **co-construction of reality** of all parties involved in a given culture. In the aftermath of 9/11, the Western symbolic interpretivism of Islam became an agreed-upon reality that the Muslim religion was mostly about "terrorism," "extremism," "intolerance," and "anti-Westernism." This practice of symbolic interpretivism is also referred to as symbolic framing. **Symbolic framing** is centered on symbolism and its interpretation within a historical or cultural context. It aims at interpreting and concentrating on the things that make symbols powerful and how they influence every aspect of human experience.[64]

Symbolism and Identity

Meaning making posits that people perceive and create reality through symbolism. Take symbolism from people, and they will have no real identity.[65] As people value the importance of symbolism, their daily life is expressed through it. Symbols communicate actions—whether big or small. They are like grammar and the alphabet, and like verbs and words; they are vital to communication and social interaction.[66] Based on these circumstances, it follows that symbolism is a form of "extended self" or an extension of a person's self-conceptualization. Furthermore, symbols not only extend the self; they also construct the self.[67]

Symbolism has long been employed to reveal the identities of cultural groups, as evident in analyses of flags and even architectural designs.[68] Symbolism personifies a nation's past, present, and future into a single descriptive part, which can be used for good or ill purposes to communicate identity subscription. Scholars have put forward the idea that elements of a people's identity—including a cultural group's history, heritage, library system, vestiges and castles, art, music, language, religion, myths, rituals, economy, politics, and cultural backgrounds—are powerful representational symbols of a cultural group, as much as existence itself.[69]

As one can see, identity begins with people and their understanding and sense of self. The latter are situated within a group's history, collective memory, and overall experience. In the context of terrorism, identity offers a reinforcing feedback loop in two ways. On the one hand, an effective terrorist attack can be a symbolic act that stimulates solidarity among people with the same interests as the terrorists'. It also fosters cohesion of identity among the victims. On the other hand, identity can also counteract a terrorist organization if it is considered an outsider or a diametrically opposed outgroup by the population.[70]

SYMBOL VERSUS SIGN

Meaning can be literal or figurative. "Literal" means that the association between an object and what it represents is direct, explicit, or fully conventional. "Figurative" means that the association between an object and that for which it stands is indirect and requires further inference or explanation, even though some level of conventionality may be involved as well, as in the case of metaphors or communication bypasses. Symbols tend to be more figurative than literal. Today, a "literal symbol" would be called a sign. A **sign** is a representation of an object that suggests a link between itself and its object. A natural sign carries a causal connection to its object; for example, thunder is a sign of storm. A conventional sign bears significance through agreement, such as how a full stop, or period, simply means the end of a sentence. This is different from a symbol, which stands for something else, such as a cross on a necklace that symbolizes Christianity for the person who wears it. That cross is more figurative than literal.[71]

Usually, the goal of using signs is to produce a response or to simply inform. This can be accomplished by marking something, presenting a message (e.g., a notice), attracting attention, showing evidence of an underlying cause (e.g., medical symptoms indicating a disease), or even enacting a bodily gesture. Signs are created for the purposes of indication and information.[72] In another comparison between sign and symbol, a red flag on the road refers to a sign that orders drivers to slow down for safe driving. However, a red flag at the forefront of a student demonstration symbolizes these students' shared beliefs, ideology, or resistance against the government, and often elicits deep emotions.[73]

Swiss psychoanalyst Carl Jung (1962),[74] who studied myths and archetypes, made a sharp distinction between symbols and signs. In Jung's view, a sign stands for something clear and requires no particular imagination, as a word represents its referent. He distinguished it from a symbol, which he used to stand for something that cannot be made clear or accurate. To Jung, a sign relates to something known or an idea. However, a symbol is infused with unconscious creativity that fundamentally requires human imagination. Typically, a sign is an element that cannot be broken down further. A bubble in a tall stem glass of champagne would be a sign (as it simply indicates that it is champagne and not water or milk). A drawing of that same tall stem glass of champagne on the windows of a café would be a symbol (as the drawing symbolizes a place where people can drink alcoholic beverages).[75]

Based on all this, it follows that **symbolic meaning** refers to open-ended meaning that is not based on a literal, direct, cause-and-effect relationship. Rather, it depends on how meaning is constituted by the sender, on the environment in which it is produced, and on how the receiver interprets the meaning. A stop sign alongside a road or a period at the end of a sentence is usually clear, simple, and closed-ended. On the other hand, the multiple possible interpretations of symbolic meanings vary according to the historical or cultural context of their use.[76]

THREE CATEGORIES OF SYMBOLS

There are three broad categories of symbols: (1) particular symbols, (2) universal symbols, and (3) multivocal symbols. These three categories serve to classify and situate the social world of various groups and interpret how they both relate to one another and determine relationships with outside groups—through a meaning-making process that is embedded in history, culture, and social structure.[77]

Particular Symbols

Particular symbols consist of objects, ideas, or events used within specific groups. Such symbols may be universally acknowledged by outside groups but are not used or shared by many of those outside groups. For example, the Union Jack and the "God Save the Queen" national anthem are traditional symbols of Great Britain and a few Commonwealth realms. They are acknowledged by most other countries but not used by them. Likewise, the First and Second Intifada in the Palestinian territories, which originated many particular Palestinian symbols, have made the world aware of the checkered keffiyeh (the Arab male headscarf); however, few non-Arabs have been spotted wearing it. Although the keffiyeh was already worn by a certain number of men in the Arab world in the 1960s, it became increasingly associated with the Arafat-led Palestinian resistance movement.[78] Other particular Palestinian symbols have included the olive tree, the Intifada rocks and stones, the burning tire, and the green-white-black-red Palestinian flag. All of these have been peculiar to the Intifada but not adopted by most outside groups.[79] Unlike universal symbols, particular symbols require more understanding, invoke more beliefs, and tend to add to one's knowledge of a specific culture, group, or theme. Consequently, particular symbols help shed light on issues that have been hidden from the public eye or underrepresented in the news media.[80]

Universal Symbols

Universal symbols are symbols shared by groups of people worldwide. They are the "gold standard" in respect to their value, and their meaning for humans is constant. The sign of the crucified Jesus on a cross represents the universal faith of Christianity.[81] The color white symbolizes purity, and the lion embodies strength or courage. In terms of human height, a tall stature tends to be seen as a sign of superiority and leadership. Fire is a universal symbol of life and death, and it has played an important role in the religious expression of these concepts. In most religions, fire also represents the manifestation of a deity or a spiritual force.[82] Universal symbols are **primordial symbols**. They are symbols that carry great psychological significance and can be seen in one form or another across all cultures. Universal symbols can acquire ordinary meaning through agreed-upon conventions.[83] For example, the peace sign was originally made for the British nuclear disarmament movement. However, pacifist movements have convinced the world that it should be used as a symbol of peace—the peace sign is an inverted "V" run through, in the middle, by a straight line (inside a circle). The AK-47 has become a cross-cultural symbol of non-Western military combat or armed resistance.

Multivocal Symbols

Multivocality is the capacity of symbols to communicate different meanings to different groups. It also suggests that the symbol may be interpreted in different ways. The power of multivocal symbolism is particularly important when leaders try to launch a movement or create group solidarity.[84] To people around the world, the American flag is a symbol for the White House and the goals of the United States. Nevertheless, this symbol has also been interpreted in other ways. Indeed, for some, it is a symbol of freedom; for others, it represents tyranny, depending on the observer's frame of mind.[85] Likewise, before Adolf Hitler rose to power, the swastika was a symbol found in American Indian, Indian, Chinese, and even African and European motifs. In the Indus Valley Civilization, it was used to represent sacred force. In Buddhist China, it evoked eternity and Buddhism. In Armenia, it was the ancient symbol of eternal light. Ever since Hitler proclaimed his ideology, however, it has become a universally understood symbol that denotes Nazism, neo-Nazism, or right-wing extremism in virtually every country on earth.[86]

PHYSICAL SYMBOLS

Communication is not limited to verbal modes of expression, such as linguistics; it also covers extralinguistic modes, such as objects and images.[87] As such, a symbol can either be a physical symbol or a nonphysical (abstract, nonmaterial) symbol. A physical symbol is a concrete object made up of physical matter or a visual such as a picture that can be referred to, labeled, or acted toward. Examples are flags, logos, buildings, systems, dress codes, and images on websites. Any event can be made visible to the entire world thanks to the strategic use of physical symbols. Giles (1977)[88] remarks that the Star of David on Israel's flag is sufficient to symbolize the nation's identity. No Ten Commandments, Six-Day War memorabilia, or menorahs need to be added to the flag. Of equal relevance are the physical symbols that individuals like to display inside their houses. For instance, they want to show who the real heroes are. When the display of physical symbols is used to generate profound levels of commitment to a movement, a terrorist cause, a religious belief, or shared values, or when the objective is to foster solidarity and in-group effort, such a display of symbols is called a **credibility-enhancing display (CRED)**.[89]

Any physical symbol can become a specific target by a terrorist organization. Banks, trade buildings, or centers of commerce may be perceived as emblems of capitalism or Western influence by anti-American militant groups.[90] Terrorist organizations themselves use logos and insignias to symbolize their ideology, mission, and objectives. These logos and insignias abound with evocative symbols that communicate the organizations' histories and messages. They also help create unique organizational cultures in the process.[91] In both national and global conflicts, the same symbol may be misused to delegitimize the enemy or advocate a separate ideology. Burning the reviled invader's flag is one method to undermine the opponent while defending one's own ideology. Appropriating another group's symbol (usually a flag, brand, or logo) and using it against that very group is a process called **meme hacking**. The message carried by the symbol (initially created for a good purpose) becomes transformed into a message that has a more evil purpose.[92] At the same time, the creation of a new flag or national anthem helps distinguish a fledging nation from the resented oppressor. In this manner, symbols can bestow legitimacy on a people's own national or ideological aims.[93]

One method of examining physical symbols, particularly visual ones, is iconography. **Iconography** looks at the classification, description, and interpretation of visible symbols: the things represented, the specific compositions, and details employed to do so. The goal is to disclose the meanings of visuals in a particular context at a particular time.[94] Iconography examines symbolic motifs associated with a certain genre through repetition. Discussing visual symbolism as iconography necessitates a critical "reading" of symbols that often tries to explore social and cultural values.[95] Websites and social media have allowed terrorists and their supporters to give them a sense of belonging. These sites are a reassurance that these members are not misfits or loners and that they have their own symbolism to cling to. Horses, flags, and sunrises become the online equivalents of scarves. Hezbollah produces souvenirs featuring logos.[96] Physical or visual symbolism can arouse powerful passions in the culture of a terrorist group. In Islamist terrorism, from using the Black Standard (the battle flag of the Prophet Muhammad), horses with riders, and swords, to using specific colors within the Islamic tradition, the iconography of symbols can be deftly crafted in order to evoke key Islamic notions of jihad. At the same time, it can stimulate the hearts and minds of soldiers as well as sympathizers and recruits.[97]

NONPHYSICAL SYMBOLS

Many symbols do not have material form. **Nonphysical symbols** can be (1) linguistic symbols, (2) behavioral symbols, (3) sociocultural symbols, and (4) ideological symbols. The psychology of symbols tells us that nonphysical symbols have as much power as physical symbols do; they can have a significant impact on the audience's mind; and they provide additional insights as to why symbolism in terrorism is a very complex phenomenon.

Linguistic Symbols

By definition, linguistic symbols are words or phrases whose meanings symbolize particular values, norms, cultural premises, and beliefs about the world. Values are beliefs about how the world looks to a specific culture. Norms are the display or enactment of values through social rules and moral imperatives—particularly in the environment in which they live. Cultural premises are accepted and unchallenged assumptions about how the world is. Beliefs are ideas that human groups assume to be true about the world. Just as a sentence can contain or communicate more meaning than a single word, so too can linguistic symbols represent more complicated relationships.[98] After the September 11, 2001, terrorist attacks, linguistic symbolism became more salient to many people, especially from a terrorism perspective. For example, "9/11" is now pronounced "nine-eleven" (not "nine-one-one"), and "Ground Zero" refers to more than just the place where a catastrophic collapse occurred. In Spain, the "Madrid train station" evokes an epicenter of terror rather than just a site for public transportation or a location to meet friends on a European tour. This is due to the Madrid train bombings perpetrated by Al Qaeda on March 11, 2004.[99]

Linguistic symbolism is manifested through stories, texts, names, labels, and so forth. In the Muslim doctrine, the linguistic symbol for Jerusalem is the Arabic *Al-Quds*. Literally, however, Al-Quds does not mean Jerusalem or, as the city is also commonly known, City of David. Rather, it means "The Holy." More precisely, it refers to the holy site that Muhammad conquered when he traveled from Mecca to Jerusalem on his white horse. That same horse allowed Muhammad to ascend to Paradise when he was in Al-Quds. Lastly, in the Muslim world, Al-Quds is the third holiest site after Mecca and Medina. Today, it is home to the Al-Aqsa Mosque and the Dome of the Rock.[100] This example illustrates that linguistic symbolism is a system of symbols that people share with others in their social world; these symbols are created for the purposes of representation, the communication of a congruence of values, and social interaction.[101]

Behavioral Symbols

Behavioral symbols refer to symbols that are enacted through rituals, ceremonies, behaviors, and performances. They help preserve kinship, affinity, relationships, and brotherhood. They serve to define and delimit the boundaries between ingroups and outgroups. Those who relate to and sanction behavioral symbols are part of the ingroup; those who do not are left out.[102] For example, before becoming an active member of the Irish Republican Army (IRA), a new terrorist recruit had to go through a "passing out ceremony." By doing this, the member became officially associated with the IRA mission.[103] Similarly, before going on their suicide mission, Hezbollah and Hamas martyrs-to-be (i.e., suicide bombers) participate in a sacred ceremony, together with the others, in fellowship and communality. This type of social connectedness is predicated upon the belief that Allah will reward these martyrs with the highest place in Paradise.[104]

Behavioral symbols also include gestures. A **gesture** is any observable bodily action that communicates thought or feeling or that has significance in symbolic action. Although they cannot be completely defined, in the context of "symbolism in terrorism," actions seen as "gestures" are usually considered "intentional," at least to a certain degree. For example, during the Bosnian War (1992–1995), Bosnian Serbs were often seen giving the three-finger salute to express Serbian nationalism and, at the same time, their superiority vis-à-vis Bosnian Muslims (i.e., Bosniaks) and Bosnian Croats.[105]

In the same vein, a certain number of Turkish extremists display a controversial hand gesture known as the Wolf Head. It is used by Turks who support or belong to the **Grey Wolves**, a Turkish ultranationalist and neo-fascist youth organization.[106] According to Turkish authorities, between 1974 and 1980, this organization perpetrated 694 fatal terrorist attacks in Turkey (their attacks included shootings, bombings, and kidnappings).[107] The Grey Wolves are named for Asena, a mythical she-wolf that led ancient Turks to freedom. Its Wolf Head symbol is also exhibited by members of the National Movement Party and similar extremist parties. The Wolf Head hand gesture consists of folding in the third and fourth fingers of the hand against the folded-in thumb, projecting the index finger and little finger upward to represent the wolf's head by its pointed ears.[108]

Overall, gestures can be performed with body parts such as the hand, head, and face. Bodily movements can reinforce speech or communicate something that speech cannot do sufficiently. Gestures that accompany speech can also express aspects of meaning that do not exist in verbal language. These forms of communication bring to light a more comprehensive view of speakers' conceptualizations. Hand signals such as the "OK" sign, the "thumbs-up" gesture, and "V for victory" are called codified forms. Secret handshakes have been adopted as interaction rituals in not just fraternities but also terrorist groups.[109] All these examples of behavioral symbols fall under the category of **nonverbal communication**, the means of sending and receiving wordless messages.[110]

Sociocultural Symbols

Every cultural group or nation (whether it is an ethnoterritorial group or an entire country) creates and uses sociocultural symbols. They fashion a sense of general connectivity among people and help them categorize their traditions and beliefs.[111] Sociocultural symbols are standards or conventions that are considered codes, like politeness codes or institutional codes of practice. The idea is that cultural groups or nations agree on what is permissible and what is taboo in specific circumstances. An example would be revealing more body parts on the beach than in church—it may be permissible or prohibited. Another instance of such a symbol is etiquette; it can dictate who eats first at the dinner table, or who is allowed to speak at that dinner table. Cultural groups are often characterized by their collective allegiance to such codes.[112]

Sociocultural symbols represent a way of life, shared identity, and philosophy whose meaning is derived and articulated through codes and traditions embedded within a nation's historically given and changing world. In the Middle East, honor killing and the beheading of religious apostates would be examples of sociocultural symbols. Adherence to such symbols creates committed, true believers and joins these believers together on themes such as life and death, good and evil, social virtues, and community relations.[113] When a symbolic movement represents a sociocultural group, symbols are created through legends and myths. Another word for this is mythology.[114] All the same, this symbolic practice can engender prejudice and stereotyping by making references to group traditions to symbolize issues (in terms of nationality, religion, or ethnic pride) that have or have not been resolved yet.[115]

Ideological Symbols

Ideological symbols are socially constructed symbols that invite or prompt action. They are communicated through nonphysical concepts, such as loyalty, respect, revenge, and justice.[116] Such nonphysical concepts are forms of meaning making that direct or incite us to react (i.e., behave) in some way or another.[117] They tend to carry out two important functions: to establish expectations and preserve order. To achieve both, they fuse historically preserved meanings with contemporary facts in order to shape the language of feeling and expressing reality.[118] From this vantage point, ideological symbols are a useful means of awakening people's consciousness and making them reject one ideological (i.e., usually religious- or politically based) reality and accept another. This form of symbolism is peculiar to oppressed groups, groups that have not experienced statehood yet (e.g., Palestinians), or groups that do not have their own successful social or political organization. Generally, stateless people long for one so strongly that they will rely on ideological symbols to transform their dream into a reality. It also goes without saying that there will always be outside nations or governments that will support a particular group's ideological symbols.[119]

It has been established that people enact ideological symbols to commemorate past events.[120] Such **collective memory** indicates that the act of remembering is a social habit in that people disclose to others the memories they have about important moments or people in their lives.[121] For example, on January 30, 1972, Bloody Sunday took place in Northern Ireland when the British Army killed thirteen unarmed civilians. It became a symbol for the IRA mission to avenge the Irish Republican community against the British aggressors. Another subsequent symbol was the internal emotional bonds among the Republican Irish.[122] These became **socially constructed emotions**—symbolic emotions experienced by individuals as a result of their membership in a specific group (usually vis-à-vis another group). Socially constructed emotions are felt, not automatically as a response to one's own life events, but more as a reaction to collective experiences of trauma or joy.[123] A synonym for ideological symbols is the notion of "soft weapons." **Soft weapons** are concepts or ideas that are easily marshaled for propaganda purposes—such as when seeking support and sanction of war and terrorism. The example of the IRA demonstrates that soft weapons can become dangerous if left alone or unresolved.[124]

SUMMARY

Symbolism is the language of symbols or the practice of representing things by symbols. As a specific method of communication, symbolism has the objective to communicate a message by channeling information between a sender and a receiver. Another purpose is to influence people to a certain degree. By and large, a symbol is (1) a medium for conveying meaning, (2) something that stands for something else, (3) a categorization of reality, (4) a communication shortcut, and (5) communication beyond language. A symbol can be a material object, a concept, an action, or an event. As such, a symbol is something that stands for something else and, in doing so, forms a causal coherence, like a cause-and-effect relationship. Because a symbol stands for something else, it carries both denotative (direct) and connotative (indirect) meanings. In a similar vein, symbolism is a discipline of anthroposemiosis, the study of human communication. Unlike animals, humans have a symbolic culture; they have created complex means of communication that are used not only to improve their survival, but also to express ideas and emotions. For this reason, the human being is a symbolic animal. As we have seen, an essential function of symbolism is meaning making, a human activity that consists of assigning meaning to the experience of life. Symbolism, then, depends on interpretation. It cannot create its own meanings; it is dependent on what is perceived. For this reason, meaning making and interpretation are social constructions of reality. Finally, there are three broad categories of symbols: (1) particular symbols, (2) universal symbols, and (3) multivocal symbols. A particular distinction was made between physical symbols (concrete objects made up of physical matter or images) and nonphysical symbols (symbols that have no material form). The latter can be linguistic, behavioral, sociocultural, or ideological symbols.

NOTES

1. Fraim, John (2003). *Battle of Symbols: Global Dynamics of Advertising, Entertainment and Media*. Einsiedeln, Switzerland: Daimon Verlag.

2. Schürmann, Reiner (1979). The Ontological Difference and Political Philosophy. *Philosophy and Phenomenological Research, 40*(1), 99–122.

3. Becker, Udo (2000). *The Continuum Encyclopedia of Symbols*. New York: Continuum.

4. Fordham, Michael (1957). Reflections on Image and Symbol. *Journal of Analytical Psychology, 2*(1), 85–92.

5. Subedi, Anant Kumar (2011). A Study on Symbols in Manjil's "Uni Kabita Zibanko Rangle Lekh." *CET Journal, 3*(1), 86–90.

6. Stein, Leopold (1957). What Is a Symbol Supposed to Be? *Journal of Analytical Psychology, 2*(1), 73–84.

7. Becker, Udo (2000). *The Continuum Encyclopedia of Symbols*. New York: Continuum.

8. Biedermann, Hans, & Hulbert, James (1994). *Dictionary of Symbolism: Cultural Icons and the Meanings behind Them*. New York: Plume.

9. Semetsky, Inna (2006). The Language of Signs: Semiosis and the Memories of the Future. *Sophia, 45*(1), 95–116.

10. Shannon, Claude, & Weaver, Warren (1949). *The Mathematical Theory of Communication*. Urbana: University of Illinois Press.

11. Schramm, Wilbur (1954). How Communication Works. In Wilbur Schramm (Ed.), *The Process and Effects of Communication* (pp. 3–26). Urbana: University of Illinois Press.

12. Berlo, David (1960). *The Process of Communication*. New York: Holt, Rinehart and Winston.

13. Laszlo, Ervin (1995). *The Interconnected Universe: Conceptual Foundations of Transdisciplinary Unified Theory*. Singapore: World Scientific.

14. Schement, Jorge Reina (1993). An Etymological Exploration of the Links between Information and Communication. In Jorge Reina Schement & Brent Ruben (Eds.), *Information and Behavior* (Vol. 4). Piscataway, NJ: Transaction.

15. Nachmani, Amikam (2001). The Palestinian Intifada 1987–1993: The Dynamics of Symbols and Symbolic Realities, the Role of Symbols, Rituals and Myths in National Struggles. *Civil Wars, 4*(1), 49–103.

16. Morgan, Gareth (1985). Spinning on Symbolism: Some Developmental Issues in Organizational Symbolism. *Journal of Management, 11*, 29.

17. Gusfield, Joseph (1981). *The Culture of Public Problems: Drinking and Driving and the Symbolic Order*. Chicago: University of Chicago Press.

18. Bandura, Albert (2001). Social Cognitive Theory of Mass Communication. *Media Psychology, 3*(3), 265–299.

19. Merriam Webster (1976). *Webster's Seventh New Collegiate Dictionary*. New York: Merriam Webster.

20. Jones, Michael Owen (1996). *Studying Organizational Symbolism*. Thousand Oaks, CA: Sage.

21. Dekmejian, Hrair (1997). Multiple Faces of Islam. In Anders Jerichow & Jorgen Simonsen (Eds.), *Islam in a Changing World* (pp. 1–12). Surrey, UK: Curzon Press; and Manger, Leif (1999). *Muslim Diversity: Local Islam in Global Contexts*. Surrey, UK: Curzon Press.

22. Arena, Michael, & Arrigo, Bruce (2005). Social Psychology, Terrorism and Identity: A Preliminary Reexamination of Theory, Culture, Self, and Society. *Behavioral Sciences and the Law, 23*, 485–506.

23. Schirch, Lisa (2005). *Ritual and Symbol in Peacebuilding*. West Hartford, CT: Kumarian Press.

24. Langer, Susanne (1996). *Philosophy in a New Key: A Study in the Symbolism of Reason, Rite, and Art*. Cambridge, MA: Harvard University Press.

25. Stryker, Sheldon (1980). *Symbolic Interactionism: A Social Structural Version*. Menlo Park, CA: Benjamin Cummings.

26. Bartlett, Frederic (1932).   *Remembering: A Study in Experimental and Social Psychology*. Cambridge: Cambridge University Press.

27. Sandstrom, Kent, Martin, Daniel, & Fine, Gary Alan (2010). *Symbols, Selves, and Social Reality: A Symbolic Interactionist Approach to Social Psychology and Sociology*. Oxford: Oxford University Press.

28. Dingley, James, & Kirk-Smith, Michael (2002). Symbolism and Sacrifice in Terrorism. *Small Wars & Insurgencies, 13*(1), 102–128.

29. Chu, Sauman (2003). Cross-Cultural Comparison of the Perception of Symbols. *Journal of Visual Literacy, 23*(1), 69–80.

30. O'Shaughnessy, Nicholas (2004). *Politics and Propaganda: Weapons of Mass Seduction*. Ann Arbor: University of Michigan Press.

31. Rhodes, Anthony (1993). *Propaganda, the Art of Persuasion: World War II*. Wigston, UK: Mayor Books.

32. Schirch, Lisa (2005). *Ritual and Symbol in Peacebuilding*. West Hartford, CT: Kumarian Press.

33. Edelman, Murray (1964). *The Symbolic Uses of Politics*. Urbana: University of Illinois Press.

34. Sebeok, Thomas, & Danesi, Marcel (2000). *The Forms of Meaning: Modeling Systems Theory and Semiotic Analysis*. Berlin: Mouton de Gruyter.

35. Kress, Gunther, & van Leeuwen, Theo (2006). *Reading Images: The Grammar of Visual Design* (2nd ed.). London: Routledge.

36. Grosz, Barbara J. (1980). Utterance and Objective: Issues in Natural Language Communication. *AI Magazine, 1*(1), 11–20.

37. Schement, Jorge Reina (1993). An Etymological Exploration of the Links between Information and Communication. In Jorge Reina Schement & Brent Ruben (Eds.), *Information and Behavior* (Vol. 4). Piscataway, NJ: Transaction.

38. Sebeok, Thomas, & Danesi, Marcel (2000). *The Forms of Meaning: Modeling Systems Theory and Semiotic Analysis*. Berlin: Mouton de Gruyter.

39. Bonner, John (1980). *The Evolution of Culture in Animals*. Princeton, NJ: Princeton University Press.

40. Dawkins, Richard (1976). *The Selfish Gene*. Oxford: Oxford University Press.

41. Geertz, Clifford (1973). Ideology as a Cultural System. In Clifford Geertz (Ed.), *The Interpretation of Cultures: Selected Essays* (pp. 193–233). New York: Basic Books.

42. Chase, Philip (1994). On Symbols and the Palaeolithic. *Current Anthropology, 35*(5), 627–629.

43. Seeley, Thomas (1995). *The Wisdom of the Hive: The Social Physiology of Honey Bee Colonies*. Cambridge, MA: Harvard University Press; and Turchin, Peter (2006). *War and Peace and War: The Rise and Fall of Empires*. New York: Penguin.

44. Deely, John (2010). Realism and Epistemology. In Paul Cobley (Ed.), *The Routledge Companion to Semiotics* (pp. 74–88). New York: Routledge.

45. Seeley, Thomas (1995). *The Wisdom of the Hive: The Social Physiology of Honey Bee Colonies*. Cambridge, MA: Harvard University Press.

46. Deely, John (2002). *What Distinguishes Human Understanding?* South Bend, IN: St. Augustine's Press.

47. Cassirer, Ernst (1946). *Language and Myth*. New York: Harper and Brothers.

48. Baumeister, Roy (1991). *Meanings of Life*. New York: Guilford Press; and Frankl, Viktor (1969). *The Will to Meaning*. New York: New American Library.

49. Proulx, Travis, & Heine, Steven Jay (2006). Death and Black Diamonds: Meaning, Mortality, and the Meaning Maintenance Model. *Psychological Inquiry, 17*, 309–318.

50. Gerbner, George (1956). Toward a General Model of Communication. *Audio-Visual Communication Review, 4*, 171–199.

51. Kellogg, Ronald (1999). *The Psychology of Writing*. New York: Oxford University Press.

52. Higgins, Tory (2000). Social Cognition: Learning about What Matters in the Social World. *European Journal of Social Psychology, 30*, 3–39.

53. Baumeister, Roy F. (1991). *Meanings of Life*. New York: Guilford Press; and Frankl, Viktor (1969). *The Will to Meaning*. New York: New American Library.

54. Sandstrom, Kent, Martin, Daniel, & Fine, Gary Alan (2010). *Symbols, Selves, and Social Reality: A Symbolic Interactionist Approach to Social Psychology and Sociology*. Oxford: Oxford University Press.

55. Idinopulos, Thomas, & Yonan, Edward (1994). *Religion and Reductionism*. Leiden: Brill.

56. Bruns, Gerald L. (1992). *Hermeneutics. Ancient and Modern*. New Haven, CT: Yale University Press; and Harris, Ray (2008). The Blood Brotherhoods: A Developmental Look at Terrorism from the Perspective of Mythos. *Journal of Adult Development, 14*, 112–121.

57. O'Hair, Dan, Heath, Robert, Ayotte, Kevin, & Ledlow, Gerald (2008). *Terrorism: Communication and Rhetorical Perspectives*. Cresskill, NJ: Hampton Press.

58. Lowe, Sid, Magala, Slawek, & Hwang, Ki-Soon (2012). All We Are Saying, Is Give Theoretical Pluralism a Chance. *Journal of Organizational Change Management, 25*(5), 752–774.

59. Geertz, Clifford (1973). Ideology as a Cultural System. In Clifford Geertz (Ed.), *The Interpretation of Cultures: Selected Essays* (pp. 193–233). New York: Basic Books.

60. White, Jonathan (2011). *Terrorism & Homeland Security* (7th ed.). Belmont, CA: Wadsworth.

61. Berger, Peter, & Luckmann, Thomas (1966). *The Social Construction of Reality: A Treatise in the Sociology of Knowledge*. Garden City, NY: Doubleday.

62. Searle, John (1997). *The Construction of Social Reality*. New York: Free Press.

63. Bakhtin, Mikhail (1965). *Rabelais and His World*. Bloomington: Indiana University Press.

64. Bolman, Lee, & Deal, Terrence (1991). *Reframing Organizations*. San Francisco: Jossey-Bass.

65. Mosse, George (1975). *The Nationalization of the Masses: Political Symbolism and Mass Movements in Germany from the Napoleonic Wars through the Third Reich*. New York: Howard Fertig.

66. Jones, Michael Owen (1996). *Studying Organizational Symbolism*. Thousand Oaks, CA: Sage.

67. Belk, Russell (1988). Possessions and the Extended Self. *Journal of Consumer Research, 15*, 139–168; and Csikszentmihalyi, Mihaly, & Rochberg-Halton, Eugene (1981). *The Meaning of Things: Domestic Symbols and the Self*. London: Cambridge University Press.

68. Stump, Roger (2000). *Boundaries of Faith: Geographical Perspectives on Religious Fundamentalism*. Lanham, MD: Rowman & Littlefield.

69. Kaiser, Colin (2002). *Personal Communication: Telephone Survey*. Sarajevo, Bosnia and Herzegovina: Chef de Bureau, UNESCO; and Osborne, Brian (2002). Corporeal Politics and the Body Politic: The Re-Presentation of Louis Riel in Canadian Identity. *International Journal of Heritage Studies, 8*(4), 303–322.

70. Paul, Christopher (2010). As a Fish Swims in the Sea: Relationships between Factors Contributing to Support for Terrorist or Insurgent Groups. *Studies in Conflict & Terrorism, 33*(6), 488–510.

71. Harman, Lesley (1986). Sign, Symbol, and Metalanguage: Against the Integration of Semiotics and Symbolic Interactionism. *Symbolic Interaction, 9*(1), 147–160.

72. Shinar, David, Dewar, Robert, Summala, Heikki, & Zakowska, Lidia (2003). Traffic Sign Symbol Comprehension: A Cross-Cultural Study. *Ergonomics, 46*(15), 1549–1565.

73. Firth, Raymond (1973). *Symbols: Public and Private*. Ithaca, NY: Cornell University Press; and Weltzer, Michael (1967). On the Role of Symbolism in Political Thought. *Political Studies Quarterly, 82*, 191–205.

74. Jung, Carl (1962). *Symbols of Transformation: An Analysis of the Prelude to a Case of Schizophrenia*. New York: Harper & Brothers.

75. Berger, Arthur Asa (1999). *Signs in Contemporary Culture: An Introduction to Semiotics*. Salem, WI: Sheffield.

76. Choudhury, Enamul (2004). The Politics of Symbols and the Symbolization of 9/11. *The American Journal of Islamic Social Sciences, 21*(1), 73–96.

77. Stryker, Sheldon (1980). *Symbolic Interactionism: A Social Structural Version*. Menlo Park, CA: Benjamin Cummings.

78. Torstrick, Rebecca (2004). *Culture and Customs of Israel*. Westport, CT: Greenwood Press.

79. Nachmani, Amikam (2001). The Palestinian Intifada 1987–1993: The Dynamics of Symbols and Symbolic Realities, the Role of Symbols, Rituals and Myths in National Struggles. *Civil Wars, 4*(1), 49–103.

80. Nachmani, Amikam (2001). The Palestinian Intifada 1987–1993: The Dynamics of Symbols and Symbolic Realities, the Role of Symbols, Rituals and Myths in National Struggles. *Civil Wars, 4*(1), 49–103.

81. Chu, Sauman (2003). Cross-Cultural Comparison of the Perception of Symbols. *Journal of Visual Literacy, 23*(1), 69–80.

82. Kaufman, Irving, Heims, Lora W., & Reiser, David E. (2010). A Re-Evaluation of the Psychodynamics of Firesetting. *American Journal of Orthopsychiatry, 31*(1), 123–136.

83. Aretxaga, Begoña (1995). Dirty Protest: Symbolic Overdetermination and Gender in Northern Ireland Ethnic Violence. *Ethos, 23*(2), 123–148.

84. Turner, Victor (1967). *The Forest of Symbols*. Ithaca, NY: Cornell University Press.

85. Schirch, Lisa (2005). *Ritual and Symbol in Peacebuilding*. West Hartford, CT: Kumarian Press.

86. Mees, Bernard (2008). *The Science of the Swastika*. Budapest, Hungary: Central European University Press.

87. Sonesson, Göran (1989). *Pictorial Concepts*. Lund, Sweden: Lund University Press.

88. Giles, Howard (1977). *Language, Ethnicity and Intergroup Relations*. London: Academic Press.

89. Atran, Scott, & Norenzayan, Ara (2004). Religion's Evolutionary Landscape: Counterintuition, Commitment, Compassion, Communion. *Behavioral and Brain Sciences, 27*, 713–730; and Cronk, Lee (1994). Evolutionary Theories of Morality and the Manipulative Use of Signals. *Zygon, 29*(1), 81–101.

90. Arrigo, Bruce (2010). Identity, International Terrorism and Negotiating Peace: Hamas and Ethics-Based Considerations from Critical Restorative Justice. *British Journal of Criminology, 50*, 772–790.

91. Borum, Randy (2004). *Psychology of Terrorism*. Tampa: University of South Florida.

92. Carvalho, Edward (2010). The Poetics of a School Shooter: Decoding Political Signification in Cho Seung-Hui's Multimedia Manifesto. *Review of Education, Pedagogy, and Cultural Studies, 32*(4), 403–430.

93. Nachmani, Amikam (2001). The Palestinian Intifada 1987–1993: The Dynamics of Symbols and Symbolic Realities, the Role of Symbols, Rituals and Myths in National Struggles. *Civil Wars, 4*(1), 49–103.

94. Giannetti, Louis (2008). *Understanding Movies*. Toronto: Pearson Prentice Hall; and Müller, Marion, & Özcan, Esra (2007). The Political Iconography of Muhammad Cartoons: Understanding Cultural Conflict and Political Action. *PS: Political Science and Politics, 40*(2), 287–291.

95. Białostocki, Jan (2003). *Iconography: Dictionary of the History of Ideas*. Charlottesville: University of Virginia Library.

96. Brown, Ian, & Korff, Douwe (2009). Terrorism and the Proportionality of Internet Surveillance. *European Journal of Criminology, 6*(2), 119–134.

97. Ranstorp, Magnus (2007). The Virtual Sanctuary of Al-Qaeda and Terrorism in an Age of Globalisation. In Johan Eriksson & Giampiero Giacomello (Eds.), *International Relations and Security in the Digital Age* (pp. 31–56). London: Routledge.

98. Hecht, Michael, Jackson, Ronald, II, & Ribeau, Sydney (2003). *African American Communication*. Mahwah, NJ: Lawrence Erlbaum.

99. Matusitz, Jonathan (2012). *Terrorism & Communication: A Critical Introduction*. Thousand Oaks, CA: Sage.

100. Dumper, Mick (1993). Jerusalem Then and Now. *Middle East Report, 182*, 2–8.

101. Sandstrom, Kent, Martin, Daniel, & Fine, Gary Alan (2010). *Symbols, Selves, and Social Reality: A Symbolic Interactionist Approach to Social Psychology and Sociology*. Oxford: Oxford University Press.

102. Nachmani, Amikam (2001). The Palestinian Intifada 1987–1993: The Dynamics of Symbols and Symbolic Realities, the Role of Symbols, Rituals and Myths in National Struggles. *Civil Wars, 4*(1), 49–103.

103. Kenney, Michael (2007). *From Pablo to Osama: Trafficking and Terrorist Networks, Government Bureaucracies, and Competitive Adaptation*. University Park: Pennsylvania State University Press.

104. Oliver, Anne Marie, & Steinberg, Paul F. (2005). *The Road to Martyrs' Square: A Journey into the World of the Suicide Bomber*. Oxford: Oxford University Press.

105. Gilberg, Trond (2000). "Yugoslav" Nationalism at the End of the Twentieth Century. In Leo Suryadinata (Ed.), *Nationalism and Globalization: East and West* (pp. 1–37). Singapore: Institute of Southeast Asian Studies.

106. Tunander, Ola (1995). A New Ottoman Empire? The Choice for Turkey: Euro-Asian Centre vs National Fortress. *Security Dialogue, 4*, 413–426.

107. Schmid, Alex, & Jongman, Albert (2005). *Political Terrorism: A New Guide to Actors, Authors, Concepts, Data Bases, Theories, and Literature*. Piscataway, NJ: Transaction.

108. Yavuz, M. Hakan (2002). The Politics of Fear: The Rise of the Nationalist Action Party (MHP) in Turkey. *Middle East Journal, 56*(2), 200–221.

109. McNeill, David (1992). *Hand and Mind*. Chicago: Chicago University Press.

110. Moore, Nina-Jo, Hickson, Mark, III, & Stacks, Don (2010). *Nonverbal Communication: Studies and Applications* (5th ed.). Los Angeles: Roxbury.

111. Coles, Robert (1986). *The Political Life of Children*. Boston: Houghton Mifflin.

112. Geertz, Clifford (1993). Thick Description. In Clifford Geertz (Ed.), *The Interpretation of Cultures: Selected Essays* (pp. 193–233). London: HarperCollins.

113. Perlmutter, Dawn (2011). The Semiotics of Honor Killing & Ritual Murder. *Anthropoetics, 17*(1), 22–34.

114. Fraim, John (2003). *Battle of Symbols: Global Dynamics of Advertising, Entertainment and Media*. Einsiedeln, Switzerland: Daimon Verlag.

115. O'Donnell, Edward Eugene (1978). *Northern Irish Stereotypes*. Dublin: College of Industrial Relations.

116. Arrigo, Bruce (2010). Identity, International Terrorism and Negotiating Peace: Hamas and Ethics-Based Considerations from Critical Restorative Justice. *British Journal of Criminology, 50*, 772–790.

117. Arena, Michael, & Arrigo, Bruce (2005). Social Psychology, Terrorism and Identity: A Preliminary Reexamination of Theory, Culture, Self, and Society. *Behavioral Sciences and the Law, 23*, 485–506.

118. Edelman, Murray (1971). *Politics as Symbolic Action: Mass Arousal and Quiescence*. Chicago: Markham.

119. Nachmani, Amikam (2001). The Palestinian Intifada 1987–1993: The Dynamics of Symbols and Symbolic Realities, the Role of Symbols, Rituals and Myths in National Struggles. *Civil Wars, 4*(1), 49–103.

120. Alexander, Jeffrey, Giesen, Bernhard, & Mast, Jason (2006). *Social Performance: Symbolic Action, Cultural Pragmatics, and Ritual*. Cambridge: Cambridge University Press.

121. Conway, Brian (2003). Active Remembering, Selective Forgetting, and Collective Identity: The Case of Bloody Sunday. *Identity: An International Journal of Theory and Research, 3*(4), 305–323.

122. Horgan, John (2005). *The Psychology of Terrorism*. New York: Routledge.

123. Smith, Eliot (1993). Social Identity and Social Emotions: Toward New Conceptualization of Prejudice. In Diane Mackie & David Hamilton (Eds.), *Affect, Cognition and Stereotyping: Interactive Processes in Group Perception* (pp. 297–315). San Diego, CA: Academic Press.

124. Whitlock, Gillian (2007). *Soft Weapons: Autobiography in Transit*. Chicago: University of Chicago Press.

Chapter Two

Interpreting Symbolism in Terrorism

A First Step

DEFINITION OF TERRORISM

Within "terrorism" lies the word "terror." **Terror** is rooted in the Latin *terrere* (i.e., "frighten" or "tremble"). When associated with the French suffix *isme* (i.e., "to practice"), it roughly means "practicing the trembling" or "causing the frightening." Trembling and frightening refer to fear, panic, and anxiety—what should be naturally called terror.[1] The word "terrorism" was used for the first time during the Reign of Terror at the end of the French Revolution (1793–1794). In the **Reign of Terror** (*Le Gouvernement de la Terreur*), the **Jacobins** (a faction of rebels led by **Maximilien Robespierre**) employed the term in reference to their own "terrorist" actions—and explanations. Indeed, the Reign of Terror was a movement of widespread violence committed by the French state; between 16,000 and 40,000 individuals were guillotined. The **guillotine** became such a standard device for decapitation that it was quickly dubbed the **National Razor**. It should also come to no surprise that, in September 1793, Robespierre declared at the French National Convention that "terror is the order of the day."[2]

Since the Reign of Terror, more than 200 definitions of terrorism have appeared in academic works and official documents. In fact, Simon (1994)[3] contends that no less than 212 different definitions of terrorism have been published worldwide; ninety of them are regularly employed by governments and other institutions. There is no common definition of "terrorism" on which all nations agree. The meanings of terrorism evolve over time. During the Reign of Terror, defenders of that regime used terrorism to refer to their own Jacobin actions and the unprecedented extremism it symbolized.[4] In the nineteenth and early twentieth centuries, the West defined terrorism as the practice of assassination and bombing by individualized rebellions against authorities and private property—sometimes called the **Golden Age of Assassination**.[5] In the mid-twentieth century, terrorism denoted civil disorder and tactics employed in nationalist and class struggles (e.g., kidnappings, skyjackings, and bank heists). During the Cold War, terrorism was the evil engendered by the Soviet Union. Today, the United States defines terrorism through several statutes (including the USA Patriot Act) as any politically or religiously motivated attack on the nation or its interests.[6]

Outside the West, definitions of terrorism are also plentiful. For example, the Chinese refer to peaceful Tibetan Buddhists as "vicious terrorists." Robert Mugabe, the Zimbabwean president, regards his democratic opposition in a similar manner.[7] In 1974, Yasser Arafat, former leader of the Palestine Liberation Organization (PLO), said in a speech before the United Nations that "one man's terrorist is another man's freedom fighter." Arafat's claim exemplifies the notion that politicians' agendas or worldviews can easily shape their definitions of terrorism. On December 21, 2001, a public opinion poll was conducted in the Palestinian territories. According to the poll, 98.1 percent of the Palestinians agreed or strongly agreed that "the killing of 29 Palestinians in Hebron by Baruch Goldstein at al Ibrahimi mosque in 1994" ought to be called terrorism, whereas 82.3 percent of the same people who were surveyed disagreed or strongly disagreed that "the killing of 21 Israeli youths by a Palestinian who exploded himself at the Tel Aviv Dolphinarium" should be referred to as terrorism.[8]

Definitions from Institutions and Scholars

Throughout the years, various institutions and scholars have attempted to define terrorism. Yet the term is so loaded with conceptual problems that a totally accepted definition of it does not exist. What comes next is a list of definitions of terrorism by some of the most distinguished institutions and scholars on the matter:

- **U.S. Joint Chiefs of Staff**: Terrorism is "the calculated use of unlawful violence or threat of unlawful violence to inculcate fear; intended to coerce or to intimidate governments or societies in the pursuit of goals that are generally political, religious, or ideological."[9]
- **Federal Bureau of Investigation (FBI)**: Terrorism is "the unlawful use of force and violence against persons or property to intimidate or coerce a government, the civilian population, or a segment thereof in furtherance of political or social objectives."[10]
- **United Nations General Assembly**: Terrorism refers to "criminal acts intended or calculated to provoke a state of terror in the general public, a group of persons or particular persons for political purposes."[11]
- **Arab Convention for the Suppression of Terrorism**: Terrorism is "any act or threat of violence, whatever its motives or purposes, that occurs in the advancement of an individual or collective criminal agenda and seeking to sow panic among people, causing fear by harming them, or placing their lives, liberty or security in danger."[12]
- **Walter Laqueur**: "Terrorism is the use or the threat of the use of violence, a method of combat, or a strategy to achieve certain targets. . . . I]t aims to induce a state of fear in the victim, that is ruthless and does not conform with humanitarian rules. . . . [P]ublicity is an essential factor in the terrorist strategy."[13]
- **David Rapoport**: Terrorism is "the use of violence to provoke consciousness, to evoke certain feelings of sympathy and revulsion."[14]
- **Bruce Hoffman**: "Terrorism is ineluctably political in aims and motives, violent—or, equally important, threatens violence, designed to have far-reaching psychological repercussions beyond the immediate victim or target, conducted by an organization with an identifiable chain of command or conspiratorial cell structure (whose members wear no uniform or identifying insignia), and perpetrated by a subnational group or non-state entity."[15]
- **Noam Chomsky**: "Terrorism is the use of coercive means aimed at populations in an effort to achieve political, religious, or other aims."[16]

Based on all of these institutional and scholarly definitions, readers can deduce that terrorist acts are never truly random. Rather, they are calculatedly perpetrated to achieve objectives, and they may be part of an agenda of events to accomplish those objectives. Nevertheless, these definitions also expose the problem of attaining a comprehensive definition of terrorism on which everyone agrees. Walter Laqueur (1987),[17] a renowned scholar on the subject, does not think that defining terrorism is actually possible. For some scholars, unless the act is lethal and involves innocent victims, it should not be called terrorism. For instance, Rigstad (2008)[18] considers terrorism a type of indiscriminate, lethal, and frightful violence that is intentionally inflicted on innocent people.

Most Universally Accepted Definition

No universally agreed-upon definition of terrorism exists. What we have, at best, is a "most universally accepted" definition of terrorism. As such, **terrorism** is the use of violence to create fear (i.e., terror and psychic fear) for (1) political, (2) religious, or (3) ideological reasons. The terror is deliberately directed toward noncombatant targets (i.e., civilians or symbols), and an important purpose is to gain the highest amount of publicity for a group, cause, or person. Speaking of ideological reasons, **ideologies** are belief systems or worldviews that frame the human mind and influence social and political conditions. The meaning of terrorism is socially constructed. In a content analysis of over one hundred definitions of terrorism, Schmid (1984)[19] discovered that the concept of violence appeared in 83.5 percent of definitions; political goals in 65 percent of definitions; causing fear and terror in 51 percent of definitions; arbitrariness and indiscriminate targeting in 21 percent of definitions; and the victimization of civilians, noncombatants, neutrals, or outsiders in 17.5 percent of definitions (see Box 2.1).

BOX 2.1: CONTENT ANALYSIS OF DEFINITIONS OF TERRORISM

Alex Schmid, a researcher at the University of Leiden (in the Netherlands), performed a content analysis of more than one hundred academic and official definitions of terrorism and examined them to identify the frequency of elements (i.e., concepts) that appeared in all those definitions. Twenty-two different elements were discovered in total, with an average of five elements per definition. The twelve most common elements are listed below:

Element	Frequency (%)
Violence or force	83.5
Political	65
Fear or terror emphasized	51
Threat	47
(Psychological) effects and (anticipated) reactions	41.5
Victim-target differentiation	37.5
Purposive, planned, systematic, organized action	32
Method of combat, strategy, or tactic	30.5
Extranormality, in breach of accepted rules, without humanitarianism	30
Coercion, extortion, or induction of compliance	28
Arbitrariness and indiscriminate targeting	21
Victimization of civilians, noncombatants, neutrals, or outsiders	17.5

Likewise, Merari (1993)[1] performed another content analysis and remarked that, in the United States, the United Kingdom, and Germany, three common elements emerge in the legal definitions of terrorism of those nations: (1) the use of violence, (2) political objectives, and (3) the objective of propagating fear in a target population.

[1] Merari, Ariel (1993). Terrorism as a Strategy of Insurgency. *Terrorism and Political Violence, 5*(4), 213–251.

The most universally accepted definition of terrorism just mentioned earlier, based on various content analyses, is also referred to as the **grammar of terrorism**—a set of linguistic rules and definitions as to what constitutes terrorism and the victims thereof.[20] This grammar of terrorism can have short- or long-term implications for political speech acts, and for the powerful or even extreme consequences of these acts. In other words, this grammar of terrorism can become embraced de facto as reliable or authoritative for policy makers.[21]

DEFINING TERRORISM WITH SYMBOLIC ELEMENTS

In chapter 1, it was postulated that humans are symbolic animals who engage in meaning making in their own symbolic cultures.[22] Consequently, humans have **symbolic power**; unlike other species, they have the power to construct reality through symbolism.[23] As we have seen, symbolic power may be exerted through a multitude of symbolic methods: physical symbols and/or nonphysical symbols (i.e., linguistic, behavioral, sociocultural, and ideological symbols). Below is a list of ten definitions of terrorism from the perspective of symbolism. These definitions come from various scholarly sources:

1. Terrorism ought to be viewed as a meaning-making tactic.[24]
2. Terrorism is a symbolic tactic that entities—individuals, communities, or nations—employ in the process of constructing their and others' identities.[25]
3. Terrorism functions to send a message from terrorists to a target audience. Symbols play a key role in this communication, through visuals that terrorist organizations use to represent themselves, as well as the meaning and significance in the selection of targets.[26]
4. "As a symbolic act, terrorism can be analyzed much like other media of communication, consisting of four basic components: transmitter (the terrorist), intended recipient (target), message (bombing, ambush) and feedback (reaction of target audience)."[27]
5. Terrorism is not an ideology, but a cruel method of communication to fulfill ideological, political, economic, or military goals.[28]
6. Terrorism is a symbolic act of which the objective is to manipulate people's political behavior.[29]
7. Terrorism is "the use or threat of use of symbolic acts of physical violence, to influence the political behavior of a given target group."[30]
8. The symbolic nature of terrorism, which differentiates it from classical forms of violence, lies in its indirect and psychological character. Terrorist attacks are ultimately created to impact one target by attacking another.[31]
9. Terrorist attacks are symbolic acts of violence committed against powerful enemy symbols in order to expose the enemy's weakness.[32]
10. Terrorism is a language of symbolic action: in the selection of victims, the selection of terrorist tactics, the dramatization created, and the multiple official reactions sought.[33]

The first two definitions evoke the notion of meaning making in groups. For example, constructing identity is a fundamental meaning-making phenomenon. The next three definitions look at terrorism from a communicative perspective. More precisely, for the terrorists, using symbolism is a form of communication. At the same time, it is a method of achieving political objectives. This is particularly evident in the sixth and seventh definitions, whereby the violent component of terrorism is underscored as being symbolic and designed to communicate a political message. It is also meant to terrorize, intimidate, and strike fear into people. The last three definitions stress the importance of selecting symbolic targets. The role of "target symbolism" is salient here because, without it, the terrorist act would have little relevance. Upon looking at the big picture, it is clear that understanding terrorism cannot be complete without understanding its symbolism. The terrorist act itself, then, should not be interpreted in merely rational "means-ends" terms. Rather, it should be interpreted as a dreadful performance of violence that has deep symbolic significance. As Juergensmeyer (2000)[34] wrote, terrorism is the "language of being noticed" (p. 139).

TERRORISM AS PERFORMATIVE VIOLENCE

Performative violence is a particular means of communication through which terrorists attempt to produce social transformations by performing symbolic acts of violence. Through a form of meaningful interaction with the audience (both the immediate victims and the public at large), terrorists shape a social reality based on symbolic actions.[35] As Blok (2000)[36] pointed out, terrorism has symbolic-expressive aspects: "rather than defining violence a priori as senseless and irrational, we should consider it as a changing form of interaction and communication, as a historically developed cultural form of meaningful action" (p. 24). Juergensmeyer (2000)[37] looked at the type of violence committed by "new world order" terrorists—sometimes with clear political goals—and concluded that they tend to engage in more destructive methods of violence than their secular counterparts. This is due to a particular type of performative violence: transformative power based on an apocalyptic agenda. The objective is to destroy the earth, replace it with a new world order, and make the audience aware of this.

Examples are Islamic fundamentalists' bombing of the World Trade Center in 1993, Aum Shinrikyo's sarin gas attack in the Tokyo subway system in 1995, and Timothy McVeigh's bombing of an Oklahoma City federal building one month later. The Oklahoma City bombing, for instance, was committed to communicate the idea that the U.S. federal government was responsible for the disastrous Waco siege that happened exactly two years before. McVeigh had read *The Turner Diaries*,[38] a novel explaining how the U.S. government is overthrown through a nuclear war. Likewise, after interviewing members of millennial religious groups and using key scriptures within each group, Juergensmeyer insisted that each group's performative violence can add knowledge to the types of tactical decisions that are possible or impossible. Performative violence, of course, is not limited to the actions committed by "new world order" or millennial religious terrorists. McCormick and Giordano (2007)[39] have identified three important effects that terrorism as performative violence has through a meticulous use of symbolism: (1) the agitation effect, (2) the provocation effect, and (3) the demonstration effect, which are discussed next.

The Agitation Effect

The **agitation effect** denotes terrorism as a vehicle of armed propaganda to communicate the presence of an emerging opposition, increase popular consciousness, and explain the terms of

the struggle. Hence, the manner in which a terrorist action is performed has symbolic meaning.[40] This can be done by employing violence against one target (the immediate victims) to
influence a different target (the audience beyond the immediate target).[41] Performative violence here is used as a propagandistic instrument to upset the status quo, galvanize the population into awareness, and create opposition to the government (at least from the terrorists'
perspective). At the end of the nineteenth century and the beginning of the twentieth century,
the agitation effect was called **Propaganda by the Deed**, a radical method whereby terrorism
became a tool of communication to stir up the populace and cause a revolution.[42] To get their
messages across, the agitators used dynamite (invented in 1866). Dynamite became the supreme democratic weapon, allowing revolutionaries to fulfill their dream of overcoming the
mighty power of the state. In fact, the propagandists labeled it the **philosophy of the bomb**:
bombing enemies was the best method for agitation effects and the creation of social change.[43]

As a symbolic action, the agitation effect produces consequences that are more far-reaching than the agitation itself. It is a method of being conspicuously visible through noisy or
controversial actions. The aim is to considerably jar the public order, to leave permanent
psychological traumas on the audience, to commit terrorist acts that carry over long distances,
and, by creating uncomfortable feelings in the audience, to impact social life.[44] Usually,
terrorist attacks with an agitation effect are very damaging and are to be used in moderation by
terrorists lest they risk losing the support or sympathy they may have obtained. For example,
the bombings perpetrated by the Provisional Irish Republican Army (PIRA) in Northern
Ireland were initially welcomed with support from the Irish Catholic population. However, as
time went by and too many civilians perished in the bombings, support diminished. Now, the
Irish Catholic population desires political solutions rather than terrorism.[45]

The Provocation Effect

The **provocation effect** denotes terrorism aimed at provoking a nation into overreacting and
taking "excessive countermeasures." In doing so, it is also designed to enhance the relative
image of the terrorist organization itself. On January 30, 1972, at a civil rights march in Derry,
Northern Ireland, British troops killed thirteen Roman Catholics—an event that became
"Bloody Sunday." Instantly, in the eyes of the Irish Catholics, British troops were no longer
protectors; they were now occupiers in Ireland. This event also contributed to the dissolution
of the Stormont Parliament and direct rule from Westminster.[46] The provocation effect led the
Catholic population to portray the Brits as aggressors and increase their admiration for the
PIRA. This process is called **symbolic frame alignment**, a phenomenon whereby the actions
of a group resonate with the symbols and beliefs of the society in which those actions are
taken.[47] Put differently, terrorists have to adapt to their social setting and the reaction of their
host societies.[48]

Gerbner (1991)[49] examined the symbolic communication of terrorism. As he explained,
"Most of what we know, or think we know, we do not personally experience. Perhaps the most
distinguishing characteristic of our species is that for all practical purposes we live in a world
erected through the stories we tell" (p. 3). Terrorism plays an essential role in this performative process. It describes social forces and meaningful interaction in conflict. As Gerbner
continued, terrorist acts "dramatize threats to human integrity and the social order. They
demonstrate power to lash out, provoke, intimidate, and control. They designate winners and
losers in an inescapably political game" (p. 3).

The Demonstration Effect

The **demonstration effect** denotes the creation of an exaggerated impression of the strength of a terrorist group and the weakness of a government. If terrorists want to gain strength, then they will try to appear strong by proving that the government is not "untouchable." Perception of relative strength is essential to mobilization and the expectation of the outcome of the struggle. An example of the demonstration effect is "Bloody Friday," which occurred on July 21, 1972, when the PIRA detonated twenty-six bombs in Belfast. Twenty-six car bombings took place within four months—as soon as the British government started to implement its direct rule. Those coordinated terrorist attacks were designed to communicate the idea that Northern Ireland was ungovernable for the Brits and that the PIRA was strong and in control.[50] The demonstration effect is also referred to as **demonstrative terrorism**, a type of terrorism performed for publicity reasons. The three publicity reasons are (1) to attract attention to protests, accusations, and grievances from soft-liners on the other side; (2) to draw the attention of third parties that might pressure the other side; and (3) to recruit new possible terrorist recruits.[51]

Performative violence seems to be an effective method to gain public attention. The choice of a particular group as a target or the meticulous coordination of attacks can testify to this.[52] Paletz, Ayanian, and Fozzard (1982)[53] define terrorism as "politically motivated violence that strikes at symbols and figures of authority in society, seeking to achieve the goals of the perpetrators through intimidation" (p. 145). The demonstration effect is the idea that the victims of terrorism are usually a mere vehicle to make deeper statements, secure symbolic victories, or assert a particular identity for the terrorist group.[54] Performative violence reflects the notion that terrorism occurs in a symbolic context thanks to which leaders and constituents define, interpret, and comprehend the nature and outcomes of extreme violence. It is such symbolic action that makes terrorism more meaningful.[55]

TERRORISM AS A TRANSNATIONAL INJUSTICE SYMBOL

One of the most important symbolic motives that drive terrorist groups to perpetrate their extreme acts is the transnational injustice symbol. By and large, a **transnational injustice symbol** is an event or situation exploited by politicians or terrorist leaders as an excuse to avenge perceived injustices before geographically, socially, and culturally scattered audiences. The term was coined by Thomas Olesen (2011)[56] in his article entitled "Transnational Injustice Symbols and Communities," which was published in *Current Sociology*. Put differently, a leader can create a transnational injustice symbol by developing a symbolic frame alignment among various audiences across the world. The aim, of course, is to advance political goals. Nevertheless, militants who try to address transnationally dispersed audiences have to cope with a difficult communication task: what works at the national level may not work at the international level. In most cases, the transnational cultural structure does not share the exact same symbolic system as the national culture. Transnational injustice symbols may give birth to injustice communities by providing common values or traits across cultures worldwide (i.e., cultural resonance), but they are still not fixed.[57]

Indeed, symbols (and the meanings assigned to them) are never fixed. Not only can their meanings change over time,[58] but also they are open to reinterpretation or subject to differences of interpretation. In Jasper's (1997)[59] words, the "creative efforts of activists" (p. 159) can also warp the original meaning of a symbol completely. For this reason, politicians or terrorist leaders are well aware of the need for **dialectical sensitivity**. It refers to people's ability to serve as transnational communicators, understand cultural differences among com-

munities, and know how to reach out to global audiences socially, ideologically, and culturally.[60] A successful transnational injustice symbol leads to a global **sentiment pool**—a worldwide community that reaches common agreement on a specific event or situation and, ultimately, on what course of action should be taken to redress the injustice that the group has
endured.[61]

Transnational Injustice Communities

Injustice symbols are a good way to create **transnational injustice communities**, which are
networks of individuals ideologically linked through similar identities and perceptions of
shared injustice. An important corollary is that injustice communities consume and further
create additional injustice symbols. For Waters (2001),[62] the study of symbols has fundamental relevance in a transnational context because "symbolic exchanges release social arrangements from spatial referents. Symbols can be proliferated rapidly and in any locality and are
easily transportable and communicable" (p. 19). The power of militant leaders to act as
communication facilitators and reach out to global audiences (i.e.., dialectical sensitivity)
makes injustice symbols pivotal for terrorists engaged in transnational communication.[63] Once
an event or situation becomes a salient symbol in a culture, it becomes a schema in that
culture. As described in chapter 1, a schema is a mental structure that is located within a
specific culture; it is transformed into a resource that generates a symbolic frame alignment,
like an "injustice frame." An **injustice frame** typically has a moral component.[64] At least two
interrelated aspects are at play. First, an injustice frame performs binaries: it identifies an
aggressor (e.g., a state) who has committed an injustice against the activist group and its
constituents; and, second, an injustice frame tends to fall back on moral shocks.[65] **Moral
shocks** are situations that create public outrage and, consequently, smooth the progress of
recruitment to movements involved in the issue. As Jasper (1997)[66] argues, "The most effective moral shocks are those embodied in, translatable into, and summed up by powerful
condensing symbols" (p. 161).

The Ummah: The Transnational Muslim Community

The idea of a transnational community is evident in the concept of ummah. In Islam, the
ummah is the international community of all faithful Muslims: all Muslims belong to the
same transnational community.[67] As the ummah encompasses all Muslim tribes or nations
(e.g., Palestinians, Maghrebis, etc.), it assumes an **umbrella effect**, as people worldwide can
feel increasingly connected through a transnational term.[68] The "global Muslim community"
is sacred; the ummah emphasizes an Allah-given order whose framework was revealed
through the Prophet Muhammad. Later, Muhammad explained how men should coexist in an
organized structure of relationships, connected through moral obligation to other members of
the ummah, and creating peace and harmony in the process. The very word "Islam," however,
means submission (to the will of Allah). This suggests that submission has to be given to the
will of the ummah as well; only then will order and harmony be possible. An important
outcome is that whatever appears to assail or affront the ummah, such as Western individualism, is also seen as an attack on Allah.[69] Furthermore, the sacred language of the Qur'an is a
standard, nonvernacular, and cross-ethnic Arabic language. An important element that binds
Muslims within the ummah is the Qur'an, a revelation from Allah. The Muslim belief is that
the true words of Allah were in Arabic, the sacred language.[70]

So, the violence from Islam mostly stems from the perceived attack on the ummah.[71] The
global Muslim community under attack is what bestows, for instance, the Palestinian cause

such a powerful emotional and religious zeal. The way the State of Israel was founded—as the Israeli Declaration of Independence imposed borders in 1948—became not just a fight between indigenous ethnic groups but more an assault on the ummah (at both the local and pan-Islamic levels). The community has been attacked and invaded, and all Muslims are expected to feel concerned. After all, the ummah implies that all Muslims are involved in opposing the attack on Allah. It is both a direct affront to Allah and a holy war. Because it is holy, the rules that exist on earth (e.g., the law of the land) do not matter. Hence, tactics like suicide bombings and indiscriminate terrorism against all targets have been widely embraced.[72]

Guantánamo Bay: Injustice Symbol for the Ummah

Islamic terrorists have managed to position themselves as transnational actors in an increasingly globalized world.[73] Transnational injustice symbols are played up by groups like Al Qaeda so they can politicize the concept of the ummah.[74] Al Qaeda, one of the most indiscriminate and ruthless perpetrators of political violence, devotes substantial energy to rationalizing its actions to the global Muslim community. The Islamic terrorists' transnational dimension is manifest in their use of shared injustice symbols like **Guantánamo Bay**, a detainment and interrogation facility at a U.S. naval base in Cuba. As a high percentage of the Muslim community sees itself as transnational, Guantánamo Bay is a very important symbol of injustice within the ummah. Therefore, the idea of joining the fight to restore the honor of pious Muslims engenders enormous support and loyalty; it also gives additional justification for a return to pure, traditional Islam.

What is unusual about Guantánamo Bay is that this place of perceived injustice is replete with prisoners of diverse national backgrounds who were forcefully transferred there from locations across the globe. It emphasizes how the incident of Guantánamo Bay could be easily constructed as a significant transnational injustice symbol. **Ayman al-Zawahiri**, the new Al Qaeda leader since the death of Osama bin Laden, has fashioned the "evil" concept of Guantánamo Bay by astutely associating it with the immoral behavior of the United States and the West. This is reflected in the leader's comments about the detainment and interrogation facility: "historic scandal," "you hypocrites," and "dirty torture." The immorality claim is based on the United States' apparent disrespect for its own proclaimed values.[75]

The photographs of **Abu Ghraib**—another U.S. detainment and interrogation facility (this time in Iraq)—have attained the pinnacle of transnational injustice symbolism. The photographs showed U.S. troops abusing Iraqi prisoners. They became part of an era of commemorative images that have molded people's memories and opinions about the Global War on Terror. Despite the fact that the same degree of prisoner abuse has not been authenticated or exposed at Guantánamo Bay, the juxtaposition and indirect comparison between Abu Ghraib and Guantánamo Bay have created a symbolic frame of injustice to which many Muslims worldwide have subscribed. Much of this effect works through the power of visual communication. This visualization process around the Guantánamo Bay injustice symbol is efficient for two reasons: first, the global diffusion of Guantánamo-related photos fulfills Al Qaeda's mobilization attempt because it allows the group's messages and claims to exploit and activate existing "visual knowledge" of Guantánamo; and, second, the photographs themselves have also been included in video- and image-based or -supported messages.[76]

Even though the concept of a "transnational injustice symbol" has not been expressed by Al Qaeda, the group's tactics reflect serious efforts at fashioning a transnationalized sense of Muslim solidarity. Khosrokhavar (2005)[77] cleverly points in this direction when he refers to modern-day jihadists as terrorists motivated by a **humiliation by proxy**. This denotes sentiments of indignation and moral shocks resulting from the witnessing of injustices against distant "brothers" and "sisters" (with whom the jihadists obviously identify). This situation is constantly cherished by Al Qaeda leaders who persistently bring up the injustices committed against Muslims in Guantánamo Bay, as well as Palestine, Iraq, Afghanistan, Chechnya, and other nations. Worldwide, militant leaders and politicians emphasize that reacting to this injustice is the duty of every "true" Muslim. The actual meaning of this "reacting to this injustice" duty is jihad.[78]

LINGUISTIC SYMBOLISM IN TERRORISM: IRISH AND ARABIC

As both a social and individual process, linguistic symbolism is a chief symbol system in our culture. The values, attitudes, beliefs, norms, and behaviors that we see as "normative" are profoundly entrenched in our language and communicative structure.[79] Language is a type of discourse; it works through a process of communication of shared cultural symbols to various publics. As one of the many forms of linguistic symbolism, language can fulfill important propaganda purposes in conflict. It can operate as a method to reinforce solidarity; it can be employed to confound, frustrate, and terrify the enemy; it can promote defections; or it can be aimed at a third party (e.g., the audience at large) to sell the group's message.[80] This section looks at two languages used as symbolism in terrorism: Irish and Arabic.

The Irish Language as Symbolism in Terrorism

The type of discourse chosen by the elite is important because it enables mobilization. For example, the IRA and other Irish militant groups use the Irish language to boost their identity and promote nationalism. Boal and Livingstone (1984)[81] note that even graffiti and flags try to incorporate Irish words in order "to emphasize and to encourage core loyalties" (p. 172). The Irish language, then, has become another symbolic weapon in the Nationalists' fight for independence. The Irish language is manipulated as a symbol, the "vehicle for a conception," through which Irish can "render otherwise incomprehensible social situations meaningful" (Geertz, 1973, p. 208).[82] As an emblem of Irish identity and culture, the Irish language is now one of the most readily identifiable aspects of the conflict in Northern Ireland. It has arguably become one of the most crucial symbols of Irish identity for Nationalists in the South as well as in the North. In fact, the Irish language is so central to Nationalists that monoglot native English speakers who have espoused the ideology of Irish Nationalism like to consider Irish as their "own language."[83]

The Irish language is an explicitly political symbol in the sense that any demonstration of interest in the language is viewed as a declaration of political allegiance in support of Irish nationalism.[84] **Sinn Féin**, an Irish Republican party traditionally associated with the PIRA, means "we ourselves"—symbolizing the Irish willingness to be independent from the British "aggressor." In regard to the IRA itself, the Irish "Dáil Éireann" has been written as graffiti on walls in Belfast and other parts of Northern Ireland in support of the Irish terrorist group. The concept of "Dáil Éireann" denotes the assembly of the revolutionary Irish Republic from 1919 to 1922. It occurred at the time of the War of Independence in Ireland and the early militant IRA attacks. Today, "Dáil Éireann" still has symbolic importance for the very militant Irish Republicans.[85] In a similar fashion, according to Rolston (1991),[86] the Irish language is expressed considerably on Republican murals to bring together cultural and Republican identities. A well-known mural says, "Time for peace, time to go," in Irish, representing a white dove moving a British soldier away from an Irish flag toward a British flag.

The Arabic Language as Symbolism in Terrorism

Why examine the Arab language in regard to contemporary events? There are two major reasons: first, many Muslims who have a religious education have at least some knowledge of the Arabic version of the Qur'an. The language of a genuine Qur'an (i.e., standard Arabic) goes beyond national language differences and allows for communication in commonly understood phrases.[87] For example, in the *Al Qaeda Training Manual* (2001),[88] the Arabic concept of "nizam" (i.e., "order") is used multiple times and underscored as a key aim for the Muslim cause. Violence, says the manual, is to be waged to gain "order" for the ummah. In this context, "order" and "ummah" are to be used interchangeably. As the manual explains, "Islamic governments have never and will never be established through peaceful solutions and cooperative councils. They are established as they [always] have been—by pen and gun, by word and bullet." According to Sattar (1995),[89] the fundamental goal of groups like Al Qaeda and the Muslim Brotherhood is to establish a "nizam al Islam" (which means an "Islamic order"). Thus, the linguistic symbol of "order" refers to a global Islamic state.

Second, the standard Arabic version of the Qur'an is rooted in Islam's historical origins. The growth of the faith coincided with the rapid conquest of the Middle East and other places, and a vocabulary related to conflict is an integral component of Islam's texts, history, and myths.[90] Pure, classical Islam has never observed a separation of church and state. Therefore, Arabic-based religious discourse tends to have a bigger emotional impact on Muslims than it would have on non-Muslims. Given these circumstances, thanks to the Arabic language, Islamic leaders have a convenient set of symbols that they can use to frame a range of issues.[91] The 1979 Islamic Revolution in Iran indicated the first effort in modern times to impose Islamic ideology as the foundation for a political entity. It was also a chance to see the Arabic language at work. The Grand Ayatollah Khomeini, the instigator of the Iranian Revolution, established an ideology that mixed modern (e.g., technology and weapons) and traditional (e.g., Arabic language) elements of Islam, the outcome of a lifetime of thought and religious fervor.[92]

This phenomenon illustrates that a shared Arabic language worldwide becomes the language of Islam. It presents a symbolic opportunity from which political entrepreneurs can draw. By using linguistic symbols related to conflict, leaders can manipulate public opinion.[93] To this point, the **Sapir-Whorf hypothesis** rests on the premise that language shapes people's thoughts and frames the nature of social life. In other words, a particular language shapes a particular worldview by imposing a certain context and an order of reality on things.[94] In the aforementioned case, this is how a certain number of Arabic speakers come to conceptualize their world. Language, in general, is always located in context; what a speaker says is assigned meaning by the context in which the speaker expressed his or her words. Context is based on the experiences of both senders and receivers of messages.[95]

LINGUISTIC SYMBOLISM IN TERRORISM: NAME-GIVING CODES

Symbols give us templates for classifying or organizing our experiences and locating them within a larger frame of reference. We gather symbols to create concepts that we employ to arrange our sensory experiences into orderly categories. Generally, these categories take the form of **name-giving codes**: names that have shared meanings for people within a specific culture. By using these names, we are able to know and understand the world in which we live. Name-giving codes can also explain how symbolism functions in the social life of terrorist organizations.[96]

Religious Terrorist Groups

The way in which religious terrorist groups interpret the threat of secularization (both within their own society and in the world at large) can be seen through the name-giving codes they assign to their own groups. In most cases, it is an indication of their conviction that they have the total truth revealed by God. Hence, it is not surprising that some extremely violent terrorist groups tend to adopt names accordingly. Let us have a look at the significance of names for several Islamist organizations (all of them in Arabic except for the last one): [97]

- Hezbollah (Party of God)
- Hamas (Islamic Resistance Movement)
- Lashkar-e-Tayyiba (Army of the Righteous)
- Jund al-Haqq (Soldiers of Truth)
- Harakat ul-Mujahedin (Movement of Holy Warrior)
- The Taliban (Students of Religion, in Pashto)

In the eyes of the groups' followers and potential new recruits, these name-giving codes confer religious legitimacy, historical validity, and rationalization for their actions. They also offer precious insight into their harmony of purpose, agenda and goals, and level of militancy. Other name-giving codes—such as Jundallah (Soldiers of God), Eyal (Jewish Fighting Organization), and Le groupe islamique armé (Armed Islamic Group, GIA)—promise unrelenting combat and sacrifice. [98] The name of the Japanese death cult Aum Shinrikyo stems from the Sanskrit syllable *Aum*, which refers to "universe," followed by *Shinrikyo* (written in kanji), which means "religion of Truth." In English, "Aum Shinrikyo" is usually translated as "Supreme Truth." [99]

This practice of name-giving codes is a product of an idioculture. An **idioculture** is a system of shared knowledge, principles, feelings, and behaviors. For group members, such a system functions as a frame of reference and source of interaction. Groups cultivate their own symbol systems, which represent how individuals are expected to think, feel, and behave. Most terrorist groups have their own idiocultures. [100]

In a similar vein, since the independence of Pakistan in 1947, conflict between Pakistan and India has had an excessively high religious dimension. In fact, tensions have increased through the influence of Hindu and Muslim fundamentalisms. In the late 1980s and 1990s, this religious dimension was enhanced with symbolism through name-giving codes. This was particularly manifest in military nomenclature. For example, Pakistani missile systems bore names associated with the early Muslim conquests of northern India (e.g., Ghauri and Ghaznavi). Likewise, India's deployment of missile systems was named after major Vedic deities (e.g., Agni and Surya) and a Hindu hero in battles against Muslims (i.e., Prithvi). [101] This example illustrates the concept of a **vocabulary of motives**, which is a set of words or phrases created to provide "legitimate" explanations for particular actions. A vocabulary of motives is specific; it is only employed in certain situations or classes of situations. [102]

Hamas: The Zeal and the Islamic Resistance Movement

On December 8, 1987, after an Israeli truck collided with a car transporting several Palestinian workers, four persons died in the crash. The incident led to the First Intifada (uprising) when mass demonstrations, riots, and violence followed. In the aftermath of the rebellion, the Muslim Brotherhood held a meeting to determine how the violent confrontation could be exploited to trigger religious and nationalist zeal. They wrote a communiqué stipulating that "hundreds of wounded and tens of martyrs offered their lives in the path of God [in order to] uphold their nation's glory and honor [and] to restore [Palestinian] rights in [their] homeland" (Hroub, 2000, p. 265).[103] The document also insisted that the Israeli occupation be totally rejected, its land confiscated, its development of settlements blocked, and its Zionism subdued.[104] The communiqué was signed Harakat al-Muqawwamah al-Islamiyya (the Islamic Resistance Movement), and its acronym, HAMAS ("zeal" in Arabic), was attached to it. The document heralded the beginning of the Palestinian Covenant of the Islamic Resistance Movement.[105]

Hamas and affiliated Palestinian militant groups appropriated religious name-giving codes. For example, the coalition of such Palestinian militias called themselves the **Al-Aqsa Martyrs' Brigade**—associated with the Fatah movement, the largest faction of the PLO. The name was created in reference to the martyrs who died in combat when defending the Al-Aqsa Mosque in East Jerusalem (opposite the Dome of the Rock).[106] Not surprisingly, Hamas also used religious terms like "jihad" and "martyrdom" for recruitment, authenticity, and endorsement.[107] Because religious names evoke sacred places as well as institutional memories and experiences linked to them, they bring to mind intense feelings. Therefore, names "conform to the most classic definitions of symbolism" (Cohen & Kliot, 1992, p. 655).[108] In addition, this practice of name-giving code exemplifies the notion of **onomastics** (or **onomatology**). Onomastics is the study of proper names in general as well as the origins of names. The words stem from the Greek *onomastikos*, "of or belonging to naming."[109]

In the same train of thought, by taking advantage of such linguistic symbolism, politicians and terrorist leaders are able to establish a form of cultural hegemony within the groups and communities that they lead. **Cultural hegemony** refers to the domination of one cultural worldview over another in a specific society. In other words, it is a worldview that becomes imposed and accepted as the cultural norm. The concept of cultural hegemony was developed by the Italian-born Marxist intellectual Antonio Gramsci.[110] The example of the acronym "Hamas" illustrates the idea that name-giving codes bring "hegemonic structures of power and authority"[111] into the daily environment. In this fashion, they infer strong nation building and the creation of socially constructed communities.[112] Hamas and, as explained next, the Fedayeen have exploited linguistic symbolism and hegemony as empowering acts of resistance.

Fedayeen

The term "Fedayeen" refers to "those who sacrifice," or, put simply, "redeemers."[113] **Fedayeen** (in the plural form) denote several different, primarily Arab groups throughout history. Fedayeen originally referred to violent Muslims from the eighth to the fourteenth centuries known as the Hashshashin (or Assassins). The Assassins were a religious cult of Ismaili Muslims with a radical agenda. They were also believed to be active as a mystic secret sect.[114] In the twentieth century, Fedayeen became associated with Palestinian terrorist groups based in Egypt, Lebanon, and Jordan—most of them made up of refugees of the 1948 Arab-Israeli War. In the 1960s, the terrorist faction of the PLO was identified as "Fedayeen" and was responsible for terrorist violence on Israeli territories. In Iran, the Fedayeen were Marxist-Islamist groups that were active between 1971 and 1983 and were based in Tehran. They committed many political assassinations in a conflict that climaxed in 1979 with the Iranian Revolution.[115]

In a similar vein, the **Fedayeen Saddam** was a terrorist organization led by the Ba'athist government of Saddam Hussein. The Fedayeen built a very strong resistance against the Iraq invasion of U.S. troops in 2003. They had a specialized unit in terrorist warfare. Saddam Hussein operated on the premise that the use of irregular warfare would make his government invincible.[116] The name "Fedayeen Saddam" was coined to create a connection with the Palestinian predecessors. Fedayeen Saddam's ideology is much more paramilitary and secular; nevertheless, their violence has ritual and religious-based characteristics that are evocative of Islamist symbolism. The clearest reference to ritual violence is that "Fedayeen Saddam" roughly means "Saddam's Men of Sacrifice," making allusions to the original religious sect of the eighth century mentioned earlier. The Fedayeen Saddam also included a terror unit called the "death squadron." In the death squadron, hooded Fedayeen employed torture and arbitrary executions.[117] To live up to their name-giving code, the "Men of Sacrifice" released several videotapes (later found in Iraq) to demonstrate their brutality. As such, in 2004, the U.S. Department of Defense released a videotape showing several different torture scenes discovered after the collapse of the Ba'athist government. The edited video included footage of the Fedayeen Saddam members and Republican Guard troops breaking arms and wrists with big sticks, throwing humans off a high building, chopping off fingers, slashing tongues, and performing ritualized mutilations, amputations, lashings, and beheadings.[118]

TERROR GLORIFICATION: SYMBOLIC PALESTINIAN TERRORISTS

Writing the name of a terrorist on permanent structures like school buildings, street signs, and sports stadiums has a lasting and bolstering impact. In Palestinian culture, the message supporting jihadism is permanent. In their work entitled *From Terrorists to Role Models: The Palestinian Authority's Institutionalization of Incitement*, Marcus, Zilberdik, and Crook (2010)[119] analyzed the concept of **terror glorification**, an institutionalized practice of incitement whereby terrorists are systematically turned into role models. In other words, it is a practice of honoring a terrorist (whether dead or alive) by attaching his or her name to permanent structures (e.g., buildings) or events like summer camps, sports competitions, educational curricula, and graduation ceremonies. As the three authors explain, terror glorification is highly visible in Palestinian society. Honoring terrorists helps terrorism experts understand the social norms of Palestinian society. For example, Yahya Ayyash Street is an important street in Ramallah, the administrative capital of the Palestinian Authority (PA). That street is passed by thousands of people every day. Because Yahya Ayyash was a topmost bomb maker of Hamas, attaching his name to the main street strengthens the message that the person behind Palestinian suicide terrorism—which killed over 1,000 Israeli civilians—is praiseworthy and honorable.

As the three authors also explain, on the way to school, a Palestinian pupil can read a street sign bearing the name of Abu Jihad, a terrorist who led a bus hijacking that killed thirty-seven innocent people in 1978—twelve of them children. That same child can spend the whole day at a school named after Ahmad Yassin (the Hamas founder), play sports in a tournament named after Abd Al-Basset Odeh (a suicide terrorist who slayed thirty people), and end his or her day at a recreation center named after Abu Iyad (whose real name was Salah Khalaf), the head of Black September, the terrorist group that killed eleven Israelis at the Munich Olympic Games in 1972 and two U.S. diplomats.[120] According to the Palestinian media, there are at least twenty schools and over twenty other permanent structures named after terrorists in the West Bank; even kindergartens are named after terrorists. Examples are Abu Ali Mustafa, who was general secretary of the Popular Front for the Liberation of Palestine (PLFP), a terrorist group that was particularly active from the 1960s to the 1990s (it committed numerous terrorist attacks against Israeli civilians during the First Intifada); and Saddam Hussein, the former president of Iraq, who was found guilty of crimes against humanity and put to death by a special Iraqi tribunal in late 2006.[121]

When a soccer team is named after someone like Abu Jihad, the aforementioned terrorist, that name infuses pride in the child who plays on that team. The terrorist's name becomes tantamount to honor and grandeur. Based on news in the Palestinian media, over fifty events have been assigned the names of terrorists in the PA. The PA's strategy of extolling the virtues of terrorists is an extremely dangerous form of brainwashing. Not only does it praise the terrorist, but also it makes the act of killing seem commonplace. When an imam on PA television asks viewers to kill Jews, the actual murder becomes a real possibility. Although nobody has yet been killed, honoring a terrorist does not allude to a possibility but glorifies an actual terrorist act.[122]

This terror glorification in the Palestinian territories is akin to the cultural worship of Osama bin Laden in several countries in the Middle East. Al Qaeda took advantage of the cultural worship of its former supreme leader, and it had the ideal impact on its followers. Polls reveal that defense and endorsement of Al Qaeda's actions have grown in inverse relation to support for the United States.[123] In the wake of September 11, 2001, Osama bin Laden became the focus of intense worship in multiple Middle Eastern countries. Afghan traders sold special candies with bin Laden's face on them. In the contemporary Muslim world, a very popular name for baby boys is Osama. Given these circumstances, it is not surprising that, in countries like Pakistan and Afghanistan, we see many posters and stickers worshipping bin Laden.[124] After 9/11, he was lionized as a hero. His look and face were drawn on T-shirts just like tattoos of rock stars appear on human bodies. Recordings of his triumphant words were duplicated and continuously played on videos and CDs.[125] In a number of countries today, support for bin Laden remains high; examples are 60 percent in Jordan and 51 percent in Pakistan.[126]

TERROR GLORIFICATION: SYMBOLIC TIMING

The timing of a terrorist attack can be carefully selected by a terrorist group to coincide with the group's particular ideological, cultural, religious, or sacred requirements or to desecrate an enemy's sacred moments (e.g., religious holidays or observances). Choosing a specific calendar day for a symbolically based terrorist attack usually requires painstaking planning and preparation. Nevertheless, when the attack succeeds, that symbolic date becomes worthy of terror glorification. Symbolic dates are important—even if the symbolism is, at first, only obvious to the group conducting the attack. For example, the symbolic timing of religious violence was unmistakable in the Algerian GIA's hijacking of an Air France passenger jet on Christmas Day (after two Catholic priests were killed), or the February 1996 suicide bombings by Hamas against Israel precisely on the second anniversary of the Hebron massacre.[127] Likewise, the rise of Al Ikhwan Muslim militancy goes back to a date in 1979 (exactly during the Islamic year 1400), when the return of the Mahdi (the divined redeemer of Islam) was expected at the Grand Mosque in Mecca. Strong supporters of this belief raided the Grand Mosque by force that year, which coincided with a period of pilgrimage and the peak of the tourist season.[128] For millenarianist religious groups, symbolic timing is manifested through an apocalyptic date upon which something important is anticipated to happen. For example, UFO cults like Heaven's Gate become even more dangerous when the event fails to happen.[129]

Institutional Memory

Every group has an institutional memory. An **institutional memory** is akin to a collective memory, a collective set of facts or experiences held by a group of people. It is the idea that we are a "memory-carrying people."[130] Remembering is a social phenomenon in that human beings share with others their memories of important events and sacred people in their lives. As it rises above the individual, the institutional memory functions through the ongoing transmission of these memories between members of specific groups. Elements of institutional memory are particularly strong within ethnic groups, religious cults, terrorist groups, and sometimes entire cultures.[131] As a consequence, this memory does not get lost—although it may get warped somewhat. Institutional memory can last very long, as the following examples will point out, and it is not unusual for a group to construct rituals designed to "never forget" some grievances that happened decades ago.[132]

Symbolic Timing for the Madrid Train Bombings

March 11, 2004, is an example of symbolic timing for the Al Qaeda–inspired group that perpetrated the attacks on four trains in Madrid. To begin, exactly 911 days occurred between September 11, 2001, and March 11, 2004. The fact that the suicide terrorists who smashed their planes into the Twin Towers and the Pentagon also chose four targets represents another calculated correlation with the attacks on the four trains in Madrid.[133] Portraying Spain as a member of the "Crusader Alliance" led by the United States, the Al Qaeda–inspired Moroccan perpetrators knew exactly that the bomb blast occurred three days before the national elections in Spain. The terrorist attack completely dwarfed all other concerns in the election for the three following days. The March 11, 2004, tragedy, which the Spanish population interpreted as punishment for their country's support of the War in Iraq, indisputably affected the outcome of the election.[134] Indeed, José María Aznar, Spain's prime minister at that time, was still leading in the polls (by a wide margin) right before the Madrid train bombings occurred. However, after that fateful day, voters elected the opposition Socialists, led by José Luis Rodríguez Zapatero.[135]

Symbolic Timing for Al Qaeda's Beheading Rituals

The purposes of ritual are plentiful. A particularly important purpose of ritual, especially in traditions of holy war, is initiation, like a rite of passage that signals entrance or acceptance into a group or culture. For example, in Islamist culture (as in some African cultures), the male initiation ritual is a rite of passage to turn boys into robust, fierce warriors. Typically, the boy reaches "adulthood" at about 12–13 years old. Analysis of the timing of Al Qaeda's beheadings reveals that they escalate and come together at certain times. The most common symbolic timing of Al Qaeda's beheadings is usually reflected as a response to key attacks by U.S. forces and political events such as the interim Iraqi government being transferred to people hostile to Al Qaeda. However, another interpretation of the symbolic timing of the beheadings is that they symbolize initiation within the Al Qaeda organization itself. Initiation rituals and rites of "fortitude" in warrior cultures tend to be violent and involve blood. Killing an infidel is a customary method of initiation. Decapitating a person or witnessing the violence without budging is the outcome of a long-term process of discipline. Drawing a parallel, at a lower level, it is akin to a method of allegiance pledged to a fraternal organization.[136]

Symbolic Timing for Chechen Terrorism

In 2005, all three Chechen suicide attacks took place inside Chechnya. In one of these suicide bombings, three female suicide terrorists blew themselves up on May 9 (one woman in Grozny and two in Assinovskaya). The females had prepared to conduct their mission on that date because it was Victory Day, a very symbolic day upon which Russia and former Soviet states display their military might in flashy parades. Undoubtedly, coordinated suicide bombings on Victory Day tarnished this display of military pride. On the same day (May 9) a year before, in 2004, Ramzan Kadyrov, the pro-Russian Chechen president, was killed (along with his team) when the stand upon which he was watching the Russian military parade exploded under his feet. This was also a powerful message sent by the terrorists about their capacity to target Russian forces. [137] On a similar note, the infamous Moscow theater hostage crisis occurred on October 23–26, 2002. In the hostage-taking incident, at least forty Chechen terrorists were killed after holding more than 800 Russians hostage. The incident happened exactly four years after Russians targeted important Chechens in Grozny (Chechnya's capital). For example, on October 25, 1998, Chechen General Shaid Bargisev was killed in a car explosion. A day later, Akhmad Kadyrov, a key Muslim cleric in Chechnya, almost died in the midst of an attack against him. [138]

Celebrity Terrorism

In this context of symbolic timing in terrorism, **celebrity terrorism** refers to the act of committing such a devastating terrorist attack that the target audience and government will commemorate or observe the day upon which the attack was perpetrated. Naturally, to the perpetrators themselves (and those sympathizing with them), that specific day is more a glorification (i.e., celebration) than just a commemoration. [139] On November 5, 1605, aspiring terrorist **Guy Fawkes** and his conspirators attempted the Gunpowder Plot: a terrorist attack against the Protestant Parliament in England with a planned assassination of the Protestant King James. [140] Ever since the failed terrorist coup, "Bonfire Nights" have been held across the world to celebrate November 5. In fact, the film *V for Vendetta* (2005) glorifies Guy Fawkes's attack. In the minds of people, November 5 should never be—and will never be—neglected.

The way in which terrorism is remembered by audiences across the world is significant to people who want to understand the motivations, goals, and targets of terrorists. [141] Needless to say, the fifth of November is not the only date that observes an infamous terrorist or terrorist attack. Symbolic date coordinates like "9/11" (the live broadcast of the attacks on New York and Washington, DC, on September 11, 2001), "3/11" (the March 11, 2004, Madrid train bombings), and "7/7" (the July 7, 2005, bombings on London subway trains and a double-decker bus) saturate ordinary culture and guarantee that the terrorist tragedies on all those dates are to be long remembered. In the wake of "26/11" (the November 2008 terror attacks in Mumbai), critics already insinuated that terrorism has much in common with celebrity cultures. [142]

Sunday Bloody Sunday

On January 30, 1972, the **Bloody Sunday** tragedy occurred in Derry, Northern Ireland, in which thirteen Catholic civilians were killed by British paratroopers. It has brought to mind two challenging memories among the Nationalist community: an official memory and a folk memory that has been underrepresented by dominant media discourses. The official memory of Bloody Sunday is expressed in the report of the Widgery Tribunal instituted by the British government in the wake of the tragedy. A second popular memory has arisen in resistance to the official one: the folk memory encodes the remembrances of the dead's families and the Northern Irish Nationalist community at large. [143] As one would expect, the song "Sunday Bloody Sunday" by Irish rock band U2 commemorates the 1972 tragedy of Bloody Sunday. Not only has the song remained a staple of U2's live concerts, but also it has been considered among the best political protest songs of all time. As a result, many youths have had an easy time remembering the real calendar event in Derry.

SEPTEMBER 11, 1565, SEPTEMBER 11, 1683, AND SEPTEMBER 11, 1697

The event that we refer to as "September 11" or "9/11" has a past that has to be rediscovered. **September 11, 1565**, was the day upon which the Ottoman Empire lost a major battle against a coalition of Western Christian combatants in Malta (a European island in the Mediterranean Sea). September 11, 1565, marked the end of the **Great Siege of Malta**.[144] The **Ottoman Empire** was a Muslim empire that occupied much of Southeastern Europe, Western Asia, the Caucasus, North Africa, and the Horn of Africa. The empire lasted from the thirteenth to the early twentieth centuries. During the Great Siege of Malta, the Christian coalition consisted of approximately 8,000 men: the Order of Saint John, Maltese civilians, and soldiers from the Kingdoms of Spain and Sicily. On the other hand, about 40,000 Muslim fighters were led by various Ottoman admirals and commanders. The battle began in May 1565 and, after almost four months of gruesome combat, the Muslim occupiers were forced to leave the island on September 11, 1565.[145] Humiliated by this event, the Ottoman Empire vowed to retaliate against the "Crusaders," a concept that was used by Osama bin Laden more than four centuries later. Indeed, on February 23, 1998, bin Laden issued a fatwa against the West entitled "Jihad against Jews and Crusaders."[146]

September 11, 1683, was the day upon which the **Battle of Vienna** took place after the Austrian capital had been invaded by the Ottoman Empire for two months. The large-scale battle was fought between the Ottoman Empire (mostly Turkish and Muslim groups) and the Holy Roman Empire (commanded by King of Poland John III Sobieski), in alliance with the Holy League (Polish, Austrian, and German forces). The Ottoman Empire lost the battle and had to retreat on September 12, 1683. The failed Ottoman siege of Vienna in 1683 turned back the invasion of Islam in the West.[147] In fact, the battle was a turning point for the Western world; it signaled the historic end of the advance of the Ottoman Empire into Europe and, by the same token, the end of the Second Jihad (which started in 1071 in Turkey).[148] Lastly, **September 11, 1697**, was the day upon which the Ottoman Empire was defeated by the Holy League at the **Battle of Zenta** (a town located in Serbia today). About 100,000 Muslims were defeated by 50,000 Christian fighters.[149]

According to experts on Islamic terrorism and jihad, such as Simpson (2006)[150] and Spencer (2006),[151] the date of September 11, 2001, chosen by Al Qaeda was no coincidence. For example, historically, no world-changing confrontations between Islam and the West occurred on close dates such as September 10 and September 12. Based on solid evidence from both Western and Arabic/Muslim publications and documents, these two dates do not bring up any institutional memory or other type of anniversary in the Muslim world in general. However, 9/11 was revenge for the Muslims' defeat on September 11, 1683. It heralded the beginning of a very old struggle against non-Muslim infidels. Put simply, the three major events of September 11, 1565, September 11, 1683, and September 11, 1697, are deeply connected to September 11, 2001. The lost battles that Muslims suffered against the West are a major reason (among others) why tensions between Islam and the West have increased.

From a symbolic perspective, siege and battle remembrances can be examined along the lines of binary oppositions: inside/outside, defenders/attackers, good/evil, weak/powerful, or religion/irreligion.[152] September 11, 2001, was a call sign, a symbol crying out for the collapse of the United States and a "born-again" Ottoman Empire (i.e., an attempt to revive the Islamic caliphate). As expressed by Osama bin Laden himself, it was "a very good sign and a great step towards the unity of Muslims and establishing the Righteous Islamic Caliphate."[153] On the same subject, does the killing of U.S. diplomat Christopher Stevens and his team at the U.S. consulate in Benghazi, Libya (on September 11, 2012), represent another terrorist action based on symbolic timing? According to *Foreign Policy*, a global magazine of economics, politics, and ideas, the answer is "yes": the killing of the U.S. mission in Benghazi by Al Qaeda on the 9/11 anniversary was symbolic.[154]

APRIL 19, 1993

The April 19, 1995, bombing of the Alfred P. Murrah Federal Building in Oklahoma City by **Timothy McVeigh** (the convicted perpetrator) was timed, according to the terrorist himself, to commemorate the second anniversary of the FBI's attack on the Branch Davidian compound in Waco, Texas, that occurred two years earlier, on April 19, 1993 (after a fifty-day siege). Terry Nichols, McVeigh's accomplice, also made references to the FBI's actions against the Branch Davidian compound in the Waco siege (which ended with the deaths of David Koresh, the leader, and seventy-five others) as justification for committing the Oklahoma City bombing.[155] The stand-off between the Branch Davidians (a religious cult) and the FBI was fueled by the killing of agents from the Bureau of Alcohol, Tobacco, Firearms, and Explosives (ATF). These agents were in the process of executing a search warrant. On top of allegations of sexual abuse and misconduct, David Koresh and his followers were accused of amassing illegal arms like M-16 rifles, grenades, and gun powder.[156] For McVeigh, an important criterion for terrorist attack sites was that the target—which eventually became the Alfred P. Murrah Federal Building—had to contain at least two of three federal law enforcement agencies involved in the Waco siege: the aforementioned ATF, the FBI, and/or the Drug Enforcement Administration (DEA). He regarded the presence of ten other U.S. law enforcement agencies—such as the U.S. Army, the Marine Corps, the Secret Service, and the U.S. Marshals Service—as a huge plus.[157]

There is no doubt that the symbolic bombing of the federal building in Oklahoma City was retaliation against the U.S. federal government on April 19, 1995, exactly two years later. In fact, in March 1993, a month before the end of the Waco siege, Timothy McVeigh actually visited the Waco site. He went to the site again after the Branch Davidians perished. McVeigh convinced himself that a federal building should be bombed as a response to the siege.[158] What has been underemphasized in the media, however, is the fact that McVeigh also chose April 19 as a symbolic date for another reason: the Battles of Lexington and Concord (the first military engagements of the American Revolutionary War) took place on that date 220 years before, on April 19, 1775.[159] The two battles were generally celebrated as the "shot heard round the world." McVeigh thought that destroying a U.S. federal building would be another "shot heard around the world."[160] What the Oklahoma City bombing exemplifies is that McVeigh was an unusually dangerous type of domestic terrorist: a terrorist bent on using symbolism but with only very broad, indefinite goals in mind.

SUMMARY

The word "terrorism" was used for the first time during the French Revolution's Reign of Terror. Ever since then, over 200 definitions of terrorism have appeared in academic works and official documents. Unfortunately, there is no common definition of "terrorism" on which all nations agree. As such, what we have at best is a "most universally accepted" definition: terrorism is the use of violence to create fear (i.e., terror and psychic fear) for (1) political, (2) religious, or (3) ideological reasons. Among the many forms of symbolic terrorism, a particular one is performative violence: a type of meaningful interaction with the audience (both the immediate victims and the public at large). There are three important effects that terrorism as performative violence has through a meticulous use of symbolism: (1) the agitation effect, (2) the provocation effect, and (3) the demonstration effect. Likewise, a transnational injustice symbol is an event or situation exploited by politicians or terrorist leaders as an excuse to avenge perceived injustices before geographically, socially, and culturally scattered audiences. As we have seen, the idea of a transnational community is evident in the concept of ummah (i.e., the global Muslim community) and the "Guantánamo Bay" attack on the ummah. In a similar fashion, as a specific form of symbolic terrorism, linguistic terrorism can fulfill important propaganda purposes in conflict, such as the use of the Irish and Arabic languages. And the way that religious terrorist groups interpret the threat of secularization (both within their own society and in the world at large) can be seen through the name-giving codes they assign to their own groups. Examples are Hamas and the Fedayeen Saddam. Symbolic terrorism is also reflected through terror glorification, as in the symbolization of Palestinian terrorism, by attaching names of killers to permanent structures and events. Another way to express terror glorification is through symbolic timing. As such, the timing of a terrorist attack can be carefully selected by a terrorist group to coincide with the group's particular ideological, cultural, or religious requirements or to desecrate an enemy's sacred moments (e.g., religious holidays). Lastly, two of the worst days in U.S. history—April 19, 1995 (the Oklahoma City bombing), and September 11, 2001—are actually symbolic dates that were tactfully chosen by terrorists as a response to huge losses that happened years or centuries ago on exactly the same calendar dates (respectively, April 19, 1993, and September 11, 1565, 1683, and 1697).

NOTES

1. Burgess, Mark (2003). *A Brief History of Terrorism*. Washington, DC: Center for Defense Information (CDI); and Tuman, Joseph (2009). *Communicating Terror: The Rhetorical Dimensions of Terrorism* (2nd ed.). Thousand Oaks, CA: Sage.

2. Shane, Scott (2010, April 3). Words as Weapons: Dropping the "Terrorism" Bomb. *New York Times*, p. WK1; and Tuman, Joseph (2003). *Communicating Terror: The Rhetorical Dimensions of Terrorism*. Thousand Oaks, CA: Sage.

3. Simon, Jeffrey (1994). *The Terrorist Trap*. Bloomington: Indiana University Press.

4. Andress, David (2006). *The Terror: The Merciless War for Freedom in Revolutionary France*. New York: Farrar, Straus and Giroux.

5. Mahan, Sue, & Griset, Pamela (2012). *Terrorism in Perspective* (3rd ed.). Thousand Oaks, CA: Sage.

6. Mayer, Arno (2000). *The Furies: Violence and Terror in French and Russian Revolutions*. Princeton, NJ: Princeton University Press.

7. International Bar Association (2003). *International Terrorism: Legal Challenges and Responses*. Ardsley, NY: Transnational; and Moeller, Susan (2002). A Hierarchy of Innocence: The Media's Use of Children in the Telling of International News. *The International Journal of Press/Politics, 7*(1), 36–56.

8. Khalil Shikaki (2001, December 21). Palestinian Survey Research. Retrieved June 17, 2014, from http://www.pcpsr.org.survey/polls/2001/p3a.html

9. U.S. Joint Chiefs of Staff (2004). *Department of Defense Dictionary of Military Terms*. Washington, DC: U.S. Joint Chiefs of Staff.

10. Federal Bureau of Investigation (2013). *What We Investigate*. Washington, DC: Federal Bureau of Investigation.

11. United Nations General Assembly (1995). *Resolution 49/60: Measures to Eliminate International Terrorism*. Retrieved March 20, 2013, from http://www.un.org/Depts/dhl/res/resa49.htm

12. Arab Convention for the Suppression of Terrorism (1998). *Arab Convention on Terrorism*. Cairo: Council of Arab Ministers of the Interior and the Council of Arab Ministers of Justice.

13. Laqueur, Walter (1987). *The Age of Terrorism* (2nd ed.). Boston: Little, Brown, p. 143.

14. Rapoport, David (1977, November 26). The Government Is Up in the Air over Combating Terrorism. *National Journal, 9*, 1853–1856.

15. Hoffman, Bruce (2006). *Inside Terrorism* (2nd ed.). New York: Columbia University Press, p. 43.

16. Chomsky, Noam (2001). *9-11*. New York: Seven Stories Press.

17. Laqueur, Walter (1987). *The Age of Terrorism* (2nd ed.). Boston: Little, Brown.

18. Rigstad, Mark (2008). The Senses of Terrorism. *Review Journal of Political Philosophy, 6*(1), 10–21.

19. Schmid, Alex (1984). *Political Terrorism: A Research Guide to Concepts, Theories, Data Bases and Literature*. Amsterdam: North-Holland.

20. Makarychev, Andrey (2006). The Grammar of Terrorism: Rethinking the Concept of Assymetric Threats. In Robert Orttung & Andrey Makarychev (Eds.), *National Counter-Terrorism Strategies: Legal, Institutional, and Public Policy Dimensions in the US, UK, France, Turkey and Russia* (pp. 58–68). Lansdale, PA: IOS Press.

21. Rigstad, Mark (2008). The Senses of Terrorism. *Review Journal of Political Philosophy, 6*(1), 10–21.

22. Cassirer, Ernst (1944). *An Essay on Man*. New Haven, CT: Yale University Press.

23. Bourdieu, Pierre (1977). *Outline of a Theory of Practice*. London: Cambridge University Press; Bourdieu, Pierre (1989). Social Space and Symbolic Power. *Sociological Theory, 7*(1), 14–25; and Bourdieu, Pierre (1991). *Language and Symbolic Power*. Cambridge: Polity Press.

24. Stump, Jacob, & Dixit, Priya (2012). Toward a Completely Constructivist Critical Terrorism Studies. *International Relations, 26*(2), 199–217.

25. Dixit, Priya, & Stump, Jacob (2011). A Response to Jones and Smith: It's Not as Bad as It Seems; Or, Five Ways to Move Critical Terrorism Studies Forward. *Studies in Conflict & Terrorism, 34*(6), 501–511.

26. O'Hair, Dan, Heath, Robert, Ayotte, Kevin, & Ledlow, Gerald (2008). *Terrorism: Communication and Rhetorical Perspectives*. Cresskill, NJ: Hampton Press.

27. Karber, Philip (1971). Urban Terrorism: Baseline Data and a Conceptual Framework. *Social Science Quarterly, 52*, 527–533, p. 529.

28. Antonello, Pierpaolo, & O'Leary, Alan (2009). Introduction. In Pierpaolo Antonello & Alan O'Leary (Eds.), *Imagining Terrorism: The Rhetoric and Representation of Political Violence in Italy 1969–2009* (pp. 1–15). London: Legenda.

29. Tuman, Joseph (2009). *Communicating Terror: The Rhetorical Dimensions of Terrorism* (2nd ed.). Thousand Oaks, CA: Sage.

30. Neumann, Peter, & Smith, M. L. R. (2005). Strategic Terrorism: The Framework and Its Fallacies. *Journal of Strategic Studies, 28*(4), 571–595, p. 574.

31. McCormick, Gordon (2003). Terrorist Decision Making. *Annual Review of Political Science, 6*, 473–507.

32. Halfmann, Jost (2003). *Fundamentalist Terrorism: The Assault on the Symbols of Secular Power*. Berkeley: Institute of European Studies, University of California Berkeley.

33. O'Shaughnessy, Nicholas, & Baines, Paul (2009). Selling Terror: The Symbolization and Positioning of Jihad. *Marketing Theory, 9*(2), 227–241.

34. Juergensmeyer, Mark (2000). *Terror in the Mind of God: The Global Rise of Religious Violence*. Berkeley: University of California Press.

35. Juris, Jeffrey (2005). Violence Performed and Imagined: Militant Action, the Black Bloc and the Mass Media in Genoa. *Critique of Anthropology, 25*(4) 413–432.

36. Blok, Anton (2000). The Enigma of Senseless Violence. In Goran Aijmer & Jon Abbink (Eds.), *Meanings of Violence* (pp. 23–38). Oxford: Berg.

37. Juergensmeyer, Mark (2000). *Terror in the Mind of God: The Global Rise of Religious Violence*. Berkeley: University of California Press.

38. MacDonald, Andrew (1980). *The Turner Diaries*. Washington, DC: National Alliance.

39. McCormick, Gordon, & Giordano, Frank (2007). Things Come Together: Symbolic Violence and Guerrilla Mobilization. *Third World Quarterly, 28*(2), 295–320.

40. Paletz, David, & Schmid, Alex (1992). *Terrorism and the Media*. London: Sage.

41. Hoffman, Bruce, & McCormick, Gordon (2004). Terrorism, Signaling, and Suicide Attack. *Studies in Conflict and Terrorism, 27*(4), 243–281.

42. Landauer, Gustav (2005). *Anarchism in Germany*. Montreal: Black Rose.

43. Carlson, Joseph (1995). The Future Terrorists in America. *American Journal of Police, 14*(3), 71–91.

44. Simonson, Peter (2001). Social Noise and Segmented Rhythms: News, Entertainment, and Celebrity in the Crusade for Animal Rights. *Communication Review, 4*(3), 399–420.

45. McCormick, Gordon, & Giordano, Frank (2007). Things Come Together: Symbolic Violence and Guerrilla Mobilization. *Third World Quarterly, 28*(2), 295–320.

46. McCormick, Gordon, & Giordano, Frank (2007). Things Come Together: Symbolic Violence and Guerrilla Mobilization. *Third World Quarterly, 28*(2), 295–320.

47. Tarrow, Sidney (1988). National Politics and Collective Action: Recent Theory and Research in Western Europe and the United States. *Annual Review of Sociology, 14*, 421–440.

48. Clapham, Christopher (1998). Introduction: Analysing African Insurgencies. In Christopher Clapham (Ed.), *African Guerrillas* (pp. 1–18). Oxford: James Currey.

49. Gerbner, George (1991). Symbolic Functions of Violence and Terror. In Yonah Alexander & Robert Picard (Eds.), *In the Camera's Eye: News Coverage of Terrorist Events* (pp. 3–9). Washington, DC: Brassey's.

50. McCormick, Gordon, & Giordano, Frank (2007). Things Come Together: Symbolic Violence and Guerrilla Mobilization. *Third World Quarterly, 28*(2), 295–320.

51. Pape, Robert (2003). The Strategic Logic of Suicide Terrorism. *American Political Science Review, 97*(3), 343–361.

52. Paletz, David, & Schmid, Alex (1992). *Terrorism and the Media*. London: Sage.

53. Paletz, David, Ayanian, John, & Fozzard, Peter (1982). Terrorism on Television News: The IRA, the FALN, and the Red Brigades. In William Adams (Ed.), *Television Coverage of International Affairs* (pp. 143–165). Norwood, NJ: Ablex.

54. Schmid, Alex, & De Graaf, Janny (1982). *Violence as Communication: Insurgent Terrorism and the Western News Media*. Beverly Hills, CA: Sage.

55. Altheide, David (1987). Format and Symbols in TV Coverage of Terrorism in the United States and Great Britain. *International Studies Quarterly, 31*(2), 161–176; and Edelman, Murray (1971). *Politics as Symbolic Action: Mass Arousal and Quiescence*. Chicago: Markham.

56. Olesen, Thomas (2001). Transnational Injustice Symbols and Communities: The Case of Al-Qaeda and the Guantanamo Bay Detention Camp. *Current Sociology, 59*(6), 717–734.

57. Olesen, Thomas (2001). Transnational Injustice Symbols and Communities: The Case of Al-Qaeda and the Guantanamo Bay Detention Camp. *Current Sociology, 59*(6), 717–734.

58. Alexander, Jeffrey (2004). From the Depths of Despair: Performance, Counterperformance, and "September 11." *Sociological Theory, 22*(1), 88–105.

59. Jasper, James (1997). *The Art of Moral Protest: Culture, Biography, and Creativity in Social Movements*. Chicago: University of Chicago Press.

60. Carr, Adrian (2006). What It Means to Be "Critical" in Relation to International Business: A Case of the Appropriate Conceptual Lens. *Critical Perspectives on International Business, 2*(2), 79–90.

61. Collins, Kathleen (2007). Ideas, Networks, and Islamist Movements Evidence from Central Asia and the Caucasus. *World Politics, 60*, 64–96.

62. Waters, Malcolm (2001). *Globalization*. London: Routledge.

63. Olesen, Thomas (2001). Transnational Injustice Symbols and Communities: The Case of Al-Qaeda and the Guantanamo Bay Detention Camp. *Current Sociology, 59*(6), 717–734.

64. Gamson, William, Fireman, Bruce, & Rytina, Steve (1982). *Encounters with Unjust Authority*. Chicago: Dorsey Press.

65. Alexander, Jeffrey (2004). From the Depths of Despair: Performance, Counterperformance, and "September 11." *Sociological Theory, 22*(1), 88–105.

66. Jasper, James (1997). *The Art of Moral Protest: Culture, Biography, and Creativity in Social Movements*. Chicago: University of Chicago Press.

67. Armstrong, Karen (2001). *Islam: A Short History*. London: Phoenix.

68. Tuman, Joseph (2009). *Communicating Terror: The Rhetorical Dimensions of Terrorism* (2nd ed.). Thousand Oaks, CA: Sage.

69. Ahmed, Akbar (1999). *Islam Today*. London: I. B. Taurus.

70. Lewis, Bernard (2002). *Islam in History*. Chicago: Open Court.

71. Pratt, Douglas (2005). *The Challenge of Islam*. Aldershot, UK: Ashgate.

72. Dingley, James (2011). Terrorism, Religion and Community. *Defense & Security Analysis, 27*(4), 325–340.

73. Roy, Olivier (2004). *Globalised Islam: The Search for a New Ummah*. London: Hurst and Company.

74. Mandaville, Peter (2003). *Transnational Muslim Politics: Reimagining the Umma*. New York: Routledge.

75. Olesen, Thomas (2001). Transnational Injustice Symbols and Communities: The Case of Al-Qaeda and the Guantanamo Bay Detention Camp. *Current Sociology, 59*(6), 717–734.

76. Olesen, Thomas (2001). Transnational Injustice Symbols and Communities: The Case of Al-Qaeda and the Guantanamo Bay Detention Camp. *Current Sociology, 59*(6), 717–734.

77. Khosrokhavar, Farhad (2005). *Suicide Bombers: Allah's New Martyrs*. London: Pluto Press.

78. Olesen, Thomas (2001). Transnational Injustice Symbols and Communities: The Case of Al-Qaeda and the Guantanamo Bay Detention Camp. *Current Sociology, 59*(6), 717–734.

79. Kirk, Mary (2009). Language as Social Institution: The Male-Centered IT Culture. In Mary Kirk (Ed.), *Gender and Information Technology: Moving beyond Access to Co-Create Global Partnership* (pp. 119–142). Hershey, PA: IGI Global.

80. Radnitz, Scott (2006). Look Who's Talking! Islamic Discourse in the Chechen Wars. *Nationalities Papers: The Journal of Nationalism and Ethnicity, 34*(2), 237–256.

81. Boal, Frederick, & Livingstone, David (1984). The Frontier in the City: Ethnonationalism in Belfast. *International Journal of Political Science Review, 5*(2), 161–179.

82. Geertz, Clifford (1973). Ideology as a Cultural System. In Clifford Geertz (Ed.), *The Interpretation of Cultures: Selected Essays* (pp. 193–233). New York: Basic Books.

83. O'Reilly, Camille (1999). *The Irish Language in Northern Ireland: The Politics of Culture and Identity*. New York: Palgrave Macmillan.

84. Cormack, Mike (2000). Minority Languages, Nationalism and Broadcasting: The British and Irish Examples. *Nations and Nationalism, 6*(3), 383–398.

85. O'Brien, Brendan (1999). *The Long War: The IRA and Sinn Féin*. Syracuse, NY: Syracuse University Press; and O'Brien, Eugene (1999). The Epistemology of Nationalism. *Irish Studies Review, 5*(17), 15–20.

86. Rolston, Bill (1991). *Politics and Painting: Murals and Conflict in Northern Ireland*. Cranbury, NJ: Associated University Presses.

87. Esposito, John (2002). *Unholy War: Terror in the Name of Islam*. New York: Oxford University Press; and Firestone, Reuven (1999). *Jihad: The Origin of Holy War in Islam*. New York: Oxford University Press.

88. *Al Qaeda Training Manual* (2001). Retrieved March 22, 2013, from http://www.usdoj.gov/ag/manual-part11.pdf

89. Sattar, Noman (1995). Affairs "Al Ikhwan Al Muslimin" (Society of Muslim Brotherhood) Aims and Ideology, Role and Impact. *Pakistan Horizon, 48*(2), 7–30.

90. Chubin, Shahram, & Tripp, Charles (1988). *Iran and Iraq at War*. Boulder, CO: Westview Press.

91. Lewis, Bernard (1993). *Islam and the West*. New York: Oxford University Press.

92. Ayubi, Nazih (1991). *Political Islam: Religion and Politics in the Arab World*. New York: Routledge.

93. Radnitz, Scott (2006). Look Who's Talking! Islamic Discourse in the Chechen Wars. *Nationalities Papers: The Journal of Nationalism and Ethnicity, 34*(2), 237–256.

94. Leavitt, John (2011), *Linguistic Relativities: Language Diversity and Modern Thought*. Cambridge: Cambridge University Press.

95. Sapir, Edward, & Swadesh, Morris (1946). American Indian Grammatical Categories. *Word, 2*, 103–112.

96. Sandstrom, Kent, Martin, Daniel, & Fine, Gary Alan (2010). *Symbols, Selves, and Social Reality: A Symbolic Interactionist Approach to Social Psychology and Sociology*. Oxford: Oxford University Press.

97. Ranstorp, Magnus (1996). Terrorism in the Name of Religion. *Journal of International Affairs, 50*(1), 41–63; Tsfati, Yariv, & Weimann, Gabriel (2002). www.terrorism.com: Terror on the Internet. *Studies in Conflict & Terrorism, 25*(5), 317–332; and Turk, Austin (2004). Sociology of Terrorism. *Annual Review of Sociology, 30*, 271–286.

98. Ranstorp, Magnus (1996). Terrorism in the Name of Religion. *Journal of International Affairs, 50*(1), 41–63.

99. Lifton, Robert Jay (2000). *Destroying the World to Save It: Aum Shinrikyo, Apocalyptic Violence, and the New Global Terrorism*. New York: Picador.

100. Sandstrom, Kent, Martin, Daniel, & Fine, Gary Alan (2010). *Symbols, Selves, and Social Reality: A Symbolic Interactionist Approach to Social Psychology and Sociology*. Oxford: Oxford University Press.

101. Stump, Roger (2005). Religion and the Geographies of War. In Colin Flint (Ed.), *The Geography of War and Peace: From Death Camps to Diplomats* (pp. 149–173). Oxford: Oxford University Press.

102. Sandstrom, Kent, Martin, Daniel, & Fine, Gary Alan (2010). *Symbols, Selves, and Social Reality: A Symbolic Interactionist Approach to Social Psychology and Sociology*. Oxford: Oxford University Press.

103. Hroub, Khaled (2000). *Hamas: Political Thought and Practice*. Washington, DC: Institute for Palestinian Studies.

104. Caplan, Neil (2009). *Israel-Palestine Conflict: Contested Histories*. London: Wiley-Blackwell.

105. Mishal, Shaul, & Sela, Avraham (2000). *The Palestinian Hamas: Vision, Violence, and Coexistence*. New York: Columbia University Press.

106. Yousef, Mosab Hassan (2009). *Son of Hamas*. Carol Stream, IL: Tyndale House.

107. Stout, Mark E. (2009). Transnational Movements and Terrorism. *Global Strategic Assessment, 6*, 119–144.

108. Cohen, Saul, & Kliot, Nurit (1992). Place-Names in Israel's Ideological Struggle over the Administered Territories. *Annals of the Association of American Geographers, 82*, 653–680.

109. Grimaud, Michel (1977). Hermeneutics, Onomastics and Poetics in English and French Literature. *MLN, 92*(5), 888–921.

110. Gramsci, Antonio (1992). *Prison Notebooks*. New York: Columbia University Press.

111. Azaryahu, Maoz (1996). The Power of Commemorative Street Names. *Environment and Planning D: Society and Space, 14*, 311–330.

112. Anderson, Benedict (1983). *Imagined Communities: Reflections on the Origin and Spread of Nationalism*. London: Verso.

113. Rea, Tony, & Wright, John (1993). *The Arab-Israeli Conflict*. Oxford: Oxford University Press.

114. Gartenstein-Ross, Daveed (2005, January 31). Christians on Pal Talk Chat Service Tracked by Radical Islamic Web Site. *New York Sun*.

115. Perlmutter, Dawn (2005). Mujahideen Blood Rituals: The Religious and Forensic Symbolism of Al Qaeda Beheading. *Anthropoetics, 11*(2), 10–21.

116. Renard, Thomas, & Taillat, Stéphane (2008). Between Clausewitz and Mao: Dynamic Evolutions of the Insurgency and Counterinsurgency in Iraq (2003–2008). *Small Wars Journal, 4*, 1–10.

117. Perlmutter, Dawn (2005). Mujahideen Blood Rituals: The Religious and Forensic Symbolism of Al Qaeda Beheading. *Anthropoetics, 11*(2), 10–21.

118. U.S. Department of State (2002). *Report on Iraq: A Population Silenced*. Washington, DC: U.S. Department of State. Retrieved March 22, 2013, from http://www.state.gov/g/drl/rls/15996.htm

119. Marcus, Itamar, Zilberdik, Nan Jacques, & Crook, Barbara (2010). *From Terrorists to Role Models: The Palestinian Authority's Institutionalization of Incitement*. Jerusalem: Palestinian Media Watch.

120. Marcus, Itamar, Zilberdik, Nan Jacques, & Crook, Barbara (2010). *From Terrorists to Role Models: The Palestinian Authority's Institutionalization of Incitement*. Jerusalem: Palestinian Media Watch.

121. Marcus, Itamar, Zilberdik, Nan Jacques, & Crook, Barbara (2010). *From Terrorists to Role Models: The Palestinian Authority's Institutionalization of Incitement*. Jerusalem: Palestinian Media Watch.

122. Marcus, Itamar, Zilberdik, Nan Jacques, & Crook, Barbara (2010). *From Terrorists to Role Models: The Palestinian Authority's Institutionalization of Incitement*. Jerusalem: Palestinian Media Watch.

123. Bergner, Daniel (2003, July 20). Where the Enemy Is Everywhere and Nowhere. *New York Times Magazine*, 14–15; and Kitfield, James (2002, November 23). Breaking Al Qaeda Means Getting Bin Laden. *National Journal*, p. 3496.

124. Abrahms, Max (2005). Al Qaeda's Miscommunication War: The Terrorism Paradox. *Terrorism and Political Violence, 17*, 529–549.

125. Alexander, Jeffrey (2004). From the Depths of Despair: Performance, Counterperformance, and "September 11." *Sociological Theory, 22*(1), 88–105.

126. Bernstein, R. (2005, July 15). Muslim Approval of Terror Drops, Poll Finds. *New York Times*, p. A8.

127. Ranstorp, Magnus (1996). Terrorism in the Name of Religion. *Journal of International Affairs, 50*(1), 41–63.

128. Dekmejian, Hrair (1995). *Islam in Revolution: Fundamentalism in the Arab World*. Syracuse, NY: Syracuse University Press.

129. O'Connor, Thomas (2008). The Criminology of Terrorism: Theories and Models. In Kevin Borgeson & Robin Valeri (Eds.), *Terrorism in America* (pp. 17–35). Burlington, MA: Jones & Bartlett.

130. Falconer, Alan, & Liechty, Joseph (1998). *Reconciling Memories*. Dublin, Ireland: Columba, p. 104.

131. Greaves, Ian (2001). Terrorism: New Threats, New Challenges? *Journal of the Royal Army Medical Corps, 147*, 142–146.

132. O'Connor, Thomas (2008). The Criminology of Terrorism: Theories and Models. In Kevin Borgeson & Robin Valeri (Eds.), *Terrorism in America* (pp. 17–35). Burlington, MA: Jones & Bartlett.

133. Alonso, Rogelio, & Reinares, Fernando (2006). Maghreb Immigrants Becoming Suicide Terrorists: A Case Study on Religious Radicalization Processes in Spain. In Ami Pedahzur (Ed.), *Root Causes of Suicide Terrorism: The Globalization of Martyrdom* (pp. 179–197). New York: Routledge; American Free Press (2004). *Terror: 911 Days after 9/11*. American Free Press. Retrieved March 23, 2013, from http://www.infowars.com/print/Madrid/311.htm; and Times of India (2004, March 13). 3/11 Happened 911 Days after 9/11. *Times of India*, p. A1.

134. Gerwehr, Scott, & Hubbard, Kirk (2007). What Is Terrorism? Key Elements and History. In Bruce Bongar, Lisa Brown, Larry Beutler, James Breckenridge, & Philip Zimbardo (Eds.), *Psychology of Terrorism* (pp. 87–100). New York: Oxford University Press.

135. Sanger, David (2004, March 15). Blow to Bush: Ally Rejected. *New York Times*, p. A1.

136. Perlmutter, Dawn (2005). Mujahideen Blood Rituals: The Religious and Forensic Symbolism of Al Qaeda Beheading. *Anthropoetics, 11*(2), 10–21.

137. Speckhard, Anne, & Akhmedova, Khapta (2006). The New Chechen Jihad: Militant Wahhabism as a Radical Movement and a Source of Suicide Terrorism in Post-War Chechen Society. *Democracy and Security, 2*(1), 103–155.

138. Szaszdi, Lajos (2008). *Russian Civil-Military Relations and the Origins of the Second Chechen War*. Lanham, MD: University Press of America.

139. Cornish, Paul (2008, November 30). The Age of Celebrity Terrorism. *BBC News*.

140. Williams, Clive (2004). *Terrorism Explained: The Facts about Terrorism and Terrorist Groups*. Sydney: New Holland.

141. Howie, Luke (2011). *Terror on the Screen: Witnesses and the Reanimation of 9/11 as Image-Event, Popular Culture and Pornography*. Washington, DC: New Academia Publishing.

142. Colen, Alexandra (2008). Paris Hilton Terrorism. *The Brussels Journal*. Retrieved March 22, 2013, from http://www.brusselsjournal.com/node/3673; and Cornish, Paul (2008, November 30). The Age of Celebrity Terrorism. *BBC News*.

143. Conway, Brian (2003). Active Remembering, Selective Forgetting, and Collective Identity: The Case of Bloody Sunday. *Identity: An International Journal of Theory and Research, 3*(4), 305–323.

144. Bradford, Ernle (1984). *The Great Siege Malta 1565*. New York: Penguin.

145. Cassola, Arnold (1999). *The 1565 Great Siege of Malta and Hipolito Sans's La Maltea*. San Gwann, Malta: Publishers Enterprises Group.

146. Bamford, James (2005). *A Pretext for War: 9/11, Iraq, and the Abuse of America's Intelligence Agencies*. New York: Anchor.

147. Stump, Roger (2005). Religion and the Geographies of War. In Colin Flint (Ed.), *The Geography of War and Peace: From Death Camps to Diplomats* (pp. 149–173). Oxford: Oxford University Press.

148. Stoye, John (2007). *The Siege of Vienna: The Last Great Trial between Cross & Crescent*. Berkeley, CA: Pegasus.

149. Findling, John, & Thackeray, Frank (1999). *Events That Changed the World in the Seventeenth Century*. Westport, CT: Greenwood.

150. Simpson, David (2006). *9/11: The Culture of Commemoration*. Chicago: University of Chicago Press.

151. Spencer, Robert (2006). *War Is Deceit*. In Gregory M. Davis & Bryan Daly (Dirs.), *Islam: What the West Needs to Know*. United States: Quixotic Media.

152. Forker, Martin, & McCormick, Jonathan (2009). Walls of History: The Use of Mythomoteurs in Northern Ireland Murals. *Irish Studies Review, 17*(4), 423–465.

153. bin Laden, Osama (2003, February 14). *Messages to the World*. Retrieved March 24, 2013, from http://www.claremont.org/publications/pubid.47/pub_detail.asp

154. Pack, Jason (2012, September 14). Honoring Chris Stevens. *Foreign Policy, 43*, 5.

155. Hoffman, David (1996). *The Web of Hate: Extremists Exploit the Internet*. New York: Anti-Defamation League.

156. Reavis, Dick (1998). *The Ashes of Waco: An Investigation*. Syracuse, NY: Syracuse University Press.

157. Key, Charles (2001). *The Final Report on the Bombing of the Alfred P. Murrah Building*. Oklahoma City: Oklahoma Bombing Investigation.

158. Michel, Lou, & Herbeck, Dan (2001). *American Terrorist: Timothy McVeigh and the Oklahoma City Bombing*. New York: Harper.

159. Chidsey, Donald Barr (1966). *The Siege of Boston: An On-the-Scene Account of the Beginning of the American Revolution*. New York: Crown.

160. Morris, Travis, & Crank, John (2011). Toward a Phenomenology of Terrorism: Implications for Research and Policy. *Crime, Law and Social Change, 56*, 219–242.

Chapter Three

Symbolic Targets

TARGETS OF TERRORISM

Terrorist attacks are a tactic of communication involving victims, spectators, and wrongdoers. Generally, attacks are not interpreted as just violent acts; rather, they also represent statements that send a particular message. Since the communication is mostly visual (although some terrorist attacks go along with claims of responsibility and even justification), symbols play a pivotal role in creating meaningful messages and, thus, become essential to the purpose and success of terrorism.[1] Terrorism has been personified through extreme violence against public buildings (e.g., the Oklahoma City bombing on April 19, 1995), public transportation (e.g., the Aum Shinrikyo subway attack on March 20, 1995), military fixtures (e.g., the suicide bombings at the U.S. Marine barracks in Beirut on October 23, 1983), historic landmarks (e.g., the attack on the Grand Mosque in Mecca on November 20, 1979), economic symbols (e.g., the attacks on the World Trade Center on February 26, 1993, and September 11, 2001), political leadership (e.g., the attempted assassination of George H. W. Bush on April 14, 1994), and what is certainly the most relevant symbol of all: human life itself.[2] As Lule (2001)[3] explains,

> Terrorists actually want the victim to symbolically represent the audience. The terror—as opposed to disgust over the slaughter or grief over the loss—resides in a personal, primarily unconscious understanding that the victim is a symbol of the self: It could have been me. (p. 57)

Nevertheless, the victim of terrorism is not necessarily the principal symbol in the communication of terrorism. The success of a terrorist act is not captured by the destruction of its target, but by the realization of a symbolic act that has far-reaching repercussions. As Kalyvas (2004) explains, "Coercion fails if it destroys the target whose compliance is sought" (p. 101).[4] The goal is to create a spectacle in which the symbolism is more salient than the physical value. The symbolism of targets, then, matters more than the target value—the eminence, size, or visibility of buildings. As such, targets are strategically selected to both annihilate and fashion symbols that communicate a specific message and create an effect on the audience.[5] What this also means is that terrorist victims are not merely individuals and institutions within the realm of civil society; the giant victim is civil society itself.[6]

When it is a **soft target**, the target is an unarmed target that can be easily destroyed (e.g., an assembly of people). When it is a **hard target**, it is a battle tank or a well-defended structure. The symbolic selections of terrorist targets are designed to reflect the grander symbolic rhetoric of terrorism overall. Terrorism does not operate on a strategy of accomplishing ideological victory through one act only.[7] What could be more deplorable than the killing of hundreds of children at Beslan (Russia) by the Chechens? In reality, however, the primary target of terrorism is the victim, who is particularly rich in symbolic meaning.[8] Crelinsten (1989)[9] corroborates this idea by arguing that the choice of victims is symbolically instrumental: victims are selected because of the larger entity that they represent and because their victimization will be deeply felt within multiple audiences.

Guilt by Association

Guilt by association refers to a form of symbolic linkage whereby terrorists connect individuals to the larger entities that they want to target. In some cases, it is the company-that-you-keep fallacy; in other cases, it is purely based on stereotyping. For example, it is evident that the Israeli athletes and coaches massacred at the 1972 Munich Olympic Games by Palestinian terrorists were not attacked on account of being athletes and coaches. Instead, they were killed because they represented the State of Israel at an international event. Therefore, the tragedy in Munich was a politico-terrorist conflict between the terrorist organization (i.e., Black September) and the State of Israel. In addition, the subsequent covert Israeli operation seeking to eliminate those who killed Mossad agents is to be considered the obverse of the initial interaction.[10] **Mossad** is the Israeli national intelligence agency.

For terrorists, guilt by association plays an important role in their justification for perpetrating their violent acts. For instance, the 2004 Madrid train bombings were committed by an Al Qaeda–inspired terrorist group. One of the reasons was Spain's participation in the Iraq War. Likewise, since decolonization in large regions of Africa and South America, the West has been targeted by terrorists because it has been accused of turning local minorities (who had been already Westernized) into comprador ruling elites. **Comprador ruling elites** are Third World leaders considered to have been put in power by the West (in spite of their incompetence and their corrupt, bloody past). In return, those elites satisfy the economic needs of the West. Because they are so Westernized (e.g., holding Ivy League degrees), the comprador ruling elites are very similar—from a cultural standpoint—to Western leaders. Consequently, the latter are held accountable for the weak nature of Third World governance because of the collaboration between crooked Third World elites and their supporters in the West.[11]

Guilt by association frequently involves the notion of citizenship. In the context of terrorism, **citizenship** alludes to mainstream people who are representative of an enemy state. For example, an anti-American terrorist group would target U.S. citizens by virtue of their attachment to U.S. soil. The criterion of representation is the main determining factor in the choice of a particular target. In other words, is the target connected to the nation-state that the terrorist organization wants to target?[12] As Goodwin (2006)[13] adds, citizenship is not the only representation procedure; various terrorist groups will cut the representational pie in various ways. Whereas some groups consider all citizens of the nation-state as potential victims (more expected to occur in democratic nations), others use an overlapping list of criteria in which citizenship is necessary but not enough (e.g., a Marxist-Leninist terrorist organization that targets mostly Western-oriented or capitalistic institutions).

Violent True Believers (VTBs)

A **violent true believer** (VTB) is a person devoted to an ideology or belief system championing massacre and suicide as logical means of advancing their cause. VTBs have very specific targets in mind and are strongly committed to their beliefs; they will disregard any objections or alternative views. VTBs generally relate to like-minded others or those who share the same violent passion. Of course, they can also operate as lone wolves.[14] Terrorists like Timothy McVeigh, Major Nidal Hasan, and Anders Behring Breivik were notable VTBs. Additionally, according to Baudrillard (1993),[15] the VTB wants his or her cause to be known the world over. Because VTBs embrace their ideology or belief system with such resoluteness, their actions are framed through the logic of symbolic selection: choosing targets to make them go from a status of nothingness to a status of world notoriety—a fetish for which no alternative is possible. Put differently, from this perspective, terrorism is an act that moves the perpetrator from the status of anybody to the status of sacred substance. In fact, VTBs fulfill our most mysterious and frightening needs: to gain death but also to give death (symbolically, these extremes are reversible).

Nacos (2002)[16] views terrorism as symbolic publicity; it tends to receive "saturation coverage," making "the perpetrators of mass-mediated political violence excellent candidates for celebrity status" (p. 89). It goes without saying that media broadcasts of terrorist incidents contribute to this publicity of terrorism. This was particularly demonstrated with the September 11, 2001, attacks (which had a global audience of three billion viewers) and the Oklahoma City bombing. In regard to the latter, the reporting led up to the terrorist's—Timothy McVeigh's—execution: "saturation coverage of terrorist spectaculars makes the perpetrators of mass-mediated political violence excellent candidates for celebrity status, just like O.J. Simpson or Princess Diana" (p. 89).

IMPACT ON THE AUDIENCE

The most essential tenet of any communication act is to understand the audience. By definition, an **audience** is a group of individuals involved in an event, either passively (e.g., by simply watching a spectacle or attending to a message conveyed by a sender) or actively (e.g., by intentionally taking part in the event or giving feedback to the one who sent the message). In both passive and active situations, the audience represents an interpretive community responding to a message.[17] In chapter 2, the argument was made that terrorism is a form of symbolism. With each terrorist act, terrorists create a type of symbolic interaction with an audience; generally, it is an audience beyond the direct targets. The intent of the message may change based on the audience, even within the context of only one terrorist act.[18]

Terrorist acts are messages sent to a specific audience. The audience can be one person, a whole group, or even the entire world. At the same time, the immediate victims represent the audience in its entirety.[19] Creating a dialogue with an audience means that terrorists seek to promote change. For example, they may wish to affect policies, to influence a particular action or set of actions, to postpone or block enactment of policy, to stimulate support or sympathy, to cause people to behave in certain ways, or to cripple the audience into inertia. Terrorists "speaking" to audiences can be considered optimistic in that they expect their message to be received, understood, and acted upon. To accomplish this, terrorists rely on public contact with the audience.[20]

The audience, then, becomes the **public character of terrorism**. Terrorism is a conspicuously public endeavor targeting the psychological and emotional state of the audience who witnesses the disaster. The aim is to engender, in the audience, a sense of anxiety and horror. The audience constitutes both the **second party** (direct target of the message) and the **third party** (target beyond the direct target of the message) of terrorism. Needless to say, terrorist attacks can also be purposely committed against third parties that are totally unrelated to the terrorists' goals. The intentions of terrorist groups are to coerce governments or other institutions into meeting the terrorists' demands.[21] As one can see, the goal of terrorism is to produce fear and signs of fear. Generally, terrorist attacks create fewer casualties than what was planned, but the attacks imprint scars, messages, and images on our psyches. An important objective of terrorism is not only to kill but also to change—something in the audience's behavior or beliefs that needs to change.[22] Since the aim of terrorism is to impact multiple audiences, it can be deduced that terrorist acts are means of persuasion. **Persuasion** is a type of influence whereby the sender wants to make the receiver accept or change a belief, attitude, or action through rational or symbolic processes.[23]

According to Williams (1998),[24] there are two levels of audience: (1) the closer, immediate, or direct audience; and (2) the farther, delayed, or indirect audience. The first type is the target of terrorist violence, commonly innocent civilians. The second type is the intended audience of terrorism. Statistically, the intended audience never gets hit by terrorism physically; in other words, the audience is not a victim in and of itself. However, the power of terrorism is such that the audience always fears to become the victim. It is this fear that grants terrorism the supreme power of multiplication effect, called the **amplification effect**.[25] The amplification effect is the unique character of terrorism, one that sends a powerful message of fear and change. For instance, the **Red Brigades**, a Marxist-Leninist terrorist group based in Italy that was particularly active in the 1970s and 1980s, used the tactic of **kneecapping** (i.e., firing a shot in the back of the knee joint, thereby making the victim unable to walk adequately again). This had an amplification effect on all Italian citizens, including journalists. They, too, knew they could become the next victim of kneecapping—or killing, especially after the Red Brigades' assassination of Italian Prime Minister Aldo Moro.[26] Not surprisingly, the Red Brigades managed to keep the entire country of Italy in constant fear and intimidation as they knew the media were broadcasting their terrorist acts on a regular basis—a process called **mass-mediated terrorism**.[27]

ATTACKING SACRED SYMBOLS: ICONOCLASM

Iconoclasm refers to hostility to religious images that leads to a public or terroristic act of their destruction. Iconoclasm involves an attack upon a sacred symbol that appears to mediate or stand between humanity and a deity, or even appropriates the place or status of a deity.[28] Terrorism brings to light a regular feature of all definitions of extreme violence: its attacks on symbolic representation. The most fundamental form of such attacks is iconoclasm in the proper sense of the term: the hatred and obliteration of icons that function as figurative mediation.[29] In this regard, iconoclasm is synonymous with **desecration**, the defilement of things holy and the act of robbing things of their sacred character. Generally, this refers to the violation of sacred places or sacred objects; it also includes the entire domain of the holy.[30]

Examples of sacred places or sacred objects that have been the target of iconoclasm or desecration include religious buildings, religious artifacts (e.g., statues, holy scriptures, etc.), museums, heritage sites, historical monuments or sites, cemeteries, political memorials or sites, archaeological sites, natural heritages, and even athletic events. All these things represent an outgroup's collective memory. In ex-Yugoslavia, the destruction of cemeteries was a symbolic action that served to rewrite history by removing physical evidence that the enemy was ever there. The objective, of course, was to prevent claims to restore the land that was stolen as well as claims to other types of property.[31] During the Bosnian War, the town of Foča was not only a site of mass killings; it was also a target of cultural terrorism. When

Serbian paramilitary troops engaged in search-and-destroy missions, they renamed the town "Serbinia."[32]

Cultural Terrorism

Cultural terrorism refers to the physical damage of cultural sites or artifacts (that belong to the enemy) or, sometimes, the physical displacement of the enemy's cultural activities.[33] One example that is classified as iconoclastic terrorism is the symbolic destruction of the Bamiyan Buddhas, which was a major event that described the Taliban's relationship with the past. The Bamiyan Buddhas were two colossal statues of standing Buddhas carved into a cliff in the Bamiyan valley (in central Afghanistan). They were built in the sixth century CE. The decision was driven by Islamist ideology that urges the destruction of all non-Muslim graven images. On February 26, 2001, Mullah Mohammed Omar, the Taliban leader, pronounced that the statues "should be destroyed so that they are not worshipped now or in the future."[34] As a result, the Taliban terrorists destroyed all such pre-Islamic treasures and ancient sculptures in central Afghanistan. They used strategically placed bombs, tanks, and anti-aircraft weapons to blow them apart (onlookers photographed the explosions).[35] Cultural terrorism is also called **cultural cannibalism**, the intentional elimination of symbolic landscapes that represent a culture.[36]

Although the Convention for the Protection of Cultural Property in the Event of Armed Conflict was adopted in The Hague in 1954, instances of cultural terrorism have been plentiful.[37] In the late 1980s, Romanian dictator Nicolae Ceaușescu pursued his dream of imposing communism across the country by sending troops throughout the countryside and erasing more than 7,000 villages. By removing the heritage of Romania's countryside, Ceaușescu also sought to remove—and, therefore, rewrite—Romanian history. That is an example of cultural terrorism.[38] By engaging in cultural terrorism, iconoclasts resort to acts of destruction to create situations that incite fear and submission among their target audience, and that send particular ideological messages. The president and chairman of the **World Monuments Fund (WMF)**, a private, global, and nonprofit institution committed to the preservation of cultural heritage sites worldwide,[39] declared that weapons of mass destruction are not always directed at cities or military installations; they also target the cultural icons that connect and inspire communities across the globe, underscoring the importance of WMF to protect cultural landmarks against terrorist attacks.[40] For this reason, "our landmarks—the Mostar Bridge in Bosnia-Herzegovina, the Bamiyan Buddhas in Afghanistan, and the World Trade Center in the U.S.—have become prized targets for terrorists" (Perry & Burnham, 2001, p. 3).[41] Such landmarks define the cultures, principles, and achievements of the groups of people who generate them, use them, and live with them.

In some contexts, cultural terrorism is also referred to as sympathetic magic. **Sympathetic magic** is a rudimentary tradition of magical thinking whereby one can hurt, humiliate, or murder another simply by destroying a cultural symbol of the victim. This is a book model of iconoclasm: demolish the statues of power, and you will overthrow their control.[42] As we have seen, terrorists select targets based on their symbolic value. Prestigious, sentimental, or similar symbolic targets are chosen with the anticipation that the target's constituents will be deeply affected.[43] As Ranstorp (2006)[44] explains, the targets are frequently symbolic and meticulously selected to inflict maximum psychological trauma on the enemy and, at the same time, enhance the religious or ideological credentials of the terrorists among their own followers. This is manifest from the terrorists' selection of cultural landmarks and attractions as these embody the nucleus of their foes.

Another important consideration is mutual cultural terrorism. **Mutual cultural terrorism** is a practice whereby a group damages or desecrates an enemy's cultural landmark in retaliation for the latter's desecration of that group's own cultural landmark in the past. For example, during the preparation for the 2014 Winter Olympics in Sochi (Russia), terrorist attacks—to be perpetrated at the Olympic site—were foiled by the Russian secret service. It turns out that the cultural symbol within "2014 Winter Olympics" was not just the "Olympic" part. Indeed, the target was more than a cultural landmark (as was the case with the Boston Marathon bombings a year earlier); it was also "2014," the year marking the 150th anniversary of the desecration of Circassian cultural landmarks by Tsarist Russia.[45] The **Circassians** are a Muslim ethnic group that was defeated and forced out of the Sochi area by the Russian Empire in 1864. More importantly, the Russian Empire also engaged in a massive genocide against the Circassians.[46] In fact, up to 1.5 million of them may have perished during that ethnic cleansing. The bloodiest episode of genocide, which Circassians call their "last stand," occurred in 1864 in the area where the Olympic site is located today. Entire tribes were slaughtered. The Circassians refer to the tragedy as the first modern genocide.[47]

Asian Iconoclasm

From the time when China's military invaded and occupied Tibet in 1950, the Chinese government has unrelentingly attempted to exterminate Tibetan Buddhism as a source of influence in the region. The annihilation of Buddhist monasteries, the incarceration of monks and nuns, and other affirmations of Chinese control spurred intermittent guerrilla warfare in the 1950s and, eventually, caused a popular rebellion in 1959. During that year, the Dalai Lama, the head monk and supreme leader of Tibetan Buddhism, escaped to northern India to institute a Tibetan government in exile. China's violent repression of the 1959 uprising was accompanied by a more pervasive clampdown on Tibetan culture, including all religious endeavors considered by Chinese authorities as associated with political dissent or Tibetan nationalism.[48] In India, religious terrorists have taken advantage of authoritative symbolism to inflame the enemy. For example, to incite violent reactions from the enemy, Dal Khalsa activists (i.e., a radical political organization of the Sikh nation) severed cows' heads outside two Hindu temples in Amritsar. This event caused massive conflicts between Sikhs and Hindus in April 1982. Two years later, in June 1984, within the premises of the Golden Temple in Amritsar, the State of India launched a raid on its own citizens. The tragedy occurred on a very sacred day of the Sikh calendar: the martyrdom day of Guru Arjun. It is usually a day upon which the Golden Temple contains the highest number of Sikh devotees.[49] On October 14, 2001, hundreds of rightist Hindu terrorists attacked the Taj Mahal by defacing the white marble walls with graffiti. Nevertheless, this attack was widely underrepresented in Western media.[50] In Sri Lanka, Tamil radicals have resorted to violence against sacred sites in a symbolic stratagem of disheartenment. This was particularly reflected though assaults on the Temple of the Tooth, a central Buddhist shrine with a remnant of the Buddha.[51]

Islamic Iconoclasm

For Islamists, violence is rooted in a deeply entrenched tradition of restoring honor, wreaking vengeance, maintaining purity, upholding customs, and saving face. Iconoclasm is seen as a justifiable tactic to diminish the enemy's power and to inflict shame, public humiliation, and a loss of face. In short, the enemy must be physically and symbolically shattered. "False gods" venerated by other religions must have their body parts removed because they symbolize other traditions that threaten Islam.[52] In the past, Mohamed ibn Abd al Wahhab, the founder of

Wahhabism (an ultraconservative Islamic movement originating in Saudi Arabia in the eighteenth century), requisitioned the destruction of sacred tombs and monuments.[53] Already in the twelve century, massive iconoclasm of Hindu monuments had occurred during the Ottoman Empire, when Turkish armies invaded India. If truth be told, several of the first Muslim warlords were vigorous iconoclasts and ordered the construction of mosques on the ashes of destroyed Hindu temples. In some cases today, visitors can still notice the disfigured sculptures of their Hindu predecessors. This iconoclasm continued sporadically as Sultans swept across India during the thirteenth and fourteenth centuries. Overall, zealous Indo-Muslim states defiled at least 60,000 Hindu temples.[54]

In this day and age, Islamic iconoclasm is still widely practiced on the same religious and political grounds. It is expressed through the destruction of sacred sites like those in Afghanistan, where 70 percent of the 100,000 relics in the Kabul Museum were ransacked and about 3,000 pieces were hacked to pieces by the mujahedin. Islamic iconoclasm today is also expressed through the violent reactions to visual controversies like the Danish publication of twelve Muhammad cartoons in 2005 and the *South Park* TV episode in which Muhammad was the subject of a few jokes (in 2010).[55] In Islamic ideology, desecration is so important that a terrorist group in Iraq was specifically dedicated to the practice. The group was called "The Brigades for the Defense of Holy Shrines," a faction of the Mahdi Army, a Shia terrorist group. A large part of the damage to non-Muslim monuments is carried out by rival factions that are generally ignored in the mainstream media establishment.[56]

The aforesaid faction of the Mahdi Army, also referred to as "The Squadrons Defending Holy Places," engages in iconoclasm to meet the spiritual demands of pure Shia Islam, such as is found in al-Najaf. Al-Najaf is the city where the shrine of Imam Ali is located. In Shia Islam, Imam Ali was the founder of the Shia movement, which makes al-Najaf a supremely holy site for the Shi'ites.[57] The majority of Muslims worldwide are either Sunnis or Shi'ites. The Shi'ites are usually more euphoric in their religious observance and have messianic hopes that a future prophet—the Mahdi—will come back on earth to restore justice. The main contention between the Shi'ites and the Sunnis today stems from the seventh-century dispute over the succession of Muhammad after he died. The Shi'ites believe that Ali (Muhammad's cousin and son-in-law) should have been the designated heir to Muhammad. In turn, Ali's descendants should have been the successive leaders in Islam.[58]

Lastly, during the 2008 Mumbai terrorist attacks (also called "26/11"), eleven coordinated attacks were committed by Pakistani Muslim terrorists in Mumbai, India's largest city.[59] Eight of the attacks took place in South Mumbai, particularly at Chhatrapati Shivaji Terminus, a historic railway station and a World Heritage Site of **UNESCO** (the United Nations Educational, Scientific and Cultural Organization). By attacking Chhatrapati Shivaji, Muslims unambiguously attacked one of Hindus' most memorable symbols.[60] In 2008, this tragic incident of iconoclasm was classified by U.S. senator John McCain as "India's 9/11."[61]

CLASH OF CIVILIZATIONS

Most examples of iconoclasm typically reflect major clashes of civilizations. Developed by Harvard professor Samuel Huntington (1996),[62] the concept of the **Clash of Civilizations** postulates that cultural and religious differences between global civilizations are a major source of terrorism today. Terrorists seek to create a Clash of Civilizations by attacking anybody or anything that conflicts with their ideology or mores. The Clash of Civilizations is analogous to the **War of Ideas**, a paradigm explaining that major differences of ideals between the West and the Muslim world tend to clash. Islam continues to resist Western political forms like democracy.[63] Another feature of the Clash of Civilizations is the model of **Jihad versus McWorld**, which was developed by political theorist Benjamin Barber (1995).[64] The model illustrates the fight between jihad and "McWorld" (i.e., the economic and political process of multinational corporations [MNCs]). For example, in 2002, in Pakistan, many Islamist groups plundered or destroyed Kentucky Fried Chicken and McDonald's franchises, and burned U.S. flags.[65]

In recent years, the Clash of Civilizations between the West and Islam was properly demonstrated through the conflict between "host" and "guest" in Egypt. Particular tourist behaviors (e.g., consumption of pork, drinking, gambling, clubbing, and enacting Western dress and codes of behavior) incompatible with Islamic cultural values have led to terrorist attacks against "guests." In Egypt, when tourism is perceived as a threat to ingrained Islamic norms, traditions, value systems, and beliefs, the fervent aspiration to protect these can deplorably manifest itself in terrorism.[66] Tourists are also targeted for their symbolic value as indirect representatives of "hostile" Western or Westernized governments.[67] Hence, terrorists try to find symbol-rich targets, often locations of transience and intercultural mélange such as Cairo, Alexandria, and Luxor.[68]

In general, symbolic targets are those that have the least connections to any active subjugation or cruelty toward the terrorist's supporters. For this reason, tourism becomes not only the message but also the medium of communication introduced by terrorists. Choosing the tourist as a target is not accidental: for terrorists, the symbolism, significance, and news value of the visitor or guest are worth too much to be left unexploited. In addition, terrorists can also target tourists to meet religious mandates, which can be explained through the framework of the Clash of Civilizations.[69] This was intensely illustrated in the hijacking of the MS *Achille Lauro* (a cruise ship) by Palestinian terrorists in 1985. The fact that the only passenger they killed was also the only Jewish American on board is anything but coincidental.[70]

Lastly, the Clash of Civilizations can also be expressed through the **David and Goliath metaphor**.[71] This metaphor is twofold: first, the two men came from two different tribes, and their beliefs were diametrically opposed (on the one hand, there was a Philistine warrior worshipping Baal; and, on the other hand, there was the young David, the future king of Israel, worshipping the Lord of Abraham). Second, the David and Goliath metaphor exemplifies the fact that the "sizes" of the two parties were diametrically opposed as well; David was alone, facing a huge army of Philistines led by a 9'9" warrior. In the context of present-day terrorism, this clashing difference would be called **asymmetric warfare**, the use of extreme but sporadic violence by a weaker group (i.e., a terrorist or guerrilla group) against a stronger power (i.e., a military, government, or even whole society) to achieve specific objectives. Asymmetrical warfare is waged between highly unequal sides. The weaker side does not attack the more powerful one under traditional rules of war because it cannot win by doing so.[72]

THE WORLD TRADE CENTER AS A SYMBOLIC TARGET

The destruction of the World Trade Center wiped out approximately twelve million square feet of Class A office space and cost $16 billion in damage.[73] The act itself is also a powerful reminder that there are many terrorist groups across the globe that hate the West and the American way of life.[74] So, to them, it seems natural to target the symbolic heart of their enemy. To some people, it is difficult to visualize a more revealing example of intense symbolic terrorism than the attack on the Twin Towers, an immense symbol of what Al Qaeda considers America's blasphemous usurpation of Allah's role in the world.[75] As Osama bin Laden himself observed, "Those awesome symbolic towers that speak of liberty, human rights, and humanity have been destroyed. They have gone up in smoke,"[76] along with the arrogance they symbolized. It is worth noting that, here, Osama bin Laden's emphasis is not only on a triumph over Western imperialism or Zionism, but also on the symbolic obliteration of the institutional values that make Western society possible.

The World Trade Center attacks did not just represent an act of **Clausewitzian terror**—terrorism used as a strategic weapon to wreak psychologically debilitating effects on mainstream citizens. Rather, 9/11 was mostly a symbolic spectacle, a grand ritual exhibiting the power of Allah, a parade designed to communicate a message not only to the American people but also to the ummah.[77] No one who was horrified upon watching the Twin Towers crashing into pieces on September 11, 2001, second-guessed what the real target of the Al Qaeda terrorist attack was: U.S. global hegemony. Al Qaeda terrorists, militants of the same kind, and Islamic sympathizers have said as much. Massive buildings like the Twin Towers are selected to symbolically demonstrate that the powers-that-be are the enemy.[78] The value of the World Trade Center as the enemy symbol is reflected through discussions that are still going on about them today: the North and South Towers symbolized Western power, wealth, materialism, and modernism. Of course, their stature—both had over a hundred stories and ninety-nine elevators, and overlooked the New York City skyline—also made them a great target. Their loss was equally visible.[79]

All things considered, Al Qaeda is a terrorist organization that has been fully aware of the power of symbolism and the symbolism of power. On Tuesday, September 11, 2001, its nineteen deputies transformed four aircrafts (symbols of globalization and modernism) into weapons and smashed them into the World Trade Center, the epitome of global trade. Below is a list of ten scholarly statements regarding the destruction of the World Trade Center as an act of symbolism:

- "It is the Islamists' spectacular attack on the World Trade Center, that great symbol of contemporary American global superiority and advanced international commercial and financial reckoning" (Azm, 2005, p. 9).[80]
- "As a symbol of U.S. capitalism and culture, the World Trade Center's destruction was an affront to the country's claim to economic and military supremacy" (Beauregard, 2004, p. 139).[81]
- "The attacks of 9/11 targeted some of the primary symbols of America's strength, power, and world status. The World Trade Center stood as the symbol of our financial wealth and enterprise" (Denton, 2006, p. 7).[82]
- "The World Trade Center and other buildings presented a rhetorical vision of the power and brilliance of, at least, our systems" (Farmer, 2002, p. 135).[83]
- "The World Trade Center was targeted because it was a symbol of the USA and the financial system that underpins the nation" (Lew, 2007, p. 537).[84]
- "The World Trade Center was not just a symbol of American prosperity. It was an economic nerve center" (Lule, 2002, p. 277).[85]
- "The Twin towers of the WTC stood as the very image of globalization, capitalism, and Western economic superiority" (O'Hair, Heath, Ayotte, & Ledlow, 2008, p. 51).[86]
- "The targets of these attacks were major symbols of American culture" (Prewitt et al., 2004, p. 138).
- "On September 11, 2001, within just a few dozen minutes, the symbol of the world's business and trade ceased to exist" (Stankiewicz, 2005, p. 683).[87]
- "Al Qaeda's attacks on 9/11 are presented as attacks on symbols of American power, on towers and buildings, thus ignoring the death of thousands of innocent civilians" (Weimann, 2008, p. 80).[88]

Upon looking at these ten statements, it is undeniable that the World Trade Center was targeted by Al Qaeda because it was a symbol of wealth, global capitalism, power, modernism, and the heart of U.S. culture and heritage. To Osama bin Laden, the World Trade Center was worth destroying. One cannot say the same about many other landmarks. To the Al Qaeda chief, most things were not worth destroying. Only oeuvres of prestige merited that fate.[89] According to a detailed Al Qaeda manual for would-be terrorists in Al Qaeda's training camps, holy warriors were required to strike "sentimental landmarks," such as the Statue of Liberty in New York, Big Ben in London, and the Eiffel Tower in Paris, because their demolition would "generate intense publicity" (Weimann, 2008, p. 72).[90] On a side note, inscribed on the sides of the metallic bodies of the fatal aircrafts, the words "United" and "American"—brand names and symbols of national dignity—were obliterated as they entered the sides of the Twin Towers, which also represented brands and symbols. In brief, the buildings exuded the same values as the airline logos.[91] An important conclusion is that Al Qaeda had calculatedly planned to destabilize the grand themes of American life by attacking the symbols that personify them.[92] Another conclusion is that the meaning of extreme violence (i.e., of attacking the World Trade Center as opposed to a site like the Grand Canyon) is essential to terrorism, because terrorism focuses on symbolic targets to coerce an enemy into making a political, ideological, or religious surrendering.[93]

BLOWBACK THEORY

Coined by Johnson (2000),[94] **blowback theory** posits that the global hegemony of empires—at both the end of the twentieth century and the beginning of the twenty-first century—and the additional global military presence of the United States have prompted resistance in the form of terrorism and attacks on symbolic targets like the Twin Towers in New York City.[95] In a nutshell, blowback theory argues that the global expansion of "empires"—usually associated with Western (economic, cultural, and militaristic) imperialism—inevitably blows back onto territories and symbols of those empires.[96] The theory, then, is analogous to "backfire" with a delayed fuse. A certain number of international policies and decisions have generated unanticipated—and sometimes disastrous—consequences for later generations. Two frequent examples in the literature include the crowning of Shah Mohammed Reza Pahlavi in Iran in 1953, now largely regarded as a long-term trigger to the Ayatollah-led anti-American revolution in Iran in 1979; and the equipping and support of Saddam Hussein's military as a protection against Iranian revolutionary ardor in the 1980s (the heavy U.S. endorsement actually empowered Iraq to attack Kuwait in late 1990).[97]

Crenshaw (2001)[98] argues that "terrorism should be seen as a strategic reaction to American power" (p. 425). The powerful international standing of the United States, especially its ability to bolster despotic undemocratic regimes, produces a greater volume of Islamic terrorism as a result. The causal structure here is that the presence of mammoth military power can lead to subsequent terrorist reactions as "retaliation for previous American imperial actions" (Johnson, 2000, p. 9).[99] From the standpoint of blowback theory, 9/11 is predominantly a counterattack on U.S. global hegemony; this really pertains to the costs and consequences of the U.S. empire. Some blowback theorists argue that twenty-first-century world politics are determined largely by the negative outcomes of U.S. foreign policy in regions like the Middle East.[100] That the 9/11 perpetrators committed these terrorist attacks as a result of their gazillion grievances over U.S. foreign policy and the American way of life, and that they did this to satisfy Allah, made the threat to our cultural comfort all the more distressing.[101]

Many modern acts of religious-based terrorism have occurred in a way that differs from the old forms of holy war. They seem to be reactions to a recurrent topic in the world's political and social life: secular globalization. The World Trade Center represented Osama bin Laden's abhorrence of two features of secular globalization—a particular form of modernization and a particular form of globalization—despite the fact that the Al Qaeda network was both modern and globalized itself. Indeed, Al Qaeda terrorists were—and still are—very sophisticated and technically trained professionals. Its network consists of followers of many different countries who have moved smoothly from location to location with no apparent nationalist schema or allegiance. Thus, they are not necessarily against modernity and globalization, inasmuch as it fits their own agenda. However, they detest the Western type of modernity that they think is being forced upon them through secular globalization.[102] The *9/11 Commission Report* (2004)[103] itself categorically confirmed the nineteen hijackers' affiliations with Al Qaeda and described their motivations: to "hit the U.S. back" for what they perceived as secular wrong-doings against Islam. Again, the terrorists chose American Airlines and United Airlines because of their symbolic names.

LIQUID MODERNITY

Developed by Zygmunt Bauman (2000),[104] the theory of **liquid modernity** rests on the premise that late modernity and postmodern consumerism lead to ambiguity and increasing uncertainty within individual souls in society. It is like the frenzied outcome of modernity, where one can quickly move from one social status to another in a "fluid" manner—hence, the term "liquid." Nomadism and instability, an increasing push for constant mobility, become common traits of the liquid modern soul as this person flows through life like a perpetual traveler, changing locations, jobs, partners, values, and even more (e.g., political or sexual orientation). In liquid modernity, the person is constructed against the backdrop of a "world of fragmented and incommensurate identities and personae" (Craik, 1994, p. 8),[105] something entirely associated with the growth of "lifestyle cultures."

Liquid Life

The experience of life within liquid modernity becomes liquid life. **Liquid life** refers to rampant individualism (as a result of unfettered capitalism) and a rapid destabilization of social bonds.[106] Bauman (2000)[107] stressed that liquid modernity and consumer chic have brought profound changes to "the human condition . . . the burden of pattern-weaving and the responsibility for failure falling primarily on the individual's shoulders" (p. 8). Liquid life is typified by ceaseless change, uncertainty, and lack of trust in general. Our abilities, then, can quickly grow into liabilities; our skills become obsolete and make the future more unpredictable by reflecting on the past. A type of survival-and-gratification consumerism assumes the appearance of "creative destruction." Across all facets of life, those at the top of the pyramid are free; they are free to move, to choose, to change identity, and to take part in a process of becoming. At the bottom of the pyramid, individuals, facing disruptive pressures, hang on to the few elements of the identity they have. Those people are perceived as losers or flawed consumers. Their frustration with their choices as consumers (e.g., to be seen with a cell phone that is now old-fashioned) contributes to permanent self-criticism and reflection. The uncertainty that accompanies such a fall from postmodern consumerism adds intensity to their desire to consume. It is by way of consumption that people construct their identity, so that what they are and what they are seen to consume tend to converge.[108]

Liquid Modernity and Social Marginalization in Britain

Liquid modernity seems to be a frequent indicator in the upbringing of most jihadist terrorists in countries like Britain. Intense individualism undoubtedly creates a separation between winners and losers. The latter often feel marginalized by those who are supposed to assist them financially and socially. **Social marginalization** is the process of becoming or feeling marginal in society. When one feels socially marginalized, one feels downgraded or shuffled off to a lower social status or standing.[109] It is reasonable to say that Muslims in the West tend to experience more disadvantage—regardless of whether it is just or unjust. As compared with the British population on the whole, there are as three times as many unemployed Muslims as unemployed non-Muslim Britons. This is due to the fact that there are more Muslims than non-Muslim Britons who are unqualified and live in deprived communities. Muslims are also significantly underperforming in high schools and higher education. Slightly over a third of the British population overall is unqualified, as compared with 43 percent of Muslims. Taking all these levels of disadvantage into account, it is not surprising that many Muslims tend to regard themselves as unfairly marginalized as a result of liquid modernity. Once Muslim communities feel rejected from mainstream society, they lose much enthusiasm to respect or identify with that society.[110]

Liquid Modernity and 7/7 London Bombers

On July 7, 2005 (now referred to as "7/7" or the **July 7, 2005, London bombings**), four homegrown Al Qaeda suicide bombers detonated bombs aboard London Underground trains and a double-decker bus. As a result, fifty-six people died and over 700 others were injured.[111] Based on a narrative analysis of martyrdom videos recorded by the 7/7 Al Qaeda suicide bombers (and eight other martyrs-to-be standing in British courts for planning to bomb international airliners with homemade explosives), Shaun Best (2010)[112] discovered a solid list of altruistic motivations that drive Islamic martyrs to attack symbols of liquid modernity. Liquid modernity seems to be a major reason for Islamic martyrs who hate the instant postmodern, individualist consumerism. For people who appreciate liquid modernity, such a stance is unfathomable and irrational. Within the framework of liquid modernity, there is no reason for altruistic fundamentalism to exist. However, the reality is that Islamic martyrs are individuals who oppose the instant survival-and-gratification consumerism for more important communal goals; as such, according to the martyrs' narratives, group well-being (e.g., altruistic motivations or collectivism) should come before individual satisfaction. Put simply, whereas the martyrs' collectivist stance is unfathomable and irrational for the liquid modernists, the latter's individualist stance makes no sense to the martyrs themselves.[113]

From this perspective, Islam is not just a traditional faith; it is also a "collective identity" movement. In terms of altruistic motivations, the 7/7 suicide bombers have also been said to harbor deep-seated local grievances upon which they wanted to impose a global meaning.[114] According to Bauman (2004),[115] we should not be astonished at the growth of Islamic fundamentalism and religious fanaticism, as it gives a sense of certainty and security. Fundamentalism is not just a religious phenomenon; it derives its strength from several sources. As Bauman (2004) explains, fundamentalism must be considered "against a background of the new global inequality and the untamed injustice reigning in the global space" (p. 87). Fundamentalism guarantees more confidence, trust, and self-assurance to individuals who would otherwise be "stripped of human dignity and humiliated—people who can do little more than watch with a mixture of envy and resentment the consumer revelry" (p. 86).

WESTOXIFICATION

Westoxification refers to the state of being inebriated with Western culture and ideas. From *Gharbzadegi* (in Persian, which also means **West-struck-ness** or **Occidentosis**),[116] Westoxification is used as a symbol for anti-Western sentiment and militancy against Western influences, which represent cultural, economic, or political threats to communities, particularly those located in the Middle East and Central Asia.[117] The term was used for the first time by Ahmad Fardid (a professor at the University of Tehran in the 1940s) and later by the Grand Ayatollah Khomeini in 1979 during the Islamic Revolution in Iran, when the leader galvanized the population under the banner of anti-Western hatred: the Ayatollah accused the West of imposing its economic exploitation, political culture, and secularization on Islamic society. The Ayatollah also accused educated Iranians of having capitulated to Westoxification. The numerous violent movements of religious fundamentalism that have emerged around the world in the decades following the Iranian Revolution have expressed this anti-Western sentiment. In essence, this sentiment was a resistance to a certain form of modernism that is secular, individualistic, and uncertain (i.e., liquid modernity). At the same time, by embracing the modern philosophy of the nation-state as well as the technological and financial apparatuses of modern society, many similar movements of religious fundamentalism have articulated a form of modernity on their own behalf.[118] In the 1985 Hezbollah Manifesto, Khomeini made it clear that the United States and the West were behind all Islam's catastrophes and the source of all evil.[119] Perhaps even more distressing was the message that terrorist attacks had to convey: that there are humans who hate the United States and the West so much that they will not hesitate to sacrifice their lives to cause harm and that, arguably, millions of individuals around the world support and even applaud such activities.[120]

Diverse Incidents of Westoxification

On February 15, 1894, the Royal Greenwich Observatory in London experienced an attempted terrorist attack. This was perhaps the first "international terrorist" episode in Britain. Fortunately, the bomb accidentally exploded in the hand of Martial Bourdin, a twenty-six-year-old French anarchist, in Greenwich Park, close to the observatory building. He died about half an hour later. The observatory was a momentous symbol of British scientific supremacy and the best international system of time calculation at that time.[121] In 1901, Leon Czolgosz, a young anarchist, killed President William McKinley because he believed there was great injustice in U.S. society, an inequality that allowed wealthy people to indulge in Western lifestyles and enrich themselves by exploiting the poor.[122]

Later in the twentieth century, the Red Brigades were violently opposed to Italy's Western-influenced foreign and labor policies and NATO membership. In the spring of 1970, the early Red Brigades brochures, featuring the group's symbol of the five-pointed star, began to circulate in Milan. Westoxification was reflected through the burning of vehicles that belonged to directors of MNCs, the kidnapping of high-profile figures with Westernized tendencies, and striking against wealthy Italian citizens who were occupying entire neighborhoods. In March 1972, in Milan, the Red Brigades kidnapped Idalgo Macchiarini, the Siemens boss.[123] Lastly, the recent killing of Peruvian Mormon missionaries by the Shining Path (i.e., Sendero Luminoso) may be even more disturbing as it indicates that Latin American terrorist groups may target church representatives as symbols of Westoxification even when the victims themselves are not from the North American continent.[124]

Islamic Anti-Western Sentiment

For Islamic terrorists, anti-Western sentiment is the logical consequence of Western politico-economic oppression and sociocultural secularization within the Muslim world.[125] The West is accused of practicing all these things (with its Israeli friends) and showing categorical support for un-Islamic and "evil" governments in Arab regions. For these reasons, neo-Islamic movements and terrorist groups have gradually thrust themselves to the forefront as the true advocates of the oppressed and downtrodden Muslims, as the only true driving force against Israel's perpetual occupation of a sacred Muslim territory, and as the only true groups capable of resisting Western presence and interference in the Muslim world.[126] Al Qaeda's stance is a combination of two important factors: one is a total opposition to U.S. global hegemony (a view shared by many Third World political movements); the other is an exceptionally Islamic fundamentalist resistance to Western cultural imperialism. Such Islamic fundamentalist opposition is to Western-liberal secularism, materialism, and sinfulness. As witnessed within many Third World groups, Al Qaeda has expressed a sense of victimhood. Western hegemony is considered to have been forced upon them. An example of this Western hegemony is the imposition of Western political schemes and ideologies. The end result is a political victimhood in the Muslim world and serious concerns about Western cultural imperialism. For Al Qaeda, opposition to the latter is entangled with a concern that Muslim purity and morality have been polluted by Western secularism (ungodliness, sinfulness, and debauchery) and materialism (liquid modernity and its postmodern consumerism).[127]

Given all these circumstances, Islamic violence is an important conduit for the preservation of the ummah. As exemplified by jihadists in Britain (i.e., "7/7"), a certain number of Muslims (both in and outside the Western world) are not taking the experience of individualist modernity well, which is often seen as a negative influence. Westernized cities are looked down upon as anomic, chaotic cities with mass unemployment. The state has frequently failed to offer the kind of social infrastructures needed to keep up with modernity.[128] From an Islamic fundamentalist's outlook, the general message is that Islam provides and the West does not provide. While science is now the bastion for truth in the West, it has assumed the opposite appearance for a large part of Islam. This, in turn, foments imperative questions of truth and ontology (i.e., the study of existence or being): whereas Western truth is a material one, Islamic truth is a spiritual and nonmaterial one. As explained through the lens of the Clash of Civilizations, the two views on truth are diametrically opposed; one automatically rejects the other. So, allowing opposing truths into the community causes tremendous harm and threatens the authority of Allah. It also reaps disharmony and does violence to the ummah.[129]

Rejection of Modernism

Today, movements against Westoxification and modernism are growing like mushrooms after the rain. Yet, the rejection of modernism is tantamount to the rejection of humanist achievements since the Enlightenment. Contemporary ideas like the inherent worth of the human being, freedom of conscience, and the rule of law are dismissed as Western or "colonial" values that should be resisted at all levels.[130] After the abolishment of the Ottoman Empire in 1923 and the subsequent establishment of the secular Turkish regime in 1924, Mustafa Kemal (aka Atatürk) believed that the road to progress was modernism. For him, this could only be achieved by mimicking the European model of secularism. As Sayyid (2003)[131] explains, "Islam was no longer linked with state power. Mustafa Kemal repeatedly described Islam as 'the symbol of obscurantism;' as 'a purified corpse which poisons our lives;' as 'the enemy of civilization and science'" (p. 64). Unfortunately, to Islamists today, at the heart of this philosophy is the idea that modernization equals Westernization. They also cite problems (whether true or not) like corruption, incompetence, and despotic power concentration. Hence, the Islamists say they have been chosen to answer a call or fulfill a duty: the duty to create a new social and political development.

The RAND statistics (in Box 3.1) expose the fatal results of Westoxification. The fact that, in 2000–2010, 96 percent of the victims of terrorism in the Western world were victims of Islamic terrorism sends a clear message: to the eyes of Islamists, the Western way of life should not be the existing order.

BOX 3.1: THE RAND CORPORATION

The **RAND Corporation** is a nonprofit global policy institution based in Santa Monica, California. Since the 1970s, it has been a frontrunner in terrorism and counterterrorism studies. RAND (which stands for "Research and Development") is largely regarded as the yardstick of measure for comprehensive data on international and homegrown terrorism. According to the RAND Database of Worldwide Terrorism Incidents, the number of casualties from terrorism in Europe and North America from 2000 to 2010 was 4,873. Of those 4,873 casualties, 4,703 were casualties of Islamic terrorist attacks. That is more than 96 percent. Upon closer examination, in the United States, 3,000 people were killed by Muslim terrorists; in Russia and Eastern Europe, the number of casualties was 1,452; and in Western Europe, the number was 251. Only 170 terrorism casualties in the United States, Russia, Eastern Europe, and Western Europe were not caused by Islamic terrorism. Even if we take out the September 11, 2001, attacks from this RAND statistic, the percentage of casualties as a result of Islamist terror is still 90 percent.[1]

[1]RAND (2011). *RAND Database of Worldwide Terrorism Incidents*. Santa Monica, CA: RAND Corporation. Retrieved April 6, 2011, from http://www.rand.org/nsrd/projects/terrorism-incidents.html.

ANTIGLOBALIZATION

Globalization not only represents the highest achievement of Western civilization and cultural imperialism; it also embodies the most recent stage of modernism. By and large, **globalization** refers to interconnections between individuals through the removal or reduction of space and time barriers. It also implies a freer flow of technology, capital, products, and services, as well as cultures, ideas, and laws, across the world. In short, globalization brings the world closer together and sets a new global standard: the nature of secular, Westernized urban society is now found not only in developed countries but also in many nations of the Third World today—and it is contemplated by critics as vestiges of colonialism.[132]

Grobalization

When this new global standard of Westernization is pushed to the extreme, it is called grobalization (no, there is no spelling error). **Grobalization** is a hybrid of the words "growth" and "globalization" (thus, the term *gro*balization). It refers to the imperialistic ambitions and needs of MNCs, or even entire countries, to plant themselves into various areas of the world to allow their power, influence, and revenues to grow even more. As a form of unrestrained capitalism and cultural imperialism, grobalization is synonymous with standardization, universalization, and homogenization. By imposing the global, grobalization also tends to eliminate the local: it engages in a delocalization and ultrapenetration of local cultures, it is one-directional and deterministic, and it is a one-way information flow and intentional cultural domination of an MNC on local cultures.[133] Wal-Mart, McDonald's, Kentucky Fried Chicken, Coca-Cola, and Disney are examples of MNCs that have grobalized the world.

This extreme form of globalization denotes the idea that unbounded globalization has challenged the modern idea of the state by creating nonlocal and global forms of economic, social, and cultural interaction. For many local communities, then, globalization erodes their sense of ethnic identity and unity. In fact, they think that it has seriously undermined secular nationalism and the nation-state by wearing them out economically (not only through the global reach of MNCs, but also by the global character of their workforce, currency, and financial methods).[134] When **value bases** (important moral resources for those ethnic identities and nation-states)[135] are ruined, as witnessed by globalization processes, Habermas (1973)[136] argues, local communities and cultures will naturally undergo a deficiency in values, or a "legitimation crisis."

The Lexus and the Olive Tree

As Friedman (2000)[137] puts it, the **Lexus** (the epitome of what is modern, technological, and global) and the **olive tree** (the epitome of what is traditional and parochial) are in deep conflict. The Lexus and the olive tree are, again, a symbol of the Clash of Civilizations. It is the long-standing struggle between the old and the new, tradition and modernity, status quo and upheaval, and global and local. It is not surprising that some antiglobalization movements have been global themselves. Fervent movements for ethnic and religious nationalism have emerged in regions where local leaders have felt subjugated by globalization, unable to gain military power against what they consider the comprador ruling elites (i.e., corrupt leaders placed in government by the United States), and invaded by symbols of Western popular culture on TV, the internet, and movies.[138] There are many olive trees but hardly any Lexuses in Egypt. In the early 1990s, this was reflected in the 43 percent drop in the country's tourism as a direct result of terrorist attacks. It also demonstrates how terrorists can express their antiglobalization outlook. When tourism symbolizes global capitalism, attacking tourists is tantamount to attacking the Western governments that the terrorists are actually fighting. This also makes those governments look weak.[139] Terrorism against tourists can stem from tensions that develop when poor locals are forced to live together with international tourists enjoying luxuries that they will probably never have. Travel styles can reflect globalization, excessive capitalism, and conspicuous consumption—that is, the Western culture of tourists and their countries.[140]

The Bali bombing in 2002 was perpetrated by a radical group called Jemaah Islamiyah. The group used Islamist values like jihad to substantiate its acts of terrorism. They maintained that globalization and capitalism are symbols of colonization championed by Western countries to the detriment of the Third World and Muslim countries.[141] In Sri Lanka, the Tamil Tigers have conducted many suicide attacks against soldiers, government officials, and civilians in Colombo, particularly against the World Trade Center, the Temple of the Tooth, and the international airport. Many of their attacks have been aimed at symbols of globalization.[142] **Baader-Meinhof** (also called the **Red Army Faction [RAF]**), a German Marxist terrorist group in the 1960s and 1970s, described Deutsche Bank as a symbol of globalization and the leader of the fascistic capital structure that planned to imperil Eastern Europe to the danger of capitalist exploitation. In November 1989, Alfred Herrhausen, the chairman of Deutsche Bank, was killed in a terrorist attack.[143]

ANTI-MULTICULTURALISM

Multiculturalism refers to the existence of multiple cultures in a community or country. The term denotes both cultural diversity (i.e., as related to the demographic composition of a particular community, institution, city, or nation) and the ideology or political philosophy that promotes such diversity (also called **institutionalization**). Multiculturalism promotes the model of the "salad bowl" or "cultural mosaic" instead of the "melting pot" theory (i.e., **cultural adaptation**).[144] Multiculturalism has also been the target of terrorism throughout history. Let us look at one specific tragedy that happened recently.

On July 22, 2011, a Norwegian terrorist killed a high number of innocent civilians based on his perception of "too much multiculturalism" in Western Europe. Indeed, **Anders Behring Breivik**, then only thirty-two years of age, committed two successive terrorist acts on the Norwegian government, civilians, and a training camp for youths in southern Norway (around the Oslo area). A total of seventy-seven individuals died, and another 151 were wounded. This was the most fatal tragedy on Norwegian soil since World War II. In his 1,500-page manifesto, *2083: A European Declaration of Independence*,[145] not only did Anders Behring Breivik modify his name to "Andrew Berwick," but also he explained why he took fatal actions against what he called Europe's "real enemies." One of the reasons, he said, was "the rise of cultural Marxism/multiculturalism in Western Europe." His views are reflected in the following excerpt:

> Multiculturalists/cultural Marxists usually operate under the disguise of humanism. A majority are anti-nationalists and want to deconstruct European identity, traditions, culture and even nation states. As we all know, the root of Europe's problems is the lack of cultural self-confidence (nationalism). Most people are still terrified of nationalistic political doctrines thinking that if we ever embrace these principles again, new "Hitler's" will suddenly pop up and initiate global Armageddon. . . . Needless to say; the growing numbers of nationalists in Western Europe are systematically being ridiculed, silenced and persecuted by the current cultural Marxist/multiculturalist political establishments. This has been a continuous ongoing process which started in 1945. This irrational fear of nationalistic doctrines is preventing us from stopping our own national/cultural suicide as the Islamic colonization is increasing annually. This book presents the only solutions to our current problems. You cannot defeat Islamisation or halt/reverse the Islamic colonization of Western Europe without first removing the political doctrines manifested through multiculturalism/cultural Marxism.

The "rise of cultural Marxism/multiculturalism" is somewhat related to "antiglobalization" (as discussed in the previous subsection) in that the latter is highly correlated with U.S. imperialism. In this particular case of anti-multiculturalism, one will quickly notice—just by examining the identity of victims killed by the Norwegian terrorist—that most of them were not Muslims or Arabs themselves. Rather, they were Norwegian youths who had left-wing tendencies. Breivik's reason to kill them, then, could be that it all had to do with a form of "guilt by association." From this perspective, it is not only Islamic immigrants who are jeopardizing the preservation of European values, but also those in favor of Muslim immigration. Hence, the excerpt above demonstrates that Breivik wanted to target the very symbol of left-wing domination: multiculturalism, or what he called **cultural Marxism**. According to him, "cultural Marxism" will ultimately cause "national/cultural suicide." Lastly, racism was another reason for Anders Behring Breivik to carry out his "final solution."

SUMMARY

Terrorism is violence perpetrated against a specific target with the objective of influencing multiple audiences. The success of a terrorist act is not captured by the destruction of its target, but by the realization of a symbolic act that has far-reaching repercussions. Because the most fundamental tenet of any communication act is to understand the audience, terrorists are well aware that a terrorist attack represents a symbolic interaction with an audience beyond the direct targets. The audience can be an individual, a nation, or even the whole world. Ultimately, the objective of terrorism is to create fear and signs of fear, and it works well through a process called "mass-mediated terrorism," a phenomenon whereby the media broadcast terrorist acts on a regular basis. Another important concept in this chapter was iconoclasm, which involves an attack upon an enemy's sacred or religious symbols (i.e., cultural terrorism). Third, the theory of Clash of Civilizations posits that cultural and religious differences between global civilizations (generally Islam and the West) are a major source of terrorism today. For example, the World Trade Center was targeted by Al Qaeda because it was a symbol of wealth, global capitalism, power, modernism, and the heart of U.S. culture and heritage. To substantiate these arguments, blowback theory posits that the global hegemony of empires—at both the end of the twentieth century and the beginning of the twenty-first century—and the additional global military presence of the United States have prompted resistance in the form of terrorism and attacks on symbolic targets like the World Trade Center. Of equal relevance, liquid modernity rests on the premise that late modernity and postmodern consumerism lead to ambiguity and increasing uncertainty within individual souls in society. Liquid modernity contributes to more jihadist incidents in countries like Britain. A particular form of liquid modernity is Westoxification (the state of being inebriated with Western culture and ideas). As we have seen, Westoxification is reflected through anti-Western sentiment, modernism, globalization, grobalization, and the Lexus (vs. the olive tree). Finally, multiculturalism has also been the target of terrorism throughout history. The specific case study of the Norwegian massacre perpetrated by Anders Behring Breivik exemplifies hatred against what the latter called "cultural Marxism."

NOTES

1. Martin, Gus (2010). *Understanding Terrorism: Challenges, Perspectives, and Issues*. Thousand Oaks, CA: Sage.

2. Boyns, David, & Ballard, James David (2004). Developing a Sociological Theory for the Empirical Understanding of Terrorism. *American Sociologist, 35*(2), 5–25.

3. Lule, Jack (2001). *Daily News, Eternal Stories*. New York: Guilford Press.

4. Kalyvas, Stathis (2004). The Paradox of Terrorism in Civil War. *The Journal of Ethics, 8*, 97–138.

5. O'Hair, Dan, Heath, Robert, Ayotte, Kevin, & Ledlow, Gerald (2008). *Terrorism: Communication and Rhetorical Perspectives*. Cresskill, NJ: Hampton Press.

6. Bendle, Mervyn (2006). Existential Terrorism: Civil Society and Its Enemies. *Australian Journal of Politics and History, 52*(1), 115–130.

7. O'Hair, Dan, Heath, Robert, Ayotte, Kevin, & Ledlow, Gerald (2008). *Terrorism: Communication and Rhetorical Perspectives*. Cresskill, NJ: Hampton Press.

8. O'Shaughnessy, Nicholas, & Baines, Paul (2009). Selling Terror: The Symbolization and Positioning of Jihad. *Marketing Theory, 9*(2), 227–241.

9. Crelinsten, Ronald (1989). Terrorism and the Media: Problems, Solutions and Counterproblems. *Political Communication and Persuasion, 6*, 311–339.

10. Goodwin, Jeff (2006). A Theory of Categorical Terrorism. *Social Forces, 84*, 2027–2046.

11. Louw, Eric (2003). The "War against Terrorism": A Public Relations Challenge for the Pentagon. *Gazette: The International Journal for Communication Studies, 65*(3), 211–230; and Lulat, Y. G.-M. (2005). *A History of African Higher Education from Antiquity to the Present: A Critical Synthesis*. Santa Barbara, CA: Praeger.

12. Goodwin, Jeff (2006). A Theory of Categorical Terrorism. *Social Forces, 84*, 2027–2046.

13. Goodwin, Jeff (2006). A Theory of Categorical Terrorism. *Social Forces, 84*, 2027–2046.

14. Meloy, Redi, Mohandie, Kris, Hempel, Anthony, & Shiva, Andrew (2001). The Violent True Believer: Homicidal and Suicidal States of Mind (HASSOM). *Journal of Threat Assessment, 1*(4), 1–14.

15. Baudrillard, Jean (1983). *Simulations*. New York: Semiotext.

16. Nacos, Brigitte (2002). *Mass-Mediated Terrorism: The Central Role of the Media in Terrorism and Counter-terrorism*. Lanham, MD: Rowman & Littlefield.

17. Comer, Jonathan, & Kendall, Philip (2007). Terrorism: The Psychological Impact on Youth. *Clinical Psychology: Science and Practice, 14*, 179–212.

18. Gressang, Daniel (2001). Audience and Message: Assessing Terrorist WMD Potential. *Terrorism and Political Violence, 13*(3), 83–106.

19. Lule, Jack (1991). Sacrifice and the Body on the Tarmac: Symbolic Significance of the U.S. News about a Terrorist Victim. In Yonah Alexander & Robert Picard (Eds.), *In the Camera's Eye: News Coverage of Terrorists Events* (pp. 30–48). Washington, DC: Brassey's.

20. Gressang, Daniel (2001). Audience and Message: Assessing Terrorist WMD Potential. *Terrorism and Political Violence, 13*(3), 83–106.

21. Vasilenko, V. I. (2005). The Concept and Typology of Terrorism. *Statutes and Decisions, 40*(5), 46–56.

22. Matusitz, Jonathan (2012). *Terrorism & Communication: A Critical Introduction*. Thousand Oaks, CA: Sage.

23. Cialdini, Robert (2001). *Influence: Science and Practice* (4th ed.). Boston: Allyn & Bacon.

24. Williams, John (1998). The Failure of Terrorism as Mass Communication. *Turkish Journal of Police Studies, 1*(4), 37–52.

25. Freedman, Lawrence (1983). Why Does Terrorism Terrorize? *Terrorism, 6*(3), 389–401.

26. Williams, John (1998). The Failure of Terrorism as Mass Communication. *Turkish Journal of Police Studies, 1*(4), 37–52.

27. Nacos, Brigitte (2002). *Mass-Mediated Terrorism: The Central Role of the Media in Terrorism and Counter-terrorism*. Lanham, MD: Rowman & Littlefield.

28. Jennings, Margaret, & Kilcoyne, Francis (2003). Defacement: Practical Theology, Politics, or Prejudice: The Case of the North Portal of Bourges. *Church History: Studies in Christianity and Culture, 72*(2), 276–303.

29. Colas, Dominique (1997). *Civil Society and Fanaticism*. Stanford, CA: Stanford University Press.

30. Perlmutter, Dawn (2006). Mujahideen Desecration: Beheadings, Mutilation & Muslim Iconoclasm. *Anthropoetics, 12*(2), 1–8.

31. Viejo Rose, Dacia (2007). Conflict and the Deliberate Destruction of Cultural Heritage. In Helmut Anheier & Yudhishthir Raj Isar (Eds.), *Conflicts and Tensions* (pp. 102–116). Thousand Oaks, CA: Sage.

32. Commission on Security and Cooperation in Europe (1998). *Briefing on Bosnia by Region*. Washington, DC: U.S. Helsinki Commission.

33. Petras, James (1994). Cultural Imperialism in Late 20th Century. *Economic and Political Weekly, 29*(32), 2070–2073.

34. Meskell, Lynn (2002). Negative Heritage and Past Mastering in Archaeology. *Anthropological Quarterly, 75*(3), 557–574.

35. Perlmutter, Dawn (2011). The Semiotics of Honor Killing & Ritual Murder. *Anthropoetics, 17*(1), 22–34.

36. Mehatg, Sarah Jane (2001). Identicide and Cultural Cannibalism: Warfare's Appetite for Symbolic Place. *Peace Research Journal, 33*(3), 89–98.

37. Viejo Rose, Dacia (2007). Conflict and the Deliberate Destruction of Cultural Heritage. In Helmut Anheier & Yudhishthir Raj Isar (Eds.), *Conflicts and Tensions* (pp. 102–116). Thousand Oaks, CA: Sage.

38. Gamboni, Dario (1997). *The Destruction of Art: Iconoclasm and Vandalism since the French Revolution*. London: Reaktion Books.

39. Winter, Tim (2007). *Post-Conflict Heritage, Postcolonial Tourism: Culture, Politics and Development at Angkor*. New York: Routledge.

40. Meskell, Lynn (2002). Negative Heritage and Past Mastering in Archaeology. *Anthropological Quarterly, 75*(3), 557–574.

41. Perry, Marilyn, & Burnham, Bonni (2001). A Critical Mission: The World Monuments Watch. *World Monuments Watch: 100 Most Endangered Sites, 7*, 3–4.

42. Perlmutter, Dawn (2011). The Semiotics of Honor Killing & Ritual Murder. *Anthropoetics, 17*(1), 22–34.

43. Martin, Gus (2010). *Understanding Terrorism: Challenges, Perspectives, and Issues*. Thousand Oaks, CA: Sage.

44. Ranstorp, Magnus (1996). Terrorism in the Name of Religion. *Journal of International Affairs, 50*(1), 41–63.

45. Noida, Ghia (2013). Georgian Policy towards the North Caucasus: Old Dilemmas, New Trends. In A. Ergun & H. Isaxanli (Eds.), *Security and Cross-Border Cooperation in the EU, the Black Sea Region and Southern Caucasus* (pp. 137–151). Amsterdam: IOS Press.

46. Richmond, Walter (2013). *The Circassian Genocide*. New Brunswick, NJ: Rutgers University Press.

47. Martin, Frankie (2014, January 23). *The Olympics' Forgotten People*. Retrieved January 26, 2014, from http://www.cnn.com/2014/01/23/opinion/martin-olympics-circassians/

48. Stump, Roger (2005). Religion and the Geographies of War. In Colin Flint (Ed.), *The Geography of War and Peace: From Death Camps to Diplomats* (pp. 149–173). Oxford: Oxford University Press.

49. Pettigrew, Joyce (1991). Songs of the Sikh Resistance Movement. *Asian Music, 23*(1), 85–118.

50. Ghazaleh, Pascale (2002, January 31). Who Owns the Past? *Al-Ahram Weekly Online*. Retrieved June 27, 2014, from http://weekly.ahram.org.eg/2002/571/li1.htm

51. Stump, Roger (2005). Religion and the Geographies of War. In Colin Flint (Ed.), *The Geography of War and Peace: From Death Camps to Diplomats* (pp. 149–173). Oxford: Oxford University Press.

52. Perlmutter, Dawn (2011). The Semiotics of Honor Killing & Ritual Murder. *Anthropoetics, 17*(1), 22–34.

53. Speckhard, Anne, & Akhmedova, Khapta (2006). The New Chechen Jihad: Militant Wahhabism as a Radical Movement and a Source of Suicide Terrorism in Post-War Chechen Society. *Democracy and Security, 2*(1), 103–155.

54. Eaton, Richard (2000). Temple Desecration and Indo-Muslim States. In David Gilmartin & Bruce B. Lawrence (Eds.), *Beyond Turk and Hindu: Rethinking Religious Identities in Islamicate South Asia* (pp. 246–281). Gainesville: University Press of Florida.

55. Perlmutter, Dawn (2011). The Semiotics of Honor Killing & Ritual Murder. *Anthropoetics, 17*(1), 22–34.

56. Perlmutter, Dawn (2006). Mujahideen Desecration: Beheadings, Mutilation & Muslim Iconoclasm. *Anthropoetics, 12*(2), 1–8.

57. National Consortium for the Study of Terrorism and Responses to Terrorism (2013). *Brigades for the Defense of Holy Shrines*. College Park, MD: START.

58. Nasr, Vali (2006). When the Shiites Rise. *Foreign Affairs, 85*(4), 58–74; and Norton, August Richard (2007). The Shiite "Threat" Revisited. *Current History, 10*, 434–439.

59. Cannon, Charles Master (2012). *Forgiving the Unforgivable: The True Story of How Survivors of the Mumbai Terrorist Attack Answered Hatred with Compassion*. New York: SelectBooks.

60. Rabasa, Angel, Blackwill, Robert, Chalk, Peter, Cragin, Kim, & Fair, Christine (2009). *The Lessons of Mumbai*. Santa Monica, CA: RAND.

61. Bishop, Ryan, & Roy, Tania (2009). Mumbai: City-as-Target: Introduction. *Theory, Culture & Society, 26*(7), 263–277.

62. Huntington, Samuel (1996). *The Clash of Civilizations and the Remaking of World Order*. New York: Simon & Schuster.

63. Rich, Andrew (2004). *Think Tanks, Public Policy, and the Politics of Expertise*. Cambridge: Cambridge University Press.

64. Barber, Benjamin (1995). *Jihad vs. McWorld*. New York: Crown.

65. Jandt, Fred (2010). *An Introduction to Intercultural Communication: Identities in a Global Community* (6th ed.). Thousand Oaks, CA: Sage; Le Feber, Walter (2002). The Post September 11 Debate over Empire, Globalization, and Fragmentation. *Political Science Quarterly, 117*(1), 9–10; and Zirinski, Roni (2005). *Ad Hoc Arabism: Advertising, Culture, and Technology in Saudi Arabia*. New York: Peter Lang.

66. Aziz, Heba (1995). Understanding Terrorist Attacks on Tourists in Egypt. *Tourism Management, 16*, 91–95; and Wahab, Salah (1996). Tourism and Terrorism: Synthesis of the Problem with Emphasis on Egypt. In Abraham Pizam & Yohel Mansfeld (Eds.), *Tourism, Crime and International Security Issues* (pp. 175–186). New York: John Wiley.

67. Richter, Linda (1983). Tourism Politics and Political Science: A Case of Not So Benign Neglect. *Annals of Tourism Research, 10*(3), 313–315.

68. O'Shaughnessy, Nicholas, & Baines, Paul (2009). Selling Terror: The Symbolization and Positioning of Jihad. *Marketing Theory, 9*(2), 227–241.

69. Hall, Colin, & O'Sullivan, Vanessa (1996). Tourism, Political Stability and Violence. In Abraham Pizam & Yohel Mansfeld (Eds.), *Tourism, Crime and International Security Issues* (pp. 175–186). New York: John Wiley.

70. Sönmez, Sevil, Apostolopoulos, Yiorgos, & Tarlow, Peter (1999). Tourism in Crisis: Managing the Effects of Terrorism. *Journal of Travel Research, 38*, 13–18.

71. Nacos, Brigitte (2002). *Mass-Mediated Terrorism: The Central Role of the Media in Terrorism and Counterterrorism*. Lanham, MD: Rowman & Littlefield.

72. Mansdorf, Irwin, & Kedar, Mordechai (2008). The Psychological Asymmetry of Islamist Warfare. *Middle East Quarterly, 15*(2), 37–44.

73. International Monetary Fund. (2001, December 18). World Economic Outlook: The Global Economy after September 11 (Press release). Washington, DC: Author.

74. Pyszczynski, Tom (2004). What Are We So Afraid of? A Terror Management Theory Perspective on the Politics of Fear. *Social Research, 71*(4), 827–848.

75. Bendle, Mervyn (2006). Existential Terrorism: Civil Society and Its Enemies. *Australian Journal of Politics and History, 52*(1), 115–130.

76. Al Jazeera (2002, February 5). Transcript of Bin Laden's October Interview. Retrieved on March 29, 2013 from http://articles.cnn.com/2002-02-05/world/binladen.transcript_1_incitement-fatwas-al-qaeda organization/4?_s=PM:asiapcf.

77. Harris, Lee (2004). *Civilization and Its Enemies: The Next Stage in History*. New York: Simon & Schuster.

78. Juergensmeyer, Mark (2004). Holy Orders: Opposition to Modern States. *Harvard International Review, 25*(4), 10–21.

79. Jones, Jonathan (2011, September 2). The Meaning of 9/11's Most Controversial Photo. *The Guardian*, p. A1; and Nouriani, Steven (2011). The Defensive Misappropriation and Corruption of Cultural Symbols. *Jung Journal: Culture and Psyche, 5*(1), 19–30.

80. Azm, Sadiq Jalal (2005). Islam, Terrorism, and the West. *Comparative Studies of South Asia, Africa and the Middle East, 25*(1), 6–15.

81. Beauregard, Robert (2004). Mistakes Were Made: Rebuilding the World Trade Center, Phase 1. *International Planning Studies, 9*(2), 139–153.

82. Denton, Robert (2006). *Language, Symbols, and the Media: Communication in the Aftermath of the World Trade Center Attack.* Piscataway, NJ: Transaction Publishers.

83. Farmer, David John (2002). The Rhetoric of Public Administration. *Administration & Society, 34*(2), 135–140.

84. Lew, Marshall (2007). Design of Tall Buildings in High-Seismic Regions. *The Structural Design of Tall and Special Buildings, 16*, 537–541.

85. Lule, Jack (2002). Myth and Terror on the Editorial Page: *The New York Times* Response to September 11, 2001. *Journalism & Mass Communications Quarterly, 79*(2), 275–293.

86. O'Hair, Dan, Heath, Robert, Ayotte, Kevin, & Ledlow, Gerald (2008). *Terrorism: Communication and Rhetorical Perspectives.* Cresskill, NJ: Hampton Press.

87. Stankiewicz, Wojciech (2005). International Terrorism at Sea as a Menace to the Civilization of the 21st Century. *American Behavioral Scientist, 48*(6), 683–699.

88. Weimann, Gabriel (2008). The Psychology of Mass-Mediated Terrorism. *American Behavioral Scientist, 52*(1), 69–86.

89. Baudrillard, Jean (2003). *The Spirit of Terrorism and Other Essays.* New York: Verso.

90. Weimann, Gabriel (2008). The Psychology of Mass-Mediated Terrorism. *American Behavioral Scientist, 52*(1), 69–86.

91. Smith, Anthony (2003). *Chosen Peoples.* New York: Oxford University Press.

92. Martin, Gus (2010). *Understanding Terrorism: Challenges, Perspectives, and Issues.* Thousand Oaks, CA: Sage.

93. Leheny, David (2002). Symbols, Strategies, and Choices for International Relations Scholarship after September 11. *Dialog-IO*, 57–70.

94. Johnson, Chalmers (2000). *Blowback: The Costs and Consequences of American Empire.* New York: Henry Holt and Company.

95. Brooks, Stephen, & Wohlforth, William (2002). American Primacy in Perspective. *Foreign Affairs, 81*, 20–33.

96. Hartnett, Stephen (2003). The Rhetorical Dialectics of Citizenship, Deception, Violence, and Empire. *Rhetoric & Public Affairs, 6*(1), 161–178.

97. Han, Peter (2002). Comment: 9/11 and the American Way of Life: The Impact of 12/7 Revisited. *Diplomatic History, 26*(4), 627–634.

98. Crenshaw, Martha (2001). Why America? The Globalization of Civil War. *Current History, 14*, 425–432.

99. Johnson, Chalmers (2000). *Blowback: The Costs and Consequences of American Empire.* New York: Henry Holt and Company.

100. Khan, Shamsul (2007). "Islamic Fundamentalism" in the Asia Pacific Region: Failures of Civil Societies or Backlash against U.S. Hegemony. In Edward Linden (Ed.), *Focus on Terrorism* (pp. 181–228). Happauge, NY: Nova Science Publishers.

101. Pyszczynski, Tom (2004). What Are We So Afraid of? A Terror Management Theory Perspective on the Politics of Fear. *Social Research, 71*(4), 827–848.

102. Juergensmeyer, Mark (2004). Holy Orders: Opposition to Modern States. *Harvard International Review, 25*(4), 10–21.

103. National Commission on Terrorist Attacks upon the United States (2004). *9/11 Commission Report.* Washington, DC: 9/11 Commission.

104. Bauman, Zygmunt (2000). *Liquid Modernity.* Cambridge: Polity.

105. Craik, Jennifer (1994). *The Face of Fashion: Cultural Studies in Fashion.* London: Routledge.

106. Bauman, Zygmunt (2005). *Liquid Life.* Cambridge: Polity.

107. Bauman, Zygmunt (2000). *Liquid Modernity.* Cambridge: Polity.

108. Bauman, Zygmunt (2004). *Identity.* Cambridge: Polity.

109. Mullaly, Bob (2007). Oppression: The Focus of Structural Social Work. In Bob Mullaly (Ed.), *The New Structural Social Work* (pp. 252–286). Don Mills, ON: Oxford University Press.

110. National Statistics Online (2007). *Labour Market.* Retrieved March 29, 2013, from http://www.statistics.gov.uk/cci/nugget.asp?id979; and Silke, Andrew (2008). Holy Warriors: Exploring the Psychological Processes of Jihadi Radicalization. *European Journal of Criminology, 5*(1), 99–123.

111. Lankford, Adam (2013). *The Myth of Martyrdom: What Really Drives Suicide Bombers, Rampage Shooters, and Other Self-Destructive Killers.* New York: Palgrave Macmillan.

112. Best, Shaun (2010). Liquid Terrorism: Altruistic Fundamentalism in the Context of Liquid Modernity. *Sociology, 44*(4), 678–694.

113. Best, Shaun (2010). Liquid Terrorism: Altruistic Fundamentalism in the Context of Liquid Modernity. *Sociology, 44*(4), 678–694.

114. Aly, Waleed (2007, September 19). *Liquid Terror: The Dynamics of Homegrown Radicalisation.* Presentation given at the Lowy Institute for International Policy, Sydney, Australia.

115. Bauman, Zygmunt (2004). *Identity*. Cambridge: Polity.

116. Al-e Ahmad, Jalal (1983). *Occidentosis: A Plague from the West*. Berkeley, CA: Mizan Press.

117. Kramer, Martin (1994). The Jihad against the Jews. *Commentary, 38*–42.

118. Juergensmeyer, Mark (2004). Holy Orders: Opposition to Modern States. *Harvard International Review, 25*(4), 10–21.

119. Norton, Augustus Richard (1987). *Amal and the Shi'a: Struggle for the Soul of Lebanon*. Austin: University of Texas Press.

120. Prewitt, Kenneth, Alterman, Eric, Arato, Andrew, Pyszczynski, Tom, Robin, Corey, & Stern, Jessica (2004). The Politics of Fear after 9/11. *Social Research, 71*(4), 1129–1146.

121. Al-Azm, Sadik (2004). Islam, Terrorism and the West Today. *Die Welt des Islams, 44*(1), 114–128.

122. Rauchway, Eric (2004). *Murdering McKinley: The Making of Theodore Roosevelt's America*. New York: Hill and Wang.

123. Henninger, Max (2006). The Postponed Revolution: Reading Italian Insurrectionary Leftism as Generational Conflict. *Italica, 83*(3), 629–648.

124. Young, Lawrence (1994). Confronting Turbulent Environments: Issues in the Organizational Growth and Globalization of Mormonism. In Marie Cornwall, Tim Heaton, & Lawrence Young (Eds.), *Contemporary Mormonism: Social Science Perspectives* (pp. 43–63). Urbana: University of Illinois Press.

125. Wurmser, David (1993). The Rise and Fall of the Arab World. *Strategic Review, 33*–46.

126. Ranstorp, Magnus (1996). Terrorism in the Name of Religion. *Journal of International Affairs, 50*(1), 41–63.

127. Louw, Eric (2003). The "War against Terrorism": A Public Relations Challenge for the Pentagon. *Gazette: The International Journal for Communication Studies, 65*(3), 211–230; and Shari'ati, Ali (1980). *Marxism and Other Western Fallacies: An Islamic Critique*. Berkeley, CA: Mizan Press.

128. Pratt, Douglas (2005). *The Challenge of Islam*. Aldershot, UK: Ashgate.

129. Lewis, Bernard (2003). *The Crisis of Islam*. London: Weidenfield and Nicolson.

130. Taheri, Amir (2004). Fascism in Muslim Countries. *American Foreign Policy Interests, 26*(1), 21–30.

131. Sayyid, Bobby (2003). *A Fundamental Fear: Eurocentrism and the Emergence of Islamism*. London: Zed Books.

132. Chanda, Nayan (2007). *Bound Together: How Traders, Preachers, Warriors and Adventurers Shaped Globalization*. New Haven, CT: Yale University Press.

133. Ritzer, George (2007). *The Globalization of Nothing 2*. Thousand Oaks, CA: Pine Forge Press.

134. Juergensmeyer, Mark (2004). Holy Orders: Opposition to Modern States. *Harvard International Review, 25*(4), 10–21.

135. Baumeister, Roy (1991). *Meanings of Life*. New York: Guilford Press.

136. Habermas, Jürgen (1973). *Legitimation Crisis*. Boston: Beacon Press.

137. Friedman, Thomas (2000). *The Lexus and the Olive Tree: Understanding Globalization*. London: HarperCollins.

138. Juergensmeyer, Mark (2004). Holy Orders: Opposition to Modern States. *Harvard International Review, 25*(4), 10–21.

139. Hall, Colin, & O'Sullivan, Vanessa (1996). Tourism, Political Stability and Violence. In Abraham Pizam & Yohel Mansfeld (Eds.), *Tourism, Crime and International Security Issues* (pp. 175–186). New York: John Wiley; and Sönmez, Sevil, Apostolopoulos, Yiorgos, & Tarlow, Peter (1999). Tourism in Crisis: Managing the Effects of Terrorism. *Journal of Travel Research, 38*, 13–18.

140. Aziz, Heba (1995). Understanding Terrorist Attacks on Tourists in Egypt. *Tourism Management, 16*, 91–95.

141. Prayudi, Prayudi (2008). Mass Media and Terrorism: Deconstructing the Relationship. *Jurnal Ilmu Komunikasi Terakreditasi, 6*(2), 113–120.

142. Moghaddam, Fathali (2008). *How Globalization Spurs Terrorism*. Westport, CT: Praeger.

143. Wegner, Adam (1991). Extraterritorial Jurisdiction under International Law: The Yunis Decision as a Model for the Prosecution of Terrorists in U.S. Courts. *Law and Policy in International Business, 22*, 409–438.

144. Kim, Young Yun (2000). *Becoming Intercultural: An Integrative Theory of Communication and Cross-Cultural Adaptation*. Thousand Oaks, CA: Sage; and Murphy, Michael (2009). *Multiculturalism: A Critical Introduction*. New York: Routledge.

145. Breivik, Anders Behring (2011). *2083: A European Declaration of Independence*. Retrieved December 18, 2011, from http://www.kevinislaughter.com/wp-content/uploads/2083+-+A+European+Declaration+of+Independence.pdf.

Chapter Four

The Symbolic Culture of Terrorism

CULTURE: DEFINITION

Culture is the social construction and historical transmission of patterns of symbols, denotations, connotations, ideologies, values, beliefs, norms, traditions, and artifacts from generation to generation. These are shared to a certain degree by members of a specific community and become internalized when individuals are in interaction with each other.[1] As cultural beings, humans are born into an interconnected system of such symbols, meanings, values, norms, and so forth that will mostly determine how they will come to interpret the world around them.[2] As appositely worded by the late anthropologist Clifford Geertz (1973),[3] culture is "a system of inherited conceptions expressed in symbolic forms by means of which men communicate, perpetuate, and develop their knowledge about and attitudes toward life" (p. 89). Swidler (1986)[4] extends this view by asserting that culture is a "'tool kit' of symbols, stories, rituals, and worldviews, which people may use in varying configurations to solve different types of problems" (p. 273).

In line with these contentions, culture is a mental model that is disseminated and shared among members of a group over a period of time.[5] It consists of ideas that circulate effectively and perpetually within a population.[6] Above all, culture is the transmission of ideas from one generation to the next. Scholars generally apply the word **idea** in reference to any substance of the mind, including perceptions of how things are or how they should be. For instance, some cultures may share the idea that Western countries have joined forces in a surreptitious war against Islam. Their minds may also encompass the idea that imported Western principles, such as the separation between religion and state, are largely negative and should be forestalled. Ideas are frequently considered independent units by scholars, or classified together into categories of belief for simplicity.[7] When culture is viewed in terms of the ideas that are broadly disseminated throughout a population, it is called **cultural epidemiology**.[8]

Cultural Model

A **cultural model** is an external representation of a culture created by the main agents of that culture (e.g., leaders, scholars, clerics, etc.). It embodies a consensus of the mental models for a specific group. Put simply, it is a formal description of the knowledge held by members of a group and describes how the world is understood by those people. Sometimes, the term **cultural knowledge** is used to refer to networks of causally interconnected ideas—ideas for which there is some point of agreement among members of a group.[9] Such causally interconnected ideas become activated within specific situations to direct our thinking and decision making, and they can be altered under suitable conditions. In a nutshell, a cultural model functions as a mental template for understanding the world and organizing knowledge about each domain.[10] It functions as a **thinking mode**; that is, a type of mental model or cognitive system that helps a particular cultural group to categorize things. For example, a thinking mode can include folk theories about how human existence should be interpreted. This, in turn, shapes our worldview.

A **worldview** is a formal or informal schema of beliefs that frames our perception of the universe, especially our relationship with the world and the sacred. In essence, a worldview identifies our position in the world relative to other groups (e.g., those who are not members of the ingroup of believers) and the sacred. A worldview is also shared within a community of believers with the same or similar mental model of human existence, but on a much larger level. In other words, it is also a shared system of beliefs that determines a nation's position vis-à-vis other nations.[11] A worldview defines an individual's (1) **orienting system**[12] (a general outlook on the world that includes beliefs, feelings, habits, and relationships from religious, personality, and social spheres), (2) **ideology**[13] (a system of concepts, theories, or themes that make up a social or political agenda of a group or community; it is a frame for social or political action to reach a particular end state), and (3) **values**[14] (the standards that people use to define worth, importance, or correctness).

Cultural Group

The term "cultural group" has been mentioned several times already. On the whole, a **cultural group** is a group of people with a shared system of symbols and ideas, unlike a **social group**, which simply consists of people interacting with one another.[15] Social groups can be found in many different areas, including being neighbors, doing the same work, and taking part in the same social and religious activities.[16] A cultural group is also somewhat different from a demographic group. A **demographic group** is based on nationality, educational status, and so on in that the demographic descriptions pertaining to such a group are contingent upon how prevalent the cultural ideas of interest are. For instance, differences between Sunni and Shia Muslims will matter little if the idea of interest is "There is no god but Allah, and Muhammad is His prophet." Conversely, if the relevant shared beliefs include those relating to the Twelfth Imam (i.e., the ultimate savior of humankind in the Shia doctrine, which is not embraced by Sunnis), then that demographic does become significant. Hence, the relevant cultural group for a study will be determined by the cultural domain, that is, the particular area of interest.[17] When cultural groups form long-lasting or permanent collaborations, they become hybrid cultures. **Hybrid cultures** develop naturally over time as groups come together on a shared process of interacting. They are based on a simplified range of shared assumptions, norms, expectations, and procedures that allow cross-cultural groups to function efficiently.[18]

SYMBOLIC INTERACTIONISM

It is important to understand how the mindset of terrorists is shaped by their own construction of reality, their everyday cultures, and their social interactions. A theory that can explain all this is symbolic interactionism. **Symbolic interactionism** postulates that human beings are able to communicate through shared meanings (e.g., symbols, words, visuals, signs, roles, etc.). Because meaning is transmitted and received within the specific culture in which one lives, meaning becomes symbolic through social interactions happening in that culture. In addition, symbolic interactionism posits that human beings shape and delineate their own meaning of behavior as well as their own social constructions of reality.[19] From this vantage point, meaning involves the interpretation of symbols and their physical and/or abstract connections to our behavior. For Blumer (1969),[20] "the use of meanings by the actor occurs through a process of interpretation" (p. 5). George Herbert Mead (1934)[21] is widely considered the originator of symbolic interaction theory. For Mead, interaction is communication through significant symbols. Meltzer (1975)[22] expanded on Mead's model by claiming the following: symbolic interaction is linked to behavioral interpretation and is created within a particular culture.

Symbolic interactionism is a form of socialization. **Socialization** is a process through which we construct a social self and a feeling of attachment to social systems. This can be achieved through our participation in these social systems and our interaction with others.[23] Symbolic interactionists believe that socialization is a continuous process that entails the attainment of shared meanings emerging through symbolic systems of groups and the behaviors of group members. For a potential recruit of a terrorist organization, agents of socialization may include terrorist recruiters, spiritual mentors, teachers, schools, friends, parents, and ethnic or cultural collectives. Some terrorist groups may implement an artificial form of socialization, such as an institutionalized practice of indoctrination whereby people are exposed to the fundamental beliefs, attitudes, and norms of a particular terrorist group.[24]

Symbolic interaction also depends on the actors' (i.e., agents') cultural backgrounds and interpretive understandings of the beliefs, attitudes, and norms of a cultural group. As described by Blain (2009),[25] thanks to this model of symbolic interaction (see Figure 4.1), group members acquire knowledge through their interactions with other (knowledgeable) members of the group. A symbolic culture develops through such symbolic interactions. These, in turn, are socially transmitted from generation to generation, which makes them quite long-lasting. In order to participate in understandable interaction, the actor and the audience must share a common cultural background. Both the verbal and nonverbal reactions of the audience are constructed based on the message of the original speaker and how that message was sent. Put simply, symbolic interaction develops between the actor and the audience when both share mutual knowledge of the signs and symbols of society and status, and their connected norms and values. Examining symbolic interactionism within this framework is indispensable for an understanding of human conduct. Of course, the cultural background of the actor and the audience will also affect the **scene** (i.e., the setting, social context, or environment) in which the symbolic interaction occurs.[26]

The Social Construction of Culture

How is culture socially constructed? How is it transmitted to future generations? How does it survive? According to Kanagy and Kraybill (1999),[27] in *The Riddles of Human Society*, symbolic interactionism can explain how cultures are socially constructed over time, and it is a four-step process: (1) construction, (2) objectivation, (3) internalization, and (4) renovation. In the first phase, **construction**, a culture is constructed by people through symbolic interaction. It is the "building" stage of social life. Members of societies are the framers and producers of social life. We invent weapons, form beliefs, organize groups, elect leaders, and create rituals. We also wage wars and develop methods of torture and slavery. In the **objectivation** phase, cultural patterns, as time goes by, solidify like water and ice. For example, people are expected to adopt certain dress codes when appearing in public. When did the norm about style of dress emerge? Whether it is ancient or new, it has become a real cultural fact. A neonate is

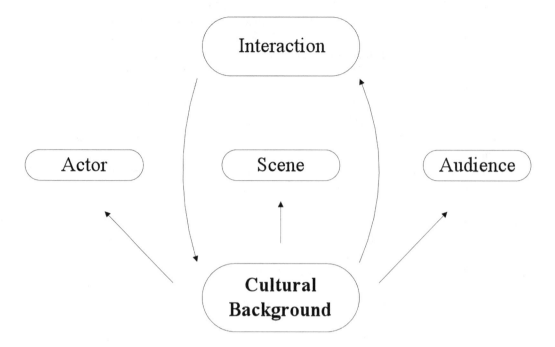

Figure 4.1.   Model of Symbolic Interaction. Blain, Michael (2009). *The Sociology of Terrorism: Studies in Power, Subjection, and Victimage Ritual*. Boca Raton, FL: Universal Publishers, p. 14.

raised into an already constructed culture, of which the foundations were laid out centuries ago. The social construction of culture has already been, in part, established.

In the **internalization** phase, the culture "out there" becomes personal. It becomes "mine" or "ours." Social reality is now subjective reality. Internalization is the development through which the values and ideas of the culture in which we live become anchored in our mind and penetrate our consciousness. What is normal or deviant in the culture becomes second nature to us. Childhood sets the stage for internalization. Our parents may instill in us attitudes of love or hatred toward certain groups of people, and by the time we become adults, this love or hatred has become an internalized habit. We internalize essential aspects of our culture through important agents of socialization such as parents, teachers, friends, neighbors, and the media, all of whom pass on language, values, and expected behavior into our minds through words and actions.

Lastly, whereas construction, objectivation, and internalization can show how culture has the power to shape our self-concept, humans can also shape their culture—a process called **renovation**. Symbolic interaction is dialectical; it is a give-and-take, back-and-forth activity. We tend to take in and regurgitate values of our society, but we can also modify them through renovation. The child of a jihadist suicide bomber is not destined to join a suicide mission team if, for example, he or she leaves his or her religion or reinterprets key principles of the religion. Ground Zero used to refer to the World Trade Center; now, it is only used in reference to the September 11, 2001, terrorist attacks. In short, renovations do happen thanks to individuals' ability to interact with each other and explore alternative courses of action and the consequences of each action. Symbolic interaction allows us to assess a situation and make choices. The scene for interaction is culture, and culture accumulates through the interconnected patterns of interaction and action.[28]

Umwelt and Lebenswelt

Jakob von Uexküll's (1957)[29] concept of **Umwelt** suggests that human beings live in a world that is constructed out of their own symbols. In German, Umwelt means "environment" or "surroundings"; it is understood as the social and physical sphere in which the living human subject is placed. Over time, our Umwelt becomes a solid social pattern; we ground our actions on deep-rooted, sometimes stereotyped, mental assumptions about events, places, and individuals that have special meaning to us. A similar term is **Lebenswelt**, Edmund Husserl's (1970)[30] notion of "lifeworld." It is a type of horizon; the world as it is encountered in daily life and conceived through our direct and immediate experiences. In symbolic interactionism, Lebenswelt refers to the world of shared human experience that produces symbolic systems, organizational cultures, cults, rituals, and religions. These "lifeworlds" allow new ideas to be cultivated and tested against the legacy of our species. In this sense, both Umwelt and Lebenswelt are analogous to **contextualism**, a view holding that truth only has meaning when it is situated within a definite context. Contextualism is any view that puts great emphasis on the significance of context for interpretation. It is a worldview according to which any event is to be related to an ongoing act within its current and historical context and in which a peculiar, functional approach to truth and meaning is adopted. Truth and meaning, then, are to be determined by society or a cultural group.[31]

Social Objects and Cultural Frames

Social objects are created "as people engage in social acts. Social acts depend upon social interaction and interpretation. That is, in order for individuals to cooperate with one another in the creation of social objects, they must orient their conduct to one another" (Hewitt, 1976, p. 49).[32] According to symbolic interactionism, meaning enters every social object and act found within an individual's environment. Because meaning is anchored in every social object and act, it is also anchored in human behavior and is neither fixed nor unchanging. Rather, it is defined in conduct as people act toward objects. Because social acts depend upon social interaction and interpretation, meaning is linked to action through cultural frames. **Cultural frames** are "interpretive devices that people use to make sense of the raw data of experience" (Babb, 1996, p. 1034).[33] These cultural frames can unite terrorists and shed light on their behavior, as in the case of Hamas.

Social identity for Hamas is profoundly embedded within their religious-based cultural frames, permeating every facet of the group members' cultural and social life. Religion gives Hamas loyalists "a sense of self-worth and self-importance by teaching them that they are special to Allah and to the movement" (Arena & Arrigo, 2005, p. 151).[34] This meaning provides a rationale for collective behavior, including the support and use of terrorist violence. Moreover, as both members and sympathizers insist, jihad is the only way to secure a Palestinian state.[35] Both the notions of social object and cultural frame are conveyed in the popular adage "To raise the banner of Allah over every inch of Palestine" (Mishal & Sela 2000, p. 42).[36] As Hamas terrorists construe the symbols of their religious and social existence, proceeding to assign meaning to the social objects and acts that corroborate this, they arrive at the conclusion that freeing the Palestinian territories and reviving an Islamic nation are the duty of every true Muslim. Thus, participating in jihad and related behaviors helps Hamas terrorists feel a sense of purpose in their lives, which, regrettably, have been plagued by political contention, relative deprivation, and ethno-religious discrimination.[37]

ORGANIZATIONAL CULTURE

A terrorist group is generally like an organizational culture. An **organizational culture** refers to a social energy that directs how members should act. Culture is to the organization what personality is to the member—a unifying code that gives meaning, direction, and a feeling of strength.[38] An organizational culture reflects the shared and learned values, beliefs, and attitudes of an organization's members.[39] It justifies the rationale for the phrase "That's the way things are done here." Based on the third step of the aforementioned social construction of culture, the organizational culture becomes so entrenched that the assumptions driving behavior have become internalized. They become second nature; no member thinks about them anymore.[40] An organizational culture matures when members share knowledge and expectations in order to develop methods of coping with external adaptation and survival as well as internal integration. These are two major challenges that every organization faces. **External adaptation and survival** refer to how the organization is able to "familiarize itself" by living up to its constantly changing external environment. This method involves mission and tactics, goal management, means, and measurement. **Internal integration** refers to the formation and upholding of effective relationships among the members of an organization. This method includes language and symbols, group boundaries, power and status, role taking and role making, and both positive and negative cults.[41]

Terrorist Socialization

In an organizational culture, two kinds of social identity exist: hereditarian social identity and/ or convictional social identity. **Hereditarian social identity** is founded in natural (i.e., determined) orders that do not depend on conviction or belief. It is "geneological rather than doctrinal" and is "not subject to volition" (Black, 1992, p. 42).[42] Although this type of social identity can be reduced or minimized, it cannot be repudiated. According to Black (1992),[43] cultures based in natural orders are "independent of conviction" and have "no correspondingly inherent need of rhetorical activity" (p. 46). The values and foundations of identity are unquestionable, over which no disagreement should emerge, because they are neither "acquired through" nor "dispossessed through persuasion" (p. 47). In layperson's terms, the chance of altering one's hereditarian social identity is rather thin.

On the other hand, **convictional social identity** is based on conviction and belief, which means that they operate on the principle of volition and choice. Convictions and beliefs are not based on a natural or determined order. Instead, they require learning through symbolic interaction, and, based on the fourth step of the social construction of culture, they are subject to renovation—amendment, correction, and even rejection. Moral choice is at the nucleus of convictional social identities: organizational members can choose from a myriad of destinies. Given the variety of choices available, symbolic activity becomes the drive for symbolic change and mutation.[44] Convictional social identities contribute to **terrorist socialization**, an ongoing, interactive process through which individuals develop terrorist social identities and learn the ways of thinking, feeling, and acting through symbolic interaction in their terrorist culture.[45]

From the perspective of terrorist socialization, the **terrorist self** is situated in interaction with society. The terrorist and his or her society cannot be understood in isolation because the terrorist self is constantly constructed through symbolic interaction with like-minded others in their cultural group. In other words, the terrorist self is a product of social interaction, developed and refined through an ongoing process of participation in a given Umwelt or Lebenswelt. This also means two things: the nature of the terrorist self is subject to change rather than fixed in one form or status,[46] and because it is constructed through social interaction, the terrorist self is like the social self.[47]

Social Roles in Terrorist Groups

By definition, **role** refers to the total of all behavioral expectations of a social system toward the role owner. The role owner assumes a particular position tht is associated with tasks and functions.[48] Roles provide a terrorist group with a certain level of stability and predictability, as each terrorist is expected to perform in a predefined manner once he or she assumes a role. Occupying a decided role facilitates role relationships in kinships, human relations, and role sets. Such roles usually exist before the recruit actually joins the terrorist group itself; that is, roles can be socially and culturally based. For example, let us look at the role of child terrorists and child soldiers. To begin, between October 2000 and March 2004, at least nine suicide attacks involving Palestinian children were documented. This type of social role can be found in many Islamist groups and does not tend to change. Thanks to such predictability and organization, the activities of a terrorist group are safer and more orderly. In the Palestinian territories, terrorist roles have remained static since the First Intifada in the late 1980s.[49]

About 100,000 children are currently involved in active combat roles in the Sudan (especially the Autonomous Region of Darfur)—which has also been a relatively unchanged practice since the 1980s.[50] In Uganda, the intense use of child soldiers has skyrocketed since 1987, which coincides with the creation of the **Lord's Resistance Army**, a new religious movement and terrorist cult in northern Uganda and South Sudan.[51] Because of their lack of maturity and experience, child soldiers undergo higher casualties than adults. Trained only in war, they are generally attracted to crime (when a conflict is over) or become easily recruited by other terrorists.[52] All these anecdotes illustrate three points: (1) roles give terrorist groups an underlying framework for establishing responsibilities and shared meanings, (2) roles are perceived to be socially recognized categories embraced by members of terrorist groups, and (3) placing so much emphasis on roles also reinforces organizational culture overall. As such, it provides the terrorist group with the aforementioned capacity for "external adaptation and survival" and "internal integration."

Role Taking and Role Making

If a member acts in line with the expectations set by the terrorist group, we call it **role taking**, as demonstrated through the examples about child terrorists and child soldiers. Role taking is related to expectations, which can potentially come from sanctions imposed on the role owner. In brief, role taking implies that the member fulfills a role that already exists in the group or that is new but has been created by the group, not the individual member. What this means is that role taking requires that the individual examine his or her own conduct from the group's point of view. This can be achieved through symbolism and meaning making, whereby individuals anticipate the responses of other group members in order to recognize the different possibilities for their own behavior.[53] As Stryker (1980)[54] illustrates, to effectively engage in terrorism, "one must anticipate the responses of the enemy in the same manner as a parent must anticipate the responses of a child when seeking to aid the child through a crisis" (p. 62). Role taking can lead to **role embracement**, a process whereby one immerses oneself in a role and allows it to shape how one thinks, feels, acts, and communicates with others.[55]

In contrast, **role making** characterizes how a person interprets a role in terms of what he or she does with that role. The role owner expresses a certain attitude toward the role and can digress from what the original expectations were. Turner (1962)[56] coined the term "role making" to explain this practice of creating a new role. As explained by Sandstrom, Martin, and Fine (2010),[57] role making is a process in which group members invent some aspects of their behavior in order to develop a role performance. While this role performance fits with the performances of other group members, it also remains in sync with the individual's personal goals and inclinations. Put simply, role making allows a member to change parameters or examples that describe his or her role. Upon looking at both role taking and role making, four conclusions can be deduced: (1) both are embedded in specific forms of social interaction; (2) both influence how the terrorist defines his or her position within the terrorist group and society and, subsequently, the development and organization of the terrorist self;[58] (3) both emphasize how individuals can diverge in the manner by which they view the appropriate interpretation of symbols, the definition of circumstances, and the elements of the roles they experience or assume;[59] and (4) both are usually the product of convictional social identities in that joining a terrorist group is often a function of volition and choice—although sometimes people are forced to participate in terrorism, as in the case of children who have been kidnapped by groups like the Lord's Resistance Army and transformed into killing machines.

Case Study: Role Taking and Role Making in Hamas

Since the founding of Hamas in 1987, important roles for its militants have evolved and been transformed. This has contributed to reshaping Palestinian identity. Role making has occurred through changes in doctrine and Islamic service. For example, some extremist Hamas members have met with members of Fatah (the rival faction in the Palestinian territories)—which had never happened before. This also means that Hamas members have infused their own individual meanings into their long-established roles. Because individual autonomy is now seen as more acceptable, allegiance to Hamas has changed too. For Mishal and Sela (2000),[60] symbolic of these changes in identity construction is the group's calculated movement "away from dogmatic positions in a quest for innovative and pliable modes of conduct, the opposite of doctrinaire rigidity, ready to respond or adjust to fluid conditions without losing sight of their ultimate objectives" (p. 7).[61] Indeed, at the same time, Hamas militants continue to commit terrorist attacks against unarmed Israeli civilians and fire hundreds of missiles into Israel.[62] Such role-taking activity has always been constant: Hamas terrorist activities occur in the present and apply previous experiences to predicted future events. The reason that role taking still exists lies in the fact that Hamas wants to seize the perspective of the universal other for the Muslim government, Palestinians living in refugee camps and, to a smaller extent, the Palestinian Authority (PA). Thus, both role-taking and role-making activities of Hamas members advance an image of a would-be Palestinian state that can break away from certain traditions but also maintain its long-term objectives, clear-cut boundaries, and firm, well-established preferences. This is precisely how Hamas has managed to muster support in the Palestinian territories and to act as an emerging decision maker for the general Palestinian population.[63]

POSITIVE CULT VERSUS NEGATIVE CULT

A **cult** is a system of ritual practices. The word was used for the first time in the early seventeenth century to denote respect paid to a deity and was borrowed from the French *culte* (from Latin *cultus*, for "worship").[64] In the eyes of Emile Durkheim (1915),[65] a French sociologist, a group can be organized around a high level of moral cohesion. What strengthens the "cult" structure of groups is a direct outcome of rituals. For Durkheim, cults are groups of individuals structured through shared beliefs and united through systems of traditions and routines. A cult is a type of hypermovement. A **hypermovement** is a movement to which an organization is symbiotically connected. It is subject to obedience to rules and widespread institutionalization over time.[66] From cult stems the notion of **cultic milieu**, the type of mind linked to a hypermovement's observance of unconventional, or rejected, knowledge.[67] The term implies a distinctive and eccentric social construction of ideas. This way of interpreting the universe gives an antithetical image of accepted knowledge (i.e., with which the general public identifies) and its sources. Whereas traditional religion, the government, institutions of higher learning, and the media generate information and ideas that are acknowledged by the world at large, these sources are dismissed as corrupted and misleading in the cultic milieu and, therefore, outright forbidden. In the cultic milieu, the standards for conventional knowledge are rejected based on the belief that "the truth" lies within more remote and secretive locations. In this fashion, conspiracy theories, the occult, and pseudoscience become elevated to a higher level of importance; the level measures up with the role assumed by orthodox knowledge in mainstream society.[68]

Positive Cult versus Negative Cult: Description

Durkheim developed his theory of ingroup cohesion in cults around two central concepts: the positive cult and the negative cult. The **positive cult** is a system of norms that impose the rules for group-based, normative behavior. It is a system of rites that rally group members closer to the sacred. It is the observance through which humans "have always believed that they upheld positive and bilateral relations with religious forces" (Durkheim, 1915, p. 326).[69] The positive cult serves two purposes: to revitalize group members' commitment to collective values and to bring back the power of cultural symbols over the members' consciousness.[70] The positive cult restores the moral force of the group, underlining the importance of integration and mobilization of members based on common faith.[71] Particularly included in a positive cult is sacrifice, as well as rites of commemoration and atonement.[72] Another example is the ritual ingesting or feasting of the totemic animal, which is regarded as highly bestowed with totemic energy. This "alimentary communion" enables group members to soak up that energy into themselves.[73]

On the other hand, the **negative cult** represents the core of the group's sanctions as well as its legal institutions. It is symbolized by a structure of restrictions, which can be observed in ascetic rituals (e.g., fasting)—usually done for purposes of ingroup cohesion. Ingroup cohesion rests upon the concept of negative cult, too. The negative cult embodies the cultural taboos and prohibitions from which individuals must abstain if they want to be regarded as group members. These taboos and prohibitions are the basis of punishments and are crucial to group dynamics because they function as the yardstick of measure for delineating group membership. The idea of the negative cult stems from the fact that, in essence, a sacred thing is divorced from its profane counterpart. Accordingly, there is a discontinuity between them. Negative cults are notorious for imposing rules of abstinences upon group members.[74] They are, plainly, systems of abstentions.[75] The sacred is what is to be embraced, and the profane is taboo. Taboos are often the most fundamental element of the ideological and religious aspects of many groups. After all, religion, for Durkheim, mostly consists of the separation between the sacred and the profane. Taboos are precisely the representation of that separation.[76]

Both positive and negative cults are efficient in that they infuse cultural symbols with a moral and emotional thrust. They create an atmosphere of sanctity around social objects, social events, and ideas that would otherwise be viewed as ordinary. Thus, these cults work to reiterate the sacred quality of those social objects, social events, and ideas, stipulating both how they should be treated and how deviant behavior should be proscribed. In this way, both the positive and negative cults are crucial to the foundational establishment of group dynamics and the preservation of its continuity over time.[77] A similar analogy is that between presentational and avoidance rituals. **Presentational rituals** are rituals that incorporate acknowledgments, invitations, compliments, and similar services for each new recruit. Through these, the new recruit is told that he or she will no longer be alone, others will be involved with him or her, and dedication to the group is of utmost importance. **Avoidance rituals** are rituals that cause group members to stay away from an individual and apply rules regarding privacy and separateness.[78]

Positive Cult versus Negative Cult in Terrorism

The description of both positive and negative cults is critical to understanding how the organizational culture of terrorists exploits cultural or religious values for their benefit. The positive cult is universally used to compare the sacred with the profane.[79] A big challenge that terrorist leaders have to face is the guarantee that group members remain trustworthy and do not abandon the cause.[80] The positive cult does not just describe what is sacred; it also creates the sacred. For example, holy water is not merely water that is found to be holy, or water that has been qualified as liquid with special qualities. Instead, it is water that has been passed by a spiritual leader and transformed through ritual. For terrorist recruits who have taken part in cults, the cognitive process associated with what has been blessed and sacred diverges from that for the profane.[81]

When a positive cult becomes an authenticated custom or a custom centered on a long-established and bureaucratic charismatic leadership, it is called **routinization**. For Weber (1946),[82] routinization can enhance the authority and status of terrorist groups within their environments. Schiffman and Kanuk (2004)[83] contend that learning or attitude formation has more chances of succeeding through repetition of messages and passive processing of nonverbal or visual cues (e.g., ritualistic symbols). Terrorist leaders take advantage of cults to connect emotions with sanctified symbols and initiate group commitments. These sacred symbols are emotionally appealing and motivationally compelling, all of which engender in-group solidarity, trust, and cooperation. Religious beliefs, including the assurance of rewards in Paradise, smooth the progress of in-group commitment by embellishing the payoffs of deadly actions, including suicide missions.[84] For example, Marshall Applewhite, leader of **Heaven's Gate**, a religious doomsday cult in San Diego, California, persuaded thirty-eight adherents to kill themselves so that their souls could board a spacecraft. In 1997, Applewhite led them to believe that, upon dying, the spacecraft would lift up their souls to a level of existence far above the human level (a new life that would be both physical and spiritual).[85]

As one would expect, the negative cult can also play a decisive role within the organizational culture of terrorist groups. Terrorist leaders are notorious for creating long lists of taboos in order to achieve ultimate objectives. For example, this can be done through deprivation (fasting for a long period of time is not uncommon)[86] or the **depluralization** of potential recruits. Regarding the latter, new members get sequestered within isolated environments. If new recruits accept living in these isolated situations, it will be easier for them to disown their membership in their former groups or friendship circles, even including their own families (i.e., also known as **replacement of relationships**). This zeal to establish a "milieu control" operates on the rationale that previous group affiliations and identities would obviate the total commitment required by the terrorist group. A group cannot successfully indoctrinate new recruits unless the group becomes their unique affiliation.[87] In a similar manner, **self-deindividuation** can eliminate a terrorist's individual identity, both externally and internally. This can be seen in the way new terrorist recruits do away with civilian clothes and start wearing uniforms. Internally, all new members must renounce values, beliefs, attitudes, or behaviors that deviate from the terrorist group's values and expectations.[88] This process is called **doctrine over existence**.[89]

Case Study: Aum Shinrikyo

Aum Shinrikyo is a deadly Japanese cult that is bent on destroying the world and listed as a terrorist organization by many countries (see chapter 7 for more detail). The group's doctrine, a mélange of Hindu, Buddhist, and yogic beliefs, is rooted in meditation, asceticism, and absolute devotion to **Shoko Asahara**, Aum's Supreme Leader. In terms of positive cult, Aum Shinrikyo engaged in numerous magical ritual practices, particularly in the 1990s. For example, they focused on the alteration of mind and body, the increase of psychic powers through science, and kundalini (i.e., "awakening" that leads to deep meditation, enlightenment, and bliss) through a mixture of yoga and esoteric Buddhism. Taken as a whole, the group's positive cult aimed at producing a progression to a level of super-humankind through spiritual training.[90] Aum Shinrikyo promoted a radical transformation of the national-state system, so much so that Shoko Asahara even considered it necessary to exterminate Japan, and the whole world, in an effort to purify it and replace it with a better society. Such elements in the positive cult were in line with the model of Aum Shinrikyo itself. In 1994, the organization established a structure of government ministries, attempting to become a self-sufficient, alternative enclave or microcommunity.[91]

What else did Aum Shinrikyo do to create a positive cult? The technique was pneumopathology. By definition, **pneumopathology** refers to spiritual insanity, as opposed to psychopathology (which denotes a psychological disorder). The difference between the two is that psychopaths do not usually separate good from evil (if they even know it), whereas pneumopaths can tell the difference. They will make sure they can hide what they know by employing religious symbols and language to trap themselves into oblivion (in regard to what they know).[92] In layperson's terms, pneumopathology is a practice whereby a leader creates an environment of "spiritual sickness" in order to deform reality itself. Reality can be deformed through symbolism and any other method to get all members "taken in." Ultimately, this deformation of reality will fit the system and agenda of the group's leader.[93]

In terms of negative cult, once recruits become members of Aum Shinrikyo, they find it very difficult to leave. The group has been known to use a variety of control techniques, including the killing of innocents and an extremely rigorous regimen like sleep deprivation, drugs, diet, and so on. The purpose of the latter was to groom members into accepting the Supreme Leader's teachings with respect to spiritual transcendence. Other control techniques included wacky methods like small electric shocks administered to the head, discouraging disagreement, and strengthening the group's norms and the uncontested authority of the Supreme Leader.[94] Secluded psychologically and geographically from the external world, Aum members were forced to believe that their group's "end of times" philosophy is of utmost importance and is in fact the only way to save the world and replace it with an ideal one. Nevertheless, this aspect of negative cult was good for Aum Shinrikyo in that the group's constant use of threats through a strong belief in an "end of times" philosophy was usually unintelligible to outsiders. This technique also served as a self-imposed barrier that allowed Aum Shinrikyo to become an elite community of believers. Lastly, this adherence to supernatural forces has enabled Aum Shinrikyo to turn increasingly inward (away from the "evil," misguided population) and lock itself into its own symbolic culture.[95]

RITUAL

A **ritual** is a symbolic act that is formal or recurrent in a tradition.[96] Carl Jung (1964)[97] referred to ritual as **canalization**, the idea that ritualistic behavior builds a canal, guiding psychic energy to stream from its regular randomness toward a mythic goal—here, it is renewal. Most rituals reinforce such mythic goals by shaping the group members' worldviews, identities, and relationships. Other rituals signal and aid in the process of change.[98] To draw upon Heidegger's (1962)[99] concept, rituals are an act of **poeisis**; that is, they bring forth a new existence by transforming a current one. Rituals as poeisis perpetuate the Lebenswelt (i.e., lifeworld) that a cultural group has collectively built. This section looks at ritual from five different perspectives. As such, ritual is (1) a symbolic act, (2) communication, (3) a rite of purity, (4) tribalism, and (5) legitimizing cultural violence.

Ritual as a Symbolic Act

Indeed, a ritual is a symbolic act. Symbolic acts are physical or nonphysical actions that require interpretation. The message of a symbolic act is nonreferential; it does not directly refer to the people, things, or ideas at hand. Rather, the message is permeated with symbols, myths, and metaphors that invoke multiple interpretations. Rituals use symbolic acts to communicate the forming or transforming of a message in unique scenes (i.e., settings, social contexts, or environments).[100] Because rituals operate mostly on the symbolic level, they also enact other individual and social purposes. Rituals are present when there is a necessity to manipulate human emotions. Thus, they play an important part in religious and public ceremonies, which have the power to manage, reduce, or direct aggression. At the same time, rituals create a social glue, improve organization overall, and foster a sense of community.[101]

The ability of rituals to stimulate both positive and negative emotional responses within members provides the keystone for the formation of motivational communal symbols. Symbols can be infused with such deep emotional significance that they effortlessly create a shared symbolic system that, in due course, influences members' choices and motivates behavior.[102] Most rituals allow control of self and the environment. Psychologically, they increase uncertainty and reassurance within inner initiates.[103] Because ritual is a symbolic act, it also helps create secret knowledge. **Secret knowledge** is to be understood as a collection of secrets successively unveiled to inner initiates who have stood the test of trustworthiness. The special knowledge of the adepts is regarded as sacred and symbolic; possession of the secrets exudes feelings of power, thereby cementing the ties within the fragile community. Naturally, the symbolism of ritual is so strong that any suspicion of an adept's betrayal or defection could not only jeopardize the cohesion of the group but also be deemed a capital offense.[104]

Ritual as Communication

Ritual as communication refers to a sacred ritual in which people come together in fellowship and a great speech or communicative event takes place.[105] This is seen when examining the motives of Islamic martyrs to participate in suicide terrorism. Martyrs and sympathizers within Muslim communities learn in fellowship that a great reward for jihadists will be granted by Allah. In the ritual, before the martyr actually carries out the suicidal mission, he or she performs a self-eulogy that is videotaped and that will be disseminated across Muslim circles after the jihadist becomes a martyr (i.e., a hero who died in holy war). A leader said to a female terrorist that one day that she will gain "a very special status among the women suicide bombers" and she will be "a real heroine." In the Palestinian territories, to make sure that

Islamic martyrs are seen as heroes, videos of their self-eulogy are available for purchase and, in many cases, parents dress their babies and infants in "suicide bomber" costumes and take photos of them.[106] Deplorably, the killing of Americans is also celebrated in those rituals. In the wake of the *Columbia* shuttle catastrophe in 2003, Ali Al-Timimi, an Islamic activist, said, "There is no doubt that Muslims were overjoyed because of the adversity that befell their greatest enemy. Upon hearing the news, my heart felt certain good omens that I like to spread to brothers."[107] In Lebanon, dead victims' bodies are abused in the name of Allah: sometimes, members of Islamist groups tie the bodies of fallen enemies behind their vehicles and drag them through the dirt. The message they send (to onlookers) is to please Allah.[108]

Ritual as a Rite of Purity

A **rite of purity** is a form of ritual that emphasizes the cleanliness (i.e., virtue and innocence) of the group (or the cause) in contrast with that of the evil (i.e., unclean) enemy or outside world. This process relies on repetitive symbolic conditioning (i.e., indoctrination techniques) that uses phrases, images, and symbols to glorify themes that resonate throughout the cultural life of the group. So, repetitive symbolic conditioning works through the astute manipulation of such phrases, images, and symbols that emphasize the clean-unclean distinction. A rite of purity can also include cleansing that is both physical and spiritual, stringent regimens, and the identification of natural bodily functions as intrinsically impure. In regard to the latter, the result is that the human body is to be considered a source of shame, replete with impurities that must be concealed and constantly purified. Purity symbolizes both the morality of the symbolic culture and an absence of immorality in human character. It serves to implant and enforce tribal codes and taboos, and it is typified by loyalty, righteousness, honor, and cleanliness.[109]

Rites of purity are found in most symbolic cultures across the world and imply, in one way or another, that the inner essence of the human being is either pure or defiled. For this reason, leaders of extremist groups will use rites of purity as a method to instill fears of disease, expulsion, and eternal punishment, and as a way to associate taboo with terror (and to associate the unclean with targets to be killed). A rite of purity is a type of positive cult; its purpose is to inculcate a visceral shaming code in group members, prevent any form of dissent or difference, create social control to prevent assimilation to other cultures, demarcate territory as sacred land, and prompt warfare when that sacred land has been invaded by polluting outsiders. This can be achieved by systematically identifying specific behaviors as impure and designating the Other as a filthy infidel who fouls the purity of true believers and sacred territories. For example, within the Islamist symbolic code, impurity is generally seen as a corruption of the ummah and a violation of the land by the Other. In order to achieve a state of purity and good moral standing, Islamists will impose rituals such as daily ablutions (ritual cleansing), prayer, the avoidance of people or things that are impure (i.e., *najis*), and total adherence to all aspects of the Islamic code.[110]

Ritual as Tribalism

Tribalism is the foundation of ritual; it delineates social and physical boundaries and is an important contributing factor to a group's collective identity. Tribalism is characterized by blood ties, common ancestry, steadfast loyalty, solidarity, conformity, and often an "us versus them" philosophy (i.e., an "in-group vs. out-group" mentality).[111] As Pryce-Jones (2002)[112] puts it, tribalism is "a closed order. Those within the tribe are deemed to be relations by blood, a family, by virtue of which they are to be protected and secured; those outside are strangers, and therefore suspected to be enemies" (p. 21). Every custom, ritual, habit, and taboo are determined by the tribe's symbolic culture. For example, although Islamists live in many non-Muslim countries, rely on modern weapons, and keep abreast with new developments in a global technological universe, they are fundamentally tribal. They abide by a code of honor and are willing to sacrifice their lives to uphold their symbolic culture. Their tribe teaches them to dominate a territory, defend sacred land, and follow an ideology to which many like-minded others subscribe. If one person is targeted, the whole tribe feels targeted, too; if one person is honored, the entire tribe feels respected, too; humiliation and honor are felt by every tribal member. This contrasts with the Western philosophy that treasures individualism and freedom of expression.[113] Many humans still perceive their association with smaller groups as more important to their lives than allegiance to society at large.[114]

Ritual as Legitimizing Cultural Violence

In this context, cultural violence refers to certain symbolic properties of our existence—epitomized by religion and dogma, language and art, and experimental and formal science (e.g., logic and mathematics)—that can be used to rationalize terrorist violence.[115] Cultural violence is often accompanied by bodily procedures, dress codes, and iconic symbols, all of which help constitute particular terroristic styles.[116] A ritual that legitimizes cultural violence can also be interpreted as a symbolic culture with four B's: (religious) beliefs, behavior (rituals), badges (e.g., religious attire), and bans (taboos). The four B's enable terrorists to serve as reliable and authentic symbols of group commitment. Particularly those committed to the group will be ready to sustain the time, energy, and opportunity costs of ritualistic creed and performance. Thus, ritual leaders can attain a real benefit from effective collective action on the part of members.[117] Ritual is clearly defined by Baudrillard (1993)[118] as collective sacrifice often related to cultural violence. **Collective sacrifice** is controlled violence that is culturally or socially driven. It is a completely artificial action that is antinatural, calculated, and, above all, shared by members of the terrorist cultural group. Thus, terrorism is behavior that is both created and upheld by humans within a cultural environment.[119]

RITUAL TERRORISM

Ritual terrorism refers to terrorism committed against people as a human sacrifice to a deity.[120] Ritual terrorism is essentially a purification rite that removes specifically marked uncleanness. The rationale for committing ritual terrorism always has to do with a defilement of purity, which requires killing or mutilation to restore honor. Although the violence is ritualized, the modus operandi does not involve a purifying agent like water, fire, earth, or sacrificial blood to purify the stain of uncleanliness. Ritual impurity dirties not just the body but also the soul. For this reason, it cannot be cleansed with water and soap. It must be washed away through ritual terrorism. One should not miscalculate the power of impurity; it compares to the power of evil. The targets to be killed are not only labeled as impure; they are also considered the symbol of evil, a sign of contagious contamination or waste that disseminates through sin and corruption.[121]

   Often driven by religious convictions, ritual terrorism is an ancient method of creating terror. The names of religious-based terrorist groups like the Jewish Zealots, Muslim Assassins, and Hindi Thugs have entered our vocabulary as a way to describe terrorists.[122] Knowledge about ritual terrorism is crucial to understanding the ideology of a terrorist cultural group. In 1971, during the Bangladesh Liberation War, a war of independence between West Pakistan and India-allied East Pakistan, over 2.5 million Hindus alone were killed by Muslims. According to Burns (1994),[123] the author of *Wrath of Allah*, the mutilation was appalling: eyes were gouged out, pregnant women were gutted and exenterated, male organs were severed, and women's breasts were amputated. In addition, many Muslim children have been indoctrinated into committing ritual terrorism. This explains unfathomable extreme acts of violence such as children remorselessly taking part in the dismemberment of bodies and posing for photos in front of mutilated bodies.[124] This section examines two case studies of ritual terrorism that occurred in the twentieth century: the Arab-Israeli War and the Mumbai terrorist attacks.

Case Study I: Arab-Israeli War

During the 1948–1949 Arab-Israeli War (also known as the Israeli War of Independence), Jewish fighters, including female combatants captured by Arab insurgents, were frequently tortured and mutilated in the most inhumane fashion. Many Palestinians subscribe to a philosophy that has been labeled **shame culture**; they feel easily humiliated and are ready to strike back against what they perceive as insults. By mutilating their Jewish prisoners, the Palestinians symbolically robbed them of their manhood or human-like character. For this reason, the particular targets of mutilation were the Jews' heads and sexual organs. Pregnant females were found with their abdomens struck or gutted. For those who identify with a shame culture, the objective of ritual terrorism is to expose the weakness and "femininity" of the enemy, and in so doing to transfer the tormentor's buried shames onto the enemy. At the same time, ritual terrorism allows torturers to co-opt their "bravery" and toughness—the "masculinity"—that they have given up, screamed away, under the sword or blade.[125] Ritual terrorism has many similarities with the honor-shame model of the Islamist symbolic code. Dishonor is reflected through female characteristics. Therefore, castrating the foe is the fundamental symbol of emasculation. According to Gilligan (1996),[126] symbolically, "shame dwells not only in the eyes but also the genitals. The relationship between shame and genitals is so close and inextricable that the words for the two are identical in most languages" (p. 83). Ritual terrorism wipes away the polluting organs, the sexual organs that symbolize masculinity, strength, and the reproduction of more infidels.[127]

Case Study II: Mumbai Terrorist Attacks

The 2008 **Mumbai terrorist attacks** were perpetrated by **Lashkar-e-Taiba**, a Pakistan-based terrorist group. Approximately 165 people died, and over 300 others were wounded.[128] Among the killing of those 165 people, many acts of torture and mutilation were perpetrated. During the mission, which occurred between November 26 and November 29, 2008, ten Pakistani terrorists unashamedly engaged in sexual humiliation, torture, and mutilation on a certain number of the hostages before killing them with their firearms. Particularly targeted were Jews and foreigners. The doctors who were at the hospital (to which the victims were taken) said it was clear that many of the dead had been mutilated. During the attack, six occupants of Mumbai's Chabad House (a Jewish outreach center), including twenty-nine-year-old Rabbi Gavriel Noach Holtzberg and his six-month-pregnant wife, Rivka, were sexually attacked and their genitalia mutilated before being shot. Their two-year-old son, Moshe, survived after being been beaten by the terrorists (his back was covered in marks consistent with ritual terrorism). Other reports said that the rabbi was castrated and the baby was taken out of the body of Rivka.[129]

The purpose of ritual terrorism is to make terrorism a symbol of **expiation**, the act of making atonement in order to please a deity. Blood washes away shame, and killing is the catharsis. The Islamists' ritual terrorism was constructed to deepen feelings of shame, scorn, and contempt that could only be relieved through ritual violence.[130] The ten Pakistani jihadists in Mumbai were born and trained in Pakistan, a nation with a long-established record of religious cruelty, ethnic extermination, and ritual mutilations. Although the terrorists may have been too young to have observed or partaken in these atrocities, the "trainers" who assigned them to Mumbai were well aware of the strategic and symbolic benefits of ritual terrorism. The ten Pakistani jihadists were trained by retired combat and marine officers of the Pakistan Army and were exposed to jihadist indoctrination that included telling recruits every-thing about the alleged barbarisms against Muslims in India.[131]

Ajmal Kasab, the only terrorist survivor of the Mumbai attacks, was indoctrinated by the hate-India propaganda, which led him to believe that his actions would guarantee him the highest place in Paradise (from the Quranic verse 9:111). Specific reports said that Kasab believed that Allah asked him to fulfill the Mumbai mission. Hence, he expressed no remorse about the attacks, maintained that they were not against Islam, and, upon being interrogated, did not lose his composure or self-control. Kasab was even convinced that his trainers were sent by Allah to help the brave warriors fulfill His will.[132] In less than twelve months, Islamist leaders transformed a poor, marginalized boy into a killing machine who believed that his actions were righteous.[133]

The Islamist code stipulates that mutilation is not a barbaric deed. Thus, barbarism sanc-tifies ritual terrorism. It is converted into a ritual that purifies sin through carnage. For Kasab, killing was not immoral but virtuous and justifiable blood vengeance to restore honor to his fellow brothers and sisters in his Pakistani community. Kasab was indoctrinated into believing that murder and mutilation would bestow him strength, assuage dishonor, and attain heroic status as a cold-blooded mujahedin. Mass murder was an initiation ritual that transported him from an innocent village youth to a pious jihadist respected by the ummah. There is no question that the Mumbai terrorist attacks constituted a martyrdom operation. It was a suicide mission by jihadists who put into practice the Islamist code of blood rituals. This code of honor not only served as symbolic warfare; it also served as *actual* warfare through both purification rituals and warrior initiation rituals.[134]

HONOR KILLING

Honor killing has many similarities with ritual terrorism, although not all honor killings are terrorist acts. In fact, even these days, in many areas of the Middle East and Southeast Asia, honor killing tends to be perceived as legitimate within local communities. Generally, **honor killing** refers to the murder of a relative or even an entire group of people based on the perpetrators' belief that the victim has caused dishonor to the family or culture.[135] In and of itself, **honor** embodies the righteousness and purity of the code; it serves to define status, respect, and reputation for the person, family, and community. It controls every part of indi-vidual and group conduct.[136]

According to Chesler (2009),[137] 90 percent of honor killings that took place in Europe and the United States in 1998–2008 were committed by Muslims. By extension, in April and May 2010, over 1,000 Egyptians were surveyed (about honor killing) by the U.S.-based Pew Research Center. According to this massive survey, 84 percent believe apostates from Islam should face the death penalty, 82 percent believe adulterers should be stoned to death, and 77 percent believe thieves should be flogged or have their hands amputated. Because honor is everything to Islamists, shame, disgrace, and dishonor are to be avoided by any means what-soever. For Pryce-Jones (2002),[138] "Honor is what makes life worthwhile: shame is a living death, not to be endured, requiring that it be avenged" (p. 35). The Western construct of honor (i.e., uprightness, justice, integrity, sincerity, and honesty) has little conceptual equivalence with its Islamist counterpart. Whereas Westerners view peace as freedom, Islamists view it as honor. The Islamist symbolic code is so entrenched in Muslims that even moderate ones who have tried to assimilate to Western culture have a high probability of reverting back to violence when their manhood is threatened.[139]

Occupation of Muslim Lands as Honor Violation

A **mujahedin**, a "person doing jihad" or a **soldier of Allah (SoA)**, achieves honor through warrior initiations, endurance rituals, and cruelty in combat. Martyrdom in suicide missions is a very high honor. The U.S. and European presence in the Persian Gulf, Iraq, and Afghanistan and the very existence of Israel are categorically considered as unpardonable occupation of Muslim territory, desecration of sacred land, and dishonor in general. Consequently, this unbearable humiliation represents an honor violation that must be met with merciless punishment. It is a moral obligation for mujahedin to strip infidels of sacred land and restore the honor of the ummah through vengeance. When a person has an attachment and an obligation to individuals and groups that, in part, constitute his or her identity, that person becomes an **encumbered self**. In contrast, an **unencumbered self** is a person whose identity makes no fundamental reference to other individuals or groups.[140] Mujahedin are very concerned about fear of disgrace and preserving the ummah. This is particularly true for those militant Muslims in countries that they deem to be occupied by infidels. Occupation is likened to dishonor. In fact, many things equate to dishonor. For instance, honor killing is so ingrained in the Islamist symbolic code that women who are suspected of dishonoring their family (even without real evidence) must be killed to preserve the honor of the Muslim community. Therefore, emotions of weakness, powerlessness, and dishonor are located just below the surface, generated or sparked off by a hypersensitivity to any actual act of humiliation. Even a glance perceived as inappropriate can be seen as endangering manhood.[141]

Facework

In sociology and psychology, **face** refers to an alleged feeling of favorable social self-worth that an individual or a cultural group wants others to have of them. It is a susceptible identity-based resource because it can be boosted or jeopardized in any ambiguous social situation. **Facework** refers to specific verbal and nonverbal strategies that help preserve and repair face loss. It also helps maintain and honor face gain for an individual or a cultural group.[142] In the Islamist symbolic code, facework is a form of honor that strengthens Islamists as men and is done by conforming to traditional masculine virtues, from being a mujahedin to procreating future soldiers of Allah (sons above all). Islamists' construct of honor and face is peculiar to Arab culture and uses visual symbolism to describe these concepts. As such, Arabs either "whiten" the face (i.e., save face) or "blacken" the face (i.e., lose face). Face is the external, visible appearance of honor, the front-stage persona that a man wants to preserve even if, in reality, he has committed a shameful act. In Arab culture, "honor" and "face" are so intertwined that the words are used interchangeably. Thus, "face" is "honor"; it is so anchored in the Arab mind that a true Muslim has the right to fall back on deceit and falseness in order to "whiten," or save, the face of his own self, his brothers and sisters, and even the entire ummah itself. The Arab mind is constantly moving—working hard against things that "blacken" the face (lose face) and jumping through hoops in order to "whiten" the face (save face).[143]

The Two Humps on the Camel's Back

In *Islamikaze: Manifestations of Islamic Martyrology*, Raphael Israeli (2003)[144] describes an interesting form of symbolism used in Islamic honor killing: the image of balance between the two humps on the camel's back. The concept is rooted in "social justice." In Arabic, the term for "social justice" is *'adalah*, or *'adl*. In the Muslim mind, *'adalah* represents the idea of balance between the two humps on the camel's back. Without such balance, the camel would not be able to march for a long time. Justice is directly tied to honor; the preservation of honor rests on the ability to protect one's property and ummah, and the willingness and capacity to restore them upon violation. Otherwise, a man's reputation is permanently damaged. For this reason, a true Muslim's honor is always at stake; it is tested by his bravery in the service of this honor. A Muslim who subscribes to that philosophy will not relent until the challenge has been answered or the wrong redressed. Only when honor is restored will justice be served. What differs dramatically from Western thinking is that there are no objective standards to determine what is right or wrong, or the parameters of violation of one's honor. Rather, the standards depend on the subjective determination of the wronged Muslim person or whole community.

Central to the Muslims' burning reasons for restoring honor is their belief that they have fallen prey to conspiracies and plots against them. When they use symbolism to explain away things and justify their demands for social justice, then they instinctively transcend the domain of rationality.[145] For example, Sayyid Qutb, one of the leading members of the Muslim Brotherhood and a fundamentalist still respected by many Muslims today, identified the Jews as the enemies of Islam and the unrepentant ally of the United States and the West. In his book *Social Justice in Islam*,[146] he cautioned readers against the global subversion of Islam by the Jews, and urged Muslims to rebel against the powers-that-be, stimulate Islamic revivals world-wide, and restore honor by wreaking revenge and destruction on the enemy.

Blood Feud

A **blood feud** is a long-running conflict between social groups of people. In simple terms, blood feud is akin to vengeance. Vengeance epitomizes the justice of the code; it rationalizes terrorist violence and dictates social order. It is reflected through acts of retribution, bloodshed, and sacrifice. When land has been polluted through invasion and the tribe has been attacked, jihadists must avenge their death. Blood feud is the imperative to commit murder in retribution for the death of a member of one's clan.[147] For Pryce-Jones (2002),

> In tribal society, violence is a mechanism of social control. Should life be lost, the tribe is diminished and must exact retribution. The blood feud begins. The feud is not simply primitive barbarism but also a mediating process by which groups constrain each other to constrain their own members, by wreaking vengeance indiscriminately, anonymously, on any members of the rival group.[148]

Based on these circumstances, Islamists do not discriminate between civilians and enemy targets. It is indiscriminate terrorism: all are pigeonholed as members of the enemy group. Islamists uphold the pre-Islamic tribal ritualism of blood feuds, according to which extreme violence is not only justified but also mandatory because bloodshed is the only way to restore honor. Such extreme violence includes killing enemies, martyrdom through suicide bombings, and honor killing by killing relatives. Symbolically, a blood feud is a purification ritual of utmost significance. For true believers, blood disinfects shame, murder washes away disgrace, and violence expunges humiliation. From their perspective, justice is served, purity is regenerated, and face is saved. [149]

Value Sphere

Honor killing is an example of a value sphere. A **value sphere** refers to a system of values dominated by its own inherent Nomos (i.e., laws). In each value sphere, choices are guided by the ultimate values of that sphere. [150] Value spheres are the realm of the Weberian Kulturmensch, endowed "with the capacity and the will to deliberately take a position on the world and ascribe a meaning to it" (Weber, 1949, p. 81). [151] In each value sphere, ultimate values are also value positions. Hence, choices always stand on something. [152] A **Kulturmensch** is a "cultural being" who takes a position in his or her value sphere; the cultural being makes decisions based on cultural values and lives off of them as well. [153] In a similar vein, honor killing is also a manifestation of the **significance quest**. The idea here is that various "sacred carriers," such as blood feud, are being exploited as defense mechanisms in the ongoing fight against infidels. Sacred carriers are used to diffuse the values and beliefs of a group. [154] Consequently, an important conclusion is that the domain of ideology coincides with the domain of symbolic culture. They equate to each other. Not only is symbolic culture present; ideology is present too. [155]

SUMMARY

Culture is a socially created and historically transmitted pattern of symbols, meanings, and ideas from one generation to the next. A cultural model is a formal description of the knowledge held by members of a particular group. It shapes our worldview. A theory that can explain all this is symbolic interactionism. The theory postulates that human beings are able to communicate through shared meanings (e.g., symbols, words, visuals, signs, and roles). Because meaning is transmitted and received within the specific culture in which one lives, meaning becomes symbolic through social interactions happening in that culture. Cultures are socially constructed over time, and it is a four-step process: (1) construction, (2) objectivation, (3) internalization, and (4) renovation. Another term for understanding symbolic interactionism is Umwelt (or Lebenswelt), which suggests that human beings live in a world that is constructed out of their own symbols. In line with these contentions, a terrorist group is generally like an organizational culture, that is, a social energy that directs how members should act. For this reason, the concept of terrorist socialization emerges. Terrorist socialization includes the notions of role taking and role making. Role taking implies that the member fulfills a role that already exists in the group or that is new but has been created by the group, not the individual member. Role making allows a member to change parameters or examples that describe his or her role. Another important consideration in this chapter was the comparison between the positive cult and the negative cult. The positive cult is a system of norms that impose the rules for group-based, normative behavior. On the other hand, the negative cult embodies the cultural taboos and prohibitions from which group members must abstain. In many terrorist groups, rituals are of utmost importance. As we have seen, a ritual is (1) a symbolic act, (2) communication, (3) a rite of purity, (4) tribalism, and (5) legitimizing cultural violence. Ritual terrorism refers to terrorism committed against people as a human sacrifice to a deity. It is essentially a purification rite that removes specifically marked uncleanness. Particularly examined were two case studies of ritual terrorism that occurred in the twentieth century: the Arab-Israeli War and the Mumbai terrorist attacks. Finally, honor killing, predominantly in the Middle East and Southeast Asia, is the murder of a relative or even an entire group of people based on the perpetrators' belief that the victim has caused dishonor to the family or culture; one example is the belief that occupation of sacred Muslim land equates to dishonor and should be met with cruel punishment. The ultimate objective is to "save face."

NOTES

1. Herskovits, Melville (1948). *Man and His Works: The Science of Cultural Anthropology*. New York: Alfred A. Knopf.

2. Sebeok, Thomas, & Danesi, Marcel (2000). *The Forms of Meaning: Modeling Systems Theory and Semiotic Analysis*. Berlin: Mouton de Gruyter.

3. Geertz, Clifford (1993). *The Interpretation of Cultures: Selected Essays*. New York: Basic Books.

4. Swidler, Ann (1986). Culture in Action: Symbols and Strategies. *American Sociological Review, 51*, 273–286.

5. Berger, Jonah, & Heath, Chip (2005). Idea Habitats: How the Prevalence of Environmental Cues Influences the Success of Ideas. *Cognitive Science, 29*(2), 195–221.

6. Sperber, Dan (1996). *Explaining Culture: A Naturalistic Approach*. Malden, MA: Blackwell.

7. Sieck, Winston (2011). A Cultural Models Approach for Investigating the Cognitive Basis of Terrorism. *Journal of Terrorism Research, 2*(1), 3–15.

8. Sperber, Dan (1996). *Explaining Culture: A Naturalistic Approach*. Malden, MA: Blackwell.

9. Sieck, Winston, Smith, Jennifer, Grome, Anna, & Rababy, David (2010). Expert Cultural Sensemaking in the Management of Middle Eastern Crowds. In Kathleen Mosier & Ute Fischer (Eds.), *Informed by Knowledge: Expert Performance in Complex Situations* (pp. 105–121). New York: Taylor & Francis.

10. Sieck, Winston, Smith, Jennifer, Grome, Anna, & Rababy, David (2010). Expert Cultural Sensemaking in the Management of Middle Eastern Crowds. In Kathleen Mosier & Ute Fischer (Eds.), *Informed by Knowledge: Expert Performance in Complex Situations* (pp. 105–121). New York: Taylor & Francis.

11. Palmer, Gary (1996). *Toward a Theory of Cultural Linguistics*. Austin: University of Texas Press.

12. Pargament, Kenneth (1997). *The Psychology of Religion and Coping*. New York: Guilford Press.

13. Lilla, Mark (2007). *The Stillborn God: Religion, Politics, and the Modern West*. New York: Alfred A. Knopf.

14. Schwartz, Stephen, & Bilsky, W. (1990). Toward a Theory of the Universal Content and Structure of Values. *Journal of Personality and Social Psychology, 58*, 878–891.

15. Mueller, Shane, & Veinott, Elisabeth (2008). *Cultural Mixture Modeling: Identifying Cultural Consensus (and Disagreement) Using Finite Mixture Modeling*. Washington, DC: Proceedings of the Cognitive Science Society.

16. Sieck, Winston, Smith, Jennifer, Grome, Anna, & Rababy, David (2010). Expert Cultural Sensemaking in the Management of Middle Eastern Crowds. In Kathleen Mosier & Ute Fischer (Eds.), *Informed by Knowledge: Expert Performance in Complex Situations* (pp. 105–121). New York: Taylor & Francis.

17. Sieck, Winston (2011). A Cultural Models Approach for Investigating the Cognitive Basis of Terrorism. *Journal of Terrorism Research, 2*(1), 3–15.

18. Sieck, Winston, Smith, Jennifer, Grome, Anna, & Rababy, David (2010). Expert Cultural Sensemaking in the Management of Middle Eastern Crowds. In Kathleen Mosier & Ute Fischer (Eds.), *Informed by Knowledge: Expert Performance in Complex Situations* (pp. 105–121). New York: Taylor & Francis.

19. Goffman, Erving (1959). *The Presentation of Self in Everyday Life*. Garden City, NY: Anchor Press; and Plummer, Ken (1991). *Symbolic Interactionism: Foundations and History*. Hants, UK: Edward Elgar Press.

20. Blumer, Herbert (1969). *Symbolic Interactionism: Perspective and Methods*. Englewood Cliffs, NJ: Prentice Hall.

21. Mead, George Herbert (1934). *Mind, Self and Society*. Chicago: University of Chicago Press.

22. Meltzer, Bernard (1975). *Symbolic Interactionism: Genesis, Varieties, and Criticism*. London: Routledge.

23. Shott, Susan (1979). Emotion and Social Life: A Symbolic Interactionist Analysis. *American Journal of Sociology, 84*(6), 1317–1334.

24. Lauer, Robert, & Handel, Warren (1983). *Social Psychology: The Theory and Application of Symbolic Interactionism*. Englewood Cliffs, NJ: Prentice Hall; and Arena, Michael, & Arrigo, Bruce (2005). Social Psychology, Terrorism and Identity: A Preliminary Reexamination of Theory, Culture, Self, and Society. *Behavioral Sciences and the Law, 23*, 485–506.

25. Blain, Michael (2009). *The Sociology of Terrorism: Studies in Power, Subjection, and Victimage Ritual*. Boca Raton, FL: Universal Publishers.

26. Hewitt, John (1976). *Self and Society: A Symbolic Interactionist Social Psychology*. Boston: Allyn & Bacon.

27. Kanagy, Conrad, & Kraybill, Donald (1999). *The Riddles of Human Society*. Thousand Oaks, CA: Pine Forge Press.

28. Crooks, Dauna (2001). The Importance of Symbolic Interaction in Grounded Theory Research on Women's Health. *Health Care for Women International, 22*(1), 11–27.

29. von Uexküll, Jakob (1957). A Stroll through the World of Animals and Men. In Claire H. Schiller & Karl S. Lashely (Eds.), *Instinctive Behavior* (pp. 5–80). New York: International Universities Press.

30. Husserl, Edmund (1970). *The Crisis of European Sciences and Transcendental Philosophy*. Evanston, IL: Northwestern University Press.

31. Lerner, Richard, & Kauffman, Marjorie (1985). The Concept of Development in Contextualism. *Developmental Review, 5*(4), 309–333.

32. Hewitt, John (1976). *Self and Society: A Symbolic Interactionist Social Psychology*. Boston: Allyn & Bacon.

33. Babb, Sarah (1996). A True American System of Finance: Frame Resonance in the U.S. Labor Movement, 1866 to 1886. *American Sociological Review, 61*(6), 1033–1052.

34. Arena, Michael, & Arrigo, Bruce (2005). Social Psychology, Terrorism and Identity: A Preliminary Reexamination of Theory, Culture, Self, and Society. *Behavioral Sciences and the Law, 23*, 485–506.

35. Kepel, Gilles (2002). *Jihad: The Trail of Political Islam*. Cambridge, MA: Harvard University Press.

36. Mishal, Shaul, & Sela, Avraham (2000). *The Palestinian Hamas: Vision, Violence, and Coexistence*. New York: Columbia University Press.

37. Arrigo, Bruce (2010). Identity, International Terrorism and Negotiating Peace: Hamas and Ethics-Based Considerations from Critical Restorative Justice. *British Journal of Criminology, 50*, 772–790.

38. McNeal, Gregory (2009). Organizational Theory and Counterterrorism Prosecutions: A Preliminary Inquiry. *Regent University Law Review, 21*, 307–329.

39. Hellriegel, Don, & Slocum, John (2010). *Organizational Behavior*. Cincinnati, OH: South-Western College Publishing.

40. McNeal, Gregory (2009). Organizational Theory and Counterterrorism Prosecutions: A Preliminary Inquiry. *Regent University Law Review, 21*, 307–329.

41. Hellriegel, Don, & Slocum, John (2010). *Organizational Behavior*. Cincinnati, OH: South-Western College Publishing.

42. Black, Edwin (1992). *Rhetorical Questions*. Chicago: University of Chicago Press.

43. Black, Edwin (1992). *Rhetorical Questions*. Chicago: University of Chicago Press.

44. Frank, David (2000). The Mutability of Rhetoric: Haydar 'Abd Al-Shafi's Madrid Speech and Vision of Palestinian-Israeli Rapprochement. *Quarterly Journal of Speech, 86*(3), 334–353.

45. Sandstrom, Kent, Martin, Daniel, & Fine, Gary Alan (2010). *Symbols, Selves, and Social Reality: A Symbolic Interactionist Approach to Social Psychology and Sociology*. Oxford: Oxford University Press.

46. Jeon, Yun-Hee (2004). The Application of Grounded Theory and Symbolic Interactionism. *Scandinavian Journal of Caring Sciences, 18*(3), 249–256.

47. Morris, Monica (1977). *An Excursion into Creative Sociology*. New York: Columbia University Press.

48. Biddle, Bruce, & Thomas, Edwin (1966). *Role Theory: Concepts and Research*. New York: John Wiley & Sons.

49. Child Soldiers International (2004). *Global Report 2004*. London: Child Soldiers International.

50. Hartjen, Clayton, & Priyadarsini, S. (2012). *The Global Victimization of Children: Problems and Solutions*. New York: Springer.

51. Doom, Ruddy, & Vlassenroot, Koen (1999). Kony's Message: A New Koine? The Lord's Resistance Army in Northern Uganda. *African Affairs Volume, 98*(390), 5–36.

52. Human Rights Watch (2006). *Children's Rights: Child Soldiers*. New York: Human Rights Watch World Report.

53. Arena, Michael, & Arrigo, Bruce (2005). Social Psychology, Terrorism and Identity: A Preliminary Reexamination of Theory, Culture, Self, and Society. *Behavioral Sciences and the Law, 23*, 485–506.

54. Stryker, Sheldon (1980). *Symbolic Interactionism: A Social Structural Version*. Menlo Park, CA: Benjamin Cummings.

55. Sandstrom, Kent, Martin, Daniel, & Fine, Gary Alan (2010). *Symbols, Selves, and Social Reality: A Symbolic Interactionist Approach to Social Psychology and Sociology*. Oxford: Oxford University Press.

56. Turner, Ralph (1962). Role-Taking: Process versus Conformity. In Arnold Rose (Ed.), *Human Behavior and Social Processes* (pp. 20–40). Boston: Houghton-Mifflin.

57. Sandstrom, Kent, Martin, Daniel, & Fine, Gary Alan (2010). *Symbols, Selves, and Social Reality: A Symbolic Interactionist Approach to Social Psychology and Sociology*. Oxford: Oxford University Press.

58. Arena, Michael, & Arrigo, Bruce (2005). Social Psychology, Terrorism and Identity: A Preliminary Reexamination of Theory, Culture, Self, and Society. *Behavioral Sciences and the Law, 23*, 485–506.

59. Stryker, Sheldon (1980). *Symbolic Interactionism: A Social Structural Version*. Menlo Park, CA: Benjamin Cummings.

60. Mishal, Shaul, & Sela, Avraham (2000). *The Palestinian Hamas: Vision, Violence, and Coexistence*. New York: Columbia University Press.

61. Arena, Michael, & Arrigo, Bruce (2005). Social Psychology, Terrorism and Identity: A Preliminary Reexamination of Theory, Culture, Self, and Society. *Behavioral Sciences and the Law, 23*, 485–506.

62. Marino, Tom (2012, November 27). *In Support of the Nation of Israel* [Speech]. Washington, DC: U.S. House of Representatives.

63. Mishal, Shaul, & Sela, Avraham (2000). *The Palestinian Hamas: Vision, Violence, and Coexistence.* New York: Columbia University Press.

64. Bainbridge, William Sims (1997). *The Sociology of Religious Movements.* New York: Routledge.

65. Durkheim, Emile (1915). *The Elementary Forms of Religious Life.* New York: Free Press.

66. Kinsella, John (2009). Coda. *Angelaki: Journal of the Theoretical Humanities, 14*(1), 165–174.

67. Campbell, Colin (1972). *The Cult, the Cultic Milieu, and Secularization: A Sociological Yearbook of Religion in Britain.* London: SCM Press.

68. Barkun, Michael (2007). Appropriated Martyrs: The Branch Davidians and the Radical Right. *Terrorism and Political Violence, 19*(1), 117–124; and Whitsel, Bradley C. (2000). Catastrophic New Age Groups and Public Order. *Studies in Conflict & Terrorism, 23*(1), 21–36.

69. Durkheim, Emile (1915). *The Elementary Forms of Religious Life.* New York: Free Press.

70. Brow, James (1981). Class Formation and Ideological Practice: A Case from Sri Lanka. *The Journal of Asian Studies, 40*(4), 703–718.

71. Aboboaie, Cristina (2010). Research and Analysis of the Phenomenon of International Terrorism: Issues, Challenges and Weaknesses. *Scientific Bulletin of the Mihail Kogalniceanu University, 19*, 111–124.

72. Bois, H. (1916). A Sociological View of Religion. *International Review of Mission, 5*(3), 449–460.

73. Durkheim, Emile (1915). *The Elementary Forms of Religious Life.* New York: Free Press.

74. Jones, Robert Alun (1980). Myth and Symbol among the Nacirema Tsigoloicos: A Fragment. *The American Sociologist, 15*(4), 207–212

75. Tannen, Deborah (1987). Conversational Style. In Hans Dechert & Manfred Raupach (Eds.), *Psycholinguistic Models of Production* (pp. 251–267). Norwood, NJ: Ablex.

76. Zuesse, Evan (1974). Taboo and the Divine Order. *Journal of the American Academy of Religion, 42*(3), 482–504.

77. Boyns, David, & Ballard, James David (2004). Developing a Sociological Theory for the Empirical Understanding of Terrorism. *American Sociologist, 35*(2), 5–25.

78. Goffman, Erving (1967). *Interaction Ritual: Essays on Face-to-Face Behavior.* Garden City, NY: Doubleday.

79. Eliade, Mircea (1959). *The Sacred and the Profane: The Nature of Religion.* New York: Harcourt Brace Jovanovich.

80. Bloom, Mia (2005). *Dying to Kill: The Global Phenomenon of Suicide Terror.* New York: Columbia University Press.

81. Rappaport, Roy (1999). *Ritual and Religion in the Making of Humanity.* Cambridge: Cambridge University Press.

82. Weber, Max (1946). *Essays in Sociology.* New York: Oxford University Press.

83. Schiffman, Leon, & Kanuk, Leslie (2004). *Consumer Behavior.* Upper Saddle River, NJ: Prentice Hall.

84. Sosis, Richard, & Alcorta, Candace (2008). Militants and Martyrs: Evolutionary Perspectives on Religion and Terrorism. In Raphal Sagarin & T. Taylor (Eds.), *Natural Security: A Darwinian Approach to a Dangerous World* (pp. 105–124). Berkeley: University of California Press.

85. Lalich, Janja (2004). *Bounded Choice: True Believers and Charismatic Cults.* Berkeley: University of California Press.

86. Hassan, N. (2001, November 19). An Arsenal of Believers: Talking to the "Human Bombs." *The New Yorker, 77*, 36–41.

87. Singer, Margaret Thaler, & Lalich, Janja (1995). *Cults in Our Midst: The Hidden Menace in Our Everyday Lives.* San Francisco: Jossey-Bass.

88. Akhtar, Salman (1999). The Psychodynamic Dimension of Terrorism. *Psychiatric Annals, 29*(6), 350–355.

89. Martin, Walter, & Zacharias, Ravi (2003). *The Kingdom of the Cults.* Grand Rapids, MI: Bethany House.

90. Susumu, Shimazono (1995). In the Wake of Aum: The Formation and Transformation of a Universe of Belief. *Japanese Journal of Religious Studies, 22*(3), 381–415.

91. Gardner, Richard (2002). The Blessing of Living in a Country Where There Are Senryū: Humor in the Response to Aum Shinrikyō. *Asian Folklore Studies, 61*, p. 37.

92. Cooper, Barry (2007). "Jihadists" and the War on Terrorism. *The Intercollegiate Review, 42*(1), 27–36; and Day, Jerry (2003). *Voegelin, Schelling and the Philosophy of Historical Existence.* Columbia: University of Missouri Press.

93. von Heycking, John (2009). Post 9/11 Evocations of Empire in Light of Eric Voegelin's Political Science. In David Edward Tabachnick & Toivo Koivukoski (Eds.), *Enduring Empire: Ancient Lessons for Global Politics* (pp. 185–214). Toronto: University of Toronto Press.

94. Cameron, Gavin (1999). Multi-Track Microproliferation: Lessons from Aum Shinrikyo and Al Qaida. *Studies in Conflict & Terrorism, 22*(4), 277–309.

95. Whitsel, Bradley (2000). Catastrophic New Age Groups and Public Order. *Studies in Conflict & Terrorism, 23*(1), 21–36.

96. Mach, Zdzislaw (1993). *Symbols, Conflict, and Identity: Essays in Political Anthropology.* Albany: State University of New York Press; and Schirch, Lisa (2004). *Ritual and Symbol in Peacebuilding.* West Hartford, CT: Kumarian Press.

97. Jung, Carl (1964). *Man and His Symbols.* New York: Doubleday.

98. Schirch, Lisa (2004). *Ritual and Symbol in Peacebuilding.* West Hartford, CT: Kumarian Press.

99. Heidegger, Martin (1962). *Being and Time*. London: SCM Press.

100. Schirch, Lisa (2004). *Ritual and Symbol in Peacebuilding*. West Hartford, CT: Kumarian Press.

101. Lorenz, Konrad (1963). *On Aggression*. New York: Harcourt, Brace & World.

102. Damasio, Antonio (1994). *Descartes' Error: Emotion, Reason, and the Human Brain*. New York: Avon Books.

103. Pruyser, Paul (1968). *A Dynamic Psychology of Religion*. New York: Harper & Row.

104. Douglas, Mary, & Mars, Gerald (2003). Terrorism: A Positive Feedback Game. *Human Relations, 56*(7), 763–786; and Urban, Hugh (1998). The Torment of Secrecy: Ethical and Epistemological Problems in the Study of Esoteric Traditions. *History of Religions, 27*(3), 209–248.

105. Carey, James (1992). *Communication as Culture: Essays on Media and Society*. New York: Routledge.

106. Oliver, Anne Marie, & Steinberg, Paul (2005). *The Road to Martyrs' Square: A Journey into the World of the Suicide Bomber*. Oxford: Oxford University Press.

107. Tanenbaum, Robert (2006). Preaching Terror: Free Speech or Wartime Incitement? *American University Law Review, 55*, 785–819.

108. Yungher, Nathan (2008). *Terrorism: The Bottom Line*. Upper Saddle River, NJ: Prentice Hall.

109. Perlmutter, Dawn (2011). The Semiotics of Honor Killing & Ritual Murder. *Anthropoetics, 17*(1), 22–34.

110. Perlmutter, Dawn (2011). The Semiotics of Honor Killing & Ritual Murder. *Anthropoetics, 17*(1), 22–34.

111. Perlmutter, Dawn (2011). The Semiotics of Honor Killing & Ritual Murder. *Anthropoetics, 17*(1), 22–34.

112. Pryce-Jones, David (2002). *The Closed Circle: An Interpretation of the Arabs*. Chicago: Ivan R. Dee.

113. Perlmutter, Dawn (2011). The Semiotics of Honor Killing & Ritual Murder. *Anthropoetics, 17*(1), 22–34.

114. Sebeok, Thomas, & Danesi, Marcel (2000). *The Forms of Meaning: Modeling Systems Theory and Semiotic Analysis*. Berlin: Mouton de Gruyter.

115. Galtung, Johan (1990). Cultural Violence. *Journal of Peace Research, 27*(3), 291–305.

116. Hebdige, Dick (1979). *Subculture*. London: Methuen.

117. Sosis, Richard (2006). Religious Behaviors, Badges, and Bans: Signaling Theory and the Evolution of Religion. In Patrick McNamara (Ed.), *Where God and Science Meet: How Brain and Evolutionary Studies Alter Our Understanding of Religion* (pp. 61–86). Westport, CT: Praeger.

118. Baudrillard, Jean (1993). *Symbolic Exchange and Death*. Thousand Oaks, CA: Sage.

119. Hawdon, James, & Ryan, John (2009). Hiding in Plain Sight: Community Organization, Naive Trust and Terrorism. *Current Sociology, 57*(3), 323–343.

120. Modjeska, Nicholas (1990). Hall of Mirrors: Ritualized Homosexuality in Melanesia. *Reviews in Anthropology, 15*(1), 41–57.

121. Perlmutter, Dawn (2011). The Semiotics of Honor Killing & Ritual Murder. *Anthropoetics, 17*(1), 22–34.

122. Rapoport, David (1984). Fear and Trembling: Terrorism in Three Religious Traditions. *American Political Science Review, 78*(3), 658–677.

123. Burns, Robert (1994). *Wrath of Allah*. Calcutta: Arvind Ghosh.

124. Perlmutter, Dawn (2011). The Semiotics of Honor Killing & Ritual Murder. *Anthropoetics, 17*(1), 22–34.

125. Hogan, Matthew (2001). The 1948 Massacre at Deir Yassin Revisited. *Historian, 63*(2), 309–334.

126. Gilligan, James (1996). *Violence, Our Deadly Epidemic and Its Causes*. New York: Grosset/Putnam.

127. Perlmutter, Dawn (2011). The Semiotics of Honor Killing & Ritual Murder. *Anthropoetics, 17*(1), 22–34.

128. Bishop, Ryan, & Roy, Tania (2009). Mumbai: City-as-Target. *Theory, Culture & Society, 26*(7), 263–277.

129. Mishra, Santosh (2008, December 25). Terrorists Sexually Humiliated Guests before Killing Them. *Mumbai Mirror*, p. A1; and Robbins, Liz, & Healy, Jack (2008, November 28). Brooklyn Couple Killed in Attacks. *New York Times*, p. A1.

130. Gilligan, James (2001). *Preventing Violence*. New York: Thames & Hudson.

131. Qasab's Full Confession. (2008, December 10). *Mid Day News*, p. A1.

132. Unnikrishnan, C. (2009, January 5). Kasab Thought He Was on Mission Kashmir. *Times of India*, p. A1.

133. Wonacott, Peter, & Anand, Geeta (2008, December 4). Sole Captured Suspect Offers Grim Insights into Massacre. *Wall Street Journal*, p. A1.

134. Perlmutter, Dawn (2011). The Semiotics of Honor Killing & Ritual Murder. *Anthropoetics, 17*(1), 22–34.

135. Pope, Nicole (2011). *Honor Killings in the Twenty-First Century*. New York: Palgrave Macmillan.

136. Bowman, James (2007). *Honor: A History*. New York: Encounter Books.

137. Chesler, Phyllis (2009). Are Honor Killings Simply Domestic Violence? *Middle East Quarterly, 16*(2), 61–69.

138. Pryce-Jones, David (2002). *The Closed Circle: An Interpretation of the Arabs*. Chicago: Ivan R. Dee.

139. Perlmutter, Dawn (2011). The Semiotics of Honor Killing & Ritual Murder. *Anthropoetics, 17*(1), 22–34.

140. Wenz, Peter (2007). *Political Philosophies in Moral Conflict*. New York: McGraw-Hill.

141. Perlmutter, Dawn (2011). The Semiotics of Honor Killing & Ritual Murder. *Anthropoetics, 17*(1), 22–34.

142. Ting-Toomey, Stella, & Kurogi, Atsuko (1998). Facework Competence in Intercultural Conflict: An Updated Face-Negotiation Theory. *International Journal of Intercultural Relations, 22*(2), 187–225.

143. Patai, Raphael (1983). *The Arab Mind*. New York: Hatherleigh Press.

144. Israeli, Raphael (2003). *Islamikaze: Manifestations of Islamic Martyrology*. New York: Routledge.

145. Israeli, Raphael (2003). *Islamikaze: Manifestations of Islamic Martyrology*. New York: Routledge.

146. Qutb, Sayyid (2000). *Social Justice in Islam*. North Haledon, NJ: Islamic Publications International.

147. Boehm, Christopher (1984). *Blood Revenge: The Anthropology of Feuding in Montenegro and Other Tribal Societies*. Lawrence: University of Kansas Press.

148. Pryce-Jones, David (2002). *The Closed Circle: An Interpretation of the Arabs*. Chicago: Ivan R. Dee, p. 22.

149. Perlmutter, Dawn (2011). The Semiotics of Honor Killing & Ritual Murder. *Anthropoetics, 17*(1), 22–34.

150. Oakes, Guy (2001). The Antinomy of Values: Weber, Tolstoy and the Limits of Scientific Rationality. *Journal of Classical Sociology, 1*(2), 195–211.

151. Weber, Max (1949). The Meaning of "Ethical Neutrality" in Sociology and Economics. In Edward Shils & Henry Finch (Eds.), *The Methodology of the Social Sciences* (pp. 1–47). New York: Free Press.

152. Oakes, Guy (2003). Max Weber on Value Rationality and Value Spheres: Critical Remarks. *Journal of Classical Sociology, 3*(1), 27–45.

153. Weber, Max (1958). Science as a Vocation. In Hans Gerth & Charles Wright Mills (Eds.), *From Max Weber: Essays in Sociology* (pp. 196–244). New York: Oxford University Press.

154. Moghaddam, Fathali M. (2008). *How Globalization Spurs Terrorism*. Westport, CT: Praeger.

155. Voloshinov, Valentin (1973). *Marxism and the Philosophy of Language*. Cambridge, MA: Harvard University Press.

Chapter Five

Myth in Symbolic Terrorism

MYTH: DESCRIPTION

Myths are present across all human societies. They represent a highly charged form of symbolism, often of remarkable heroic and national consequence.[1] A myth can be looked at from three different perspectives: (1) myth as narrative, (2) myth as magic, and (3) myth as social cohesion.

Myth as Narrative

A myth is an ideology in narrative form.[2] It is a narrative that a culture tells about itself in order to perpetuate itself; it is the echo of a culture's internal dialogue.[3] Mythic discourse deals in grand categories that have multiple referents: levels of the universe, terrestrial geographies, logical categories, and the like. A typical mythic discourse serves to establish the relations among these categories and support a hierarchy among them, instituting the rightness (or at least the necessity) of a group and the evilness of another group.[4] A myth may emerge as either a truthful depiction or an overelaborated description of historical events. Nevertheless, in the culture in which it is told, a myth is usually seen as a true reflection of the remote past. By telling or resurrecting myths, societies are able to distance themselves from the present.[5] As Tudor (1973)[6] explains it, "A myth is an interpretation of what the myth-maker (rightly or wrongly) takes to be hard fact. It is a device men adopt in order to come to grips with reality" (p. 52). Tudor continues, "We can tell that a given account is a myth, not by the amount of truth it contains, but by the fact that it is believed to be true" (p. 52).

According to Malinowski (1954),[7] a myth "is not merely a story told but a reality lived" (p. 100) that satisfies "deep religious wants, moral cravings, [and] social submissions" (p. 100), and "expresses, enhances, and codifies belief," and "safeguards and enforces morality" (p. 101). From this perspective, myth "is not an idle tale, but a hard-worked active force" that serves as a "pragmatic charter of primitive faith and moral wisdom" (p. 101). In other words, **myth** both symbolizes ideology and provides a sacred story that directs our faith and shapes our conduct.

Myth as Magic

In addition, a myth is more than just a narrative; it is a *sacred* narrative explaining how the world or humankind became what it is now.[8] A myth functions as a highly ordered strategy that transforms the real world into a magical world. Without a doubt, myth does not transform the world itself but the way we interpret the world. By changing our attitude toward the world, myth gives us magical solutions to real conflicts. It should come as no surprise, then, that an enormous appeal to myths exists for the consciousness of a "tyrannized" or "invaded" people.[9] Both myth and ritual pertain to the creation of magic and sacredness. Nevertheless, a distinction needs to be made between myth and ritual. According to Schöpflin (1997),[10] myth is a narrative, a set of ideas, whereas:

> Ritual is the acting out, the articulation of myth; symbols are the building blocks of myth and the acceptance or veneration of symbols is a significant aspect of ritual. A ritual generally observes the procedures with which a symbol is invested, which a symbol compels. Thus, myths are encoded in rituals, liturgies and symbols, and reference to a symbol can be quite sufficient to recall the myth for the members of the community without need to return to ritual. (p. 20)

Religious movements tend to use the new in order to extend the sacred. For instance, suicide terrorism is framed as a new way to wage jihad, the ultimate act of piousness in Islam. To be in line with a group's collective identity, the source—though not necessarily the form—of what is "new" is to be discovered in the past.[11] Mircea Eliade (1971)[12] referred to this type of magical thinking as **eternal return**. He wrote, "Here again we find the motif of repetition of an archetypal gesture projected onto all planes—cosmic, biological, historical, human. The past is but a prefiguration of the future. No event is irreversible and no transformation is final" (p. 89). Some of the most effective myths are devised for the effect of "eternal return." Take, for instance, the magic of a golden age: when leaders of terrorist groups exploit themes of conquest, defeat, calamity, massacre, suffering, military prowess, and renewal, such myths can shape very powerful and inflammable foundations for militant action.[13]

Myth as Social Cohesion

Last, myths are essential for social cohesion. Because social rift can be the result of the collapse of myths, the latter can serve as a symbolic guarantee of social order, thereby buttressing social cohesion and cultural unity by exploiting and validating the traditional order. Myths remind a group of its own identity. Whether or not members of a cultural group believe in the irrational content of myth matters little, for myths have symbolic value and perform a key social function in upholding the given social order.[14] Those who excel at devising myths to maintain the social order are called myth entrepreneurs. **Myth entrepreneurship** is the astute appropriation of symbolic content from a mass of cultural properties.[15] Skilled propagandists figure out their myths judiciously; for a myth to effectively organize and mobilize public opinion, it must have cultural resonance with a given group or society. The myth that fails to produce a response will be dismissed right away.[16]

For Tyrrel and Brown (1991),[17] myths are relations intrinsic to a community's value system. They symbolize, in imaginary form, a model to inspire people. They describe the destructive forces at work in society that, if left unanswered, could break the social cohesion. By appealing to myths when core values are lost, they remind people of what is culturally valued, and, in that way, they can assert the status quo. To ensure the survival of a cultural system, it is necessary to keep myths alive. For instance, the Roman emperors worked to make ordinary people believe that Rome was still ruled by those ordinary people (and the Senate). Therefore, the emperors constantly used the slogan "Senatus Populusque Romanus" (SPQR; i.e., the legionnaires' motto).[18] Such methodical practice is called "mythomoteur." **Mythomoteur** (a combination of the French words for "myth" and "engine") is a myth that bestows a group its sense of purpose. A mythomoteur gives shape and direction to a movement's or group's cause. Hence, a terrorist group's mythomoteur constitutes the driving force for its identification and formation.[19]

SYMBOLIC DNA OF TERRORISM

A concept developed by Rowland and Theyes (2008),[20] the **symbolic DNA of terrorism** is a mythic-symbolic design that acts as both a persuasive and an epistemic scheme. Terrorists do not go through some form of satanic metamorphosis and suddenly become villains. In actuality, the most dangerous terrorist groups, particularly those determined to kill innocent targets massively, use a mythic-symbolic scheme rooted in religion or an ideological-mythic scheme resembling religion. This design functions as a symbolic representation that rationalizes terrorism, turning it into sacramental aggression. The symbolic DNA of terrorism is also located within the acronym DNA itself. Religious terrorist movements that perpetrate massive terrorist attacks, and groups that embrace an ideological-mythic scheme resembling religion, are driven by a mythic philosophy that consists of three elements: a sense that their identity and existence have been **denied** and risk being shattered by some group, a complete **negation** of the identity of individuals who pose the threat, and **affirmation** of a new identity through an essential myth associated with the group's origin or a utopian myth about the idyllic life that the group will relish in the future.

To outsiders, the symbolic DNA of terrorism may seem irrational, but for a community of believers driven by such a strong ideology, it functions as a "reality lived," transforming mainstream citizens into a divinely motivated army.[21] The symbolic DNA may lead to **group delirium**—collective dreams that electrify individuals in a movement's cause or religion. The most systematic, elaborate designing and killing may be machinated from such delirium.[22] For Kenneth Burke (1966),[23] such a well-engineered feat is a terministic compulsion that automatically produces violence. The symbolic DNA has been observed in terrorist groups whose religious views are linked to major faiths. Much attention on this topic has been paid to Al Qaeda (i.e., the epitome of the symbolic pattern). Nevertheless, all religious-ideological and mythic-symbolic terrorist groups have a tendency to tell a mythic narrative about how the group, whose very identity is threatened by destruction, can regain its strength, safeguard its culture, and defeat the evil enemy it faces by adopting the sacred idea of eternal return; that is, by returning to the heroic virtues that existed before the terrorist group was formed or that existed at the infancy of the group's identity.

SYMBOLIC CONVERGENCE THEORY

Symbolic convergence theory (**SCT**) was developed by Ernest Bormann (1972).[24] The theory rests on the premise that sharing group fantasies produces symbolic convergence. Examples of fantasies are jokes, stories, metaphors, and human interpretations of events—fantasies also bring to mind how group members' feelings and moods transpire after these events. When humans have a good time together or have it rough together, they tend to increase group cohesion. This is what is referred to as symbolic convergence.[25] The "symbolic" in SCT relates to fantasy, language, and symbolic facts. The "convergence" part has to do with its fundamental proposition; it depicts the process of communication in which groups share fantasies to develop their symbolic world. The fundamental unit of analysis in SCT is the fantasy theme. **Fantasy themes** are created to meet rhetorical or psychological needs and can be used to construe a collective's past, present, or future. Similar to myth making, a fantasy theme can be just a word, a phrase, a sentence, or even a long paragraph.[26] Fantasies born out of small-group interactions become incorporated later in public speeches, then employed by the mass media, and eventually diffused to larger publics. In this manner, the phenomenon of group fantasizing influences and is applicable to persuasive events on a very large scale.[27]

Although the concept of fantasy frequently relates to elves, fairies, or dragons, in SCT fantasy tends to refer to a world distinct from reality, created by language and communication. The reality shaped by a terrorist organization matters as much as its motivation. The world in which terrorists live is the world in which they can have determination if they have the disposition and ability to create change. Without the symbolic world in which terrorist recruits live, the terrorist group's efforts may fail completely. Thanks to fantasy themes, however, the average Joe or Jane may be convinced to ardently join a cause and protest actively for it.[28] According to Panda and Gupta (2001),[29]

- What matters about an event is not what happened, but what meaning a terrorist group makes of it.
- Events and meanings are not highly correlated: the meaning of an event can vary from one terrorist group to another. This is due to differences in the framework they use to interpret the event.
- Major events experienced by terrorist groups are often ambiguous or undefined. It is usually difficult to understand what happened, why it happened, or what will happen in the future.
- When confronted with ambiguity and uncertainty, terrorist groups produce symbols to assuage misunderstanding, enhance predictability, and provide guidance. Events, in and of themselves, may remain irrational or meaningless, but symbols make them look otherwise.
- Many events are more important for what they symbolize than what they produce: they are symbols, myths, rituals, and sagas that help terrorists find meaning and organize their experience.

Analogous to the process of fantasy themes, Lévi-Strauss (1966)[30] used the term bricolage. **Bricolage** is the method of creating a new social identity by adopting or "stealing" symbols and artifacts from various customs and cultures. This practice happens a lot within terrorist groups or movements as well. In Islam, bricolage is the jihadists' decision to exploit it as a tool for bolstering their actions against "the establishment." The overuse of symbols—for group identity and propaganda—to churn out new Muslim killing machines, support jihad, or galvanize sympathizers for a cause is an example of bricolage.[31] Along with fantasy themes and bricolage, there are three additional concepts related to SCT: symbolic cue, fantasy type, and saga.

SYMBOLIC CUE, FANTASY TYPE, AND SAGA

A **symbolic cue** is a brief or condensed signal like a symbol, sign, or word that represents a fantasy theme. Having one's closed fist held with the thumb up (i.e., the "thumbs up") is an example of a symbolic cue. Terrorist groups regularly use flags, images, or other identification signals that contain symbols. Some symbolic cues are religious based, others are rooted in a group's history, and others are simply slogans or mottos. Each symbol has a unique meaning to a group and represents justification for that group to ensure group cohesion.[32] In Islamic culture, the horse is a very potent symbol. The horse symbolizes the first generation of Muslims and their successful jihadist crusades. The animal calls to mind the traditional notions of purity and the belief that the Prophet Muhammad and his first followers practiced the authentic version of Islam. In the early 2000s, Osama bin Laden was pictured on a white horse. Muslims believe that Muhammad's horse was white; it was the one that he mounted on his trip from Mecca to Jerusalem. Hence, Osama bin Laden on a white horse symbolized his desire for conquest. Furthermore, after Muhammad died, he ascended to Paradise on the back of his white horse.[33]

A **fantasy type** is a standard script using a prominent, spectacular template to explain new events. It is a broad term for a set of recurrent, related fantasy themes in a standard scenario. These fantasy themes are repeated over and over again by the same or similar characters and are characterized by recognizable script lines, events, settings, and representations of people.[34] In the fantasy type, there is a process of imitation, where old events are assigned new meaning, even though the historical facts do not totally reflect reality—if they reflect reality at all.[35] For instance, for the Tamil Tigers in Sri Lanka, many symbols play an important part in their identities. A particularly salient symbol is the series of discriminatory measures adopted by the Sinhalese-dominated government; a second symbol was all the anti-Tamil massacres that happened in 1956, 1958, 1977, 1981, and 1983.[36] As another example of a fantasy type, Baader-Meinhof, a German terrorist group active in the 1960s and 1970s, used Bertolt Brecht's play *The Measures Taken* (*Die Massnahme*) as one of their standard scripts of inspiration.[37]

A **saga** is a description or chronicle of the achievements of a key individual, group, society, organization, or even country. It is a prominent concept in close-knit groups that progressively form a coherent unit with a compelling vision.[38] At the height of Muhammad's conquests, militant jihad was the main device for turning Dar al-Harb (i.e., the infidels and immoral societies across the globe) into Dar al-Islam (the divinely perfect and righteous house of true Muslims). People who resisted the rapid diffusion of Islam had to fight or die until they either became Muslims or were killed by them.[39] Similarly, members of Aum Shinrikyo, the deadly Japanese cult, eventually came to believe that (1) their self-aggrandizing leader, Shoko Asahara, was both God and their savior; (2) many rituals and machines could replicate Asahara's brainwaves; (3) planet Earth was on its way to Armageddon; (4) the cult itself could save the human race from its depravity by causing Armageddon; and (5) Aum Shinrikyo members could be born again after the apocalypse.[40]

Another general saga is one in which terrorists picture themselves as soldiers. The image that terrorists project about themselves (i.e., as soldiers on a mission or answering a higher call) can be a strategy to elude responsibility for terrorist attacks. In this manner, the "soldiers'" saga is a form of self-presentation, self-perception, or even self-deception. It allows them to better handle the notion of danger and the emotional consequences of killing others. "Soldier" sounds better than "terrorist"; it implies participation in a joint endeavor that has been externally approved. In the 1970s, the Red Brigades (i.e., left-wing Italian terrorists) imagined themselves to be waging a war with the Italian administration. Their saga was a crucial fantasy scheme that made their resolution to violence more acceptable.[41]

CASE STUDY OF SCT: EARTH LIBERATION FRONT (ELF)

The **Earth Liberation Front (ELF)** traces its origin to Brighton, England, with the creation of Earth First! a radical environmental advocacy group. In 1992, infighting within Earth First! led to the formation of a militant offshoot, the ELF. The newly formed group consisted of members who resorted to extreme violence in order to gain publicity and affirm their thirst of justice. The ELF insisted that people across the world become "ecocentric" by cherishing the well-being of the environment over experiences or contacts with nature leading to environmental destruction.[42] The ELF, also known as **Elves** or **The Elves**, is the collective designation for autonomous individuals or covert terrorist cells that, according to Holden (2011),[43] use "economic sabotage and guerrilla warfare to stop the exploitation and destruction of the environment" (p. C5). The letdown of peaceful protests to attain environmental protections had disenchanted Earth First! members. As a result, a militant movement of environmentalism emerged. The ideology of the ELF makes it clear that liberation is necessary for those who do not have the power to liberate themselves from malevolent humans bent on environmental destruction.[44] Today, the ELF is a terrorist organization with actions reported in seventeen countries, and it is widely regarded as closely associated with the Animal Liberation Front (ALF) because of the relationship and joint efforts between the two.[45]

The actions of the ELF are equivalent to ecoterrorism. **Ecoterrorism** refers to acts of violence or sabotage perpetrated in favor of ecological or environmental causes, against individuals or their property.[46] Ecoterrorism "should be reserved for incidents in which the environment itself is disrupted or threatened by the perpetrator as a symbol that elicits trepidation in the larger population over the ecological consequences of the act" (Schwartz, 1998, p. 484).[47] Ecoterrorists are sometimes called eco-anarchists or green anarchists. They take part in various actions toward these ends. The extreme actions taken by ecoterrorists are referred to as **monkey wrenching** (or **ecotage**, a portmanteau of the "eco" prefix and "sabotage").[48] Typically, the ELF carries out ecotage operations against facilities involved in logging, genetic engineering, genetically modified crops, deforestation, SUV sales, rapid urbanization, rural grouping and residential developments with larger homes, and energy production and distribution. When it comes to defending "Mother Earth," ELF militants want no compromise. They center their movement's identity around the "ecological self" and the "wild within."[49] By the 1990s, the ELF already claimed that monkey wrenching should be performed to liberate humanity from capitalism—which was viewed as harming or threatening the natural environment.[50]

Symbolic Cues

The ELF logo is totally green. It symbolizes the organization's origins and lessons in life by putting its acronym in front of a giant tree. Thus, the ELF seeks to personify "green anarchism"; it even considers itself as part of a global anarchist movement. In its literature, its ideological slant appropriates common symbols, like the "circle a" and black flags that are diagonally split by plain red or green. Many ELF symbols make political pleas for unity with the global anarchist movement and use other framing tactics to recruit new members.[51] In addition, many symbols of plants and animals can be seen on the organization's pamphlets and internet communiqués. The importance of plants, animals, and humans must be made equal, and people's interests in nature must be as ardent as their interests in their own friends and relatives. Once this philosophy is widely embraced, the demise of a plant or animal will arouse the same intense reaction as that of a human, and, based on these emotions, any act of retaliation will seem righteous. In line with these contentions, in terms of linguistic symbolism, of equal relevance is the spelling of "elves" throughout the movement's brochures and websites. Using the letter "v" instead of "f" (as in "ELF") unquestionably alludes to a specific image: the mythological creatures depicted in J.R.R. Tolkien's *The Hobbit*, *The Lord of the Rings*, and *The Silmarillion*. Lastly, elves symbolize lower-status beings in society; drawing a parallel, many ELF members come from lower-class backgrounds and seek to oppose the "oppression" and "exploitation" of the powers that be, particularly in terms of their environmental decision making.[52] Overall, through its symbolism, the ELF's aspirations to protect the environment are elevated from a simple plea to a powerful need, which can help create a frame of mind unashamed of using violence to achieve its ends.[53]

Fantasy Type

A fantasy type is a standard script repeated time and again by the same or similar characters. The script usually consists of recurrent and recognizable fantasy themes. The first ELF communiqué was published in 1997:

> We take inspiration from . . . the little people—those mischievous elves of lore. Authorities can't see us because they don't believe in elves. We are practically invisible. We have no command structure, no spokespersons, no office, just many small groups working separately, seeking vulnerable targets and practicing our craft. Many elves are moving to the Pacific Northwest and other sacred areas. Some elves will leave surprises as they go. Find your family! And let's dance as we make ruins of the corporate money system.[54]

According to Baldo (2010),[55] the leaders of the ELF transform their recruits and sympathizers into elves—those mysterious and fantastical creatures. By constantly referring to activists as "elves" (instead of humans), this script character associates the movement with fantasy. Subconsciously, ELF activists progressively identify as important players in this new reality. When they operate as "elves" rather than environmentalists or anarchists, they can get rid of feelings of responsibility or shame that would put a damper on their choices and behaviors. Moreover, as elves are generally considered immortal beings of nature and "invisible" to the eyes of their adversaries, ELF activists can now position themselves as (1) creatures above morality; (2) creatures that will never be apprehended, charged, or imprisoned; and (3) creatures united with nature rather than human civilization. So, as mysterious elves capable of resisting the established order, the protestors can afford to overlook the consequences they must face for using extreme violence. Even on its own, the ecoterrorist organization's name suggests a great fantasy theme; a movement shaping a new world in which extreme violence no longer represents a concern of moral or legal consequences. Rather, violence is a cleverly used "skill" that serves to safeguard a fabulous, epic world that engulfs the activists themselves.

As one would expect, the best method to live up to this philosophy is **personification**, the transmission of human traits to nonhuman beings. The personification of these symbols is important because it functions as a form of victimage, portraying the "oppression" and "exploitation" of the established order. As Stewart, Smith, and Denton (2007)[56] write, "Activists are willing to sacrifice their security, dignity, and social status for other innocent victims" (p. 61). Personification forges ties between ELF activists and the environment by influencing the way they see the environment and deepening their emotions about it. Consequently, this more compassionate relationship with nature produces emotions that make extreme violence seem justified. Deforestation becomes viewed not only as an unpardonable act of greed but also as the genocide of sentient beings. Terrorism is the natural retribution to restore the honor of the environment.

Because ELF activists see environmental degradation through the eyes of unworldly, innocent Middle Earth creatures, the morality called into question carries a more immature tone, stressing the blunt nature of good and evil usually associated with such an immature perspective. By regarding human-induced environmental degradation as the innocent concept of pure evil, adult followers might possibly embrace this new perception of the universe and, by the same token, make extremely violent actions seem more rational and ethical. In this way, not only can personification serve as a fantasy type to forge bonds between the narrator and nature, but also it can forge bonds between the audience and nature. These emotional relationships are an important drive for the ecoterrorist movement; the activists come to believe that they can save the lives of sentient beings capable of feeling pain and forging unprecedented bonds.[57]

Saga

A major saga of the ELF is centered on the life, achievements, and writings of Aldo Leopold. **Aldo Leopold** was a U.S. writer, scientist, ecologist, and forester. He influenced other ecoterrorist groups as well.[58] Leopold's writing is notable for its creative attacks on those harming natural systems and claiming ownership over the environment. In *Thinking like a Mountain*, Leopold (2008)[59] wrote an article narrating the incident of Jesmond Dene, a massive ecological direct-action protest in 1997. In the article, Leopold, too, identified the protestors as magical creatures: "July 22nd: Last night the fairies must have frolicked—this morning locks on security cabins and tools have stopped working, and graffiti has appeared on them; e.g. 'Jihad,' 'Counsel Scum,' and 'Remember the Earth goddess.'" Here, the characters are not elves but fairies. The classic idea of fairies includes many of the same qualities that the ELF literature lists about elves. Examples of such qualities are smallness, magical powers, ties to nature, and an aura of mystery.[60] Another major saga is centered on the life and writings of J.R.R. Tolkien himself. The ecoterrorist movement exalts Tolkien as a true role model of environmentalism that everyone should emulate. In regard to the ELF, James Bell (2002),[61] in "Lord of Machines," contends that the author of *The Lord of the Rings*, J.R.R. Tolkien, has become "a sort of patron saint of neo-luddites. One [must] wonder if Tolkien would have approved of today's 'elves'—those of the Earth Liberation Front." To the eyes of ELF activists, the mythological characters created by J.R.R. Tolkien and the philosophical foundations that characterized his environmentalism have offered those activists concrete ideas based on which they can take action.

CASE STUDY OF SCT: HEZBOLLAH

Hezbollah (from Arabic, "Party of God") is a Shia terrorist organization that was founded in Lebanon in 1982 with the assistance of the **Islamic Revolutionary Guards Corps (IRGC)**—also called the Army of the Guardians of the Islamic Revolution, the Revolutionary Guards, or (in Farsi) the Pasdaran. The IRGC is Iran's well-trained military wing established to protect the country's Islamic system. Hezbollah adheres to a radical interpretation of Shia Islam that was championed by the Grand Ayatollah Khomeini. Hence, the terrorist organization receives much of its financial and political support from Iran. According to the U.S. Treasury Department, the IRGC gives Hezbollah $100–200 million in funding every year and has also taught Hezbollah fighters how to use extreme military tactics. In the early 1980s, the group led the way in the use of suicide bombings in the Middle East.[62] Today, Hezbollah is so popular that it has secured a certain number of seats in the Parliament of Lebanon.[63] Whereas Hezbollah is deemed a resistance movement across much of the Muslim world, it is considered a terrorist organization by the United States, many European nations, Canada, and Australia.[64]

Symbolic Cues

To reinforce the Shia doctrine and enlarge its organizational structure, Hezbollah resorts heavily to symbolism. Hezbollah symbols are evoked daily, not just in times of struggle. They can be seen in religious ceremonies and events organized by the organization worldwide.[65]

The image used by the organization shows a bright yellow background, with green Arabic wording (for the organization's name) in the center, which means "The Party of God." Surfacing from the wording is a fist clutching an AK-47, beneath which lie a Qur'an, a globe, and a seven-leafed branch. The red writing above signifies, "The Party of God, they are the triumphant ones." This Islamic verse, lifted verbatim from the Qur'an, shores up support for Allah-directed actions—it is a verse that commends Islamic warriors. In the text below, it is written, "The Islamic Resistance in Lebanon."[66] Furthermore, the color green, which has represented Islam since its inception, is important in Hezbollah's symbolism. Accordingly, the green coloring of the central image leaves no doubts about Hezbollah's identification with Islam. In the vein of the symbolism employed by Al Qaeda in Iraq, the rifle symbolizes allegiance to militancy, while the globe is a sign of worldwide involvement and ambition to live up to the Shia doctrine. The Qur'an denotes both a foundation in Islam and Hezbollah's goal to establish a caliphate, starting in Lebanon and Israel.[67]

Fantasy Type

Azani (2007)[68] examined, at length, the role of symbolism in Hezbollah's terrorism. The author remarked that these Shia militants use fantasy types for social mobilization. By doing so, such a method allows their support base to expand, recruit new activists, and further stimulate proactive actions that meet the interests of like-minded terrorist groups. Below is a list of eight frequent events and phenomena that have made up Hezbollah's standard script since the early 1980s:

- **Calendar of events**: Hezbollah's calendar of events includes symbolic dates (e.g., religious memorial dates) that are exploited to create a culture of resistance and recruit new members into the terrorist group.[69] For example, World Jerusalem Day (Al-Quds Day) has become one of the most important symbolic calendar events in Islam's struggle—for Hezbollah, the city's sacred location is still identified as a place of residence and worship for the Palestinian people. On November 29, 2012, now a symbolic date in Hezbollah militancy, the United Nations voted to elevate the status of the Palestinian Authority (PA) to that of a nonmember observer state.[70] In the eyes of Hezbollah, this is a triumph for the Muslim world at large.
- **World Jerusalem Day**: the ceremony was promulgated by Khomeini to achieve the Sunnis' and Shi'ites' mutual goal of conquering Israel and delivering Jerusalem. Hezbollah's brochures on Jerusalem evoke its significance in Islam, blame Israel for the fire that almost burned the Al-Aqsa mosque to the ground in 1969, and conclude with extracts from speeches and writings made by Khomeini, Imam Musa Sadr, and Hasan Nasrallah (the current Supreme Leader of Hezbollah). In addition, Hezbollah follows Iran's steps in hailing World Jerusalem Day (i.e., Al-Quds Day) as a day of unity "for Sunni and Shi'ite, for Lebanese Muslims, and Palestinian Muslims," and for "Arab, Ajam, and Turk," because Al-Quds Day is celebrated by the ummah against its adversaries.[71]
- **Month of Ramadan**: the objective is to bring Muslims closer to Islam and enlarge the support for the struggle against social injustice and discrimination. One way to bring Muslims closer to Islam is by observing Ramadan. Ramadan is intended to teach people about fortitude, spirituality, humbleness, and submissiveness to Allah.
- **Definition of enemies**: the Great Satan has been defined as the United States, and the Little Satan as Israel. These concepts were used by Khomeini and Mahmoud Ahmadinejad (president of Iran from 2005 to 2013, and also an avid fan of Hezbollah).

- **Social justice**: Hezbollah's history is overloaded with the same standard script illustrating the dichotomy between oppressors (the evil West) and oppressed (the Shi'ites) and the crucial concern for social justice. The concept of social justice is a symbol that is socially constructed. As a result, it steers or stimulates people to react (i.e., behave) in a certain way.[72]
- **Individual self-sacrifice**: it is the disposition to sacrifice one's life in holy war against Islam's foes. The purpose is to honor Allah. By instituting this principle, Khomeini laid the groundwork on which the tradition of suicide bombing is based.[73]
- **Ashura procession**: this is a tradition to bolster Shia activism. The Ashura procession commemorates the day Imam Hussein ibn Ali (Muhammad's successor, according to the Shi'ites) died in battle. Every year, the Shi'ites celebrate the tragedy through mourning ceremonies in which they reenact the battle. A certain number of participants in the procession flog themselves until they bleed. The goal is to experience the pain that Hussein ibn Ali endured in the battle. In Shia doctrine, the battle symbolizes the core of the hatred between the Sunnis and the Shi'ites. In January 2009, Hezbollah took advantage of the Ashura procession in Lebanon to galvanize its supporters against Israel. Countless Hezbollah sympathizers marched the streets of the southern districts of Beirut (the capital city) to pay homage to the martyrdom of Imam Hussein.[74]
- **Matams**: these are public congregations in which Shi'ites assemble for sacred purposes (e.g., to mourn the loss of a family member) and to meet before or after a religious procession. On top of being meeting places for Shi'ite religious tributes, matams are also social and political gathering places.[75] The big issue is that they are not just used to develop social and political bonds among the Shi'ites or improve Shia identity; they also serve as hotbeds for Hezbollah terrorists, as is the case in Bahrain.[76]

Shia symbolism has proved to be an astute tactic for Hezbollah. Its fantasy type is a standard scenario that has become an ingrained, well-established template to define events and, ultimately, live up to its long-term agenda. In Hezbollah's terrorism, exploiting these eight frequent events and phenomena allows the group to enlist Shia society and impart in them themes such as the willingness to make self-sacrifices for the prolongation of jihad.[77]

Saga

A major saga of Hezbollah is centered on the image of **Ruhollah Khomeini** (the Grand Ayatollah who became the First Supreme Leader of Iran). During the 1979 Islamic Revolution in Iran, Khomeini, who had been exiled from the country since 1963, became a major source of inspiration for Hezbollah. His mesmeric sermons and beguiling fatwas were diffused through audiotapes that were later transcribed and photocopied en masse. His messages infiltrated Iran in a "new media" form and, once in Iran, diffused internally in a more old-fashioned and paper-form medium.[78] Khomeini was soon turned into a semidivine figure. The first Khomeini worshippers were "children of the Revolution," dubbed by Khomeini himself as "an army of twenty million."[79] These worshippers granted him the title of "leader of the dispossessed masses of the world" because, under his supervision, Iran actively endorsed national liberation movements in other Islamic countries.[80] Today, posters of the Ayatollah can still be found almost everywhere in Iran and Lebanon—two countries where Hezbollah is very active. Images of the leader on billboards sometimes read, "Down with USA."[81]

Until his death in 1989, during the time Khomeini was leading Iran, he enjoyed quasi-veto powers over most government policies, control over the IRGC, and the title of Supreme Leader (which meant that he was an Ayatollah far above all others). The adoration of Khomeini extended to the title he was given by the public and regime: Imam. Imam with a capital "I" is a title reserved exclusively for the twelve successors to Muhammad. This title was not used for any Shia leader before or since, and it implied Khomeini's semidivine nature. As a matter of fact, many Iranians believed that Khomeini would herald the return of the Mahdi, the prophesied redeemer of Islam.[82] All things considered, the saga surrounding Khomeini was tantamount to a personality cult; it was like a veneration of the chief in which he became a key symbol. This is epitomized by his image carved into massive rocks. His fatwas have remained legitimate forever, and slogans such as "Khoda, Koran, Khomeini" ("God, Koran, Khomeini") are still some of Hezbollah's most important battle cries.[83]

SYMBOLIC TRINITY

The theory of **symbolic trinity** was developed by Nicholas O'Shaughnessy (2004).[84] By and large, the symbolic trinity is a three-part framework that consists of symbolism, rhetoric, and myth. The first part, symbolism, has already been defined at length in this book. The second part, **rhetoric**, refers to discourse in which source encoders (i.e., message senders) aim at informing, persuading, or motivating particular message receivers in specific situations. In a nutshell, rhetoric is the practice of communicating efficiently and influentially through language.[85] The power of rhetoric lies, in part, in the power of metaphor. For optimal effects, rhetoric must have cultural resonance with the target. An easy way to reach that target is by relaying rhetoric through the media.[86] The third part, myth, functions as a narrative or event that illuminates the principal values of some group, culture, or society: the narrative or event can be real or fictional, but, most likely, imagination will have embellished them. The myth maker, thus, draws from the current repertoire of mythologies but can add to them as well.[87]

The theory of symbolic trinity differs from symbolic convergence theory in that the former focuses more on the rhetorical side of things. It examines important components of a cultural system, often manifested through rhetoric and myth. The trinity deals mostly with the expression of the core concerns and preoccupations of a culture; that is, the themes that emerge or become the most recurrent in a culture.[88] A major premise is that logic, in and of itself, rarely frames human perceptions. Rather, emotions and myths are the pathways to conviction. Therefore, the symbolic trinity is akin to emotional persuasion. In order to convince a target audience to relate to the cause of a terrorist group, it is important that terrorist communicators speak to them in their own language. The symbolic trinity can achieve this because it is necessarily ingrained in specific cultural paradigms shared with the target audience.[89] As O'Shaughnessy (2004)[90] points out, the trinity of symbolism-rhetoric-myth is the conceptual framework of propaganda. The symbolic trinity is a type of rhetorical trope. A **rhetorical trope** is a figure of style, an analogy, a myth, or a metaphor. Rhetorical tropes are essential for any meaningful act of persuasion.[91]

Symbolic Trinity and Propaganda

Together with symbolism and myths, rhetoric plays a crucial role in propaganda, and the three are interconnected.[92] As a particular form of rhetoric, **propaganda** refers to public communication aimed at a group of people and created to influence attitudes and behavior in times of crisis. Propaganda is communication that uses a variety of rhetorical strategies and cognitive heuristics to make particular declarations.[93] As philosophers John Austin (1962)[94] and John Searle (1969)[95] explained, the purpose of language is not only to communicate. In their **speech act theory**, Austin and Searle explained that speakers employ language to achieve intended actions, and, in this manner, hearers deduce or interpret intended meanings from what is expressed by speakers. Hence, language is used not only to explain the world, but also to fulfill additional purposes and actions. Propaganda can be framed as speech act theory. Problems related to human speech acts arise, such as styles of indirect speech, contextual concerns, and the multifunctionality of language.[96]

Propaganda is filled with symbolic appeals that allude to myths. News itself has a lot to do with myth. News stories are not crafted with neutral methods but with symbolic devices and the concoction of myths. In truth, the pervasion of myths in a culture represents a certain selective perception of the world. Selective perception has the ability to introduce a characteristic interpretation to phenomena.[97] Myth is a conceptual keystone of propaganda, and it would be difficult to imagine any propaganda without myths because they are convenient and can be easy to understand. Myths are effective because they are organized and told as stories that incorporate meaningful facts into a persuasive context.[98]

Symbolic Trinity and Myth Fabrication

Myths can be easily fabricated to alter perceptions; nowadays, it is a communicative practice often referred to as "spin." This is a throwback to the concept of myth entrepreneurship. **Spin** is a method of offering an interpretation of an event to sway public opinion in favor of or against a particular group or person. While traditional public communicators may also fall back on an imaginative presentation of the facts, "spin" usually implies dishonest, deceiving, or manipulative tactics. Political leaders are often blamed by their opponents for using spin. To be more precise, they pretend to be honest and strive for objectivity while employing spin tactics to sway public opinion.[99] Propaganda is like spin; it is the support of slanted interpretations and myths over others. Because very few situations only offer one fixed and absolute interpretation, the possibility of embroidering reality to some degree will always be there. Defeat can be framed as victory, and the genius is to use persuasion in lieu of logic.[100]

Another way to fabricate myths is through myth resurrection. **Myth resurrection** is the notion that symbols can frequently articulate, embellish, simplify, or resurrect myths. Old symbols can be made to come back because symbols tend to be plastic and malleable; they can be easily changed and recast for modern purposes. Propaganda discards intellectual challenge and hides behind the framework of old myths. Just as old myths can be re-created, new myths can also be devised. Myths have had a deep influence on the fate of history. Since the fabrication of myths is a constant activity, myths remain important even though some myths become extinct—but they are easily replaceable. The progress of humankind is replete with myths. Therefore, propaganda becomes the sagacious restoration of old myths, but it also operates on the creation of new ones.[101]

CASE STUDY OF THE SYMBOLIC TRINITY: NAZISM

Nazism, or **National Socialism**, was the ideology of the Nazi Party in Germany. A major Nazi theme is the domination of society by human beings considered as racially superior, while cleansing society of people declared inferior (in terms of health, intelligence, etc.) and deemed to pose a risk to national survival. The Nazi symbolic trinity was constructed as a structure of collectively held notions, beliefs, premises, ideas, dispositions, and rhetorical strategies that favored pan-Germanicism. **Pan-Germanicism**, the ultimate agenda of the Third Reich, was an ideology that promoted the unity of the Germanic and Aryan peoples worldwide.[102]

Symbolism

In Freudian psychology, violent symbols provoke, and in so doing, they release violent impulses. By allowing people to fully express their emotional states of hatred toward members of outgroups, symbols of violence allow ingroups to solidify their social cohesion.[103] At the heart of Nazi symbolism stood the "Blood" (Blut); then came the "People" (Volk) as the principal carrier of the blood; the "Soil" (Boden), the land that feeds the people; the "Empire" (Reich), in which the Volk find their political realization; the "Führer" as the leader of the Volk and Reich; and the "Reich War Flag" (Reichskriegsflagge; the official German Nationalist flag) as the holiest physical symbol.[104] Naturally, the Jew was the scapegoat. The Jew came to represent the evils of rationalization and capitalism, and the fortunes and misfortunes of the world. The entire Nazi culture aimed to exclude this alienated individual from the organic unit of the Volk. Therefore, Nazi symbols brought to mind solidarity, rooted in common Aryan ancestry.[105] Taken as a whole, Nazi symbolism separated the world into two categories: those who belonged and those who did not (or insiders and outsiders). Further, the symbol of the swastika, the hymns and rituals of worship, and similar quasi-religious symbols of Nazism provided a feeling of certainty in a realm of confusion.[106] The swastika was something to behold: it showed that the Nazi party and its symbol were seen as inseparable.

Rhetoric

Although Nazism may have been unifying, dominance and interest were unmistakably at work. The ruling elite deliberately used propaganda to control the Volk.[107] From this vantage point, the importance about myths in propaganda is that they are not only long established or resurrected; they can also be fabricated from scratch. The maestros of Nazi propaganda consciously created myths. Goebbels manufactured the myth of Horst Wessel, an unintelligent young ruffian killed in a drunken fight. Goebbels made Wessel a Nazi saint. He also invented the myths of an "Era of Struggle," the Old Comrades, and so on. The purpose was to exaggerate the political barriers and communist violence the Nazis had to defeat in their rise to power, and all of it was enmeshed with syrupy and overemotional sentimentality. Goebbels was arguably the most influential myth maker of the twentieth century. Yet he was certainly not the only one. The impact of myth fabrication is everywhere. The powerful impact of myth fabrication is noticeable in the history of oppressive regimes. Examples are the March on Rome and communism's similar narratives with its *Battleship Potemkin*, Long March, and others.[108]

Even when myths are factually incorrect, they can still survive and wield tremendous authority. Truth rarely matters—what matters is what is believable. Myths can be easily manipulated or warped because of their significance.[109] For example, Hitler and Goebbels framed the Jews as the ones responsible for the economic hardships in Germany. Perspectives can be so effortlessly changed by rhetoric. Words are never neutral. Dictatorial Nazi ideology was achieved through a propaganda machine built for total domination and the controlling of thoughts and actions. Nazi culture was exploited by the elite to warrant imperialist expansion.[110] As one can see, a function of rhetoric can be to make the killing of man by man more acceptable—a man who one has never encountered and with whom one had no prior disagreement.

Myth

Myths can have devastating effects. They can uphold a current feeling of superiority by alluding to a more glorious past. They can propagate falsehoods and the resulting "social iniquities." The myth created by the German General Staff in 1919 to absolve themselves from blame (i.e., the myth of the stab in the back) had appalling consequences after being accepted by the German people.[111] The stab in the back comes from the outcome of the Treaty of Versailles. Whereas the treaty ended the war between Germany and the Allies, it also unnecessarily punished the German military—at least to the eyes of the German General Staff. Subsequently, after the Nazis took power in 1933, a certain number of Nazi myths became victor myths: those of the subjugated were to die out or lead a heinous, substandard life. When cleverly fashioned, myths are widely regarded as depicting the objective truth. As such, the Nazis referred to the Jews as "bacilli," "parasites," "plague," "disease," and so on. Although killing another human may be unconscionable, "exterminating a disease" is not.[112]

National Socialism in Germany worked hard to create a cult of death.[113] A **cult of death** is a glorification of death as part of a major plan to promote a movement and transform the world.[114] Nazi culture was soaked by a type of death fixation—a movement that eventually became responsible for the deaths of innumerable millions. The cult of death was a hallmark of *Triumph of the Will*, a movie directed by Leni Riefenstahl (a female director working for the Third Reich). The movie is dominated by the passing of President Hindenburg (who died in 1934, one year before the movie's release), the salutation to the German fallen of World War I, and the grave and somber march of the Führer to the flaming podiums. The funereal character of Nazi propaganda is one of its many peculiar facets. Yet, what most Germans did not know is that this "cult of death" propaganda was devised for two reasons: (1) to come to terms with the past, particularly with the enormous casualties of World War I; and (2) to pave the way for the preparation and acceptance of the immense life sacrifices that Hitler was now demanding. Hitler centered his myth making on the blood of the martyrs, thereby corroborating his claim that one can serve a supreme power only in heroic attire. In his frenzied ideological world rooted in racial struggle, heroic death was so much better than life itself.[115]

An important mythic date in Nazi symbolism is November 9, 1923. On that day, the **Beer Hall Putsch**, led by Hitler, was an unsuccessful attempt by the Nazis at seizing power in Munich. During the rebellion, sixteen Nazis died. This event became the foundation for Nazi mythology: on that fateful day, the original sixteen Immortals sacrificed their souls for a "reawakened Germany." According to Nazi mythology, their souls were resurrected to join the combat units of SA, SS, and Hitler Youth, thus ensuring the victory of National Socialism. For Hitler, the tragedy of November 9, 1923, became the Germanic Passion. The Führer drew analogies to Golgotha, the Crucifixion, the Resurrection, and the Return. Such myths represent a common cultural denominator, they unite and advance both a cause and movement, they eschew the necessity for complex verbal explanation, and they can be used with a very low level of pictorial reference and rendered through symbolism. Once Hitler came to power, November 9 became a sacred day of commemoration in the Nazi calendar. Put simply, the Beer Hall Putsch marked the rise of the Nazi Party as a key player on Germany's political landscape.[116]

CASE STUDY OF THE SYMBOLIC TRINITY: MAHARASHTRIAN TERRORISM

Mumbai is the capital city of the state of Maharashtra in Western India. Between 2001 and 2011, thirteen terror attacks took place in Maharashtra, leaving over 500 people dead.[117] The symbiotic relationship between propagandist cultural identity, myth, and symbolism presupposes great significance in Maharashtrian terrorism. Shivaji Maharaj, the forefather of the Maratha kingdom in the seventeenth century, occupies a key position in the lives of Maharashtrians.[118] As a noble of the royal Bhosle clan, Shivaji led an insurgency to liberate the Maratha people from the Mughal Empire and instituted a "self-rule" of Hindu people. He modernized rules of military combat, establishing the "Shiva sutra" or ganimi kava (guerrilla tactics), and formed a redoubtable force of 100,000 warriors.[119]

Symbolism

A particular militant movement active in the state of Maharashtra today is **Hindutva terrorism**, a movement advocating Hindu nationalism.[120] Hindutva terrorists consider Shivaji both a great pro-Hindu hero and the symbol of native pride of the Maharashtrian cultural group. After all, Shivaji was an authentic military leader who guided the Maharashtra people against the Mughal Empire in the seventeenth century. The appropriation of the symbol of Shivaji by Hindu terrorist groups serves to strengthen the cultural and political power of Maharashtrians. The whole Indian state represents a category for the deployment of chauvinistic power.[121] Shivaji festivals and rituals are celebrated by various groups in the region. The main logo used by one of the Hindutva terrorist groups is a roaring tiger, evoking the Shivaji epic.[122] As a well-grounded symbol of Maharashtrian history, culture, and identity construction, the image of Shivaji arouses curiosity regarding its path and evolution, thereby making its existence a vital element of the history of Western India.[123]

Maharashtrian terrorism is a clear example of Indian subnationalism, as Hindutva terrorism is mostly located in that region. In Maharashtra today, Shivaji remains the most important of all heroes. For this reason, Shivaji symbolism was a prime target in the 2008 Mumbai terrorist attacks. Eight of the eleven attacks perpetrated by the Pakistani jihadists occurred in South Mumbai, notably at Chhatrapati Shivaji Terminus. Chhatrapati Shivaji is another name for Shivaji. Islamists clearly assaulted one of Hindus' most treasured symbols.[124] Shivaji symbolism represents a continual repetition of the idea of Hinduism under threat, the need to save it from the disgrace inflicted by Islam, and, consequently, the necessity for a firmer and more aggressive resistance.

Rhetoric

Upon examining identity construction and the development of a group's political consciousness, it becomes critical to look at the diverse images of Shivaji popularized by the different ideological perspectives as the "chosen pasts."[125] Shivaji has enjoyed a status of supremacy in Maharashtrian folk culture. The cogent and already existing emotional affinity with the exploits of Maharashtra's past has enabled ideologues and political leaders to exploit the image of Shivaji in order to sway different social groups.[126] A famous leader of Maharashtrian terrorism in the nineteenth century was Jyotirao Phule. He is most known for transforming lower castes and the masses into insurgents ready to eliminate those opposing their views.[127] To most Indians, Jyotirao Phule was a social revolutionary; to outsiders, he was rather a terrorist leader. Shivaji was an important symbol in Phule's rhetoric. As Phule (1869)[128] wrote himself, "Shivaji, as a king, is identified with non-brahmin identity formation, as he is credited with uplifting the downtrodden and significantly giving the sacred thread to the kunbis" (p. 1).

In a similar fashion, it is important to take into consideration the variety of rhetorical channels used, from traditional oral channels to modern methods of printing and publishing to the mainstream methods of mass gatherings, speeches, and festivals. Shivaji is still used as a symbol through the classic oral medium of ballads (called "povadas"). The povada is a ballad usually invoking themes of heroism and valor. It is essentially a declaration to attribute local cultural tradition to lower-class people. Shivaji is also brought up in literature and journalism; publishing information on Shivaji confers on ideas and views of Maharashtrian militancy a certain degree of legitimacy and firmness, and a wider circulation and readership.

Myth

Demonstrating a profound understanding of the Maharashtrian region and its culture, Jyotirao Phule was able to associate the imagery of the Western Indian landscape with the heroic exploits of Shivaji to bestow povadas the required emotive strength. Povadas about Maharashtra start with the topography of the state, depicting it as tough and correspondingly fitting a hardy people. Therefore, from the outset, it can invoke pride and forge a robust bond between the land and the people. [129] In 1906, revolutionary terrorism in Maharashtra reached a pinnacle. The terrorist movement in Maharashtra was inspired by the "Hindu right to revolt," which was akin to the Chinese philosophy of the "mandate from heaven." With these anecdotes, it is not difficult to see that Shivaji has come to symbolize an aggressive spirit of resistance and resurgent nationalism—with unique and overt Hindu penchants. [130] In the past, many Maharashtrian subnationalists were inspired by religious and mythological sources; Kali, the Hindu goddess of empowerment and death, became the mythic reference for terrorists who targeted British and pro-British officials for assassination. "Vande matram," the idolatrous song of made-up thugs, and embodying another myth capable of inspiring revolts against Muslim rulers, was named after a fictitious character of a novel. Nevertheless, it became the national song in Maharashtra. [131]

Whether in conventional folk culture, popular imagination, or contemporary politics, tales of Shivaji's life, as well as his military prowess and valor, still remain a strong emotive force for those who live in Maharashtra. [132] In ethnic and national revivals, and in nationalism and subnationalism, history often induces a romantic "golden age," where the ancestors are believed to have flourished and prospered in all aspects of human activity. Essential to this Maharashtrian theme is the concept of linear development, which climaxes in a downward trend, following the same top-down trajectory from the Indian "golden age" to the present. In regard to the aforementioned subnationalist leaders, objectivity is not one of their main concerns. The goal is to retell the past in a way that would enthuse the community not only to take steps in a chosen direction, but also to shed light on their current condition and prescribe remedies. [133]

SUMMARY

A myth represents a highly charged form of symbolism, often of remarkable heroic and national consequence. A myth can be examined from three different perspectives: (1) myth as narrative, (2) myth as magic, and (3) myth as social cohesion. One method of looking at both myth and terrorism is the symbolic DNA of terrorism. This is a mythic design that rationalizes terrorism, turning it into sacramental aggression. The symbolic DNA may lead to group delirium—collective dreams that electrify individuals in a movement's cause or religion. A more mainstream theory is symbolic convergence theory (SCT). SCT postulates that sharing group fantasies produces symbolic convergence. When humans have a good time together or have it rough together, they tend to increase group cohesion. This is what is referred to as symbolic convergence. The fundamental unit of analysis in SCT is the fantasy theme. Fantasy themes are created to meet rhetorical or psychological needs, and they can be used to construe a collective's past, present, or future. Three important concepts are related to SCT: symbolic cue, fantasy type, and saga. A symbolic cue is a brief or condensed signal like a symbol, sign, or word that represents a fantasy theme. A fantasy type is a standard script using a prominent, spectacular template to explain new events. A saga is a description or chronicle of the achievements of a key individual, group, society, organization, or even country. Using the three-part framework of symbolic cue, fantasy type, and saga, two case studies of SCT were used in this chapter: one of the Earth Liberation Front (ELF) and one of Hezbollah. Finally, another three-part framework is the theory of symbolic trinity, consisting of symbolism, rhetoric, and myth. Rhetoric is the art of communicating efficiently and influentially through language. Myths can be easily fabricated; they can also be resurrected. The symbolic trinity was applied in two case studies: Nazism and Maharashtrian terrorism.

NOTES

1. Goody, Jack (1960). Religion and Ritual: The Definitional Problem. *British Journal of Sociology, 12,* 159–160.

2. Lincoln, Bruce (2006). An Early Moment in the Discourse of "Terrorism": Reflections on a Tale from Marco Polo. *Comparative Studies in Society and History, 48*(2), 242–259.

3. O'Shaughnessy, Nicholas (2004). Persuasion, Myth and Propaganda. *Journal of Political Marketing, 3*(3), 87–103.

4. Lincoln, Bruce (2006). An Early Moment in the Discourse of "Terrorism": Reflections on a Tale from Marco Polo. *Comparative Studies in Society and History, 48*(2), 242–259.

5. Eliade, Mircea (1967). *Myths, Dreams and Mysteries.* New York: Harper & Row.

6. Tudor, Henry (1973). *Political Myth.* London: Macmillan.

7. Malinowski, Bronislaw (1954). *Magic, Science and Religion and Other Essays.* Garden City, NY: Doubleday.

8. Dundes, Alan (1984). *Sacred Narrative: Readings in the Theory of Myth.* Berkeley: University of California Press.

9. Kearney, Richard (1988). *Transitions: Narratives in Modern Irish Culture.* Manchester, UK: Manchester University Press.

10. Schöpflin, George (1997). The Functions of Myth and a Taxonomy of Myths. In Geoffrey Hosking & George Schöpflin (Eds.), *Myths and Nationhood* (pp. 19–35). London: Hurst.

11. Ness, Cindy (2005). In the Name of the Cause: Women's Work in Secular and Religious Terrorism. *Studies in Conflict & Terrorism, 28*(3), 353–373.

12. Eliade, Mircea (1971). *The Myth of the Eternal Return: Cosmos and History.* Princeton, NJ: Princeton University Press.

13. Githens-Mazer, Jonathan (2006). *Myths and Memories of the Easter Rising: Cultural and Political Nationalism in Ireland.* Dublin: Irish Academic Press.

14. Overing, Joanna (1997). The Role of Myth: An Anthropological Perspective. In Geoffrey Hosking & George Schöpflin (Eds.), *Myths and Nationhood* (pp. 1–18). London: Routledge.

15. O'Shaughnessy, Nicholas (2004). Persuasion, Myth and Propaganda. *Journal of Political Marketing, 3*(3), 87–103.

16. Schöpflin, George (1997). The Functions of Myth and a Taxonomy of Myths. In Geoffrey Hosking & George Schöpflin (Eds.), *Myths and Nationhood* (pp. 19–35). London: Hurst.

17. Tyrrel, Blake, & Brown, Frieda (1991). *Athenian Myths and Institutions.* Oxford: Oxford University Press.

18. O'Shaughnessy, Nicholas (2004). Persuasion, Myth and Propaganda. *Journal of Political Marketing, 3*(3), 87–103.

19. Curta, Florin (2001). *The Making of the Slavs: History and Archaeology of the Lower Danube Region.* Cambridge: Cambridge University Press; and Smith, Anthony (1986). *The Ethnic Origins of Nations.* Oxford: Blackwell Publishing.

20. Rowland, Robert, & Theye, Kirsten (2008). The Symbolic DNA of Terrorism. *Communication Monographs, 75*(1), 52–85.

21. Malinowski, Bronislaw (1954). *Magic, Science and Religion and Other Essays.* Garden City, NY: Doubleday.

22. Piven, J. S. (2007). Psychological, Theological, and Thanatological Aspects of Suicidal Terrorism. *Case Western Reserve Journal of International Law, 39*(3), 731–758.

23. Burke, Kenneth (1966). *Language as Symbolic Action: Essays on Life, Literature, and Method.* Berkeley: University of California Press.

24. Bormann, Ernest (1982). Fantasy and Rhetorical Vision: Ten Years Later. *Quarterly Journal of Speech, 68*, 288–305.

25. Bormann, Ernest (1972). Fantasy and Rhetorical Vision: The Rhetorical Criticism of Social Reality. In Bernard Brock (Ed.), *Methods of Rhetorical Criticism* (pp. 211–222). Detroit, MI: Wayne State University Press; and Bormann, Ernest (1985). Symbolic Convergence Theory: A Communication Formulation. *Journal of Communication, 35*, 128–138.

26. Bormann, Ernest, Cragan, John, & Shields, Donald (2001). Three Decades of Developing, Grounding, and Using Symbolic Convergence Theory (SCT). In William Gudykunst (Ed.), *Communication Yearbook 25* (pp. 271–313). Mahwah, NJ: Lawrence Erlbaum; and Bormann, Ernest, Cragan, John, & Shields, Donald (2003). Defending Symbolic Convergence Theory from an Imaginary Gunn. *Quarterly Journal of Speech, 89*, 366–372.

27. St. Antoine, Thomas, Althouse, Matthew, & Ball, Moya (2005). Fantasy-Theme Analysis. In Jim Kuypers (Ed.), *The Art of Rhetorical Criticism* (pp. 212–240). Boston: Pearson Education.

28. Stewart, Charles, Smith, Craig, & Denton, Robert E., Jr. (2007). *Persuasion and Social Movements* (5th ed.). Long Grove, IL: Waveland.

29. Panda, Abinash, & Gupta, R. K. (2001). Understanding Organizational Culture: A Perspective on Roles for Leaders. *Vikalpa, 26*(4), 3–19.

30. Lévi-Strauss, Claude (1966). *The Savage Mind*. Chicago: University of Chicago Press.

31. Tattarini, Mirko (2007). Kamikaze Cyberpunk: Threats and Alternatives in the Age of Viral Power. In Boaz Ganor, Katharina Von Knop, & Carlos Duarte (Eds.), *Hypermedia Seduction for Terrorist Recruiting* (pp. 188–198). Amsterdam: NATO Science for Peace and Security Series.

32. Bormann, Ernest, Cragan, John, & Shields, Donald (2001). Three Decades of Developing, Grounding, and Using Symbolic Convergence Theory (SCT). In William Gudykunst (Ed.), *Communication Yearbook 25* (pp. 271–313). Mahwah, NJ: Lawrence Erlbaum; and Klatch, Rebecca (1998). Of Meanings and Masters: Political Symbolism and Symbolic Action. *Policy, 21*(1), 137–154.

33. Eljahmi, Mohamed (2006). Libya and the U.S.: Qadhafi Unrepentant. *Middle East Quarterly, 13*(1), 11–20; and Tuman, Joseph (2010). *Communicating Terror: The Rhetorical Dimensions of Terrorism*. Thousand Oaks, CA: Sage.

34. St. Antoine, Thomas, Althouse, Matthew, & Ball, Moya (2005). Fantasy-Theme Analysis. In Jim Kuypers (Ed.), *The Art of Rhetorical Criticism* (pp. 212–240). Boston: Pearson Education.

35. Bormann, Ernest, Cragan, John, & Shields, Donald (1996). An Expansion of the Rhetorical Vision Component of the Symbolic Convergence Theory: The Cold War Paradigm Case. *Communication Monographs, 63*, 1–29.

36. Ponnambalam, Satchi (1983). *Sri Lanka: The National Question and the Tamil Liberation Struggle*. London: Zed; and Tamil Information Centre (2001). *Tamils of Sri Lanka: The Quest for Human Dignity*. London: Tamil Information Centre.

37. Wessendorf, Markus (2005). Culture of Fear: Uncomfortable Transactions between Performance, Theatre and Terrorism. *International Journal of the Humanities, 3*(3), 217–228.

38. Bormann, Ernest, Cragan, John, & Shields, Donald (2001). Three Decades of Developing, Grounding, and Using Symbolic Convergence Theory (SCT). In William Gudykunst (Ed.), *Communication Yearbook 25* (pp. 271–313). Mahwah, NJ: Lawrence Erlbaum.

39. Gendron, Angela (2010). Confronting Terrorism in Saudi Arabia. *International Journal of Intelligence and CounterIntelligence, 23*(3), 487–508.

40. Lifton, Robert Jay (2000). *Destroying the World to Save It: Aum Shinrikyo, Apocalyptic Violence, and the New Global Terrorism*. New York: Picador.

41. Ferracuti, Franco, & Bruno, Francesco (1983). Italy: A Systems Perspective. In Arnold Goldstein & Marshall Segall (Eds.), *Aggression in Global Perspective* (pp. 287–312). Elmsford, NY: Pergamon Press.

42. Liddick, Donald (2006). *Eco-Terrorism: Radical Environmental and Animal Liberation Movements*. Westport, CT: Praeger.

43. Holden, Stephen (2011, June 21). If a Tree Falls: A Story of the Earth Liberation Front. *The New York Times*, p. C5.

44. Morris, Travis, & Crank, John (2011). Toward a Phenomenology of Terrorism: Implications for Research and Policy. *Crime, Law and Social Change, 56*, 219–242.

45. Best, Steven, & Nocella, Anthony J. (2006). *Igniting a Revolution: Voices in Defense of the Earth*. Oakland, CA: AK Press.

46. Leader, Stefan, & Probst, Peter (2003). The Earth Liberation Front and Environmental Terrorism. *Terrorism and Political Violence, 15*(4), 37–58.

47. Schwartz, Daniel (1998). Environmental Terrorism: Analyzing the Concept. *Journal of Peace Research, 35*(4), 484.

48. Plows, Alexandra, Wall, Derek, & Doherty, Brian (2004). Covert Repertoires: Ecotage in the UK. *Social Movement Studies, 3*(2), 199–219.

49. Ingalsbee, T. (1996). Earth First! Activism: Ecological Postmodern Praxis in Radical Environmentalist Identities. *Sociological Perspectives, 39*, 263–276.

50. Liddick, Donald (2006). *Eco-Terrorism: Radical Environmental and Animal Liberation Movements*. Westport, CT: Praeger.

51. Williams, Dana (2009). Red vs. Green: Regional Variation of Anarchist Ideology in the United States. *Journal of Political Ideologies, 14*(2), 189–210.

52. Wall, Derek (1999). *Earth First! and the Anti-Roads Movement: Radical Environmentalism and Comparative Social Movements*. New York: Routledge.

53. Baldo, Shannon (2010). Elves and Extremism: The Use of Fantasy in the Radical Environmentalist Movement. *Young Scholars in Writing, 13*, 108–115.

54. Earth Liberation Front (1997). *Beltane*. Portland, OR: Earth Liberation Front Press Office (ELFPO).

55. Baldo, Shannon (2010). Elves and Extremism: The Use of Fantasy in the Radical Environmentalist Movement. *Young Scholars in Writing, 13*, 108–115.

56. Stewart, Charles, Smith, Craig, and Denton, Robert E., Jr. (2007). *Persuasion and Social Movements* (5th ed.). Long Grove, IL: Waveland.

57. Baldo, Shannon (2010). Elves and Extremism: The Use of Fantasy in the Radical Environmentalist Movement. *Young Scholars in Writing, 13*, 108–115.

58. Flader, Susan (1974). *Thinking like a Mountain: Aldo Leopold and the Evolution of an Ecological Attitude toward Deer, Wolves, and Forests*. Columbia: University of Missouri Press.

59. Leopold, Aldo (2008, February 13). *Thinking like a Mountain*. Retrieved April 11, 2013, from http://www.eco-action.org/dt/thinking.html.

60. Baldo, Shannon (2010). Elves and Extremism: The Use of Fantasy in the Radical Environmentalist Movement. *Young Scholars in Writing, 13*, 108–115.

61. Bell, James (2002). *Lord of the Machines*. Retrieved April 14, 2013, from http://yeoldeconsciousness-shoppe.com/art100.html

62. Bartell, Dawn, & Gray, David (2012). Hezbollah and Al Shabaab in Mexico and the Terrorist Threat to the United States. *Global Security Studies, 3*(4), 100–114.

63. American Chronicle (2010, March 28). Iran Massively Rearming Hezbollah in Violation of UN Security Council Resolution. Retrieved February 1, 2014, from http://www.americanchronicle.com/articles/view/148262

64. Elie Alagha, Joseph (2011). *Hizbullah's Documents: From the 1985 Open Letter to the 2009 Manifesto*. Amsterdam: Amsterdam University Press; and Shehata, Samer (2012). *Islamist Politics in the Middle East: Movements and Change*. New York: Routledge.

65. Matusitz, Jonathan (2012). *Terrorism & Communication: A Critical Introduction*. Thousand Oaks, CA: Sage.

66. Abdul-Hussain, Hussain (2009). Hezbollah: A State within a State. *Current Trends in Islamist Ideology, 8*, 68–81.

67. Schleifer, Ron (2009). Psyoping Hezbollah: The Israeli Psychological Warfare Campaign during the 2006 Lebanon War. *Terrorism and Political Violence, 21*(2), 221–238.

68. Azani, Eitan (2007). Islam & Political Symbolism: Hezbollah as a Case Study. In Boaz Ganor, Kathrina von Knop, & Carlos Duarte (Eds.), *Hypermedia Seduction for Terrorist Recruiting* (pp. 14–34). Amsterdam: IOS Press.

69. Sharara, Waddah (1996). *Hizbullahi State: Lebanon, Islamic Society*. Beirut: Dar al-Nahar.

70. Bronner, Ethan, & Hauser, Christine (2012, November 29). U.N. Assembly, in Blow to U.S., Elevates Status of Palestine. *The New York Times*, p. A1.

71. Khalili, Laleh (2007). "Standing with My Brother": Hizbullah, Palestinians, and the Limits of Solidarity. *Comparative Studies in Society and History, 49*(2), 276–303.

72. Arena, Michael, & Arrigo, Bruce (2005). Social Psychology, Terrorism and Identity: A Preliminary Reexamination of Theory, Culture, Self, and Society. *Behavioral Sciences and the Law, 23*, 485–506; and Bahry, Louay (2000). The Socioeconomic Foundations of the Shiite Opposition in Bahrain. *Mediterranean Quarterly, 10*, 129–143.

73. Azani, Eitan (2007). Islam & Political Symbolism: Hezbollah as a Case Study. In Boaz Ganor, Kathrina von Knop, & Carlos Duarte (Eds.), *Hypermedia Seduction for Terrorist Recruiting* (pp. 14–34). Amsterdam: IOS Press.

74. Antelava, Natalia (2009, January 9). Hezbollah Woos Crowds at Ashura Rally. *BBC News*. Retrieved April 12, 2013, from http://news.bbc.co.uk/2/hi/7816675.stm; and Jones, Toby Craig (2010). *Desert Kingdom: How Oil and Water Forged Modern Saudi Arabia*. Cambridge, MA: Harvard University Press.

75. Pinault, David (1992). *The Shiites: Ritual and Popular Piety in a Muslim Community*. New York: Palgrave Macmillan.

76. Arena, Michael, & Arrigo, Bruce (2005). Social Psychology, Terrorism and Identity: A Preliminary Reexamination of Theory, Culture, Self, and Society. *Behavioral Sciences and the Law, 23*, 485–506; and Bahry, Louay (2000). The Socioeconomic Foundations of the Shiite Opposition in Bahrain. *Mediterranean Quarterly, 10*, 129–143.

77. Ranstorp, Magnus (1996). Terrorism in the Name of Religion. *Journal of International Affairs, 50*(1), 41–63.

78. Tehranian, Majid (1980). Communication and Revolution in Iran: The Passing of a Paradigm. *Iranian Studies, 13*(1), 5–30.

79. Khosravi, Shahram (2009). *Young and Defiant in Tehran*. Philadelphia: University of Pennsylvania Press.

80. Ramazani, Ruohallah (1986). *Revolutionary Iran*. Baltimore: Johns Hopkins University Press.

81. Cohen, Jared (2008). *Children of Jihad: A Young American's Travels among the Youth of the Middle East*. New York: Gotham; and Lucic, Ante (2009). Hezbollah: An Iranian Project? *National Security and the Future, 1*(10), 77–88.

82. Moin, Baqer (1999). *Khomeini: Life of the Ayatollah*. New York: St. Martin's Press.

83. Oksnevad, Roy (2012). BMB Discipleship: An Investigation into the Factors Leading to Disharmony within the Iranian Churches in the Diaspora. *St Francis Magazine, 8*(4), 397–434.

84. O'Shaughnessy, Nicholas (2004). *Politics and Propaganda: Weapons of Mass Seduction.* Ann Arbor: University of Michigan Press.

85. van Eemeren, Frans, & Grootendorst, Rob (2004). *A Systematic Theory of Argumentation: The Pragmadialectical Approach.* Cambridge: Cambridge University Press.

86. Schwartz, Tony (1973). *The Responsive Chord.* New York: Basic Books.

87. O'Shaughnessy, Nicholas (2004). Persuasion, Myth and Propaganda. *Journal of Political Marketing, 3*(3), 87–103.

88. O'Shaughnessy, John, & O'Shaughnessy, Nicholas (2003). *The Marketing Power of Emotion.* New York: Oxford University Press.

89. Blain, Michael (1988). Fighting Words: What We Can Learn from Hitler's Hyperbole. *Symbolic Interaction, 11*(2), 257–276.

90. O'Shaughnessy, Nicholas (2004). Persuasion, Myth and Propaganda. *Journal of Political Marketing, 3*(3), 87–103.

91. Markovits, Elizabeth (2013). The Politics of Sincerity: Plato, Frank Speech and Democratic Judgment. *Contemporary Political Theory, 12*, e5–e9.

92. O'Shaughnessy, Nicholas (2004). Persuasion, Myth and Propaganda. *Journal of Political Marketing, 3*(3), 87–103.

93. Pratkanis, Anthony R., & Aronson, Elliot (1991). *Age of Propaganda: The Everyday Use and Abuse of Persuasion.* New York: W. H. Freeman.

94. Austin, John (1962). *How to Do Things with Words.* Oxford: Oxford University Press.

95. Searle, John (1969). *Speech Acts: An Essay in the Philosophy of Language.* Cambridge: Cambridge University Press.

96. Gumperz, John (1982). *Discourse Strategies.* Cambridge: Cambridge University Press.

97. Bird, Elizabeth, & Dardenne, Robert (1988). Myth, Chronicle and Story: Exploring the Narrative Qualities of News. In James Carey (Ed.), *Media, Myths, and Narratives: Television and the Press* (pp. 67–86). Newbury Park, CA: Sage.

98. O'Shaughnessy, Nicholas (2004). Persuasion, Myth and Propaganda. *Journal of Political Marketing, 3*(3), 87–103.

99. Safire, William (1996, December 22). The Spinner Spun. *The New York Times*, p. A1.

100. O'Shaughnessy, Nicholas (2004). Persuasion, Myth and Propaganda. *Journal of Political Marketing, 3*(3), 87–103.

101. O'Shaughnessy, Nicholas (2004). *Politics and Propaganda: Weapons of Mass Seduction.* Ann Arbor: University of Michigan Press.

102. Adams, Ian (1993). *Political Ideology Today.* Manchester, UK: Manchester University Press.

103. Juergensmeyer, Mark (2008). Martyrdom and Sacrifice in a Time of Terror. *Social Research, 75*(2), 417–434.

104. Vondung, Klaus (2005). National Socialism as a Political Religion: Potentials and Limits of an Analytical Concept. *Totalitarian Movements and Political Religions, 6*(1), 87–95.

105. Mosse, George (1966). *Nazi Culture.* New York: Grosset and Dunlap.

106. Phillips, Peter (1969). *The Tragedy of Nazi Germany.* New York: Praeger.

107. Klatch, Rebecca (1988). Of Meanings & Masters: Political Symbolism & Symbolic Action. *Polity, 21*(1), 137–154.

108. O'Shaughnessy, Nicholas (2004). Persuasion, Myth and Propaganda. *Journal of Political Marketing, 3*(3), 87–103.

109. O'Shaughnessy, Nicholas (2004). Persuasion, Myth and Propaganda. *Journal of Political Marketing, 3*(3), 87–103.

110. Neumann, Franz (1944). *Behemoth: The Structure and Practice of National Socialism 1933–1944.* New York: Oxford University Press.

111. O'Shaughnessy, Nicholas (2004). Persuasion, Myth and Propaganda. *Journal of Political Marketing, 3*(3), 87–103.

112. Matusitz, Jonathan (2012). *Terrorism & Communication: A Critical Introduction.* Thousand Oaks, CA: Sage.

113. Preston, Paul (1995). *Franco.* London: Fontana Press.

114. Buruma, Ian, & Margalit, Avishai (2004). *Occidentalism: The West in the Eyes of Its Enemies.* New York: Penguin.

115. O'Shaughnessy, Nicholas (2004). Persuasion, Myth and Propaganda. *Journal of Political Marketing, 3*(3), 87–103.

116. Baird, Jay Warren (1992). *To Die for Germany: Heroes in the Nazi Pantheon.* Bloomington: Indiana University Press.

117. India Today (2011, July 17). Maharashtra Terror History: 13 Attacks, 500 Deaths in a Decade. *India Today*, p. A1.

118. Vartak, Malavika (1999). Shivaji Maharaj: Growth of a Symbol. *Economic and Political Weekly, 34*(19), 1126–1134.

119. Jackson, William Joseph (2005). *Vijayanagara Voices: Exploring South Indian History and Hindu Literature.* Farnham, UK: Ashgate Publishing; and Sardesai, H. S. (2002). *Shivaji, the Great Maratha.* Nasik, India: Cosmopolitan Publishing.

120. Bidwai, Praful (2008). Confronting the Reality of Hindutva Terrorism. *Economic and Political Weekly, 43*(47), 10–13.

121. Misra, Sanghamitra (2006). Interrogating the "Region." *MisraEconomic and Political Weekly, 41*(25), 2542–2544.

122. Heuzé, Gérard (2000). Populism, Religion, and Nation in Contemporary India: The Evolution of the Shiv Sena in Maharashtra. *Comparative Studies of South Asia, Africa and the Middle East, 20*(1), 3–43.

123. Vartak, Malavika (1999). Shivaji Maharaj: Growth of a Symbol. *Economic and Political Weekly, 34*(19), 1126–1134.

124. Rabasa, Angel, Blackwill, Robert, Chalk, Peter, Cragin, Kim, & Fair, Christine (2009). *The Lessons of Mumbai.* Santa Monica, CA: RAND.

125. Vartak, Malavika (1999). Shivaji Maharaj: Growth of a Symbol. *Economic and Political Weekly, 34*(19), 1126–1134.

126. O'Hanlon, Rosalind (1983). Maratha History as Polemic: Low Caste Ideology and Political Debate in Late Nineteenth Century Western India. *Modern Asian Studies, 17*(1), 1–33.

127. Keer, Dhananjay (1997). *Mahatma Jotirao Phooley: Father of the Indian Social Revolution.* Mumbai, India: Popular Prakashan.

128. Phule, Jyotirao (1869). *Shivajicha Powada.* Pune, India: Oriental Press.

129. Vartak, Malavika (1999). Shivaji Maharaj: Growth of a Symbol. *Economic and Political Weekly, 34*(19), 1126–1134.

130. Wolpert, Stanley A. (1977). *Tilak and Gokhale: Revolution and Reform in the Making of Modern India.* Berkeley: University of California Press.

131. Qureshi, Imran (1948). The Founder of Pakistan. *Pakistan Horizon, 1*(3), 144–165.

132. Vartak, Malavika (1999). Shivaji Maharaj: Growth of a Symbol. *Economic and Political Weekly, 34*(19), 1126–1134.

133. Smith, Anthony (1986). *The Ethnic Origins of Nations.* Oxford: Blackwell Publishing.

Chapter Six

Symbolic Place and Territory in Terrorism

PLACE AND TERRITORY AS SYMBOLISM

A spatial-symbolic approach to terrorism can add fresh, new insights to the definition of terrorism. According to Walter (2003),[1] the most intractable conflicts of the second half of the twentieth century were those fought over places and territories. Places and territories are often overflowing with symbolism because they represent spatial or territorial consciousness, something that defines community or ethnic boundaries.

Place

Place refers to an area with definite boundaries, with which a particular group identifies, and where a series of events happens. The notion of place is a combination of nature and culture based on a history recollected within individual and/or collective memories. In many cases, symbolism and meaning are what make a place unique or sacred. Places function as narratives of collective memory that reinforce group cohesion and identity. They play a role in the mythology of cultures and are the foundational blocks of identity.[2] For example, without a sense of place, there would have been no Irish Republican Army (IRA). The growth of the IRA was tied to several locations. Those places were chosen because of their symbolism. Local Catholic churches were crucial to the organizing of the IRA. Gaelic clubs, offices, workshops, and sports teams were also instrumental to the building of social networks that would develop into the IRA. By attaching meaning and symbolism to various places, IRA members and potential recruits were able to choose how they wanted to be identified as a group. To the extent that **social identity** refers to the characteristics shared by individuals in small or large groups, it is also the result of the conditions that constitute place, as well as the behavior, ideas, actions, and rituals occurring in those places.[3]

Territory

Territory refers to possession and/or control of land. "Territory" differs from "place" in that the former denotes an area controlled and defended by an individual, a group, or an entire country. Human beings are territorial animals and seek to protect their space. Unlike place, territory points toward an emphasis on physical or material possession. There are three categories of territory: (1) public territories, (2) home territories, and (3) interactional territories. **Public territories** are zones or areas where any citizen can go (e.g., a national forest). **Home**

territories are zones or areas in which entrance is restricted to members, such as temples, sacred sites, or even an entire holy land. Home territories offer a sense of social, cultural, or religious intimacy (and, therefore, control over the area). In many instances, home territory is synonymous with homeland. **Interactional territories** are zones or areas in which people meet informally for the social outlet (e.g., lounges or local gyms). Parties or social gatherings are other examples of interactional territories. An interactional territory tends to claim boundary maintenance for the specific period of interaction.[4]

The second category, home territory, has often been the source of both internal and international conflicts when the territory was deemed to be encroached by invaders. **Territorial encroachment** can be of three forms: violation, invasion, or contamination. **Violation** is unjustified use of territory. Violators are those who have rebuffed or circumvented those who denied them access. **Invasion** occurs when people, with no right to entrance or use, cross the boundaries anyway. At the same time, they take possession of or change the social meaning of the territory. An invasion may be temporary or enduring. **Contamination** refers to pollution or infection. Contamination requires that something be made impure in terms of its definition and usage. Home territories may be contaminated by pollution or corruption of the symbols of sacred sites.[5]

ETHNONATIONALISM

Many ethnic groups have made claims to real or imaginary home territories. **Ethnonationalism**, also called **ethnic nationalism**, refers to a category of nationalism characterized by the desire of an ethnic group to have absolute authority over its own territory and its own political and cultural affairs. Put simply, it refers to the pursuit of statehood on the part of an ethnic group. Ethnonationalist movements also imply that the ethnic group's interests are not being recognized or respected under the current political or national regime.[6] The word *ethnic* gave rise to the word *ethnie*. **Ethnie** designates a specific population with a myth of common ancestry, common historical memories, many elements of a shared culture, a strong connection to a homeland, and a strong social cohesion among a certain number of its members.[7] In today's media, the most recurrent theme of ethnonationalist terrorism is the one involving Palestinian militant groups against Jewish targets in Israel and the Palestinian territories.

Separatist Terrorism

Separatist terrorism refers to terrorism motivated by ethnonationalism. Separatist terrorists fight to establish their own independent, sovereign state (separatism) for which they would obtain full autonomy. They clash with what they see as occupying, imperial, or unlawful powers.[8] Generally, separatist terrorism is perpetrated as a result of threats against cultural or religious symbols and the type of control that an ethnic group aspires to exercise over its historic homeland. The expectation is that declining control over a homeland endangers the safeguarding and maintenance of national identity.[9] Consequently, movements that endorse ethnonationalism are often violent. They oppose the involvement of outsiders and their ideologies and, with the likelihood of being intolerant, gratify their ethnic and cultural bases and impose strict social boundaries.[10] They support the idea of an irredenta. An **irredenta** is a territory that is culturally or historically linked to one nation but is controlled by a foreign government.[11]

Ethnonationalist terrorism is often linked to religiously motivated terrorism. This phenomenon is also called **sacral nationalism**, a type of nationalism in which ethnic or cultural groups use religious imagery and symbolism to advance their political agenda.[12] History tells us that the larger national military often wins against the ethnonationalist minority. The latter tends to see itself as a laager culture. A **laager culture** is a metaphor for an ethnonationalist minority that considers itself under siege. In military history, a laager was a mobile fortification that was vulnerable to attacks. The Roman Catholic Irish Republicans felt like a laager culture that had to constantly defend itself against the more powerful British-backed Loyalist oppressor.[13]

The following are examples of ethnonationalist groups that, in many countries, have been considered terrorist groups: ETA (a Basque militant group), PKK (the Kurdistan Workers' Party), ASALA (Armenian Secret Army for the Liberation of Armenia), Front de libération du Québec (FLQ), the Provisional IRA, Chechen separatists, and the Tamil Tigers in Sri Lanka.

Inscape

Home territories are a predominant theme of liberation movements as they are historically attached to a people and have increasingly become a powerful component of identity. A term that captures the essence of this statement is inscape. Coined by Osborne (1996),[14] **inscape** suggests that the homeland is transformed as a sacred reason for living up to the fight, something to be engaged visually day in and day out. Inscape is a combination of "inside" and "landscape." A key objective of ethnonationalism is to internalize the homeland as a landscape with deep symbolic meaning. People load the landscape with symbols, which "serve to punctuate time, focus space, and figure the landscape, converting it into a psychic terrain" (Osborne, 1996, p. 25).[15] The ultimate outcome of this internalization of homeland symbolism is a **landscape of identity**, the notion that identity is territory bound. It alludes to the sacred land envisioned by individuals with a common ancestry and way of life. By loading particular symbols onto a sacred land, people define the meaning of their identities, both individually and as groups. Landscapes of identity develop over time, and symbolism separates and influences the import of the "land" and its intended ethnonationalist uses.[16]

Basque Ethnonationalism

Basque ethnonationalism is a separatist movement advocating full independence of the Basque Country. The **Basques** are an ethnic group inhabiting regions bordering Spain and France. Basque ethnicity (Euskadi) and Basque language (Euskera) are not Indo-European and are considered archaic. This implies that Basque ethnonationalism has constantly been considered, by Spain and France, as culturally exclusive for countless generations. This distinction influences reluctance from Basques to recognize a shared ancestry with other populations and views Euskera as key to unifying Euskadi as a determinedly non-Spanish or non-French nation.[17] The Euskera word for Basque, "Euskal," refers to speakers of Euskera; it characterizes Basque identity in the context of ethnonationalist symbolization. Shabad and Llera Ramo (1995)[18] assert that, for many decades, "numerous segments of Basque society perceived threats to their collective identity coming from both Madrid and from new groups within the Basque Country itself" (p. 418).

The main organization of the Basque ethnonationalist movement, and the principal player in the Basque conflict, is **ETA**, an acronym for Euskadi Ta Askatasuna ("Basque Homeland and Freedom"). ETA is considered a terrorist organization by the United States and many European countries. Since 1968, ETA has been held accountable for killing over 800 individuals, wounding thousands, and carrying out dozens of kidnappings.[19] In the mid-twentieth century, the precipitous regression of the Basque language, to the point where only one

Basque out of four could speak it, became a pivotal ethnonationalist symbol and rallying point for the Basques.[20] This is, in part, the reason why ETA was created. ETA was ethnically inclusive. The terrorist group redefined Basque identity. Originally, ETA was a labor movement; later, it evolved into a key symbol of Basque nationalism. ETA subscribed to Marxism and attracted widespread support from the labor class. In the 1960s, adopting Marxism was common among separatist terrorist groups. Other groups such as the Popular Front for the Liberation of Palestine (PFLP) and the IRA used radical leftist rhetoric at a time when nationalist movements framed themselves as communist revolutions.[21]

Still to this day, the Basques consider themselves as an ethnically exclusive group and feel exceptionally sensitive to threats against their ethnic identity. With the emergence of ETA, Basque ethnocultural symbolism has been reinforced even more and has led to violent symbolic attachments and an intense need to preserve them. Euskera and ancestral homeland are two sacred symbols that play a crucial role in Basque nationalism, which supports Euskera diffusion, separation from Spain and France, and irredenta of the Basque homeland. These factors are justifiable reasons for organizing a separatist movement: they form the basis for a nostalgic determination to restore and safeguard cultural identity.[22]

TERRA SANCTA

There is a general agreement among scholars and policy makers, notwithstanding their approach, that, among conflicts over territories, those involving sacred lands are the most problematic.[23] Sacred lands are at the nucleus of many past and current violent conflicts such as Israel-Palestine, Kashmir, Chechnya, Sri Lanka, Northern Ireland, and the Basque Country. Dispute over sacred land, it seems, cannot be resolved by negotiation or compromise. Quite simply, the drive of many terrorist missions is a dispute over land, a contaminating encroacher that must be taken off the homeland. These circumstances are ripe for religious symbolism, and, as a result, homelands in such contexts are continually perceived as sacred.[24]

Terra Sancta: Definition

Terra sancta (from Latin, meaning "sanctified land" or "sacred land") is hallowed territory. It symbolizes a believer's lifelong, holy goal to recapture the homeland from any violators, invaders, or contaminators. Whereas territory, in and of itself, is divisible, terra sancta is not. The price of terra sancta is invaluable, its meaningfulness is unfathomable, and the resolve to regain it is nonnegotiable.[25] Symbolically, terra sancta is the land where the nation's purity was preserved before any contact with outsiders was made.[26] In 1996, Osama bin Laden proclaimed his fatwa (i.e., his declaration of jihad) against the United States, saying,

> Our Muslim brothers throughout the world: your brothers in the country of the two sacred places [Saudi Arabia] and in Palestine request your support. They are asking you to participate with them against their enemies, who are also your enemies—the Israelis and the Americans—by causing them as much harm as can be possibly achieved. (Cited in Bergen, 2002, p. 97)[27]

Osama bin Laden's direct emphasis on the two Muslim sacred places and Palestine as terra sancta testifies to the immense importance and symbolic value that Islamists attach to specific territories. They represent a shared and contested history. The complex symbolism of territory that emerges in this context has serious political implications by informing a global movement's raison d'être.

In Guernica, a Basque city in northern Spain, the relationship between terra sancta and history is symbolized through the physical environment of the place. Of particular importance is the famous Tree of Guernica (Arbol de Guernica), under which Basque leaders assembled to exercise their rights. Today, the remains of the tree, well maintained in front of the Basque Assembly House (Casa de Juntas), represent their attempt at gaining autonomy.[28] The old tree of Guernica is terra sancta because it symbolizes the old Basque laws and liberties.[29] Similarly, in Sri Lanka, Sinhalese Buddhist Nationalists (i.e., those fighting the Tamil Tigers) want to define the modern state not just as the core of Sinhalese identity but also as terra sancta—a sacred land where Buddhism will endure forever and in its purest form. Religious perceptions of national territory can have extreme ramifications for warfare. For example, they can resist the legitimacy of compromise vis-à-vis territorial control. Being blessed with terra sancta is seen as a sacred necessity and a long-deserved right. This is plainly how Sinhalese Buddhist Nationalists have approached the question of Sri Lanka's postcolonial identity.[30]

Al-Quds: The Muslim Jerusalem

In regard to the issue of terra sancta, Palestinian concerns have centered on both territories and local places. One of these sacred local places is Al-Quds. **Al-Quds** is what Arabic speakers call Jerusalem. In the Muslim world, the exact name for Jerusalem is Al-Quds al-Sharif (i.e., the Noble Holy Place). For Muslims, Al-Quds is the third terra sancta in order of importance—the first two being the holy cities of Mecca and Medina. Although not cited in the Qur'an, Al-Quds is sacred for its profound connection with the Prophet Muhammad. In Islamic symbolic culture, Al-Quds was founded on Muhammad's night journey to Jerusalem from Mecca. Jerusalem was the first *qibla* (direction of prayer) in Islam, but later Muhammad switched the *qibla* to Mecca. Tradition also has it that, before ascending to Paradise, Muhammad tethered Buraq, his white horse that had wings, to the fragments of the Herodian wall that once enclosed the Jewish temple, thus turning that site into a sign of conquest over the archenemy: the Jewish people.[31]

The site of the Jewish temple is called the **Temple Mount**, the holiest site in Judaism. In the Islamic world, the Temple Mount is referred to as the Haram al-Sharif and includes the two sacred sites of Al-Quds: the Al-Aqsa Mosque and the Dome of the Rock. The Al-Aqsa Mosque marks the furthest point on Muhammad's night journey from Mecca, and the Dome of the Rock is the site from which he ascended to Paradise. For all these reasons, Al-Quds is the third holiest site in Islam and has become a commendable "second leg" of the required pilgrimage to Mecca. Al-Quds had found such an important place in Islamic theological and political discourse that the desire to keep Jerusalem Muslim is now a popular rallying cry for those brothers and sisters who have suffered the violations, invasions, and contaminations of Judaism and Christendom.[32] Many Islamic regimes, like the Saudi and Jordanian regimes, consider themselves the stewards and gatekeepers of the Noble Holy Place.[33]

The Islamic Republic of Iran has created the **Al-Quds Force** ("Jerusalem Force"), a special terrorist unit of the Islamic Revolutionary Guards Corps (IRGC). The Al-Quds Force has been tasked with the liberation of Muslim lands, and Al-Quds in particular. It has created strong bonds with Hezbollah, Hamas, and the Islamic jihad.[34] In terms of logistics, the Al-Quds Force has the mission to organize, train, equip, and put money into Islamic revolutionary movements across the world. It does so by creating and maintaining contacts with underground Islamic terrorist organizations in over forty countries. The Al-Quds Force reports directly to the current Supreme Leader of Iran, the Ayatollah Ali Khamenei.[35] Hezbollah's first anti-Jewish suicide mission was Operation Khaybar. Khaybar is a throwback to the Battle of Khaybar, an oasis in northwestern Saudi Arabia where the Prophet Muhammad and his army conquered a Jewish tribe.[36]

PERSUASIVE CARTOGRAPHY

Persuasive cartography is a countermapping practice, a method whereby a group diffuses its doctrine by altering a map. This can be done by distorting the borders on the map, changing the names of cities or sites, or even removing them altogether. This can also be done through **map symbolization** (or **geographic symbolism**)—the selection of symbols, for propagandistic purposes, in order to inform the map reader what is relevant and what is not. In this context, a map becomes a human-subjective creation whereby a group packages or markets spatial knowledge.[37] As Wood and Fels (2008) explain, "The map is a vehicle for creating and conveying authority about, and ultimately over, territory" (p. 27).[38] To the outside world, persuasive cartography can also help convince the world community that they should recognize the projected nation-state as it is.[39]

Cartographic Propaganda

Persuasive cartography is an example of cartographic propaganda. **Cartographic propaganda** denotes the creation of maps for propagandistic intent; it is a conscious attempt to advance an ideological vision of geographical expansionism through false claims.[40] Cartographic propaganda has been studied in many contexts. For instance, in German schools in 1935, Adolf Hitler's map of "Deutschland" was showing all the German-speaking areas surrounding Germany without borders, as if they were part of the Third Reich. It looked like the Reich stretched over Austria and the German-speaking regions of Poland, Czechoslovakia, and even France.[41] During the Cold War, the Soviet Union intentionally falsified most public maps of the country by misplacing streets, misrepresenting boundaries, and removing geographical features. The Soviet secret police were the ones who ordered this. According to Western experts, the maps were garbled to avoid aerial bombing or foreign attacks.[42]

Likewise, the official maps of India and Pakistan continue to abjure political and geographical reality by presenting the highly contested region of Kashmir as under their control.[43] When ethnonationalist groups clash with each other, they have maps and countermaps that differ conspicuously from each other (e.g., by referring to different territories or fabricating new ones). A typical Basque map presents a map of "the seven provinces," torn from Spain and France, to portray the Basque terra sancta as a single unit. The Tamil Tigers' map claims the areas along the northern coast of Sri Lanka as "Tamil Eelam." This, of course, is very different from the official map of Sri Lanka as a single state. Nationalist (Irish Republican) maps picture the entire Ireland as just one territory with no political separations, whereas Loyalists (Northern Irish Protestants) are pleased about looking at their maps of Northern Ireland as a British area, with the rest of the island often missing altogether.[44]

The method of cartographic propaganda has often been used in ethnonationalism because countermapping is a **geopolitical code**, a practice whereby ethnonationalist groups offer an alternative map to achieve their long-term agenda. After all, it is the separatists' or irredentists' objective to gratify their constituents by accommodating them with a great vision. A great vision can be offered through the redrawing of internal and external borders, as well as the creation of larger countries, autonomous regions, or nation-states that are geographically separated. Such countermapping practices affirm their aspiration for a nation-state.[45] All the aforementioned cases of persuasive cartography make the typical altered map a kind of logo-map. A **logo-map** is a map on which an ethnonationalist group incorporates celebrated cultural icons, changes the name of the cities, adds new things, or subtracts existing things. It is a visual depiction molding the geographical imagination of the nation as a **geo-body**, the idea that the newly shaped image of the nation's territory will be clearly recognizable by anybody belonging to the group.[46] As a geo-body, the map is a privileged symbol because it contributes to discourses of national memory, history, and identity. These discourses rely on geographical notions of terra sancta, but they are not exclusively territorial. Hence, the meaning of the map is not intrinsic to its discursive context but rather dependent on it.[47]

A Palestinian Map versus Israeli Map

In his article titled "Trapped in Mirror-Images," Wallach (2011)[48] examined the persuasive cartography of both the Palestinians and Israelis in detail. The Palestinian and Israeli homelands are depicted in maps that are similar in shape. Although both ethnoreligious groups come from extremely unequal positions, they celebrate maps as a conspicuous instrument of persuasion. These maps present a land shaped in a sliver and located between the Mediterranean Sea and the River Jordan. So the land has an iconic "knife shape," and its blade points downward. While Palestinians refer to it as "Palestine" or "historical Palestine," the Jews call it the "Land of Israel" or "Greater Israel."[49]

In spite of these similarities, both maps differ greatly in many ways. For example, as opposed to Palestinian maps, Israeli maps include the Golan Heights. Internationally recognized as Syrian territory, this region in the Levant has been occupied and controlled by Israel since 1967. Additionally, Israeli and Palestinian maps differ through visual and textual cues like legends, place names, and coloring. Each of the two ethnoreligious groups has also kept on referring to the same controversial landlocked territory by a different name. In this case, the intention of both groups is to indicate their exclusive ownership of the land. Thus, the Palestinians insist on calling it "West Bank," while Israel insists on calling it "Judea and Samaria."[50] Many maps in Palestinian textbooks do not even mention Israel or Jewish-Israeli cities. However, the same textbooks describe places within Israel, like Haifa and the Galilee, as located in Palestine. The removal of Israel from the Palestinian maps is perceived as strongly reflecting the Palestinian national agenda.[51]

What is peculiar to the Palestinian-Israeli conflict is that the same "logo-map" is used by two clashing ethnoreligious groups; the same "geo-body" inhabits two nations. In that protracted conflict, each map has been repeatedly shown to be taken for factuality. Although the two sides are diametrically opposed on matters of history and justice, Israelis and Palestinians seem in accord about the "objectivity" of their own maps and their success at presenting factual truth. A pro-Palestinian website states that "the maps tell the real story. Israel is the aggressor—a nation eager to conquer lands which do not belong to it."[52] Through their persuasive cartography, both Palestinians and Israelis practice a form of rejectionism. **Rejectionism** describes a long-established attitude or policy of rejection toward some group. It is usually used by commentators on both sides of the controversy as a label for Palestinian opposition to the existence of the State of Israel, and as a label for Israeli opposition to the recognition of the Palestinian State.[53]

In present-day Palestinian culture, the map is one of the most recognizable and celebrated symbols, often juxtaposed with the Palestinian flag and the Dome of the Rock. These three omnipresent symbols shape the Palestinian symbolic landscape, and they are employed to underscore nationalism in daily surroundings. The map can be seen on most streets, in public spaces, on posters, and through graffiti and wall paintings. It is also a sacred sign of Palestinian individual identity. Palestinians wear their map on necklaces, on T-shirts, and even as a form of wallpaper for their mobile phones. Yasser Arafat, the later chairman of the Palestine Liberation Organization (PLO), famously shaped his keffiyeh (headgear) to resemble the map of Palestine. The Palestinian map is not just an abstract symbol; it is also a symbol of presence performed through visual, material, and tactile ways.[54]

In Palestinian commemoration, the map is a very prominent motif that plays a part in the sacralization of Palestinian cartography. The map often appears in Palestinian commemoration sites, from monuments sponsored by the Palestinian Authority (PA) to grassroots commemoration plaques. Memorials for Palestinian martyrs who died in holy war against the Israelis often feature the map. Upon commemorating the Deir Yassin massacre (when Zionist forces killed over one hundred people in a Palestinian-Arab village), the map of Palestine is stabbed with a knife; the terra sancta becomes the main victim of the massacre. Palestinian families whose children died in the conflict regularly create their own commemoration portraits, with the picture of their child juxtaposed with symbolic nationalist symbols, such as the Palestinian map.[55] Lastly, the Palestinian map is often supplemented with photos of refugees expecting to return to Palestine. The map is a visual representation of the Palestinian "Right of Return," which is one of the building blocks of Palestinian nationalism and the linchpin of Palestinian political ideology.[56]

TERRORIST MURALS

A **terrorist mural** is any piece of artwork (mostly graffiti) or writing created on a wall, ceiling, or large permanent structure by a terrorist group or people supporting the cause of a militant group. A terrorist mural tends to air grievances related to an ongoing conflict with a neighboring state, enemies worldwide, or even adversaries within the state itself. Hence, such a mural tells people who the group is and why they should stop and take notice. Most terrorist murals are created by youths who are familiar with the meaning of the crisis or conflict in question. Murals are a good way for them to share their interpretation of the world.[57] Terrorist murals are evidence of an attempt to offer a voice and produce a public sphere. For Habermas (1991),[58] the **public sphere** is a domain in which public opinion can be formed; it is also "an ideal speech situation in which discursive communication takes place" (p. 398). In some places, terrorist murals have become so famous that tourists flock to see them. **Conflict tourism** illustrates the popularity that past (and sometimes current) conflict sites enjoy for tourism and travel. For example, in Belfast, terrorist murals are photographed by people from all over the world. In West Belfast particularly, walls stretch to a distance of about 21 km (13 miles). Some walls can be 8 meters (25 feet) high and are composed of diverse materials: steel, metal slabs, or brick.[59]

Terrorist Murals as Territorial Markers

A **territorial marker** is any symbol used by people to identify their territory (mostly walls). In this case, terrorist murals are markers of territoriality. A wall is not a simple separation; it also acts as a border fence. When terrorist murals are territorial markers, they symbolize an expression of control of public space through graffiti or writings on walls. Control of public space is central to commitment and devotion to one's group.[60] Terrorist murals are territorial markers analogous to street maps with territorial demarcations. Just by looking at the symbolism on the walls, readers know which areas are controlled by whom.[61] Shirlow and Murtagh (2006)[62] write that "muralists use defined spaces within which to operationalize a propaganda-conditioning perspective that encompasses signals of territorial demarcation" (p. 68).

What terrorist murals often symbolize is that two ethnic or religious communities refuse to coexist peacefully. Such murals can even lead to territorial competitiveness between two paramilitaries.[63] With such a terrorist signature on a wall, a mural features a cultural landscape that acutely divides clashing communities. The wall itself acts as a territorial marker not only to divide two incompatible groups, but also to separate their respective commercial areas altogether. It seems like the two communities live in two different worlds. Those few residents who live on both sides of the wall would admit that the "other side" is a dreaded landscape, in spite of formal peace agreements.[64]

When two groups hate each other so much that they would push each other into the sea, it is called territorial purification. **Territorial purification** describes what is reflected in the way of ethnic or religious territorialization.[65] Under this type of **activity segregation**, groups not only live in different areas but also avoid any interaction with each other. Terrorist murals can express the daily activity segregation of distinctive groups, which leads to mutual exclusiveness.[66] A terrorist mural is also an example of **symbolic totemism**, a symbol of group belonging and sentiment. In this case, it can be an elaborate painting or a graffiti signature. These are declarations of presence and control in a district. Symbolic totemism allows decision makers to mobilize people in areas where risky actions need to be anticipated or undertaken.[67]

Terrorist Murals as Political Communication

When terrorist murals are used for purposes of political communication, it is not only on walls that graffiti and writings are made, but also on the sides of buildings (commercial and residential) and ceilings of public buildings. Such murals are akin to inscapes or landscapes of identity in that they contain political significance and often send messages to the international community. They help convey a group's cultural identity by investing symbolic meaning in those inscapes. They expose the experiential and challenged ideologies of that group. They disseminate directives for both fighting occupation and turning oneself into a real fighter in the process. As an instrumental device of communication, a terrorist mural is made to speak to multiple audiences. The violence that surrounds its creation and reading underscores the significance of symbols themselves as sites of potential future revolutions. This also means that both the production and interpretation of terrorist murals are cultural and historical practices situated in a social context.[68]

Specifically because of their importance as ubiquitous repositories for memory, murals are places to which people should go if they forget an important part of their culture's history. At the same time, for those who favor the peace process, murals can be easily defaced, destroyed, or removed. A few have been defaced by youths, rival groups, and police forces.[69] While each message addressed in a terrorist mural may be unique in some ways, it can certainly be interpreted in more than one way. Nevertheless, in most cases, the message is straightforward: terrorist murals illustrate political views, and they voice a group's political allegiances in the same way that fluttering flags and bunting are used to express nationalistic pride.[70] They act as a credendum. A **credendum** is a doctrine to be believed by the public, and it is expressed through the symbolism and language of struggles or political movements.[71] Many terrorist murals worldwide depict violent credenda: the dissention, extreme deaths, paramilitary actions, and human suffering linked to ethnic or religious clashes.[72] In Northern Ireland and the Palestinian territories, several murals replicate renowned newspaper photos, such as the image of young men with gas masks, Molotov cocktails, and AK-47s. Many murals also portray recurrent motifs of suppression by aggressors and resistance to invaders.[73]

CASE STUDY I: MURALS IN NORTHERN IRELAND

Ulster, one of Ireland's four historic regions, is composed of nine counties. In 1921, six counties were partitioned and controlled by Great Britain, giving birth to Northern Ireland. The majority of Northern Irish are Protestant and descendants of the Plantation of Ulster in the seventeenth century. The Catholics in Belfast aspire to be included in the Republic of Ireland, or Southern Ireland (some Belfast commentators call it the Republic). The Protestants, on the other hand, are mostly Scots and English who want to stay loyal to Great Britain. Because of this loyalty, the Protestants are designated as Loyalists, while the Catholics are called Nationalists. Belfast's identity as a city that is divided between Catholics and Protestants was born out of intense conflicts in the past few decades. The harsh conflicts essentially stem from these two communities that cannot coexist peacefully. The result is the development of distinct and segregated residential districts. Since the early 1980s in Northern Ireland, there has been an upsurge in murals portraying paramilitary images and symbols.[74]

Nationalist Murals

Nationalist murals experienced an increase in Catholic areas during and after the hunger strikes of 1981, at which time Bobby Sands died and when the Nationalists' social movement adopted the practice of creating murals. The first Nationalist murals appeared seventy-three years after the first Loyalist ones were made. Their purpose was to let the world know what their protests were created for. From the beginning, Nationalist murals were loaded with various themes: electoral support for Sinn Féin (the Republican Party), Irish history and folklore, and cases of state repression.[75] Many other murals, however, are militaristic and show sympathy for militant activities. One commemorates the armed struggle of the IRA; another celebrates the Proclamation of the Irish Republic against Britain following the 1916 Easter Rising. A third one pays homage to the 1920 victims murdered by the Royal Irish Constabulary and the Gibraltar victims (three Irish men killed by undercover SAS agents in 1988).[76] Unlike Loyalist murals, Nationalist murals tend to center on more specific political or historical events, such as particular battles or riots, martyrs or hunger strikers, and the Easter Rising. Other Nationalist murals vibrantly depict gigantic hands bound by barbed wire, prison strip searches, deportation of Irish prisoners of war, confinement, plastic bullets, censorship, and other Irish Republican campaigns.[77]

Of equal relevance is the high emphasis on the use of international symbolism. Indeed, this international consciousness is something to behold. Irish Nationalists are still on the side of Palestinians today. For instance, at the annual West Belfast Festival, the area is decorated with Palestinian flags, and there are events inviting Palestinian spokespersons. In addition, Palestine represented the first identifiable international theme on a Nationalist mural. Painted in 1982, it illustrated two militant men, from the PLO and IRA, holding aloft, together, a Russian rocket-propelled grenade mortar, a device used by both groups. Underneath, the slogan read, "One struggle."[78] This strong identification with the Palestinian cause symbolizes a resistance to "ethnic victimization." **Ethnic victimization** designates the safety of a group being jeopardized by violence and conflict. Its human and civil rights are not honored, and repeated attacks on the victim group constitute a constant threat that engenders a fear of destruction of the group.[79]

Figure 6.1 is a Nationalist mural created as an apparatus for propaganda and as a means of refuting the influence of Loyalist political dominance. Figure 6.1 shows a mural replicating the newspaper image of a Nationalist boy with a gas mask and a Molotov cocktail.[80] This mural is located in Derry, the second-largest city in Northern Ireland. The image symbolizes the struggle between disaffected Nationalists and the British-backed Loyalist "aggressors." In this case, it was the **Battle of the Bogside** (a district outside the city walls of Derry), which took place in August 1969. It was a violent fight between the local Nationalist residents of the Bogside and the Royal Ulster Constabulary (RUC), the British-backed police force in Northern Ireland.

The ideology of Irish Republican Nationalism is replete with political metaphors and symbolism. Indeed, the nationalistic pride and focus are like an **imagined community**; it occurs at the mental and emotional levels and assumes the lifeblood or substance of a metaphysical being. An imagined community differs from an actual community in that the former is not (and cannot be) based on everyday face-to-face interactions between its members. The formation of imagined communities has become much more possible thanks to the printing press, new media, and other forms of communication. Capitalist entrepreneurs have published books and employed new media in the vernacular—rather than elite script languages such as Latin—in order to make their circulation much larger.[81] Others refer to imagined communities as **fictive kin**, a situation in which people who do not know each other personally cultivate emotional ties on the basis of social identification, particularly in times of crisis or suffering.[82]

Loyalist Murals

After the expansion of Nationalist murals, Loyalist murals started to reappear, embracing similar militaristic symbolism.[83] Belfast Loyalist murals have placed emphasis on narrower themes. Examples are martyrdom, heroism in hard struggles, and Northern Irish history. This thematic narrowness, nonetheless, allowed for a rich multiplicity of representations; various images and icons were incorporated in the paintings. Loyalist murals tend to pay homage to the dead. Many historical events that have marked Protestant or British history and paramilitary activities of the Ulster Defence forces are portrayed as well. Other compelling and vivid militaristic murals (although much fewer in number) also communicate messages about Loyalism and Northern Irish collective memory.[84]

Just like Nationalists extol the virtues of the Palestinian cause, Loyalists align themselves with the Israeli cause. As a result, Nationalists have created anti-Semitic murals. For example, Rossville Street, the main street in the Nationalist Bogside area outside of Derry, is overpowered by a series of murals created by a group of three local men called the Bogside Artists (2001).[85] A Star of David was painted on the front of an enemy military vehicle. A second mural portrays a British soldier with a sledgehammer breaking down a door. Again, the Bogside Artists added a Star of David, but this time on the end of the sledgehammer. When Loyalists paint the Israeli flag on their murals, it is usually about getting even with Nationalists for flying the Palestinian flag. It is not so much about creating heated political arguments.[86]

Of equal importance in Loyalist murals is the Red Hand of Ulster. The Red Hand is seen on many Loyalist murals and is even used by the Loyalist paramilitary. After Northern Ireland was formed in 1921, Loyalist groups began to use it as a pervasive symbol. Examples of these groups are the Red Hand Commandos, Red Hand Defenders, and Ulster Defence Association.[87]

Figure 6.2 shows a Loyalist mural located in the Shankill community, on the eastern side of Belfast. The marksman is pointing a gun at the audience; no matter where the viewer is positioned vis-à-vis the mural, the marksman is aiming at you. Also displayed are many flags. For instance, on the far right, the Union Jack (the flag of the United Kingdom) and, next to it, the Northern Irish flag (with the white background) are displayed in an attempt to convince the

Figure 6.1.   Mural in a Nationalist Community. Tony Crowley, Claremont Colleges Library.

Figure 6.2.   Mural in a Loyalist Community. Tony Crowley, Claremont Colleges Library.

audience that Northern Ireland should, indeed, remain part of Great Britain forever. It serves to reinforce their vision of the nation. [88]

CASE STUDY II: MURALS IN THE PALESTINIAN TERRITORIES

After the Six-Day War in 1967, the Israelis occupied the West Bank. Twenty years later, in 1987, the Palestinians joined forces to put the kibosh on the Israeli occupation of the West Bank and Gaza. Within Palestinian society itself, the agreement was that the objective of a Palestinian uprising was to expunge the Israelis. The Palestinian uprising has come to be seen as a symbolic reaction to Muslim humiliation and therefore has reverberated not only in the Middle East but also within the ummah across the world. [89] Known as the **Intifada**, the Palestinian uprising occurred between 1987 and 1993 (another Intifada occurred between 2000 and 2005). As Friedman (1995)[90] notes, Intifada connotes "to shake, to shake off, to shake out, to rid oneself of something, to refuse to have anything to do with something, to break with someone" (p. 375). As the emblem of redemption and deliverance, the Intifada marked the end of Palestinian impassiveness and anguish. It was also a symbol of confidence and hope, a sign of a brighter future. [91]

During the Intifada, Palestinian militant murals emerged in the West Bank and Gaza. Paintings of Palestinian youths throwing rocks at the IDF (Israel Defense Forces) and their armored vehicles—a pertinent reminder of the David-Goliath struggle—became one of the Intifada's most loaded and unforgettable symbols. [92] Graffiti symbolized an act of resistance to Israeli domination, a means of repossessing occupied territory, a statement to harmonize conflicting Palestinian factions, a means of deprecating collaborators, and a rite of passage for young boys and girls joining the Palestinian uprising.[93] **Graffiti** exemplify "minor media." They often present signs or images that are hastily written, brief, and fragmentary—much like the Intifada itself. The Intifada graffiti are fairly simplistic, using mainly language and a limited range of symbols to express social and political determination.[94] As cultural symbols of resistance, graffiti are not passive or lifeless. Reading Intifada graffiti is an active process for graffiti and language functioning as a "carrier of relationships."[95]

Last Communication Option

Within the context of the Intifada, which happened before the advent of the internet, writing on the wall was the last communication option for most Palestinians. Censorship undercut the use of other media. With the other channels being difficult to access, murals and the time-honored medium of graffiti were opportunities for Palestinians to communicate their ideas and symbols. "We have no other way" was what some of the scribblers themselves wrote on the store façades, telephone poles, cemetery walls, and homes. Murals were just an easy way for youths to promote their cause (and the cause of their parents).[96] Wall writing was an egalitarian and vitalized Palestinian public space. Graffiti allowed anybody to bypass denial of voice. They represented what Foster (1985)[97] refers to as "a response of people denied response" (p. 48). They were meant to be public and worked as a type of billboard for Palestinians. Wall writing contested Israeli claims to surveillance, representing a loophole in the Israeli state's ability to detect and control everything. In eschewing censorship and establishing a direct relationship with both a local and global public, graffiti incited an active response from readers.

Even today, for Palestinians, murals continue to symbolize a type of equalizer. As cultural artifacts, they express a widespread effort to overthrow the Israeli hierarchy; they constitute Palestinian voices. They are not monolithic voices; they are multiple voices in constant flux; they serve to record history and to define and redefine relationships as a type of cultural production. In the Intifada, they are to be distinguished from other types of cultural production, like embroidery or the use of colors of the Palestinian flag in ornamental objects. Through graffiti, the Palestinian community can think "out loud." Matters of gender, religion, and politics are debated wide open and in broad daylight.[98] More importantly, Palestinian murals can express the people's victimization, as illustrated in the following slogans: "Death to the settlers wherever they are—PFLP [Popular Front for the Liberation of Palestine]"; "Our people are stronger than all modes of repression—PFLP"; "Let us seek complete freedom—UNL [Unified National Leadership]"; and "No to occupation."[99]

Symbolism in Palestinian Murals

Specific symbols of the Palestinian resistance movement have included the clenched fist, the V sign, the rifle, the Palestinian flag, and the aforementioned map of Palestine. The clenched fist and the V sign have been globally recognizable symbols of insurgency and resistance for several decades now. Since the Intifada, they have acquired an additional meaning. For example, the fist is now used by holy warriors to symbolize the popular armies, the underground military units that are called the "striking hands" or "striking fists" of the Palestinian uprising. The fist also epitomizes unwavering, strong, even violent action, and it is generally depicted holding a gun, standard, or knife. In Gaza, where Hamas serves as the watchdog of personal integrity, the one-way sign on walls—a fist and heaven-flung finger—represents both a territorial marker and a warning to anybody who would deviate from the path of Islam.[100]

In one mural, the letters "fth" (for Fatah) cross a map of Palestine. The northern part of the map becomes a human figure that carries the Palestinian flag. The mural was painted in the colors of the flag—white, red, green, and black—and signed by "qd" ("quwwat al-darb," the Strike Forces, a wing of Fatah). The color red in the flag symbolizes the blood of martyrs, green represents the fertility of Palestinian terra sancta (for true Muslims, green is also the color of Islam), white means peace, and black refers to the occupation. From a general standpoint, the flag and the colors convey the message, to all publics, of the justification for launching the Intifada.[101]

A mural that is addressed to two specific types of audience, such as the Israeli occupier and the Palestinian people, is **polysemic**; it prompts multiple readings and electrifies readers for further actions. This caricature of the Palestinian map on the wall is both antagonistic toward the IDF (Israel Defense Forces) and favorable toward the Palestinian people.[102] To be more precise, such a mural is polysemic because it shows it can carry a double message. On the one hand, it is powerful enough to challenge the Israeli status quo (e.g., claims to surveillance and control of Palestinian public spaces); on the other hand, the graffiti leave a reinforcing mark for Palestinians—that they can make claims to the same space.[103]

Symbolic Mathematical Equations

In "The Writing on the Walls: The Graffiti of the Intifada," Julie Peteet (1996)[104] describes political attempts at reaching pan-Arabic support for specific movements in the Middle East. Interesting is the message (like a political commentary) encoded in mathematical equations that are expressed through graffiti: "Fahd + Assad = a mouse." In Arabic, "fahd" means "panther" and was the king of Saudi Arabia's first name (he died in 2005). "Assad" means "lion" and is the name of the president of Syria. This equation warns Palestinians to look outside the Arab world for help, exposing its weaknesses and its impossibility of being more than a "mouse," even though leaders of key Islamic countries are purportedly endowed with powerful (lion and panther) qualities. In brief, the political commentary in question connotes the abdication of reliance on help from powerful Arab leaders and, rather, points toward communal self-sufficiency and autonomy.

Likewise, Julie Peteet also examines historical events that marked the transformation of the Palestinian people, like events in which they were granted centrality in declaring Palestinian national sentiment and identity. The communication of the mural was also a symbolic mathematical equation: "1948 + 1967 = All Palestine." The reference to 1948 indicates a historical consciousness of decisive moments in time and place in which the Palestinian people were shattered by the 1948 Palestine war. As a result, over 700,000 of them had to flee their own sacred land. The other date, 1967, was the year during which the Israelis captured key Palestinian territories. These two defining historical moments—1948 and 1967—are metonyms. A **metonym** is a figure of speech consisting of a thing or concept that is not called by its own name; rather, it is called by the name of something closely related to that thing or concept.[105] For example, "Washington" is the U.S. capital. However, the word is used metonymically to refer to the U.S. government. The two dates—1948 and 1967—are metonyms for the loss and resultant transformation of Palestine and the shattering of its people.

The Written

Notwithstanding the importance of these symbols, most of the Intifada graffiti are made up of slogans and written messages. They should probably be understood as manifestations of the Muslim concept of *al-maktub* (i.e., "the Written"). Originating from a pre-Islamic belief that the written word was filled with magic and power, what is written still has high respect today. The word "Allah" is seen everywhere; it is blazingly painted on the side of buses or hiding in some dark corner. While writing the name of Allah is prevalent in Muslim countries where "Allah" serves as an amulet bringing down the Divine Presence, the practice became a political act during the Intifada. The "Allah" wall writing works as a claim to identity and a territorial marker. It is not unusual to find pompous statements such as "Hamas does not fear bullets" or "We are stronger than the *mukhabarat* [the Arabic name for secret police]," or, simply, "Palestine is Free." Merely writing these words could somehow work miracles. Hamas slogans attain a strong resonance by using the sacred Muslim language. The credo of Islam—"la 'illah illa Allah Muhammad Rasul Allah" ("There is no god but Allah; Muhammad is Allah's messenger")—is written everywhere as well. Hamas often uses symbols of the Qur'an and the Dome of the Rock, sometimes alongside Palestinian flags or knife-wielding fists.[106]

SUMMARY

Places and territories are often loaded with symbolism. Place refers to an area with definite boundaries, with which a particular group identifies, and where a series of events happen. Territory, on the other hand, refers to an area controlled and defended by an individual, a group, or an entire country. The three categories of territory are public territories, home territories, and interactional territories. Territory can be encroached through violation, invasion, or contamination. Many ethnic groups have made claims to real or imaginary home territories, a phenomenon called ethnonationalism. When terrorism is motivated by ethnonationalism, it is called separatist terrorism. A case study about this was the Basques' lifelong struggle to secede from Spain and France. Terra sancta refers to sacred land or hallowed territory. It symbolizes the lofty, holy goal to recapture the homeland from violators, invaders, or contaminators. For example, in the Islamic world, Al-Quds (Jerusalem) is the third terra sancta in order of importance, after Mecca and Medina. The importance attached to sacred land is evident in persuasive cartography. Persuasive cartography is a countermapping practice, a method whereby a group diffuses its doctrine by altering a map. This can be done through map symbolization (or geographic symbolism). Persuasive cartography is an example of cartographic propaganda, the creation of maps for propagandistic intent. For example, we have seen that Palestinian and Israeli maps differ in many ways. Both sides, of course, want to pursue their own national agenda. Lastly, terrorist groups (or their sympathizers) can express their attachment to land and ancestry through murals. A terrorist mural is any piece of artwork (mostly graffiti) or writing created on a wall, ceiling, or large permanent structure made by a person to convey the mission of a terrorist cause or air grievances about an ongoing conflict. Terrorist murals can serve as territorial markers or political communication. Two striking case studies in this chapter were murals in Northern Ireland and murals in the Palestinian territories. In Northern Ireland, both Nationalists and Loyalists have painted walls to make political statements and commemorate important events in their respective histories. In the Palestinian territories, murals and wall writing have been the last communication options for most people. They are also ways to express their resistance to Israeli occupation.

NOTES

1. Walter, Barbara (2003). Explaining the Intractability of Territorial Conflict. *International Studies Review, 5,* 137–153.

2. Connerton, Paul (1989). *How Societies Remember*. Cambridge: Cambridge University Press.

3. Hart, Peter (2005). *The IRA at War, 1916–1923*. Oxford: Oxford University Press.

4. Moore, Nina-Jo, Hickson, Mark, III, & Stacks, Don (2010). *Nonverbal Communication: Studies and Applications* (5th ed.). Los Angeles: Roxbury.

5. Moore, Nina-Jo, Hickson, Mark, III, & Stacks, Don (2010). *Nonverbal Communication: Studies and Applications* (5th ed.). Los Angeles: Roxbury.

6. Connor, Walker (1993). *Ethnonationalism*. Princeton, NJ: Princeton University Press.

7. Hutchinson, John, & Smith, Anthony (1996). *Ethnicity*. Oxford: Oxford University Press.

8. Post, Jerrold M. (2005). When Hatred Is Bred in the Bone: Psycho-cultural Foundations of Contemporary Terrorism. *Political Psychology, 26*(4), 615–636.

9. Smith, Anthony (1991). *National Identity*. Reno: University of Nevada Press.

10. Juergensmeyer, Mark (2004). Holy Orders: Opposition to Modern States. *Harvard International Review, 25*(4), 10–21.

11. Wolters, O. W. (1963). China Irredenta: The South. *The World Today, 19*(12), 540–552.

12. O'Brien, Conor (1994). *Ancestral Voices: Religion and Nationalism in Ireland*. Dublin: Poolbeg.

13. Moore, Ronnie, & Sanders, Andrew (2002). Formations of Culture: Nationalism and Conspiracy Ideology in Ulster Loyalism. *Anthropology Today, 18*(6), 9–15.

14. Osborne, Brian (1996). Figuring Space, Marking Time: Contested Identities in Canada. *International Journal of Heritage Studies, 2*(1), 23–40.

15. Osborne, Brian (1996). Figuring Space, Marking Time: Contested Identities in Canada. *International Journal of Heritage Studies, 2*(1), 23–40.

16. Larsen, Svend Erik (2004). Landscape, Identity, and War. *New Literary History, 35*(3), 469–490.

17. Clark, Robert (1984). *The Basque Insurgents: ETA, 1952–1980*. London: University of Wisconsin Press.

18. Shabad, Goldie, & Llera Ramo, Francisco (1995). Political Violence in a Democratic State: Basque Terrorism in Spain. In Martha Crenshaw (Ed.), *Terrorism in Context* (pp. 410–472). University Park: Pennsylvania State University Press.

19. Collins, Roger (1987). *The Basques*. New York: Basil Blackwell.

20. Cohen, Irwin, & Corrado, Raymond (2003). A Future for the ETA? In Dilip Das & Peter Kratcoski (Eds.), *Meeting the Challenges of Global Terrorism: Prevention, Control, and Recovery* (pp. 271–288). New York: Lexington Books.

21. Laqueur, Walter (1999). *Terrorism and History*. Oxford: Oxford University Press.

22. Alexander, Yonah, & Meyers, K. A. (1982). *Terrorism in Europe*. New York: St. Martin's Press; and Hooper, John (1995). *The New Spaniards*. New York: Penguin.

23. Toft, Monica (2003). *The Geography of Ethnic Conflict: Identity, Interests, and the Indivisibility of Territory*. Princeton, NJ: Princeton University Press.

24. Pape, Robert (2005). *Dying to Win: The Strategic Logic of Suicide Terrorism*. New York: Random House.

25. Bloom, Mia (2006). Dying to Kill: Motivations for Suicide Terrorism. In Ami Pedahzur (Ed.), *Root Causes of Suicide Terrorism: The Globalization of Martyrdom* (pp. 25–53). New York: Routledge.

26. Forker, Martin, & McCormick, Jonathan (2009). Walls of History: The Use of Mythomoteurs in Northern Ireland Murals. *Irish Studies Review, 17*(4), 423–465.

27. Bergen, Peter L. (2002). *Holy War, Inc.: Inside the Secret World of Osama bin Laden*. New York: Touchstone.

28. Raento, Paulina, & Watson, Cameron (2000). Gernika, Guernica, Guernica? Contested Meanings of a Basque Place. *Political Geography, 19*(6), 707–736.

29. Aulestia, Gorka (1981). Poetry and Politics: Basque Poetry as an Instrument of National Revival. *World Literature Today, 55*(1), 48–52.

30. Stump, Roger (2005). Religion and the Geographies of War. In Colin Flint (Ed.), *The Geography of War and Peace: From Death Camps to Diplomats* (pp. 149–173). Oxford: Oxford University Press.

31. Dumper, Mick (1993). Jerusalem Then and Now. *Middle East Report, 182*, 2–8.

32. Dumper, Mick (1993). Jerusalem Then and Now. *Middle East Report, 182*, 2–8.

33. Albin, Cecilia (1997). Securing the Peace of Jerusalem: On the Politics of Unifying and Dividing. *Review of International Studies, 23*, 117–142.

34. Wright, Robin (2008). *Dreams and Shadows: The Future of the Middle East*. New York: Penguin.

35. Wunderle, William, & Lajeunesse, Gabriel (2009). *Countering Iranian Malign Influence: The Need for a Regional Response*. Chapel Hill, NC: American Diplomacy Publishers.

36. Khatib, Lina (2012). *Hizbullah's Image Management Strategy*. Los Angeles: Figueroa Press.

37. Black, Jeremy (1997). *Maps and Politics*. Chicago: University of Chicago Press.

38. Wood, Denis, & Fels, Jon (2008). *The Natures of Maps: Cartographic Constructions of the Natural World*. Chicago: University of Chicago Press.

39. Zeigler, J. (2002). Post-Communist Eastern Europe and the Cartography of Independence. *Political Geography, 21*(5), 671–686.

40. Barber, Peter, & Harper, Tom (2010). *Magnificent Maps: Power, Propaganda, and Art*. London: The British Library.

41. Barber, Peter, & Harper, Tom (2010). *Magnificent Maps: Power, Propaganda, and Art*. London: The British Library.

42. Monmonier, Mark (1996). *How to Lie with Maps*. Chicago: University of Chicago Press.

43. Monmonier, Mark (1996). *How to Lie with Maps*. Chicago: University of Chicago Press.

44. Wallach, Yair (2011). Trapped in Mirror-Images: The Rhetoric of Maps in Israel/Palestine. *Political Geography, 30*, 358–369.

45. Sparke, Matthew (2005). *In the Space of Theory: Postfoundational Geographies of the Nationstate*. Minneapolis: University of Minnesota Press.

46. Cornell, Svante (2002). Autonomy as a Source of Conflict: Caucasian Conflicts in Theoretical Perspective. *World Politics, 54*(2), 245–276.

47. Wallach, Yair (2011). Trapped in Mirror-Images: The Rhetoric of Maps in Israel/Palestine. *Political Geography, 30*, 358–369.

48. Wallach, Yair (2011). Trapped in Mirror-Images: The Rhetoric of Maps in Israel/Palestine. *Political Geography, 30*, 358–369.

49. Wood, Denis (2010). *Rethinking the Power of Maps*. New York: Guilford Press.

50. Nachmani, Amikam (2001). The Palestinian Intifada 1987–1993: The Dynamics of Symbols and Symbolic Realities, the Role of Symbols, Rituals and Myths in National Struggles. *Civil Wars, 4*(1), 49–103.

51. Pina, Aaron (2005). *Palestinian Education and the Debate over Textbooks*. Washington, DC: Library of Congress Congressional Research Service.

52. Winichakul, Thongchai (1994). *Siam Mapped: A History of the Geo-Body of a Nation*. Honolulu: University of Hawaii Press.

53. Kaas, Ilana, & O'Neill, Bard (1996). Rejectionism, Reversibility and Realism: The Middle East Peace Process in Perspective. *Comparative Strategy, 15*(4), 309–333.

54. Aburish, Said (1998). *Arafat from Defender to Dictator*. London: Bloomsbury; and Ramadan, Adam (2009). A Refugee Landscape: Writing Palestinian Nationalisms in Lebanon. *Acme, 9*, 69–99.

55. Wallach, Yair (2011). Trapped in Mirror-Images: The Rhetoric of Maps in Israel/Palestine. *Political Geography, 30*, 358–369.

56. Bowker, Robert (2003). *Palestinian Refugees: Mythology, Identity, and the Search for Peace*. London: Lynne Rienner; and Peretz, Don (1993). *Palestinians, Refugees, and the Middle East Peace Process*. Washington, DC: U.S. Institute of Peace Press.

57. Jarman, Neil (1997). *Material Conflicts: Parades and Visual Displays in Northern Ireland*. New York: Berg.

58. Habermas, Jürgen (1991). The Public Sphere. In Chandra Mukerji & Michael Schudson (Eds.), *Rethinking Popular Culture, Contemporary Perspectives in Cultural Studies* (pp. 398–404). Berkeley: University of California Press.

59. Brunn, Stanley, Byrne, Sarah, McNamara, Louise, & Egan, Annette (2010). Belfast Landscapes: From Religious Schism to Conflict Tourism. *Focus on Geography, 53*(3), 81–91.

60. MacRaild, Donald (2000, May 15). "The Bunkum of Ulsteria": The Orange Marching Tradition in Late Victorian Cumbria. *The Irish Parading Tradition, 87*, 44–59.

61. Ley, David, & Cybriwsky, Roman (1974). Urban Graffiti as Territorial Markers. *Annals of Association of American Geographers, 64*, 491–505.

62. Shirlow, Peter, & Murtagh, Brendan (2006). *Belfast: Segregation, Violence and the City*. London: Pluto.

63. Boal, Frederick (2008). Territoriality on the Shankill-Falls Divide, Belfast. *Irish Geography, 41*(93), 3349–3366.

64. Mitchell, Audra (2010). *Transformation and Ongoing Conflict in Belfast*. Belfast: Queen's University of Belfast.

65. Boal, Frederick, & Livingstone, D. (1984). The Frontier in the City: Ethnonationalism in Belfast. *International Journal of Political Science Review, 5*(2), 161–179.

66. Boal, Frederick (1969). Territoriality on the Shankill-Falls Divide, Belfast. *Irish Geography, 6*(1), 30–50.

67. Baudrillard, Jean (2003). *The Spirit of Terrorism and Other Essays*. New York: Verso.

68. Peteet, Julie (1996). The Writing on the Walls: The Graffiti of the Intifada. *Cultural Anthropology, 11*, 139–159.

69. Rolston, Bill (1991). *Politics and Painting: Murals and Conflict in Northern Ireland*. London: Associated Universities Press.

70. Brunn, Stanley, Byrne, Sarah, McNamara, Louise, & Egan, Annette (2010). Belfast Landscapes: From Religious Schism to Conflict Tourism. *Focus on Geography, 53*(3), 81–91.

71. Laswell, Harold, & Kaplan, Abraham (1950). *Power and Society: A Framework for Political Inquiry*. New Haven, CT: Yale University Press.

72. Masev, Victor, Shirlow, P., & Joni, D. (2009). The Geography of Conflict and Death in Belfast, Northern Ireland. *Annals of the Association of American Geographers, 99*(5), 893–903.

73. Cashman, Ray (2008). Visions of Irish Nationalism. *Journal of Folklore Research, 45*(3), 361–381.

74. Shirlow, Peter, & Murtagh, Brendan (2006). *Belfast: Segregation, Violence and the City*. London: Pluto.

75. Rolston, Bill (2009). "The Brothers on the Walls": International Solidarity and Irish Political Murals. *Journal of Black Studies, 39*(3), 446–470.

76. Brunn, Stanley, Byrne, Sarah, McNamara, Louise, & Egan, Annette (2010). Belfast Landscapes: From Religious Schism to Conflict Tourism. *Focus on Geography, 53*(3), 81–91.

77. Forker, Martin, & McCormick, Jonathan (2009). Walls of History: The Use of Mythomoteurs in Northern Ireland Murals. *Irish Studies Review, 17*(4), 423–465.

78. Rolston, Bill (2009). "The Brothers on the Walls": International Solidarity and Irish Political Murals. *Journal of Black Studies, 39*(3), 446–470.

79. Montville, Joseph (1990). The Psychological Roots of Ethnic and Sectarian Terrorism. In Vamik Volkan, Demetrios Julius, & Joseph Montville (Eds.), *The Psychodynamics of International Relationships: Unofficial Diplomacy at Work* (163–180). Lexington, MA: Lexington Books.

80. Cashman, Ray (2008). Visions of Irish Nationalism. *Journal of Folklore Research, 45*(3), 361–381.

81. Anderson, Benedict (1983). *Imagined Communities: Reflections on the Origin and Spread of Nationalism.* London: Verso.

82. Carsten, Janet (2000). *Cultures of Relatedness: New Approaches to the Study of Kinship.* Cambridge: Cambridge University Press.

83. Forker, Martin, & McCormick, Jonathan (2009). Walls of History: The Use of Mythomoteurs in Northern Ireland Murals. *Irish Studies Review, 17*(4), 423–465.

84. Brunn, Stanley, Byrne, Sarah, McNamara, Louise, & Egan, Annette (2010). Belfast Landscapes: From Religious Schism to Conflict Tourism. *Focus on Geography, 53*(3), 81–91.

85. Bogside Artists. (2001). *Murals.* Derry, Ireland: Guildhall Press.

86. McKay, Susan (2000). *Northern Protestants: An Unsettled People.* Belfast: Blackstaff Press.

87. Wack, Daniela (2005). *Give My Head Peace: Analysis of a Political Sitcom in Northern Ireland.* Santa Cruz, CA: GRIN Verlag.

88. Brunn, Stanley, Byrne, Sarah, McNamara, Louise, & Egan, Annette (2010). Belfast Landscapes: From Religious Schism to Conflict Tourism. *Focus on Geography, 53*(3), 81–91.

89. Nachmani, Amikam (2001). The Palestinian Intifada 1987–1993: The Dynamics of Symbols and Symbolic Realities, the Role of Symbols, Rituals and Myths in National Struggles. *Civil Wars, 4*(1), 49–103.

90. Friedman, Thomas (1995). *From Beirut to Jerusalem.* New York: Anchor Books.

91. Nachmani, Amikam (2001). The Palestinian Intifada 1987–1993: The Dynamics of Symbols and Symbolic Realities, the Role of Symbols, Rituals and Myths in National Struggles. *Civil Wars, 4*(1), 49–103.

92. Nachmani, Amikam (2001). The Palestinian Intifada 1987–1993: The Dynamics of Symbols and Symbolic Realities, the Role of Symbols, Rituals and Myths in National Struggles. *Civil Wars, 4*(1), 49–103.

93. Feldman, Jackie (2011). Abraham the Settler, Jesus the Refugee: Contemporary Conflict and Christianity on the Road to Bethlehem. *History & Memory, 23*(1), 62–95.

94. Fischer, Michael, & Abedi, Mehdi (1990). *Debating Muslims: Cultural Dialogues between Tradition and Postmodernity.* Madison: University of Wisconsin Press.

95. Davis, Natalie Zemon (1991). Printing and the People. In Chandra Mukerji & Michael Schudson (Eds.), *Rethinking Popular Culture: Contemporary Perspectives in Cultural Studies* (pp. 65–96). Berkeley: University of California Press.

96. Oliver, Anne Marie, & Steinberg, Paul (1990). A Geography of Revolt. *Public Culture, 3*(1), 139–144.

97. Foster, Hal (1985). *Recordings: Art, Spectacle, Cultural Politics.* Port Townsend, WA: Bay Press.

98. Peteet, Julie (1996). The Writing on the Walls: The Graffiti of the Intifada. *Cultural Anthropology, 11*, 139–159.

99. Rolston, Bill (1987). Politics, Painting and Popular Culture: The Political Wall Murals of Northern Ireland. *Media, Culture and Society, 9*, 5–28.

100. Oliver, Anne Marie, & Steinberg, Paul (1990). A Geography of Revolt. *Public Culture, 3*(1), 139–144.

101. Hiro, Dilip (1999). *Sharing the Promised Land: The Tale of Israelis and Palestinians.* New York: Olive Branch Press.

102. Peteet, Julie (1996). The Writing on the Walls: The Graffiti of the Intifada. *Cultural Anthropology, 11*, 139–159.

103. Zawawi, Zahraa, Corijn, Eric, & Van Heur, Bas (2012). Public Spaces in the Occupied Palestinian Territories. *GeoJournal, 5*, 10–21.

104. Peteet, Julie (1996). The Writing on the Walls: The Graffiti of the Intifada. *Cultural Anthropology, 11*, 139–159.

105. Barcelona, Antonio (2003). *Metaphor and Metonymy at the Crossroads.* Berlin: De Gruyter.

106. Oliver, Anne Marie, & Steinberg, Paul (1990). A Geography of Revolt. *Public Culture, 3*(1), 139–144.

Chapter Seven

Symbolism in Religious Terrorism

General Perspectives

RELIGIOUS TERRORISM

There is a long-established and profound relationship between terrorism and religion. Terrorism has surfaced episodically in various religions, particularly Islam, Christianity, Judaism, Hinduism, and Sikhism. The relationship between terrorism and religion has increasingly taken on powerful symbolic dimensions that have been revealed both in the specific concerns of terrorists and in their resultant actions. Religious terrorism is triggered by theological requirements. Because many religious terrorists participate in a cosmic struggle to change the world, and because they seek to cleanse the world through apocalyptic methods, they are invested in conveying their message to specific audiences. Furthermore, religious terrorists tend to be rather centralized, using a shared experience and faith as well as direct contact with leaders and fellow members.[1]

Religious Fundamentalism

Terrorism motivated by religious fundamentalism can be persistent and lethal. According to Kimball (2003),[2] religious fundamentalism operates on the basis of five key principles. These principles are as follows: means to justify the end, holy war, blind obedience, absolute truth claims, and the ideal times. **Religious fundamentalism** is the belief that religious doctrines or texts contain the fundamental, straightforward, intrinsic, absolute truth about humanity and deity; that this essential truth is diametrically opposed to forces of evil, which must be fought until the end; that this truth must be embraced immediately (based on the central, rigid practices of the past); and that those who have faith in these fundamental teachings and adhere to them have a special connection with the deity.[3] By and large, religious fundamentalism is a dimension or kind of religiosity that is theoretically present within any belief system. It has been shown to correlate with various types of hatred, prejudice, and discrimination more strongly than any other dimension of religiosity.[4]

Religious fundamentalists profess strong commitments to their beliefs and are regarded as unbending and resistant to change. Due to their religious commitments, there is no prospect for any compromise or other types of negotiation. The statements of many religious-based terrorist groups seem to validate such inflexibility. For instance, Osama bin Laden's mentor,

Abdullah Azzam, often reiterated his trademark slogan, "Jihad and the rifle alone: no negotiations, no conferences, and no dialogues."[5] This statement implies two things. First, religious fundamentalism engenders an in-group commitment more than any other terrorist endeavor (in regard to group dynamics). Second, religious fundamentalism does not need much intellectual mediation.

Junk Terrorism: Hijacked Religion

Religious groups create rituals and symbols that serve to evoke and commemorate local heroes by granting them an otherwise unreachable status that is also eternal.[6] However, when the use of religious terrorism is centered on an ideological and fanatical interpretation of selected religious scriptures, it is called **junk terrorism**, the idea that religious violence can be the result of the hijacking of a religion.[7] Junk terrorism sometimes operates on **truth claims**, meaning that even fundamental teachings of a religion can be interpreted in multiple ways or, as Kimball (2003) asserts, can allow diverse interpretations to emerge.[8] The resolute "truth claims" championed by religious terrorists allow them to use "religious structures and doctrines, almost like weapons" (p. 32) for their cause. Jihad, for instance, has been interpreted in many different ways, not all of them involving war. Whereas the **greater jihad** represents the struggle that someone has within him- or herself to fulfill what is right, the **lesser jihad** symbolizes the external, physical effort to defend Islam (including terrorism) when the ummah is under threat.[9] Another way to describe junk terrorism is by comparing "intrinsic faith" with "extrinsic faith." An **intrinsic faith** is a principal motive in life, an end in itself, a religion to be deeply lived and experienced from within. In contrast, an **extrinsic faith** tends to use religion for ulterior motives, a means to an end, a religion to be used rather than lived and experienced.[10] Lastly, the concept of "exaptation" can further illustrate this point. **Exaptation** is the use of adaptation for specific purposes other than those for which they were initially created (i.e., adapting religious symbols to fulfill the objectives of a terrorist group).[11]

FIVE PRINCIPLES OF RELIGION

In 2012, an international Gallup poll reported that 59 percent of the world's population was religious, 23 percent not religious, and 13 percent atheist.[12] The word "religion" is sometimes used interchangeably with "faith" or "belief system." Religion can be classified into five different categories. These categories should rather be called principles: (1) a connection with the divine, (2) social glue, (3) a cultural system, (4) a symbolic representation of society, and (5) an emotional state.

Religion as a Connection with the Divine

The first principle is that religion is a veneration of God or gods, and a careful contemplation of divine matters. The term "divine" refers to anything that is godlike (whether it is a concrete deity or not) to which a person feels urged to respond with earnestness and depth.[13] Argyle and Beit-Hallahmi (1975) corroborate this idea when they write that religion is "a system of beliefs in a divine or superhuman power, and practices of worship or other rituals directed towards such a power" (p. 1).[14] Likewise, for O'Collins and Farrugia (1991), religions are "systems of belief in and response to the divine, including the sacred books, cultic rituals, and ethical practices of the adherents" (p. 203).[15] Lastly, for Clark (1958), religion is "the inner experience of the individual when he senses a Beyond, especially as evidenced by the effect of this experience on his behavior when he actively attempts to harmonize his life with the

Beyond" (p. 22).[16] All these definitions point to the idea that religion is a mental representation of the existence and powers of supernatural beings. Along with the notion of divinity, we have **spirituality**, which denotes the search for and connection with that which one takes to be a holy or sacred transcendent being (a God or a higher power)—for example, by saying daily prayers.[17]

Religion as Social Glue

The very notion of religion (Latin, "religio" = bonds, relations) is highly correlated with ideas of community or society (Latin, "socio" = compassion), where compassion and bonds have strong connections with each other, particularly at the moral level and, therefore, help offer a legitimacy to the order and connections involved.[18] As expressed by Emile Durkheim (1915),[19] religion is **social glue**: it makes all individuals who follow it coalesce into a single moral community. Religion is the glue of society and the foundation of social solidarity. As social glue, religion is also made up of **sociological sticky stuff**, the glue that holds a religious group or culture together.[20] For a long time, anthropologists have observed the fundamental "faith-based" parts of religion (i.e., symbols, myths, and rituals). These parts are more able to create an in-group commitment than any other social institution. In this sense, religion implies transcending oneself and cultivating a commitment to contribute to others.[21]

A concept similar to social glue is religious development. **Religious development** refers to the child's growth within a well-defined community with shared narratives, traditions, teachings, rituals, and symbols that bring individuals closer to the sacred and improve their relationship to the community.[22] To feel that sense of community, the individual has to be able to commune with others: through bonding and compassion, and through interaction with people. This, in turn, gives more legitimacy to the religious community to impose moral regulations. Thus, religion plays a pivotal role in bestowing an order with moral legitimacy and social control. It gives people direction, resolution, and meaning beyond rudimentary power; it also offers highly practical guidelines as to how to uphold a life-supporting order so essential to existence.[23]

For religious terrorists, cohesiveness is generally nurtured by compelling religious symbols, which "often become focal points in occupations involving a religious difference" (Pape, 2005, p. 89).[24] As such, religion becomes a functional channel of shared identification that often unites an otherwise heterogeneous, fragmented community. Religious symbols help draw diverse human factions within the community, gluing them into a single united movement. In consequence, policy making and nation building are replete with symbols appropriated from various religious sources. For example, let us look at the Persian Gulf War: in the summer of 1990, just before the outbreak of the war, Saddam Hussein added the statement "There is no God but Allah" to Iraq's flag. In this manner, he was able to attract more people to join the jihad against infidels. Likewise, the battle instructions given by Hamas were loaded with religious symbolism. One decree stipulated that all Palestinian women had to wear a hijab (head covering). The order, which was in line with the masculine symbol of the bearded Palestinian man, symbolized the growing importance of unification under Islam.[25]

Religion as a Cultural System

Religion is both an individual and communal endeavor; it is experienced internally in the mind of the human being, and externally influenced by culture. A religion is a form of cultural system, an assimilated collection of meanings and behaviors shared by a society of believers. Religion is different from other forms of cultural systems in its focus on beliefs and practices that ultimately build connections with superhuman entities. These entities can be deities, natural spirits, worshipped ancestors, or perfected heroes who are deemed to have powers beyond those of ordinary people. Beliefs about the superhuman are a crucial part of religion. This is how religious adherents interpret reality and the forces that frame it. A religion's philosophy becomes a cultural system in and of itself, through the values and emotions that underlie believers' thoughts and behaviors.[26]

Religion denotes the totality of cultural systems that purport to solve problems of meaning and contingency by relating to a transcendent reality. This transcendent reality shapes daily life but cannot be directly controlled. For this reason, religious symbol systems add mythical, ethical, and ritual components as well as "salvation goods."[27] A recurrent theme that arises through historical examples of religious terrorism is the motif of holy war as a religious mandate—for example, to diffuse the truth or to protect fellow believers or sacred places from invaders or external forces. This ethos transcends the concept of the **just war**, generally described as a type of war that has been legitimized in moral or religious terms. Instead, this perspective characterizes war as a religious obligation and as a direct expression of the beliefs that it advocates or defends.[28]

Religion as a Symbolic Representation of Society

German philosopher Karl Marx likened religion to society (i.e., a nation or ethnic group), which, in turn, implied order, regularity, and pattern to movement. From this vantage point, religion is the symbolic representation of society. Religious acts are often the result of symbolic reactions to social demands, reiterating the necessity for community, cooperation, and the creation of symbolic representations of society. Religion helps establish a symbolically orientated approach to key aspects of the individual's place in the universe, especially his or her national identity. Religion plays an important role in determining a person's national experience. Therefore, religion is acted out just as one's national identity is acted out. Terrorist attacks are acted out on behalf of a whole religious community in the same way that sacrifices and rituals to the deities are enacted forms of commitment and confirmation.[29]

Religious beliefs are hierarchically structured within communities. At the summit of a community's conceptual hierarchy is what Rappaport (1999)[30] refers to as ultimate sacred symbols. Religion is the symbolic representation that both reflects and induces the zeal to eliminate impurity. History records that the worst sacrifices of all have included the massacre of innocents—as it operates on the principle that religion requires purity. Slaughtering a certain number of tough soldiers, prepared to kill, does not have the same symbolic impact. This may, for example, explain the ethnic violence and cleansing in ex-Yugoslavia, which the West, it seems, did not comprehend or effectually respond to. In a similar fashion, martyrdom occurs when a warrior sacrifices his or her life for his or her faith. Since the First Intifada in 1987, martyrdom has become a religious mandate and a symbolic representation of Palestinian society. By developing legends of heroes who are ready to sacrifice themselves in holy war and who can reach otherwise unattainable eternal status, Muslim religious factions can reinforce the symbolic traditions of a society. As Pape (2005)[31] remarks, "Suicide terrorist organizations commonly cultivate 'sacrificial myths' that include elaborate sets of symbols and rituals to mark an individual attacker's death as a contribution to the nation" (p. 29).

Religion as an Emotional State

Religion is also an emotional state that, upon being acted out in the presence of others, boosts emotional experience. The veneration of symbols, icons, or images plays a similar role, by concentrating on these, as does the enactment of ritual. By stimulating an emotional state, the adherent can now make the switch from the rational to the nonrational realm, a realm in which commonsensical explanation and legitimation are no longer necessary. Emotional states are evoked and emotions gratified through religion.[32] Religion, then, becomes a constant ceremonial or communal phenomenon, like a type of mass emotional experience that places the believer in a **trance**, a whole different emotional state.[33]

The role of emotion, so central to religion, is formative in bestowing terrorists nonrational causal reasons to commit their horrifying deeds. They redirect their resentment to other things, and this to the detriment of their traditional way of life that gave them symbolic meaning in this world.[34] A significant function of religious terrorism is the inclusion of emotionally evocative symbolism that can individually motivate and collectively amalgamate dissimilar people under a common banner.[35] For instance, the religious blood ritual is now related by the terrorists to their own blood rituals. This usually occurs through a process analogous to that of **psychoanalytic transference**, a process in which deep emotions are transferred from one object to another. It can also be a redirection of feelings from one person to another, as in the case of Islamists emulating the warlike deeds of the Prophet Muhammad.[36]

Religious terrorism can also be articulated through the recall of symbols or images—especially the recollection of a culture's ideas or way of life under threat. It is an emotional remembrance of conflated images, a symbolic representation of supernatural forces (a culture that transcends the individual). The culture itself becomes a felt, subjective experience, an emotional state of oneness between individual and society. This emotional state is felt as a divine or supernatural order (the religious experience) and relies on religious symbols to remind its members about the importance of defending that culture. Naturally, members also get the message that sacrifice and suffering are often the by-products of all this.[37]

THREAT OF SECULARIZATION

The threat of secularization from foreign influences is one of the triggers that get religious terrorists into action. Infiltration of secular values into the terrorists' world and the conspicuous presence of secular interference elicit self-defensive violence and hostility toward the sources of these evils. This is particularly the case with ill-perceived neocolonialism (i.e., Western-based colonialism) and even other religions in general. Because modernity itself clashes with tradition, most modernity is seen as an assault on religion. These defensive feelings often go hand in hand with the emergence and presence of extremist clerics. Clerical leaders espouse more activist and militant principles than mainstream believers. Clerics often start in mainstream movements as either clandestine leaders or heads of breakaway groups. As time passes, these ideologues become a centrifugal force able to draw support, reinforce the organizational mechanisms, and reframe methods of resistance (to threats of secularization) through terrorism. At the same time, they offer theological justification, which allows their adepts to fulfill the holy causes more effectively and rapidly. In this sense, clerics act as spiritual guides; ultimately, they regulate most political and military activities while sanctifying terrorist attacks. This phenomenon can be found in many religious terrorist groups.[38]

Religious terrorists espouse a radical vision of a supreme fight to resist secularization from both within and without. They chase this vision in absolutely adamant holy terms, as in the battle between good and evil. The majority of religious terrorist groups have actually been activated into existence as a result of key events. Put simply, they feel compelled to react to such key events, which either function as a symbol (catalyst or inspirational model) for the terrorist groups or aggravate the sense of threat of secularization. As we will see later in this chapter, in the case of millennial terrorist groups, there is generally a heightened perception that time is running out and action needs to be taken now. The growth and increased activism of doomsday cults stem, in part, from the belief that the looming apocalypse is awaiting them. Their self-prophetic vision of the future has caused them to accelerate the new millennium.[39]

GOOD VERSUS EVIL

Religious terrorism regularly implies a battle between good and evil, an all-out struggle against enemies. This view, in turn, legitimizes the degree and intensity of terrorist violence. The fight of religious terrorists is one defined in dialectic and cosmic terms as believers versus unbelievers, order versus chaos, and justice versus injustice. All this is reflected in the totality and categorical nature of their cause, whether that cause requires the establishment of a Zionist Israel, a global Islamic state based on sharia, or a Sikh independent Khalistan ("Land of the Pure"). The purpose and blessing of religious terrorism necessitate clearly defined enemies. The rewards for those who fight for "good" are eternal. Nevertheless, the timelines of their fight are vast; most of their struggles look for endings within the lifetimes of the actors, but religious wars can take generations to win. Today, the recently created religious terrorist groups do not appear in a vacuum and do not necessarily consist of people born into extremism. Rather, the decision to resort to religious violence and the identification of certain groups as "enemies" are based on a heightened sense of "good versus evil," a topmost struggle that needs to be waged and won.[40]

Exclusivism

Exclusivism refers to the practice of being exclusive vis-à-vis all other groups. It is a mentality typified by a disdain for opinions, ideas, and even existence other than that of one's own group. For example, this rigid position is manifest in Hamas's (1988)[41] own charter in Article 11: "The land of Palestine is an Islamic trust (waqf) to be maintained by succeeding generations of Muslims until the Day of Judgment. In this responsibility, or any part of it, no negligence will be tolerated, and no surrender." On this note, there is a great degree of similarity between the stands of Hamas and Kach, an Israeli terrorist group: both have the vision of a religious nation between the Jordan River and the Mediterranean Sea, utmost rejection of everything alien or secular (which must be eradicated from the entire land), and fervent hatred toward Western culture. The difference between the in-group and the out-group is buttressed in the daily rhetoric of these terrorist groups' clerical leaders.[42] By extension, **religious exclusivism** asserts that one religion is true and all others are wrong (and, therefore, evil).[43]

Chosen People

Various groups regard themselves as the **chosen people**; that is, people chosen by God for a specific purpose (e.g., to act as God's representatives on earth). When a group sees itself as the chosen people, it often feels superior and ethnocentric, which can be used to warrant exclusivism and terrorist violence. In the words of an extremist rabbi after the funeral of Baruch Goldstein, an Israeli terrorist who killed twenty-nine Muslims at a mosque in 1994: "There is a great difference in the punishment becoming a person who hurts a Jew and a person who hurts a gentile. The life of a Jew is worth much more than the lives of many gentiles."[44] In a second example, in 1984, Gush Emunim (an Israeli messianic terrorist movement) acted as the chosen people by planning to blow up the Dome of the Rock (Islam's third holiest site), partly for messianic reasons (to provoke a cataclysmic war between Jews and Muslims and speed up the arrival of the Messiah). In a third example, the Japanese cult leader Shoko Asahara and his followers believed they were the chosen people who had to answer a call to kill everybody on earth. So, in 1995, they perpetrated the sarin attack on Tokyo's subway system—sarin is a nerve gas—to accelerate the new millennium. This moral self-purification implies that the terrorists consider themselves divinely chosen people who are not only bestowed religious legitimacy and validation for their extreme violence; they also operate on the principle that the violence happens at a divinely sanctioned time in history.[45]

DAR AL-ISLAM VERSUS DAR AL-HARB

The September 11, 2001, terrorist attacks in New York and Washington, DC, symbolized a world divided into two radically different spheres—Western civilization and civilization inspired by extreme religious fundamentalism. Islamists saw a twofold division of the world: Dar al-Islam (the "House of Submission"; Islam means "submission") and Dar al-Harb (the "House of War"). Whereas **Dar al-Islam** refers to the divinely perfect and honorable abode of true Muslims (i.e., the area of the world ruled by Islam), **Dar al-Harb** refers to the abode of infidels and immoral societies in the world. To the eyes of devout Muslims, only those nations regulated by sharia and Islam represent the House of Submission. These are Islamic cultures in which Muslims make up most of the population and in which the government ensures them protection. The majority of Dar al-Islam regions are surrounded by other Islamic societies to guarantee public protection.[46] In *Images and Symbols*, Mircea Eliade (1961)[47] remarked that traditional societies looked at the world as two diametrically opposed realms: order and chaos. The inhabited, accustomed sphere was a well-organized one, whereas the sphere outside of that was the world of chaos, demons, ghosts, the deceased, and other inimical creatures.

Mullahs (Muslim scholars) insist that assigning the label of "Dar al-Islam" to a nation or place is contingent on the question of religious security. In other words, if a Muslim practices Islam freely in his or her place of abode (even if the place is mostly secular or un-Islamic), then he or she will be thought to live in Dar al-Islam. In Dar al-Harb, however, Muslims are considered to face intrusion, oppression, and attacks by unbelievers until the latter are defeated and forced into submission. In a nutshell, Dar al-Harb consists of those countries where sharia is not implemented, in terms of worship and protection of the faithful.[48] For Islamism, Western society is evil, depraved, and manipulative. It is Dar al-Harb, remaining outside Dar al-Islam, into which it will, one day, be included. As Osama bin Laden wrote at the end of an Al Qaeda text (*America and WWIII*), "It will end with the destruction of the Great Satan. It will end with the triumph of Islam. It will end with the annihilation of Israel and the United States of America and a return to the Muslim polity that is ruled in the purist Islamic tradition" (cited in Williams, 2002, p. 184).[49]

Taken as a whole, Dar al-Harb refers to all un-Islamic territories, and it signals that all Muslims have a religious and political duty to wage war until all such territories turn to Islam and sharia; only then will they be considered "sacred space." As a result, any Muslim land, even land that was lost centuries ago (e.g., Spain or Israel), must be restored, either by cunning deceit or by force, regardless of what the cost may be (this is known as **sacred space theology**). The objective of Dar al-Islam is to convert all nonbelievers into Muhammad followers (who are not allowed to leave the Muslim religion, risking the death penalty) and adherents of sharia throughout the world.[50] The world outside the Islamic empire was consistently perceived as an alien, dangerous, and threatening world. The distressing incursions of the Crusades (from the tenth to the twelfth centuries) and the Mongols (thirteenth century) into

Muslim sacred lands reinforced a belief in the bipolar interpretation of the world for many Muslims at that time.[51]

DEHUMANIZATION OF ENEMIES

In this "good-versus-evil" struggle, enemies become satanized, and thus compromise and negotiation become difficult. Extreme religious ideologies serve to demonize enemies and adopt ideas of cosmic war as attempts at reaching self-elevation and empowerment. The very act of murder in support of a religious code is not only morally sanctioned; it is also a political gesture. By claiming the right to take other people's lives, religious terrorists make a daring entitlement of power in aid of the powerless—a foundational principle of legitimacy for public order that, in many cases, breaks the state's monopoly.[52] Killing enemies does not happen in a vacuum; rather, many religious terrorist groups label their enemies with dehumanizing terms. Dehumanization enables killers to loosen their moral constraints, especially when using extreme acts of terrorist violence.

Dehumanization is a method by which an in-group underscores the "inferiority" of an out-group by expressing intensely derogatory statements. It is a potent weapon to distance oneself from others by depicting them as animals or beasts rather than humans. Across the globe, dehumanization has been used in the political sphere for centuries. For example, during World War II, Hitler and Goebbels dehumanized Jews and distributed or broadcasted humiliating labels to describe them. In this day and age, neo-Nazis are also degrading people of non-European descent by referring to them as "mud people." On a Palestinian wall, youths drew pigs and monkeys and included the statement "Sons of monkeys and pigs," comparing Jews with these animals. In Islam, pigs are considered unclean animals.[53] Three particular techniques of dehumanization are Othering, enemification, and evilification.

Othering is the labeling and degrading of groups other than one's own. It is like a language of oppression. The Nazis labeled Jews "bacilli," "parasites," "plague," "disease," and so on. Although killing another human is unconscionable, exterminating a disease is not. The subservience of ethnic groups became more acceptable when they were referred to as "savages."[54] **Enemification** is the portrayal of out-groups as enemies—usually a permanent label. From this viewpoint, it is easier to believe that calling enemies "pure evil" makes it easier to see these enemies as outrageously horrific. Enemification functions to identify a "legitimate" target at which rockets should be launched. It engenders a feeling of unity and conviction in objectives.[55] **Evilification** is the practice of satanizing or demonizing other groups and systematically pigeonholing them as outcasts.[56]

CONTRAST SYMBOLS AND TOTALISM

In psychology, the technique of **contrast symbols** consists of categorizing reality by contrasting the good traits of one group with the evil traits of the enemy group. The "chosen people" are encouraged to define their in-group in terms of absolute contrasts with radically degraded, unfavorable categories of outsiders. The group pictures itself as a bastion or repository of total truth, purity, and righteousness in a totally immoral, evil, and hopeless world. And it has to anticipate hostility from that world. When contrast symbols become absolute, it is called **totalism**. Totalism is a frequent strategy of mind control.[57] Totalism has also been likened to what has been termed **exemplary dualism**, an apocalyptic theme "in which contemporary sociopolitical or socioreligious forces are viewed as absolute contrast categories in terms not only of moral virtue but also of eschatology and the millennial destiny of humankind" (Anthony & Robbins, 1997, p. 268).[58]

Totalism and exemplary dualism symbolize, to true believers, a perfect, flawless system led by exemplary leaders and overflowing with values; everything in the outside world, of course, is diametrically opposed. Because totalism is absolute, there is a profound intolerance for ambiguity. Totalism, then, is a polarized self-construct that creates "divided selves." Now, young terrorists or recruits can identify with heroic leaders and the idealized values they embody. At the same time, prior feelings of weakness, failure, low self-esteem, irreverence, shame, and guilt can be rejected more easily and projected onto chosen enemies considered fundamentally inferior and abhorrent. Through the dynamics of such **projective identification**, the self-image of in-group terrorists becomes, in part, psychologically dependent on the out-group scapegoat and the contrast symbols that were projected onto people of the out-group and that are antithetical to the in-group.[59]

Projective identification is a psychological defense mechanism associated with splitting. **Splitting** reflects the notion that the enemy is *totally* different, morally weak, and worthy of extermination. Consequently, everything about the enemy is *totally* shuffled off to the "evil" category. Splitting is fundamental to totalitarian thinking and involves a strategy to divide all world nations into good and evil, saved and doomed, human and subhuman, and so on, and to switch back and forth rapidly between these polarized categories.[60] Another key aspect of totalism is **pseudospeciation**, the propensity for totalists to pigeonhole persons based on race, ethnicity, class, doctrine, religion, sexual orientation, and so on, and classify them into stigmatized categories. The ultimate objective is to make them look totally different, radically inferior—like a subhuman species or a group of nonpersons.[61] The pseudospeciation concept is convergent with the notion of the **dispensing of existence**, meaning that enemies have no legitimate claims to anything, not even any rights to life. Put differently, enemies are trapped into what they are and cannot get out of it.[62]

VIOLENT NEW RELIGIOUS MOVEMENTS

Violent new religious movements (VNRMs) are religious-based terrorist groups that strongly believe in creating a radical transformation of society that they have been called to bring—by exterminating the world, by using weapons of mass destruction (WMDs), and so forth. VNRMs are also called **millennial** (or **millenarian**) **groups**. Millennial groups claim that the existing world and its leaders are corrupt, unfair, or otherwise wrong. Therefore, these people need to be killed and replaced. VNRMs are typified by personal, or group-specific, conceptions of the sacred that consider the divine to be a supernatural entity that belongs exclusively to the group (i.e., outsiders do not have access to the sacred).[63] Hence, VNRMs espouse a dualistic worldview (i.e., dividing the world into good and evil, just and unjust, order and chaos, or sacred and profane). They identify modern society as evil, immoral, and illegitimate. Generally, this rejection of the current order takes the form of extreme violence like terrorism and mass suicide.[64]

Wessinger (2000)[65] has identified three main categories of millennial groups: (1) assaulted, (2) fragile, and (3) revolutionary. First, **assaulted millennial groups** are considered by society as dangerous and have been placed under surveillance—and, usually, they are subject to criminal investigation and prosecution—by law enforcement organizations. The Branch Davidians, a deadly Seventh-Day Adventist sect, are a real case of an assaulted millennial group. Second, **fragile millennial groups** are groups that experience long-lasting internal stressors and self-perceived threats from external forces (emanating from mainstream society). These stressors and threats endanger the group's existential concern (i.e., the achievement of salvation). Heaven's Gate, of which the members committed mass suicide in an attempt to reach a spatial shuttle, is a fatal case of a fragile millennial group. Another example is Aum Shrinrikyo, which worked hard on developing WMDs; the group committed terrorist attacks in reaction to perceptions of persecution by the outside world. Third, **revolutionary millennial groups** embrace theologies of violence, believing that only the violent overthrow and total annihilation of society can bring spiritual salvation. A certain number of white nationalist movements, hoping that a Racial Holy War (i.e., the complete obliteration of the existing social order) will lead to a new Golden Age for the Aryan race, are examples of revolutionary millennial groups.

CASE STUDY OF A VNRM: AUM SHINRIKYO

On March 20, 1995, Aum Shinrikyo, a Japanese terrorist group, launched a sarin attack on the Tokyo subway system. This was the first major use of WMDs by terrorists. A poison gas, sarin, was employed for the first time by the Nazis; Aum used a Soviet recipe. The outcome of the attack was thirteen dead (as well as over 1,000 people injured).[66] As a VNRM, **Aum Shinrikyo** has also been referred to as a Japanese dead cult or a millennial sect. The group practices **theosophy**, a complex belief system mixing Eastern religions, reincarnation, and a belief in humans' ability to become godlike.[67] Aum Shinrikyo was founded and led by Shoko Asahara, a charismatic guru who considered himself the ultimate reincarnation of God. Asahara attracted a certain number of educated, successful people looking for answers to religious needs in this postmodern world; to many of these seekers, he was able to appear as an enlightened and generous guide.[68] The members of Aum Shinrikyo were convinced that Asahara was the savior, and the plot of destruction for salvation was a divine obligation. Complete loyalty was required, and punishment of members was made to guarantee obedience for the sake of righteous purification and justice.[69] Caught by the Japanese police, Asahara was sentenced to death in 2004 (the execution has not taken place yet).

Armageddon

Aum Shinrikyo's path to violence was shaped by Asahara's obsession with the end of civilization: the apocalypse and its reverberation. The sarin attack was used as a symbol of "the weird time" ahead—a phrase Aum followers used to define the earth-shattering war between good and evil and that was believed to unfold in 1997. Aum wanted to bring about the Armageddon in order to conquer Japan first, then the entire world. In June 1994, the word "sarin" was used in Asahara's "Sermon of the sarin gas," followed by a sermon on the Armageddon, and repeated a few times. Aum's first sarin attack occurred in June 1994 in Matsumoto, a city near Tokyo. Aum drove a transformed automobile to disseminate the gas around a building in which the judges and the auxiliary personnel (examining a case referring to Aum) were located. Matsumoto was the city in which people had initiated a protest against the deadly cult.[70]

Shoko Asahara was a master of apocalyptic millennialism and messianic redemptiveness. This millennial apocalypse is based on a belief in an imminent cataclysm eradicating most of the human race, allowing the survivors to transform the world into a millennial kingdom.[71] This is why Aum Shinrikyo believed that the world would end in 1997: the depraved Japanese society would be replaced by the ideology of Aum, the sole survivor of Armageddon. It should come to no surprise, then, that the group's symbol was the Hindu god Shiva, the god of destruction and reproduction.[72] Although there was obvious, concrete symbolism to every Aum attack, it was also symbolism about the total lack of remorse regarding massive casualties. For Aum, anyone who belonged to the out-group was an enemy who deserved punishment. The group had no scruples about sudden attacks in public places and using WMDs. While mainstream political and media rhetoric about the sarin attack on the Tokyo subway system speaks of "innocent victims," in Aum's VNRM-like worldview, the world was polarized between good and evil. The absolute purity of Aum clashed with the evil world. Hence, outside the group's boundaries, "innocence" did not exist.[73]

Aum's Armageddon was a universal, inescapable, end-of-the-world motif that dominated every aspect of the group's existence. Targets belonged to two major categories. The first was the West (or non-Buddhist nations), and the second consisted of impure Buddhists (those not devoted to the movement). Again, targets were framed in terms of a religious purification code—like all non-Muslims who belong to Dar al-Harb. In the group's theosophy, non-Aum humans represented an obstacle to their utopian society, thereby thwarting the restoration of universal balance. The sarin gas attack on the Tokyo subway was the beginning of a war with Aum's archenemy and was to be expanded globally to eliminate the whole impure human race, thus heralding world peace.[74]

Poa: Altruistic Killing

The final statement of the previous paragraph, to eliminate the whole human race in order to bring world peace, is called "poa" in tantric Buddhism. Shoko Asahara had decided to *poa* the world, which, he claimed, would not only better it but also enhance the chances for a victory against the United States in an apocalyptic combat that only Aum would survive. **Poa** is a Tibetan meditative method to give good karma in the cycle of reincarnation. In the beginning, poa was used for smoothing the transition of souls to their rebirth, and was sought for liberation from karmic consequences. In other words, poa can be used to destroy the world in order to save it. In this sense, poa is "altruistic killing"; this is a throwback to the aforementioned "messianic redemptiveness." Asahara made poa an active verb and sent his adepts into action, attracting the attention of Japanese police forces, which immediately saw in the sarin attack not poa but deliberate murder.[75]

Overall, Asahara's version of poa is an example of **New Age ideology**, a syncretic mix of beliefs and attitudes that include Eastern religious thoughts, occult traditions, unconventional "healing techniques," and "consciousness-raising" maneuvers.[76] Asahara saw poa as killing to raise the status of the victim. Poa enables the dying to improve their journey to Buddhahood, that is, into the place of Buddha or the "true land." It is a belief of reincarnation present in premodern cultures: the individual soul is elevated with the collective soul, turning death into a deep connection with immortality. The individual is killed by spiritually advanced beings and raised into immortality. By improving the immortality of the victim, the killer him- or herself gains extra spirituality. Thus, one never actually kills anyone, but offers the victim poa: killing for the sake of healing.[77]

First Reality and Second Reality

Asahara rationalized his evil, unorthodox actions by warping religious scriptures and symbols. The disparity between cruel action and its justification is in accordance with what Voegelin (1990)[78] called the difference between first reality and second reality. **First reality** is reality in the three-dimensional world, the one we experience in everyday life. **Second reality** is the outcome of an initial and intentional act of the imagination. People can picture themselves as subhuman or superhuman. Against this reality of the imagination is the rational experience of being human that develops into several different but equivalent symbolizations. The purpose of developing a second reality is to cloak or ignore the first reality of human experience. The unavoidable result is a discord between commonsense reality—in the case of Aum, for example, it is thirteen casualties to be examined by the Japanese police—and the second reality of the imagination. In regard to the latter, it was Asahara's conviction that he was able to poa his fellow earthlings. More often than not, second reality is not sheer fantasy. To obscure first reality, second reality must still include a modicum of first reality to make the endeavor acceptable or palatable (especially to those individuals to whom second reality is presented). As such, Asahara was sincere in his efforts to poa others even though he knew that, nomologically speaking, it was not achievable. The moral of this anecdote is that, upon analyzing terrorist incidents, it is important to make a distinction between commonsense grievances (of which terrorists seek to take advantage) and the imaginary goals they aspire to fulfill. [79]

SUPERNATURAL FORCES IN WARFARE

Supernatural forces are phenomena that are not subject to the laws of nature or that are said to exist above and beyond nature. Divine interventions, paranormal facts, and voluntary determinations would fall under the supernatural. A certain number of religions make strange parallels between supernatural forces and successful battles. Hence, spirits tend to lay down the conditions for achieving victory in warfare. On the other hand, it is also the case that the warrior believes that he or she has to fight supernatural forces in order to conquer the enemy. This section provides several examples of supernatural forces in warfare.

Ground-Level versus Cosmic-Level Warfare

One worldview is the distinction between two types of spiritual warfare. In **ground-level warfare**, the forces that one has to face are at the horizontal level; that is, one has to confront the various spirits (demons) that possess people. To be more precise, in every society, ground-level warfare is waged against demonization on earth. The spirits or demons may take various forms: family spirits, occult spirits, and "ordinary" spirits like those associated with fear, death, and so forth. Demons are thought to operate at the ground level in ways appropriate to the culture in which they are active. They select their approach based on the problems and issues most recurrent in any given society. In **cosmic-level warfare**, one has to fight spirits at the vertical level. These spirits are territorial spirits hovering over cities, regions, and whole countries; institutional spirits, like those inhabiting churches, administrations, educational institutions, occult organizations, and obscure religions; and spirits tasked to oversee and animate special functions, including immoral or controversial behaviors like prostitution, abortion, homosexuality, gambling, pornography, and terrorism. [80]

The Jinn

In Islam, the **Jinn** are genies. Cited in the Qur'an, they are spirits who occupy an unseen world in dimensions unconceivable or unsuitable to the universe of human beings. The Jinn, along with humans and angels, comprise the three sapient creations of Allah. [81] In the Qur'an, the Jinn are a race of supernatural beings created by Allah "from the fire of a scorching wind" (Qur'an 15:27), before the first humans were actually conceived. Some Muslims believe that terrorism is caused by such supernatural forces. Now, the issue is not whether the Jinn are triggering global terrorism, but rather how some people easily attribute supernatural forces to global terrorism.[82] Some followers of the Muslim faith like to reframe current global conflicts in terms of sacred meaning. In other words, violence leads people to rely on mysticism for better coping with reality. For them, the world "out there" is a disenchanted world ruled by supernatural creatures with free will. Indeed, the Jinn have free will, which allows them to do as they please. They are invisible to humans, and human silhouettes are not clear to them either. The Jinn are able to travel large distances and very fast. They are believed to inhabit remote areas, mountains, seas, trees, and the skies, forming their own communities. Like humans, Allah will judge them on the Day of Judgment. The Jinn, then, will go to Paradise or Hell based on their deeds.[83]

9/11 as the "Last Night"

Before destroying the North Tower on September 11, 2001, **Mohamed Atta** (one of the 9/11 ringleaders) and his four Al Qaeda hijackers practiced a supernatural rite called the "last night." What they actually did was recite Qur'anic verses extolling the virtues and heroic deeds of the Prophet Muhammad's supernatural powers. The inspiration of the **last night** is based on Muhammad's campaign of holy war in order to protect Medina, where he had a ditch built around the city. He sent armed envoys to undermine the enemies (called confederates, as they were made up of a mixture of various Arab tribes). Muhammad cursed the confederates by invoking the prayer included in the "last night" (as well as other verses from the Qur'an).[84]

This practice operates on the principle that true Muslims are the ones who put themselves on the front line (while fighting the enemy), whereas traitors and apostates recoil in shame at the back rows. This interpretation of warfare allows Muslims to determine who is a "true" or "false" Muslim. True Muslims would stick their neck out and fight, but false Muslims would flee. The 9/11 hijackers' version of the "last night" comprised fifteen points for the final night of the martyrs' life on earth. These consisted of reciting various Qur'anic prayers and verses to reach spiritual and physical purity. The ultimate objective, of course, was to be better prepared for the task ahead of them. Some of these points require that the holy warrior free himself from the existence on earth and seek Paradise. Points 12–15 explain how one prepares oneself before the actual endeavor, such as blessing one's suitcases and weapons, and bathing and dressing properly.[85]

Upon looking at "last night" documents, there was no question in Mohamed Atta's mind that "martyrdom operations" are allowed in Islamic doctrine. Besides, these sets of prayers were believed to be protective. Atta and his associates were convinced that the "last night" ritual would summon supernatural succor and protection in order to smooth the progress of their mission. Put another way, for the 9/11 hijackers, the "last night" made them invisible.[86] As Cook (2002)[87] notes, "behind the constant attitude of prayer lies a complete confidence in its efficaciousness as one passing through airport security, boarding the plane, slaughtering passengers who resist and ultimately facing the target and the death of the 'martyr'" (p. 18).

SUMMARY

There is a long-established and profound relationship between terrorism and religion. When terrorism professes strong commitments to religious beliefs and is regarded as unbending and resistant to change, it is called religious fundamentalism. When the use of religious terrorism is centered on an ideological and fanatical interpretation of selected religious scriptures, it is called junk terrorism (the hijacking of a religion). Religion itself has five principles: (1) a connection with the divine, (2) social glue, (3) a cultural system, (4) a symbolic representation of society, and (5) an emotional state. It was also found that religious terrorism regularly implies a battle between good and evil, and an all-out struggle against enemies. Such practice of being exclusive vis-à-vis all other groups (i.e., exclusivism) allows various groups to regard themselves as the chosen people, that is, people chosen by God for a specific purpose (e.g., to act as God's representatives on earth). In the case of Islamism, for example, whereas Dar al-Islam refers to the divinely perfect and honorable abode of true Muslims (i.e., the area of the world ruled by Islam), Dar al-Harb refers to the abode of infidels and immoral societies in the world. One of the by-products of the "good-versus-evil" distinction is dehumanization, a method by which an in-group underscores the "inferiority" of an out-group by expressing intensely derogatory statements. Three particular techniques of dehumanization are Othering, enemification, and evilification. In a similar vein, the technique of contrast symbols consists of categorizing reality by contrasting the good traits of one group with the evil traits of the enemy group. When contrast symbols become absolute, it is called totalism, the idea that the enemy is totally different and has no right to anything, not even the right to live. Of equal relevance in this chapter is the fact that violent new religious movements (VNRMs) are religious-based terrorist groups that strongly believe in creating a radical transformation of society that they have been called to bring (i.e., by exterminating the world, by using weapons of mass destruction [WMDs], and so forth). VNRMs are also called millennial (or millenarian) groups. A good example that illustrates the power of VNRM is Aum Shinrikyo, a deadly Japanese cult that believes in Armageddon and altruistic killing in order to save the world itself. Finally, in many religions, supernatural forces are believed to play a role in warfare—for good or ill. In the case of the Jinn, it is not good, but in the case of the "last night," it is actually tantamount to supernatural reinforcement and protection.

NOTES

1. Stevens, Michael (2005). What Is Terrorism and Can Psychology Do Anything to Prevent It? *Behavioral Sciences and the Law, 23*, 507–526.
2. Kimball, Charles (2003). *When Religion Becomes Evil*. New York: Harper San Francisco.
3. Altemeyer, Bob, & Hunsberger, Bruce (1992). Authoritarianism, Religious Fundamentalism, Quest and Prejudice. *The International Journal for the Psychology of Religion, 2*, 113–133.
4. Hunsberger, Bruce (1995). Religion and Prejudice: The Role of Religious Fundamentalism, Quest and Right Wing Authoritarianism. *Journal of Social Issues, 51*(2), 113–129.
5. Rubin, Barry, & Rubin, Judith (2002). *Anti-American Terrorism and the Middle East*. New York: Oxford University Press.
6. Sosis, Richard, & Alcorta C. S. (2005). *Ritual, Emotion and Sacred Symbol: The Evolution of Religion at an Adaptive Complex, Human Nature*. New York: Maryknoll.
7. Schwartz, Stephen (2002). *The Two Faces of Islam: The House of Sa'ud from Tradition to Terror*. New York: Doubleday.
8. Kimball, Charles (2003). *When Religion Becomes Evil*. New York: Harper San Francisco.
9. Martin, Gus (2010). *Understanding Terrorism: Challenges, Perspectives, and Issues*. Thousand Oaks, CA: Sage.
10. Allport, Gordon W. (1950). *The Individual and His Religion*. New York: Macmillan.
11. Buss, David, Haselton, Martie, Shackelford, Todd, Bleske, April, & Wakefield, Jerome (1998). Adaptations, Exaptations, and Spandrels. *American Psychologist, 53*, 533–548.
12. Gallup International (2012). *Global Index of Religiosity and Atheism*. Washington, DC: Gallup International.
13. Brodd, Jeffery (2003). *World Religions*. Winona, MN: Saint Mary's Press.
14. Argyle, Michael, & Beit-Hallahmi, Benjamin (1975). *The Social Psychology of Religion*. London: Routledge.
15. O'Collins, Gerald, & Farrugia, Edward (1991). *A Concise Dictionary of Theology*. New York: Paulist Press.
16. Clark, Walter (1958). How Do Social Scientists Define Religion? *Journal of Social Psychology, 47*, 143–147.
17. Pargament, Kenneth (1997). *The Psychology of Religion and Coping*. New York: Guilford Press.
18. Turner, Bryan (1991). *Religion and Social Theory*. London: Sage.
19. Durkheim, Emile (1915). *The Elementary Forms of Religious Life*. New York: Free Press.
20. Swatos, William, Jr., & Christiano, Kevin (1999). Secularization Theory: The Course of a Concept. *Sociology of Religion, 60*(3), 209–228.

21. Atran, Scott (2003). Genesis of Suicide Terrorism. *Science, 299*, 1534–1539.

22. Pargament, Kenneth (1997). *The Psychology of Religion and Coping*. New York: Guilford Press.

23. Dingley, James (2011). Terrorism, Religion and Community. *Defense & Security Analysis, 27*(4), 325–340.

24. Pape, Robert (2005). *Dying to Win: The Strategic Logic of Suicide Terrorism*. New York: Random House.

25. Nachmani, Amikam (2001). The Palestinian Intifada 1987–1993: The Dynamics of Symbols and Symbolic Realities, the Role of Symbols, Rituals and Myths in National Struggles. *Civil Wars, 4*(1), 49–103.

26. Pals, Daniel (1996). *Seven Theories of Religion*. New York: Oxford University Press; and Stump, Roger (2005). Religion and the Geographies of War. In Colin Flint (Ed.), *The Geography of War and Peace: From Death Camps to Diplomats* (pp. 149–173). Oxford: Oxford University Press.

27. Stolz, Jörg (2009). Explaining Religiosity: Towards a Unified Theoretical Model. *The British Journal of Sociology, 60*(2), 345–376.

28. Stump, Roger (2005). Religion and the Geographies of War. In Colin Flint (Ed.), *The Geography of War and Peace: From Death Camps to Diplomats* (pp. 149–173). Oxford: Oxford University Press.

29. Dingley, James, & Kirk-Smith, Michael (2002). Symbolism and Sacrifice in Terrorism. *Small Wars & Insurgencies, 13*(1), 102–128.

30. Rappaport, Roy (1999). *Ritual and Religion in the Making of Humanity*. Cambridge: Cambridge University Press.

31. Pape, Robert (2005). *Dying to Win: The Strategic Logic of Suicide Terrorism*. New York: Random House.

32. Hamilton, Malcolm (1995). *The Sociology of Religion*. London: Routledge.

33. Durkheim, Emile (1915). *The Elementary Forms of Religious Life*. New York: Free Press.

34. Dingley, James, & Kirk-Smith, Michael (2002). Symbolism and Sacrifice in Terrorism. *Small Wars & Insurgencies, 13*(1), 102–128.

35. Atran, Scott (2003). Genesis of Suicide Terrorism. *Science, 299*, 1534–1539.

36. Bartlett, Frederic (1932). *Remembering: A Study in Experimental and Social Psychology*. Cambridge: Cambridge University Press.

37. Dingley, James, & Kirk-Smith, Michael (2002). Symbolism and Sacrifice in Terrorism. *Small Wars & Insurgencies, 13*(1), 102–128.

38. Ranstorp, Magnus (1996). Terrorism in the Name of Religion. *Journal of International Affairs, 50*(1), 41–63.

39. Delgado, Richard (1980). Limits to Proselytizing. *Society, 17*, 25–33.

40. Ranstorp, Magnus (1996). Terrorism in the Name of Religion. *Journal of International Affairs, 50*(1), 41–63.

41. Hamas (1988). *Hamas Charter: The Covenant of the Islamic Resistance Movement*. Retrieved April 26, 2013, from http://www.mideastweb.org/hamas.htm

42. Ranstorp, Magnus (1996). Terrorism in the Name of Religion. *Journal of International Affairs, 50*(1), 41–63.

43. Griffiths, Paul (2001). *Problems of Religious Diversity: Exploring the Philosophy of Religion*. New York: Blackwell.

44. Ranstorp, Magnus (1996). Terrorism in the Name of Religion. *Journal of International Affairs, 50*(1), 41–63.

45. Pollack, Andrew (1995, April 15). Cult's Prophecy of Disaster Draws Precautions in Tokyo. *The New York Times*, p. A1.

46. Schroeder, John Ross (2012). Islam vs. the West: Why the Clash of Civilizations? *The Good News, 17*(1), 4–7.

47. Eliade, Mircea (1961). *Images and Symbols: Studies in Comparative Religion*. Kansas City, MO: Sheed Andrews & McMeel.

48. Williams, Paul (2002). *Al Qaeda: Brotherhood of Terror*. New York: Alpha.

49. Williams, Paul (2002). *Al Qaeda: Brotherhood of Terror*. New York: Alpha.

50. Sookhdeo, Patrick (2005, November 12). Will London Burn too? *The Spectator*, p. A1.

51. Eliade, Mircea (1961). *Images and Symbols: Studies in Comparative Religion*. Kansas City: Sheed Andrews & McMeel.

52. Juergensmeyer, Mark (2004). Holy Orders: Opposition to Modern States. *Harvard International Review, 25*(4), 10–21.

53. Baumeister, Roy (1996). *Evil: Inside Human Violence and Cruelty*. New York: Freeman; and Oliver, Anne Marie, & Steinberg, Paul (2005). *The Road to Martyrs' Square: A Journey into the World of the Suicide Bomber*. Oxford: Oxford University Press.

54. Hillgruber, Andreas (1987). War in the East and the Extermination of the Jews. *Yad Vashem Studies, 18*, 103–132.

55. Bhatia, Aditi (2008). Discursive Illusions in the American National Strategy for Combating Terrorism. *Journal of Language and Politics, 7*(2), 201–227.

56. Lazar, Anita, & Lazar, Michelle M. (2004). The Discourse of the New World Order: "Out-Casting" the Double Face of Threat. *Discourse & Society, 15*(2), 223–242.

57. Anthony, Dick, Robbins, Thomas, & Barrie-Anthony, Steven (2002). Cult and Anticult Totalism: Reciprocal Escalation and Violence. *Terrorism and Political Violence, 14*(1), 211–240.

58. Anthony, Dick, & Robbins, Thomas (1997). Religious Totalism, Exemplary Dualism, and the Waco Tragedy. In Thomas Robbins & Susan Palmer (Eds.), *Millenium, Messiahs and Mayhem: Contemporary Apocalyptic Movements* (pp. 261–312). Berkeley: University of California Press.

59. Anthony, Dick, Robbins, Thomas, & Barrie-Anthony, Steven (2002). Cult and Anticult Totalism: Reciprocal Escalation and Violence. *Terrorism and Political Violence, 14*(1), 211–240.

60. Manfield, Philip (1992). *Split Self/Split Object: Understanding and Treating Borderline, Narcissistic and Schizoid Disorders*. London: Aronson.

61. Friedman, Lawrence (1999). *Identity's Architect: A Biography of Erik H. Erikson*. New York: Scribner's.

62. Lifton, Robert Jay (1961). *Chinese Thought Reform and the Psychology of Totalism*. New York: W. W. Norton.

63. Lifton, Robert Jay (2000). *Destroying the World to Save It: Aum Shinrikyo, Apocalyptic Violence, and the New Global Terrorism*. New York: Picador.

64. Wallis, Roy (1996). Three Types of New Religious Movements. In Lorne Dawson (Ed.), *Cults in Context: Readings in the Study of New Religious Movements* (pp. 39–72). Toronto: Canadian Scholars' Press.

65. Wessinger, Catherine (2000). *How the Millennium Comes Violently: From Jonestown to Heaven's Gate*. New York: Seven Bridges Press.

66. Cooper, Barry (2007). "Jihadists" and the War on Terrorism. *The Intercollegiate Review, 42*(1), 27–36.

67. Melton, Gordon (1989). *Encyclopedia of American Religions*. Detroit, MI: Garland.

68. Juergensmeyer, Mark (1997). Terror Mandated by God. *Terrorism and Political Violence, 9*(2), 16–23.

69. Metraux, Daniel (2000). *Aum Shinrikyo's Impact on Japanese Society*. Lewiston, NY: Edwin Mellen Press.

70. Frenţiu, Rodica (2010). Exploring the Boundary between Morality and Religion: The Shin-Shinshūkyō (New New Religions) Phenomenon and the Aum Anti-Utopia. *Journal for the Study of Religions and Ideologies, 9*(27), 46–70.

71. Reader, Ian (1996). *A Poisonous Cocktail: Aum Shirikyo's Path to Violence*. Copenhagen: Nordic Institute.

72. Campbell, James (1997). Excerpts from Research Study "Weapons of Mass Destruction and Terrorism: Proliferation by Non-State Actors." *Terrorism and Political Violence, 9*(2), 24–50.

73. Reader, Ian (2012). Globally Aum: The Aum Affair, Counterterrorism, and Religion. *Japanese Journal of Religious Studies, 39*(1), 179–198.

74. Morris, Travis, & Crank, John (2011). Toward a Phenomenology of Terrorism: Implications for Research and Policy. *Crime, Law and Social Change, 56*, 219–242.

75. Evans-Wentz, Walter (1937). *Tibetan Book of the Dead*. Oxford: Oxford University Press; Foard, James (2003). Religious Violence in Contemporary Japan: The Case of Aum Shinrikyo by Ian Reader. *History of Religions, 43*(1), 81–82.

76. Saliba, John (1995). *Understanding New Religious Movements*. Grand Rapids, MI: William Eerdmans Publishing.

77. Lifton, Robert Jay (1998). Reflections on Aum Shinrikyo. *Journal of Personal and Interpersonal Loss: International Perspectives on Stress & Coping, 3*(1), 85–97.

78. Voegelin, Eric (1990). On Debate an Existence. In Ellis Sandoz (Ed.), *The Collected Works of Eric Voegelin: Vol. 12. Published Essays, 1966–1985* (pp. 36–51). Baton Rouge: Louisiana State University Press.

79. Cooper, Barry (2007). "Jihadists" and the War on Terrorism. *The Intercollegiate Review, 42*(1), 27–36.

80. Adogame, Afe (2007). HIV/AIDS Support and African Pentecostalism: The Case of the Redeemed Christian Church of God (RCCG). *Journal of Health Psychology, 12*(3) 475–484.

81. El-Zein, Amira (2009). *Islam, Arabs, and the Intelligent World of the Jinn*. Syracuse, NY: Syracuse University Press.

82. Saniotis, Arthur (2005). Re-Enchanting Terrorism: Jihadists as "Liminal Beings." *Studies in Conflict & Terrorism, 28*, 533–545.

83. Maarouf, Mohammed (2007). *Jinn Eviction as a Discourse of Power: A Multidisciplinary Approach to Moroccan Magical Beliefs and Practices*. Leiden, the Netherlands: Brill.

84. Cook, David (2002). Suicide Attacks or Martyrdom Operations. *Contemporary Jihad Literature, 3*, 17–19.

85. Cook, David (2002). Suicide Attacks or Martyrdom Operations. *Contemporary Jihad Literature, 3*, 17–19.

86. Saniotis, Arthur (2005). Re-Enchanting Terrorism: Jihadists as "Liminal Beings." *Studies in Conflict & Terrorism, 28*, 533–545.

87. Cook, David (2002). Suicide Attacks or Martyrdom Operations. *Contemporary Jihad Literature, 3*, 17–19.

Chapter Eight

Hindu, Sikh, Christian, and Jewish Terrorism

HINDU TERRORISM

Hindu terrorist organizations have perpetrated attacks including the 2006 Malegaon blasts, the 2007 Mecca Masjid bombing (Hyderabad), the 2007 Samjhauta Express bombings, the 2007 Ajmer Sharif Dargah Blast, and the 2008 Western India bombings. For a few years, Hindu terrorism has been nicknamed "saffron terror." **Saffron terror** refers to terrorism spurred by Hindu extremist nationalism. The term comes from the association of the color saffron with Hindu nationalism.[1]

Hindutva

A principal focus of the Hindu terrorist discourse is the notion of Hindutva. **Hindutva** refers to "Hinduness" and reflects the idea that Indians (of all backgrounds and walks of life) belong to the Hindu nation and need to be unified in a single community—particularly those whose ancestors, culture, and religion are from the Indian subcontinent. Hindutva symbolizes the common identity of individuals who see this part of the world as both their "homeland" and their "holy land." For this reason, Hindutva is a conceptual promoter of Hindu terrorism. It is related to the idea that the gods and heroes of Hindu mythology are part of their heritage. Those who reject Hindutva are not only apostates; they are also traitors.[2] As explained by Rapoport (1984),[3] for the religious terrorist, an important audience is the deity itself, and based on his or her religious interpretation, it is sometimes the case that the holy terrorist does not want to have the public observe his or her deed. Hindu nationalists idealize a Hindu majority that rejects the diversity that has made up Hinduism (and the whole country of India, for that matter). Hindu fundamentalists have imposed a type of conformity that is just as tyrannical to the average Hindu as it is to minority groups. Given these circumstances, the rise of Hindu extremism based on Hindutva tends to lead to violent conflict between Hindus and Muslims (which occurred both before and after the division of the country by the British).

The God Ram

The god **Ram** is a powerful symbol that Hindu nationalists have chosen to unite Hindus—who are dissimilar in their large amounts of sects and traditions—into a self-conscious nation. Ram is one of the incarnations of Vishnu and a key figure in the Hindus' fusion of nationalism and religion. For Hindu nationalists, religion is a vehicle through which they can achieve political power and restore **Ram Rajya** (i.e., the rule of Ram, or the perfect rule of the Golden Age of Ram).[4] With the expansion of the radical Hindu fundamentalist movement in the 1980s, the site of the Babri Mosque in Ayodhya (in Uttar Pradesh, northern India) became a persistent controversial matter. Hindu tradition has it that the **Babri Mosque** was erected on the site of a Hindu temple demolished by the Moguls, a method that the Moguls used elsewhere in northern India to assert their power. Ayodhya is the alleged birthplace of Ram, and devout Hindus claim that, in the sixteenth century, Babur (the Mogul emperor) shredded the Hindu temple into pieces and built the Babri Mosque on the ashes of it.[5]

For many years, Hindu fundamentalists had been calling for the obliteration of the Babri Mosque and its replacement with a new temple dedicated to Ram. For example, in 1989, attempts by Hindu terrorist groups to destroy the mosque and to restore Hindu honor—through the erection of a new temple of Ram—triggered what became the biggest Hindu-Muslim clash since the partition of the country in 1947. Because the purpose of erecting such a temple was so central to the discourse of radical Hindu fundamentalists, the disputing of the site symbolized tensions between Hindu extremists and the Muslim minority in India (as well as peaceful Indians in favor of a secular, modern, and constitutional India). The fundamentalists' fervent pursuit of building a new temple also symbolized what was perceived as being their ultimate agenda of imposing Ram Rajya all over India. Thus, the fate of the Babri Mosque had become a contentious national issue leading to a series of violent conflicts. In 1992, the violence reached a pinnacle immediately after an immense demonstration by Hindu fundamentalists at the Babri site. During the demonstration, the mosque was destroyed and replaced by a makeshift shrine dedicated to Ram. Many other mosques were destroyed in Ayodhya as well. In the aftermath of the destruction, more than 2,000 people were killed across India. In retaliation, Islamic terrorists in Pakistan attacked or destroyed multiple Hindu temples.[6]

Thugs

In the Middle Ages, the **Thugs**, also known as the **Thuggee** terrorist cult, were Hindu assassins who traveled in groups throughout India for several centuries. They killed thousands of people each year to venerate **Kali**, the Hindu goddess of terror, destruction, empowerment, and sexuality. To be more precise, the Thugs wanted their victims to experience terror for the simple and pure pleasure of Kali. The Thugs murdered more than any terrorist group in history, in part because they were active for several hundred years.[7] For various reasons, the Thugs killed only travelers. Although they seized their victims' property, material gain was not an important concern. This was confirmed by their tradition of distinguishing their most important accomplishments not by the property they confiscated but by the number of people killed.[8]

In Hindu mythology, Kali has manifold facets. She symbolizes the energy of the universe. Hindu legend has it that Kali both sustains and destroys life. She also serves as the goddess of time by controlling endless cycles in which fundamental aspects of the life process are achieved. From this perspective, to the Thugs, Kali was seen as the Creator. The average Thug understood that his task was to supply the blood that Kali needed in order to keep the world in equilibrium. His duty was to remain alive as long as possible so that he could continue to kill. Based on various estimations, each year, a Thug killed three people on average.[9] Because Kali was the Creator, a Thug's life was governed by countless rules laid down by the goddess. The rules specified victims, means of attack, division of labor, discarding of corpses, sharing of victims' property, and training of new recruits. The Thugs did not have any choice because, in case of disobedience, Kali would retaliate through omens.[10]

Truly, in the Thugs' life world, it was clear that assassination was their main business; the death agony was intentionally prolonged to give Kali a great chunk of time to enjoy the terror screamed by the victims.[11] Thugs were convinced that death was actually good for the victim, who would certainly go to Paradise.[12] This relates to the notion of poa covered in chapter 7. Poa is the idea that the human race needs to be destroyed in order to save it and elevate it to a higher level of morality. On the other hand, those Thugs who did not comply with Kali's instructions would become weak, and their families would disappear or experience misfortune. Lastly, an examination of those people who were never attacked by the Thugs—women, vagrants, lepers, the blind, the mutilated, and certain craft artists (all considered part of Kali's lineage, like the Thugs themselves)—suggests that the Hindu cult may have had political undertones as well.[13]

TAMIL TIGERS

A modern-day Hindu faction is the Tamil ethnic group, native to India and Sri Lanka. Although almost 90 percent of Tamils are Hindus, most practice what is believed to be folk Hinduism, worshipping a large number of village deities.[14] In Sri Lanka, Tamils are very distinct (both culturally and linguistically) from the Sinhalese majority. After Sri Lanka became independent from Britain in 1948, relationships between the Sinhalese and the Tamils started to deteriorate rapidly. As a result, ethnic and political tensions, violent riots, and civilian genocides gave rise to the formation and support of separatist groups championing independence for the Tamils. One of these separatist groups today is the **Tamil Tigers**, considered a terrorist organization by over thirty countries.[15] Also known as the **Liberation Tigers of Tamil Eelam (LTTE)**, the Tamil Tigers want the Tamil people to be totally independent from the Sinhalese-led government. In other words, they want to have an autonomous, monoethnic Tamil Eelam state. In the Tamil language, Eelam refers to the Island of Sri Lanka, which the Tamil Tigers want to liberate from the Sinhalese majority.[16]

Hindu Symbols of Martyrdom

The Tamil Tigers use "Hindu symbols for purposes of recruitment and rely on the language of religious martyrdom to justify and reward the sacrifice" (Berman & Laitin, 2005, p. 28).[17] Analogous to the release of video testaments, before going on suicide missions, the Tamil Tigers have a ritual dinner with their leader in honor of Hindu gods, evidently sealing their commitment to execute the attacks.[18] In a comprehensive ethnography, Roberts (2005)[19] remarks that these rites for martyrs resemble the way "they approach the deities [and] enables those Tamils who are so inclined to appeal to the divine forces and convince themselves that their actions, and those of the LTTE, are in harmony with the cosmological arrangements" (p. 83). As Roberts (2005) continues, the Tamil Tigers cleverly use symbols and ritual to "mobilize supporters and legitimize their cause among Tamil speakers, while also cementing the loyalty of their personnel" (p. 494).

A potent symbol adopted by the Tamil martyrs-to-be is the decoration of a cyanide capsule around the neck. Considered a supreme symbol of bravery and commitment to a cause, the cyanide capsule is awarded at the closing initiation ceremony. A Tamil Tiger commando wearing the capsule must swallow it without fail in case of an unsuccessful mission. Failure to use the capsule will lead to severe capital punishment at the hands of the Tamil leaders. The capsule should also be swallowed by the female fighter if captured. Songs, poems, and martyrologies are recited and vocalized to extoll the virtues of the slow death brought by cyanide.[20]

By wearing the capsule and showing commitment to the organization, a Tamil Tiger becomes a "walking witness" through self-determination and willingness to be a martyr.[21]

Black Tigers: Suicide Commandos

Suicide is common in Hindu society, and the Tamil Tigers can be called fanatical Hindus. They have a top suicide commando unit called the **Black Tigers**. They constitute the Tamil suicide attack squad and are made up of both adults and children (as young as ten years old)— and both male and female. In fact, females are increasingly chosen to be prepared to carry out missions.[22] The importance of training the Black Tigers is, according to the Tamil Tigers' leadership, a requisite weapon in the organization's arsenal because they play a crucial role. The commemoration of Black Tigers Day, a ritual celebration, is a sign of the Tamil Tigers' appreciation of the daily reality of terrorism and conflict in northern Sri Lanka.[23] Every year on July 5, thousands are present at Black Tigers Day, honoring the martyrs, whose shrines are ornamented with flowers and shrubs.[24] Many terrorist organizations, including Hezbollah and Hamas, have been inspired by the suicide methods of the Black Tigers (i.e., their groundbreaking use of suicide belts and vests). The Tamil commandos have carried out a steady suicide terror campaign since the dawn of their separatist movement in 1987.[25] From 1987 until 2004, there were at least 200 Tamil Tigers suicide attacks, of which about thirty were perpetrated by women targeting political and military leaders.[26]

Yellow Tiger as the National Insignia

A key symbol for the Tamil Tigers is the **yellow tiger**, a culturally important creature that represents heroism, militancy, and nationalism. Created in 1977 by Vellupillai Prabaharan (the founder and leader of the Tamil Tigers), the symbol represents the Tamil Eelam national insignia and depicts a yellow tiger roaring, with its head and paws protruding out of a black circle with a red background. Two crossed rifles with bayonets overlay the circle drawn like bullets (which are black in color). The text around the tiger is in Tamil, and the one below the tiger is in English. The script reads, "Liberation Tigers of Tamil Eelam." The centrality of this image points to the desire of the Tamil Tigers to be self-determined and autonomous. The bullets and rifles signal their use of violence as a way to achieve these goals.

According to a guidebook issued by the Tamil Tigers, yellow signifies the Tamils' dream to freely control their own homeland and the virtue and morality of Tamil struggle. In Tamil culture, yellow symbolizes sacredness. The color black (i.e., the black circle mentioned previously) reminds the Tamil community that its march on the way to freedom is awash with perils, death, and destruction. The color red (i.e., the red background) characterizes the egalitarianism and revolutionary changes needed to promulgate social justice. The roaring head and paws of the yellow tiger are made to symbolize aggressiveness, whereas the rifle and bullet represent the Tamil Tigers' pledge to violence.[27]

Ingrained in Dravidian (i.e., southern Indian) culture, the yellow tiger symbol also exemplifies the battle-hardened history and national turmoil of the Tamils. It symbolizes their strength, bravery, and self-confidence. It echoes their ethnic patriotic and valorous feelings. The yellow tiger is deeply engraved on the minds of the Tamils. Thanks to this symbol, the soul of the nation is revitalized. Besides employing contemporary methods of organization, training, and discipline, the Tamil Tigers want to uphold this martial tradition through the symbol of the tiger. The "tiger" is also considered the opposite of the "lion," the long-established symbol of the Sinhalese. Consequently, the "tiger" and the "lion" are symbols of clashing nationalisms in Sri Lanka.[28]

Symbols of Oppression

A predominantly salient symbol for the Tamils is the series of discriminatory rulings passed by the Sinhalese government. Ratified in June 1956, the Sinhala Only Act was the first of multiple initiatives that harmed the Tamil people. As such, the act ensured that Sinhala would be Sri Lanka's only official language allowed in all government proceedings, including civil service, courtroom, legal cases, as well as diverse administrative reports, pleadings, judgments, and orders.[29] On account of the Sinhala Only Act, many Tamils were shattered by the government's efforts to reallocate jobs among the Sinhalese majority. The percentage of Tamils in public service precipitously dropped after the legislation was passed. Additionally, those Tamil civil servants who declined to use Sinhala—notwithstanding offers of promotion and other enticements—were instantly terminated from their positions. As one can see, the Tamil community repercussion from the Sinhala Only Act was severe.[30]

A second symbol of oppression was the anti-Tamil exterminations that occurred in 1956, 1958, 1977, 1981, and 1983 (during which the most infamous of these genocides took place). In 1983, a Sinhalese riot was sparked by the slaying of thirteen Sri Lankan Army soldiers after being ambushed by the Tamil Tigers in Jaffna at night. Throngs of Sinhalese rioters carrying axes, poles, iron rods, clubs, knives, daggers, petrol bombs, and firearms beat, killed, and sexually assaulted innocent Tamils. Moreover, hundreds of them were dispossessed, displaced, and forced into refugee camps.[31] Senaratne (1997)[32] portrays the anti-Tamil riots of 1983 as a turning point in postcolonial Sri Lankan history. The dreadful stories of victimization diffused quickly within the Tamil community: women were raped in public, passengers on minibuses were massacred or burned while being trapped inside (in spite of their cries for mercy), thousands of Tamil dwellings were looted and destroyed (while women and infants were still inside), and hundreds of thousands of Tamils became refugees. These reprehensible acts happened while Sri Lankan police officers and military personnel purportedly turned a blind eye and even partook in the pogroms of 1983.

Due to these carnages and what they symbolized, the Tamil people developed an appreciation for the Tamil Tigers' violent actions. Before the pogroms of 1983, all Tamil militant groups only had fifty active members at the most. However, after that fateful year, hundreds of young Tamils "began approaching local militant leaders whom they had shunned until then, clamoring for membership and arms. Many boys ran off from their homes, leaving terse notes that they were going away to fight for Eelam" (Swamy, 1994, p. 104).[33] The symbolic makeup of the subsequent violence against the Tamils became yet another incentive for people to support or participate in the struggle for Tamil Eelam.[34]

SIKH TERRORISM

Founded in the fifteenth century, **Sikhism** is a monotheistic religion mostly practiced in northern India. The Sikhs' main language is Punjabi, a modern Indo-European language that is also spoken by many people in Pakistan. Although Sikhs may be confused with Hindus, Sikhism is not a Hindu religion. Rather, it is a system of religious philosophy and belief in one God that prevails in everything. Sikhs are ordained to follow the teachings of the ten Sikh gurus, or enlightened leaders, as well as the pursuit of salvation through a congregational method of meditation on the name and message of God.[35] In India, Sikhism is considered a revolutionary social movement. Sikhs reject the Hindu caste system, asceticism, and holiness. They proclaim that Hindus, Muslims, and all other religious groups are equal, and that there should be no status differential between men and women.[36] The detailed description of Sikh symbolism below is an example of ethnosymbolism. **Ethnosymbolism** is a philosophy that stresses the importance of symbols, values, and traditions in the creation and preservation of a modern nation-state.[37]

The Golden Temple in Amritsar

In the early 1980s, a movement for Sikh independence gained popularity through the spellbinding sermons of Bhindranwale, a devout Sikh leader. In 1984, in a raid named Operation Bluestar, the Indian Armed Forces desecrated the Golden Temple in Amritsar. The **Golden Temple in Amritsar** is Sikhism's holiest shrine and the spiritual center for the Amritdhari Sikhs (hence, the name "Amritsar"). Prime Minister Indira Gandhi alleged that the Golden Temple was being used to launch a terrorist crusade against the Indian nation-state.[38] Bhindranwale died in the attack, but the militancy was not quelled. Operation Bluestar and the lethal Sikh retaliations became important events that spurred massive mobilization within the Sikh community worldwide to espouse this cause. Sikh terrorists assassinated Indira Gandhi and produced a cycle of extreme violence between the Sikhs and Hindus that, by 2005, had already claimed more than 20,000 lives.[39] On June 23, 1985, Air India Flight 182 was blown up in midair off the coast of Ireland. Over 320 passengers perished. The main suspects in the terrorist attack were Sikh terrorists.[40]

Amritdhari Sikhs have been oppressed more than most minorities in India. Amritdhari Sikhs are those who wear the five Sikh symbols and strongly believe in baptism (Amritdhari means "having taken Amrit [or baptism]"). The five Sikh symbols are known as the **Five Ks**. Each of the five symbols begins with the letter "k" in the Punjabi language: kirpan (a dagger), kara (an iron bracelet), kesh (unshorn hair), kacch (breeches), and kangha (a small comb in the hair).[41] The Five Ks are not just symbols; they also show commitment to the teachings of Guru Nanak Dev, the founder of Sikhism and the first of the ten Sikh Gurus.[42] In René Girard's (1989)[43] apposite words, "Victims are chosen not for the crimes they are accused of but for the signs that the victims bear, for everything that suggests their guilty relationship with the crisis" (p. 24). Not all Amritdhari Sikhs are religiously observant. However, their turbans and beards symbolize a rejection of central Indian authority.[44] As opposed to the majority of South Asian religions, Sikhs stand out. Sikhism requires that its adherents stand out. How can it be done? Through the outward symbols of their religion—the Five Ks—which are daily reminders of the importance of their faith.[45]

Various Sikh Symbols

Another fundamental aspect of the Sikh community is **Khalsa** (which means "pure"). Khalsa implies that the Sikhs are committed to the achievement of divine power and justice. The Khalsa symbol is depicted as a vertical double-edged sword, a ubiquitous insignia called **Khanda**. Khanda denotes a domesticized type of violence.[46] The double-edged sword is drawn over a quoit and edged by two crossed sabers.[47] Violence is rationalized through this doctrine; it reflects the notion that religion is to be triumphant in both the spiritual and the worldly spheres. In fact, the aforementioned Five Ks are the symbols of the Khalsa order.[48]

There are many reasons for adopting the sword as a symbol of Sikhism. Looking back in history, the experience of the Sikhs in the early days of the faith led to its exaltation of military symbols like the kirpan. The word **kirpan** is Punjabi and is roughly translated as "grace of God." It is a ceremonial sword that represents the Sikh's duty to resist oppression. Two of the ten Gurus of the faith, Guru Arjun Dev and Guru Tegh Bahadur, were brutally murdered by the Muslim Mogul rulers at that time. This tragedy catalyzed and animated the members of the Sikh faith into a militant movement. Guru Hargobind, the sixth Guru, walked with two swords around his waist, symbolizing both spiritual and temporal authority, and was bent on creating a Sikh army to counteract further intimidation from the Moguls.[49]

At the core of the Sikh terrorists' discourse is a radical interpretation of religious identity inspired by the martial traditions of Sikhism and, at the same time, the unity of Khalsa in contemporary, nationalistic terms. The ultimate focus is the establishment of an autonomous, sovereign Sikh state called **Khalistan** ("Land of the Pure"). The appalling Operation Bluestar in 1984 (and its violent and bloody consequences) undoubtedly heightened the desire, within the Sikh diaspora, for creating Khalistan. Increasingly, the globally dispersed members of the Sikh faith have seen themselves as being a "nation."[50] The territorial delineation of the "Land of the Pure" consists of the entire Punjab region (in northern India).[51] Thus, one can easily deduce that Sikh terrorism is, in part, Khalistan oriented and based on an ideal theocratic government through secession and partition of the Indian nation-state.[52] There are claims of financial support from Sikhs outside India to attract youths into pro-Khalistan terrorist groups.[53]

Gurdwara

There are several significant institutions and cultural processes—both local and global—that are necessary for both expanding and preserving the Sikh diaspora (roughly thirty million Sikhs worldwide). The diaspora has energized youths to join the Khalistan insurgency. One of these local institutions and cultural processes is the gurdwara. Actually speaking, the **gurdwara** is the physical space in which the Sikh congregation assembles in the presence of its most important holy scriptures. It is a place for organizing the Sikh community into strategic geographic locations and synchronizing various cultural responsibilities.[54] Symbolically speaking, the gurdwara is a holy site of galvanization of the Sikh diaspora for the Khalistan movement both directly through fundraising, and indirectly through propagandizing a greatly stylized version of the Sikh conflict and their history. For instance, many walls in gurdwaras often display photos of recent "martyrs" from the Sikh-Hindu conflict. The photos are often juxtaposed with portrayals of historical martyrs from the archives of Sikh history.[55] Gurdwaras strengthen connections between the diaspora and the Punjab through the soliciting and gathering of voluntary contributions for humanitarian, political, and social causes within the Sikh community. Not surprisingly, gurdwaras also serve to endorse and reinforce Sikh terrorist organizations, pro-Khalistan leaders, and any type of pro-Khalistan institutions worldwide.[56]

CHRISTIAN TERRORISM

Christian terrorism consists of terrorist attacks committed by groups or individuals who appeal to Christian motives or goals for their actions. Just like many types of religious terrorists, Christian terrorists have used unique interpretations of the principles of faith—in this case, the Bible. Christian groups have quoted both the Old Testament and New Testament to warrant killing or to try to cause the "end times" described in the Book of Revelation.[57] When Christian extremism is based on selectively used biblical verses or a reinterpretation of certain verses to create an alternate version of the Christian religion, it is called **freewheeling fundamentalism**.[58] Likewise, when Christian extremism adheres to the belief that the world should be governed through a theocratic Christian dictatorship, it is called **dominionism**.[59]

Antiabortion Violence

Antiabortion violence is a form of pro-life terrorism based on an expression of moral indignation of abortion; the pro-life terrorist considers abortion as murder. Antiabortion violence has been identified as a form of Christian terrorism.[60] In Canada, it is called **single-issue terrorism**, a category of terrorism that seeks to resolve specific issues in order to change attitudes about these issues (e.g., pro-life, animal, and antinuclear movements).[61] Antiabortion activism tends to rely on condensing symbols. Unlike the referential symbol that has a rather straightforward meaning, a **condensing symbol** strikes deeper into the unconscious and projects its emotional quality to forms of behavior or situations that are far removed from the initial or intended meaning of the symbol. For example, the fetus represents a powerful condensing symbol for the antiabortion activist; it symbolizes babies, birth, motherhood, family values, and life itself.[62]

Abortion doctors have been attacked when entering clinics. For example, in 1993, a lone terrorist killed Dr. David Gunn as he was walking into a clinic in Pensacola, Florida. Michael Griffin, the doctor's killer, felt that God instructed him to give Gunn one last warning. When Gunn dismissed the threat, Griffin shot him three times in the back. To Michael Griffin, tolerating the status quo was more evil than resorting to extreme violence in order to change behavior.[63] In a similar vein, the **Army of God (AOG)** is a Christian terrorist organization focused on antiabortion, particularly against abortion clinics in the United States. In 1985 alone, the AOG's East Coast chapter claimed responsibility for bombing seven abortion clinics in Maryland, Virginia, and Washington, DC.[64] The AOG also believes that homosexuals are "disgusting" and uses Leviticus 18:22 as a biblical foundation to target gays and lesbians.[65]

Christian Identity Movement

The **Christian Identity Movement** combines poisonous antigovernment politics with an apocalyptic, end-of-the-world vision. This ideologically and emotionally unites its adherents with one another. The very concept of **Christian Identity** is the posterity of British Israelism, a nineteenth-century philosophy based on the premise that white Christians are the real Israelites.[66] Barkun (1995)[67] identifies three key beliefs of Christian Identity. First, Christian Identity postulates that white "Aryans" are the progenies of the biblical tribes of ancient Israel, and, thus, their purpose on earth is to do God's work. Second, Christian Identity maintains that Jews have no historical connection to the Israelites; rather, they are the biological descendants of Lucifer and Eve in the Garden of Eden. Third, Christian Identity posits that the earth is on the brink of a final cleansing turning point, an apocalyptic clash between good and evil. This struggle requires Aryans to wage war against the global Zionist conspiracy. Therefore, the movement preaches that the United States is a divinely gifted white Christian holy land to be conquered through an apocalyptic battle against the Jewish-controlled U.S. government, race traitors, and deviant subgroups.

A central narrative for Christian Identity patriots is the biblical story of Phineas, who killed a tribal chief and his foreign-born concubine for not following the prohibition against interracial marriage. Thanks to this cruel murder, Phineas "cleansed" the community that had condoned "whoredom and the daughters of Moab" (Numbers 25:11–13). Christian Identity has used this biblical story as a valid source for oppressing and murdering interracial couples and other nonwhites (whom they call "mud people"). A good indicator for any group's penchant for violence is the nature of its central narrative. As Stern (1999)[68] explains it, "groups that model themselves on an avenging angel or a vindictive god (such as Christ with a sword, or

Phineas) are more likely to lash out than those whose core myth is the suffering Messiah" (p. 72). One of the by-products of the Phineas story was the creation of a Christian terrorist organization called the **Phineas Priesthood** (or **Phineas Priests**), a radical Christian Identity movement comprising white supremacists, antiabortionists, and environmental and animal rights activists.

A prominent player who champions violence in the Christian Identity Movement is **Louis Beam**. Beam, a former Ku Klux Klan (KKK) member, has developed a model for leaderless resistance among whites. **Leaderless resistance** is a strategy whereby one person (or a very small, highly cohesive unit) mounts acts of antigovernment terrorism independent of any command structure or support network. In the 1980s, Beam became a strong advocate for the overthrow of the federal state.[69] He encouraged white militants to create lone-wolf terrorist cells, small underground units ready to strike the government, thereby eliminating the need for supervision or leadership.[70] This strategy was outlined in *The Seditionist*, his newsletter, in 1992. Beam also introduced, to white racists and Identity Christians, the use of the internet for communication. In fact, he developed the first white supremacist internet site. He has been associated with numerous terrorist plots, including federal-building bombings and damages to railroads. In 1987, he was included on the FBI's Ten Most Wanted List. Beam has the shady honor of being the contact person for white anarchists bent on assassinating federal officials, civil rights leaders, blacks, homosexuals, and others.[71]

Christian Terrorism of the IRA

For IRA terrorists, their formative years and socialization are strongly ingrained within Catholicism. Many former IRA members still live in predominantly Catholic milieus. Catholicism is an essential component of IRA members' social identity and political idealism. It regulates their daily life and consciousness.[72] Although Catholic communities are rather small, homogeneous, and isolated, they are typified by strongly interconnected matriarchal families, with a very conventional, communal way of life. In rural areas, this very much resembles the social structure of peasant society, a model peasant culture that is transplanted into urban Catholic circles through the ideals of ethnic nationalism.[73] It is a religious society with many churchgoers: the priest plays a key role, and the church itself provides and regulates the school curriculum, as well as social and health facilities. The hub of the community is invariably the church building itself.[74] As Sean O'Callaghan (1999),[75] a former high-ranking IRA member, recalls,

> The Irish Catholic Church was the single most influential institution in daily life. We learned that God and Irish nationalism marched hand in hand to a tune shrouded in mystery but which was always clear to the faithful. We were taught, over and over again, as part of our daily school routine, that Irish Catholics were special to God. (p. 34)

Perhaps this is the reason why the IRA has survived, unlike the average Western terrorist group, which has a life expectancy of around two to six years.[76] Prominent Catholic icons became the symbols of Republicanism. In murals of Republican areas in Belfast, one can see the daily unification of Republican nationalism and Catholicism. The imagery of subjugated and persecuted Ireland relies on Catholic symbols, such as Mother Ireland and the Virgin Mary, suffering and supplicant.[77] As O'Callaghan (1999)[78] recalls of his schooldays, the Virgin Mary was depicted as an Irish colleen. As he continues, "Padraig Pearse and the other rebel leaders executed by the British after the Easter rising of 1916 were painstakingly interwoven with images of Christ and Catholic martyrs into a seamless mix of blood sacrifice for faith and fatherland" (p. 35).

The Irish people became the Christian soul created in God's image and likeness. National freedom bore the four marks of the Christian religion: unity, sanctity, catholicity, and apostolic succession. The **Easter Rising** of 1916, an armed insurrection mounted by Irish Republicans to end British rule in Ireland and establish an independent Irish Republic, was the most important event in Irish Republicanism.[79] The Easter Rising was created almost entirely in the sacrificial and symbolic terms of Irish Catholicism. In this framework, the act alone represented a pure and unsullied image, a non-erasable image implanted in people's minds and that carried its own message. The Easter Rising was its own act of revelation. In no way was it a guileful conspiracy of political calculation. Rather, it was a heroic and sacrificial act that provided ritual roles for players and offered an image of salvation. It was a symbolic gesture designed to evoke a spirit of rebellion by conjuring up the sacrificial image of Christ on the cross. The latter served as a role model for national redemption.[80] Each year, at Easter, Irish tricolors are hung on telephone poles and painted on walls and streets to commemorate the Easter Rising of 1916. It has remained a symbol of what could be accomplished by God-led spiritual power.[81]

In Catholicism, the **Mass** is a symbolic act in which people participate in the **Eucharist** (the act of Christ's sacrifice), or **Holy Communion**. The IRA exploited the Mass by transforming it into a ritualistic campaign for self-sacrifice. The Easter Rising propelled the cult of self-sacrifice to the forefront of twentieth-century Irish militancy in a peculiar combination of Catholicism and Republicanism. After capturing many Easter Rising Irish militants and executing sixteen of its leaders, the British government transformed them into martyrs, then secular saints. By the same token, it preserved their immortality. The executions reinforced the sacrificial motif of Mass. The very concept of Mass, then, was warped and co-opted into a cult for dead leaders and martyrs-to-be. The process was still overflowing with Catholic traditions and themes—for example, linking heroes with the sacrifice of Christ, the ageless martyrs and heroes, and the esteemed dead from previous insurgencies.[82] The objective of sacrifice is to connect the unconnected, particularly those of Catholic salvation and Republican purity. As Lévi-Strauss (1966)[83] observed, "Sacrifice seeks to establish a desired connection between two initially separate domains" (p. 225). It is also important to note that a strong relationship exists between Republican violence, Catholicism, and a pan-Celtic ethos focused on the redeeming character of blood sacrifice. Catholics in Northern Ireland often call to mind the symbolic meaning of "martyrs for the cause," or Christ-like figures. This was illustrated by the deaths of Patrick Pearse in the 1916 Easter Rising and Bobby Sands in the 1981 hunger strikes.[84]

Christian Militant Serbs

Christian militant Serbs adopted a brutal method of ethnic cleansing to remove Muslims scattered across Serb-dominated areas. This caused a civil war that claimed the lives of 200,000 people and caused 2 million people to be refugees.[85] Between 1991 and 1994, sixteen mosques were destroyed in Banja Luka, Bosnia-Herzegovina. Most of these were methodically dynamited and bulldozed, despite the fact that the Serbians encountered no resistance from the Muslims. Banja Luka was under Serb national control during the course of the war. The destruction made reconstruction unachievable. The intensified method of destruction of religious structures illustrates the significance of religious symbols as the social glue to group identity.[86]

The nationalist aspect of the Serb Christian militancy was reflected in **Christoslavism**, an ideology postulating that Slavs are intrinsically Christian.[87] A particular Christian discourse promoted by radical Serbs was based on the martyrdom of Saint Lazar, a Serbian prince killed by the Ottoman Empire at the Battle of Kosovo in 1389. Indeed, Serb Christian militancy was also observed in great depth in Kosovo, which was once part of Serbia in the Middle Ages. For Serbs, Lazar's death symbolized unpardonable defeat by the Ottoman forces. Nevertheless, Serbian nationalist discourses depicted Lazar as a fabulous, Christ-like figure. On the other hand, Lazar's opponents, including Serbs who betrayed him, were described as "Christ killers." In the 1990s, radical Serbs defined the Muslims of Kosovo and Bosnia-Herzegovina in the same terms: Christ killers. They employed this discourse to justify their atrocities against Muslims in the areas they wanted to control.[88]

Using conspicuously religious terms, Serbian Christian narratives continually represented Kosovo as the sacred site of (1) the martyrdom of Lazar, (2) the Serbian Orthodox Church itself, and (3) the Orthodox churches and monasteries overall. Consequently, in 1939, upon commemorating the 550th anniversary of Lazar's death, an Orthodox bishop stated about Kosovo, "Beside the name of Christ, no other name is more beautiful or more sacred," and another one said of the region that it was "our national Golgotha and at the same time our national resurrection" (Emmert, 1990, p. 139).[89] This religious discourse contributed tremendously to the revival of Serbian nationalism when Yugoslavia collapsed. This was obvious when Lazar's relics were relocated from Belgrade to a monastery in Kosovo in 1989. Parts of his relics were also circulating among Serbian villagers in the early 1990s. Still today, paintings of the 1389 Battle of Kosovo can be found in many Serbian homes.[90]

JEWISH TERRORISM

Symbolism in terrorism has also been used by Jewish terrorist organizations like Irgun and the Stern Gang (also known as Lehi) in the 1930s and 1940s, coinciding with the last years of the British mandate in Palestine. Assassination was an efficient tactic. For example, Lord Moyne, a member of Churchill's cabinet, was killed in 1944, and Count Bernadotte, a UN high commissioner, was killed in 1948—both by the Stern Gang. The purpose was simple: to symbolically articulate the impracticalities and inappropriateness of British rule in Palestine. The victims were chosen based on their popularity among the Brits. In other words, British public opinion, easily swayed by those killings, would call for an end to the conflict and the release of Palestine. In another instance, two British Army sergeants were abducted and found hanging. Yet, Jewish terrorists' biggest achievement was the explosion of the King David Hotel in Jerusalem in 1946 (this time, by Irgun). The British rule had its headquarters in that hotel. More than ninety people—mostly Arab, British, and Jewish—perished in that explosion.[91]

Zealots: The First Big Terrorist Organization

In the first century AD, during the Roman Empire, the **Zealots** were a Jewish terrorist group involved in violent acts against the Romans, who had occupied Israel since 63 BC, and their "collaborators." They are considered the first big organized terrorist organization in human history. As Jews, the Zealots refused to pay taxes to Rome and to acknowledge the authority of the Roman emperor. A splinter terrorist group of the Zealots were the **Sicarii**. "Sicarii" derived from the word **sica**, a small dagger to kill targets.[92] Most Zealots were Sicarii simultaneously. The Zealots reasoned that direct action through violence was the best way to facilitate the process of religious liberation. Increasingly, Romans started to defile Jewish institutions, and, as a result, more and more frustrated Jews joined the Zealots' rebellious group. As time passed, they formed an extensive web of terrorists and a major information network. This helped terrorists gash the Romans' throats.[93]

What came subsequently was a Jewish revolt in 66 AD, after Florus, the last Roman procurator, seized a large amount of silver from the Jerusalem Temple. An estimated one million Jews, inspired by Talmudic conviction, launched a mass uprising against not only the Romans but also the Greeks in Judea. As such, the Zealots ambushed Roman patrols, sabotaged military stores, stole horses, damaged roads and water works, and poisoned water wells, granaries, and other food supplies of Jerusalem.[94] Through such actions, the Zealots hoped to act as the catalysts of a long-prophesized messianic intervention. The objective of this was to cause **attrition warfare**, a strategy to wear down the enemy. In this case, the terrified Roman oppressor would either give up or show little resistance out of fear of being outnumbered. Unfortunately, history records that, in 73 AD, the Zealots retreated to Masada, a fortification overlooking the Dead Sea, and committed mass suicide upon learning that the Romans had given them no possibility of escape.[95]

Symbolic Attacks on Muslims

In regard to Jerusalem, messianic expectations have also been observed in plans by radical Jewish organizations to assault Muslim sacred sites. Already in 1948, Irgun went to the Palestinian village of Dir Yassin and killed 254 innocent Muslim villagers. Zionist symbolism was deepened with the 1969 arson attack on the Al-Aqsa mosque by Denis Michael Rohan, a pro-Zionism extremist. Later, in 1982, Jewish fanatics planned to blow up Temple Mount in order to spark a cataclysmic war between Muslims and Jews.[96] It was the most extreme terrorist attempt at wounding Muslims. The terrorists themselves were caught by Israeli police forces after having amassed explosives to destroy the mosques within al-Haram al-Sharif (Arabic for "Temple Mount"). The Temple Mount Faithful, a religious Zionist group, has proclaimed its intention to lay the foundations for a new Jewish Temple there.[97]

On February 25, 1994, the day of the second Muslim Sabbath during Ramadan (Islam's holy month), **Baruch Goldstein**, an American-born Zionist, from the settlement of Kiryat Arba, entered the well-attended Ibrahim Mosque. The mosque was located in Hebron on the West Bank. Goldstein emptied three thirty-five-shot magazines with his automatic assault rifle into the assembly of 800 Palestinian Muslims, slaying twenty-nine and wounding 150 of them, before being subdued and killed in the process.[98] A lifelong adept of the Kach movement (a radical Jewish fundamentalist group), Baruch Goldstein was driven by a complex mélange of highly desirable political and religious goals. He was fueled by fanaticism and an acute sense of betrayal as Yitzhak Rabin, the prime minister of Israel (at that time), was taking Israel out of its God-given heritage by granting large portions of land to the Palestinians.[99] Both the location and the timing of the Hebron killing were deeply soaked with religious symbolism. Hebron was the site where sixty-nine Jews were killed in 1929. In addition, the massacre took place during the Jewish holiday of Purim, which symbolically cast Goldstein as Mordechai in the Purim story. The Jewish holiday commemorates the deliverance of the Jewish people by Mordechai in the ancient Persian Empire. The story was recorded in the biblical Book of Esther. Upon looking at the big picture, the Hebron massacre could be interpreted as wreaking revenge against the enemies of the Jews.[100]

When an Israeli leader seems to be overly nice to Muslims, there may be blowback for him or her, as the Prime Minister of Israel, Yitzhak Rabin, fatally learned in 1995. On November 4, 1995, a fanatic Jewish student, Yigal Amir, killed Rabin upon acting on God's orders. Disturbed by Rabin's support of the Oslo Accords (which granted land and other concessions to the Palestinians), Yigal Amir had been inspired by militant rabbis and their selective Hebraic rulings. One of these rulings was the "Law of the Pursuer." Called *rodef* in Hebrew, the **Law of the Pursuer** is a traditional Jewish law whereby an individual must be killed by any bystander after being warned to stop an action or decision. The rule was set forth in the twelfth century by Maimonides, a Jewish scholar.[101] Yigal Amir interpreted this law as one that had to be applied against Israel's leader. Most Israelis are astonished at the idea of a Jew killing another Jew, but Rabin became the victim of a broader force characterized as one of the most dangerous and pervasive movements in the post–Cold War world: modern-day religious terrorism.[102]

SUMMARY

Hindu terrorism, also called saffron terror, thrives on the notion of Hindutva. Hindutva refers to "Hinduness" and reflects the idea that all Indians (of all backgrounds and walks of life) belong to the Hindu nation and need to be unified in a single community. A powerful symbol that Hindu nationalists have chosen to unite Hindus is the god Ram. It is such a key figure in Hindus' fusion of nationalism and religion that they destroyed the Babri Mosque in 1992 in order to erect a temple dedicated to Ram. Already in the Middle Ages, Hindu terrorists called the Thugs killed thousands of people each year to venerate Kali, the Hindu goddess of terror, destruction, empowerment, and sexuality. A modern-day Hindu faction is the Tamil ethnic group, native to India and Sri Lanka. The Tamil people want to be totally independent from the Sinhalese-led government in Sri Lanka. One of the separatist groups in support of the Tamils are the Tamil Tigers. A key symbol is the yellow tiger, a culturally important creature that represents heroism, militancy, and nationalism. The Tamil Tigers, too, use Hindu symbols in order to reinforce their nationalistic desire. For example, they have a ritual dinner with their leader in honor of Hindu gods. They also have a top suicide commando unit called the Black Tigers. In line with these contentions, Sikhism is a monotheistic religion mostly practiced in northern India. Considered a revolutionary social movement due to their rejection of the Hindu caste system, asceticism, and holiness, the Sikhs have been the target of violence, such as the desecration of the Golden Temple in Amritsar in 1984. As a result, Sikh terrorist organizations have sprung up; the ultimate objective is to establish an autonomous, sovereign Sikh state called Khalistan (which consists of the entire Punjab region). Religious terrorism has also been found in Christianity. For example, the Christian Identity Movement promotes the concept that white Christians are the real Israelites, and they need to wage war against the global Zionist conspiracy. Likewise, the actions of IRA terrorists are strongly embedded within Catholicism. In a third example, Serb Christian militancy in the late twentieth century was reflected in Christoslavism, an ideology postulating that Slavs are intrinsically Christian. As a result, many Muslims in Kosovo and Bosnia-Herzegovina were killed. Finally, Jewish terrorist organizations, like Irgun and the Stern Gang, were active in the 1930s and 1940s to eliminate British rule in Palestine. In fact, the first big organized terrorist organization in human history was Jewish: the Zealots. Today, Jewish terrorist groups have committed symbolic attacks against Muslims. A tragic example was the 1994 Hebron massacre committed by Baruch Goldstein.

NOTES

1. Bidwai, Praful (2008). Confronting the Reality of Hindutva Terrorism. *Economic and Political Weekly, 43*(47), 10–13.

2. Stump, Roger (2000). *Boundaries of Faith: Geographical Perspectives on Religious Fundamentalism.* Lanham, MD: Rowman & Littlefield.

3. Rapoport, David C. (1984). Fear and Trembling: Terrorism in Three Religious Traditions. *The American Political Science Review, 78*(3), 658–677.

4. Hardgrave, Robert (1993). India: The Dilemmas of Diversity. *Journal of Democracy, 4*(4), 54–68.

5. Hardgrave, Robert (1993). India: The Dilemmas of Diversity. *Journal of Democracy, 4*(4), 54–68.

6. Van Creveld, Martin (1993). *Nuclear Proliferation and the Future of Conflict.* New York: Free Press.

7. Rapoport, David C. (1984). Fear and Trembling: Terrorism in Three Religious Traditions. *The American Political Science Review, 78*(3), 658–677.

8. Gupta, Hiralal (1959). A Critical Study of the Thugs and Their Activities. *Journal of Indian History, 38,* 167–176.

9. Bruce, George (1968). *The Stranglers.* London: Longmans.

10. Sleeman, James (1933). *Thugs, or a Million Murders.* London: S. Low and Marston.

11. Gupta, Hiralal (1959). A Critical Study of the Thugs and Their Activities. *Journal of Indian History, 38,* 167–176.

12. Sleeman, James (1933). *Thugs, or a Million Murders.* London: S. Low and Marston.

13. Rapoport, David C. (1984). Fear and Trembling: Terrorism in Three Religious Traditions. *The American Political Science Review, 78*(3), 658–677.

14. Indrapala, K. (2005). *The Evolution of an Ethnic Identity: The Tamils of Sri Lanka.* Sydney: South Asian Studies Centre.

15. Hoffman, Bruce (2006). *Inside Terrorism.* New York: Columbia University Press

16. Schalk, Peter (2004). *Ilam-Sihala? An Assessment of an Argument.* Uppsala, Sweden: Uppsala University Press.

17. Berman, Eli, & Laitin, David (2005). *Hard Targets: Theory and Evidence on Suicide Attacks.* Cambridge, MA: National Bureau of Economic Research.

18. Gambetta, Diego (2005). *Making Sense of Suicide Missions.* Oxford: Oxford University Press.

19. Roberts, Michael (2005). Tamil Tiger "Martyrs": Regenerating Divine Potency? *Studies in Conflict & Terrorism, 28,* 493–514.

20. Schalk, Peter (1997). Resistance and Martyrdom in the Process of State Formation of Tamililam. In Joyce Pettigrew (Ed.), *Martyrdom and Political Resistance: Essays from Asia and Europe* (pp. 61–83). Amsterdam: VU University Press for Centre Asian Studies.

21. Roberts, Michael (2005). Tamil Tiger "Martyrs": Regenerating Divine Potency? *Studies in Conflict & Terrorism, 28,* 493–514.

22. Cronin, Audrey Kurth (2009). *Terrorists and Suicide Attacks.* Collingdale, PA: Diane Publishing.

23. Gunawardena, Arjuna (2006). *Female Black Tigers: A Different Breed of Cat?* Tel Aviv: The Jaffee Center for Strategic Studies.

24. Pape, Robert (2005). *Dying to Win: The Strategic Logic of Suicide Terrorism.* New York: Random House.

25. Reading, Matthew (2010). Understanding Female Suicide Terrorism in Sri Lanka through a Constructivist Lens. *Strategic Insights, 9*(1), 65–89.

26. Hoffman, Bruce, & McCormick, Gordon (2004). Terrorism, Signaling, and Suicide Attack. *Studies in Conflict and Terrorism, 27*(4), 243–281.

27. Manoharan, N. (2007). *Semiotics of Terrorism: A "Symbolic" Understanding of the LTTE.* New Delhi: Institute of Peace and Conflict Studies.

28. Manoharan, N. (2007). *Semiotics of Terrorism: A "Symbolic" Understanding of the LTTE.* New Delhi: Institute of Peace and Conflict Studies.

29. Tamil Information Centre (2001). *Tamils of Sri Lanka: The Quest for Human Dignity.* London: Tamil Information Centre.

30. Swamy, M. R. Narayan (1994). *Tigers of Lanka: From Boys to Guerrillas.* Delhi: Konark.

31. Swamy, M. R. Narayan (1994). *Tigers of Lanka: From Boys to Guerrillas.* Delhi: Konark.

32. Senaratne, Jagath (1997). *Political Violence in Sri Lanka, 1977–1990: Riots, Insurrections, Counterinsurgencies, Foreign Intervention.* Amsterdam: VU University Press.

33. Swamy, M. R. Narayan (1994). *Tigers of Lanka: From Boys to Guerrillas.* Delhi: Konark.

34. Joshi, Manoj (1996). On the Razor's Edge: The Liberation Tigers of Tamil Eelam. *Studies in Conflict and Terrorism, 19,* 19–42.

35. Singh, Khushwant (2006). *The Illustrated History of the Sikhs.* New Delhi, India: Oxford University Press.

36. Singh, Patwant (1999). *The Sikhs.* New York: Doubleday.

37. James, Paul (2006). *Globalism, Nationalism, Tribalism: Bringing Theory Back In.* Thousand Oaks, CA: Sage.

38. Gupte, Pranay (1985, August 9). The Punjab: Torn by Terror. *The New York Times,* p. A1.

39. Fair, Christine (2005). Diaspora Involvement in Insurgencies: Insights from the Khalistan and Tamil Eelam Movements. *Nationalism and Ethnic Politics, 11*(1), 125–156.

40. Kumar, Ram Narayan (1996). *The Sikh Unrest and the Indian State*. New Delhi, India: Ajanta.

41. Jakobsh, Doris (2008). 3HO/Sikh Dharma of the Western Hemisphere: The "Forgotten" New Religious Movement? *Religion Compass, 2*, 385–408.

42. Pettigrew, Joyce (1991). Songs of the Sikh Resistance Movement. *Asian Music, 23*(1), 85–118.

43. Girard, René (1989). *The Scapegoat*. Baltimore: Johns Hopkins University Press.

44. Pettigrew, Joyce (1991). Songs of the Sikh Resistance Movement. *Asian Music, 23*(1), 85–118.

45. Bagga, Rishi (2006). Living by the Sword: The Free Exercise of Religion and the Sikh Struggle for the Right to Carry a Kirpan. *Bepress Legal Series, 902*, 1–31.

46. Juergensmeyer, Mark (2000). *Terror in the Mind of God: The Global Rise of Religious Violence*. Berkeley: University of California Press.

47. Gunawardena, Sue (2000). Constructing Cybernationalism: Sikh Solidarity via the Internet. *International Journal of Punjab Studies, 7*(2), 263–322.

48. McClymond, Michael, & Freedman, David (2010). Religious Traditions, Violence and Nonviolence. In George Fink (Ed.), *Stress of War, Conflict and Disaster* (pp. 397–407). Waltham, MA: Academic Press.

49. Bagga, Rishi (2006). Living by the Sword: The Free Exercise of Religion and the Sikh Struggle for the Right to Carry a Kirpan. *Bepress Legal Series, 902*, 1–31.

50. Dusenbery, Verne (1995). A Sikh Diaspora? Contested Identities and Constructed Realities. In Peter van der Veer (Ed.), *Nation and Migration: The Politics of Space in the South Asian Diaspora* (pp. 17–42). Philadelphia: University of Pennsylvania Press.

51. Stump, Roger (2000). *Boundaries of Faith: Geographical Perspectives on Religious Fundamentalism*. Lanham, MD: Rowman & Littlefield.

52. Virupakshiah, H. M. (2009). *Terrorism Challenge Diplomacy*. New Delhi, India: Concept Publishing.

53. BBC News Channel (2008, March 4). Sikh Separatists "Funded from UK." Retrieved April 29, 2013, from http://news.bbc.co.uk/2/hi/programmes/file_on_4/7263211.stm

54. Fair, C. Christine (2005). Diaspora Involvement in Insurgencies: Insights from the Khalistan and Tamil Eelam Movements. *Nationalism and Ethnic Politics, 11*(1), 125–156.

55. Fenech, Louis (2001). *Martyrdom in the Sikh Tradition: Playing the "Game of Love."* Oxford: Oxford University Press.

56. Fair, Christine (2005). Diaspora Involvement in Insurgencies: Insights from the Khalistan and Tamil Eelam Movements. *Nationalism and Ethnic Politics, 11*(1), 125–156.

57. Juergensmeyer, Mark (2000). *Terror in the Mind of God: The Global Rise of Religious Violence*. Berkeley: University of California Press.

58. White, Jonathan (2011). *Terrorism & Homeland Security* (7th ed.). Belmont, CA: Wadsworth.

59. Worrell, Mark (2013). *Terror: Social, Political, and Economic Perspectives*. New York: Routledge.

60. Simonsen, Clifford, & Spindlove, Jeremy (2007). *Terrorism Today: The Past, the Players, and the Future*. Upper Saddle River, NJ: Prentice Hall.

61. Monaghan, Rachel (2000). Single-Issue Terrorism: A Neglected Phenomenon? *Studies in Conflict & Terrorism, 23*(4), 255–265.

62. Jasper, James (2008). *The Art of Moral Protest: Culture, Biography, and Creativity in Social Movements*. Chicago: University of Chicago Press.

63. White, Jonathan (2011). *Terrorism & Homeland Security* (7th ed.). Belmont, CA: Wadsworth.

64. Bray, Michael (1994). *A Time to Kill: A Study Concerning the Use of Force and Abortion*. Portland, OR: Advocates for Life Publications.

65. Altum, Justin (2003). Anti-Abortion Extremism: The Army of God. *Chrestomathy: Annual Review of Undergraduate Research at the College of Charleston, 2*, 1–12.

66. Hough, George (2006). American Terrorism and the Christian Identity Movement: A Proliferation Threat from Non-State Actors. *International Journal of Applied Psychoanalytic Studies, 3*(1), 79–100.

67. Barkun, Michael (1995). *Religion and the Racist Right: The Origins of the Christian Identity Movement*. Chapel Hill: University of North Carolina Press.

68. Stern, Jessica (1999). *The Ultimate Terrorists*. Cambridge, MA: Harvard University Press.

69. Kaplan, Jeffrey (1997). Leaderless Resistance. *Terrorism and Political Violence, 9*(3), 80–95.

70. Southern Poverty Law Center (1998). *Intelligence Report*. Montgomery, AL: Southern Poverty Law Center.

71. Sharpe, Tanya Telfair (2000). The Identity Christian Movement: Ideology of Domestic Terrorism. *Journal of Black Studies, 30*(4), 604–623.

72. Tonge, Jonathan (1998). *Northern Ireland: Conflict and Change*. Hemel Hempstead, UK: Prentice Hall.

73. Clark, Robert (1984). *The Basque Insurgents: ETA, 1952–1980*. London: University of Wisconsin Press.

74. Dingley, James (2001). The Bombing of Omagh, 15 August 1998: The Bombers, Their Tactics, Strategy, and Purpose behind the Incident. *Studies in Conflict & Terrorism, 24*(6), 451–465.

75. O'Callaghan, Sean (1999). *The Informer*. London: Corgi.

76. Hoffman, Bruce (1998). *Inside Terrorism*. London: Gollancz.

77. Buckley, Anthony D. (Ed.) (1998). *Symbols in Northern Ireland*. Belfast: Institute of Irish Studies, Queen's University Belfast.

78. O'Callaghan, Sean (1999). *The Informer*. London: Corgi.

79. MacDonagh, Oliver (1977). *Ireland: The Union and Its Aftermath*. Crows Nest, Australia: George Allen & Unwin.

80. MacDonagh, Oliver (1983). *States of Mind*. London: Allen & Unwin.

81. Cashman, Ray (2008). Visions of Irish Nationalism. *Journal of Folklore Research, 45*(3), 361–381.

82. Sweeney, George (1993). Self-Immolation in Ireland: Hunger Strikes and Political Confrontation. *Anthropology Today, 9*(5), 10–14.

83. Lévi-Strauss, Claude (1966). *The Savage Mind*. Chicago: University of Chicago Press.

84. Feehan, John (1986). *Bobby Sands and the Tragedy of Northern Ireland*. Dublin: The Permanent Press.

85. Lopasic, Alexander (1996). The Muslims of Bosnia. In Gerd Nonneman, Tim Niblock, & Bogdan Szajkowski (Eds.), *Muslim Communities in the New Europe* (pp. 99–114). Reading, UK: Ithaca.

86. Dodds, Jerrilynn (1998). Bridge over the Neretva. *Archaeology, 51*, 48–52.

87. Sells, Michael (1996). *The Bridge Betrayed: Religion and Genocide in Bosnia*. Berkeley: University of California Press.

88. Sells, Michael (1996). *The Bridge Betrayed: Religion and Genocide in Bosnia*. Berkeley: University of California Press.

89. Emmert, Thomas (1990). *Serbian Golgotha: Kosovo, 1389*. New York: Columbia University Press.

90. Stump, Roger (2005). Religion and the Geographies of War. In Colin Flint (Ed.), *The Geography of War and Peace: From Death Camps to Diplomats* (pp. 149–173). Oxford: Oxford University Press.

91. O'Shaughnessy, Nicholas, & Baines, Paul (2009). Selling Terror: The Symbolization and Positioning of Jihad. *Marketing Theory, 9*(2), 227–241.

92. Laqueur, Walter (1999). *Terrorism and History*. Oxford: Oxford University Press; and Smith, Morton (1971). Zealots and Sicarii: Their Origins and Relation. *Harvard Theological Review, 64*, 1–19.

93. Roth, Cecil (1959). The Zealots in the War of 66–73. *Journal of Semitic Studies, 4*, 332–355.

94. Bloom, James (2002). *The Roman-Judaeo War of 66–74 AD: A Military Analysis*. Rochester, NY: Sage.

95. Jacobson, David (2006). The Northern Palace at Masada: Herod's Ship of the Desert? *Palestine Exploration Quarterly, 138*(2), 99–117.

96. Husain, Mir Zohair (1995). *Global Islamic Politics*. New York: HarperCollins.

97. Stump, Roger (2000). *Boundaries of Faith: Geographical Perspectives on Religious Fundamentalism*. Lanham, MD: Rowman & Littlefield.

98. Ranstorp, Magnus (1996). Terrorism in the Name of Religion. *Journal of International Affairs, 50*(1), 41–63.

99. Cohen-Almagor, Raphael (1994). Vigilant Jewish Fundamentalism: From the JDL to Kach (or "Shalom Jews, Shalom Dogs"). *Terrorism and Political Violence, 4*(1), 44–66.

100. Hedges, Chris, & Greenberg, Joel (1994, February 28). West Bank Massacre: Before Killing, a Final Prayer and a Final Taunt. *The New York Times*, p. A1.

101. Ranstorp, Magnus (1996). Terrorism in the Name of Religion. *Journal of International Affairs, 50*(1), 41–63.

102. Kifner, John (1995, November 19). A Son of Israel: Rabin's Assassin. *The New York Times*, p. A1.

Chapter Nine

Islamist Terrorism

GLOBAL SUPPORT FOR ISLAMIST TERRORISM

On April 30, 2013, a Pew Research Center survey of Muslims worldwide found that many of them are deeply committed to Islam and want sharia (Islamic law) to be the only law of the land (i.e., in their personal lives, politics, and society in general). The survey involved over 38,000 face-to-face interviews (in more than eighty languages) with Muslims in Europe, Asia, the Middle East, and Africa. One question in the survey was whether they support suicide bombings and violence against civilians: 72 percent disagreed. Nevertheless, 28 percent fully agreed or did not mind terrorist violence against civilians. Mathematically speaking, 28 percent of 1.6 billion Muslims would be equivalent to about 450 million. As the study continues, in the United States, 81 percent responded that suicide bombings and similar acts against civilians are *never* justified. This means that 19 percent of U.S. Muslims are not firmly opposed to terrorist violence against civilians. [1] Below are additional statistics on support for Islamist terrorism worldwide, based on various sources:

- Forty percent of British Muslims want sharia in Britain, and 20 percent of them feel sympathy toward the Al Qaeda suicide terrorists responsible for the London bombings of July 7, 2005. [2]
- Sixteen percent of Muslim youths in Belgium consider terrorism "acceptable." [3]
- Among Muslim youths in the West, 42 percent of young Muslims in France, 35 percent in Britain, 29 percent in Spain, 26 percent in the United States, and 22 percent in Germany believe that suicide bombings against civilians are justified. [4]
- U.S. Muslims who identify more strongly with their Muslim faith are three times more likely to consider suicide terrorism against civilians a justifiable tactic. [5]
- Only 81 percent of Muslims in the United States believe that suicide terrorism against civilians is *never* justified. [6]
- Eighty-three percent of Palestinian, 62 percent of Jordanian, 61 percent of Egyptian, 42 percent of Turkish, 38 percent of Moroccan, and 41 percent of Pakistani Muslims approve of attacks on Americans. Only a minority of Muslims disagree entirely with terror attacks on Americans. And about 50 percent of those opposed to attacking Americans are nevertheless sympathetic with Al Qaeda's attacks against the United States. [7]
- Fifty-five percent of Jordanian, 45 percent of Nigerian, 43 percent of Indonesian, and 30 percent of Egyptian Muslims have a positive view of Hezbollah. [8]

- Sixty percent of Jordanian, 49 percent of Egyptian, 49 percent of Nigerian, and 39 percent of Indonesian Muslims have a positive view of Hamas.[9]

Upon looking at these staggering statistics, it is no wonder why Muslims support terrorism more than any other religious group. In chapter 3, it was mentioned that, according to the RAND Corporation, in 2000–2010, 96 percent of the victims of terrorism in the Western world were victims of Islamic terrorism. This datum sends an unequivocal message: extreme violence in Islam is not regarded as a tactic of last resort. Jenkins (2011)[10] noted that, by 2010, more than 175 individuals in the United States had already been charged, arrested, or identified as jihadists or Al Qaeda sympathizers since 9/11. This chapter examines the symbolic reasons for espousing jihad, Salafism, the idea of the caliphate, and other radical methods.

VIOLENCE AGAINST UNBELIEVERS IN THE QUR'AN

Al Qaeda and other Muslim terrorist groups point the finger at U.S. intervention in the Middle East and Israeli actions toward the Palestinians for triggering the September 11, 2001, and other terrorist attacks. Yet, until the tragic day of 9/11, the United States had sent troops to Latin America much more and for a longer time, but had caused very little terrorism to happen from there (in comparison with the Middle East). Likewise, in the 1980s, Algerian terrorists targeted foreign tourists, businesspeople, diplomats, as well as Algerian citizens themselves for being "too un-Islamic" (e.g., women not wearing a veil, people being too attracted to Western culture, etc.). And China's communist leaders are far less concerned about Tibetan Buddhists attacking Beijing than Russia's leaders fear Islamic Chechens bombing Moscow (which has happened many times). A yearning for national independence, political oppression, or Western imperialism is insufficient to explain why Islamist groups have killed far more innocent civilians than non-Muslim terrorist organizations in similar circumstances.[11]

Then, where does the violence in the Muslim doctrine come from? To what degree is the use of violence important or necessary in Islam? Is Islam determined to obliterate non-Muslim civilizations? The best answers to such questions go beyond mere opinions. Examining facts—based on content analysis and measurements—is not only the essential basis for critical thought; it also allows scholars to resolve pressing questions. By analyzing the foundational scriptures of Islam, one can measure the importance of ideas by looking at how many concepts or phrases are used. For many Muslims, the foundational text is the Qur'an. Meaning "recitation" in Arabic, the **Qur'an** is the main religious text in Islam, which Muslims believe is the verbatim word of Allah given to the Prophet Muhammad. Muslims view the Qur'an as the main miracle of Muhammad, which was revealed to him word for word through the angel Gabriel.[12] The Qur'an is used along with the hadiths to decode and apply sharia. A **hadith** is a collection of sayings by Muhammad. His sayings are acts of approval or disapproval ascribed to Muhammad.[13]

The Qur'an frequently makes claims, in its verses, that it is divinely ordained, an assertion that Muslims believe, as they argue that it is innately and naturally impossible for humans to create a text like the Qur'an. In fact, the Qur'an is the most self-referential religious text. Muslims consider it to be a guide, a reflection of Muhammad's prophecies, and the truth of the religion. In Qur'an 25:33, the holy text is "the clear truth and the best explanation"; in Qur'an 16:89, it is a revelation that was achieved "to make everything clear." According to Scruton (2002),[14] "matters which, in Western societies, are resolved by negotiation, compromise, and the laborious work of offices and committees are [under Islamic rule] the object of immovable and eternal decrees, either laid down explicitly in the holy book [the Qur'an]" (p. 91). It is also mentioned ninety-one times that Muhammad is the perfect Muslim, the divine human embodiment, and the only model acceptable to Allah.[15]

The Qur'an comprises 114 chapters of diverging lengths, each called a **sura** (chapter). Suras are categorized as either Meccan or Medinan. The early Meccan Qur'an is more peaceful, poetic, and religious. The later Medinan Qur'an is more brutal and political. This difference stems from the fact that, in Mecca, Muhammad was merely a religious leader. In Medina, he became a political and military leader as well.[16] Between the Meccan and Medinan verses, there is a drastic difference in tone, subject, and word choice between the two texts. The Qur'an devotes 64 percent of its verses to the subject of the unbeliever (called *kafir* in Arabic).[17] This suggests that the unbeliever is important in Islamic doctrine. Not only are there two Qur'ans, Meccan and Medinan, that are different in tone, subject, and word choice, but also the Qur'an has a certain number of verses that contradict each other. Below are two examples:

- **Qur'an 8:61**: "If your enemy inclines toward peace, then you too should seek peace and put your trust in Allah" versus **Qur'an 47:35**: "Do not weaken and call for peace."
- **Qur'an 109:6**: "To you your religion, and to me my religion" versus **Qur'an 2:191**: "Slay them wherever you find People of the Book [i.e., mostly Jews and Christians]."

Which verse reflects true Islam? The answer is located within the interpretation of Qur'an 2:106, called the Principle of Abrogation. The **Principle of Abrogation** is a tenet in the Qur'an to resolve the contradictions between Meccan and Medinan verses. According to that principle, in regard to any controversial topic (e.g., killing, treatment of infidels, and ethics), the later (Medinan) verse abrogates (i.e., has precedence over) the earlier (Meccan) verse. Hence, since the more violent Medinan guidelines were written after the Meccan rules, they have precedence over the more peaceful verses. The few verses of tolerance and peace are to be abrogated by the many that call for Muslims to fight and subjugate unbelievers until they choose one of three options: accept humiliation, convert to Islam, or get killed. This is exemplified in Qur'an 9:29: "Fight those who believe not in Allah . . . the People of the Book, until they pay the *jizya* ['tax' for non-Muslims] with willing submission, and feel themselves subdued."

This explanation leads scholars to focus more specifically on Islam in and of itself, and not just its "distortion" by the terrorists.[18] The Qur'an contains at least 109 verses that call Muslims to wage war with unbelievers to uphold Islamic rule. Some verses are graphic, with orders to sever heads and fingers and kill non-Muslims wherever they may be found. Muslims who do not agree to fight unbelievers are called "hypocrites" and are warned that Allah will send them to Hell. (See Box 9.1.)

BOX 9.1: IJTIHAD

By and large, **ijtihad** refers to an interpretation of the Qur'an that allows Muslims to revisit Islamic history and use it to validate their theological understandings of the Qur'an.[1] Today, it heavily influences the decision-making process in Islamic jurisprudence across the globe. Through the provision of ijtihad, the Qur'an permits Muslims to interpret its principles so that they can suit changing times and needs (both private and public) in Islamic communities. From this perspective, Islamic scholars and leaders in Muslim nations can interpret the Qur'an's more specific or outdated discourses by modifying them to fulfill regional objectives in accordance with the will of Allah. For example, ijtihad urges Muslims to find Qur'anic verses that allow them to fight un-Islamic forces (e.g., non-Muslim invasions, un-Islamic governance, and anything that threatens Islam's sovereignty) in order to bring about religious rectitude and protect full religious observance. In this process, the Qur'an encourages strict adherence to certain Medinan verses that could give credence and empowerment to violent war.[2]

Islamists use ijtihad to emphasize aspects of pure, traditional Islam that delineate the geopolitical conditions that are so necessary for upholding the foundations of Islamic law. A certain number of historical verses that are meaningful to the theological understandings and methodology of Islamists pertain to Muhammad's life as a warrior, the subhuman nature of the People of the Book, the paradisiac rewards for dying as a martyr, and the virtues of Islam's Golden Age. These verses describe how the holy warriors were used by Muhammad to overpower non-Muslims and bring Islamic dominance in Mecca and Medina. In turn, these verses have deeply influenced the propensity toward extreme violence within modern-day Muslim societies.[3] Additionally, the Golden Age is regarded as a religious condition to be emulated because the war waged by Muhammad was a central tenet of that Golden Age.[4]

[1] Hallaq, Wael (2005). *The Origins and Evolution of Islamic Law*. Cambridge: Cambridge University Press.

[2] Venkatraman, Amritha (2007). Religious Basis for Islamic Terrorism: The Quran and Its Interpretations. *Studies in Conflict & Terrorism, 30*(3), 229–248.

[3] Schwartz, Stephen (2002). *The Two Faces of Islam: The House of Sa'ud from Tradition to Terror*. New York: Doubleday.

[4] Venkatraman, Amritha (2007). Religious Basis for Islamic Terrorism: The Quran and Its Interpretations. *Studies in Conflict & Terrorism, 30*(3), 229–248.

A very high expression of violence toward infidels or non-Muslim believers is captured in the **Verse of the Sword** in the Qur'an: "When the sacred months have passed, slay the unbelievers wherever you find them, and take them captive, and besiege them, and prepare for them each ambush. But if they repent and become Muslims and pay the jizya, then leave their way free" (Qur'an 9:5). The Verse of the Sword has been a major catalyst for both ancient and modern jihad. It can be traced back to the beginnings of Muhammad-led warfare on unbelievers and People of the Book. Still today, the Qur'an is being used as the main source of inspiration by many Islamist groups and repressive regimes. For example, Osama bin Laden's intentions were unmistakable when he cited the following Qur'anic verse in a communiqué:

> The establishment of the Rule of Allah over this earth must be considered to be obligatory for the Muslims. Allah's prescripts are an obligation for the Muslims. Hence, the establishment of an Islamic state is an obligation for the Muslims, for something without which something which is obligatory cannot be carried out becomes (itself) obligatory. If, moreover, (such a) state cannot be established without war, then this war is an obligation as well. (Qur'an 24:55)

Likewise, the Iranian Constitution cites verses from the Qur'an fourteen times. Its objective is unambiguous: to promote Islamic doctrine worldwide. Its introduction states that "the mission of the Constitution" is "to create conditions conducive to the development of man in accordance with the noble and universal values of Islam" and "fulfill the ideological mission of jihad in Allah's way; that is, extending the sovereignty of Allah's law throughout the world."[19] This is in accordance with Qur'an 8:60: "Prepare against them whatever force you are able to muster, and strings of horses, to strike in the heart of your enemy."

SYMBOLIC MEANINGS OF JIHAD

Jihad is an important religious duty for Muslims. In Arabic, the word "jihad" translates as "struggle." To be more precise, it is the "struggle in the way of Allah." The word appears forty-one times in the Qur'an. Jihadist ideology animates a violent movement called jihadism (described later in this chapter).[20] Jihad has connotations of "exertion." For the individual believer, it is a spiritual exertion that makes him or her superior and more virtuous. It is a mystic ecstasy that produces a fusion with Allah. The term also possesses a sociopolitical character with aggressive overtones that emerge in specific legal definitions. Traditionally, there has been a distinction between **offensive jihad**—giving a religious cover to the violent expansion of the Islamic world, to conquest, and to the invasion of unbelievers' territories— and **defensive jihad**, a jihad decreed by the Muslim religious establishment and lawmakers (i.e., a widespread mobilization for the ummah under threat, whenever sacred lands and values are under attack from infidels).

Sunni versus Shia Views on Jihad

Most Muslims are either Sunnis or Shi'ites. Whereas Sunnis represent 85 percent of world Muslims, Shi'ites only make up 10–15 percent of Muslims globally. **Sunnis** typically follow the orthodox version of Islam, called the **Sunnah** (the normative way of life practiced and preached by Muhammad). **Shi'ites** tend to be more ecstatic (i.e., exhilarated, beatific, and frenzied) in religious practice and have messianic expectations that a messiah will bring justice on earth. Close to 40 percent of Shi'ites live in Iran. The main disagreements between Shi'ites and Sunnis have to do with disputes about leadership after Muhammad's death. Shia Muslims believe that Ali (Muhammad's cousin and son-in-law) should have been designated as Muhammad's rightful successor. In turn, Ali's descendants should have been the succeeding leaders. The most notorious Shia terrorist organization is Hezbollah, created by Iran and mostly active in Lebanon.[21] A minority of Sunni scholars consider jihad the sixth pillar of Islam—the other five pillars being the profession of faith in Allah, praying five times a day, almsgiving, fasting, and the pilgrimage to Mecca. In **Twelver Shia Islam**, the largest branch of Shia Islam, jihad is one of the ten Practices of the Religion. Generally called "Twelvers," these Shi'ites believe in twelve divinely chosen leaders, known as the Twelve Imams.[22] What the last few statements illustrate is that jihad is an important religious mandate for true Muslims.

Four Symbolic Categories of Jihad

Within traditional Islamic jurisprudence—which was developed during the first few centuries after Muhammad's death—jihad is the only form of warfare permitted in Islamic law. Under this provision, jihad may be waged against unbelievers, apostates, insurgents, thieves, and dissenters challenging the authority of Islam. In this framework, jihad has supreme authority. It can abolish fasting in Ramadan or obedience to a leader in opposition; all this is justified as a matter of survival of the community of believers. Each true Muslim under threat must participate, one way or another, in this warlike method—by arms (if not with funds) or by prayer. Jihad becomes the highest virtue and regulates the organization and deployment of all energies. Any mean justifies the end: the preservation of ummah.[23] Islamic lawmakers describe four symbolic categories of jihad:[24]

- **Jihad of the heart**: a type of "inner-struggle" jihad that consists of fighting the evil that has penetrated the self. It is the attempt to escape the devil's or infidels' persuasion to evil. This jihad of the heart is regarded as the greater jihad.
- **Jihad by the tongue**: a type of jihad concerned with propagation (speaking the truth and diffusing the word of Islam with one's tongue). By retelling stories of the glorious past, jihadists argue to Muslims that Islam is in a state of demise and must be restored through truth.
- **Jihad by the hand**: a type of jihad whereby Islamists choose to do "what is right" by resisting injustice and wrongs through action. Jihadists in this mold use the concept of humiliation to rationalize their actions. They identify the purported source of the Muslims' plight in constant attacks on and dishonor of Muslims on the part of an anti-Muslim alliance consisting of "Crusaders," "Zionists," and "Apostates."
- **Jihad by the sword**: violent armed fighting in the way of Allah (holy war) and the most common method by Salafi Muslims (described later in this chapter). Like most types of symbolic terrorism, jihadists enact a program of action (i.e., violent jihad). The main objective of jihad is not just the forced conversion of unbelievers to Islam; it is also the expansion and protection of the Islamic state.

Based on these four symbolic categories, one can logically deduce that jihad incorporates both military and nonmilitary aspects of a Muslim's duty. The last two categories, however, have been labeled jihadism—increasingly so since the September 11, 2001, terrorist attacks.

Jihadism

Jihadism is a term used to describe the renewed focus on violent warfare in Islamic fundamentalism. In this regard, it includes both mujahedin guerrilla tactics and Islamic terrorism with a global scope. Taken as a whole, jihadism is a system of propagating offensive jihad, waging it in conquest, and using it to advance Islam. In the first half of the twentieth century, it was championed by **Sayyid Qutb** (1906–1966), an Islamist intellectual and key player in the Muslim Brotherhood.[25] Hence, modern jihadism has been synonymous with **Qutbism**. The main principle of Qutbism is that the ummah has been too complacent for the past few centuries, which means that it has fallen into divine ignorance. Therefore, the ummah must be reconquered for Allah and sharia must become the sacred law of the land throughout all nations; without sharia, Islam cannot survive. Only then will peace, personal tranquility, and complete freedom from servitude be possible. The only way to achieve all these things is through offensive jihad in both Muslim and non-Muslim lands.[26]

In his book titled *Milestones*, Qutb (1964)[27] made famous the idea that the whole world was a land of war. Today, *Milestones* is seen as the bible of the global jihadist movement. Just like Qutbism, jihadism is equivalent to global Islamism. Through violent jihad, the duty of a true Muslim is to destroy anyone who has created and sustains evil. These include both the **near enemy** (apostate Muslims, apostate governments, and their warped systems of thought) and the **far enemy** (infidel, non-Muslim civilizations and the irreligious regimes they have imposed on Muslims). Because jihadists see themselves as agents of Allah's wrath, violence toward outsiders becomes second nature. Osama bin Laden's infamous **fatwa** (i.e., "Islamic decree") titled "Jihad against Jews and Crusaders," on February 23, 1998, cried out for the deaths of Americans and their allies. This attests to the sense of urgency to fulfill the utmost wish of Allah.[28] In Iran, the Grand Ayatollah Khomeini described violent jihad as "a divine blessing." Even where direct war is not feasible, usually because the chances of winning are low, it is useful to maintain the "war spirit" by inciting conflicts. It comes to no surprise that discussions of forming a "war cabinet" were frequent in Khomeinist rhetoric. In such a type of environment, jihad is a cult of war that interprets existence as an existential struggle between good and evil.[29] In Khomeini's regime, jihadism and the Islamic Revolution "executed and killed hundreds of thousands of people" (Mandaville, 2009, p. 46).[30]

Jihadist Globalism

Contemporary jihadists have framed many conflicts in religious terms. Examples are the war against the Soviet invaders in Afghanistan in the 1980s, the civil war in Bosnia in the early 1990s, and the conflict between Chechen secessionists and Russia (beginning in the mid-1990s). Regarding these conflicts as attacks on the ummah, extremists from numerous Muslim countries joined the jihad in Afghanistan, Bosnia, and Chechnya in order to safeguard Islam. Under these circumstances, **Al Qaeda** (i.e., "The Base" in Arabic) surfaced in the late 1980s as an international jihadist network targeting more dispersed, symbolic people and permanent structures in its holy war on Western adversaries. At that time, Yasser Arafat, leader of the Palestinian Liberation Organization (PLO), which became the Palestinian National Authority, regularly employed the word "jihad" to boost his influence in the Arab world.[31]

The term "jihadist globalism" is often used in relation to jihadism. **Jihadist globalism** was coined to describe modern-day jihadist violence as a reaction to Western forms of modernization—those that jihadists believe have exacerbated poverty, political instability, and daily life in Muslim society. Jihadist globalism is an intense reaction not only against market globalism but also against domestic groups that have imposed their routines on Muslim nations. Many people designate acts of terrorism, including the September 11, 2001, and the July 7, 2005, terrorist attacks, as demonstrations of jihadist globalism.[32] Suicide terror has been optimized as an exigency to fulfill the mission of jihadist globalism (e.g., in Dar es-Salaam, Iraq, Istanbul, Beirut, Buenos Aires, Casablanca, Nairobi, Russia, Chechnya, and Bali). In 2002, nightclubs were bombed in Bali. Four years before, in Tanzania and Kenya, it was U.S. embassies that were targeted. Let us not forget attacks on synagogues in Istanbul and Tunisia, an Israeli-owned hotel in Nairobi, and a Jewish club in Casablanca.[33]

Al Qaedaism

When jihadists unashamedly advertise or make an open call for the implementation of global jihad, the joining of martyrdom missions, or the killing of infidels, it is sometimes called "Al Qaedaism." **Al Qaedaism** is the symbol of a "jihad brand" that offers a political and a religious basis on which Muslims can revitalize long-established Islamist doctrine. It refers to the complex mélange of symbolical, religious, and cultural principles that provides the support on which Al Qaeda hangs its tactics and strategies. It is a justification to uphold the Al Qaeda brand in places where Islamism is badly needed.[34] Al Qaedaism seems to work effectively. It is estimated that the terrorist network has several thousand jihadist commanders in forty countries.[35] The popularity of Al Qaeda's "brand awareness" is viral. Al Qaeda has become a brand in jihad franchising: a distribution model with low financial risks but high gratification rewards. Devout warriors can exploit Al Qaedaism and replicate its behaviors.[36] For Whelan (2005),[37] the real danger posed by Al Qaedaism comes not just from Muslim countries but also from Western nations themselves. Al Qaedaism attracts the disaffected, those who believe that Western values have nothing to offer them, and who are confronted by what they consider American and European arrogance.

SALAFI SYMBOLISM

Salafism, also called the **Salafi movement** (or **Salafist movement**), is an Islamist movement adhering to a literalist, strict, and ultraconservative approach to Islam. A certain number of Salafis embrace violent jihad against civilians as a legitimate expression of Islam. Salafism is related to or includes **Wahhabism**, an ultraconservative branch of Islam advocated by fundamentalists in Saudi Arabia. The two terms are often used interchangeably.[38] In recent years, the Salafi doctrine has often been correlated with the jihad of terrorist organizations such as Al Qaeda and those groups in favor of killing innocent civilians.[39] Al Qaeda and the radical extremists that constitute the new "global jihadi movement" are not religious outliers in Islam. They belong to the broader community of Salafis.[40] Kepel (2005)[41] refers to this as **Salafi jihadism**, a way to describe self-claiming Salafi groups that have cultivated an interest in jihad since the mid-1990s. Based on the yearly report of the 2010 German domestic intelligence service, Salafism is the world's fastest growing Islamic movement.[42]

Manhaj as a Salafi Symbol

Salafism is the philosophy that the type of Islam practiced by Salafis is pure and unsullied. Therefore, one way to uphold it across the world is through jihad, until all non-Muslims convert to Islam and practice it too. "Salafism" comes from **Salaf** ("predecessors" or "ancestors"), denoting the earliest Muslims who were considered the role models of Islamic practice. Most of them were the Prophet Muhammad's companions and, later, consisted of the first three generations of Muslims. Salafis believe that because the earliest Muhammad followers learned about Islam directly from the Prophet, they had an unadulterated understanding of the faith. Unfortunately, subsequent practices were blemished by innovations in religion that contaminated the Muslim community over time. As a result, Muslims were called to purify the religion by strictly adhering to the Qur'an, the Sunnah, and the consensus of Salafi jurists. Every behavior must be authorized by these religious sources. Today, Salafis still believe that they have the purest and best understanding of Islam. However, to their eyes, too many Muslims have been corrupted by erroneous and disreputable interpretations that have misled them. Given this state of affairs, Salafis have developed a method called **manhaj**, which consists of distinguishing true from false ideas. Put simply, manhaj is the symbol of absolute Islamic truth and provides a methodology to reach it.[43]

Symbolism of Salafi Conquest

In the mentality of Salafi jihadists, the September 11, 2001, terrorist attacks symbolized a **ghazwah**, a nickname for the raid (i.e., the Battle of the Trench) led by Muhammad in 627 against pagans and Jews (called "confederates" in the Qur'an). The latter suffered substantial casualty losses. The direct relationship between the sacred past and the present is at the core of the Salafi jihadists' frame of mind.[44] If we look closely at Muslims' reactions to the attacks on the Twin Towers, there were Muslims across the globe shouting approval for the blow dealt to the United States. This was because these Muslims understood the symbolism of 9/11. To them, it was like Salafis chopping off the heads of the mighty infidels. At the ghazwah in 627, between 600 and 700 captives were beheaded by Muhammad's warriors. Islamists understand symbolism, as is also the case for the Ground Zero mosque. The name initially selected for this Islamic center was the "Cordoba House." Now, it is called Park51. Cordoba is a Spanish city where medieval Muslims destroyed a church and built a mosque on the ashes of it. The entire region surrounding the mosque became the **Caliphate of Cordoba**.[45]

Speaking of Cordoba, the city is located in the Spanish province of Andalusia, which was under Muslim rule for almost 800 years. When informed Muslims refer to Spain, they call the latter "Al Andalus," the medieval Muslim state that constituted the Caliphate of Cordoba. Spain is very appealing to Salafi jihadists because they feel called upon to repossess their old territory.[46] Indeed, Spain still represents the enemy infidel and an ancient Islamic territory. A jihadist video uploaded after the Madrid train bombings made references to a few historical facts and events, including "Al Andalus," the Crusades launched on the Iberian Peninsula against Muslims, the Spanish Inquisition, and Tariq ibn Ziyad, the Muslim general who led the conquest of Spain in 711. In line with these contentions, the Islamist bombings in Madrid on March 11, 2004, were inspired by Al Qaeda's call to punish Spain's involvement in the Iraq War—because the southern region of Spain used to belong to Muslims for almost eight centuries. Although newly elected Spanish prime minister José Luis Rodríguez Zapatero, forming his socialist government, distanced himself from the George W. Bush administration, Spain still had over 1,000 troops in the Middle East. In another terrorist video released in late 2004, Islamists threatened to keep perpetrating terrorist attacks on Spanish soil until all troops disengaged from the Middle East.[47]

It is not difficult for Salafis to fall back on the symbolism of the historical legacy of the Christian-led Crusades—representing the apogee of Christendom's clash with Islam. Not only do the Crusades symbolize Muslims' long-lasting circumstances of oppression and disinheritance; they also provide justification for extreme violence against Western encirclement and secularization. Salafis reinterpret these historic religious symbols to suit current conditions as an instrument to inspire political action and revolutionary violence against their opponents. The term "Crusaders" serves to associate a historic military campaign with a present-day enemy. Images of colonial occupation of Muslim lands and the slaying of Muslims before and after colonization from European countries (including the French in Algeria and the British in Egypt) are symbols of Salafis' plight and validations for reconquering lands.[48]

THE CALIPHATE: SYMBOL OF GLOBAL DOMINATION

A **caliphate** is a one-world Muslim government, like a grand Islamic state, led by a supreme religious and political leader called the "caliph." In the Middle Ages, "caliphate" was applied to the successions of Muslim empires in the Middle East (e.g., the Ottoman Empire) and Southwest Asia. Today, the caliphate symbolizes Muslim clerics' dream of global domination: an Islamic government ruled by a single leader. A number of Muslim political parties and mujahedin have called for the reestablishment of the caliphate by unifying all Muslim nations, through either political action or jihad. This movement seeks to (1) bring back the rule of the caliph, (2) reestablish **sharia** (Islamic law derived from the Qur'an and the hadiths) over both the community of the Muslim faithful and non-Muslim territories on earth, and (3) ultimately spread Islamic doctrine all over the world.[49]

The caliph is the symbol of Islamic unity and a single divinely chosen religious authority.[50] From the Arabic *Khalifa*, **caliph** means "successor," "substitute," or "lieutenant." It is mentioned in the Qur'an as the person establishing man's role as representative of Allah on earth and, hence, successor of the Prophet Muhammad. Indeed, the role of the caliph dates back to Muhammad in the early seventh century. Later, during the Ottoman Empire, the caliphate was moved to Turkey, where it was the rule for more than three centuries. In 1924, the Turkish government, in an effort to become a more secular nation, abolished the caliphate (after having instated many caliphs for three hundred years). Since this abolishment, restoring the caliphate has been a salient cause within Islamic movements—particularly the Muslim Brotherhood.[51]

Conventions and Gatherings on the Caliphate

On August 12, 2007, Hizbut Tahrir, a radical pan-Islamic political organization, hosted the third International Caliphate Conference in Jakarta, Indonesia. The conference attracted more than 90,000 participants from at least thirty-nine different countries. Groups in attendance ranged from nonviolent Muslim organizations to groups affiliated with Al Qaeda. Conference attendees expressed a profound desire to reinstate the caliph as a religious and political leader of a one-world Muslim government.[52] McLeod's (2008)[53] research and polling team employed several data sources to examine the popularity of the caliphate ideology. First, they conducted in-depth interviews with leaders and important members of Hizbut Tahrir in Indonesia (during the weeks preceding the 2007 Caliphate Conference in Jakarta). Second, they examined data from the 2007 START survey conducted by the Program on International Policy Attitudes (PIPA) in four Muslim countries. Overall, McLeod's team found that most Muslims in Egypt, Morocco, Indonesia, and Pakistan favor the reestablishment of the caliphate.

In chapter 7, it was mentioned that a certain number of Muslim clerics divide the world into two halves: Dar al-Islam (the House of Islam) and Dar al-Harb (the House of War).[54] The caliphate imagery is also a powerful motivator within Muslim discourse. Devout Muslims are often swayed by the idea of the caliphate when attending small study groups. Small Islamic study groups are usually called *halaqa* and *usroh*. For such Muslims, the imagery of Islam indicative of Muhammad's Golden Age is a virtue that should be pursued in terms of life goals, financial support, and personal sacrifice for the sake of Allah. This ideological struggle for conquering Dar al-Harb and imposing a caliphate is considered a struggle for "collective identity" and has no scarcity of pious volunteers willing to jump on the bandwagon.[55]

Pansurgency

A portmanteau of "pan-" ("all-") and "insurgency," **pansurgency** is a global movement seeking to instigate revolutions in order to rout Western civilization and substitute it with a new world order. In this context, it would be an Islamic new world order.[56] All Islamist movements today seek to restore the caliphate and return the caliph to the land of Muhammad—in fact, some of them even want to depose the Saudi government. These pansurgent movements have been inspired by reform movements such as Salafism. Salafis, too, desire to reestablish the caliphate. When such zealous movements fail to achieve their objective, they develop strategies to surmount the obstacles that have thwarted their plan—obstacles such as the multiple U.S. interventions in the Middle East and the establishment of moderate Muslim governments like the one in Morocco. Many Muslim internet sites describe the shame endured by their community resulting from the abolishment of the caliphate and the domination of Westernization. Social psychologists remark that such a shame is a strong motivator for extremist movements.[57] Many Salafis have identified Saudi Arabia as proof that Allah blesses those who follow pure Islam, enforce sharia, and uphold manhaj. The evidence they use is the plethora of oil-based wealth that Saudi Arabia has. They argue that if the entire ummah espoused true Salafism—the one present in much of the known world ten centuries ago—Islam would regain its Golden Age, power, and glory.[58]

Global domination is the ultimate goal of jihadists. They want to bring all nations under sharia, even now in this modernized age, and even if it means deposing all existing governments. Islamic fundamentalists resort to suicide bombings and other dreadful methods of violence to achieve their aims.[59] As a result, many in the pansurgent movement call for a global jihad, arguing that it is the obligation of every Muslim to take part in it. On the other hand, Muslims opposing these methods are nonbelievers or **apostates**, people who leave their religion—a sin punishable by death in Islam.[60] Al Qaeda revealed its grand plan toward the caliphate many times. For example, in 2005, **Abu Musab al-Zarqawi**, former leader of Al Qaeda in Iraq (AQI), released a statement for waging his terrorist campaign:

> We are not fighting to chase out the occupier or to save national unity and keep the borders outlined by the infidels intact. We are fighting because it is a religious duty to do it, just as it is a duty to take sharia [Islamic law] to the government and create an Islamic state.[61]

In a similar fashion, in the early 1990s, the Armed Islamist Group (GIA), in Algeria, proclaimed its plans to restore the caliphate and appoint a caliph. Furthermore, with Hamas's victory in the 2007 Palestinian elections, a huge gathering of supporters followed, with Hamas's spokesman extolling the virtues of the caliphate.[62] The intractable Israeli-Palestinian conflict threatens the pansurgent goal of Islamists to liberate Jerusalem. This threat has led to an increased collaboration among Islamist groups in an attempt to sabotage enemies (even those in favor of the peace process) and more confrontations with the West, Israel, and moderate Arab governments.[63]

ISLAMIC REVIVAL

The **Islamic revival** is a revival across the Muslim world of the Muslim religion, which made a significant comeback at the end of the 1970s. It is reflected in profound religious piety and an increasing espousal of Islamic culture, dress, terminology, division of the sexes, free speech and media restrictions, and overall Muslim values.[64] The present-day movement of Islamic revival has been likened to earlier Salafi efforts in the Middle-Ages: "The call to fundamentalism, centered on the sharia: this call is as old as Islam itself and yet still new because it has never been fulfilled" (Roy, 2004, p. 4).[65] Another phenomenon is **transnational Islam**, a concept developed by two French experts on Islam: Kepel (2008)[66] and Roy (2007).[67] Transnational Islam entails a feeling of a growing universalistic Muslim identity.

Islamization

Islamization refers to the process whereby a country or culture converts to Islam. In the Western world, it usually refers to the imposition of an Islamist social and political rhetoric on a nation or culture that is not Islamic or one with a more modern version of Islam. Islamist thinkers like Sayyid Qutb were crucial to the development of modern Islamic thought. A return to pure Islamic values, unlike the Westernization moves by some Arab and Asian regimes in the 1950s and 1960s, seems to be happening.[68] Davidson (1998)[69] describes four basic assumptions of the Islamic revival. First, the ummah is in a state of chaos caused by political and moral decay. This decay is the outcome of the constant failure of those in the private and public spheres to follow the dictates of Islam. Second, the political and moral degeneration of the ummah has allowed Western colonialism to infect Muslim lands with its own ignoble values, namely, principles based on secularism, materialism, and nationalism. This colonization has essentially shattered the Muslim world. Third, the method to fight this bankruptcy and infection is to re-Islamize the ummah. This requires imposing sharia and eradicating Western culture and its nefarious influence. Fourth, the only way to re-Islamize the world is to re-politicize the Muslim religion itself. As fundamentalist reasoning goes, "Islam began as a religion that preached the rejection of false gods and corrupt practices. The West and Westernizers now represent precisely these evils. Islam, representative of a total world-view, is the path to justice and socioeconomic equity" (Davidson, 1998, p. 13).

Islamic Revival to Support Terrorism

The Islamic revival is also reflected in the growing support of Islamic terrorism. Islamism is a pathological, "heretical" consequence of a process that needs to be evaluated on its own terms: an Islamic revival. In political terms, this means that the objectives of the terrorists are exactly what they relentlessly claim: to restore international forms of medieval Salafi rule, reconquer lost territory, and so on.[70] From a Western standpoint, the most significant event that inspired Islamic revival was the **Iranian Revolution** in 1979. It imposed an Islamic Republic under the Grand Ayatollah Khomeini. It also diluted the assumption that Westernization reinforced Muslim countries and was the unalterable movement of the future.[71] The Iranian Revolution imparted a radical model of Islam and inspired other Islamic movements to fundamentally oppose existing regimes at home. Later, in the 1980s, the internationalization of Islamist violence against the West and Israel buttressed Iran's determination to export the revolution abroad. It was a useful instrument to alter the foreign policies of Western nations unsympathetic toward the Islamic Republic. Muslim warriors were secured a place in Paradise as martyrs while the living would enjoy a caliphate. Moreover, the Islamic Republic demanded the elimination of "apostate" Muslims.[72]

In the same train of thought, large segments of Palestinians in the West Bank and the Gaza Strip have become more devout because of Islamic revivalism. The success of Hamas as a sustainable competitor of the nationalist camp in 1988, the popularity of Islamic groups in many universities in the West Bank and Gaza since the 1980s, and the diffusion of Islamic charity networks (especially in Gaza) have expanded the foundations and legitimacy for the Islamic revival movement.[73] The impact of Islamic groups in Gaza grew in parallel with the rise of poverty and the Second Intifada in 2000. The efforts to impose sharia continued when Hamas won most seats in the Palestinian Parliament in 2006 and started to control Gaza in 2007. By the same token, the terrorist group's popularity compelled many security forces (devoted to the secular President Mahmoud Abbas) to move to the West Bank. After the civil war was over, Hamas proclaimed the end of secularism and "heresy" in the Gaza Strip. For the first time since the 1989 Sudanese coup d'état (which allowed Colonel Omar al-Bashir to seize power), a Muslim Brotherhood militant organization governed a sizable territory. Gaza human rights groups have accused Hamas of strictly imposing Islamic rule and putting a ceiling on many freedoms.[74]

THE MUSLIM BROTHERHOOD

The **Muslim Brotherhood** (or the Society of the Muslim Brothers, or *Ikhwan* in Arabic) is one of the largest and most influential Islamic movements in the world. It is also the largest political opposition organization in the majority of Arab nations. The Muslim Brotherhood wants to depose any government that is not sufficiently Muslim.[75] The existential goal of the Brothers is to impose an "Islamic order." To many, "order" simply means "caliphate"—that is, to overthrow the existing order for the sake of a theocracy. Since the core texts of its founders and ideologues (e.g., Sayyid Qutb) are considered a guide for many Muslims, the danger posed by the Muslim Brotherhood is real. To the Brothers, an Islamic state is guaranteed thanks to three principles:[76]

- The Qur'an is the fundamental constitution.
- The government makes decisions only sanctioned by Islamic organizations.
- The executive ruler is the caliph. He is bound by Islamic teachings and traditional jurisprudence.

The Muslim Brotherhood is an Islamist movement that many Muslims see as the vanguard of their beliefs. An Islamic order would mean a resurgence of the core fundamentals of Islam. The emblem of the Muslim Brotherhood shows two crossed swords beneath a red Qur'an, both of which are located within a green circle; the circle sits in a brown square. This indicates Qur'an-guided jihad.[77] Written on the depicted Qur'an is the phrase "Truly, it is a generous Quran." Below the swords, "Be Prepared" is inscribed. The color green and the presence of a Qur'an symbolize the heavy Islamic underpinnings of the Muslim Brotherhood. The swords indicate militancy; to this point, the choice to use swords instead of guns epitomizes the Muslim Brotherhood's desire to return to pure, historic Islam. The motto "Be Prepared" references Qur'an 8:60, a verse that warns Muslims to be prepared to fight enemies of Allah. Not surprisingly, this verse is also mentioned in the Constitution of the Islamic Republic of Iran. The full official motto of the Muslim Brotherhood is "Allah is our objective; the Prophet [or Messenger] is our leader; the Qur'an is our law; Jihad is our way; dying in the way of Allah is our highest hope."[78]

Origins of the Brotherhood

Hasan al-Banna, an Egyptian scholar, founded the Muslim Brotherhood in 1928. He was dedicated to invigorating the Islamic call (dawa) by means of education and reform. In the 1930s, members of the Muslim Brotherhood were involved in the Palestinian Arab resistance and remained there to establish the Palestinian branch. During the next several decades, the Palestinian Muslim Brotherhood remained prudent, avoided military strategies, hardened its devout members in the face of Israeli rule, dedicated much effort to institution building, and slowly prepared for jihad. In 1987, when the First Intifada was launched, the Palestinian Muslim Brotherhood came out of the shadow and declared to the world that it was now Harakat al-Muqawamah al-Islamiyya (the Islamic Resistance Movement), better known by its acronym, Hamas.[79]

In Arabic, the translation for "brothers" is *ikhwan*. The **Ikhwan** were Islamic religious guerrillas comprising the principal military body of the Arabian ruler Ibn Saud and played a major role in instating him as ruler of the majority of the Arabian Peninsula (his new country of Saudi Arabia). In the 1910s and 1920s, the Ikhwan were composed of Bedouin tribes and irregular tribesmen. This religious militia of "brothers" claimed to be fully committed to the purification and unification of Islam. The Ikhwan relied primarily on traditional weapons such as swords, spears, and occasionally ancient firearms. Generally, they launched attacks in the form of raids—a style typical to Bedouins in the Arabian deserts. The Ikhwan often traveled on camels and horses. Their brutal raids in the central region of the Arabian Peninsula were ruthless. In many instances, all male captives were killed by throat cutting.[80]

Jahiliyyah

In the late 1940s, Sayyid Qutb spent a few years in the United States. Disgusted by what he considered immorality and decadence, he intensified his deep-seated, hateful rhetoric against the West upon his return to Egypt. For Qutb, Westerners were completely debauched and barbarous. In his writings, he referred to them as being in a state of **jahiliyyah**, when individuals are astray from spirituality and divine guidance and are at variance with the teachings of the Qur'an. Put simply, jahiliyyah applies to anyone who is not a pure Muslim. Qutb referred to the West as a huge bordello, awash with immorality, greed, and selfishness. His writings were appealing to Muslims who were "oppressed" and "humiliated" by Westerners—whom Qutb called "Occidentals."[81] "Jahiliyyah" is mentioned several times in the Qur'an: for example, "Do they truly desire the law of paganism? But who is fairer than God in judgment for a people firm of faith?" (Qur'an 5:50) and "For the unbelievers had planted in their hearts zealotry, the zealotry of lawlessness" (Qur'an 48:26).

Sayyid Qutb reminded Muslims that one of their tasks was to save the ummah from **fitna** (internal divisions) and to bring back the Islamic way of life. Qutbist principles represented an ideological platform for multiple interpretations of jihad. By falling back on the concept of jahiliyyah, Qutb insisted that many Muslims were in a state of divine ignorance similar to the one that existed before the Prophet Muhammad came along. He regarded democracy—in which the leader is elected by the people—as a system antithetical to Islam. In his view, laws should be derived from the Qur'an, hadiths, and traditional Islamic jurisprudence—not legislatures erected or elected by people.[82]

Today, the struggle to obliterate jahiliyyah and the illegal institutions that are corrupt to the core have become a legitimized battle plan for Islamists. They believe they must follow Allah's dictate to resist jahiliyyah and redeem the soul of humankind. It is a cosmic war for which they need to mobilize their efforts, often through violent jihad. For them, jahiliyyah is the upheaval of the modern man against Allah's supreme rule on earth.[83] Muslim leaders and organizations that champion the expansion of Islamism commonly argue that today's ummah is weak in comparison with the ummah in the old days. They rehash the same argument: Western influences and, as a result, the ummah's avoidance of practicing Islam like they did at the pinnacle of the Islamic empire are to be blamed for this degeneration.[84]

Connections to Terrorism

In the late 1980s, during the exhilaration of the Afghani victory over the Soviet Union, a global jihadist movement started to dwarf many other Islamist groups: Al Qaeda. A leading ideologue of this movement was **Abdullah Azzam**, a Palestinian man living in Saudi Arabia. Azzam, Osama bin Laden's professor of Islamic jurisprudence in Jeddah, was also a Muslim Brotherhood member in Jordan and Egypt. Azzam wrote "Join the Caravan" (1987),[85] in which he corroborated Qutb's view that the ummah was in decline and that offensive jihad was the élan vital of Islam. To make his case, Azzam used Islamic jurisprudence and historic analogy from the seventh century. A year later, Azzam (1988)[86] published, in his *al-Jihad* monthly magazine, an article titled "Al-Qa'idah al-Sulbah," or "The Solid Base," and established Al Qaeda as the instrument for this global jihadist movement.

At that time, another notorious Islamist group, Hamas, was created by Sheikh Ahmad Yassin, an Islamist ideologue who also served as a preacher for the Muslim Brotherhood in Gaza. In accordance with his teachings, Yassin (and his followers) founded Hamas as part of the Palestinian Muslim Brotherhood.[87] Today, **Hamas** still considers itself as belonging to the larger Muslim Brotherhood movement. This is actually mentioned in Article Two of the 1988

Hamas Covenant: "The Islamic Resistance Movement [Hamas] is one of the wings of the Muslim Brotherhood in Palestine."

Applying the doctrine of the Muslim Brotherhood, Hamas successfully indoctrinates new recruits via its religious and social institutions. Those who are trained in these institutions also get social welfare services that are complemented by presentations devised to indoctrinate them into the militant ideology of Hamas. The religious and social institutions of Hamas represent a very active source of indoctrination throughout all levels of Palestinian culture. If truth be told, the recruitment of martyrs-to-be (i.e., suicide bombers) takes place at universities, sports clubs, mosques, and other institutions in which Hamas has a presence. Hassan Yusuf, a top Hamas leader in Ramallah (i.e., the headquarters of the Palestinian Authority), stated, "We like to grow them—from kindergarten through college."[88]

Today, the Muslim Brotherhood has been classified as a terrorist organization in Russia. In 2004, Muhammad Aqef, the supreme guide of the Muslim Brotherhood at that time, issued a decree to all the branches of the Brotherhood worldwide. His ruling called for full commitment to the fight against Israel.[89] The Muslim Brotherhood has made headlines in the United States, too. In 2007, the U.S. Justice Department, during a massive terrorism-financing trial in Dallas, Texas, gathered evidence that the Muslim Brotherhood had planned for a "grand jihad" that called for destroying the United States from within. Defense attorneys for the Holy Land Foundation, a Muslim charitable organization charged with funding terrorism, agreed that the "grand jihad" plan was part of a genuine Muslim Brotherhood document. The document also listed twenty-nine U.S. organizations affiliated with the Brotherhood, including ISNA (the Islamic Society of North America).[90]

The Neglected Duty

In October 1981, Egyptian prime minister Anwar Sadat was assassinated by members of the Muslim Brotherhood—his own bodyguards. They left a written manifesto behind with Sadat's body; the pamphlet was titled **The Neglected Duty**. The main idea was that many Muslims worldwide had abandoned the practice of jihad. For this reason, "The Neglected Duty" provided doctrinal justification for assassinating Sadat (as he had also imprisoned many Salafis and Muslim Brotherhood members). From this perspective, jihad is a duty incumbent on all Muslims, like a "pillar of Islam," something that must be revived as a central tenet of the faith. It is an obligation for Muslims, in the same way that belief in Allah, prayer, almsgiving, fasting, and the pilgrimage to Mecca are obligations too.[91] Today, "The Neglected Duty" is the Muslim Brotherhood's symbol of Islamic revival. It is their primordial philosophy of eliminating the enemy from within. Eliminating the enemy from within is a variation on the concept of displacement of blame used by many organizations.[92]

THE MAHDI

In Islamic doctrine, the **Mahdi** ("Guided One" in Arabic) is the prophesied savior of Islam who will rule for up to nineteen years before the Day of Judgment. Many Muslims believe in the looming arrival of the Muslim messiah who will establish Islam as the world's sole religion.[93] Isa (Jesus Christ) will return to assist the Mahdi against the false messiah and his followers. After helping the Mahdi against these false people, Isa will unite humanity. It is generally believed that this idea of the Mahdi entered Islam from Judeo-Christian teachings. It was passed on from Judaism to Christianity and then Islam.[94]

SUNNI VIEWS OF THE MAHDI

The Sunnis consider the Mahdi to be the successor of Muhammad. The Mahdi will come to rule the world and restore righteousness. The Mahdi is only described in the hadiths, not the Qur'an. The Guided One is frequently described as establishing the caliphate. Some Sunnis believe that the Mahdi will be an ordinary man. According to a hadith, Muhammad said, "The world will not come to an end until the Arabs are ruled by a man from my family whose name is the same as mine and whose father's name is the same as my father's."[95] Muslim extremists subscribe to a form of **Mahdism**, the belief that humanity will end upon the return of the Muslim messiah and the establishment of the subsequent pure Islamic state. Muslim extremists even maintain that the Saudi government has become contaminated by modernization and Western influence and, consequently, does not have the authority to serve as the custodian of Islam's holy cities. A 1979 rebellion conducted by Islamic extremists in Saudi Arabia, which ultimately failed, involved toppling the Great Mosque in Mecca.[96] They intentionally focused their rebellion on the Great Mosque because it represents Islam's most important sacred site. What they did is occupy, for two weeks, the complex that surrounds the mosque as they aired their grievances. Profoundly distressed over hostages and the mosque itself, Saudi counterterrorism forces (assisted by the French) eventually overcame the fanatics, whose leaders were sentenced to death.[97]

This anecdote has a lot to do with the **Augustinian paradigm**, a concept describing how religious fanatics long for the purity and eternal peace of godly places. At the same time, they also express deep anger toward the alienation and corruption of daily life in earthly places.[98] St. Augustine's dualistic representation of a messy, chaotic civil society opposing a perfectly ordered godly city of an idyllic future is a notion that has become fundamental in Islam. St. Augustine was a Western philosopher and bishop from Roman Africa. His writings had a major influence on the development of Christianity in the West.[99] Muslim extremists tend to follow this Augustinian paradigm: they are overzealous in their use of illegal means against symbols of the Mahdi's enemy—to defend the virtues of Allah's creations.[100]

Shia Views of the Mahdi

Belief in the Mahdi is more prevalent in Shia Islam. In Shia Islam, the Mahdi is believed to be the **Twelfth Imam**, Muhammad al-Mahdi, who disappeared a long time ago and who will return from occultation. According to Shia teaching, the Twelfth Imam will not require an introduction upon his return (which means that humans do not have the power or capacity to encourage the Twelfth Imam to return). His identity will be obvious to all, or at least to those able to recognize him.[101] One Shia doctrine states that he will rule through a human agent, or maybe the agent will pave the way for the return of the Twelfth Imam (who will be the actual ruler of the world). This major agent, who has acquired a high stature through his knowledge and religious authority, is the supreme mujtahid ("striver") tasked with interpreting the will of the Imam. The mujtahid, thus, acts as a legislator in Shia Islam, and his declarations and verdicts are the law.[102] The last decades of the twentieth century witnessed a giant ideological and political leap under the Grand Ayatollah Khomeini. Khomeini took the Shi'ites' view of the Mahdi from passivity and expectation to activity and aggression. That is to say, Muslim warriors were decreed to control the "natural course of events" by eradicating the earth and, in this process, paving the way for the Mahdi to come. In Twelver Shia doctrine, the Ayatollah is the Supreme Leader who commands every aspect of the believers' life. The new activism brought about by the Islamic Revolution in Iran has created a new frame of mind for **violent**

eschatology, the doctrine that the earth must be cleansed before the second coming of a messiah.[103]

SUMMARY

According to many recent surveys, Muslim support for terrorist violence worldwide is higher than for any other religious group. The Qur'an, the foundational text of Islam, mandates violence against unbelievers—particularly the Medinan verses (after the Prophet Muhammad fled Mecca to Medina). One of these verses is 9:5 (The Verse of the Sword). The Principle of Abrogation dictates that the later (and more violent) verses have precedence over the earlier (more peaceful) verses. Likewise, ijtihad allows Muslims to interpret the Qur'an in order to validate their theological understandings of the Qur'an and to suit changing times and needs in Islamic communities. An important religious duty for Muslims is jihad ("struggle in the way of Allah"). In fact, within traditional Islamic jurisprudence, jihad is the only form of warfare permitted in Islamic law. The renewed focus on violent warfare in Islamic fundamentalism is called jihadism. There are four categories of jihad: jihad of the heart, by the tongue, by the hand, and by the sword. Similarly, Al Qaedaism is the symbol of a "jihad brand" that offers a political and a religious basis on which Muslims can revitalize the long-established Islamist doctrine. Another important phenomenon is Salafism, an Islamic movement that mandates a strict and ultraconservative approach to Islam. According to Salafis, too many Muslims have been corrupted by erroneous and disreputable interpretations of Islam. Under these circumstances, Salafis have developed a method called manhaj, which consists of distinguishing true from false ideas. Put simply, manhaj is the symbol of absolute Islamic truth. The dream of Islamic global domination is captured in the concept of the "caliphate," a one-world Muslim government led by a supreme religious and political leader (the "caliph"). To this point, pansurgency is a global movement seeking to instigate revolutions in order to oppose Western civilization and substitute it with an Islamic new world order. Islamic revival, akin to Islamization, is the process whereby a country or culture converts to Islam. It has been largely inspired by the 1979 Iranian Revolution. Islamic revival and the caliphate have been promoted by the Muslim Brotherhood, one of the largest and most influential Islamic movements in the world. It seeks to overthrow any government that is not sufficiently Muslim. Created by Hasan al-Banna in 1928, the Muslim Brotherhood was strengthened by Sayyid Qutb (an Islamist thinker and key player in the movement) when he successfully denounced the West and disloyal Muslims as being in a state of jahiliyyah (to be astray from Qur'anic spirituality and divine guidance). Not surprisingly, the Brotherhood is connected to terrorism: one just needs to read "The Neglected Duty," its manifesto on the importance of waging jihad. Lastly, in Islamic doctrine, the Mahdi ("Guided One" in Arabic) is the prophesied redeemer of Islam who will rule for up to nineteen years before the Day of Judgment. When Mahdism is taken too far, it becomes violent eschatology, the doctrine that the earth must be cleansed before the second coming of a messiah.

NOTES

1. Pew Research Center (2013, April 30). *The World's Muslims: Religion, Politics and Society.* Retrieved May 3, 2013, from http://www.pewforum.org/uploadedFiles/Topics/Religious_Affiliation/Muslim/worlds-muslims-religion-politics-society-full-report.pdf (p. 36).

2. Hennessy, Patrick, & Kite, Melissa (2006, February 19). *Poll Reveals 40pc of Muslims Want Sharia Law in UK.* Retrieved May 3, 2013, from http://www.telegraph.co.uk/news/uknews/1510866/Poll-reveals-40pc-of-Muslims-want-sharia-law-in-UK.html

3. Het Laatste Nieuws (2013, May 3). *Zestien procent moslimjongens vindt terrorisme aanvaardbaar* [16% of Young Muslims in Belgium State Terrorism Is "Acceptable"]. Retrieved May 3, 2013, from http://www.hln.be/hln/nl/1275/Islam/article/detail/1619036/2013/04/22/Zestien-procent-moslimjongens-vindt-terrorisme-aanvaardbaar.dhtml.

4. Pew Research Center (2007, May 22). *Muslim Americans: Middle Class and Mostly Mainstream*. Retrieved May 3, 2013, from http://pewresearch.org/files/old-assets/pdf/muslim-americans.pdf#page=60

5. Pew Research Center (2007, May 22). *Muslim Americans: Middle Class and Mostly Mainstream*. Retrieved May 3, 2013, from http://pewresearch.org/files/old-assets/pdf/muslim-americans.pdf#page=60

6. Pew Research Center (2011, August 30). *Muslim Americans: No Signs of Growth in Alienation or Support for Extremism*. Retrieved May 3, 2013, from http://www.people-press.org/2011/08/30/muslim-americans-no-signs-of-growth-in-alienation-or-support-for-extremism/

7. World Public Opinion (2009, February 25). *Public Opinion in the Islamic World on Terrorism, Al Qaeda, and US Policies*. Retrieved May 3, 2013, from http://www.worldpublicopinion.org/pipa/pdf/feb09/STARTII_Feb09_rpt.pdf.

8. Pew Research Center (2010, December 2). *Muslim Publics Divided on Hamas and Hezbollah*. Retrieved May 3, 2013, from http://www.pewglobal.org/2010/12/02/muslims-around-the-world-divided-on-hamas-and-hezbollah/

9. Pew Research Center (2010, December 2). *Muslim Publics Divided on Hamas and Hezbollah*. Retrieved May 3, 2013, from http://www.pewglobal.org/2010/12/02/muslims-around-the-world-divided-on-hamas-and-hezbollah/

10. Jenkins, Brian Michael (2011). *Stray Dogs and Virtual Armies: Radicalization and Recruitment to Jihadist Terrorism in the U.S. since 9/11*. Santa Monica, CA: RAND.

11. Snow, Eric (2012). The Koran and Conquest: A Look at Islamic Theology. *The Good News, 17*(1), 25–29.

12. Nelson, Kristina (1985). *The Art of Reciting the Quran*. Austin: University of Texas Press.

13. Lucas, Scott (2004). *Constructive Critics, Hadith Literature, and the Articulation of Sunni Islam*. Leiden: Brill Publishers,

14. Scruton, Roger (2002). *The West and the Rest: Globalization and the Terrorist Threat*. Wilmington, DE: Intercollegiate Studies Institute.

15. Saeed, Abdullah (2008). *The Qur'an: An Introduction*. London: Routledge.

16. Federer, William (2007). *What Every American Needs to Know about the Qur'an: A History of Islam & the United States*. St. Louis, MO: Amerisearch, Inc.

17. Center for the Study of Political Islam (2009). *Statistical Islam*. Nashville, TN: CSPI.

18. Katz, Adam (2004). Remembering Amalek: 9/11 and Generative Thinking. *Anthropoetics, 10*(2), 10–24.

19. Tamadonfar, Mehran (2001). Islam, Law, and Political Control in Contemporary Iran. *Journal for the Scientific Study of Religion, 40*(2), 205–220.

20. Habeck, Mary (2006). *Knowing the Enemy: Jihadist Ideology and the War on Terror*. New Haven, CT: Yale University Press.

21. Nasr, Vali (2006). When the Shiites Rise. *Foreign Affairs, 85*(4), 58–74; and Norton, August Richard (2007). The Shiite "Threat" Revisited. *Current History, 10*, 434–439.

22. Esposito, John (2010). *Islam: The Straight Path*. New York: Oxford University Press.

23. Kepel, Gilles (2003). The Origins and Development of the Jihadist Movement: From Anti-Communism to Terrorism. *Asian Affairs, 34*(2), 91–108.

24. Wiktorowicz, Quintan (2001). The New Global Threat: Transnational Salafis and Jihad. *Middle East Policy, 8*(4), 18–38.

25. Lappin, Yaakov (2010). *Virtual Caliphate: Exposing the Islamist State on the Internet*. Dulles, VA: Potomac Books.

26. Kepel, Gilles (2002). *Jihad: The Trail of Political Islam*. Cambridge, MA: Belknap Press of Harvard University.

27. Qutb, Sayyid (1964). *Milestones*. Chicago: Kazi Publications.

28. PBS (1998, February 23). *Al Qaeda's Second Fatwa*. Retrieved May 5, 2013, from http://www.pbs.org/newshour/updates/military/jan-june98/fatwa_1998.html

29. Taheri, Amir (2004). Fascism in Muslim Countries. *American Foreign Policy Interests, 26*(1), 21–30.

30. Mandaville, Michael (2009). *Citizen-Soldier Handbook: 101 Ways Every American Can Fight Terrorism*. Indianapolis, IN: Dog Ear Publishing.

31. Stump, Roger (2005). Religion and the Geographies of War. In Colin Flint (Ed.), *The Geography of War and Peace: From Death Camps to Diplomats* (pp. 149–173). Oxford: Oxford University Press.

32. Steger, Manfred B. (2003). *Globalization: A Short Introduction*. New York: Oxford University Press.

33. Peters, Ralph (2002, October 15). The Bali Attack Is a Sign of the Terrorists' Desperation. *The Wall Street Journal*, p. A1.

34. Burke, Jason (2004). Al Qaeda. *Foreign Policy, 142*, 18–26.

35. Cassidy, Robert (2006). *Counterinsurgency and the Global War on Terror: Military Culture and Irregular War*. Westport, CT: Praeger Security International.

36. Grillo, Beppe (2006). *Economia del Kamikaze*. Retrieved June 22, 2012, from http://www.beppegrillo.it/2005/07/economia_del_ka_1.html

37. Whelan, Richard (2005). *Al-Qaedaism: The Threat to Islam, the Threat to the World*. Dublin: Ashfield Press.

38. Bonnefoy, Laurent (2012). *Salafism in Yemen: Transnationalism and Religious Identity*. New York: Columbia University Press.

39. Meijer, Roel (2009). *Global Salafism: Islam's New Religious Movement*. New York: Columbia University Press.

40. Wiktorowicz, Quintan (2001). The New Global Threat: Transnational Salafis and Jihad. *Middle East Policy, 8*(4), 18–38.

41. Kepel, Gilles (2005). *The Roots of Radical Islam*. London: Saqi Books.

42. Assyrian International News Agency (2012, April 16). Uproar in Germany over Salafi Drive to Hand out Millions of Qurans. Retrieved May 3, 2013, from http://www.aina.org/news/20120416150547.htm

43. Wiktorowicz, Quintan (2005). A Genealogy of Radical Islam. *Studies in Conflict & Terrorism, 28*, 75–97.

44. Wiktorowicz, Quintan (2006). Anatomy of the Salafi Movement. *Studies in Conflict & Terrorism, 29*, 207–239.

45. Zumwalt, James (2010). Muslims Know the Symbolism of the Ground Zero Mosque. *Human Events, 23*, 1.

46. Sills, Ben (2007, October 31). Spanish Court to Deliver Verdict in Madrid Train Bombing Case. *Bloomberg*, 21.

47. Jordan, Javier, & Horsburgh, Nicola (2005): Mapping Jihadist Terrorism in Spain. *Studies in Conflict & Terrorism, 28*(3), 169–191.

48. Halliday, Fred (1995). *Islam and the Myth of Confrontation*. London: I. B. Tauris; and Morris, Travis, & Crank, John P. (2011). Toward a Phenomenology of Terrorism: Implications for Research and Policy. *Crime, Law and Social Change, 56*, 219–242.

49. Rodgers, Guy (2012). *Understanding the Threat of Radical Islam*. Broomall, PA: National Highlights.

50. Aly, Abd al-Monein Said, & Wenner, Manfred (1982). Modern Islamic Reform Movements: The Muslim Brotherhood in Contemporary Egypt. *Middle East Journal, 36*(3), 336–361.

51. Deliso, Christopher (2007). *The Coming Balkan Caliphate: The Threat of Radical Islam to Europe and the West*. Westport, CT: Praeger.

52. Nawab, Mohamed, & Osman, Mohamed (2009). Reviving the Caliphate in Malaysia. *Studies in Conflict & Terrorism, 32*(7), 646–663.

53. McLeod, Douglas (2008). *Support for the Caliphate and Radical Mobilization*. College Park, MD: National Consortium for the Study of Terrorism and Responses to Terrorism.

54. Saniotis, Arthur (2005). Re-Enchanting Terrorism: Jihadists as "Liminal Beings." *Studies in Conflict & Terrorism, 28*, 533–545.

55. Hairgrove, Frank, & McLeod, Douglas (2008). Circles Drawing toward High Risk Activism: The Use of Usroh and Halaqa in Islamist Radical Movements. *Studies in Conflict & Terrorism, 31*(5), 399–411.

56. U.S. National War College (2002). *Combating Terrorism in a Globalized World*. Washington, DC: U.S. National War College.

57. Gerges, Fawaz (2005). *The Far Enemy: Why Jihad Went Global*. New York: Cambridge University Press; and Mitchell, Richard (1993). *The Society of the Muslim Brothers*. New York: Oxford University Press.

58. Rodgers, Guy (2012). *Understanding the Threat of Radical Islam*. Broomall, PA: National Highlights.

59. Schroeder, John Ross (2012). Islam vs. the West: Why the Clash of Civilizations? *The Good News, 17*(1), 4–7.

60. Rodgers, Guy (2012). *Understanding the Threat of Radical Islam*. Broomall, PA: National Highlights.

61. Roggio, Bill (2005). The Anbar Campaign: A Flash Presentation. *The Long War Journal, 2*, 10–21.

62. Charfi, Mohamed, & Camiller, Patrick (2005). *Islam and Liberty: The Historical Misunderstanding*. London: Zed Books.

63. Ranstorp, Magnus (1996). Terrorism in the Name of Religion. *Journal of International Affairs, 50*(1), 41–63.

64. Lapidus, Ira (2002). *A History of Islamic Societies*. Cambridge: Cambridge University Press.

65. Roy, Olivier (2004). *The Failure of Political Islam*. Cambridge, MA: Harvard University Press.

66. Kepel, Gilles (2008). *Beyond Terror and Martyrdom: The Future of the Middle East*. Cambridge, MA: Belknap Press of Harvard University.

67. Roy, Olivier (2007). *Secularism Confronts Islam*. Columbia: Columbia University Press.

68. Lapidus, Ira (2002). *A History of Islamic Societies*. Cambridge: Cambridge University Press.

69. Davidson, Lawrence (1998). *Islamic Fundamentalism*. Westport, CT: Greenwood Press.

70. Katz, Adam (2004). Remembering Amalek: 9/11 and Generative Thinking. *Anthropoetics, 10*(2), 10–24.

71. Wright, Robin (2008). *Dreams and Shadows: The Future of the Middle East*. New York: Penguin.

72. Anderson, Sean (1992). Iran: Terrorism and Islamic Fundamentalism. In Edwin Corr & Stephen Sloan (Eds.), *Low-Intensity Conflict: Old Threats in a New World* (pp. 173–195). Oxford: Westview Press.

73. Milton-Edwards, Beverly (1996). *Islamic Politics in Palestine*. London: I. B. Tauris; and Roy, Sara (2000). The Transformation of Islamic NGOs in Palestine. *Middle East Report, 21*(4), 24–27.

74. Toameh, Khaled Abu (2007, June 15). Haniyeh Calls for Palestinian Unity. *Jerusalem Post*, p. A1.

75. Davidson, Lawrence (1998). *Islamic Fundamentalism*. Westport, CT: Greenwood Press.

76. Sattar, Noman (1995). Affairs "Al Ikhwan Al Muslimin" (Society of Muslim Brotherhood) Aims and Ideology, Role and Impact. *Pakistan Horizon, 48*(2), 7–30.

77. Besson, Sylvain (2005). *La conquête de l'Occident: Le projet secret des Islamistes*. Paris: Le Seuil.

78. Kupferschmidt, Uri (1995). Modernisation and Islamic Fundamentalism: The Muslim Brotherhood and its Ramifications. In Lieteke van Vucht Tijssen, Jan Berting, & Frank Lechner (Eds.), *The Search for Fundamentals: The Process of Modernisation and the Quest for Meaning* (pp. 41–62). Boston: Kluwer Academic Publishers.

79. Mishal, Shaul, & Sela, Avraham (2000). *The Palestinian Hamas: Vision, Violence, and Coexistence.* New York: Columbia University Press; and Mitchell, Richard (1993). *The Society of the Muslim Brothers.* New York: Oxford University Press.

80. Howarth, David (1956). *The Desert King: The Life of Ibn Saud.* New York: Collins; and Thesiger, Wilfred (1991). *Arabian Sands.* New York: Penguin.

81. Qutb, Sayyid (1981). Milestones. Cedar Rapids, IA: The Mother Mosque Foundation.

82. Rodgers, Guy (2012). *Understanding the Threat of Radical Islam.* Broomall, PA: National Highlights.

83. Juergensmeyer, Mark (2001). *Terror in the Mind of God: The Global Rise of Religious Violence* (2nd ed.). Berkeley: University of California Press.

84. Rodgers, Guy (2012). *Understanding the Threat of Radical Islam.* Broomall, PA: National Highlights.

85. Azzam, Abdullah (1987). *Join the Caravan.* Retrieved May 5, 2013, from http://archive.org/stream/JoinThe-Caravan/JoinTheCaravan_djvu.txt

86. Azzam, Abdullah (1988). Al-Qa'idah al-Sulbah. *al-Jihad, 41*, 46.

87. Frankel, Glenn (1989, December 17). Militant Islamic Movement Upstages PLO in West Bank Uprising. *The Washington Post,* p. A1.

88. Kelley, Jack (2001, July 5). Devotion, Desire Drive Youths to "Martyrdom." *USA Today,* p. A1.

89. Ya'ari, Ehud (2004, November 1). The Outer Intifada. *Jerusalem Report,* p. A1.

90. Rodgers, Guy (2012). *Understanding the Threat of Radical Islam.* Broomall, PA: National Highlights.

91. Jansen, Johannes (1986). *The Neglected Duty: The Creed of Sadat's Assassins and Islamic Resurgence in the Middle East.* New York: Macmillan.

92. Faraj, Muhammad Abd Al Salam (2001). The Neglected Duty. Excerpted in Adam Parfrey (Ed.), *Extreme Islam: Anti-American Propaganda of Muslim Fundamentalism.* Los Angeles: Feral House.

93. Momen, Moojan (1985). *An Introduction to Shi'i Islam.* New Haven, CT: Yale University Press.

94. Choueiri, Youssef (2010). *Islamic Fundamentalism: The Story of Islamist Movements.* New York: Continuum.

95. Sunan Abi Dawud, 11:370.

96. Hiro, Dilip (1989). *Holy Wars: The Rise of Islamic Fundamentalism.* New York: Routledge.

97. Stump, Roger (2005). Religion and the Geographies of War. In Colin Flint (Ed.), *The Geography of War and Peace: From Death Camps to Diplomats* (pp. 149–173). Oxford: Oxford University Press.

98. Bendle, Mervyn (2006). Existential Terrorism: Civil Society and Its Enemies. *Australian Journal of Politics and History, 52*(1), 115–130.

99. Ehrenberg, John (1999). *Civil Society: The Critical History of an Idea.* New York: New York University Press.

100. Burton, John (1997). *Violence Explained.* Manchester, UK: Manchester University Press.

101. Momen, Moojan (1985). *An Introduction to Shi'i Islam.* New Haven, CT: Yale University Press.

102. Algar, Hamid (1981). *Islam and Revolution.* Berkeley: University of California Press.

103. White, Jonathan (2011). *Terrorism & Homeland Security* (7th ed.). Belmont, CA: Wadsworth.

Chapter Ten

Symbolism in Suicide Terrorism

Suicide terrorism is an attack upon a target, in which a terrorist intends to kill others and/or create significant damage while being aware that he or she will die in the process.[1] As Pedhazur (2004)[2] puts it, suicide terrorism refers to "a diversity of violent actions perpetrated by people who are aware that the odds they will return alive are close to zero" (p. 8). For Ganor (2001), it is an "operational method in which the very act of the attack is dependent upon the death of the perpetrator" (p. 6).[3] Suicide terrorism differs from other terrorist or militant tactics in that the success of a suicide attack depends exclusively on the destruction of the attackers—for example, through a massive explosion—who are used as weapons against people and/or material entities.[4] In addition, the difference between mere suicide and suicide terrorism is that the terrorists are ready to not just risk their lives but also commit themselves to die for their cause. From a criminal law standpoint, suicide terrorism is a murderous deed with a specific **mens rea** (i.e., "guilty mind"), that is, the willingness to kill along with the willingness to die.[5]

Synonyms of suicide terrorism include suicide bombing, suicide-homicide bombing, and martyrdom operation. Suicide attacks are committed primarily in four different ways: **human-borne suicide** (also called the suicide bodysuit), **vehicle-borne suicide** (including the use of trucks, cars, and motorcycles), **marine-borne suicide** (e.g., watercraft and scuba divers), and **aerial-borne suicide** (e.g., gliders, mini-helicopters, and airplanes).[6] Due to the magnitude of devastation that these methods can generate, suicide terrorism appeals to militant groups because it can kill large numbers of people in a short amount of time.[7] Between 1980 and 2001, each suicide attack killed thirteen people on average, whereas other terrorist incidents killed only one person on average—and that is without counting September 11, 2001, which would render the death ratio much stronger.[8] Lastly, suicide attacks are comparatively economical because they cause the greatest amount of damage with the lowest number of perpetrators. Suicide terrorism does not necessitate an escape plan and leaves no one to be caught (and, therefore, no one can be tortured or inform on one's recruiters).[9]

Biopolitics

In the context of suicide terrorism, **biopolitics** reflects the idea that the body of the terrorist becomes a destructive weapon, where his or her shattered body parts turn into devastating projectiles, just like the resultant broadcast images of the terrorist act do. Put simply, biopolitics entails using one's life and body as a weapon.[10] Murray (2006)[11] observes that "the attacker's body is literally weaponized. Shards of bone become human shrapnel" (p. 207). The suicide bomber's exploding body is the hinge between his or her achieved goal and the victims' sacrifice.[12] In biopolitics, the suicide terrorist becomes a **smart bomb**, because the terrorist can choose where and when the detonation of his or her body will be. The ultimate objective is to inflict as much damage as possible to the enemy. As terrorism expert Bruce Hoffman (2003)[13] explains, the suicide bomber is "the ultimate smart bomb, or human cruise missile" (p. 3). And if the bomber is identified, he or she can detonate immediately.

Reem Riyashi, a twenty-one-year-old Palestinian terrorist, read the following words for her farewell video: "It was always my wish to turn my body into deadly shrapnel against the Zionists and to knock on Heaven's doors with the skulls of Zionists." The day after reading these words, she killed four Israelis in a suicide attack. Reem, or those who wrote her last words, believed that her suicide accomplishment would secure her admission into Paradise.[14] Smart bombs can make changes at the last minute to make sure that their operation works as planned. This is another aspect of biopolitics. The psychological effect on those observing the suicide terror act, whether friend or enemy, is powerful. Suicide terrorists convey a message to our constituency that the struggle is here to stay because they are ready to sacrifice their bodies and souls for their cause. It also communicates the message that such fatal sacrifices do not go in vain. Others must keep on carrying the torch of liberation through similar acts.[15]

Brief History and Statistics on Suicide Terrorism

In the Middle Ages, from the eleventh to the thirteenth centuries, the **Assassins**, a terrorist cult in Iran and Syria, believed that dying in the way of Allah (i.e., as a hero in battle) was the highest duty. To kill (and be killed in the process) was seen as a positive act because it was done for Allah, and it guaranteed a place in Paradise after death. As the Qur'an explains it, "Allah has purchased of the believers their persons and their goods; for theirs in return is the garden of Paradise: they fight in His cause, and slay and are slain: a promise binding on Him in truth" (Qur'an 9:111). Such belief in supreme justification and reward is widely embraced by Islamists today. The Assassins deeply influenced the modern era of Islamism.[16] The Assassins also believed that salvation was only for warriors who obeyed their leaders (i.e., imams), killed infidels, and committed ritual suicide subsequently. The only adequate weapon was the dagger. A laudable Assassin was expected to die after living up to his duty to kill others.[17]

From the mid-eighteenth century onward, other groups resorted to suicide terrorism against colonial rulers in countries like India, Indonesia, and the Philippines.[18] In the twentieth century, particularly in October 1983, during the Lebanese Civil War, two suicide terrorists from Hezbollah, a Shia terrorist organization based in Lebanon, exploded truck bombs at U.S. Marine barracks in Beirut, killing 241 U.S. and 58 French servicemen. The attack boosted the image and credibility of Hezbollah. Now, the Shia terrorist group was regarded by many as the "spearhead of the sacred Muslim struggle against foreign occupation" (Ranstorp, 1997, p. 38).[19] A few years later, Al Qaeda sent its members to Hezbollah in order to receive training on suicide bombing. This collaboration became a turning point in the diffusion of suicide attacks around the world.[20] In a nutshell, Hezbollah's suicide truck explosions gave a new face to terrorism.

In the late 1980s, the Tamil Tigers became notorious for acting like human cruise missiles in Sri Lanka. They initiated and revolutionized the use of concealed explosive belts and vests. Between July 5, 1987, and November 20, 2008, they committed 378 suicide attacks.[21] In Europe, the Provisional Irish Republican Army (PIRA) used a unique form of suicide terrorism in multiple attacks in the 1990s. The PIRA's suicide terrorism consisted of capturing British military soldiers or personnel and forcing them to drive explosive-laden vehicles into British Army checkpoints. In the worst incident, five British soldiers were killed by a British Army cook when the latter was forced to drive a 1,000-pound bomb into a checkpoint in Derry, Northern Ireland.[22]

Between October 2000 and October 2006, 218 suicide attacks occurred in Israel, Gaza, and the West Bank.[23] Suicide bombing, of course, has been heightened with the September 11, 2001, terrorist attacks (i.e., "detonating" planes by crashing them into buildings, which killed roughly 3,000 people) and the suicide bombings in London (on subway trains and a double-decker bus) on July 7, 2005 (which killed fifty-six people).[24] Statistics show that 75 percent of all suicide attacks since the mid-1980s have taken place after 9/11. Indeed, in the ten years after September 11, 2001, there were 336 suicide attacks in Afghanistan and 303 in Pakistan, while 1,003 documented suicide attacks took place in Iraq between March 20, 2003, and December 31, 2010.[25] Overall, between 1981 and 2008, more than 2,000 suicide attacks were perpetrated around the world, representing 4 percent of all terrorist attacks but over 30 percent of all terrorism-related deaths (i.e., killing more than 21,000 people and injuring 50,000 others).[26] More recently, according to the Institute for National Security Studies (2014),[27] eighteen nations experienced extreme cases of suicide terrorism in 2013. Close to 300 suicide bombings were perpetrated, leading to about 3,100 deaths. This statistic represents a 25 percent increase from the year 2012 (in the number of suicide attacks).

CASE STUDY: KURDISTAN WORKERS' PARTY

Founded in 1978, the **Kurdistan Workers' Party**, commonly known as the **PKK**, is a secular terrorist organization responsible for perpetrating numerous acts of terrorism against Turkey. Designated as an international terrorist organization by the United Nations, NATO, the United States, and the European Union, the PKK aims at seceding from Turkey in order to have its own self-governing Kurdish homeland called **Kurdistan**, a geocultural region spanning southeastern Turkey, northeastern Iraq, and parts of Syria and Iran. Up to 40 million Kurds live in that region.[28] As of June 2013, the conflict between Turkey and the PKK had already resulted in over 40,000 deaths, including PKK members, Turkish soldiers, and many civilians (both Kurdish and Turkish).[29] Historically, suicide terrorism had no tradition in Turkey. However, the PKK broke that mold.

Indeed, in the mid-1990s, the PKK began a series of fifteen suicide bombings—eleven of which were committed by women—on Turkish government and police installations, and local tourist spots. The objective was to undermine Turkish authorities by way of a long and low-intensity confrontation.[30] Few, if any, of the suicide terrorists appear to have been walk-ins. Rather, the PKK's suicide terrorists were long-established members of the organization. To be more precise, none of them, except one, ever volunteered to be a suicide terrorist. They were handpicked and trained for their mission. Each selected person was asked to carry the struggle to a higher level of efficacy. Their chivalry was commended, and they were offered an eminent place in the history of the movement. By and large, Kurdish society, from which the PKK derived its manpower and cultural values, is predominantly rural. The tradition of chivalry and armed rebellion keeps their fighting spirit alive and fired up. Based on the Kurdish code of honor, both men and women have chivalrous qualities and cannot allow themselves to be humiliated by the Turkish government, which they perceive as an oppressive and illegitimate entity.[31] Terrorism is a good way for the Kurds to preserve the virtues of their group. The essence of this worldview is captured in the concept of **pathological narcissistic terrorism**.

In this instance, it symbolizes the PKK's vehement determination to use any conceivable means—like suicide terrorism—to knock the Turks off balance.

The origins of the PKK's suicide terrorism most likely come from their narrow commitment to the group's leader, Abdullah Öcalan. Since he has been jailed, not only has Öcalan published many books, but also he has called for his followers to carry out suicide attacks as a way to force the Turkish government to release him. What this anecdote demonstrates is that suicide terrorism can be the outcome of internal group dynamics. Another conclusion is that suicide terrorism is not always due to religious obligation or devotion (i.e., the PKK is a secular group). In this particular case, suicide terrorism is an extreme strategy of national liberation. Nevertheless, as we will see, most suicide terror attacks are rooted in religion. [32]

WEAPON OF MASS PERSUASION

This case study on the PKK illustrates the potential of suicide terrorism to provoke changes, induce the Turkish government to undertake a different course of action, and act as a massive persuader. When suicide terrorism becomes this massive persuader, it is generally called a "weapon of mass persuasion." A **weapon of mass persuasion** refers to any method designed to influence the mind and behavior of the targeted population. As a form of propaganda, it is a psychological mechanism that provides a perspective and manipulates salience in order to shape subsequent judgment. [33] Suicide terrorism involves the audience in the persuasive process, making it a powerful instrument to influence and change minds. Of all the symbols of terrorist propaganda, suicide terrorism has been the most dramatic and effective weapon of mass persuasion known to humankind. Adopted or supported by various ideological groups across the continuum of the political spectrum, by numerous religious organizations, and even by secular ones, the appeal of suicide terrorism has reached a universal scope. The objective of war and violent resistance is to impose our will on the enemy. Many different terms could be used to express this function. In ancient China, the philosophy of Sun Tzu (1963), [34] a military strategist, was to "subdue the enemy" or "break the enemy's resistance." Suicide terrorism as a weapon of mass persuasion also reflects the notion of asymmetric warfare, a phenomenon whereby suicide attacks are a result of an imbalance of power, in which groups with insignificant power use suicide bombing as a method to destabilize the group with significant power: the enemy government and its leaders (see chapter 3). [35]

Influence Operations

In military jargon, weapons of mass persuasion are called influence operations. **Influence operations** are actions taken with the main goal of influencing the actions, behavior, attitudes, or opinions of others. [36] After all, the enemy is made up of individuals. There are many ways to influence an individual. On one side of the spectrum, a person may be killed. On the other side of the spectrum, that same person can be persuaded to accept, and hopefully adopt, an important policy—changing the individual's attitudes, behavior, opinions, and, in due course, actions. [37] Similarly, Hoffman and McCormick (2004) [38] put forward the notion that suicide terrorism is a type of **strategic signaling** whereby terrorists communicate (to their audience) their intention and determination. For example, Pape (2006) [39] attributes more than 90 percent of attacks before the Iraq Civil War to an objective of withdrawal of U.S. military forces. On the other hand, Atran (2006) [40] claims that, since 2004, the vast majority of suicide bombers have been driven by Islamist ideology and that Islamist suicide attacks have been much more numerous. In only two years (2004–2005), more suicide attacks occurred—indeed, about 600 more—than Pape's entire sample.

Acting Out

Suicide terrorists do not merely commit suicide or murder. They exploit their own and their victims' death as a symbolic gesture. As a symbol itself, death acts as a channel for the communication of ideas and ideologies. Deprived of a clear message, the act is all there is; it explains it all. In the absence of efficient or significant communication, the event unfolds everything through its own "eventness." It becomes what psychoanalysts call "acting out." The symbolism is fully located within the act itself; death becomes its tool and its meaning.[41] **Acting out** is a defense mechanism whereby one communicates emotional conflict and feelings through actions rather than words. "Acting out" literally means acting out (i.e., expressing) the desires that are craved by the id. The "id" is that part of human personality that contains our primitive drives and operates mostly based on the pleasure principle. The **pleasure principle** is a principle that has two key objectives: the seeking of pleasure and the avoidance of pain. It has no authentic rationality and wants to satisfy its needs through what Sigmund Freud referred to as the "primary processes" that control the lives of infants, including satisfaction and self-protection.[42]

CATEGORIES OF SUICIDE TERRORISM

According to Durkheim (1951),[43] suicide is death that comes directly or indirectly from a positive or negative act of the individual him- or herself, who is aware that it will produce this result. Durkheim's work on suicide describes four categories of suicide: anomic, fatalistic, egoistic, and altruistic. In the twentieth century, these categories were considered the best foundation for understanding suicide and, to a great extent, deviant behavior. The last two categories—egoistic and altruistic suicide—fit our framework of suicide terrorism. Whereas egoistic terrorism gives one rewards in the afterlife, altruistic terrorism leads one to kill numerous people on behalf of one's group. This is also ascertained by the constructs of instrumental rationality and value rationality (see the "Durkheim's Categories" subsection).

Durkheim's Categories

Anomic suicide is a type of suicide whereby the victim is incapable to cope with a crisis in a rational way and chooses suicide in order to solve the problem. Put differently, anomic suicide is triggered by the erosion of one's capacity to navigate through difficult times. **Anomie** is a condition stemming from a lack of norms and moral guidelines in society. Anomic individuals generally feel alienated, disconnected, and powerless. Anomie is a condition or malaise within people that is characterized by an absence or decrease of standards or values. When related to a government or society, anomie denotes social unrest, which is akin to the use of the term "anarchy." It is a negative response toward or a withdrawal from the regulatory control of society.[44]

Fatalistic suicide is a type of suicide caused by disproportionate social regulation that fundamentally restricts an individual's freedom on a daily basis. People who take their own lives in this manner see their future as blocked or their passions as dammed by unfair discipline. The normative or moral demands placed on the person are too overbearing. Based on all this, individuals experience serious and persistent duress that contributes to a sense of downright hopelessness.[45] **Fatalism** refers to an extremely regulated existence "with futures pitilessly blocked and passions violently checked by oppressive discipline" (Durkheim, 1951, p. 276).[46]

Egoistic suicide is a type of suicide based on an individual's desire to reap the rewards of a better life in another world. He or she no longer finds a basis for existence in life; hence, life on earth is not worth living. Egoistic suicide occurs when a person sees him- or herself as superior to what society has to offer, like a transcendence of societal norms of belief and behavior that no longer seem to be self-evident and binding.[47] In this context, **egoism** is not only an excessive or extravagant sense of self-importance; it is also an individual's ability to assert him- or herself as a result of endless self-gratifying opportunities and excessive individualism.

Altruistic suicide is a type of suicide whereby a person is significantly integrated into a group so that he or she believes that no sacrifice is too great. **Altruism** is the principle that promotes the survival chances of others to the detriment of one's own; it is self-sacrifice for the sake of others.[48] Typically, altruistic suicides are characterized by cultural approval and advance the social order. Examples are the Japanese kamikaze pilots in World War II and Islamist martyrs who blow themselves up while killing enemies in the process. Altruistic suicide is less likely to occur in contemporary Western societies in which the individual's personality is increasingly liberated from a collective personality.[49]

Instrumental Rationality versus Value Rationality

Rationality is reasoned action or assessment as a basis for decision making. Such an assessment can be founded on self-interest or larger values.[50] Two such larger values are instrumental rationality and value rationality. **Instrumental rationality** implies a firm cost-benefit calculus in regard to goals, which requires the rejection or modification of goals if the costs of achieving them are too high. **Value rationality** is a type of decision making based on a conscious ethical, religious, or other belief, regardless of its chances of success. Both types of rationality are manifestations of goal-directed behavior, but their conceptions of costs widely differ. Instrumental rationality implies self-interest, whereas value rationality has more to do with altruism.[51]

The first one would mean that suicide terrorists gain more from dying than from living. In this context, a vehement belief in Paradise is unmistakably an asset for Islamists strapping on an explosive belt: many physical and similar rewards are lying ahead. In the second case, suicide terrorists would hold themselves to be acting altruistically on behalf of others in their group. They believe their fatal sacrifices will benefit their kin and social group.[52] Pedahzur, Perliger, and Weinberg (2003)[53] observed that, between 1973 and 2002, at least eighty Palestinian suicide terrorists were acting out of altruistic motives for their group. Their deaths were seen as necessary for the salvation of the Palestinian collectivity. A conclusion is that both instrumental rationality and value rationality are good incentives for engaging in suicide terrorism.

MARTYRDOM

A particular type of suicide terrorism is martyrdom. **Martyrdom** refers to heroic death, usually in battle, that is sanctified by a deity or Supreme Being. Death in battle gives immortality, and the deceased is hailed as a martyr. The martyr is generally not self-made; martyrdom operations are rarely, if ever, the product of lone nuts. For example, in the Palestinian territories, Hamas, the Palestinian Islamic Jihad (PIJ), and other Palestinian groups recruit, indoctrinate, and train their future suicide bombers. Hence, the martyr is a product of his or her society. His or her creation depends, in part, on the nature of the social environment as well as other important catalysts. There is a growing trend to embrace martyrdom as a symbol of resistance and terrorism. On rare occasions, when a suicide terrorist kills him- or herself as part of a jihad against enemies, but does it all by him- or herself, it is called **predatory martyrdom**. Predatory martyrs are less common. They are usually indoctrinated by emails, revolutionary books, extremist websites, and their own admiration for radical teachers and leaders with terrorist agendas. [54]

In Arabic, the martyr is called the **shahid** ("shuhada" in the plural). Hamas public announcements that claim responsibility for martyrdom operations (along with other terrorist attacks) are itemized on the official internet site of the movement, the Palestine Information Center. In Arabic, the document is entitled "Sijil Al-Majid," or the "Record of Glory." Each terrorist who perpetrates a martyrdom operation is unapologetically called a "shahid." Hamas posts a memorial page for each shahid on its website. The memorial section is entitled "Shuhada' wa mu'ataqalun" ("Martyrs and Prisoners"). [55]

Why Martyrdom?

There are four major reasons why martyrdom is used by terrorist groups. To begin, martyrdom represents a vehicle to uphold one's religious values and affirm one's self-worth. To the eyes of potential militants and their sympathetic backers, it turns brutal terror into sacred missions. In this context, martyrdom is akin to "cosmic war" (as explained, in detail, in the next subsection). Second, as Pape (2006)[56] suggests, psychological explanations cannot justify why more than 95 percent of incidents occur as part of well-organized crusades by groups of individuals who do not fit the conventional stereotype of "normal" suicidal people. Suicide martyrs are peculiar. Fewer than 20 percent of people committing "ordinary" suicides leave a suicide note or a letter that is very personal and intended for friends and relatives. The martyr, on the other hand, symbolizes a renunciation without compensation of the human's most basic appetite—the instinct of self-preservation. The suicide terrorist becomes a martyr in the service of transcendence (in a word, theism), as opposed to the adjournment of appetite in the service of nonviolent exchange (in a word, humanism). [57]

Third, as Atran (2010)[58] acutely remarks, the "jihad fights with the most primitive and elementary forms of human cooperation, tribal kinship and friendship, in the cause of the most advanced and sophisticated form of cultural cooperation ever created: the moral salvation of humanity" (p. 35). In a survey of support for suicide bombings in the Palestinian territories, results indicate that support was rooted in a belief of a sense of injustice—an injustice committed against the group (e.g., by Israelis or Americans). This belief of perceived injustice explains why Islam sanctions martyrs. Fourth, although the use of martyrdom by radical groups can be explained by the increased sense of threat to the groups, it can also be explained by a growing level of globalization between groups—in terms of contact, similarity of causes, and examples of suicide tactics. This is particularly evident among Islamist groups. For example, many Algerian, Egyptian, and Palestinian Muslim extremists have participated alongside the mujahedin warriors in the Soviet war in Afghanistan. They trained with these Afghan fighters and buttressed them (both physically and ideologically) in a war "as much about the forging of a new and revolutionary social order as about national liberation" (Davis, 1993, p. 327). [59]

Cosmic War

Leaders of suicide terrorist groups and martyrs-to-be answer to transcendent authorities (i.e., like deities or Supreme Beings). Based on well-informed, ill-informed, or even selective readings of religious texts, they argue that, because they are called to fulfill the commands of a transcendent authority, they are neither limited by, nor to be evaluated by, human standards. Killing the enemy is a step closer to gratifying and accomplishing a divine mission.[60] Juergensmeyer (2000)[61] refers to this condition as **cosmic war**, a spiritual struggle that symbolizes the fight between good and bad, and between truth and evil. In cosmic war, the rules and objectives of conflict do not have an earthly or rational basis. Terrorist leaders inspire their holy warriors to engage in self-destructive acts by manipulating holy scriptures. The young suicide recruits are indoctrinated into believing that, in this process of religious struggle, dying does not mean the end of life; rather, it is the beginning of eternal life. What holy warriors are guaranteed are the rewards of martyrdom.

In these circumstances, the existence of both the terrorist and victim has no real meaning. Religious terrorists do not trouble themselves with negotiation. Instead, their only aim is to eliminate their enemies in order to fulfill their mission. If an enemy civilian were to be killed, then it is good. Due to the growing popularity of the concept of "cosmic war," terrorists engage more conspicuously in martyrdom operations. As we have seen, these come in many shapes and forms: exploding human-driven vehicles, self-detonated bombs strapped to people, and massive killings in places where the terrorist will inexorably be gunned down by police forces.[62]

Martyrdom Videos

The majority of martyrs-to-be leave videotaped statements for public consumption (i.e., martyrdom videos). A **martyrdom video** is a video recording, mostly from Islamist activists, championing the participation in a suicide attack and extolling the virtues of dying as a hero in holy war. The video consists of a speech by the martyr-to-be, who is preparing to die for the cause. Although most videos are of substandard quality, some of them incorporate text, music, and soppy or emotional segments—a term called **emotive narratives**.[63] The martyr's statements are somewhat personal; in order to boost community approval, they also provide a more general justification for the deadly action.[64] The text for the video testament is carefully written before the filming. The filming itself is done right before the suicide mission, which the martyrs themselves watch to intensify their determination. Photos of them are taken and later appear on propaganda posters. These videos generally include weapons, the Qur'an, and other Islamic symbols. In fact, the future martyr sits or stands before a black Islamic standard. These disparate items are combined into a single inclusive message: the religious significance of martyrdom and its violent aspects.[65]

When all these things are done, the group's leaders assign their foot soldiers to pre-identified targets.[66] A martyrdom video truly represents a type of iconographic art of suicide terrorism. This imagery is commonly used by Palestinian terrorists. The videos they create for their loved ones are also used by their operators as a type of legacy or educational method to recruit others.[67] As such, martyrdom videos can amplify the actual power of jihadist groups and their supporters. These videos not only help immortalize the martyrs and their cause among followers; they also create rock-solid contracts. Backpedaling on a mission—particularly after making a videotaped proclamation of one's intentions—would lead to deep social and presumably spiritual costs.[68] Some martyrdom videos simultaneously claim and disclaim responsibility because they are created before a suicide mission and watched only after the mission is over (when the hero is dead).[69]

ISTISHHAD

For Kobrin (2010),[70] Islamic suicide terrorism is a type of group-assisted mass murder through suicide bombings. It is the result of a group-held fantasy of killing infidels (Jews, Christians, and sometimes even fellow Muslims). Martyrdom operations have been justified as a commendable approach to mortality at the hands of the enemy, and as a legitimate tactic for the will of Allah. Among other arguments, some terrorist leaders claim that Allah, and not the suicide bomber, decides whether the latter will die, and whether women and children will go down with the martyr.[71] The essence of this paragraph can be captured in one concept: istishhad. **Istishhad** is the Arabic word for martyrdom, a martyr's death, or a heroic death. When translated verbatim, it actually means "self-chosen martyrdom."[72]

As a religious term, istishhad symbolizes the ultimate giving of one's life to Allah. In common parlance, the term has come to accentuate heroism in the performance of sacrifice rather than victimization in war. It has developed into the military and political tactic of martyrdom operations.[73] A person performing istishhad is called an "istishhadi" (which is the same as a shahid). The origins of modern istishhad come from Shia Islam in Iran during the Iran-Iraq War of 1980–1988. One of the first occurrences of this was Iranian children walking through minefields to detonate buried landmines. The objective was to pave a safe way for adult soldiers. Mohammed Hossein Fahmideh, a thirteen-year-old boy soldier in the Iran-Iraq War, is said to be the very first martyr to have partaken in contemporary istishhad. In November 1980, he fastened rocket-propelled grenades to his body and exploded himself under an Iraqi tank. The Grand Ayatollah Khomeini made Fahmideh a national hero and inspiration for new recruits for istishhad.[74]

Hamas

In recent years, Hamas terrorism has been highly correlated with istishhad. The shahid can achieve high standing when he or she becomes a suicide bomber. In Hamas jargon, the term "suicide bomber" is not used; instead, the group brings up the very concept of istishhad.[75] One of the key Hamas founders, Abdul Aziz Rantisi, suggests that the "suicide bomber" label points toward an impulsive action by a deranged person. However, for Hamas, the supreme act of martyrdom is purposeful and deftly chosen, springing from profoundly felt religious obligation. Thus, when a person sacrifices his or her life in holy war, the individual is bestowed permanent symbolic immortality. Indeed, the shahid is raised to a higher spiritual platform and sits with Allah in Paradise.[76]

Already in early 1994, when Hamas performed martyrdom attacks for the first time—by strapping bombs to the belly or chest of the mission carrier—in the Israeli villages of Afula and Khidara, it described these operations as "martyrdom operations" rather than the more secular "suicide bombing." Today, "istishhad" is the most commonly used word to refer to sacrificial acts in the Palestinian resistance movement. Between April 6, 1994, and March 4, 1996 (after the Hebron massacre), an unprecedented spree of thirteen Hamas martyrdom attacks took place inside Israel, killing 136 people. On October 4, 2003, twenty-nine-year-old Hanadi Tayseer Jaradat, a lawyer and new member of the Palestinian Islamic Jihad (PIJ), walked into Maxim, a renowned restaurant in Haifa, and detonated herself. Nineteen people were killed in that tragedy, and more than fifty were wounded. [77] In a note left to her family, she wrote,

> I know that there is no possible way for me to restore Palestine. I know this for sure. Yet I also know that this is my duty, which I have already completed towards Allah. I have accepted his calling by upholding the principles of my religion. And now I avow in front of you that I will achieve, if God permits, what Allah has promised me and all who would take this path. He has promised us paradise where we shall live forever. As I sincerely believe in all these things, how would you think that I be willing to accept all the temporary seductions of this world? How would I live on this earth while my soul has bonded with the Almighty God? (Cited in Stadler, 2006) [78]

The terms istishhadi, shahid, and martyr have recently been referred to as **Islamikaze**, a portmanteau of "Islam" and "kamikaze." "Islamikaze" is the new brand of Islamic suicide terrorists. It is now clear that labeling such people as mere "suicide terrorists" is not sufficiently precise. "Islamikaze" denotes the Islamic martyrs' existential concern to kill all enemies—by using any means, including being absolutely willing to sacrifice their own lives in the process. [79]

Martyrdom in Islamic Scriptures

At the beginning of this chapter, the point was made that a sharp difference exists between suicide and suicide terrorism. In Arabic, suicide is *intihar*, a practice that is caused by personal distress and prohibited in Islamic teachings. [80] The Qur'an is unequivocal about suicide: "Do not kill yourselves, for truly Allah has been to you Most Merciful" (Qur'an 4:29). On the other hand, there is another side to this story: the same action of taking one's own life, when used as a method to advance jihad, elevates the person to the status of a martyr. [81] In this case, martyrdom becomes synonymous with death in holy war and in the way of Allah, which, of course, earns eternal bliss: "Think not of those who are slain in Allah's way as dead. Nay, they live, finding their sustenance in the presence of the Lord" (Qur'an 3:169). The jihadist dying in the way of Allah does not really die but secures eternal life in Paradise. [82] By extension, according to the Qur'an, mujahedin (i.e., jihadists) who fight in the name of Allah and Muslim believers who do not fight in His name are not treated by Allah in the same manner:

> Not equal are those believers remaining [at home]—other than the disabled—and the mujahedin, [who strive and fight] in the cause of Allah with their wealth and their lives. Allah has preferred the mujahedin through their wealth and their lives over those who remain [behind], by degrees. And to both Allah has promised the best [reward]. But Allah has preferred the mujahedin over those who remain [behind] with a great reward. (Qur'an 4:95)

This verse exemplifies the idea that Allah prefers mujahedin over nonviolent Muslims. By the same token, a similar notion is expressed clearly in Qur'an 49:15: "The believers are only the ones who have believed in Allah and His Messenger and then doubt not but strive with their properties and their lives in the cause of Allah. It is those who are the truthful." The Qur'anic framework for the martyrs' rewards in Paradise is also expanded in the hadith and has been amply examined by generations of scholars.

The absolute willingness to submit to the will of Allah, to the point of dying for Him, is called **Karbala**, which implies the notion that rewards will be abundant after life on earth. [83] Consequently, Islamic martyrs go to their deaths, in countless bodily pieces, expecting to meet the Prophet Muhammad and finally see the real Allah. They are told that the first drop of blood shed by a martyr, upon carrying out their sacrificial act, immediately cleanses them of sin.

This means that, on the Day of Judgment, they will face no reckoning and suffer no punishment of the tomb.[84] They will make a transition that puts them alongside other shahids and next to Allah.[85] They will have the honor of accompanying prophets, saints, and righteous believers; they will be able to intercede for their relatives on the Day of Resurrection; they will live in the middle of rivers of wine and sweet honey; they will be married to seventy-two huris (black-eyed virgins).[86]

As one can see, for suicide jihadists, there is probably no better self-gratification than the belief that they will have the highest reward for their sacrifice: eternal life in Paradise, or the **Heavenly Garden (janna** in Arabic). In Arabic, the word used to allude to Paradise also means "garden." Mentioned in the Qur'an, it denotes the Garden of Paradise for Muslims who have lived particularly compliant and pious lives (i.e., Muslims who have died as martyrs). In Islamic discourse, "janna" is a meaningful and well-developed notion. By and large, it brings to mind all aspects associated with earning the supreme reward, including the escorting of the huris. In contrast, the concept of **jahanam** ("Hell" in Arabic) is often used in jihadist propaganda to disgrace enemies and highlight the notions of good (Islam) and evil (enemies of Islam). "Hell" in Islam is comparable to the notion in Christianity. It is a place of interminable suffering and fire for the sinful, the oppressive, and the unjust.[87]

The Smile of Joy

After a suicide bombing occurs in Israel or the Palestinian territories, many survivors, upon being interviewed, recall that the suicide jihadist had a smile on his or her face before detonating him- or herself and killing the target in the process. The **smile of joy** comes from "bassamat al-farah" in Arabic. It symbolizes the suicide jihadist's indoctrination into believing that he or she will now be rewarded by Allah with eternal life in the Heavenly Garden. This is why the suicide killer expresses his or her cheering attitude before the final act.[88] In regard to the aforementioned vehicle-borne suicide at the U.S. Marine barracks in Beirut, Lebanon, in October 1983, one of the survivors, a young U.S. guard, caught a glimpse of the Islamist terrorist driving the truck full of explosives toward the barracks. The guard said that the man had a huge smile on his face. He said that the smile was almost exhilarated.[89] In Islamic martyrdom tradition, just moments before the terrorist's impending martyrdom, his or her fellow members (sometimes, members of the same suicide squad) will say, "Your face has the smile of a martyr." Without a doubt, this is an aspect of religious fervor that motivates them. In parts of the Muslim world, "The Smile of Joy" even became a sonnet (i.e., short poem or song) written after the destruction of the Twin Towers in New York on September 11, 2001.[90]

Uncertainty Avoidance: Key to Paradise

As a cultural dimension, **uncertainty avoidance** indicates the degree of intolerance for risk or uncertain situations in a given culture. Hofstede's (1980)[91] construct explains how a cultural group avoids stress and anxiety within its own society. On the whole, cultures experiencing greater anxiety create groups that reinforce their needs for stability. Occasionally, such groups develop into terrorist groups because they include like-minded individuals sharing the same experiences, feelings, and values. Hence, they are more easily geared toward communal group behavior. Wiedenhaefer and his colleagues (2007)[92] looked at terrorism from the framework of uncertainty avoidance. Upon examining roughly 2,200 terrorist attacks from the late 1960s to the late 1970s, the authors concluded that uncertainty avoidance is typical of terror-producing countries. When uncertainty avoidance is very high in terror-producing countries, there is a strong facilitating effect of cultural stress and anxiety that contributes to group-driven terrorism.

In the Palestinian territories, many martyrs-to-be are interviewed before getting ready for their ultimate mission. Some who have been caught have been interviewed in Israeli prisons. A common denominator, in the Islamists' narratives, is that they express high uncertainty about life on earth. Some of this has to do with poor economic conditions and stressful living situations. According to the World Bank (2001),[93] more than 33 percent of the Palestinian population, about 1 million people, live below the poverty line of $2.10 a day. At the same time, martyrs-to-be are convinced that, by blowing themselves up (and other people in the process), they are secured the safest place in Paradise: "He who fights in the cause of Allah and is killed or achieves victory, we will bestow upon him the greatest reward" (Qur'an 4:74). They believe that a true Muslim should sacrifice his or her life for Allah. Only then will an authentic and dignified life be awarded to him or her.

Commitments to a sacred and superior cause lead Islamists to achieve greater sacrifice than what is achievable on earth (i.e., the traditional reward system based on material incentives). Abhorring life on earth, they reason that it is better for them to die in glory than living in humiliation. Before going on a suicide mission, many suicide recruits are separated from women in the weeks preceding their last day; they are also shown porn movies because they are led to believe that they will have sex with seventy-two perpetual virgins in Paradise (they will also enjoy the presence of 80,000 servants).[94] Achieving istishhad is the Key to Paradise. The **Key to Paradise** is to be taken both literally and metaphorically. Literally, if the suicide bomber changes his or her mind at the last minute by not detonating a grenade, then he or she takes the other option: by pressing the black button to stop the detonation. The other button on the grenade, the green button, is the detonation and, therefore, the Key to Paradise. Metaphorically, it is the ultimate objective of the shahid: to enjoy the highest place in Paradise.[95] When one strongly believes in this whole concept, one is said to **marry for Allah**; that is, to join a suicide mission team in order to die for Allah.[96]

STATUS SYMBOL

A **status symbol** is a type of societal recognition that can be material and/or social. It is a visible symbol of one's social position and a perceived indicator of one's social status.[97] In many Muslim cultures, people regard martyrdom as a status symbol. The few lucky ones who are selected for istishhad are lionized as heroes. A whole cultural structure made up of friends, relatives, teachers, religious leaders, reporters, and politicians shares and diffuses a strong belief in the status symbol of martyrdom.[98] A theory that clearly illustrates the phenomenon of martyrdom as a status symbol is symbolic self-completion theory. Developed by Wicklund and Gollwitzer (1982),[99] **symbolic self-completion theory** rests on the premise that individuals who experience status anxiety may engage in self-symbolization. They do so by attempting to gain some type of status symbol in order to bolster their identity or compensate for their own inadequacies. Put another way, self-symbolization occurs when someone's status is legitimized by others who see particular symbols as valid status markers.[100] In the Palestinian territories, becoming a martyr for Allah is a status symbol that appeals to many disaffected youths.

More Power to the Martyr

The martyr is the one who sacrifices him- or herself and is depicted as carrying symbols of power. [101] Identifying the hero as a martyr elevates the person's death to an exalted level. [102] For the shahid, "self-chosen martyrdom" is hailed as the most honorable of acts. As Sayed Abu Musamah, the editor-in-chief of the Hamas newspaper, *Al-watan*, explained, istishhad "is the highest form of courage" (Bartholet, 1995, p. 42). [103] To the Palestinians, istishhad is *the* symbolic act of sacrifice: by killing any Israeli, shahids enact a type of ritual in which they elevate their status and prove themselves invincible over their victims. Through such pious acts, many of their Palestinian brethren feel for them. [104] Upon being interviewed on their last day (before detonating their grenades or pulling their suicide belts), suicide bombers often say that they want their wives and children to do the same. It is the highest honor for a martyr's family. The phenomenon whereby the martyr's relatives are encouraged to become martyrs too (in order to gain such a status symbol) is called an **associational catalyst**: a set of constant reminders about the greatness of being elevated as a martyr. Such reminders are reflected through well-known and easily recognizable symbols. Thanks to associational catalysts, people are more receptive to the value of martyrdom overall. [105]

Celebrating the Martyr's Life

Proponents of martyrdom craft posters, websites, and public exhibits to honor their heroes and expose their heroic sacrifice. Calendars are depicted with the "martyr of the month." Paintings exalt the martyrs in Paradise, victorious beneath a flock of green birds. This symbol stems from a saying of the Prophet Muhammad: the soul of a martyr is given to Allah amid the green birds of Paradise. A biography of a martyr describes how his soul was lifted up to the sky on a fragment of a bomb. [106] Often, the writing includes the name of the dead hero and when he or she was killed. The image shows the mosque or shrine, the quote, and the martyr's pseudonyms (if there were any). Of equal significance is the fact that the image shows the deceased's bloody face. At al-Najah University in Nablus (in the West Bank), a place that has generated numerous martyrs, many posters of the deceased are hung on almost every wall and door entrance. Imams' sermons are devoted to commemorating the martyrs' lives and raving about their great accomplishments. [107]

According to sharia, anyone who dies in defense of Islam has the right to a Muslim burial without the traditional ablution or purification process, or the change of clothing—normally required in the case of corpses of people who did not become martyrs. The status symbol of martyrdom makes a corpse legally pure. In a similar vein, by framing the picture of a specific martyr, Islamist discourse is able to arouse notions of familial sentimentality. Islamists employ this method for both innocent martyrs and those who died in action. These portraits are designed to remind viewers of their own family portraits, communicating the idea that these are average people who sacrificed their lives in heroic acts that constitute a reasonable option for anyone—anyone who is strong enough to do it. [108] On that note, organizers of martyrdom operations also honor the martyrs' mothers and fathers by granting them the title of "umm al-shahid" (mother of the martyr) or "abu al-shahid" (father of the martyr). [109]

Material and Financial Support

A terrorist group like Hamas acclaims its operatives who perpetrate istishhad and provides them with a myriad of status symbols. Hamas also covers the material needs of the martyr's family. [110] The total cost of a single martyrdom operation is $140–150. In the beginning of the

First Intifada against Israel, the price of a Palestinian shahid was about $2,000. To be more precise, those who volunteered to partake in suicide bombing attacks were guaranteed that their families would receive $2,000 after the mission was accomplished—an excessively large sum of money in that culture.[111] According to Hassan (2001),[112] after a martyrdom operation, Hamas covers the material needs of the heroes' families by giving them even more money: between $2,800 and $5,000 for each family. Academic scholarships for Palestinian siblings and compensation for their families' resettlement (if the Israelis destroy their homes) are promised.[113] In contrast, in Iraq, the estimation of a suicide bomber's life has been reported to be much higher. Before his demise, Saddam Hussein allegedly increased the financial reward for suicide bombers' families from $10,000 to $25,000. In some cases, this financial increase was the catalyst for many people to join martyrdom operations; the suicide bombers asserted that this was the best method for improving their families' lifestyles.[114]

CULTURE OF DEATH

By definition, **culture of death** refers to the purposeful devaluation of human life leading to murder and/or self-murder.[115] Committed to a culture of death (with the anticipation to enter Paradise upon dying), terrorists consider their enemies as weak because they adhere to a "culture of life."[116] A synonym for "culture of death" is martyropathy. **Martyropathy** is a perspective that "is the result of an inversion born of resentment. The goal is no longer to realize an ideal, but to take leave of life by destroying the enemy in an apocalyptic vision that will put an end to life" (Khosrokhavar, 2005, p. 60).[117] Put another way, martyrs-to-be regard death, not life, as their goal. As Shehzad Tanweer, one of the 7/7 London suicide bombers, said in a videotaped statement that justified his actions, "We are 100% committed to the cause of Islam. We love death the way you love life."[118]

A characteristic of many extremist movements—including Nazism—is the cult of death. From the "Viva la Muerte" motto of the Phalangists to the Nazi reverence of the scalp symbol, from Heaven's Gate's devotion to entering an alien afterlife to the passion of the Iranian fundamentalists for martyrdom, there is a profound love of death at work. The martyr knows that he or she immediately goes to Paradise. Iranian boys and girls were given Taiwan-made plastic keys to hang from their necks when sent to the minefields during the 1980–1988 war with Iraq. These were called "keys to paradise." The martyr would rapidly have access to seventy-two virgins upon arrival to the Heavenly Garden. Khomeini's most favored dictum was "To kill and get killed are the supreme duties of Muslims."[119] The martyr-to-be is often spotted wearing a shroud in street demonstrations to show his or her readiness to die at any time. No street or permanent structure is named after a living person; only the deceased heroes are honored in this fashion. For instance, the street of the Egyptian embassy in Tehran is named after Khalid Showqi al-Islambouli (President Anwar Sadat's killer). On the other hand, Naguib Mahfouz, an Egyptian laureate of the Nobel Prize for Literature, is never mentioned except when he is insulted.[120]

According to Ali Khamenei, the current supreme leader of Iran, it is "by dying for his faith that a Muslim becomes truly alive" (Tehran Radio broadcast, February 11, 1988). In other words, my life only has meaning if I die. At the time Khamenei expressed these words, he was already president of the Islamic Republic of Iran. One of Osama bin Laden's favorite poems is entitled "The Sweet Nectar of Death"; to motivate his young recruits, bin Laden used **death cult language**, a type of discourse focusing on the glorification of death. The objective, of course, is to change the whole world and establish a caliphate. In his death cult language, bin Laden uttered the following statements: "The Crusader army became dust," "Death is truth and the ultimate destiny," and "Courageous youth of Islam fear no danger." Human sacrifice had a preeminent place in bin Laden's world. Unlike Christian martyrs experiencing torture and death for their faith, Muslim martyrs are vigorous warriors like Japanese kamikazes. It is the notion that they will be accepted into Paradise after killing infidels and dying in the way of Allah. Such death cult language goes back to early terrorist cults in the Muslim world. The Assassins asserted that salvation was only secured for people who submitted to their leaders (e.g., imams), killed enemies, and committed ritual suicide subsequently. [121]

SACRIFICE

Martyrdom is about virtuous, magnanimous sacrifice by strong-willed people. In this context, **sacrifice** refers to selfless noble deeds. [122] Regarded symbolically as an ultimate act of faith rather than a standard act of violence, martyrdom is to be viewed as a suicide terrorist's self-sacrificing conduct. Self-sacrificial suicide upholds a faith-based identity formation. [123] In sacrifice, there is less risk at work because organizers are not too concerned about perpetrators being captured. Suicide operations are also much cheaper and more unfailing than many other types of terrorist tactics. Suicide terrorist organizations generally develop a **sacrificial myth**, a system of beliefs incorporating a complex set of symbols and rituals to magnify the suicide attackers' potential to cause harm and attract more recruits in the process (see the sections on myths and rituals in chapter 4). Thanks to sacrificial myths, any terrorist group can fashion reliable symbols to make powerful statements. [124] Repeated ritual performances foster and internalize complex beliefs and concepts. An example would be a system of rewards and punishments, including prospects for afterlife activities. This notion of sacrificial myth functions as a useful method for fostering and strengthening the commitment of suicide recruits to any cause advocated by terrorist groups. [125]

Blood Sacrifice

One of the most important symbolic acts is that of blood sacrifice, whereby terrorist acts have strong connections with religion and humankind's collective being. [126] **Blood sacrifice** refers to the sacrifice of one's life for a nation; it means death for a fatherland or motherland, or even a party or movement. In many cases, it alludes to the martyrs' death for a particular cause. Blood sacrifice is simply death as a sacrifice for the greater good. It is used as "an avenue by which certain rewards are obtained" (Vernon, 1970, p. 40). [127] Terrorism succeeds when it can elicit a joint response from the terrorists' own constituency. It works by exploiting shared cultural messages that draw on a cultural group's sacrificial myths. This is why the role of blood sacrifice and suffering as a martyr is important in this discourse on symbolism. In many societies, the shedding of blood arouses a strong emotional response that borrows from important cultural mechanisms. These mechanisms send cultural messages that impact the emotional state of those living in the culture and, therefore, shape their attitude and behavior (both socially and politically). If one were to repudiate the blood-shedding symbolism, there would be no cultural message available. [128] One of the perks of engaging in istishhad is the very benefit of blood sacrifice: the first drop of blood shed by a martyr in holy war washes away his or her sins instantly. [129]

Redemption

It is very clear, by now, that in places like the Palestinian territories, terrorist groups planning martyrdom operations foster an enticing culture of death to attract volunteers for suicide missions. Such groups have managed to frame self-destructiveness as a meaningful act of redemption. **Redemption** is the act of saving oneself (and others) from sin that could bring about eternal damnation. In this regard, redemption is about being committed to one's values and fulfilling the criteria entailed in those values. Rather than avoiding the challenge, some strong-willed people elect to redeem their identity through heroic and self-sacrificial acts—for example, by taking remarkable measures to save their nation from existential threats. Martyr-dom groups often implore people to participate in violence to live up to their own values, relatives, friends, ethnic group, or religion. Failing to do so creates dissonance because it is perceived as a betrayal of one's principles, loved ones, nation, God, or even sense of viril-ity.[130]

HUNGER STRIKE AS MARTYRDOM

A **hunger strike** (or **hunger protest**) is a form of pressure in which individuals fast as an act of political protest or to induce feelings of guilt in others, generally with the hope of achieving a goal (e.g., a policy change). In this sense, a hunger strike is a weapon of mass persuasion in which the body becomes an effective form of speech capable of expressing displeasure with the patriarchal structures of power. It can also act as a symbolic gesture of suicide.[131] The body is essential to personal and political expression. It becomes a social text, and, when deliberately starved and disciplined beyond its capacity, it produces a powerful symbolic territory for the formulation of dissent against social or political oppression.[132]

Hunger strikes have long-established roots in Irish society. Hunger strikers are willing to sacrifice their lives to draw attention to an injustice and, in so doing, force authorities into adopting a solution. The 1981 **Irish hunger strike** was the peak of a five-year protest by Irish Republican prisoners in Northern Ireland. The hunger strikers relied on identity cues to bolster Irish Republican resistance to Great Britain. Many of them let their hair grow very long; their beards were becoming long and disheveled. They discarded their prison-issue clothing to wear blankets in robe-like fashion. At the same time, they became infirm and thin, projecting themselves as committed young warriors—physically weak but spiritually loyal to their cause, and maltreated by a heartless, imperialist power. Their plea for martyrdom, publicized across the world, had very much in common with that of Christianity's most hailed martyr: Jesus Christ. The hunger strike articulated values of self-sacrifice, suffering, and a resolute commit-ment to the principles of truth and justice. All of these values were ingrained within the IRA movement.[133]

For the Irish Republican movement, the 1981 Irish hunger strike became synonymous with symbolic sacrifice. It led to a major disgrace of the Thatcher administration, global profile raising of the IRA's plight, and better communal solidarity within Catholic communities. More importantly, it intensified terrorism in Northern Ireland.[134] The martyrdom message glued supporters together and played on a common understanding and emotional response. The injured dying body was now a source of electoral harmony and, of course, a token of recognition and appreciation for the martyr. In Republican wall murals (in the Catholic ghettos of Belfast), the Madonna was depicted as blessing the injured body of the departed hunger striker. This meant that a vote against him was tantamount to a vote against the Madonna. The best reward is the honor that the martyrs (and, by extension, their families) receive—which bestow them a sense of individual immortality. That is the ultimate prize for the hunger striker.[135] The first IRA volunteer to become a martyr as a result of the 1981 Irish hunger strike was **Bobby Sands**. He fasted for sixty-six days. His death resulted in an escalation of

IRA recruitment and activity, the recognition of the Irish hunger strike as religious-political martyrdom, and, unfortunately, an increase in other volunteers who took the same deadly path.

Like modern-day Islamist shahids, hunger strikers are playing out an ancient religious drama as contemporary politics. This is certainly true at the level of the participants' own community and their internal social dynamics (but not outside the community). The hunger strikers' community is given new meaning through the acting out of the ancient drama and its sacrifices so that it can preserve its raison d'être and keep asserting its values. Through a reenactment of known stories, the martyrdom of hunger strikers represents a form of revival of old communal consciousness, as observed in traditional religious ceremonies. [136] In practical terms, in a hunger strike, martyrdom and religious symbolism fuse together in order to wield a significant electoral impact (in terms of garnering support from sympathizers). [137]

SUMMARY

Suicide terrorism is an attack upon a target, in which a terrorist intends to kill others and/or create significant damage while being aware that he or she will die in the process. Using one's life and the body as a weapon is also called biopolitics. Suicide terrorism is a weapon of mass persuasion, which other scholars call "influence operations" and "strategic signaling." A weapon of mass persuasion is any method designed to influence the mind and behavior of a targeted population. Durkheim's work on suicide describes four categories of suicide: anomic, fatalistic, egoistic, and altruistic. The last two categories fit our framework of suicide terrorism. On a similar note, instrumental rationality and value rationality are good incentives for engaging in suicide terrorism. The first type of rationality implies that suicide terrorism is committed out of self-interest (i.e., reaching Paradise). The second type entails killing oneself altruistically on behalf of one's group. A particular type of suicide terrorism is martyrdom. Martyrdom refers to heroic death, usually in battle, that is sanctified by a deity or Supreme Being. Death in battle grants immortality, and the deceased one is hailed as a martyr. Four major reasons exist as to why martyrdom is used by terrorist groups. One of these reasons is cosmic war, a spiritual struggle that symbolizes the fight between good and bad, and between truth and evil. The Arabic word for martyrdom is istishhad. When translated verbatim, it means "self-chosen martyrdom." Although Islam forbids suicide, taking one's own life for advancing jihad and dying in the way of Allah is recommended. Of equal importance is the fact that istishhad should be looked at as the Key to Paradise, a practice also called "marrying for Allah." By detonating the green button on a grenade (or pulling a suicide belt), the ultimate objective of the shahid (i.e., martyr) is to avoid uncertainty on earth and enjoy the highest place in Paradise. Terrorist groups acclaim martyrs who have carried out suicide missions successfully by granting them a myriad of status symbols. Examples are special Muslim burials, posters, websites, public exhibits, and, of course, final rewards for their families. Martyrdom reflects the notion of "culture of death," also called martyropathy. It denotes a constant focus on eternal life in Paradise, which can only be achieved through honorable death. For this reason, Osama bin Laden relied on death cult language a lot. Regarded symbolically as an ultimate act of faith rather than a standard act of violence, martyrdom is to be viewed as a suicide terrorist's self-sacrificing conduct. This is enabled, in part, thanks to the phenomenon of sacrificial myth, a system of beliefs incorporating a complex set of symbols and rituals to magnify the suicide attackers' potential to cause harm and attract more recruits in the process. Shedding blood for a nation or a cause is also called "blood sacrifice." Finally, a hunger strike is a form of pressure in which individuals fast as an act of political protest or to induce feelings of guilt in others, generally with the hope of achieving a particular goal. The 1981 Irish hunger strike turned IRA volunteers into martyrs deserving the highest rewards.

NOTES

1. Pedahzur, Ami (2006). *Root Causes of Suicide Terrorism: The Globalization of Martyrdom*. New York: Routledge.

2. Pedahzur, Ami (2004). *Suicide Terrorism*. New York: Polity.

3. Ganor, Boaz (2001). *Countering Suicide Terrorism: An International Conference*. Herzliya, Israel: ICT.

4. Baloch, Qadar Bakhsh (2010). Suicide Missions: Power of the Powerless and Powerlessness of the Powerful. *The Dialogue, 2*(2), 45–66.

5. Alvanou, Maria (2006). *Criminological Perspectives on Female Suicide Terrorism*. Tel Aviv: The Jaffee Center for Strategic Studies.

6. Falk, Ophir (2009). Introduction: Overview and Historical Account of the Weapon. In Ophir Falk & Henry Morgenstern (Eds.), *Suicide Terror: Understanding and Confronting the Threat* (pp. 1–30). New York: Wiley.

7. Mitchell, Jolyon (2013). *Martyrdom: A Very Short Introduction*. New York: Oxford University Press; and Stover, William James (2005). A Dialog of Faith: Reflections on Middle East Conflict from Jewish, Muslim and Christian Perspectives. *Journal of Beliefs & Values: Studies in Religion & Education, 26*(1), 65–75.

8. Pape, Robert (2005). *Dying to Win: The Strategic Logic of Suicide Terrorism*. New York: Random House.

9. Hafez, Mohammed M. (2006). Dying to Be Martyrs: The Symbolic Dimension of Suicide Terrorism. In Ami Pedahzur (Ed.), *Root Causes of Suicide Terrorism: The Globalization of Martyrdom* (pp. 54–80). New York: Routledge.

10. Hardt, Michael, & Negri, Antonio (2005). *Multitude: War and Democracy in the Age of Empire*. London: Hamish Hamilton.

11. Murray, Stuart (2006). Thanatopolitics: On the Use of Death for Mobilizing Political Life. *Polygraph: An International Journal of Politics and Culture, 18*, 191–215.

12. Douzinas, Costas (2008). July 2, July 7 and Metaphysics. In Angharad Closs Stephens & Nick Vaughan-Williams (Eds.), *Terrorism and the Politics of Response* (pp. 190–210). Abingdon, UK: Routledge.

13. Hoffman, Bruce (2003). The Logic of Suicide Terrorism. *The Atlantic Monthly, 291*(5), 1–10.

14. Marcus, Itamar, & Crook, Barbara (2012). *Kill a Jew: Go to Heaven*. Jerusalem: Palestinian Media Watch.

15. Hafez, Mohammed (2006). Dying to Be Martyrs: The Symbolic Dimension of Suicide Terrorism. In Ami Pedahzur (Ed.), *Root Causes of Suicide Terrorism: The Globalization of Martyrdom* (pp. 54–80). New York: Routledge.

16. Anderson, Sean, & Sloan, Stephen (2003). *Terrorism: Assassins to Zealots*. Lanham, MD: Scarecrow Press; and Lewis, Bernard (1987). *The Assassins: A Radical Sect in Islam*. New York: Oxford University Press.

17. Buruma, Ian, & Margalit, Avishai (2004). *Occidentalism: The West in the Eyes of Its Enemies*. New York: Penguin.

18. Martyrdom and Murder. (2004, January 8). *The Economist, 388*, 10.

19. Ranstorp, Magnus (1997). *Hizb'allah in Lebanon: The Politics of the Western Hostage Crisis*. New York: Palgrave Macmillan.

20. Horowitz, Michael (2010). Nonstate Actors and the Diffusion of Innovations: The Case of Suicide Terrorism. *International Organization, 64*, 33–64.

21. Ministry of Defence of Sri Lanka (2011). *Humanitarian Operation Factual Analysis: July 2006–May 2009*. Colombo: Ministry of Defence of Sri Lanka.

22. McCauley, Clark, & Moskalenko, Sophia (2011). *Friction: How Radicalization Happens to Them and Us*. New York: Oxford University Press.

23. Schweitzer, Yoram (2007). Palestinian Istishhadia: A Developing Instrument. *Studies in Conflict & Terrorism, 30*(8), 667–689.

24. Atran, Scott (2006). The Moral Logic and Growth of Suicide Terrorism. *The Washington Quarterly, 29*(2), 127–147.

25. Amir Mir (2011, September 6). Pakistan: The Suicide-Bomb Capital of the World. *Asia Times Online*. Retrieved July 7, 2014, from http://www.atimes.com/atimes/South_Asia/MI16Df04.html

26. Wright, Robin (2008, April 18). Since 2001, a Dramatic Increase in Suicide Bombings. *The Washington Post*, p. A18.

27. Rosner, Yotam, Yogev, Einav, & Schweitzer, Yoram (2014). *A Report on Suicide Bombings in 2013*. Tel Aviv: Institute for National Security Studies.

28. Marcus, Aliza (2007). *Blood and Belief: The PKK and the Kurdish Fight for Independence*. New York: New York University Press.

29. Letsch, Constanze (2013, May 7). Kurds Dare to Hope as PKK Fighters' Ceasefire with Turkey Takes Hold. *The Guardian*, p. A1.

30. Matovic, Violeta (2007). *Suicide Bombers: Who's Next?* Belgrade, Yugoslavia: The National Counter Terrorism Committee.

31. Ergil, Doğu (2000). Suicide Terrorism in Turkey. *Civil Wars, 3*(1), 37–54.

32. Pape, Robert (2006). *Dying to Win: Why Suicide Terrorists Do It*. London: Gibson Square.

33. Corman, Steven, Trethewey, Angela, & Goodall, Harold (2008). *Weapons of Mass Persuasion*. Bern, Switzerland: Peter Lang.

34. Sun Tzu (1963). *The Art of War* (Trans. Samuel B. Griffith). London: Oxford University Press.

35. Mansdorf, Irwin, & Kedar, Mordechai (2008). The Psychological Asymmetry of Islamist Warfare. *Middle East Quarterly, 15*(2), 37–44

36. Hebert, Adam (2005). Information Battleground. *Air Force Magazine, 7*, 64–67.

37. Kagan, Frederick (2003). War and Aftermath. *Policy Review, 12*, 10–21.

38. Hoffman, Bruce, & McCormick, Gordon (2004). Terrorism, Signaling, and Suicide Attack. *Studies in Conflict and Terrorism, 27*(4), 243–281.

39. Pape, Robert (2006). *Dying to Win: Why Suicide Terrorists Do It*. London: Gibson Square.

40. Atran, Scott (2006). The Moral Logic and Growth of Suicide Terrorism. *The Washington Quarterly, 29*(2), 127–147.

41. Douzinas, Costas (2008). July 2, July 7 and Metaphysics. In Angharad Closs Stephens & Nick Vaughan-Williams (Eds.), *Terrorism and the Politics of Response* (pp. 190–210). Abingdon, UK: Routledge.

42. Freud, Sigmund (1949). *The Ego and the Id*. London: Hogarth Press.

43. Durkheim, Emile (1951). *Suicide: A Study in Sociology*. New York: Free Press.

44. Kanagy, Conrad, & Kraybill, Donald (1999). *The Riddles of Human Society*. Thousand Oaks, CA: Pine Forge Press.

45. Bearman, Peter (1991). The Social Structure of Suicide. *Sociological Forum, 6*, 510–524.

46. Durkheim, Emile (1951). *Suicide: A Study in Sociology*. New York: Free Press.

47. Berk, Bernard B. (2006). Macro-Micro Relationships in Durkheim's Analysis of Egoistic Suicide. *Sociological Theory, 24*(1), 58–80; and Johnson, Kathryn (2010). Durkheim Revisited: "Why Do Women Kill Themselves?" *Suicide and Life-Threatening Behavior, 9*(3), 145–153.

48. Kanagy, Conrad, & Kraybill, Donald (1999). *The Riddles of Human Society*. Thousand Oaks, CA: Pine Forge Press.

49. Stack, Steven (2004). Emile Durkheim and Altruistic Suicide. *Archives of Suicide Research, 8*, 9–22.

50. Putnam, Hilary (1981). *Reason, Truth and History*. New York: Cambridge University Press.

51. Varshney, Ashutosh (2003). Nationalism, Ethnic Conflict and Rationality. *Perspectives on Politics, 1*(1), 85–86.

52. Vittori, Jodi (2008). *Idealism Is Not Enough: The Role of Resources in the Autonomy and Capability of Terrorist Groups*. Ann Arbor, MI: ProQuest.

53. Pedahzur, Ami, Perliger, Arie, & Weinberg, Leonard (2003). Altruism and Fatalism: The Characteristics of Palestinian Suicide Terrorists. *Deviant Behavior, 24*(4), 405–423.

54. Barlow, Hugh (2007). *Dead for Good*. New York: Paradigm Publishers.

55. Independent Media Review Analysis (2004). *A Chronology of Terrorist Attacks Carried out by Hamas since September 2000*. Kfar Saba, Israel: Independent Media Review Analysis.

56. Pape, Robert (2006). *Dying to Win: Why Suicide Terrorists Do It*. London: Gibson Square.

57. Katz, Adam (2004). Remembering Amalek: 9/11 and Generative Thinking. *Anthropoetics, 10*(2), 10–24.

58. Atran, Scott (2010). *Talking to the Enemy: Faith, Brotherhood, and the (Un)Making of Terrorists*. New York: HarperCollins.

59. Davis, Anthony (1993). Foreign Combatants in Afghanistan. *Jane's Intelligence Review*, p. 327.

60. O'Boyle, Garrett (2002). Theories of Justification and Political Violence: Examples from Four Groups. *Terrorism and Political Violence, 14*(2), 23–46.

61. Juergensmeyer, Mark (2000). *Terror in the Mind of God: The Global Rise of Religious Violence*. Berkeley: University of California Press.

62. Lentini, Pete, & Bakashmar, Muhammad (2007). Jihadist Beheading: A Convergence of Technology, Theology, and Teleology? *Studies in Conflict & Terrorism, 30*(4), 303–325.

63. Olson, Lester, Finnegan, Cara, & Hope, Diane (2008). *Visual Rhetoric: A Reader in Communication and American Culture*. Thousand Oaks, CA: Sage.

64. Leenaars, Antoon (1988). *Suicide Notes*. New York: Human Sciences Press; and Maris, Ronald (2000). *Comprehensive Textbook of Suicidology*. New York: Guilford Press.

65. Combating Terrorism Center (2006). *The Islamic Imagery Project: Visual Motifs in Jihadi Internet Propaganda*. West Point, NY: Combating Terrorism Center.

66. *The Economist* (2004, January 8). Martyrdom and Murder. *The Economist, 388*, 10.

67. Israeli, Raphael (2002). A Manual of Islamic Fundamentalist Terrorism. *Terrorism and Political Violence, 14*(4), 23–40.

68. Atran, Scott (2003). Genesis of Suicide Terrorism. *Science, 299*, 1534–1539.

69. Bourg, Julian (2010). Humanity: An International Journal of Human Rights. *Humanitarianism, and Development, 1*(1), 137–154.

70. Kobrin, Nancy Hartevelt (2010). *The Banality of Suicide Terrorism: The Naked Truth about the Psychology of Islamic Suicide Bombing*. Dulles, VA: Potomac Books.

71. *The Economist* (2004, January 8). Martyrdom and Murder. *The Economist, 388*, 10.

72. Juergensmeyer, Mark (2000). *Terror in the Mind of God: The Global Rise of Religious Violence*. Berkeley: University of California Press.

73. Lewis, Bernard, & Churchill, Buntzie Ellis (2008). *Islam: The Religion and the People*. Philadelphia: Wharton School Publishing.

74. Baer, Robert (2006, September 3). The Making of a Suicide Bomber. *Sunday Times*, p. A1.

75. Juergensmeyer, Mark (2000). *Terror in the Mind of God: The Global Rise of Religious Violence*. Berkeley: University of California Press.

76. Kushner, Harvey (1996). Suicide Bombers: Business as Usual. *Studies in Conflict and Terrorism, 19*, 329–337.

77. Bilsky, Leora (2004). Suicidal Terror, Radical Evil, and the Distortion of Politics and Law. *Theoretical Inquiries in Law, 5*(1), 131–161.

78. Stadler, Nurit (2006). Terror, Corpse Symbolism, and Taboo Violation: The "Haredi Disaster Victim Identification Team in Israel" (Zaka). *Journal of the Royal Anthropological Institute, 12*, 837–858.

79. Israeli, Raphael (2002). A Manual of Islamic Fundamentalist Terrorism. *Terrorism and Political Violence, 14*(4), 23–40.

80. Hudson, Rex (1999). *The Sociology and Psychology of Terrorism: Who Becomes a Terrorist and Why?* Washington, DC: Library of Congress.

81. MacEoin, Denis (2009). Suicide Bombing as Worship: Dimensions of Jihad. *Middle East Quarterly, 16*(4), 15–24.

82. Myers, Joseph (2009). The Quranic Concept of War. In Joseph Morrison Skelly (Ed.), *Political Islam from Muhammad to Ahmadinejad: Defenders, Detractors, and Definitions* (pp. 72–87). Westport, CT: Praeger.

83. Aghaie, Kamran Scot (2004). *The Martyrs of Karbala: Shi'i Symbols and Rituals in Modern Iran*. Seattle: University of Washington Press.

84. Dellios, Hugh (2001, August 27). His Father's Son: The Making of a Bomber. *Chicago Tribune*, p. A1.

85. Kushner, Harvey (1998). *Terrorism in America: A Structured Approach to Understanding the Terrorist Threat*. Springfield, IL: C. C. Thomas.

86. Martyrdom and Murder. (2004, January 8). *The Economist, 388*, 10.

87. Combating Terrorism Center (2006). *The Islamic Imagery Project: Visual Motifs in Jihadi Internet Propaganda*. West Point, NY: Combating Terrorism Center.

88. Yungher, Nathan (2008). *Terrorism: The Bottom Line*. Upper Saddle River, NJ: Prentice Hall.

89. Richardson, Louise (2007). *What Terrorists Want: Understanding the Enemy, Containing the Threat*. New York: Random House.

90. Bartow, Charles (2002). Bassamat Al-Farah (The Smile of Joy). *Theology Today, 58*, 567.

91. Hofstede, Geert (1980). *Culture's Consequences: International Differences in Work-Related Values*. Newbury Park, CA: Sage.

92. Wiedenhaefer, Robert, Dastoor, Barbara Riederer, Balloun, Joseph, & Sosa-Fey, Josephine (2007). Ethno-Psychological Characteristics and Terror-Producing Countries: Linking Uncertainty Avoidance to Terrorist Acts in the 1970s. *Studies in Conflict & Terrorism, 30*, 801–823.

93. World Bank (2001). *Poverty in the West Bank and Gaza*. Washington, DC: West Bank.

94. Pennell, Richard, Stinson, Emmett, & Pryde, Pam (2011). *Banning Islamic Books in Australia*. Melbourne: Melbourne University Publishing.

95. Patterson, David (2010). *A Genealogy of Evil: Anti-Semitism from Nazism to Islamic Jihad*. Cambridge: Cambridge University Press.

96. Rehov, Pierre (2006). *Suicide Killers*. New York: City Lights Pictures.

97. Cherrington, David (1994). *Organizational Behavior*. Boston: Allyn & Bacon.

98. Caracci, Giovanni (2002). Cultural and Contextual Aspects of Terrorism. In Chris Stout (Ed.), *The Psychology of Terrorism: Theoretical Underpinnings and Perspectives* (pp. 57–83). London: Praeger.

99. Wicklund, Robert, & Gollwitzer, Peter (1982). *Symbolic Self-Completion*. Hillsdale, NJ: Lawrence Erlbaum.

100. Gollwitzer, Peter, & Wicklund, Robert (1985). Self-Symbolizing and the Neglect of Others' Perspectives. *Journal of Personality and Social Psychology, 48*, 702–715.

101. Kimhi, Shaul, & Even, Shemuel (2006). The Palestinian Human Bombers. In Jeffrey Ivan Victoroff (Ed.), *Tangled Roots: Social and Psychological Factors in the Genesis of Terrorism* (pp. 308–323). Landsdale, PA: IOS Press.

102. Barkun, Michael (2007). Appropriated Martyrs: The Branch Davidians and the Radical Right. *Terrorism and Political Violence, 19*(1), 117–124.

103. Bartholet, Jeffrey (1995, April 24). A Guaranteed Trip to Heaven. *Newsweek, 125*(17), 42.

104. Hareven, Alouph (1983). Victimization: Some Comments by an Israeli. *Political Psychology, 4*(1), 145–155.

105. Edelman, Murray (1964). *The Symbolic Uses of Politics*. Urbana: University of Illinois Press.

106. Hassan, Nasra (2001, November 19). An Arsenal of Believers: Talking to the "Human Bombs." *The New Yorker*, pp. 36–41.

107. Hafez, Mohammed (2006). Dying to Be Martyrs: The Symbolic Dimension of Suicide Terrorism. In Ami Pedahzur (Ed.), *Root Causes of Suicide Terrorism: The Globalization of Martyrdom* (pp. 54–80). New York: Routledge.

108. Combating Terrorism Center (2006). *The Islamic Imagery Project: Visual Motifs in Jihadi Internet Propaganda*. West Point, NY: Combating Terrorism Center.

109. Hafez, Mohammed (2006). Dying to Be Martyrs: The Symbolic Dimension of Suicide Terrorism. In Ami Pedahzur (Ed.), *Root Causes of Suicide Terrorism: The Globalization of Martyrdom* (pp. 54–80). New York: Routledge.

110. Saad, Rasha (2001, December 13). Weapons of the Weak. *Al-Ahram Weekly*, p. A1.

111. Charny, Israel (2007). *Fighting Suicide Bombing: A Worldwide Campaign for Life*. Westport, CT: Praeger.

112. Hassan, Nasra (2001, November 19). An Arsenal of Believers: Talking to the "Human Bombs." *The New Yorker*, pp. 36–41.

113. Kelly, Michael (1994, November 29). In Gaza, Peace Meets Pathology. *The New York Times*, p. 56.

114. Charny, Israel (2007). *Fighting Suicide Bombing: A Worldwide Campaign for Life*. Westport, CT: Praeger.

115. Mahan, Sue, & Griset, Pamela (2012). *Terrorism in Perspective* (3rd ed.). Thousand Oaks, CA: Sage.

116. Halfmann, Jost (2003). *Fundamentalist Terrorism: The Assault on the Symbols of Secular Power*. Berkeley: Institute of European Studies, University of California Berkeley.

117. Khosrokhavar, Farhad (2005). *Suicide Bombers: Allah's New Martyrs*. London: Pluto Press.

118. Khosrokhavar, Farhad (2005). *Suicide Bombers: Allah's New Martyrs*. London: Pluto Press.

119. Taheri, Amir (2004). Fascism in Muslim Countries. *American Foreign Policy Interests, 26*(1), 21–30.

120. Taheri, Amir (2004). Fascism in Muslim Countries. *American Foreign Policy Interests, 26*(1), 21–30.

121. Buruma, Ian, & Margalit, Avishai (2004). *Occidentalism: The West in the Eyes of Its Enemies*. New York: Penguin.

122. Carter, Jeffrey (2003). *Understanding Religious Sacrifice*. New York: Continuum.

123. Arena, Michael, & Arrigo, Bruce (2005). Social Psychology, Terrorism and Identity: A Preliminary Reexamination of Theory, Culture, Self, and Society. *Behavioral Sciences and the Law, 23*, 485–506.

124. Pape, Robert (2005). *Dying to Win: The Strategic Logic of Suicide Terrorism*. New York: Random House.

125. Sosis, Richard (2003). Why Aren't We All Hutterites? Costly Signaling Theory and Religion. *Human Nature, 14*, 91–127.

126. Dingley, James, & Kirk-Smith, Michael (2002). Symbolism and Sacrifice in Terrorism. *Small Wars & Insurgencies, 13*(1), 102–128.

127. Vernon, Glenn (1970). *Sociology of Death: An Analysis of Death-Related Behaviour*. New York: The Ronald Press Company.

128. Dingley, James (2008). *Combating Terrorism in Northern Ireland*. New York: Routledge.

129. Hassan, Nasra (2001, November 19). An Arsenal of Believers: Talking to the "Human Bombs." *The New Yorker*, pp. 36–41.

130. Hafez, Mohammed M. (2006). Dying to Be Martyrs: The Symbolic Dimension of Suicide Terrorism. In Ami Pedahzur (Ed.), *Root Causes of Suicide Terrorism: The Globalization of Martyrdom* (pp. 54–80). New York: Routledge.

131. Pye, Lucian (1990). Tiananmen and Chinese Political Culture: The Escalation of Confrontation from Moralizing to Revenge. *Asian Survey, 30*(4), 331–347.

132. Ellmann, Maud (1993). *The Hunger Artists: Starving, Writing, and Imprisonment*. Cambridge, MA: Harvard University Press.

133. Arena, Michael, & Arrigo, Bruce (2005). Social Psychology, Terrorism and Identity: A Preliminary Reexamination of Theory, Culture, Self, and Society. *Behavioral Sciences and the Law, 23*, 485–506.

134. Reischer, Erica, & Koo, Kathryn (2004). The Body Beautiful: Symbolism and Agency in the Social World. *Annual Review of Anthropology, 33*, 297–317.

135. Dingley, James, & Marcello Mollica (2007). The Human Body as a Terrorist Weapon: Hunger Strikes and Suicide Bombers. *Studies in Conflict & Terrorism, 30*(6), 459–492.

136. Dingley, James, & Marcello Mollica (2007). The Human Body as a Terrorist Weapon: Hunger Strikes and Suicide Bombers. *Studies in Conflict & Terrorism, 30*(6), 459–492.

137. Arthur, Paul (1984). *Political Realities: Government & Politics of Northern Ireland*. Essex, UK: Longman Group.

Chapter Eleven

Symbolism of Terrorist Weapons

TERRORIST WEAPONS: GENERAL PERSPECTIVES

From a symbolic perspective, a terrorist weapon is both an artifact and a social object. An **artifact** is, from Latin, "something made" with a particular cultural function in mind. A social object (see chapter 4) is an object of which the meaning is shared by a community. For example, as we will see, the sword in Islamism is a social object.[1] An important aspect of the trend toward terrorist violence is the growing availability of **weapons of war**, light or small arms that were initially designed and procured for use by armed forces. Increasingly, these weapons are made available to and obtained by a diversity of substate actors and organizations such as criminal and terrorist groups.[2]

Defensive Weapons versus Offensive Weapons

Weapons are generally classified into two categories: defensive weapons and offensive weapons. **Defensive weapons** are lighter weapons and weapons with a limited range and potential for damage (e.g., handguns, rifles, and swords). **Offensive weapons** (e.g., weapons of mass destruction [WMDs]) pose a greater threat to a country's stability—and even the whole world's stability—because they necessitate a coordinated response from potential targets. Defensive weapons can be replaced by offensive weapons. When that happens, the new weapon becomes a replacement symbol. A **replacement symbol** is a weapon that acts as a game changer, something that can alter the outcome of the conflict. To the eyes of many leaders of hostile governments, WMDs are ideal replacement symbols; their essence is to wreak extreme damage.[3] Naturally, the conventional distinction between offensive and defensive weapons is not always clear; it can be based on how the weapons are actually used and for what purpose. For example, the distinction between offensive and defensive weapons can be difficult for nuclear weapons, since some of the purely defensive arms (e.g., antiballistic missile systems) can pose a significant threat to an enemy, if they are used along with offensive weapons (e.g., nuclear missiles).[4]

Symbolism of Modern Weapons

Modern weapons, such as rifles and rocket-propelled grenades (RPGs), exemplify the violent character of jihadist fighting and symbolize the exploitation of Western military technology to gain power and achieve goals. They can also be perceived as a symbol of intimidation and unremittingness; in this sense, jihadists' use of modern weapons exaggerates the power of their own military technology. By extension, modern weapons are reminders that successful jihadist resistance—such as the expulsion of the Soviets from Afghanistan—can be strong enough to accomplish modern victories (or perceived victories). Modern weapons, then, embody the intrinsic capacity of the jihadist movement to overcome Western or Westernized military dominance. On an equally important note, modern weapons are used by Islamist soldiers and martyrs to associate themselves with violent Islamic extremism. Individuals pose with them (for photos) to ascertain their connection with and loyalty to the jihadist movement. This helps them build their identities as key players in jihad. As such, they are regarded as heroic symbols of participation in resistance to attacks on the ummah. [5]

Weapons as Prestige Symbols

To a terrorist group, their weapons (e.g., WMDs, hand grenades, and AK-47s) are "prestige symbols" that indicate or communicate what the group is able to do with them. A **prestige symbol** is an object or artifact that reinforces the group's belief in its power and influence. It is perceived as a valuable commodity. [6] Having a prestige symbol tends to shape the mind and behavior of the particular possessor of the weapon. [7] Nevertheless, as we will see, terrorist weapons are not just artifacts and social objects. They can also be reflected in the terrorist practices themselves: examples are beheadings and gender communal terrorism (i.e., war rape). One way to represent terrorist weapons as prestige symbols is through weapons combination. **Weapons combination** is the practice of joining weapons in different combinations. An example of this is the symbolic motif in Islamist terrorism that combines premodern and modern weapons. When a jihadist fighter combines a sword and a rifle, the connotations of both premodern Muslim history and modern jihadist successes are called to mind. In this manner, swords can be used to bestow modern weapons (e.g., rifles) a more honorable connotation, and associate them with Salafi notions of the Prophet Muhammad's followers and their successful jihadist operations against infidels. [8] In common parlance, this situation also exemplifies the idea that "old wine can fit into new bottles."

EXAMPLES OF SYMBOLIC TERRORIST WEAPONS

Weapons can arouse profound sentiments by suggesting a terrorist group's participation in, or support of, a radical movement. Whether the weapon is weak or strong matters little; the essence of their use is to destroy the enemy. Over time, terrorist organizations' symbolic weapons become their signature weapons (as reported in various media outlets). For example, let us start by examining the symbolism of Irish militants' weapons.

Irish Militants' Weapons

In traditional Irish society, the shillelagh was associated with Irish pride. A **shillelagh** is an Irish fighting stick, club, or cudgel usually made from a sturdy knotty stick with a big knob at the top. By the nineteenth century, the shillelagh had become such a symbol of Irish warrior culture that it was likened to the popularity of the sword as a symbol of the Japanese samurais' warrior culture. During the Easter Rising in 1916, shillelagh fights took place between the IRA and the Royal Irish Constabulary. More recently, the MGM-51 antitank missile in Ireland was baptized as the "Shillelagh." Officers of the Irish Guards are given shillelaghs upon graduating—just like Irish Regiments of the British Army in the past. [9] In a similar fashion, the IRA used to associate fetishistic importance to guns and specific types of guns. Some guns had nicknames, such as "Peter the Painter," and members would even fight for turns to use these symbolic guns.[10] They also created a brand loyalty for weapons. For example, the Thompson submachine gun company was kept in business thanks to, in part, its admiration within the IRA. It should be mentioned that this admiration had nothing to do with effectiveness, as the Thompsons were not as good as other firearms. This symbolic fetish with weaponry was a large motivator for the IRA to carry out its armed struggle.[11] Lastly, the **barrack buster** became the IRA's favorite homemade mortar (fabricated since the 1970s). Barrack busters symbolized the anxious resistance of the IRA (typically poor and outnumbered) against the wealthy and powerful British in Northern Ireland.[12] Yet the homemade mortar was effective: the escalation of the IRA's "barrack buster" campaign in the late 1980s forced British authorities to increase the number of troops in Northern Ireland.[13]

Ku Klux Klan's Weapons

The **Ku Klux Klan** (also known as the **KKK** or the **Klan**), an extremist white supremacist group active in the United States, was so closely attached to specific weapons that, during the Reconstruction Era (1865–1877), a tax on their favorite weapons was one of the many anti-Klan bills. In particular, the anti-Klan legislature was targeting pistols and bowie knives.[14] A bowie knife is a fixed-blade fighting knife with a crossguard and a clip point. In the second half of the twentieth century, other symbolic KKK weapons included the rifle, sawed-off shotgun, and Thompson submachine gun. All of these played a role in William Wilkinson's incarnation of the Klan. William Wilkinson was the imperial wizard of the Invisible Empire Knights of the KKK from the mid-1970s until 1981.[15] Of course, let us not forget the weapon that has been the most associated with the KKK: **cross burning**, the Klan's practice of burning crosses on hillsides or close to the homes of people who they wish to intimidate.

Shining Path's Weapons

In Peru, the Shining Path considered dynamite one of its most important weapons. The **Shining Path** (or **Sendero Luminoso**) is a leftist terrorist organization seeking to replace bourgeois democracy with Maoism (i.e., hoping to impose communist rule through a pure proletariat). This reflects an ideology that advocates a return to pre-capitalistic South American farming practices—those that pertain to quasi-total self-reliance (and little to no trade with neighboring communities). From 1981 to 1988, as a result of Shining Path insurrection, the death toll caused by the group was between 30,000 and 50,000.[16] Fortunately, since the capture of its leader Abimael Guzmán in 1992, the activities of the Shining Path have declined.[17] Dynamite is seen as the weapon of the weak, like a great equalizer. For this reason, dynamite attacks against the Peruvian government's power grids have been used to destroy infrastructures and accentuate Shining Path propaganda. These attacks also symbolize a drastic step, in the disaffected areas of the country, toward the terrorist organization's economic agenda of autarky (i.e., a communist, self-sufficient economic system) of its "liberated zones."[18]

AK-47: Game Changer in Terrorist Violence

Developed in the Soviet Union in the late 1940s, the **AK-47** (also known as the **Kalashnikov** or **Kalash**) is a selective-fire, gas-operated assault weapon. By 2007, more than 100 million AK-47s had already been manufactured. About half of them are counterfeit; close to a million a year are produced without a license. After the collapse of the Soviet Union, AK-47s were sold both openly and on the black market to anybody who had cash, including drug gangs and dictatorial governments. More recently, they have been used by Islamist groups such as the Taliban and Al Qaeda in Afghanistan and Iraq, as well as the FARC and Ejército de Liberación Nacional (National Liberation Army) in Colombia.[19] On this note, the AK-47 inventor, Mikhail Kalashnikov, made the following statement: "I'm proud of my invention, but I'm sad that it is used by terrorists."[20]

The AK-47 has been the backbone of terrorist attacks due to its militant history and ease to maintain. It has proved ideal and very reliable for fighting in the jungle or the desert—effortlessly assembled and able to continue firing in sandy or wet conditions that would cram or clog a U.S.-made M-16.[21] During the Soviet war in Afghanistan, the CIA supplied mujahedin with Chinese and Polish AK-47s. The AK-47 has ascertained itself as the most pervasive instrument of destruction on earth. Part of the reason is that the assault rifle quickly became a symbol of resistance, defiance, and anti-Western creeds.[22] Notwithstanding its limitations, the AK-47 has had an incredible impact on the battlefield across the full spectrum of warfare. When a weapon evolves into a cultural or national symbol, it makes a social statement. It is a culture's or group's way of paying tribute to the weapon that bought its liberty or that shoved its leaders into power, for good or ill.[23]

In many cases across the world, an individual's act of swearing allegiance to a movement or terrorist group has been rewarded and solidified by presenting an AK-47. Even in the twenty-first century, in many Third World countries, especially those that have a tribal or clan culture, a young person's purchase or presentation of an AK-47 symbolizes his or her attainment of adulthood. It has created a "Kalashnikov culture" in which an adult male or female was not an actual adult until he or she had an AK-47.[24] Taken as a whole, **Kalashnikov culture** refers to the attitudes and behavior that are characteristic of a particular belligerent cultural group, one that stresses the importance of resolving political disputes through assault rifles. It also refers to the wide ownership of such firearms, even among children.[25]

IMPROVISED EXPLOSIVE DEVICES

An **improvised explosive device (IED)** is a homemade bomb mainly deployed in terrorist attacks. It tends to be made of conventional military explosives (like an artillery round) connected to a detonating mechanism. Roadside bombs are a customary use of IEDs. The daily role of IEDs in terrorism is relatively new. Until the twenty-first century, IEDs only made front-page news in major but periodic terrorist attacks such as the bombing of the U.S. Marine barracks in Beirut in 1983, the Oklahoma City bombing in 1995, and the bombing of the USS *Cole* in Yemen in 2000. In the Iraq War, IEDs were used considerably against U.S.-led Coalition forces, and, by the year 2007, they had become responsible for approximately 60–65 percent of Coalition deaths (in Iraq alone). Insurgent groups use them in Afghanistan, which, since 2001, has caused over 65 percent of the Coalition casualties in the war.[26]

IEDs as Weapons of Mass Persuasion

IEDs have been used as weapons of mass persuasion by insurgents in many countries—particularly Iraq and Afghanistan. They are deployed to achieve strategic influence; they are used as a propaganda tool to coerce changes in policies of nation-states. By targeting civilians, they have the ability to spark and fuel civil wars, further destabilizing nation-states.[27] IEDs are weapons of mass persuasion because they can influence the strategies and decision-making processes of senior military leadership as well. For example, they have the power to compel the redeployment of troops away from the defense lines. Yarger (2006)[28] defines **strategy** as "the art and science of developing and using the political, economic, social-psychological, and military powers of the state in accordance with policy guidance to create effects that protect or advance national interests relative to other states, actors, or circumstances" (p. 1).

IEDs are functional weapons; they are "effects based" and, thereby, produce psychological effects on top of the more observable physical effects. They are weapons that effectively complement the tactics of terrorism and insurgency, allowing militants to confront a much stronger military force with the least possible resources and personnel, while coercing the populace into active or implicit support. As Hammes (2006)[29] puts it, IEDs allow terrorists to "stay in the fight until the coalition gives up and goes home" (p. 183). IED attacks are not random acts of terror; rather, they are perpetrated against two types of targets: the "target of attack" and the "target of influence." The target of attack is selected to convey a message to the target of influence. Successful influence of the target audience results in behavior change that, in turn, helps achieve short- and long-term objectives.[30]

IEDs as Symbolic Weapons

At their nucleus, IEDs are symbolic weapons. The consequences of their explosions rise above the immediate targets to cause terror and the anticipation of further attacks. As symbolic weaponry, IEDs are especially well suited as weapons for not only terrorist organizations but insurgent groups as well (i.e., IEDs help achieve the strategic and political goals of such insurgent groups). In contrast to conventional weapons, IEDs are deployed through not only three-dimensional physical space but also social space. Both physical space and social space play a major symbolic role. The physical space is the space where the adversaries show that they control the physical terrain; in the social space, the adversaries show that they control the human terrain as well.[31]

IEDs, which are more efficient than many other weapons, represent the great equalizer for various militant groups and guerrillas through "symbolic violence and the manipulation of violent images" (McCormick & Giordano, 2007, p. 295).[32] IEDs are symbolically powerful in that they enable terrorists to upset a militarily superior force while using the mass media to wear down support for the conflict at home. For example, according to a poll in the *Washington Post* in October 2001, 94 percent of the respondents favored Bush's invasion of Afghanistan. By July 2008, that same *Washington Post* poll only showed 51 percent support for the War in Afghanistan.[33] Truly, IEDs are weapons that empower the weak as never witnessed before. They represent an unprecedented mobilization of support (both locally and internationally) for holy war against the West. Their message has recurrent motifs: we are in control of the terrain and the people, we are growing, and we will conquer. These statements exemplify the terrorists' belief that the power of IEDs will not fade easily. Speaking of the power of IEDs, a simple picture or reference to the U.S. Marine barracks in Beirut or the firefighter holding the dead child in front of the Oklahoma City federal building brings to mind a range of emotions for witnesses, victims, and the public at large—long after the terrorist attack itself has occurred.[34]

WEAPONS OF MASS DESTRUCTION

A **weapon of mass destruction (WMD)** is a weapon that can kill and bring significant harm to a large number of humans (and other life forms) and/or cause great damage to permanent structures. Terrorists who possess (or want to possess) WMDs in order to wreak massive havoc are referred to as **postmodern terrorists**.[35] The use of chemical and toxic agents by terrorists is not new. In antiquity, the Zealots-Sicarii contaminated Jerusalem's water supply (around 70 AD) as part of their terrorist campaign against the Roman invaders.[36] In 1995, Aum Shinrikyo, the Japanese dead cult, released sarin gas in the Tokyo subway. Today, a very recurrent example of a WMD is the **nuclear weapon**, an explosive device of which the destructive force comes from nuclear reactions. Terrorism using WMDs is sometimes called **superterrorism**.[37]

Three Models of Nuclear Weapons

Like many weapons, nuclear weapons are not just instruments of national security; they are also artifacts and political objects of great significance in domestic debates and internal bureaucratic skirmishes. Scott Sagan (1996)[38] offers three theoretical frameworks as to why nations decide to build or refrain from building nuclear weapons: the **security model**, according to which nations develop nuclear weapons to improve national security against foreign hazards (nuclear threats in particular); the **domestic politics model**, which foresees nuclear weapons as political tools to advance narrow-minded domestic and bureaucratic interests; and the **norms model**, under which decisions about nuclear weapons are based on weapons acquisition (or restraint in weapons development). This idea of weapons acquisition confers a significant normative symbol to a nation's image of modernity. Thus, in regard to the norms model, having nuclear weapons can play an important symbolic role in a nation's self-image and identity.[39] It may be the case that the symbolic functions of nuclear weapons are the major reason for North Korea to develop its nuclear weapons program. On April 24, 2006, the **Korean People's Army** (**KPA**), the largest military organization in the world (with about 9,500,000 active, reserve, and paramilitary personnel, as of 2013),[40] officially declared that "the development of nuclear weapons is a great achievement that matchlessly glorifies the country's dignity and the nation's pride" (cited in Scobell & Sanford, 2007).[41]

Nuclear Grandeur

Greenwood, Feiveson, and Taylor (1977)[42] contend that nuclear weapons are regarded as a symbol of global standing. Nations attempt to build or acquire nuclear weapons to represent or enhance their overall prestige. This philosophy is what Thomas Friedman (1995)[43] calls **nuclear grandeur**. Nuclear weapons are often presumed to gratify functions of "grandeur" in a similar way as flags, airlines, and Olympic teams do for a nation; they constitute what many nations believe they must have in order to earn universal credibility, validate their status as leading-edge states, and claim a "great-power" role in international affairs. From this vantage point, nations enduring a perceived status of inferiority or those seeking to be authenticated as innovative and powerful states are strong candidates in the nuclear arms race.[44] There is a high symbolic connotation to the procurement of nuclear weapons. Immediately after World War II, nuclear weapons incarnated a healing remedy to compensate for the trauma and humiliation experienced in a war that claimed the lives of more than fifty million people. Nuclear weapons were even more desired by those developed countries whose colonial powers disappeared in the 1960s. An example was France. President Charles de Gaulle's legendary statement that "France cannot be France without greatness" captured the essence of this ambition for prestigious status, rhetorically validating the procurement of nuclear weapons as a personification of grandeur.[45]

Nuclear Progress

In many cases, nuclear weapons are also conferred a symbolic meaning of progress. They become precious political status symbols, particularly symbols of economic and scientific progress.[46] For example, in 2006, stressing the symbol of progress that a nuclear Iran would project, Khamenei (the current Ayatollah of Iran) claimed that many nations "neither understand nuclear energy nor understand that it is their inalienable right. Our people understand that nuclear energy is a great and palpable indicator of progress. If a nation does not possess this it would be in trouble" (quoted in Parsi & Yetiv, 2008, p. 31).[47] For many years, Iran has worked hard to position the state's nuclear program as a symbol of economic progress and scientific advancement. By putting the nuclear symbol on its banknotes and extolling the virtues of "nuclear technology day," Iran highlights a technological achievement of which its denizens should be proud. The result is that it has struck a chord with the Iranian people. There is a predominant feeling among those living in the Gulf region that the West is intentionally trying to prevent Muslim nations from developing modern technology overall. Hence, for some governments, becoming nuclear can be a "shortcut to credibility." It also shows a state's capacity to handle economic challenges and offer "modern" solutions by filling the technology gap between the West and Muslim states.[48]

THE SWORD IN ISLAMIST CULTURE

Weapons carry important symbolic meanings in Islamist culture and are frequently used as motifs in jihadist propaganda. In Islamist culture, the sword is a premodern weapon that alludes to the violent reality of the jihadist fight. The symbol of the sword connects that struggle to early Muslims' history and the first generation of warriors. Regarded as a noble weapon, the sword personified the purity, nobility, and overall uprightness that are connected to the Prophet Muhammad, his companions, other early Islamic heroes, and their successful military campaigns. Therefore, the sword signals a desire to associate the current jihadist movement and its aims to those of early Islamic ancestors. In so doing, it legitimizes and portrays today's jihadist activities as the contemporary extensions of the successful campaigns of early jihadists. Thus, the sword gives modern-day Islamists an aura of strength and credibility.[49] Many of the **Taliban**, an Islamist movement active in Afghanistan since 1979, have been seen carrying a sword with one hand and a Qur'an with the other. Their objective is to present themselves as militant Islamic reformists—hoping to revive the caliphate as it was in the old days.[50] Four symbolic themes describe blood spilled as a result of the sword. The themes are the bloody sword itself, the bloody martyr, the bleeding text, and bloody hands.[51]

Bloody Sword

Blood symbolizes violence, cruelty, martyrdom, sacrifice, inequality, oppression, and triumph in battle. As shown in some photos, blood drips from the sword of a Muslim holy warrior, calling to mind both the literal violence integral to jihad and the potentials of a military victory. The blood accentuates the strength and power of the jihadist and provides him with an inflated image (that of a strong, successful combatant). The jihadist's sword and outfits also link him (and, thereby, the greater jihadist struggle) to notions of Islam's past, particularly to the first generation of Muslims and their conquest in jihad. From this perspective, blood dripping from a sword has profound Salafi connotations.[52]

Bloody Martyr

The bloody sword can also be the symbol of the sacrifice and martyrdom of holy warriors. Naturally, today, very few fights are waged with the sword. Allegorically, swords speak to the ongoing jihad in the Middle East and Central Asia. For example, the "crossed swords" monument in Iraq (called the "Swords of Qādisīyah"), which consists of a pair of giant triumphal arches in central Baghdad, evokes the deaths of Iraqi martyrs during the Iran-Iraq War in the 1980s—soldiers who were slain like many of their ancestors in early campaigns of Islamic history. Both ancient and recent Muslim martyrs did not die in vain; rather, they *sacrificed* their lives. The principal symbol of the martyr is blood or red, which is associated with Islam's vital force and warlike qualities. In Islam (as was the case in pre-Muhammad Arabia), blood has much to do with contrition and expiation, such as paying for an offense or sin with blood. This speaks to the gargantuan sacrifice required for the attainment of jihad and brings to mind associations of warlike qualities and martyrdom, as well as paradisiac rewards for those who sacrifice their lives. [53]

Bleeding Text

A common but less important theme in jihadist imagery is the theme of **bleeding text**, or text dripping with blood. A particular example is the death of Hussein, the son of Ali (considered by the Shi'ites as the rightful successor to Muhammad). Hence, in Shia Islam, the name "Hussein" is often seen dripping with blood (e.g., in wall murals and paintings in private residences). This image has a special connotation to Shi'ites in that it alludes to the martyrdom of Imam Hussein. In this regard, the blood also symbolizes the oppression, cruelty, and injustice surrounding not only Hussein but also his followers in the seventh century, as well as the overall subjugation of Shia Muslims under Sunni regimes. Although the blood glorifies Hussein's martyrdom in particular, it also elevates martyrdom in general. [54]

Bloody Hands

Bloody or bleeding hands are generally connected to an item or a gesture: for example, a bloody hand carrying a sword, pointing, or represented as a raised fist. The element of blood often instills the notion of bloody hands with added meaning. It can evoke sacrificial battles. It can also represent forced conversion to Islam through the sword. By the same token, the symbol of bloody hands represents the violent Crusades, an important period of the clash between Christendom and Islam. [55] Lastly, bloody hands have much to do with cutting off the heads of infidels with a sword, a method that has not been discontinued as a form of execution and is still widely practiced as ritual terrorism around the world.

ISLAMIST BEHEADINGS

In many cultures, beheading is capital punishment. Within **capital punishment** lies the word "capital," derived from the Latin *capitalis* (meaning "head"). In ancient times, capital punishment usually meant that the offender had his or her head cut off. As opposed to ritual murder or human sacrifice, capital punishment follows the rule of law. It symbolizes the supreme decision of power over the human being—the taking of life itself. [56] Islamist beheadings are a specific form of capital punishment. Because it is not easy to completely understand Islamist beheadings from a Western perspective, they are usually reduced to acts of savagery and psychological warfare. They constitute the most obvious and prevailing examples of religiously sanctioned Islamist killings. The symbolism of today's Islamist beheadings is both political and religious. Whereas the political aspects are to cause fear, the religious aspects are to morally sanction murder.

Beheading videos have confirmed the terrorizing impact of decapitating someone with a dagger, then holding the severed head for the camera.[57] A **beheading video** is a U.S. colloquial concept that became standardized during President George W. Bush's Global War on Terror. Beheading videos are videos created by Islamist groups that show a Muslim beheading an individual who is kneeling and making his or her last plea. The most notorious cases are the beheadings of Daniel Pearl and Nick Berg in 2002 and 2004, respectively. Although Islamist beheadings are a cogent form of psychological warfare, they also carry a much deeper meaning to jihadists and have a long history in Islamic theology. Islamist beheadings are like beheading rituals; they are replete with symbolism that places the perpetrators closer to Islam's roots (when the best way of winning a battle was through the sword). Today, these decapitation rituals reinforce the essence or paradigm that they are in the same holy war that Muhammad and the early Muslims were fighting. In addition, beheading videos have recruitment appeal to Muslim youths who see evidence that the global Salafi movement is strong and pure.[58] Islamists justify the beheading of prisoners with Qur'anic scriptures. Qur'an 47:4 says, "When you encounter the unbelievers on the battlefield, strike off their heads until you have crushed them completely; then bind the prisoners tightly." For centuries, prominent Islamic scholars have interpreted this verse literally. As Furnish (2005)[59] explains,

> Islam is the only major world religion today that is cited by both state and non-state actors to legitimize beheadings. . . . In contradiction to the assertions of apologists, both Muslim and non-Muslim, these beheadings are not simply a brutal method of drawing attention to the Islamist political agenda and weakening opponents' will to fight. Zarqawi and other Islamists who practice decapitation believe that God has ordained them to obliterate their enemies in this manner. (p. 57)

Chechen Islamists have decapitated ethnic Russians, non-Muslim Chechens, and foreigners throughout the First and Second Chechen Wars. The Abu Sayyaf Group in the Philippines has also beheaded hostages (using their special knife, called a "boco"), as have multiple Algerian groups and the Taliban.[60] The mujahedin have not established a cult of human sacrifice or offerings to Allah; rather, they have gone back to a pure form of Islam, as they repeatedly claim.[61] Islamists are also inspired by Muslim theology and religious symbolism in order to validate their actions. An important point is the Islamists' chanting of "Allahu Akbar" as they slowly cut off the head of a hostage. **Allahu Akbar** is an Arabic phrase meaning "Allah is greater" or "Allah is [the] greatest." Today, it is still the mujahedin's most repeated battle cry; it was shouted by the 9/11 hijackers a few seconds before hitting the Twin Towers. Shouted and heard by millions for centuries, this battle cry clearly evinces the religious nature of Islamist methods and objectives. Al Qaeda has released a certain number of beheading videos. Beheadings in the terrorist network's videos meet all the criteria to be labeled ritualistic murders—more precisely, ritual terrorism in the category of holy war. **Ritualistic murder** refers to any violent act characterized by a sequence of repeated physical, sexual, and/or psychological assaults, along with a methodical use of symbols, ceremonies, and/or machinations. The necessity to repeat such acts can be cultural, sexual, economic, psychological, and/or religious.[62]

FOUR CATEGORIES OF BEHEADING

Symbolic interpretations of beheadings are plentiful. In her book titled *Losing Our Heads: Beheadings in Literature and Culture*, Regina Janes (2005)[63] created four main categories of traditionally severed heads: judicial, sacrificial, presentational, and trophy. The **judicial category** of severed heads is best illustrated by the present-day method of public execution in Saudi Arabia: decapitation by sword. Under a firm and exacting Wahhabist interpretation of Islam, individuals guilty of murder, drug trafficking, rape, burglary, witchcraft, and apostasy can be beheaded in public. It is important to mention that, while decapitation may appear as a barbaric system of formal execution, it is not a symbol of desecration. Islamist beheadings (pre- and postmortem) are manifested as the other three categories: sacrificial, presentational, and trophy heads.[64]

The **sacrificial category** is best illustrated by the videotaped ritualistic murders of Daniel Pearl and Nick Berg by Muslim terrorist groups. Beheading videos are symptomatic of decapitation in the performance of a religious ritual. What makes the sacrificial head different from other forms of severed heads is that the beheading is a communal blood ritual. With the introduction of modern technology, the categories of beheading are not always diametrically opposed. For instance, the videotaped beheadings made by al-Zarqawi (a former key Al Qaeda leader) originate as sacrificial heads, the outcome of a ritualized communal event with strict premeditated violence (a jihadist symbol of warrior brotherhood). When the head is held aloft and presented to the cameras (as was the case with Daniel Pearl's head), it is not a sacrificial head any longer; rather, it falls into the category of presentational heads.[65]

The **presentational category** is reduced from a symbol to a sign. No superior power lies in the head or is granted to the taker from it. The taker "expects reward or recognition from the person to whom he presents the head" (Janes, 2005, p. 15).[66] In his videos, al-Zarqawi presented decapitated heads to the world and received incredible recognition from both friends and foes of Islam. In Afghanistan, Al Qaeda–linked terrorists and pro-Taliban tribal insurgents have beheaded many tribesmen accused of spying for the United States and Afghanistan. Often, they leave written notes on the corpses as warning signs to others. One note even said that the beheaded body was a gift for Hamid Karzai, Afghanistan's president.[67] Severed heads are also presented to fellow terrorists or sympathizers; they are used to strengthen friendship, make new friends, and make up with enemy clans. To the West, they symbolize the escalation of hatred and hostilities.[68]

The **trophy category** is the most common type of jihadist desecration. The trophy head is an intricate, irrepressible, and long-established icon of death, motif of war, sign of the fighter, and symbol of life. A cultural sign of individual martial bravery, the trophy head is a ritualized, widely distributed, and terror-provoking symbol of victory. The head is coveted by others by virtue of the power that the head bestows (and continues to possess) even after it is cut off. This power can be taken, possessed, and transmitted to the taker. Nevertheless, the head is also sought after as a symbol of the warrior's success (as compared to other warriors).[69]

GENDER COMMUNAL TERRORISM

Gender communal terrorism is mass terrorism committed against another gender. In most cases, it is a situation in which a large number of men—from various types of terrorist organizations, insurgent groups, or military forces—rape a large number of women. Overall, gender communal terrorism is the systematic rape of women, and the forceful impregnation of females exploited as a weapon of war. It is also referred to as **sexual terrorism**, **sexual-based terrorism**, **mass rape**, and (more commonly) **war rape**.[70] This form of terrorism aims at eliminating ethnicity (in the victims' offspring) and constitutes a form of ethnocide (i.e., ethnic cleansing). It is a weapon of war because it has a mass intimidatory impact and is often broadly publicized.[71] There is a growing use of gender communal terrorism in modern-day armed conflict. Typically, the victim is a civilian (not a warrior) and a woman (not another male combatant).[72] According to Korac (1996),[73] "Rape in war, ethnic-national war in particular, becomes a powerful symbolic weapon against the 'enemy'" (p. 137).

War Rape in History

Gender communal terrorism has plagued the history of humankind. Cases of war rape were reported in the Bangladesh Liberation War, in the anti-Chinese riots of Indonesia, and, on an immense scale, in the Second Sino-Japanese War, when Japanese soldiers occupied China.[74] In regard to the latter, in December 1937, during a six-week campaign, the Japanese seized Nanking, the capital city of China at that time. Between 200,000 and 300,000 Chinese were killed. Roughly 20,000 to 80,000 Chinese women and girls were raped by those Japanese troops. Thousands of women and girls became either comfort women (i.e., sex slaves) or "performers" in which they had to participate in perverse sex shows and pose for pornographic photos as entertainment for Japanese soldiers. Foreign missionaries issued reports of war rapes: at least ten gang rapes a day. The rapes reached such a magnitude that the media, in response, started to refer to the tragedy not as the capture of Nanking, but the **Rape of Nanking**.[75] Similarly, in 1943, Moroccan mercenaries fighting with the Free French Army were given full permission to plunder enemy territory and rape women. Consequently, widespread mass rapes occurred in Italy, leading to pregnancies. In the second half of the twentieth century, during the large-scale campaign against enemy civilians in Bosnia-Herzegovina, insurgents and regular forces targeted the female population in particular. Between 20,000 and 50,000 women and girls were systematically raped, most of whom were Bosnian Muslims.[76] More recently, in the Sudan, the government transformed all of Darfur into a rape camp.[77] The **War in Darfur** is largely a campaign of ethnic cleansing perpetrated by Sudanese Muslim militias (of Arab ethnicity) against Darfur's non-Arabs.[78] Lastly, according to Benhabyles (2005),[79] in Algeria, many women and children have been the victims of sexual terrorism. They have been the targets of a fatwa that sanctions the massacre of a segment of the population. Females, from little girls to women, have suffered the worst forms of sexual terrorism. The fatwa itself describes rape as a "pure act."

War Rape as Identicide

Identity is a very salient social factor that can produce the highest degree of ambivalence and struggle between peoples. Some groups have gone very far to forcefully annihilate other groups' cultural places and practices.[80] **Identicide** is a strategy of warfare that intentionally annihilates a group's identity. It achieves this by deliberately targeting and destroying cultural elements through various means in order to attain the eventual acculturation, removal, and/or complete destruction of a specific identity group—including its "controversial" signs, symbols, behaviors, morals, places, and accomplishments.[81] Identicide is the killing of the relatedness between individuals and place; it removes the bond that buttresses individual, community, and national identity. Identicide, then, is violence against people and the negotiated consequences of cultural identity. Its meaning comes from the combination of "identity" and the epithet "-cide." Taken literally, identicide is the intentional destruction of everything that is included under the term "identity." Because any given culture includes women (and all the female roles assigned by that culture), hurting women sexually is the same as hurting the identity of that culture. Women are raped, sexually abused, and brutalized because of their ethnic ties with the Other. Lastly, identicide comprises the categories of killing that add to the genocide discourse, and it provides a way to define the antecedent to genocide as something in and of itself, with impacts of its own.[82]

TWELVE SYMBOLIC REASONS FOR WAR RAPE

Like many forms of rape, war rape is more an aggressive act than a sexual act. It is used to inflict harm upon entire communities. Twelve symbolic reasons for war rape have been identified. This list is to be considered a typology that can be used as a framework for better understanding the symbolic impact of war rape across the world:

- **Punishment**: rape can be used to punish women, families, and communities for belonging to or allegedly supporting the enemy group. As such, war rape is akin to **punitive rape**, a type of rape used to punish in order to produce silence and control.[83] A forceful invasion into the interior of a person's body constitutes the most severe punishment conceivable upon the intimate self and the self-esteem of a human being. By any measure, it is evidence of harsh torture. In war, sexually punishing the enemy's women is considered absolute humiliation and a stamp of absolute conquest. It is, for the male enemy whose female compatriots are being targeted, a castrating experience that serves to expose the impotence of the enemy.[84] Victims are forced to break the constitutive prohibitions that have defined their identity as human beings. In some cases, a father is forced to rape his daughter or a son must rape his mother. In other cases, prisoners must perform oral sex on each other, or they must bite off each other's testicles.[85]
- **Proof of manhood**: in extreme conflict, masculinity is largely tantamount to militarized aggression. As a result, men are under constant pressure to ascertain their manhood by joining terrorist groups and engaging in a variety of violent acts, including sexual terrorism. As women are considered precious jewels of the enemy, their bodies become territories to be taken and exploited.[86] War rape is a sexual expression of male aggression. In the offender's mind, there is no sexual purpose, but what matters is the demonstration of rage, violence, and dominance over a woman.[87] In this context, proof of manhood is analogous to **patriarchal terrorism**, the meticulous use of violence by men in a serious attempt to control women. Rape becomes a sign of the clash between power and powerlessness based on relatively fixed conventional views of masculinity and femininity.[88]
- **Planting alien seeds**: as a symbol of the nation, the woman represents the motherland as a spatial metaphor, a personified femaleness. Raping the female's body/nation, by planting alien seeds, upsets the preservation of the collective. This principle leads to understandings of rape as terroristic harm. War rape has the objective to impregnate women of an enemy group; in this manner, it achieves forced pregnancy and poisons the womb of the enemy.[89] During the Bosnian War, women in some camps were constantly raped until a gynecologist established pregnancy, and then were held hostage until abortion was not possible anymore.[90]
- **Abjection**: abjection means pollution or contamination. Rape turns women into abjects. The **abject** is an object that elicits disgust. For example, the smell and sight of a rotten body keep people at bay, in the same way that excreta and bodily waste jeopardize our corporeal

and spiritual purity. Human reactions toward abjected matter are all rooted in the distinction between purity and impurity. We stay away from filth and most things related to impurity.[91]

- **Ritual**: from the perspective of the war rapist, rape can be a ritual of initiation, a ritualistic bond, and a sign of one's fidelity to the mission of an armed group or a nation. Being forced to rape women, Serbian soldiers or paramilitary men were compelled into a brotherhood of guilt; it was like a form of baptism. Those who rejected the raping of women were humiliated and sometimes castrated or even killed.[92] As Card (1996)[93] explains, "Paramilitary groups are using rapes 'to build up a kind of solidarity' among the rapists, to teach who is 'good' and who is 'contemptible,' and to destroy bonds of friendship that had existed between former neighbors" (p. 10).

- **Fantasy**: war rape fulfills fantasies. It can relax all prohibitions and allow terrorists to enter an erotic nirvana. Men are given a very tantalizing charge in possessing supreme sexual power in their hands.[94] Fantasies are situations of excess and transgressions of social roles, customs, and laws. A common fantasy is that of a dominant man taking a female against her will. The taking and the resisting are, in this framework, viewed as part of a game: from this viewpoint, she desires to be taken.[95]

- **Conquering territory**: when a woman is raped in conflict, her womb and body become "occupied" territory.[96] When women are raped to be impregnated, this is a direct assault on contested homes and societies. The very logic of gender communal terrorism is predicated upon the use of gender as a way to control communication and exacerbate the boundaries between two conflicting groups.[97] Sexual terrorism has also been used to subdue populations as a way to access valuable or scarce assets. Such assets can be national resources (e.g., diamonds, gold, and timber) or domestic possessions like money, cars, jewels, clothing, and even livestock.[98] Conquering territory through war rape is analogous to the notion of a **symbolic footprint**, which consists of establishing an interaction with and even claiming a territory in one way or another.[99]

- **Ethnic cleansing**: in this context, war rape serves to destroy a nation. It has the same goals as genocide; it damages social cohesion and, in so doing, breaks down the infrastructures of enemy groups.[100] Going back to the Bosnian War, ethnic cleansing had particularly dreadful consequences for women. Interviews with Bosnian rape survivors (and their families) revealed that the purpose of the mass rapists was to "taint" the Bosnian ethnic stock. A key foundation of war rape is to destroy an ethnic group by killing it, unsettling it, or eliminating it from its own soil.[101] During the occupation of Tibet in 1950, Chinese troops raped and impregnated Tibetan women as a systematic means of ethnic cleansing.[102]

- **Wounded femininity**: through the infringement on women's bodies and control of their existence, war rape is a severe onslaught on women's rights to reproductive self-determination. When a woman's inner space is aggressively conquered, it has the same effect as torture does. It leads to physical pain, loss of self-worth, an attack on her identity, and a lack of self-determination over her own body.[103] The penetration leaves a mark of disgrace on her body and her "self," which cannot be erased, making her feel like a morally inferior person. The body's inner space is considered one's most private and intimate part. As Miller (1997)[104] puts it, "The vagina is a gateway inside, the gate to the woman's soul by which act of entry property in her body is claimed" (p. 102). During the Second Congo War (1998–2003), because Congolese women's dignity was so closely tied to virginity, wifehood, and bearing children, rape often resulted in "social murder."[105]

- **Wounded masculinity**: raping women "belonging to the enemy" communicates an essential message from men to men. It tells men of the opposite side that they are not capable of protecting their women. Hence, sexual terrorism against women results, at the symbolic level, in wounded masculinity, stigmatizing men as "incompetent" in their roles as guardians of "their" women.[106] Etymologically, rape comes from the Latin *rapere*, meaning "to steal, seize, or carry away." The rapist appropriates wealth that, in his eyes, belongs to another man.[107] In some instances, relatives, friends, and even strangers are forced to watch or perform the act of rape—this is to make sure that the men feel humiliated. During the Bosnian War, male enemies were described as "pussies" and homosexuals; they were also forced to wear women's garments.[108]

- **Wounded community**: the main aim of sexual terrorism is not the destruction of the individual. Rather, the atrocities committed by the terrorists are against an entire community, because through the individual, the whole community endures the terror. Owing to the fact that terrorism launches attacks on social ties and structures, communities risk not being able to live up to their usual role: adapting and offering support and comfort for its members. As a result, terrorism produces a loss of confidence in oneself, in other people, in the institutions, and in the representatives of the nation. This contributes to an overall mistrust that undermines society as a whole. The chief objective of war rape is to cause trauma and, ultimately, tear down family ties and communal solidarity within the enemy camp. Avoidance of fields and markets—sites where rapes usually take place—has led to soaring malnutrition and economic loss.[109]

- **Rejection from family**: in many cultures, because virginity and chastity before marriage are treasured, rape renders the victim unbefitting for marriage or motherhood. Social stigma as a consequence of war rape has left many victims (and children born out of rape) excluded by their own families. In addition, numerous cases of HIV and other infections continue to be untested and untreated.[110] Under these circumstances, the rape victim suffers twice: first at the hands of the rapist(s), and second by her own family. In Algeria, over and above the sexual, physical, and moral abuse that women have experienced, their own families castigate and ostracize them. This, in turn, makes them more prone to depression, drug use, prostitution, and suicide.[111]

SUMMARY

A terrorist weapon is both an artifact and a social object; it can be both a defensive weapon (e.g., a handgun or rifle) and offensive weapon (e.g., a weapon of mass destruction [WMD]); and it can be a prestige symbol (an object or artifact that reinforces the group's belief in its power and influence). Over time, the symbolic weapons of terrorist organizations become their signature weapons. For Irish militants, it was the shillelagh, Thompson submachine gun, and barrack buster; for the KKK, it was the bowie knife and cross burning; and for the Shining Path, it was dynamite. The most popular terrorist weapon, however, has been the AK-47. Likewise, an improvised explosive device (IED) is a homemade bomb mainly deployed in terrorist attacks. IEDs are both weapons of mass persuasion and symbolic weapons. A WMD is a weapon that can kill and bring significant harm to many people and/or cause great damage to permanent structures. An example of a WMD is the nuclear weapon. Three theoretical frameworks were offered as to why nations decide to build or refrain from building nuclear weapons: the security model, the domestic politics model, and the norms model. Nuclear weapons also symbolize grandeur and progress. In Islamist culture, the sword is a premodern weapon that carries important meaning: it alludes to the violent reality of the jihadist fight. Four symbolic themes describe blood spilled as a result of the sword: the bloody sword itself, the bloody martyr, the bleeding text, and bloody hands. In the context of the sword, of particular importance is the Islamist beheading, which is rooted in Muslim theology and ritualistic murder. Four main categories of traditionally severed heads were described: judicial, sacrificial, presentational, and trophy. In a similar fashion, commonly known as war rape, gender communal terrorism is mass terrorism committed against another gender. In most cases, it is a situation in which a large number of men rape a large number of women. The most famous incident of war rape in history was the Rape of Nanking committed by Japanese soldiers against Chinese women. War rape is also a form of identicide, a method that intentionally annihilates a group's identity. Finally, there are twelve reasons for committing war rape. These reasons are punishment, proof of manhood, planting alien seeds, abjection, ritual, fantasy, conquering territory, ethnic cleansing, wounded femininity, wounded masculinity, wounded community, and rejection from family.

NOTES

1. Sebeok, Thomas, & Danesi, Marcel (2000). *The Forms of Meaning: Modeling Systems Theory and Semiotic Analysis*. Berlin: Mouton de Gruyter.
2. Smith, Christopher (1996). Light Weapons and the International Arms Trade. In United Nations Institute for Disarmament Research (UNIDIR) (Eds.), *Disarmament and Conflict Resolution Project, Small Arms Management and Peacekeeping in Southern Africa* (pp. 41–48). New York: UNIDIR.
3. Galtung, Johan (1984). Transarmament: From Offensive to Defensive Defense. *Journal of Peace Research, 21*(2), 127–139.
4. Fischer, Dietrich (1984). Weapons Technology and the Intensity of Arms Races. *Conflict Management and Peace Science, 8*(1), 49–69.
5. Combating Terrorism Center (2006). *The Islamic Imagery Project: Visual Motifs in Jihadi Internet Propaganda*. West Point, NY: Combating Terrorism Center.
6. McNall, Scott (1974). Value Systems That Inhibit Modernization: The Case of Greece. *Studies in Comparative International Development, 9*(3), 46–63.
7. Göle, Nilufer (2003). The Voluntary Adoption of Islamic Stigma Symbols. *Social Research, 70*(3), 809–828.
8. Combating Terrorism Center (2006). *The Islamic Imagery Project: Visual Motifs in Jihadi Internet Propaganda*. West Point, NY: Combating Terrorism Center.
9. Hurley, John (2007). *Shillelagh: The Irish Fighting Stick*. Philadelphia: Caravat Press.
10. Bradley, Gerry, & Feeney, Brian (2008). *Insider: Gerry Bradley's Life in the IRA*. Dublin: The O'Brien Press.
11. Hart, Peter (2005). *The IRA at War, 1916–1923*. Oxford: Oxford University Press.
12. Martin, Gus (2010). *Understanding Terrorism: Challenges, Perspectives, and Issues*. Thousand Oaks, CA: Sage.
13. Ripley, Tim, & Chappel, Mike (1993). *Security Forces in Northern Ireland (1969–92)*. Oxford: Osprey Publishing.
14. Trelease, Allen (1995). *White Terror: The Ku Klux Klan Conspiracy and Southern Reconstruction*. Baton Rouge: Louisiana State University Press.
15. Chalmers, David (1987). *Hooded Americanism: The History of the Ku Klux Klan*. Durham, NC: Duke University Press.
16. Bellamy, Alex (2011). *Mass Atrocities and Armed Conflict: Links, Distinctions, and Implications for the Responsibility to Prevent*. Muscatine, IA: The Stanley Foundation.
17. Rochlin, James (2003). *Vanguard Revolutionaries in Latin America: Peru, Colombia, Mexico*. Boulder, CO: Lynne Rienner Publishers.
18. Harmon, Christopher (2001). Five Strategies of Terrorism. *Small Wars & Insurgencies, 12*(3), 39–66.
19. Kahaner, Larry (2007). *AK-47: The Weapon That Changed the Face of War*. New York: Wiley.
20. Connolly, Kate (2002, July 29). Kalashnikov: "I Wish I'd Made a Lawnmower." *The Guardian*, p. A1.
21. Associated Press (2007, July 6). *AK-47 Inventor Doesn't Lose Sleep over Havoc Wrought with His Invention*. Retrieved May 12, 2013, from http://www.foxnews.com/story/0,2933,288456,00.html
22. Lawuyi, O. B. (1998). Acts of Persecution in the Name of Tradition in Contemporary South Africa. *Dialectical Anthropology, 23*, 83–95.
23. Rottman, Gordon (2011). *The AK-47: Kalashnikov-Series Assault Rifles*. Oxford: Osprey Publishing.
24. Rottman, Gordon (2011). *The AK-47: Kalashnikov-Series Assault Rifles*. Oxford: Osprey Publishing.
25. Cohn, Martin Regg (2001, April 11). Talking Tough on Guns in Pakistan. *World Press Review*, p. A1.
26. Wilson, Clay (2007). *Improvised Explosive Devices (IEDs) in Iraq and Afghanistan: Effects and Countermeasures*. Washington, DC: Congressional Research Service.
27. Martin, James Kennedy (2009). *Dragon's Claws: The Improvised Explosive Device (IED) as a Weapon of Strategic Influence*. Monterey, CA: Naval Postgraduate School.

28. Yarger, Harry (2006). *Strategic Theory for the 21st Century: The Little Book on Big Strategy*. Carlisle, PA: U.S. Army War College.

29. Hammes, Thomas (2006). *The Sling and the Stone: On War in the 21st Century*. St. Paul, MN: Zenith Press.

30. Hoffman, Bruce, & McCormick, Gordon (2004). Terrorism, Signaling, and Suicide Attack. *Studies in Conflict and Terrorism, 27*(4), 243–281.

31. Martin, James Kennedy (2009). *Dragon's Claws: The Improvised Explosive Device (IED) as a Weapon of Strategic Influence*. Monterey, CA: Naval Postgraduate School.

32. McCormick, Gordon, & Giordano, Frank (2007). Things Come Together: Symbolic Violence and Guerrilla Mobilization. *Third World Quarterly, 28*(2), 295–320.

33. Morin, Richard, & Deane, Claudia (2001, October 8). Public Support Is Overwhelming: Poll Finds 94% Favor Bush's Ordering Strikes on Afghanistan. *The Washington Post*, p. A5; and *The Washington Post* (2013, May 13). Afghanistan. Retrieved January 22, 2014, from http://www.pollingreport.com/afghan.htm

34. Martin, James Kennedy (2009). *Dragon's Claws: The Improvised Explosive Device (IED) as a Weapon of Strategic Influence*. Monterey, CA: Naval Postgraduate School.

35. Campbell, James (1997). Excerpts from Research Study "Weapons of Mass Destruction and Terrorism: Proliferation by Non-State Actors." *Terrorism and Political Violence, 9*(2), 24–50.

36. Laqueur, Walter (1977). *The Age of Terrorism*. Boston: Little, Brown.

37. Mahan, Sue, & Griset, Pamela (2012). *Terrorism in Perspective* (3rd ed.). Thousand Oaks, CA: Sage.

38. Sagan, Scott (1996). Why Do States Build Nuclear Weapons? Three Models in Search of a Bomb. *International Security, 21*(3), 54–86.

39. Sagan, Scott (2000). Rethinking the Causes of Nuclear Proliferation: Three Models in Search of a Bomb? In Victor Utgoff (Ed.), *The Coming Crisis: Nuclear Proliferation, U.S. Interests, and World Order* (pp. 17–50). Cambridge, MA: MIT Press.

40. Crisis Watch Network (2013). *North Korea Weapons Aftermath*. Retrieved May 13, 2013, from http://www.crisiswatch.net/international/NorthKoreaWeaponsAftermath.html

41. Scobell, Andrew, & Sanford, John (2007). *North Korea's Military Threat: Pyongyang's Conventional Forces, Weapons of Mass Destruction, and Ballistic Missiles*. Carlisle, PA: Strategic Studies Institute.

42. Greenwood, Ted, Feiveson, Harold, & Taylor, Theodore (1977). *Nuclear Proliferation: Motivations, Capabilities, and Strategies for Control*. New York: McGraw-Hill.

43. Friedman, Thomas (1995, October 4). Foreign Affairs: The French Ostrich. *The New York Times*, p. A1.

44. Singh, Sonali, & Way, Christopher (2004). The Correlates of Nuclear Proliferation: A Quantitative Test. *Journal of Conflict Resolution, 48*(6), 859–885.

45. Jasper, Ursula, & Portela, Clara (2010). EU Defence Integration and Nuclear Weapons: A Common Deterrent for Europe? *Security Dialogue, 41*(2), 145–168.

46. Müller, Harald (1979). Nuclear Exports and Nuclear Weapons Proliferation: The Quest for a German Non-Proliferation Policy. *Bulletin of Peace Proposals, 10*(1), 128–137.

47. Parsi, Mani, & Yetiv, Steve (2008). Unequal Contest: Iranian Nuclear Proliferation between Economic and Value Symmetry. *Contemporary Security Policy, 29*(2), 31.

48. Stracke, Nicole (2007). Nuclear Development in the Gulf: A Strategic or Economic Necessity? *Insights, 7*, 4–10.

49. Bonner, Michael (2008). *Jihad in Islamic History: Doctrines and Practice*. Princeton, NJ: Princeton University Press.

50. Matinuddin, Kamal (2000). *The Taliban Phenomenon Afghanistan 1994–1997: With an Afterword Covering*. New Delhi: Lancer Publishers

51. Combating Terrorism Center (2006). *The Islamic Imagery Project: Visual Motifs in Jihadi Internet Propaganda*. West Point, NY: Combating Terrorism Center.

52. Lockhart, Laurence (2009). The Persian Army in the Ṣafavī Period. *Der Islam, 34*(1), 89–98.

53. Cook, David (2007). *Martyrdom in Islam*. Cambridge: Cambridge University Press.

54. Combating Terrorism Center (2006). *The Islamic Imagery Project: Visual Motifs in Jihadi Internet Propaganda*. West Point, NY: Combating Terrorism Center.

55. Kaeuper, Richard (2000). *Violence in Medieval Society*. Woodbridge, UK: Boydell & Brewer.

56. Jones, Ronald (2005). *Terrorist Beheadings: Cultural and Strategic Implications*. Carlisle, PA: Strategic Studies Institute.

57. Perlmutter, Dawn (2005). Mujahideen Blood Rituals: The Religious and Forensic Symbolism of Al Qaeda Beheading. *Anthropoetics, 11*(2), 10–21.

58. Perlmutter, Dawn (2005). Mujahideen Blood Rituals: The Religious and Forensic Symbolism of Al Qaeda Beheading. *Anthropoetics, 11*(2), 10–21.

59. Furnish, Timothy (2005). Beheading in the Name of Islam. *The Middle-East Quarterly, 12*(2), 51–57.

60. Filler, Alfredo (202). The Abu Sayyaf Group: A Growing Menace to Civil Society. *Terrorism and Political Violence, 14*(4), 131–162; and Tishkov, Valery (2003). *Chechnya: Life in a War-Torn Society*. Berkeley: University of California Press.

61. Perlmutter, Dawn (2003). *Investigating Religious Terrorism and Ritualistic Crimes*. Boca Raton, FL: CRC Press.

62. State of California Office of Criminal Justice (1989). *Occult Crime: A Law Enforcement Primer*. Sacramento: State of California Office of Criminal Justice.

63. Janes, Regina (2005). *Losing Our Heads: Beheadings in Literature and Culture*. New York: New York University Press.

64. Perlmutter, Dawn (2006). Mujahideen Desecration: Beheadings, Mutilation & Muslim Iconoclasm. *Anthropoetics, 12*(2), 1–8.

65. Perlmutter, Dawn (2006). Mujahideen Desecration: Beheadings, Mutilation & Muslim Iconoclasm. *Anthropoetics, 12*(2), 1–8.

66. Janes, Regina (2005). *Losing Our Heads: Beheadings in Literature and Culture*. New York: New York University Press.

67. Shah, Miran (2006, August 30). Pakistani Militants Allegedly Behead Islamic Cleric, Afghan Refugee. *USA Today*, p. A1.

68. Janes, Regina (2005). *Losing Our Heads: Beheadings in Literature and Culture*. New York: New York University Press.

69. Janes, Regina (2005). *Losing Our Heads: Beheadings in Literature and Culture*. New York: New York University Press.

70. Martin, Gus (2010). *Understanding Terrorism: Challenges, Perspectives, and Issues*. Thousand Oaks, CA: Sage; and U.S. Agency for International Development (2004). *Sexual Terrorism: Rape as a Weapon of War in Eastern Democratic Republic of Congo*. Washington, DC: U.S. Agency for International Development.

71. Benton, Sarah (1995). Women Disarmed: The Militarisation of Politics in Ireland 1913–1923. *Feminist Review, 50*, 148–172.

72. Diken, Bülent, & Bagge Laustsen, Carsten (2005). Becoming Abject: Rape as a Weapon of War. *Body & Society, 11*(1), 111–128.

73. Korac, Maja (1996). Understanding Ethnic-National Identity and Its Meaning: Questions from Women's Experience. *Women's Studies International Forum, 19*(1), 133–143.

74. Watts, Charlotte, & Zimmerman, Cathy (2002). Violence against Women: Global Scope and Magnitude. *Lancet, 359*(9313), 1232–1237.

75. Seifert, Ruth (1994). War and Rape: A Preliminary Analysis. In Alexandra Stiglmayer (Ed.), *Mass Rape: The War against Women in Bosnia-Herzegovina* (pp. 54–72). Lincoln: University of Nebraska Press.

76. Salzman, Todd (1998). Rape Camps as a Means of Ethnic Cleansing: Religious, Cultural, and Ethical Responses to Rape Victims in the Former Yugoslavia. *Human Rights Quarterly, 20*(2), 348–378.

77. Kristof, Nicholas (2008, June 15). The Weapon of Rape. *The New York Times*, p. C3.

78. Hagan, John, & Rymond-Richmond, Wenona (2008). *Darfur and the Crime of Genocide*. Cambridge: Cambridge University Press.

79. Benhabyles, Saïda (2005). Terrorism in Algeria: The Impact on Children and Adolescents. In Jill Donnelly (Ed.), *Developing Strategies to Deal with Trauma in Children* (pp. 23–24). Washington, DC: IOS Press.

80. Guntram, Herb, & Kaplan, David (1999). *Nested Identities: Nationalism, Territory and Scale*. Lanham, MD: Rowman & Littlefield.

81. Meharg, Sarah Jane (2001). Identicide and Cultural Cannibalism: Warfare's Appetite for Symbolic Place. *Peace Research Journal, 33*(3), 89–98.

82. Gourgouris, Stathis (2004). Transformation, Not Transcendence. *Boundary, 31*(2), 55–79.

83. Penn, Michael, & Nardos, Rahel (2003). *Overcoming Violence against Women and Girls: An International Campaign to Eradicate a Worldwide Problem*. Lanham, MD: Rowman & Littlefield.

84. Brownmiller, Susan (1988). *Against Our Will: Men, Women and Rape*. London: Penguin.

85. Askin, Kelly (1997). *War Crimes against Women: Prosecution in International War Crimes Tribunals*. The Hague: Martinus Nijhoff.

86. Korac, Maja (1998). Ethnic Nationalism, Wars and the Patterns of Social, Political and Sexual Violence against Women: The Case of Post-Yugoslav Countries. *Identities, 5*(2), 153–181.

87. Seifert, Ruth (1994). War and Rape: A Preliminary Analysis. In Alexandra Stiglmayer (Ed.), *Mass Rape: The War against Women in Bosnia-Herzegovina* (pp. 54–72). Lincoln: University of Nebraska Press.

88. Johnson, Michael (1995). Patriarchal Terrorism and Common Couple Violence: Two Forms of Violence against Women. *Journal of Marriage and the Family, 57*, 283–294.

89. Korac, Maja (1998). Ethnic Nationalism, Wars and the Patterns of Social, Political and Sexual Violence against Women: The Case of Post-Yugoslav Countries. *Identities, 5*(2), 153–181.

90. Salzman, Todd (1998). Rape Camps as a Means of Ethnic Cleansing: Religious, Cultural, and Ethical Responses to Rape Victims in the Former Yugoslavia. *Human Rights Quarterly, 20*(2), 348–378.

91. Bataille, Georges (1993). *The Accursed Share*. New York: Zone Books.

92. Diken, Bülent, & Bagge Laustsen, Carsten (2005). Becoming Abject: Rape as a Weapon of War. *Body & Society, 11*(1), 111–128.

93. Card, Claudia (1996). Rape as a Weapon of War. *Hypatia, 11*(4), 5–18.

94. Ignatieff, Michael (1993). *Blood and Belonging: Journeys into the New Nationalism*. London: Macmillan.

95. Diken, Bülent, & Bagge Laustsen, Carsten (2005). Becoming Abject: Rape as a Weapon of War. *Body & Society, 11*(1), 111–128.

96. Korac, Maja (1998). Ethnic Nationalism, Wars and the Patterns of Social, Political and Sexual Violence against Women: The Case of Post-Yugoslav Countries. *Identities, 5*(2), 153–181.

97. Meznaric, Silva (1994). Gender as an Ethno-Marker: Rape, War, and Identity Politics in the Former Yugoslavia. In Valentine Moghadam (Ed.), *Identity Politics and Women: Cultural Reassertions and Feminism in International Relations.* Boulder, CO: Westview.

98. United Nations (2001). *Report of the Panel of Experts on the Illegal Exploitation of Natural Resources and Other Forms of Wealth of the Democratic Republic of Congo.* New York: United Nations.

99. Williams, Carol (1993, November 12). A Bridge Too Many: Destruction of Bosnia Landmark Sparks Outrage from All Sides. *Montreal Gazette,* p. B5.

100. Nikolic-Ristanovic, Vesna (1996). War and Violence against Women. In Jennifer Turpin & Lois Ann Lorentzen (Eds.), *The Gendered New World Order: Militarism, Development and the Environment* (pp. 195–210). New York: Routledge.

101. Diken, Bülent, & Bagge Laustsen, Carsten (2005). Becoming Abject: Rape as a Weapon of War. *Body & Society, 11*(1), 111–128.

102. Brownmiller, Susan (1988). *Against Our Will: Men, Women and Rape.* London: Penguin.

103. Seifert, Ruth (1994). War and Rape: A Preliminary Analysis. In Alexandra Stiglmayer (Ed.), *Mass Rape: The War against Women in Bosnia-Herzegovina* (pp. 54–72). Lincoln: University of Nebraska Press.

104. Miller, William (1997). *The Anatomy of Disgust.* Cambridge, MA: Harvard University Press.

105. Penn, Michael, & Nardos, Rahel (2003). *Overcoming Violence against Women and Girls: An International Campaign to Eradicate a Worldwide Problem.* Lanham, MD: Rowman & Littlefield.

106. Seifert, Ruth (1994). War and Rape: A Preliminary Analysis. In Alexandra Stiglmayer (Ed.), *Mass Rape: The War against Women in Bosnia-Herzegovina* (pp. 54–72). Lincoln: University of Nebraska Press.

107. Diken, Bülent, & Bagge Laustsen, Carsten (2005). Becoming Abject: Rape as a Weapon of War. *Body & Society, 11*(1), 111–128.

108. Goldstein, Joshua (2001). *War and Gender: How Gender Shapes the War System and Vice Versa.* Cambridge: Cambridge University Press.

109. Belarouci, Latéfa (2005). Terrorist Violence: Attack on Community Attachments. In Jill Donnelly (Ed.), *Developing Strategies to Deal with Trauma in Children* (pp. 25–31). Washington, DC: IOS Press.

110. U.S. Agency for International Development (2004). *Sexual Terrorism: Rape as a Weapon of War in Eastern Democratic Republic of Congo.* Washington, DC: U.S. Agency for International Development.

111. Benhabyles, Saïda (2005). Terrorism in Algeria: The Impact on Children and Adolescents. In Jill Donnelly (Ed.), *Developing Strategies to Deal with Trauma in Children* (pp. 23–24). Washington, DC: IOS Press.

Chapter Twelve

Symbolism in Female Terrorism

FACTS ON FEMALE TERRORISM

Female terrorism is on the rise and is expected to increase. Since 2002, women have directly participated in about forty national and international terrorist organizations.[1] According to Harmon (2000),[2] "More than 30 percent of international terrorists are women, and females are central to membership rosters and operational roles in nearly all insurgencies" (p. 212). In South America, two of the most famous groups designated as terrorist organizations by the U.S. Department of State, the FARC (in Colombia) and the Shining Path (in Peru), have increasingly included women into their groups. Statistics on total female membership within the FARC alone vary between 20 and 40 percent.[3]

In regard to suicide terrorism, out of roughly seventeen terrorist organizations that have started using suicide bombings and martyrdom operations, women have been active in more than 50 percent of them.[4] In addition, more than one third of all suicide attacks conducted since 1985 in Chechnya, Sri Lanka, Israel, the Palestinian territories, Lebanon, Morocco, Egypt, and Iraq have been carried out by women. Women have perpetrated at least one third of all suicide bombings, and, owing to that, their important roles cannot be denied.[5] Between 1985 and 2006, 225 female suicide bombers acting on behalf of many different terrorist organizations were reported, and dozens of women were caught (i.e., female terrorists whose suicide missions failed).[6]

Generally, female terrorists tend to be older. Part of this age difference is due to the fact that they are widows of men killed by the state or the military. According to international research, the nature of female participation in terrorist groups has changed as a result of different recruitment efforts by religious organizations. Women have increasingly taken part in religious-based groups in ways and capacities never seen before. Examples include their participation on the battlefield and as martyrs for the cause.[7] Some Palestinian terrorist organizations have increasingly used women, calling to mind fresh religious sophisms to rationalize martyrdom. The Tamil Tigers, the PKK, and Chechen terrorists have given preference to female bombers, because they draw, or used to draw, less suspicion. What this also means is that, internationally, the terrorist or suicide bomber does not have a clear profile.[8]

GENDER ROLE REVERSAL

Gender refers to a collection of physical, mental, and behavioral characteristics that make masculinity different from femininity. Gender is to be looked at as an act and norm—not as a noun. By and large, gender is an act that requires repetitive performance "of a set of meanings already socially established; it is the mundane and ritualized form of their legitimation" (Butler, 1999, p. 178).[9] Traditionally, women have played supporting roles. They tend to be seen as "life givers" rather than "life takers." The traditional assignment of fixed roles to women in society is an example of **homosocial reproduction**, a term coined by Rosabeth Kanter (1977)[10] to describe the process whereby descriptive characteristics of societal power structures are perpetuated across several generations. Through its body of rules and various institutions, society has typically prescribed women's roles outside the boundaries of militancy. Providing help through subordinate roles is greeted and encouraged. Conversely, fighting in war or violent conflict is not.[11] Hence, for centuries, the underrepresentation of women in terrorism was not the outcome of women refusing to commit themselves to violent extremism but rather the outcome of homosocial reproduction.[12]

This traditional view of gender roles is also referred to as **cultural feminism** (or **gynocentric feminism**), which theorizes femininity as nonviolent mostly due to women's role as actual and/or potential mothers.[13] Women are conceptualized as wardens of traditional culture, which, in effect, locks women into traditional roles within the private spheres of home and married life. Those females who break these established boundaries and, thereby, jeopardize the order and stability of the culture are said to engage in **gender role reversal**.[14] Based on their violent conduct and actions, female terrorists personify a transgression of gender and sexuality that transcends the simple performance of masculinity. Instead, they symbolize a type of gender outside the "normal" expressions of man and woman. In this context, gender role reversal will be explained through the lens of female terrorists' "fight for equality" and their "girl militancy."

Fighting for Equality

The phrase "fighting for equality" is a product of **standpoint feminism**. Standpoint feminists postulate that women's experiences of the world fundamentally differ from men's; therefore, they are in a better position to observe and evaluate this system.[15] Women who become terrorists as a way to reach "equality" have traditionally been linked to left-wing terrorism, principally as a factor of the terrorist group's developed ideology. This philosophy usually entails racial and gender equality or the conviction that such movements can create social change. Terrorist groups may also employ women to foster group solidarity and greater acceptance of females. In Europe and Latin America, left-wing groups have gone to universities and rallies to actively recruit women.[16] In addition, although women may become suicide bombers as a consequence of a personal tragedy, some also think that they can bring change to society's gender norms by means of militant involvement. A difference exists between male and female suicide attackers: for women, combat is a method of escaping the preordained life that is expected of them. When women become human bombs, their objective is to make a statement not only on behalf of a nation, religion, or leader but also on behalf of their gender.[17]

In line with these contentions, a woman can join a terrorist organization because she has been a victim of her surroundings and put into a contextual atmosphere that motivates her to be more equal with her male counterparts. In many instances, the female terrorist is a creation of her society and her personal story. She will tend to employ this as a motivational factor.

Many female Tamil Tigers, for example, claim to have joined the Tigers after their brothers, husbands, and fathers were killed in battle or disappeared at the hands of Sri Lankan security forces. "Equality" can even be "equality in death." The Tamil Tigers case is interesting because it illustrates a situation in which the female fighters have reached the greatest equality: they carry out exactly the same tasks as their male counterparts, even though they are separated from men in their camps and are categorically prohibited from seeing their male companions. The female Tigers are also viewed as the supreme symbol of women's liberation.[18] Samarasinghe (1996)[19] has portrayed this equal possibility of death for men and women within the Tamil Tigers as the "the teacher of equality in life" (p. 5).

Girl Militancy: A Threat to Body Politic

Historically, the woman has come to represent the guardian of tradition, an indication of motherhood and life. Then, how can she, as contradictory to this as it seems, devote her life to violence and death? The answer to this question is captured in the concept of "girl militancy." **Girl militancy** refers to the ultimate transgression of traditional femininity and, through political violence, evokes a more extreme form of feminism that calls for the end of patriarchal oppression. Political violence used by women is the result of violence suffered at the hands of the government or military (i.e., women are resisting, not suddenly or accidently turning violent).[20] Through their girl militancy, female terrorists pose a threat to the body politic. **Body politic** is a metaphor explaining how a nation is to be viewed as a corporate entity, being compared to a human body. A body politic, including all the individuals in a particular country, is considered a single human block and follows the same cultural norms.[21]

A violation of body politic means that women are no longer defined according to their gendered roles. In this context, participation in terrorism is an option thanks to which females can practice a misinterpreted understanding of women's liberation or emancipation. Owing to the absence of other role models, militant women sincerely believe that gender equality is tantamount to being as violent as militant men. By quitting the house and by becoming a first-line terrorist, women break a powerful social taboo.[22] As they underscore female physical prowess as a way to reject femininity, they break an important cultural mold. This act is also called **amazon feminism**, which opposes the idea that certain characteristics or interests are fundamentally masculine.[23]

Case Study I: Palestinian Female Terrorists

In the Palestinian territories, women have resorted to terrorism in order to escape the rigid constraints of traditional roles. In this manner, they can become, in some ways, equal to men.[24] During the First Intifada, the long-established symbol of motherhood developed a new meaning. Now, motherhood was more than just raising children and taking care of the family and the house; it also meant taking to the streets and protecting the youth against the Israeli occupiers. Throughout the Intifada, Palestinian women often challenged, verbally and physically, soldiers on their way to arrest Palestinian men or teenagers.[25]

Palestinians have had a set of norms that define and delineate gender roles (although the first mobilizations of Palestinian women started to emerge in the 1960s). These rules have decreed the separation of the sexes and limited women to the private domain—particularly in agricultural or remote areas. By way of violence, women have put themselves on the frontlines, in public, and even among males to whom they are not related. This has created a double task for female militant Palestinians—persuading society that their militant contributions are valid and, at the same time, refashioning the normative standards of society. With respect to suicide terrorism, the involvement of Palestinian women in martyrdom operations has had a profound effect on the cultural norms of Palestinian society.[26]

Indeed, in Palestinian society, one of the best ways to become a heroine is by carrying out a suicide attack. On January 27, 2002, Wafa Indris, a twenty-six-year-old Palestinian woman, entered a shopping mall in Jerusalem and blew herself up while killing one Israeli and wounding 131 fellow mall shoppers. Earlier that day, Yasser Arafat, then chairman of the Palestinian Liberation Organization (PLO), addressed a large crowd of Palestinian women. Highlighting their invaluable role in the Intifada, he proclaimed, "You are my army of roses that will crush Israeli tanks." He continued, "You will sacrifice the way you, women, have always sacrificed for your family" (Victor, 2003, p. 19).[27] Not only was Wafa Indris Arafat's first "rose"; she was now the Palestinians' heroine. The **Palestinian Liberation Organization (PLO)** is an organization whose purpose is to establish an independent State of Palestine. It is considered a terrorist organization by the United States and Israel.

Case Study II: German Female Terrorists

At the zenith of female terrorism in the 1960s and 1970s, German media were described as "Männerpresse" ("male press"). **Männerpresse** is a metaphor describing the obsession of the German male-controlled media with the female body, which was clearly considered an object of the hungry male gaze. This idea resonates with the fact that the feminine ideals of "Kinder, Küche, Kirche" form the foundation of German cultural discourse. **Kinder, Küche, Kirche (or three Ks)** is a German catchphrase meaning "children, kitchen, church." When Adolf Hitler came to power in 1933, he used this antiquated female role model as a massive motivator for creating the ideal German family: while the Nazi husband is in combat, his wife is at home raising kids and taking care of house chores. The irony is that the more active German female terrorists were, the more obsessed Männerpresse was. Taken as a whole, Männerpresse denotes the mass hysteria about female terrorism in the 1960s and 1970s in Germany. Women in terrorist groups like Baader-Meinhof (or the Red Army Faction) and "Movement 2. June" (Bewegung 2. Juni) stimulated a gendered discourse echoing the cultural nervousness about women participating in extreme violence; the media disseminated notions that conceptualized female terrorists as "unnatural" women. In West German media, articles and news columns castigated them as "terrorist girls" and "wild furies."[28]

On July 30, 1977, Jürgen Ponto, CEO of Dresdner Bank, one of West Germany's greatest banks, was killed in his house in Oberursel by Baader-Meinhof. One of the terrorist group's members, a young woman named Susanne Albrecht (who personally knew the Ponto family), shocked the world as she helped the whole group gain access to the house. The media focused primarily on her "deviant" behavior rather than the brutal killing. By underlining the stereotypical feminine deception that enabled a female terrorist to enter Ponto's home, the media generated a highly gendered representation of the terrorist act.[29] This also destabilized gender conventions; it was a deviance (a violent female terrorist) within a framework that was already deviant in and of itself (terrorism). This disruption of gender norms became noticeable in the unwarranted media coverage of women active in left-wing terrorist groups in the second half of the twentieth century. This case study also demonstrates that violent female terrorists challenge conventional gender roles and drastically damage the body politic of the German nation by totally surpassing their feminine socialization.[30] The next five sections examine, in detail, five overarching symbols of female terrorism. As such, female terrorism is a symbol of continuity of the fight, strategic desirability, revenge, restoration of honor, and change.

FEMALE TERRORISM AS CONTINUITY OF THE FIGHT

Female participation in terrorism communicates a powerful message: it is a symbol of an entire group's or culture's continuity of the fight—thereby reinforcing that fight. In hypothesizing the dense connections between women and the nation, Anthias and Yuval-Davis (1993)[31] argue that nationalist movements perceive women in five fundamental ways: as symbols of the nation, as biological reproducers of the nation, as spreaders of national culture, as boundary protectors between nations, and as dynamic actors in the nationalist struggle.

In Ireland, although the hero or soldier tends to be represented as male, the "woman as a national symbol" becomes "the guardian of the continuity and immutability of the nation, the embodiment of its respectability" (Mosse, 1985, p. 18).[32] It was obvious that the female Irish Republicans themselves deliberately used their femininity. By participating in Republican demonstrations and rituals wearing military attire, women situated themselves very conspicuously in organized public events. Their uniforms of skirts and tunics symbolized their femininity and militarism at the same time.[33] Likewise, among Sikh militants, women have played an assortment of roles, including warriors in battle. Sikh women's support of their husbands and sons has increased their capability of fighting and dying for the nation. Their roles as mothers engendering future warriors for that nation are also acknowledged.[34]

In the context of Islamism, women are also an essential symbol, as demonstrated by the co-optation of female militants by Islamist movements since the 1980s. In the nationalist Palestinian discourse, women occupied a central place during the First Intifada. During its early phases, women became one of the Palestinian movement's most outstanding symbols. Just by marching in demonstrations against the Israeli occupiers, or through personal acts of resistance, Palestinian women helped determine and expose the revolutionary nature of the Intifada. They participated in almost all Intifada-related events. A few hundred women were accused of extreme acts such as terrorism, subversion, and sabotage, and they were thrown in Israeli state jails. They attempted to prevent Palestinian boys and men from being detained. Some women even made the drastic decision to turn in their own sons to the PLO, in case they were collaborators with the Israelis. The women's passionate, at time disproportionate, commitment to the Palestinian national cause was loudly and wholeheartedly admired.[35]

The Israeli and Palestinian media have crafted different versions of reality. On the one hand, the Israeli press has fashioned a version of reality that was chauvinistic—that is, by exposing the machismo of Islamic society and describing the female Palestinian suicide terrorist in a fairly positive light, in comparison with the male suicide terrorist. This narrative positions her as weak and the victim of manipulation by a chauvinist society; it concentrates on personal and social aspects, and does not take nationalist motives into account. On the other hand, the Palestinian press cultivates the feminist dimension, depicting the Palestinian female suicide terrorist as consciously involved in the jihad for independence, while paying less attention to personal aspects.[36] Expressions such as "daughter of Palestine" and "Palestinian's bride" have been used to allude to the loyalty of female martyrs-to-be to the Palestinian struggle. Palestinian terrorists use these terms to further validate their actions against the Israelis and as propaganda for full conscription of women into suicide missions.[37]

FEMALE TERRORISM AS STRATEGIC DESIRABILITY

Gender stereotypes affect the tactical moves and decisions of terrorist groups as well as the behavior of female terrorists. Consequently, intelligence and law enforcement agencies involved in the successful accomplishment of antiterrorism and counterterrorism operations would benefit greatly from understanding and stressing the big canyon that exists between the stereotypical female terrorist and the reality of gender roles in terrorist groups.[38] Concerns about thorough searches, especially of women's bodies, may get in the way of stricter scrutiny. A woman's ability to become pregnant and the resultant changes to her body allow her to hide weapons and bombs using maternity outfits; this further hinders inspection because of impropriety concerns.[39] All these things point toward a concept called **strategic desirability**. The idea, here, is that the woman can symbolize the dangerous gentle sex. Considering the gendered behavioral norms and women's second-class status in the cultures where terrorist attacks occur, women are less likely to raise suspicion when used as terrorists.[40] According to Fighel (2003),[41] "terrorist organizations have been quick to see the advantages of using females to perpetrate terrorist attacks, especially inside Israeli cities. Women are often perceived as 'the gentle sex,' and are less likely to arouse suspicion than men are" (p. 2).

The ability for Palestinian female terrorists to "Westernize" their looks and blend in right in the middle of Jerusalem makes them a serious threat to consider. A certain number of terrorist organizations consider women priceless suicide bombers because of the pervasive cliché that women are innately nonviolent. For instance, women can circumvent Israeli checkpoints and border police more easily. These checkpoints have worked well against Palestinian terrorists inside the occupied territories. Since the mid-1990s, it has been virtually impossible for single males under the age of forty to obtain permits in order to cross the border into Israel. Women, on the other hand, do not raise as much suspicion and can blend in well with Israeli civilians.[42] The sad reality is that women have attacked and tried to kill Israeli soldiers as much as men have. The Second Intifada (2000–2005) witnessed an increasing number of stabbing attempts committed by Palestinian women—some of which succeeded. It was relatively easy for a woman to conceal a dagger in her roomy attire, taking advantage of Israeli soldiers who were very disinclined to frisk or pat down Palestinian women. In general, the soldiers were also less distrustful of women. By extension, if arrested, Palestinian women are incarcerated for shorter periods than their male counterparts and are usually freed under bail or with a fine.[43]

Already at the beginning of the twenty-first century, about 50 percent of Tamil Tigers are women. Females receive equivalent training and combat experience, and they play equally important roles in the Tamil Tigers' organization and structure. As is the case with Palestinian women, Tamil women's usefulness as suicide bombers comes from the lesser attention paid to them by police and security forces. Given these circumstances, women can better bypass scrutiny and reach their targets. The 1991 assassination of Rajiv Gandhi, the sixth prime minister of India, by a Tamil female terrorist, who bent down to touch his feet and detonated a belt filled with 700 grams of explosives hidden under her dress, testifies to the power of female terrorism as strategic desirability.[44]

FEMALE TERRORISM AS REVENGE

A certain number of women choose to join terrorist organizations because they are seeking revenge, usually owing to the fact that the men (i.e., husbands, fathers, and brothers) have died as a result of state oppression, counterterrorism, failed missions, or successful suicide missions (in which, of course, they lost their lives).[45] Because widows or relatives seek revenge, entire communities can be victimized.

Remarks on Revenge

By definition, **revenge** is a destructive action against an individual or group in response to a grievance, whether real or imaginary. It is also called **vengeance**, **retaliation**, **retribution**, and **payback**.[46] Within the framework of terrorism, the national tradition and even the obligation, driven by religious-based ideology, to avenge a friend or relative can offer a type of psychological remedy; the remedy is the killing of the enemy, which allows the grieved terrorist to "get even." Logically, this psychological remedy can be short-lived if the grieved one turns into a suicide bomber.[47] Consider, for instance, females who become Tamil Tigers. The Sri Lankan government has been responsible for organized violence against the Tamils in a methodical campaign of abductions, rape, checkpoint searches, and torture—as well as the obliteration of entire villages in rural areas. Moreover, in the midst of conflict, the Sri Lankan forces have not discriminated civilians from combatants and militants when opening fire.[48] Many grieved Tamils have become Tamil Tigers as a result.

In a longitudinal study of 653 clinical subjects who suffered war traumas, Akhmedova (2003)[49] found that subjects who experienced the highest degree of posttraumatic effects were more "transformed" in this regard. In close to 40 percent of the cases, they advocated revenge and no longer considered it as applicable when the victim's family had been harmed. Rather, the feeling of revenge was generalized to inflict harm on the ethnic group from which the evildoer came. The higher the trauma was, the more generalized and acceptable the revenge was. Positive correlations also existed between the support for revenge and higher levels of religiosity, violence, suspiciousness, and negativism.

Case Study: Black Widows in Chechnya

From 1994 to 1996, the First Chechen War occurred when Russian forces attempted to take back the breakaway southern republic of Chechnya. The war resulted in thousands of Chechen civilian deaths and massive damage to Chechnya's infrastructure. In turn, this war engendered deep feelings of resentment toward Russia. This resentment, along with a yearning to attain full independence from Russia, led many Chechen rebels to resort to terrorism against the Russian government and its civilians.[50] Some of these Chechen rebels included (and still include) **Black Widows** (or **shahidka**), a term for Islamist female suicide bombers in Chechnya willing to be martyrs in the name of Allah. The name "Black Widows" most likely comes from the fact that many of these women are widows of men slain by Russian forces in Chechnya. The toxic reference to black widow spiders is also at work.[51]

Von Knop (2007)[52] argues that Black Widows retaliate against Russians as a result of their own experience of rape by Russian troops and for the killings of their husbands, male relatives, and friends. In October 2002, at least forty Chechen terrorists seized the crowded Dubrovka Theater, an event commonly known as the **Moscow theater hostage crisis**. All forty terrorists were killed by Russian counterterrorist forces, but 130 hostages died from the toxic substance used by the Russians. What has been less reported in the media, in regard to that tragedy, is that nineteen Black Widows appeared in black Arab-style burqa clothes with bombs strapped to their bodies. A **burqa** is an outer garment covering the entire body.[53]

Seeking revenge for the killing of a family member is deeply ingrained within Chechen culture. In that culture, the traditional concept of revenge for social injustices done toward families is what Islamist Chechens live by. It is a code of revenge stipulating that, upon the death or harm of a loved one, it is the duty of the family members to locate the perpetrator and exact due repayment. This situation exemplifies the concept of blood feud, whereby the relatives of a person who has been killed or hurt seek revenge by killing or physically punishing the evildoers (and/or their families) (see chapter 4).[54] This ideology of revenge is methodical and usually does not go beyond seeking out the originator of the wrong. Recently, however, due to massive attacks on the part of Russian forces, traumatization, bereavement, and the indoctrination of a terrorist mentality, revenge has become generalized in the hearts and souls of many.[55]

FEMALE TERRORISM AS RESTORATION OF HONOR

Women can also turn to terrorism in order to reclaim their personal or family honor. Female terrorism as restoration of honor should be examined through six different themes that symbolize the attributes of the female terrorist: the role model, emancipated woman, raped woman, infertile woman, pregnant woman, and divorcee.

- **Role model**: female terrorists can represent powerful role models for other women who may try to emulate their heroine's actions. By the same token, female terrorism can boost male recruitment because men may feel shamed into joining when their female equivalents appear to be taking their dominant role in conflict.[56] Palestinian suicide bombers, whose child- or husband-warriors have been killed by the IDF (Israel Defense Forces), have become role models for many would-be terrorists in the Palestinian territories.
- **Emancipated woman**: when women join terrorist organizations, they may do so out of a drive for deliverance from state oppression or traditional societal restrictions. In other words, female terrorism may be driven by female emancipation. This was cited as the reason why female Tamil Tigers have been nicknamed **Freedom Birds**. This concept symbolizes the achievements and results of the Tamils' liberation struggle: freedom from political and social "servitude." In Hinduism, traditions such as the caste and dowry systems are viewed as female bondage by Tamils. The ethos of the Tamil Tigers does not acknowledge or allow caste-based restrictions and the dowry system.[57]
- **Raped woman**: a certain number of female Chechens have been raped by Russian troops. Likewise, during the Indian-led peacekeeping operation in Sri Lanka (1987–1990), rape of Sri Lankan Tamil females was widespread. Subsequent to a rape, Tamil women are regarded as "damaged goods" and social customs do not permit them to get married. This has led Tamil females to join the Tamil Tigers for both security and a chance to wreak vengeance against the Sri Lankan state. Their participation in terrorism also allows them to restore their personal and familial pride.[58]
- **Infertile woman**: in many Third World cultures, the shame caused by sexual violation is amplified by the humiliation of not being able to get married and, hence, fulfill childbearing duties. For the Tamil Tigers, the self-sacrifice of female suicide terrorists becomes an extension of the idea of motherhood in Tamil society. In this highly male-controlled culture, Tamil mothers sacrifice themselves for their sons every day. They feed them before themselves and the girl children, and serve them in the same manner. Transforming oneself into a human bomb is a well-embraced offering for a woman who will never become a mother.[59]
- **Pregnant woman**: the concept of "pregnant woman" is something to behold, particularly when it comes to restoring honor. As we have seen, in Israel, pregnant women tend not to be frisked or patted down at security checkpoints. What was not mentioned, however, is that, recently, many of these women have been denied entry at many security checkpoints out of fear that they may be carrying a bomb instead of a child. This makes Palestinians angry and resentful. The idea of Israelis having control over the physical bodies of Palestin-

ian females is powerful; it has a strong impact on helping terrorist organizations recruit women to become suicide bombers. When they choose to become suicide bombers, it is a supreme tactic for them to restore control over the sacredness of their body, a value that is of utmost importance in the Muslim world. [60]

- **Divorcee**: for some women, terrorism also emerges out of a failure to fulfill an expected feminine role—that of wife and mother. In the Palestinian territories, three female suicide bombers were divorced from their husbands because they were unable to have children. Another Palestinian woman became a suicide bomber after being traumatized by a miscarriage and subsequent divorce from her husband. [61]

What all six themes illustrate is that terrorism is sometimes seen as a viable option by women who have experienced various shocks and pains. Whether the objective is to become a role model for other women who have lost their husbands in holy war or to fulfill duties that the woman could not fulfill as a wife, this analysis shows how women can reclaim their personal or family honor through a whole range of personality attributes.

FEMALE TERRORISM AS CHANGE

Female terrorism can also be a symbol of change. In this section, change is analyzed from several perspectives: the new sensation experienced as a result of joining a terrorist organization, social change, new interpretations of holy scriptures, and even a reversal of the power structure. For example, when a woman joins a terrorist group, the latter prescribes (and proscribes) new behaviors inherent to the group and expects full dedication to a meaningful life. Symbols of belonging include pursuing a new lifestyle and wearing certain clothing. Female terrorism can represent change by sheer virtue of a woman joining a terrorist group; it fills a vacuum for the victim who has been traumatized by the loss of important family members and who, in the heart of war and occupation, has lost direction in life. [62]

In a similar fashion, in regard to social change, upon analyzing the operational role of women in Italian terrorist organizations in the 1960s and 1970s, several key tendencies were identified. Although Italian women only accounted for 20 percent of terrorist members during these two decades, the few women who joined terrorist organizations were disproportionately attracted to leftist and nationalist movements. This coincided with a period of widespread social change, as demonstrated in various domains such as divorce, abortion, education, and employment. All these social changes made it easier for the Italian Left to recruit and rally the country's women. [63]

Within Muslim circles, calls for Islamic revival worldwide have led to new forms of militant Islam, including the acceptance of female warriors in jihad. Scholars view the new radical interpretation of Islam (e.g., in places like Chechnya and the Palestinian territories) as one that suits a general societal need to react to the violent, bereaving, and traumatic events that women have endured. In joining violent groups and subscribing to Islamist ideology, a new worldview develops within would-be suicide bombers in which materialism is rejected, death as a martyr is exalted, and terrorist violence is warranted as a way of fulfilling the jihad. Naturally, the afterlife is considered a worthwhile recompense for sacrificing one's life. [64] Speaking of the afterlife, whereas the male martyr enjoys seventy-two virgins in Paradise, the female warrior gets to choose the most attractive man to marry. [65]

Lastly, female terrorism also symbolizes a reversal of the power structure. For example, among Chechen terrorists, the advent and rise of Black Widows represent a new worldview that has been likened to a total change of mentality and lifestyle. This also means a change in power structure. Traditionally, Chechen terrorist organizations (which are totally Islamic) are male run, with women being confined to submissive and traditional roles: cooking, cleaning, healing the wounded, and so on. However, some of the worst terrorist attacks—including suicide bombings in Moscow—have been committed by Chechen women. And, in many cases, leftist terrorist groups or operations (particularly in Europe) have frequently been led by women. An example is Baader-Meinhof: Ulrike Marie Meinhof, a woman, was one of its leaders.[66]

BEAUTIFUL FEMALE TERRORISTS

Female terrorists are likely to attract more media attention than their male counterparts because the thought of those who bring forth life actually annihilating it is troubling. The mere idea of women turning to violent extremism goes completely against expectations of femininity. So images of female terrorists garner massive publicity and, in the process, diffuse the terrorist organization's message to a larger audience.[67] Especially in regard to suicide terrorism, a growing number of terrorist organizations have taken advantage of the fact that female suicide bombing, especially when perpetrated by young girls and beautiful women, will make the audience stop and watch—both in the West and in the Middle East. Statistically speaking, attacks by women receive eight times more media coverage than attacks by men; again, this is mostly due to the expectation that women are nonviolent. Aware of this, the Palestinian Al-Aqsa Martyrs' Brigade has designed an enormous propagandist campaign to lionize its female bombers (e.g., their posters are shown on the walls of Ramallah).[68]

Fitting Western Standards

Media images of female terrorists work as useful propaganda tools. Many terrorist organizations cleverly recruit women for strategic purposes: women who murder or threaten to murder are "hot news."[69] The female terrorist becomes exploited by the world at large—particularly the Western world. She tends to be portrayed as a superheroine, amazon, or warrior princess—like G.I. Jane, Catwoman, or Wonder Woman. She becomes a goddess or virago. A **virago** is a beautiful woman who oozes commendable and heroic qualities. The word comes from the Latin word *vir* (i.e., "virile" or "man"). Female terrorists are more likely to be described in terms of appearance, age, and stereotypical negative traits (e.g., that they tend to use their looks for deceptive purposes). An interesting aspect of the media depiction of female terrorists is the high emphasis on their corporeal traits and sexuality.

With respect to female suicide bombers, examples of corporeal traits and sexuality described in the media are (1) **sensuality** (i.e., her beautiful and voluptuous body does not serve to gratify men, but it is used to detonate bombs); (2) **virginity** (i.e., female terrorists represent precious human capital that is sacrificed for an ideal); (3) **pregnancy** (i.e., the woman's belly is particularly mentioned when discussing the "demographic war" between the Israelis and Palestinians, and when describing female suicide bombers disguising their explosive belts as bulging bellies); and (4) **motherhood** (i.e., choosing the path of martyrdom has been extended, by the Arab press, to a "generalized Palestinian motherhood").[70] On that note, Arab newspapers frequently describe female suicide terrorists as pure wives and "mothers of the revolution." This obsession with female terrorists' bodies is proof that media portrayals of female terrorists use a gendered representation of them that fits Western standards, which results in a considerably deluded image of female suicide bombers.[71]

Case Study I: Wafa Idris

A newspaper article about **Wafa Idris**, the very first female Palestinian suicide bomber, opened with the following sentence: "She was an attractive, auburn haired graduate who had a loving family and likes to wear sleeveless dresses and make-up" (Walter, 2002, p. B1).[72] In another article, Idris was depicted as a female with "long, dark hair tied back with a black-and-white keffiyeh" (National Public Radio, 2002).[73] She was also the centerpiece of a story about the upsurge of "Palestinian women strapping explosives to their bodies and becoming martyrs"; this story, on the website of the Christian Broadcasting Network, was entitled "Lipstick Martyrs: A New Breed of Palestinian Terrorists" (CBN, 2003).[74] After she exploded herself in 2002, her photo was used on posters throughout the Palestinian territories. The political and cultural elites celebrated her memory, and an Egyptian TV program broadcast her story across the Muslim world. The beautiful Idris became a symbol of heroism and sacrifice, and inspired other female youths to commit suicide terrorism as well. A Fatah leader said, "Wafa's martyrdom restored honor to the national role of the Palestinian woman." The editor of *Al-Arabi*, a weekly Kuwait-based magazine, wrote, "She is Joan of Arc, Jesus Christ and the Mona Lisa" (quoted in Victor, 2003, p. 25).[75]

Case Study II: The Tigress

From 1986 to 1994, **Idoia López Riaño** (under the pseudonym of **the Tigress**) was a very active female terrorist for ETA, the Basque terrorist group. During those years, she was responsible for a Madrid explosion in which twelve Civil Guards were killed in 1986, a car bomb that killed five more that year, and the killing of several individual police officers and four soldiers.[76] What is interesting, however, is the way the media have portrayed Idoia. For example, in 1995, a year after the Tigress was arrested and condemned to 1,500 years in jail, Anne McElvoy (1995)[77] reported in the *Times of London* that the Tigress looked like a Mediterranean movie star and was "one of the few women who manages to look good even in a police shot" (p. A1). She was also described as "wearing hefty eye make-up, fuchsia lipstick and dangling earrings that tinkle as she tosses her hair of black curls" (p. A1).

Case Study III: Ulrike Marie Meinhof

Ulrike Marie Meinhof was the cofounder and co-leader of Baader-Meinhof (or the Red Army Faction). In May 1976, after many active years as a terrorist, she was found dead in prison—apparently as a result of suicide. A *Bild* (1976)[78] article, published in the aftermath of Ulrike Meinhof's alleged suicide, made the following statements: "She made herself look beautiful one more time and then ripped a towel into strips" (p. 2). Making herself look beautiful may not have been the first thing on Meinhof's mind before committing suicide, if indeed she did take her own life. The article was accompanied by two pictures of Meinhof, one of which had a clear glamor shot appeal. On that photo, Meinhof was wearing lipstick, smiling, and demurely looking back at the camera over her right shoulder. A very high amount of interest was also produced by Meinhof's clothing. As Lampe (1972)[79] informed us, "Wearing a designer dress, she would discuss Marx and Lenin at bourgeois parties" (p. 3). Similarly, *Der Spiegel* (1972)[80] revealed that Meinhof was the rock star of the Hamburg scene, as someone who would attract anyone's attention; "she decorated herself for society and wore hand-crafted Skoluda pendants along with her Gloria designer dresses" (p. 64).

SUMMARY

Statistics show that, on average, female membership in terrorist organizations is 30 percent. Female terrorism symbolizes an opposition to homosocial reproduction (i.e., the traditional assignment of fixed roles to women in society). This is also referred to as "gender role reversal," "amazon feminism," and "girl militancy." Five overarching symbols of female terrorism were described. The first symbol, "continuity of the fight," communicates the message that female participation in terrorism is a symbol of an entire group's or culture's continuity of the struggle—thereby, reinforcing that struggle. The second symbol, "strategic desirability," reinforces the idea that the woman is a symbol of the dangerous gentle sex. Considering the gendered behavioral norms and women's second-class status in the cultures where terrorist attacks occur, women are less likely to raise suspicion when used as terrorists. The third symbol, "revenge," explains how terrorism can be a destructive action against an individual or group in response to a grievance (also called "blood feud"). For example, Chechen Black Widows have become suicide bombers for that reason. The fourth symbol, "restoration of honor," describes how women can turn to terrorism in order to reclaim their personal or family honor. In this regard, female terrorism can be examined through six different themes that symbolize the attributes of the female terrorist: role model, emancipated woman, raped woman, infertile woman, pregnant woman, and divorcee. The fifth symbol, "change," can be looked at from several perspectives: the new sensation experienced as a result of joining a terrorist organization, social change, new interpretations of holy scriptures, and even a reversal of power structure. Finally, female terrorists are more likely to attract media attention than their male counterparts because the mere idea of women turning to violent extremism goes completely against expectations of femininity. With respect to female suicide bombers, the media tend to focus on the corporeal traits and sexuality of the female terrorist. Examples are her sensuality, virginity, pregnancy, and motherhood. The case studies of Wafa Idris, the Tigress, and Ulrike Marie Meinhof confirm this.

NOTES

1. Jordan, Kim, & Denov, Myriam (2007). Birds of Freedom? Perspectives on Female Emancipation and Sri Lanka's Liberation Tigers of Tamil Eelam. *Journal of International Women's Studies, 9*(1), 42–62.

2. Harmon, Christopher (2000). *Terrorism Today*. London: Frank Cash.

3. Cunningham, Karla (2003). Cross-Regional Trends in Female Terrorism. *Studies in Conflict & Terrorism, 26*(3), 171–195.

4. Bloom, Mia (2007). Female Suicide Bombers: A Global Trend. *Dædalus, 136*(1), 94–102.

5. Bloom, Mia (2005). *Dying to Kill: The Global Phenomenon of Suicide Terror*. New York: Columbia University Press.

6. Von Knop, Katharina (2007). The Female Jihad: Al Qaeda's Women. *Studies in Conflict & Terrorism, 30*(5), 397–414.

7. Cook, David (2005). Women Fighting in Jihad. *Studies in Conflict and Terrorism, 28*(5), 375–384.

8. Martyrdom and Murder. (2004, January 8). *The Economist, 388*, p. 10.

9. Butler, Judith (1999). *Gender Trouble: Feminism and the Subversion of Identity*. New York: Routledge.

10. Kanter, Rosabeth (1977). *Men and Women of the Corporation*. New York: Basic Books.

11. Bloom, Mia (2007). Female Suicide Bombers: A Global Trend. *Dædalus, 136*(1), 94–102.

12. Ferber, Abby, & Kimmel, Michael (2008). The Gendered Face of Terrorism. *Sociology Compass, 2*, 870–887.

13. Hackett, Elizabeth, & Haslanger, Sally (2005). *Theorizing Feminisms: A Reader*. Oxford: Oxford University Press.

14. Ryan, Louise (2002). "Furies" and "Die-hards": Women and Irish Republicanism in the Early Twentieth Century. *Gender & History, 11*(2), 256–275.

15. Ticker, Ann (2004). The Growth and Future of Feminist Theories International Relations. *Brown Journal of World Affairs, 10*(2), 47–56.

16. Eager, Paige (2008). *From Freedom Fighters to Terrorists: Women and Political Violence*. Burlington, VT: Ashgate Publishing.

17. Beyler, Clara (2003). *Messengers of Death: Female Suicide Bombers*. Herzliya, Israel: ICT.

18. Bokhari, Laila (2007). Women and Terrorism—Passive or Active Actors? Motivations and Strategic Use. In the Centre of Excellence Defence against Terrorism (Ed.), *Suicide as a Weapon* (pp. 51–63). Ankara, Turkey: Centre of Excellence Defence against Terrorism.

19. Samarasinghe, Vidyamali (1996). Soldiers, Housewives and Peace Makers: Ethnic Conflict and Gender and Sri Lanka. *Ethnic Studies Report, 14*(2), 203–227.

20. Melzer, Patricia (2009). "Death in the Shape of a Young Girl": Feminist Responses to Media Representations of Women Terrorists during the "German Autumn" of 1977. *International Feminist Journal of Politics, 11*(1), 35–62.

21. Olwig, Kenneth (2002). *Landscape, Nature, and the Body Politic*. Madison: University of Wisconsin Press.

22. Von Knop, Katharina (2007). The Female Jihad: Al Qaeda's Women. *Studies in Conflict & Terrorism, 30*(5), 397–414.

23. Tandon, Neeru (2008). *Feminism: A Paradigm Shift*. New Delhi: Atlantic Publishers.

24. Victor, Barbara (2003). *Army of Roses: Inside the World of Palestinian Women Suicide Bombers*. Emmaus, PA: Rodale Books.

25. Nachmani, Amikam (2001). The Palestinian Intifada 1987–1993: The Dynamics of Symbols and Symbolic Realities, the Role of Symbols, Rituals and Myths in National Struggles. *Civil Wars, 4*(1), 49–103.

26. Bloom, Mia (2007). Female Suicide Bombers: A Global Trend. *Dædalus, 136*(1), 94–102.

27. Victor, Barbara (2003). *Army of Roses: Inside the World of Palestinian Women Suicide Bombers*. Emmaus, PA: Rodale Books.

28. Melzer, Patricia (2009). "Death in the Shape of a Young Girl": Feminist Responses to Media Representations of Women Terrorists during the "German Autumn" of 1977. *International Feminist Journal of Politics, 11*(1), 35–62.

29. Steinseifer, Martin (2006). Terrorism as Media Event in Fall 1977: Strategies, Dynamics, Representations, Interpretations. In Klaus Weinhauer, Jörg Requate, & HeinzGerhard Haupt (Eds.), *Terrorism in West Germany* (pp. 351–381). Frankfurt am Main: Campus Verlag.

30. Melzer, Patricia (2009). "Death in the Shape of a Young Girl": Feminist Responses to Media Representations of Women Terrorists during the "German Autumn" of 1977. *International Feminist Journal of Politics, 11*(1), 35–62.

31. Anthias, Floya, & Yuval-Davis, Nira (1993). *Racialised Boundaries*. London: Routledge.

32. Mosse, George (1985). *Nationalism and Sexuality*. Madison: University of Wisconsin Press.

33. Ryan, Louise (2002). "Furies" and "Die-hards": Women and Irish Republicanism in the Early Twentieth Century. *Gender & History, 11*(2), 256–275.

34. Mahmood, Cynthia (1996). *Fighting for Faith and Nation: Dialogues with Sikh Militants*. Philadelphia: University of Pennsylvania Press.

35. Nachmani, Amikam (2001). The Palestinian Intifada 1987–1993: The Dynamics of Symbols and Symbolic Realities, the Role of Symbols, Rituals and Myths in National Struggles. *Civil Wars, 4*(1), 49–103.

36. Issacharoff, Avi (2006). *The Palestinian and Israeli Media on Female Suicide Terrorists*. Tel Aviv: The Jaffee Center for Strategic Studies.

37. Brunner, C. (2005). Female Suicide Bombers: Male Suicide Bombing? Looking for Gender in Reporting the Suicide Bombings of the Israeli Palestinian Conflict. *Global Society: Journal of Interdisciplinary International Relations, 19*(1), 29–48.

38. Nacos, Brigitte (2005). The Portrayal of Female Terrorists in the Media: Similar Framing Patterns in the News Coverage of Women in Politics and in Terrorism. *Studies in Conflict & Terrorism, 28*(5), 435–451.

39. Cunningham, Karla (2003). Cross-Regional Trends in Female Terrorism. *Studies in Conflict & Terrorism, 26*(3), 171–195.

40. Friedman, Barbara (2008). Unlikely Warriors: How Four U.S. News Sources Explained Female Suicide Bombers. *Journalism & Mass Communication Quarterly, 85*(4), 841–859.

41. Fighel, Yoni (2003). *Palestinian Islamic Jihad and Female Suicide Bombers*. Herzliya, Israel: ICT.

42. Bloom, Mia (2007). Female Suicide Bombers: A Global Trend. *Dædalus, 136*(1), 94–102.

43. Nachmani, Amikam (2001). The Palestinian Intifada 1987–1993: The Dynamics of Symbols and Symbolic Realities, the Role of Symbols, Rituals and Myths in National Struggles. *Civil Wars, 4*(1), 49–103.

44. Cunningham, Karla (2003). Cross-Regional Trends in Female Terrorism. *Studies in Conflict & Terrorism, 26*(3), 171–195.

45. Von Knop, Katharina (2007). The Female Jihad: Al Qaeda's Women. *Studies in Conflict & Terrorism, 30*(5), 397–414.

46. Schivelbusch, Wolfgang (2004). *The Culture of Defeat: On National Trauma, Mourning, and Recovery*. New York: Picador.

47. Speckhard, Anne, & Akhmedova, Khapta (2006). *Black Widows: The Chechen Female Suicide Terrorists*. Tel Aviv: The Jaffee Center for Strategic Studies.

48. Bloom, Mia (2007). Female Suicide Bombers: A Global Trend. *Dædalus, 136*(1), 94–102.

49. Akhmedova, Khapta (2003). Fanaticism and Revenge Idea of Civilians Who Had PTSD. *Social and Clinical Psychiatry, 12*(3), 24–32.

50. Garrison, Carole (2006). Sirens of Death: Role of Women in Terrorism Past, Present, and Future. *Varstvoslovje, 8*(3), 332–339.

51. Ahmed, Akbar (2013). *The Thistle and the Drone: How America's War on Terror Became a Global War on Tribal Islam*. Washington, DC: Brookings Institution Press.

52. Von Knop, Katharina (2007). The Female Jihad: Al Qaeda's Women. *Studies in Conflict & Terrorism, 30*(5), 397–414.

53. Speckhard, Anne, & Akhmedova, Khapta (2006). *Black Widows: The Chechen Female Suicide Terrorists*. Tel Aviv: The Jaffee Center for Strategic Studies.

54. Grutzpalk, Jonas (2002). Blood Feud and Modernity: Max Weber's and Émile Durkheim's Theories. *Journal of Classical Sociology, 2*(2), 115–134.

55. Speckhard, Anne, & Akhmedova, Khapta (2006). The New Chechen Jihad: Militant Wahhabism as a Radical Movement and a Source of Suicide Terrorism in Post-War Chechen Society. *Democracy and Security, 2*(1), 103–155.

56. Von Knop, Katharina (2007). The Female Jihad: Al Qaeda's Women. *Studies in Conflict & Terrorism, 30*(5), 397–414.

57. Balasingham, Adele (2003). *The Will to Freedom: An Inside View of Tamil Resistance*. Mitcham, UK: Fairmax Publishing; and Gunawardena, Arjuna (2006). *Female Black Tigers: A Different Breed of Cat?* Tel Aviv: The Jaffee Center for Strategic Studies.

58. McDowell, Chris (1996). *A Tamil Asylum Diaspora: Sri Lankan Migration, Settlement and Politics in Switzerland*. New York: Berghahn Books; and Samarasinghe, Vidyamali (1996). Soldiers, Housewives and Peace Makers: Ethnic Conflict and Gender and Sri Lanka. *Ethnic Studies Report, 14*(2), 203–227.

59. Gunawardena, Arjuna (2006). *Female Black Tigers: A Different Breed of Cat?* Tel Aviv: The Jaffee Center for Strategic Studies.

60. Brunner, C. (2005). Female Suicide Bombers: Male Suicide Bombing? Looking for Gender in Reporting the Suicide Bombings of the Israeli Palestinian Conflict. *Global Society: Journal of Interdisciplinary International Relations, 19*(1), 29–48; and Garrison, Carole (2006). Sirens of Death: Role of Women in Terrorism Past, Present, and Future. *Varstvoslovje, 8*(3), 332–339.

61. Friedman, Barbara (2008). Unlikely Warriors: How Four U.S. News Sources Explained Female Suicide Bombers. *Journalism & Mass Communication Quarterly, 85*(4), 841–859.

62. Speckhard, Anne, & Akhmedova, Khapta (2006). *Black Widows: The Chechen Female Suicide Terrorists*. Tel Aviv: The Jaffee Center for Strategic Studies.

63. Weinberg, Leonard, & Eubank, William Lee (1987). Italian Women Terrorists. *Terrorism: An International Journal, 9*(3), 241–262.

64. Friedman, Barbara (2008). Unlikely Warriors: How Four U.S. News Sources Explained Female Suicide Bombers. *Journalism & Mass Communication Quarterly, 85*(4), 841–859; and Von Knop, Katharina (2007). The Female Jihad: Al Qaeda's Women. *Studies in Conflict & Terrorism, 30*(5), 397–414.

65. Alvanou, Maria (2008). Palestinian Women Suicide Bombers: The Interplaying Effects of Islam, Nationalism and Honor Culture. *The Homeland Security Review: A Journal of the Institute of Law & Public Policy, 1*(1), 1–28.

66. Gultekin, Kubra (2007). Women Engagement in Terrorism: What Motivates Females to Join in Terrorist Organizations? In Suleyman Orezen, Ismail Dincer Gunes, & Diab Al-Badayneh (Eds.), *Understanding Terrorism: Analysis of Sociological and Psychological Aspects* (pp. 167–175). Amsterdam: IOS Press.

67. Von Knop, Katharina (2007). The Female Jihad: Al Qaeda's Women. *Studies in Conflict & Terrorism, 30*(5), 397–414.

68. Nacos, Brigitte (2005). The Portrayal of Female Terrorists in the Media: Similar Framing Patterns in the News Coverage of Women in Politics and in Terrorism. *Studies in Conflict & Terrorism, 28*(5), 435–451.

69. Alvanou, Maria (2006). *Criminological Perspectives on Female Suicide Terrorism*. Tel Aviv: The Jaffee Center for Strategic Studies.

70. Brunner, C. (2005). Female Suicide Bombers: Male Suicide Bombing? Looking for Gender in Reporting the Suicide Bombings of the Israeli Palestinian Conflict. *Global Society: Journal of Interdisciplinary International Relations, 19*(1), 29–48

71. Bloom, Mia (2005). Mother. Daughter. Sister. Bomber. *Bulletin of the Atomic Scientists, 61*(6), 54–62.

72. Walter, Christopher (2002, January 31). Twisted by Anger, She Turned to Terror. *Times of London*, p. B1.

73. National Public Radio (2002, February 7). *All Things Considered*. Washington, DC: National Public Radio.

74. Retrieved November 4, 2012, from http://www.cbn.com

75. Victor, Barbara (2003). *Army of Roses: Inside the World of Palestinian Women Suicide Bombers*. Emmaus, PA: Rodale.

76. Moran, Lee (2011, November 27). The Tigress Terrorist. *The Sunday Times*, p. A1.

77. McElvoy, Anne (1995, September 9). The Trapping of a Tigress. *Times of London*.

78. Die Wahrheit über den Selbstmord von Ulrike Meinhof. (1976, May 14). *Bild*, p. 2.

79. Lampe, Bernd (1972, June 19). Ulrike Meinhof—von der überzeugten Pazifistin zur Anarchistin der Tat. *Die Welt*, p. 3.

80. *Der Spiegel* (1972, June 26). Wer sich nicht wehrt, stirbt: Ulrike Meinhof—von Engagement zu Engagement. *Der Spiegel*, pp. 62–67.

Chapter Thirteen

Brand Management in Terrorism

PUBLIC COMMUNICATION

Before discussing brand management in detail, it would be useful to define a more overarching term: public communication. **Public communication** is a purposive effort to inform or affect the behaviors of large audiences within a specific time using a coordinated set of communication activities.[1] In chapter 3, a large section was devoted to the role of the audience in terrorism. Particularly emphasized was the audience's reaction to a terrorist act: each terrorist attack involves a sender (i.e., the terrorist him- or herself) and a receiver (i.e., the public and the media). In this chapter, however, public communication will not be examined from the audience's perspective; rather, what will be analyzed is the communication of the terrorist organization itself, mainly how it positions itself and fashions its "brand" or image. Often, the public image of a terrorist organization is important to them. It is almost like engaging in **public relations**, in which the organization practices a type of impression management. As such, public relations consists of controlling the dissemination of information to the public; the goal is to uphold a particular point of view about the organization (i.e., its members, leaders, decisions, and actions overall).[2]

Another term to explain this is public identity. The **public identity** of a terrorist organization comprises certain characteristics of the organization that its members see as central, distinctive, and enduring. More precisely, public identity consists of attributes that members believe are fundamental to (central) and exclusively descriptive of (distinctive) the organization and that gradually remain within the organization (enduring). The public identity is the reality and individuality of the organization, which is inherently linked to its external image, status, and reputation through communication and symbols.[3] Balmer and Wilson (1998)[4] have identified multiple types of public identity. In this context, three types are deemed relevant to the identity of terrorist organizations:

- **Desired identity** (or **ideal identity**): the idealized image that the leaders have of the terrorist organization and what it should become under their leadership. In this sense, it is well understood that public communication is communication with laypeople.
- **Perceived identity**: the public opinion about the terrorist organization; that is, the set of attributes that are viewed as representative of the terrorist organization (in the eyes of the public). The public is a crucial reference group of public communication.

- **Projected identity**: the appearance (i.e., signs or indications) that the terrorist organization conveys to the public—both consciously and unconsciously—through communication and symbols. As we will see, public communication can be easily manipulated by terrorists.

What these three types demonstrate is that the public identity of a terrorist organization is a form of knowledge-producing scheme that follows specific rules for establishing image. Public identity is also a form of mediation between the organization and the public. Of course, the initial identity that the terrorist organization creates about itself may not be received (by the public) as it was anticipated.

BRAND MANAGEMENT

Brand management is a communication function that consists of examining and planning how a brand should be positioned in the world, to what type of audience the brand should be targeted, and how the ideal reputation of the brand should be preserved.[5] Indeed, the best way for an organization to maintain its public identity is through brand management. Historically, the first brands appeared in ancient Greece. They served as names, symbols, or trademarks for quick recognition. As Debord (1994)[6] argues, the ability of an organization to effectively publicize its mission and identity through its brand lends credibility to the reality that brand management plays a large role in creating the aforementioned "desired identity" (or "ideal identity").

Definition of Brand

A **brand** is a symbol that differentiates one product or service from another. It serves to elicit a specific style or genre in the viewers' mind and is generally easily recognizable. Instead of looking for brand names, viewers are familiar with, and search for, symbols as visual shortcuts. Brands represent particularly important means of identification, as well as key portrayals of organizations' verbal and visual promotion strategies.[7] They act as communication intermediaries between organizations and various publics. A brand differs from a logo in that the latter is exclusively the materialistic representation of an entity. A **logo** is a graphic symbol that portrays the true values of an organization; it also includes typography, color, and slogan.[8]

Like many other symbol systems (e.g., words, images, numbers, and language), brands are tools for sending and receiving information; they can act as a visual front for the connection between the sender and the receiver.[9] They can also serve as instant identification through their use on billboards, building walls, signposts, and outdoor displays.[10] Thanks to increased brand exposure, positive emotions produced by the brand can be developed over time. The brand must be capable of creating, in the viewers' minds, a whole range of emotions and images that the organization symbolizes—emotions and images that the organization may have taken years to establish as the foundation of its desired public identity. Brands that project these images and feelings can successfully earn loyalty to the organization by being evocative of a positive public image.[11]

Three Traits of Successful Brands

It is clear by now that the design of a recognizable brand is of utmost importance to many organizations. One purpose of brands is that they "imply social rapport and social power" (Baudrillard, 1983, p. 88).[12] They allow individuals to fashion a cognitive map of their environment. Three traits can make a brand successful: differentiation, credibility, and authenticity.[13] By evaluating an organization's strengths in each area, one can see how brand value is built, communicated, and delivered.

- **Differentiation**: a successful brand tends to represent an alternative. The objective of the brand is to differentiate itself from other brands, and position itself as a better option for the audience. The brand's visual identity plays a crucial role in helping audiences recognize this difference and believe in it.
- **Credibility**: a successful brand represents an icon of trust and credibility. Its aim is to engender faith and loyalty among viewers, thereby creating brand zealots. An organization can achieve credibility by living up to its promise(s).
- **Authenticity**: successful organizations are well aware that they need to go beyond support from individuals who are directly concerned with the issue. Instead, they need to provide efforts to draw a wider audience. Successful brands walk the talk: they say what they do and do what they say.

For the terrorist-propagandist, brands are an enormously cost-effective method of gaining recognition, capable of infinite duplication. They also possess intrinsic plasticity: they can be reinvented, faked, and bequeathed with new meanings.[14] What comes subsequently is an examination of Hezbollah's brand and how the Shia terrorist organization has crafted a multi-faceted communicative strategy to portray its image and mission across the Muslim world.

CASE STUDY: THE BRAND OF HEZBOLLAH

Hezbollah is one of the most important "ambassadors" of the Islamic Republic of Iran in Lebanon. The official Shia doctrine was established in 1979 in the Islamic government of the Grand Ayatollah Khomeini in Iran (the current ayatollah is Khamenei, a different person and different spelling). Hezbollah's leaders vehemently believe that the daily supervision of the Shia Lebanese people (around a Khamenei-like system) will improve the establishment of a collective identity, which will ultimately lead to a better society. This allows Shia Islam to exist as a coherent system of government capable of implementing the actions that it preaches.[15] The Iranian influence on Hezbollah's brand has been reflected in two major ways: (1) through Hezbollah's use of heroic videos and (2) through its self-proclaimed protection and liberation of all Muslims worldwide.

Differentiation

Hezbollah's brand differentiates itself from other terrorist groups' brands for several reasons. For example, Hezbollah is the first Islamist organization to record its "martyrdom operations" on video. In fact, already in the 1970s, the Grand Ayatollah Khomeini, while living incognito in Paris, was able to sneak his Islamist brand into Iran: audiotapes of his entrancing sermons and future plans for Muslims to sacrifice their lives for Allah.[16] Unlike old-fashioned and paper-form media at that time, the new brand of Shia extremism was based on a "new media" form.[17] Khomeini was the one who instigated the creation of Hezbollah. Aaker (1995)[18] notes that the power of brands lies in brand awareness. **Brand awareness** is the degree to which a brand is recognized by the general audience and associated with a specific product. Hezbollah was the first Islamist organization to use suicide bombings systematically, as a result of Khomeini's spellbinding sermons. Suicide bombings became Hezbollah's signature product, later emulated by other Islamist groups. Nevertheless, brand awareness does not pertain only to recognition of a brand, but also its supremacy in people's minds over other brands. Hezbollah managed to achieve this through repetition of its victory messages in the entire media establishment, which transformed slogans like "the most honorable of people" (alluding to **Hassan Nasrallah**, the current Hezbollah leader) and "The Divine Victory" (alluding to the 2006 war) into daily expressions and common parlance.[19] The 2006 war was actually a major conflict that broke out between Israel and Hezbollah (in Lebanon) in the summer of 2006.

Hezbollah has an "information unit" that manipulates the display of its brand. In many streets and public spaces of Lebanon, the brand displays images of martyrs and religious leaders, and Palestinian symbols (to appeal to the Palestinian people as well). Overall, Hezbollah's brand management is focused on depicting the fundamental elements of Hezbollah's resistance society: martyrdom, Shi'ism, and the Israeli invasion of Palestine.[20] On this note, Hezbollah differentiates itself on several levels. For example, the group speaks for the Shi'ites in Lebanon, representing a viable alternative to past and present Christian and Sunni administrations. This differentiation has characterized Hezbollah from the start; it is a source of identification for its constituency. Hezbollah has branded itself as a counterforce to Israel, the "evil" superpower supported by the United States. This resistance has made the organization admired by non-Shia communities as well.[21] In addition, most brands have graphic and visual elements, which help viewers to identify these brands and identify *with* these brands. Hezbollah's flag has a yellow background; the organization's logo is colored in green, and its major slogans are in red. One of these slogans includes the letters "Party of God" (i.e., "Hezbollah" in Arabic) and shows an arm holding a rifle, which symbolizes Shia military resistance. All these things have made Hezbollah's logo, in the minds of Shia and non-Shia Muslims alike, a cogent symbol that portrays the true principles of the organization.[22]

Credibility

The color green is seen on Hezbollah's official logo and many of its iconographic symbols. In the eyes of the ummah, it lends more credibility to the terrorist group. By and large, the color green is often linked to Muhammad because it was the color used by the Prophet's tribe on its flags. The actual dome that is built above Muhammad's tomb in Medina is called the "Green Dome" (i.e., after the color of the dome).[23] As one can see, green is synonymous with Islam itself, and it is used universally in the Islamic world: in the adornment of mosques, the bindings of Qur'ans, the silken covers for the crypts of Sufi saints, and the flags of various Muslim countries. Although the practice of "coloring" a state (or a flag, a person, or a symbol) green may seem simple and of low significance, it should be noted that the color green matters very much across all sectors of the Islamic world. Coloring specific symbols in green is an openly political and explicitly Islamic statement.[24] The color is also linked to jihadist doctrine; it is thought that, while the bodies of jihadist martyrs lay in their tombs, their souls are transferred to the bodies of green birds that drink from the waters of the Garden of Eden and eat from its fruits.[25]

In a similar vein, slogans, logos, and colors were plentiful in Hezbollah's 2006 campaign in Lebanon. In that campaign, all Hezbollah billboards had a red background, with the words "The Divine Victory" inscribed in white and green. This was a direct reference to the colors of the Lebanese flag. The billboards also contained a logo written in a contemporary Arabic font that spelled the slogan "Victory from God" at the bottom. The same slogan, logo, and colors were also featured on Al-Manar (Hezbollah's satellite television station), on its websites, and on a whole range of products. Choosing those specific words was intentional: in April 2006, Hassan Nasrallah promised to crush Israel and release the Lebanese prisoners from Israeli jails (hence, on July 12, 2006, he named Hezbollah's mission "Operation Truthful Pledge"). Nasrallah's cognomen literally means "Victory from God."[26] Overall, Hezbollah has shown efforts to live up to its promises by vowing to destroy Israel and branding its objectives through various symbols.

Hezbollah was keen to buttress people's loyalty by rallying thousands of people to take part in its victory celebrations. In exchange, loyalty was shown by the Shia community through a cultivation of an expression of sacrifice to Hassan Nasrallah. Those Lebanese whose homes were destroyed or who lost relatives and friends during the 2006 war were now convinced that their losses were worthwhile inasmuch as Nasrallah prevailed. It was a symbol of paramount loyalty to the brand, regardless of how ominous the circumstances were.[27] Nasrallah's rhetoric made him a very credible leader. His rhetoric is also what distinguishes him from most other Muslim leaders. He is not just the leader of an institution whose power comes from coercion; he is also a leader followed by many because they "want to." In turn, this strong identification with Nasrallah reinforces Hezbollah's brand association, which denotes the emotional bonds that link a "consumer" to a brand.[28]

Authenticity

Hezbollah's brand management authenticity is an example of Blumenthal's (1980)[29] concept of **permanent campaign**. A permanent campaign is "a process of continuing transformation. It never stops, but continues once its practitioners take power" (p. 8). The objective of a permanent campaign is to maintain legitimacy and credibility. To achieve this, Hezbollah follows Blumenthal's statement: "Credibility is verified by winning, staying in power. And legitimacy is confused with popularity" (p. 7). So how does Hezbollah win, remain in power, and sustain its legitimacy? The answer is reflected in the group's practice of what it preaches. Subsequent to the Israeli invasion of Lebanon in 1982, Hezbollah established an anti-Israeli Islamist militia. Its brand management was filled with Palestinian and Iranian references. The Iranian influence was particularly obvious in the visual style of Hezbollah's billboards that it used to diffuse its ideological and military messages. Because Hezbollah is a product of the Iranian Republican Guard Corps (IRGC), it has relied on the same Iranian institutions and support.[30] As a result of its successful brand management campaign, many Shi'ites have joined Hezbollah and perpetrated attacks on Israeli targets. Examples are the Israeli embassy attack in Buenos Aires, Argentina, killing twenty-nine people (in 1992), and the bombing of a Jewish cultural center, also in Buenos Aires, killing eighty-five people (in 1994).[31]

Hezbollah's most infamous expression of its "authentic brand," however, occurred at the heart of the Lebanese Civil War. In October 1983, two Hezbollah suicide bombers detonated truck bombs at U.S. Marine barracks located in Beirut, taking the lives of 241 U.S. and 58 French servicemen. This attack boosted the prestige and growth of Hezbollah. Now, the Shia terrorist group was regarded by many as the "spearhead of the sacred Muslim struggle against foreign occupation" (Ranstorp, 1997, p. 38).[32] This attack authenticated Hezbollah as an organization capable of creating a new world order. Following the attack, recruitment within Hezbollah became much easier and increased at a fast pace, particularly from local populations in regions where the group had networks on the ground. In the Soviet Union, Hezbollah terrorists recruited Palestinian students who were studying at Soviet universities, while in Uganda they recruited Muslim students and sent them to Iranian universities. At those universities, these Muslim students learned the ropes of Islamism; together with Lebanese recruits, they received military training and were taught how to use small arms, make explosives, and resist interrogation techniques.[33]

APPROPRIATION OF SYMBOLS

A useful method for a terrorist organization to promulgate its brand is appropriation. **Appropriation** is the practice whereby a group borrows symbolic elements from other groups to create something new. In this process, a sign acquires a new meaning.[34] The appropriation of symbols by a terrorist organization enables it to create a new brand and shape its public identity.[35] For example, according to Bergen (1996),[36] Nazi symbolism is "replete with Christian notions of sacrifice and redemption. Even committed National Socialists clung fiercely to cultural manifestations of their religious tradition—the celebration of Christmas, favorite hymns, the symbol of the cross" (p. 9). Two specific types of appropriation are symbolic manipulation and symbolic transformation.

Symbolic Manipulation

Symbolic manipulation is a technique whereby a group appropriates preexisting symbols and adjusts them to promote a movement, cause, or doctrine.[37] In and of itself, **manipulation** is a form of social influence that can change individuals' perception of reality by distorting reality or deceiving. Manipulation is both a social and cognitive phenomenon. It is a social phenomenon because it necessitates interaction and power abuse between individuals in a social setting—be it small or large. It is a cognitive phenomenon because it inherently implies the manipulation of people's minds. It should be added that manipulation can also be a discursive-symbolic phenomenon because it is usually applied through verbal and/or visual messages.[38] Symbols are malleable; they can be tweaked or reinvented.

Manipulating symbolism is a key component for the successful brand management of a terrorist group. When terrorist leaders exploit symbolism, manipulate feelings of urgency, and isolate members from the outside world, their mission can be fulfilled more easily.[39] Manipulators do things that are in line with the manipulator's interests.[40] Manipulating people entails manipulating their beliefs, such as their knowledge, opinions, and ideologies. This ultimately controls their actions. Manipulation may also be achieved thanks to pictures, images, movies, and other media.[41] Generally, the process of symbolic manipulation is carried out by propagandists and other manipulators whose plans differ from the public's own. In this sense, manipulation is about not only power but also abuse of power (i.e., distortion of reality and shaping of people's minds).[42]

Symbolic Transformation

Symbolic transformation is the technique of modifying one's own group's existing symbols to clarify relationship messages. Transforming existing symbols (or symbolic strategies) is an important component of the propagandist's task.[43] The symbolic transformation of an extremist movement is generally related to the transformation of symbols.[44] Guru Nanak (1469–1538), the founder of Sikhism in northern India, was famous for his kind soul. However, the religious movement progressively became more violent; the violence coincided with symbolic transformation.[45] For example, in the 1980s, an old symbol gained more prominence within the ever-evolving symbolism of Sikh ethnicity: Khalistan. Initially, the Khalistan movement was not to be embraced with violence. However, it became the utmost existential symbol for many Sikhs: an ideal Punjabi nation-state for which they would sacrifice their lives.[46] Under such circumstances, an image enhancement crusade can produce positive image change for a terrorist group. As we will see in the two following case studies, both symbolic manipulation and symbolic transformation can be useful in garnering support from people who are not associated with terrorism in any way (i.e., usually people whose relatives or ancestors have suffered from the "oppressive elite").

Time can play an important role in the interpretation and modification of symbols. Symbols can help people understand the past, present, and future because symbols are created within the frameworks and aspirations of cultures in different eras of history. So, the meanings of symbols can evolve over time.[47] New symbols are generated when people consider existing symbols unable to encapsulate or confer expression to their experiences, feelings, or beliefs. This is expected to happen when people face dramatic moments or major transformations in the natural, social, or political environment. In these conditions, a symbol may emerge naturally from the reality of the situation.[48] As Lauer and Handel (1983)[49] argue, "To understand how people define situations, then, is to understand the meaning that the situation has for them and thereby to understand why they behave as they do in the situation" (p. 129).

CASE STUDY I: ISLAMIST TERRORISM

Islamist groups are usually efficient at increasing support among their sympathizers. These measures include transforming older Muslim symbols and appropriating symbols from groups with similar agendas. For example, to make Palestinians support Hezbollah, the latter has appropriated and circulated many Palestinian national icons. Palestinian symbols—particularly symbols about the Dome of the Rock—are among the images garnishing Hezbollah-run districts in Beirut. Hezbollah has also made extensive use of commemorative markers of the infamous Sabra and Shatila massacre—still deeply entrenched in Palestinians' memories.[50] The **Sabra and Shatila massacre** took place in 1982. It was the slaughter of close to 3,500 Palestinian and Lebanese Shia civilians by a Lebanese Christian militant group in the Palestinian refugee camps of Beirut.[51] Because the massacre is so significant to Palestinian nationalist symbolism, Hezbollah has exploited it as a turning point in its recruiting campaign. When Hezbollah makes references to the tragedy, it speaks to the whole collectivity concerned by that tragedy (i.e., Palestinian and Lebanese) and to the ummah as a larger constituency: "our fathers, children, women, and brothers." Hezbollah's gesture of spokespersonship is both ideological and utilitarian. On the one hand, the terrorist group purports to speak for the oppressed among the Shi'ites. On the other hand, it takes advantage of symbolic-rich Islamic concepts in order to lay claim to a morality captured through symbols of internationally recognized suffering.[52] On September 17, 2002, on the twentieth anniversary of the Sabra and Shatila massacre, Hezbollah hosted the commemorative event and organized a memorial on the site of the tragedy. By taking such actions, Hezbollah can judiciously promote its anti-Israel agenda, which many Palestinians share.[53]

Other well-known cases of symbolic appropriation by Islamists have been recorded. To begin, in 1990, Saddam Hussein added the words Allahu Akbar ("Allah is greater") to the Iraqi flag and proclaimed his invasion of Kuwait as a holy war. Yet Saddam's hero was no Muslim; it was Joseph Stalin. In fact, a decade earlier, Saddam had Iraq's leading Islamic cleric and his sister assassinated. His Ba'ath Party in Iraq was based on Arab nationalism, Soviet-style socialism, and anti-imperialism—not on the Qur'an or hadiths. Likewise, in Syria, the Assad-led government—dominated by the **Alawites**, a Shia Muslim minority group in Syria—has appropriated certain Islamic symbols to cover the face of its repressive regime toward Sunni Muslims. For instance, in 2000, after assuming power, one of Assad's earliest steps was to repeal the long-established law forbidding the wearing of headscarves by women in the educational system of Syria. Assad's objective, of course, was to ascertain his legitimacy within the Sunni majority in Syria.[54] Thus, appropriation conferred his regime a sense of convenience and freedom of political action to a degree that was unprecedented in Syria. However, his policies (as well his father's) have been plagued with brutalities committed against Sunnis. One of them was the Hama massacre: in 1982, Syria's government troops killed between 10,000 and 40,000 people in an attempt to wipe out a center of Sunni Muslims; Assad's family is Shi'ite.[55]

Lastly, many pictures and drawings used by jihadist propagandists are not the original creations of the propagandists; rather, they have been taken from other websites and other media sources. As we will see in chapter 14, jihadist propagandists have appropriated these images to bolster their own agenda. They also tend to modify their own symbols by adding them, for instance, to a terrorist logo, the name of a city, or even the name of an individual. In short, in terms of symbolic creation, pure innovation rarely matters to a given Islamist group, as long as they can get people to participate in global jihad.[56]

CASE STUDY II: SHINING PATH

Founded by Professor Abimael Guzmán in 1980, the Shining Path (or Sendero Luminoso) intensely disseminated its brand of communist ideology during Guzmán's tenure at the National University of San Cristóbal de Huamanga in Peru.[57] The terrorist group claimed to represent the voice of people's disgruntlement and hoped for Peru's total switch to the Left. For this reason, the group distributed thousands of Communist Party pamphlets with red flags and hammers and sickles.[58]

Appropriating Mao

The Shining Path appropriated many ideas from Mao Zedong, the leader of the Cultural Revolution. The **Cultural Revolution** was a social-political movement (1966–1976) bent on enforcing communism in China by eradicating capitalist, traditional, and cultural elements from Chinese society. Pupils and students were told to kill their own teachers. Through massacres, persecution, and famine, the Cultural Revolution caused the deaths of about twenty million people.[59] The Shining Path regarded youths as susceptible to the teachings of the group's Maoist doctrine because they had little political past—if they had any at all. As one document states, youths were recommended to participate in the armed struggle against the elite and espouse the creed of the proletariat. The hope was that Peruvian youths would take part in the popular war and, in turn, spread the revolution across future generations.[60]

In the early 1980s, the Shining Path instituted "popular schools" throughout the Ayacucho Region in southern Peru (where the group was operating). The group also allegedly built many education camps for children classified as "orphans of the revolution."[61] These popular schools were designed to be forums to raise class consciousness among farmers, the proletariat, and students. Ultimately, these schools spread Shining Path's ideology "by emphasizing the failures and inadequacies of the present state, the unjust and corrupt nature of the existing socioeconomic order, and José Carlos Mariátegui's Marxist interpretation of Peruvian reality" (Tarazona-Sevillano, 1994, p. 197).[62] In the 1980s and early 1990s, the Shining Path repeatedly attacked evangelical Protestants and Roman Catholics; these attacks were driven by Maoist disapproval of religion in general and its resentment toward evangelicals as symbols of U.S. colonization and expansionism.[63]

Appropriating Inca Symbols

Another important method to promote the Shining Path brand was through the appropriation of Inca symbols. By using Inca symbols, the Shining Path stirred up long-standing Indian resentment toward the wealthy and educated white Spanish elites, who, as conquistadors' descendants, are considered blameworthy for the gradual wreckage of Indian culture.[64] It is important to mention that close to half of the population in Peru (45 percent) is indígena (of Indian descent, generally living in the countryside), mestizos (people of mixed Indian and Caucasian ancestry) account for 37 percent of the population, 15 percent are white, and the remaining 3 percent are black as well as Japanese and Chinese.[65] The Inca symbols appropriated by the Shining Path were mostly Incan revolutionary symbols. An example is **sasachacuy** (an ancient pre-Hispanic word that means "difficult times"). For the Shining Path, it was important to convince poor Peruvian peasants that overthrowing bureaucratic capitalism through armed struggle is their duty. Sasachacuy is a concept evoking ancestral community practices—when peasants lived happily and peacefully (before the invasion of conquistadors that caused those difficult times). In other words, sasachacuy was used by the peasants to illustrate their experiences of demise and social disintegration.[66]

An additional Inca symbol appropriated by the Shining Path was the dog. In Inca culture, this animal symbolizes the age-old racial discrimination by the white Spanish elites in Peru. The dog image is often depicted as a poor Indian peasant, emblematic of the inner struggle sensed by the group.[67] One of the very first actions of the Shining Path was to express disdain for the bourgeoisie by hanging a dead dog in front of the Chinese embassy in Lima.[68] To be more precise, in the 1980s, the day after Christmas, the terrorist group hanged dog corpses to public lighting posts in Lima. They crammed dynamite into their mouths and hanged leaflets comparing them to Deng Xiaoping, the capitalist Chinese head of state (1982–1987) whose imperialistic gang let the Cultural Revolution down. The leaflets stated that a dead dog is an Indian symbol of a dictator sentenced to capital punishment by his own people. The Shining Path was even able to cause the entire city of Lima to be in total darkness on New Year's Day (in 1982) and during Pope John Paul II's visit (in 1985).[69]

TERRORISTS' DRESS CODE AS BRAND MANAGEMENT

A **dress code** is a set of written or unwritten rules about clothing. A dress code is a visual sign of difference and belonging. "Dress" comes from Old French *dresser* (meaning "to arrange, set up"). Across all layers of society, the separate items of clothing conform symbolically to each of these layers. Hence, each societal layer has its own dress signifier, a visual sign of difference and belonging that informs how to present oneself in society. A dress code has specific connotative meanings that lay the foundations for the symbolism related to the clothes worn during certain social settings (e.g., ceremonies and rituals). For a terrorist group, a dress code is also an opportunity to advertise its brand. By looking at how terrorists dress, audiences worldwide have a better idea of what a particular terrorist group advocates.[70]

Brand management through style of dress becomes a type of cultural knowledge that can fit a specific agenda (e.g., militarization of the rural poor, anti-Western hatred, anticapitalism, and a revival of ancient values and practices). In this respect, dress code is synonymous with social code. A **social code** bestows the terrorist group the symbolic resources for making statements about itself and for controlling interpersonal activities among members. A social code also drives the symbolically guided social behaviors that characterize daily interactions in a specific terrorist culture. Social codes create an all-encompassing set of regulations based on a symbolic system. Individuals can even be punished for violating the social code.[71] In this section, three case studies describe terrorists' dress codes.

Case Study I: The FARC

The **Revolutionary Armed Forces of Colombia** (better known as the **FARC**) are a Colombian Marxist-Leninist terrorist group that has been clashing with the Colombian government since the 1960s. The FARC see themselves as an army and claim to represent the poor in Colombia (against the "evil" capitalist elite).[72] As levels of FARC violence increased throughout the 1970s and 1980s, many FARC terrorists underwent what Bell (1990)[73] calls a "paramilitarization" of dress code. Paramilitarization is characterized, among several things, by a more aggressive style of dress and conduct. As a result, FARC terrorists have often been photographed wearing military fatigues and carrying sidearms or assault rifles.[74] This was also witnessed within other guerrilla groups in Latin America. The FARC are known for holding prisoners and hostages in distant jungle camps. As the FARC brand themselves as an army, they look at hostages as "prisoners of war." By the same token, when held by the Colombian government, the FARC also refer to themselves as "prisoners of war."

The FARC's training camps are something to behold. According to Human Rights Watch (2005),[75] about 20 to 30 percent of FARC recruits are minors; most of them are forced to go through terrorist training camps. In these training camps, the compulsory military dress code reveals that a new recruit is experimenting with (or has already completed) a development of radicalization; that is, a development in which the individual assimilates extremist values and becomes a militant in an individual manner (i.e., of their own volition). By forcing new recruits to wear military fatigues, the FARC are successfully inculcating ideas, particularly within young minds, that they will fight the "evil" government as soldiers—not as rebels or terrorists.[76]

Case Study II: Anti-Western Fashion

Islamist terrorists passionately oppose Western political dominance, and they totally condemn U.S. and European foreign policy in the Middle East. A conspicuous symbol of their anti-Western stance is their refusal to wear suits and ties, which represent key symbols of the Western world.[77] Osama bin Laden, Muammar Gaddafi, and Ayman al-Zawahiri (the new Al Qaeda leader), have exemplified anti-Western hatred through their style of dress. In the 1930s and 1940s, the Grand Mufti of Jerusalem was Haj Amin al-Husseini. A friend of Adolf Hitler, he collaborated with the Führer by recruiting Muslim soldiers for Nazi battalions, including three SS units of Yugoslavian Muslims.[78] During the Mufti's leadership in Palestine, Palestinians who did not adhere to his anti-Western dress code were immediately killed.[79]

In the 1980s in Pakistan, a few years after Muhammad Zia-ul-Haq became the president, the fashion scene went through a tremendous change. Anti-Western dress propaganda became full-fledged; Western style of dress was regarded as plainly offensive to tradition. Pakistani fashion designers re-created a stylish repertoire that was evocative of the Mogul empire. From the sixteenth to the nineteenth centuries, the Mogul emperors were Muslims and direct progenies of both Genghis Khan and Tamerlane; the Moguls conquered Central and Southeast Asia and decimated millions of Hindus.[80] In short, by forcing Pakistani Islamist men to wear Mogul-style battle dress uniforms (BDUs) and the woman to wear the hijab and Iranian-style chador, the Pakistani fashion scene was extolling the virtues of the old Mogul days and the flamboyance of the early jihadists. The overall purpose was to make sure that such a form of counterdiscourse (i.e., anti-Western hatred) could facilitate support for Islamism.[81]

Case Study III: Mullah Mohammed Omar

Mullah Mohammed Omar is the spiritual leader of the Taliban and considered an international terrorist by the U.S. Department of State. In 1994, Omar took a sacred garment—regarded by many Afghans as the original cloak of the Prophet Muhammad—from its sanctuary in Kandahar (a city in Afghanistan). The cloak of Muhammad had been placed in a padlocked chest in the royal crypt of Kandahar. One day, Omar stood on top of the mosque in the city and was wearing the cloak. Until this episode of religious drama, Omar had been a "nobody." However, his stunt branded him as an Allah-chosen leader with mystical powers (at least according to 90 percent of the Pashtuns, who are generally illiterate). Omar was now proclaimed the "Leader of the Faithful"—not just of the Afghans but also of the entire ummah. His new title, "Leader of the Faithful," had not been bestowed to any Muslim worldwide for almost 1,000 years.[82] On a similar note, the Taliban have been forcing all men to dress like the Prophet Muhammad. Men have been required to conform to a strict dress code, avoid Western clothing, and abstain from shaving their facial hair.[83]

Keffiyeh: Brand of Palestinian Resistance

A **keffiyeh** (also known as **kufiya** and **ghutrah**) is an old-fashioned Arab headdress made from a square scarf (typically cotton). It is often worn by Arab men.[84] After the Palestinian insurgencies of the 1960s and the keffiyeh's world-famous adoption by Yasser Arafat (his had a black-and-white checkered pattern), it became an intensely used symbol. In regard to Arafat, the keffiyeh was his trademark symbol: the Palestinian leader was rarely spotted without his well-arranged scarf.[85] Notwithstanding historical contexts, the headdress has consistently symbolized Palestinian solidarity for full independence from Israel. In the 1980s, during the First Intifada, the keffiyeh was exploited even more as a symbol of resistance; it epitomized the Palestinians' conspicuous challenge to Israeli presence. The keffiyeh had the power to awaken emotions, thoughts, and reactions, which allowed Palestinian leaders to galvanize local populations into fighting for the Palestinian State.[86]

Means of Identification

The keffiyeh was also a symbolic means of identification and a mark of national identity (like other long-existing Arab garments, such as the hijab for Muslim women). Such method of identification is also referred to as a **cultural metaphor**, an image seen to represent a culture.[87] Besides, by dressing in traditional Arab attire, the Palestinians exhibited and, if truth be told, flaunted their pride in their nation and tradition. This was, in part, a reaction to the Israeli (and Western) propensity to disparage and ridicule Palestinian and Muslim values and civilization. The importance attached to traditional Arab garments and customs also indicated that the Palestinians were fighting on behalf of a much larger entity: the Arab nations and the entire ummah. From this vantage point, Arab and Muslim attire and customs function as flags and symbols of unity.[88]

The keffiyeh has been shown to personify an international attitude larger than any of the groups that use it. To this point, it is worth mentioning that, during the two Intifadas (and even today), a keffiyeh on the dashboard of an Israeli licensed vehicle branded the driver as either Palestinian or an Israeli supporting the Palestinian cause. As a practical routine, it was also an "agreed-upon" symbol: by looking at the keffiyeh, militants could abstain from throwing rocks at the vehicle; they would deduce that, although the car had an Israeli yellow number plate, it was driven by either a Palestinian living in East Jerusalem or an Israeli sympathizer.

Imagespeak

Understanding brand management through such highly visible headdress can be captured in the concept of "imagespeak." **Imagespeak** describes how individuals produce forms of shared symbolic language to assign contextual symbolism to an object (something that can be seen). A unique Palestinian imagespeak surfaced and created permanent cultural meanings for an object such as the keffiyeh.[89] In 1993, when the First Intifada ended, Palestinians made little political gains, despite the agreement made by Yasser Arafat and the U.S.-Israeli alliance. Because of the failure of the agreement (called the Oslo Accords), disgruntled Palestinians donned the keffiyeh (as a symbol of nationalism) even more. The keffiyeh has been increasingly co-opted by Palestinian terrorist groups such as Hamas and the Palestinian Islamic Jihad (PIJ).[90]

Today, many people worldwide consider the keffiyeh a symbol heavily associated with Islamic terrorism. To go back to Lederman's (1992)[91] definition of "imagespeak," symbolism works only if the general public can collectively make sense of the symbol from "a personal fount of knowledge" (p. 184), and, as he remarks, "it takes times to build that memory bank" (p. 184). As a well-established militant organization, Hamas's exploitation of the keffiyeh seems to be systematic; the headdress is worn by leaders and mainstream people at rallies, and it is displayed on political posters everywhere. By means of the keffiyeh, Hamas can tap the already-materialized national consciousness of the object in order to fashion an apparently continuous and larger discourse of nationalism. Hence, even though Hamas has a different doctrinal foundation than the Palestinian Authority (PA), both groups can draw on the symbolic power of the keffiyeh in the same ways and without incongruity.

TERRORIST CHIC

Terrorist chic refers to the appropriation of objects and/or symbols of terrorist groups or individuals; these objects and/or symbols are used in popular culture or fashion.[92] Terrorist chic is the belief that terrorism is cool. It has also been referred to as **fear fashion**, **hate couture, radical chic**, or **militant chic**.[93] When governments label a devious or extremist organization as a terrorist organization, they may—involuntarily—cause the public to identify with and even support a terrorist movement. In this case, the public appropriates the brand of a terrorist group and reconstructs that brand in various ways. In the 1970s, **Carlos the Jackal** (born Illich Ramirez Sanchez), a Venezuelan-born Palestinian terrorist, became a media celebrity as the world's most glamorous terrorist (rather than a dangerous killer). Likewise, in the *Washington Post*, Smiley (2005)[94] describes the lives of stylish young people in Berlin sporting outfits with "Prada Meinhof" on them. Prada Meinhof is a direct reference to Baader Meinhof, the German terrorist group that remonstrated the Vietnam War and global capitalism in the 1960s and 1970s. In recent years, Baader Meinhof has seen its brand's popularity soar thanks to an outbreak of terrorist chic. It has generated books, films, and paraphernalia like Prada Meinhof T-shirts and bags displaying the German group's Heckler and Koch machine gun logo. These two examples illustrate that terroristic chic is a result of the **multiplier effect**: terrorist objects and/or symbols become culture as a commodity, and they are exported to nonterrorist cultures.[95]

Islamist Chic

Islamist chic, also called **jihadist chic**, is the practice of appropriating politically loaded Islamist symbols and giving them a new meaning—often a personal meaning. For example, in the *Los Angeles Times*, Hernandez (2006)[96] describes the lifestyle of a twenty-nine-year-old painter and musician in Los Angeles. Every day, the artist puts on a keffiyeh with a checkered pattern, reminiscent of Yasser Arafat and Islamists. The man is not Arab or Muslim. Since 2005, the keffiyeh has been increasingly seen on the streets, appearing everywhere across Europe, in hip quarters of New York City, and in the Hollywood, Silver Lake, and Echo Park areas of Los Angeles. In the past, it was worn mostly by Middle Eastern men. Today, it has become a symbol with undertones ranging from individual self-determination to sympathy toward terrorism. To many, the keffiyeh still remains a politically loaded symbol, even after hipsters and teens all over the Western world have begun to wear it as a new trend.[97] The keffiyeh is usually accompanied by draping scarves, military prints, and heavy boots. Two other Western men, Raf Simons and Bernhard Willhelm, also sport keffiyehs and other Middle Eastern prints on a daily basis. They wear hoods and scarves that conceal their faces, as well as pointy head coverings that bring to mind the most stomach-turning moments of the Abu Ghraib prison scandal.[98]

Nazi Chic

Nazi chic describes the use of Nazi-themed images, styles, and paraphernalia in popular culture and fashion. Nazi chic attire and items include actual or reproduced Nazi uniforms, headgear, helmets, boots, and belts, as well as the symbols, insignias, and other official elements that stood for the Nazi Party.[99] The punk generation, represented by youths who are barely aware of Nazi atrocities and World War II crimes, do not look at the swastika with the same disgust as their parents and grandparents did. Instead, since the 1970s, punks have used the swastika as a mighty symbol of their opposition to the postwar establishment, Western culture, and political and economic imperialism.[100] The swastika and other Nazi symbols have been displayed on clothes made and sold by two of the most prominent British designers of punk in the 1970s: Malcolm McLaren and Vivienne Westwood. Their punk style was designed exclusively to be worn to express resistance to British establishment, create hullabaloo, and draw attention. McLaren and Westwood's Nazi chic fashion quickly became popular in the punk rock scene.[101]

Today, a widespread trend of Nazi chic is witnessed in Asia and appears to be gaining popularity. MacIntyre (2000)[102] reports the widespread use of Nazi-style furniture, ornamental art, and themes as interior designs in South Korean bars, restaurants, and various public places. One bar, called the Fifth Reich, has an interior that is adorned with Third Reich symbols, including photos of Hitler; the waitstaff sport swastika arm badges. Patrons sit at booths that are flanked by sculptures of golden eagles, Romanesque columns, and massive glass display cases of SS emblems. Next to the cash register, Nazi pins and Iron Crosses can be purchased. It appears that a specific segment of the South Korean bar scene unashamedly pays tribute to those who killed six million Jews in the Holocaust.

SUMMARY

Brand management is a communication function that consists of examining and planning how a brand should be positioned in the world, to what type of audience the brand should be targeted, and how the ideal reputation of the brand should be preserved. Brand management is an example of public communication. Public communication is a purposive effort to inform or affect the behaviors of large audiences within a specific time using a coordinated set of communication activities. A related term is public identity. Three types of public identity are deemed relevant to the identity of terrorist organizations: desired identity, perceived identity, and projected identity. A brand is a symbol that differentiates one product or service from another. Three traits can make a brand successful: differentiation, credibility, and authenticity. The case study of Hezbollah's brand sheds light on how a terrorist organization can grow rapidly and recruit new volunteers more easily through a massive "brand awareness" campaign. For example, by using certain slogans, logos, and colors, Hezbollah has been able to convince many people that the fight against the "evil" Israelis is worthwhile. Another important term in this chapter was appropriation. Appropriation is the practice whereby a group borrows symbolic elements from other groups to create something new. Two specific types of appropriation are symbolic manipulation and symbolic transformation. Whereas symbolic manipulation is a technique whereby a group appropriates preexisting symbols and adjusts them to promote a movement, cause, or doctrine, symbolic transformation is a technique of modifying one's own group's existing symbols to clarify relationship messages. For example, the first case study of Islamist terrorism explains how Hezbollah manipulates key Palestinian symbols to increase support for the Shia terrorist group. Likewise, the second case study of the Shining Path describes how the Peruvian terrorist group appropriated symbols from Maoist ideology and from the Inca tradition. In line with these contentions, a dress code is a visual sign of difference and belonging. As a social code, the dress code bestows the terrorist group the symbolic resources for making statements about itself and for controlling interpersonal activities among members. Three case studies served to illustrate terrorists' dress codes: the FARC in Colombia, anti-Western fashion within Islamism, and Mullah Mohammed Omar in Afghanistan. As a particular social code, the keffiyeh, an old-fashioned Arab headdress made from a square scarf (typically cotton), is a symbol of Palestinian resistance and a mark of their national identity. Finally, terrorist chic refers to the appropriation of objects and/or symbols of terrorist groups or individuals; these objects and/or symbols are used in popular culture or fashion. Terrorist chic is the belief that terrorism is cool. Examples are Islamist chic and Nazi chic.

NOTES

1. Rogers, Everett, & Storey, Douglas (1987). Communication Campaigns. In Charles Berger & Steven Chaffee (Eds.), *Handbook of Communication Science* (pp. 817–846). Newbury Park, CA: Sage.

2. Seitel, Fraser (2007). *The Practice of Public Relations.* Upper Saddle River, NJ: Pearson Prentice Hall.

3. Pratt, Michael, & Foreman, Peter (2000). Classifying Managerial Responses to Multiple Organizational Identities. *Academy of Management Review, 25*(1), 18–42.

4. Balmer, John, & Wilson, Alan (1998). Corporate Identity: There Is More to It than Meets the Eye. *International Studies of Management & Organization, 28*(3), 12–31.

5. Keller, Kevin Lane (2012). *Strategic Brand Management* (4th ed.). Upper Saddle River, NJ: Prentice Hall.

6. Debord, Guy (1994). *The Society of the Spectacle.* New York: Zone Books.

7. Selame, Elinor (1988). *Developing a Corporate Identity: How to Stand Out in the Crowd.* Cambridge, MA: Cambridge Books.

8. Heilbrunn, Benoit (1997). Representation and Legitimacy: A Semiotic Approach to the Logo. In Winfried Nöth (Ed.), *Semiotics of the Media: State of the Art, Projects, and Perspectives* (pp. 175–189). Berlin: Mouton de Gruyter.

9. Alberto, Paul, Fredrick, Laura, Hughes, Melissa, McIntosh, Laura, & Cihak, David (2007). Components of Visual Literacy: Teaching Logos. *Focus on Autism and Other Developmental Disabilities, 22*(4), 234–243.

10. Considine, David, & Haley, Gail (1992). *Visual Messages.* Englewood, CO: Teacher Ideas Press.

11. Selame, Elinor (1988). *Developing a Corporate Identity: How to Stand Out in the Crowd.* Cambridge, MA: Cambridge Books.

12. Baudrillard, Jean (1983). *Simulations.* New York: Semiotext.

13. Beverland, Michael (2005). Crafting Brand Authenticity: The Case of Luxury Wines. *Journal of Management Studies, 42*(5), 1003–1029.

14. O'Shaughnessy, Nicholas (2004). *Politics and Propaganda: Weapons of Mass Seduction.* Ann Arbor: University of Michigan Press.

15. Harb, Mona, & Leenders, Reinoud (2005). Know Thy Enemy: Hizbullah, "Terrorism" and the Politics of Perception. *Third World Quarterly, 26*(1), 173–197.

16. Lin, Chin-Huang, Liou, Dian-Yiang, & Wu, Kang-Wei (2007). Opportunities and Challenges Created by Terrorism. *Technological Forecasting and Social Change, 74*(2), 148–164.

17. Tehranian, Majid (1980). Communication and Revolution in Iran: The Passing of a Paradigm. *Iranian Studies, 13*(1), 5–30.

18. Aaker, David (1995). *Building Strong Brands*. New York: Free Press.

19. Khatib, Lina (2012). *Hizbullah's Image Management Strategy*. Los Angeles: Figueroa Press.

20. Harb, Mona, & Leenders, Reinoud (2005). Know Thy Enemy: Hizbullah, "Terrorism" and the Politics of Perception. *Third World Quarterly, 26*(1), 173–197.

21. Melnick, Michael (2007). Brand Terror: A Corporate Communication Perspective for Understanding Terrorism. In Boaz Ganor, Kathrina von Knop, & Carlos Duarte (Eds.), *Hypermedia Seduction for Terrorist Recruiting* (pp. 199–206). Amsterdam: IOS Press.

22. Byers, Ann (2002). *Lebanon's Hezbollah*. New York: Rosen Publishing Group.

23. Petersen, Andrew (1999). *Dictionary of Islamic Architecture*. New York: Routledge.

24. Friedland, Roger, & Hecht, Richard (2000). *To Rule Jerusalem*. Berkeley: University of California Press.

25. Combating Terrorism Center (2006). *The Islamic Imagery Project: Visual Motifs in Jihadi Internet Propaganda*. West Point, NY: Combating Terrorism Center.

26. Khatib, Lina (2012). *Hizbullah's Image Management Strategy*. Los Angeles: Figueroa Press.

27. Quilty, Jim, & Ohrstrom, Lysanda (2007). The Second Time as Farce: Stories of Another Lebanese Reconstruction. *Middle East Report, 243*, 31–48.

28. Hunt, Sonja (1984). The Role of Leadership in the Construction of Reality. In Barbara Kellerman (Ed.), *Leadership: Multidisciplinary Perspectives* (pp. 157–178). Englewood Cliffs, NJ: Prentice Hall; and Kellerman, Barbara (1984). Leadership as a Political Act. In Barbara Kellerman (Ed.), *Leadership: Multidisciplinary Perspectives* (pp. 63–90). Englewood Cliffs, NJ: Prentice Hall.

29. Blumenthal, Sidney (1980). *The Permanent Campaign: Inside the World of Elite Political Operatives*. Boston: Beacon.

30. Khatib, Lina (2012). *Hizbullah's Image Management Strategy*. Los Angeles: Figueroa Press.

31. Harmon, Christopher C. (2000). *Terrorism Today*. New York: Routledge.

32. Ranstorp, Magnus (1997). *Hizb'allah in Lebanon: The Politics of the Western Hostage Crisis*. New York: Palgrave Macmillan.

33. Levitt, Matthew (2005). *Iranian State Sponsorship of Terror: Threatening U.S. Security, Global Stability, and Regional Peace*. Washington, DC: U.S. House of Representatives.

34. Young, James, & Brunk, Conrad (2012). *The Ethics of Cultural Appropriation*. New York: Wiley-Blackwell.

35. Giddens, Anthony (1994). Living in a Post-Traditional Society. In Anthony Giddens, Ulrich Beck, & Scott Lash (Eds.), *Reflexive Modernization: Politics, Tradition, and Aesthetics in the Modern Social Order* (pp. 56–109). Cambridge: Polity Press.

36. Bergen, Doris (1996). *Twisted Cross: The German Christian Movement in the Third Reich*. Chapel Hill: University of North Carolina Press.

37. Radnitz, Scott (2006). Look Who's Talking! Islamic Discourse in the Chechen Wars. *Nationalities Papers: The Journal of Nationalism and Ethnicity, 34*(2), 237–256.

38. Van Dijk, Teun (2006). Discourse and Manipulation. *Discourse & Society, 17*(3), 359–383.

39. Welner, Michael (2007). Psychopathy, Media and the Psychology at the Root of Terrorism and Mass Disasters. In Matthias Okoye & Cyril Wecht (Eds.), *Forensic Investigation and Management of Mass Disasters* (pp. 189–220). Tucson, AZ: Lawyers & Judges Publishing.

40. Martín Rojo, L. M., & Van Dijk, Teun A. (1997). There Was a Problem, and It Was Solved: Legitimating the Expulsion of Illegal Migrants in Spanish Parliamentary Discourse. *Discourse & Society, 8*(4), 523–566.

41. Van Leeuwen, Theo (2005). *Introducing Social Semiotics*. London: Routledge.

42. Barkun, Michael (2007). Appropriated Martyrs: The Branch Davidians and the Radical Right. *Terrorism and Political Violence, 19*(1), 117–124.

43. O'Shaughnessy, Nicholas (2004). *Politics and Propaganda: Weapons of Mass Seduction*. Ann Arbor: University of Michigan Press.

44. Arena, Michael, & Arrigo, Bruce (2005). Social Psychology, Terrorism and Identity: A Preliminary Reexamination of Theory, Culture, Self, and Society. *Behavioral Sciences and the Law, 23*, 485–506.

45. McClymond, Michael, & Freedman, David (2010). Religious Traditions, Violence and Nonviolence. In George Fink (Ed.), *Stress of War, Conflict and Disaster* (pp. 397–407). Waltham, MA: Academic Press.

46. Fair, Christine (2005). Diaspora Involvement in Insurgencies: Insights from the Khalistan and Tamil Eelam Movements. *Nationalism and Ethnic Politics, 11*(1), 125–156.

47. Chu, Sauman (2003). Cross-Cultural Comparison of the Perception of Symbols. *Journal of Visual Literacy, 23*(1), 69–80.

48. Elder, Charles, & Cobb, Roger (1983). *The Political Uses of Symbols*. New York: Longman.

49. Lauer, Robert, & Handel, Warren (1983). *Social Psychology: The Theory and Application of Symbolic Interactionism*. Englewood Cliffs, NJ: Prentice Hall.

50. Kapeliouk, Amnon (1983). *Sabra/Shatila: Inquiry into a Massacre*. Belmont, MA: Association of Arab-American University Graduates; and Schiff, Zeev, & Ya'ari, Ehud (1984). *Israel's Lebanon War*. New York: Simon & Schuster.

51. Bregman, Ahron (2002). *Israel's Wars: A History since 1947*. London: Routledge.

52. al-Hout, Bayan (2004). *Sabra and Shatila, September 1982*. Ann Arbor: University of Michigan Press.

53. Khalili, Laleh (2007). "Standing with My Brother": Hizbullah, Palestinians, and the Limits of Solidarity. *Comparative Studies in Society and History, 49*(2), 276–303.

54. Zisser, Eyal (2005). Syria, the Ba'th Regime and the Islamic Movement: Stepping on a New Path? *The Muslim World, 95*(1), 43–65.

55. Seale, Patrick (1989). *Asad: The Struggle for the Middle East*. Berkeley: University of California Press.

56. Combating Terrorism Center (2006). *The Islamic Imagery Project: Visual Motifs in Jihadi Internet Propaganda*. West Point, NY: Combating Terrorism Center.

57. McClintock, Cynthia (1984). Why Peasants Rebel: The Case of Peru's Sendero Luminoso. *World Politics, 37*, 48–84.

58. Revilla, Vicente (1989). Descendants of the Incas. *Society, 26*(5), 77–80.

59. Chirot, Daniel (1996). *Modern Tyrants: The Power and Prevalence of Evil in Our Age*. Princeton, NJ: Princeton University Press.

60. Strong, Simon (1992). *Shining Path: The World's Deadliest Revolutionary Force*. London: HarperCollins.

61. Niksch, Larry, & Sullivan, Mark (1993). *Peru's Shining Path: Background on the Movement, Counterinsurgency Strategy, and U.S. Policy*. Washington, DC: Library of Congress.

62. Tarazona-Sevillano, Gabriela (1994). The Organization of Shining Path. In David Scott Palmer (Ed.), *The Shining Path of Peru* (pp. 189–208). New York: St. Martin's Press.

63. Stump, Roger (2005). Religion and the Geographies of War. In Colin Flint (Ed.), *The Geography of War and Peace: From Death Camps to Diplomats* (pp. 149–173). Oxford: Oxford University Press.

64. Špičanová, Lenka (2006). The Shining Path: Peruvian Guerilla Still Alive. In Jan Klíma (Ed.), *KIAS Papers: Yearbook 2006* (pp. 71–86). Hradec Králové, Czech Republic: University of Hradec Králové.

65. Springerová, Pavlína (2008). Guerrilla and State Terror in Peru between 1980 and 2000. In Pavlína Springerová & Jan Haisman (Eds.), *KIAS Papers: Yearbook 2008* (pp. 78–93). Hradec Králové, Czech Republic: University of Hradec Králové.

66. Gamarra, Jefrey (2000). Conflict, Post-Conflict and Religion: Andean Responses to New Religious Movements. *Journal of Southern African Studies, 26*(2), 271–287.

67. Milton, Cynthia E. (2009). Images of Truth: Art as a Medium for Recounting Peru's Internal War. *Contra Corriente, 6*(2), 63–102.

68. Starn, Orin (1991). Missing the Revolution: Anthropologists and the War in Peru. *Cultural Anthropology, 6*(1), 63–91.

69. Špičanová, Lenka (2006). The Shining Path: Peruvian Guerilla Still Alive. In Jan Klíma (Ed.), *KIAS Papers: Yearbook 2006* (pp. 71–86). Hradec Králové, Czech Republic: University of Hradec Králové.

70. Sebeok, Thomas A., & Danesi, Marcel (2000). *The Forms of Meaning: Modeling Systems Theory and Semiotic Analysis*. Berlin: Mouton de Gruyter.

71. Sebeok, Thomas A., & Danesi, Marcel (2000). *The Forms of Meaning: Modeling Systems Theory and Semiotic Analysis*. Berlin: Mouton de Gruyter.

72. Dudley, Steven (2004). *Walking Ghosts: Murder and Guerrilla Politics in Colombia*. New York: Routledge.

73. Bell, Desmond (1990). *Acts of Union: Youth and Sectarian Culture in Northern Ireland*. London: Macmillan.

74. Bajak, Frank (2007, January 27). Militias Grab Colombia's Best Land. *The Washington Post*, p. A1.

75. Human Rights Watch (2005). *Colombia: Armed Groups Send Children to War*. New York: Human Rights Watch.

76. Eccarius-Kelly, Vera (2012). Surreptitious Lifelines: A Structural Analysis of the FARC and the PKK. *Terrorism and Political Violence, 24*(2), 235–258

77. Zuhur, Sherifa (2008). Wars of Our Own Creation. *Home, 2*(1), 10–21.

78. Mattar, Philip (1992). *The Mufti of Jerusalem: Haj Amin al-Husseini and the Palestinian National Movement*. New York: Columbia University Press.

79. Schiller, David (1982). *Palästinenser zwischen Terrorismus und Diplomatie*. Munich: Bernard & Graefe.

80. Richards, John (1996). *The Mughal Empire*. Cambridge: Cambridge University Press.

81. Dedebant, Christèle (2001). "Mughal Mania" under Zia ul-Haq. *Counter-Discourses, 8*(1), 11.

82. Johnson, Thomas, & Mason, Chris (2007). *Terrorism, Insurgency, and Afghanistan*. Monterey, CA: Naval Postgraduate School.

83. Sultana, Aneela (2009). Taliban or Terrorist? Some Reflections on Taliban's Ideology. *The Politics and Religion Journal, 1*, 7–25.

84. Torstrick, Rebecca (2004). *Culture and Customs of Israel*. Westport, CT: Greenwood.

85. McRay, Michael, & Camp, Lee (2013). *Letters from Apartheid Street: A Christian Peacemaker in Occupied Palestine*. Eugene, OR: Cascade Books.

86. Nachmani, Amikam (2001). The Palestinian Intifada 1987–1993: The Dynamics of Symbols and Symbolic Realities, the Role of Symbols, Rituals and Myths in National Struggles. *Civil Wars, 4*(1), 49–103.

87. Watson, James, & Hill, Anne (2006). *Dictionary of Media and Communication Studies* (7th ed.). Don Mills, ON: Hodder Arnold.

88. Firth, Raymond (1973). *Symbols: Public and Private*. Ithaca, NY: Cornell University Press.

89. Lederman, James (1992). *Battle Lines: The American Media and the Intifada*. New York: Henry Holt.

90. Smith, Charles (2007). *Palestine and the Arab-Israeli Conflict*. Boston: Bedford/St. Martin's Press.

91. Lederman, James (1992). *Battle Lines: The American Media and the Intifada*. New York: Henry Holt.

92. Selzer, Michael (1979). *Terrorist Chic: An Exploration of Violence in the Seventies*. New York: Hawthorn Books.

93. Bradley, Linda Arthur (2011). Culture, Gender and Clothing. *Paideusis: Journal for Interdisciplinary and Cross-Cultural Studies, 5*, A1–A6; and Mercer, Kobena (1987). Black Hair/Style Politics. *New Formations, 3*, 33–54.

94. Smiley, Shannon (2005, February 20). Germany Debates "Terrorist Chic." *The Washington Post*, p. A25.

95. Watson, James, & Hill, Anne (2006). *Dictionary of Media and Communication Studies* (7th ed.). Don Mills, ON: Hodder Arnold.

96. Hernandez, Daniel (2006, April 9). "Terrorist Chic" and Beyond. *Los Angeles Times*, p. A1.

97. Bradley, Linda Arthur (2011). Culture, Gender and Clothing. *Paideusis: Journal for Interdisciplinary and Cross-Cultural Studies, 5*, A1–A6.

98. Hernandez, Daniel (2006, April 9). "Terrorist Chic" and Beyond. *Los Angeles Times*, p. A1.

99. Kidd, Laura (2011). Goose-Stepping Fashion: Nazi Inspiration. *Paideusis: Journal for Interdisciplinary and Cross-Cultural Studies, 5*, C1–C29.

100. Marko, Paul (2007). *The Roxy London WC2: A Punk History*. London: Punk 77 Books.

101. Kidd, Laura (2011). Goose-Stepping Fashion: Nazi Inspiration. *Paideusis: Journal for Interdisciplinary and Cross-Cultural Studies, 5*, C1–C29.

102. MacIntyre, Donald (2000, June 5). They Dressed Well. *Time*, p. A5.

Chapter Fourteen

Visual Motifs in Islamist Terrorism

VISUAL MOTIFS

A **visual motif** is a visual theme or pattern that represents a certain subject or category of subjects. Visual motifs help create symbolic cohesion by means of setting, background, color, intensity of light, images, and organization of text.[1] As Jones (1987)[2] puts it, visual motifs deal with the grammar of pictorial or graphic art. For example, many designs in Islamic mosques are motifs, such as those of the sun, moon, animals, plant life, and sceneries. Motifs can have emotional impacts and be employed for propaganda.[3] In this chapter, a thorough analysis of visual motifs in Islamist terrorism is conducted. More precisely, the analysis is twofold: the first part is an analysis based on Conceptual Metaphor Theory (using the three categories of metaphors [structural, orientational, and ontological metaphors]), and the second part examines Islamist motifs based on Edward T. Hall's (1976)[4] distinction between low context and high context.

Islamist visual motifs are a form of guerrilla communication. **Guerrilla communication** refers to political activism achieved through the manipulation of photos, cartoons, or words. It is an attempt to create subversive outcomes through interventions in the process of communication. Guerrilla communication differs from other genres of political action in the sense that it is not based on the analysis of the dominant discourses; rather, it is based on the interpretation of the signs in a different manner. Its chief aim is to make an essential nonquestioning of the existing.[5] Visual motifs accomplish several objectives for Islamists. First, they articulate identification with key traditions in Islam. They are able to conjure feelings and emblematize particular Islamic beliefs and ideas. Second, they produce a mental conception of reality for their viewers. The use of meticulously edited images brings to mind emotional or historical memories, stimulating an emotional reaction that may be conscious or subconscious. Third, they allow the propagandist to convey a message—usually a visual argument in favor of or against something. Imagery, often accompanied by texts, offers interactive methods for Islamists to engage the ideology itself.[6] Hence, visual motifs are akin to visual propaganda.

In this analysis, many examples of Islamist pictorial or graphic art appear to be more than just images; they are also accompanied by symbolic messages that can communicate ideas just as efficiently and explicitly as images do.[7] This analysis was inspired, in part, by the work of experts at the Combating Terrorism Center. What is missing in their research, however, is a thorough academic analysis of Islamists' motives for (1) using visual motifs to recruit jihadists and martyrs-to-be and (2) using particular images (so dear to Islam) instead of others. Their research is merely describing the images themselves based on Islamic documents, but no critical analysis is offered. Overall, in this chapter, an important deduction from Islamist visual motifs is that metaphors are the Islamists' predominant conceptual system, in terms of which they think and act. Metaphors are their principal method to perceive and experience much of the universe. They structure what they see in this world and how they relate to each other as well as to outside groups (e.g., infidels). Edward T. Hall's low-context versus high-context distinction is another method that can elucidate Islamists' structure and perception of the world.

The **Combating Terrorism Center** is an academic institution at the U.S. Military Academy (USMA), in West Point, New York, specializing in terrorism and counterterrorism studies. The center (2006)[8] examines Islamist imagery as an important channel for the communication and diffusion of jihadist ideas. Islamist imagery is a communicative conduit used by ideologues, extremists, terrorist organizations, and sympathetic propagandists that plays to the specific religious and cultural experiences of their base. Consequently, understanding how Islamist visual motifs work, what ideas they communicate, why they are used, and what reactions they trigger is essential to our fight against the influence of Islamism and the violence it produces.

CONCEPTUAL METAPHOR THEORY

Metaphors are vehicles or processes of communication that allow understanding of one thing in terms of another or as concepts of communication that make sense of one concept by mentioning another, often unrelated, concept. Metaphors are a central tool that individuals use to make sense of the universe in which they live. They give us the mental frameworks for our thinking, our perceptions, and our communication with others. They lend meaningful form to constructs and offer structure for experiences that are not very structured by their own terms.[9] Metaphor is analogous to conceptual mapping; the quality of metaphors is conceptualization. Straightforward concepts are often employed to understand and perceive abstract and difficult concepts.[10] A metaphor possesses both emotive import and discursive content. In brief, it is conferred meaning that transcends, and cannot be reduced to, rational discourse or emotive utterance. The outcome is that knowledge consists of more than just facts and information; it is an affective state that arouses cognition and, at the same time, creates a significant sensory response.[11]

Metaphors enable terrorist propagandists to strike a responsive chord within their constituency. They facilitate shared meaning and consensus among the terrorists' audience. They are a type of meaningful communication of experience and offer clues to the advancement of ideology.[12] Generally, they work well because they can conceptualize events, structure cognition, and produce abstract concepts. Abstract reasoning would be barely possible without metaphors. They play a highly important role in human thought, understanding, and the production of our social, cultural, and psychological reality. In short, they shape not only the way we communicate, but also the way we think and act. In large part, trying to understand metaphors is like attempting to understand the world in which we live.[13] According to **Conceptual Metaphor Theory**, metaphors are part of our everyday life and are deeply engrained in our conceptual system. Our concepts structure the world (and how we function in it) through three categories of metaphors: structural, orientational, and ontological metaphors.[14]

Structural Metaphors

Structural metaphors perform the function of highlighting the characteristics of one structured experience or activity to the detriment of other experiences or activities.[15] Examples are "Argument is war," "Time is money," and "Religion is the opium of the people." These metaphors are daily phrases reflecting the reality that we do not just mention certain topics in a metaphorical way; we also play the part defined by the metaphor, producing a whole discourse according to its direction. An important feature of structural metaphors is the highlighting or hiding dichotomy. This means that certain aspects of a phenomenon receive special attention, whereas other ones tend to be ignored. In the example of "Argument is war," the feature of conflict is highlighted, but cooperation, which can also be a feature of war (e.g., the attempt to end war), is hidden. Therefore, the concept is metaphorically structured, action is metaphorically structured, and, hence, language is metaphorically structured, resulting in a metaphorically structured mindset within people.[16] In regard to Islamist visual motifs, an example of a structural metaphor is a drawing of Jinn killing Jews wherever they can be found (based on Qur'an 2:191: "Kill them wherever you find them"). This illustrates a clear highlighting-hiding phenomenon: although, in real life, Jews can be given a second chance by Muslims (i.e., to repent or convert to Islam) when found hidden behind a rock, the visual motif reduces all possibilities to one option only. Put differently, for the jihadist or jihadist-to-be, the visual motif becomes metaphorically structured into a false dilemma in which pure Muslims have only one choice: "Kill them."

Orientational Metaphors

Orientational metaphors pertain to our orientation in space, usually with respect to polar oppositions such as "up" versus "down," "central" versus "peripheral," and "front" versus "back." "Up" is generally positive, and "down" is negative. Likewise, "happy" is up, and "sad" is down. These are abstract concepts rooted and conceptualized in terms of our bodily experience in the three-dimensional world. Often, orientational metaphors are used by groups that see themselves as the center of the world, including significant objects and events in their context. Hierarchy, power, and uprightness become inherently associated with the goodness, growth, and happiness of such groups. For example, "Control is up" (i.e., we have power over the enemy).[17] This is similar to the "in-group versus out-group" distinction. Thus, in an Islamist visual motif, ideal human social relationships can be conceptualized as points in space: a map of an imaginary Palestinian State shows a large territory encompassing the entire nation of Israel, with Muslims placed at the center of the map. Jews, on the other hand, are pushed into the Mediterranean Sea (shuffled off to peripheral areas). Similarly, to return to the "up-versus-down" distinction, "up" shows Islamist martyrs enjoying eternal life in Paradise, and "down" shows Americans burning in Hell.

Ontological Metaphors

Ontological metaphors help propagandists interpret life by using common objects and substances that are frequently personified. Such metaphors consist of projecting entity characteristics onto areas of life that have a different status—whether physical or nonphysical. Thus, nonthings like ideas become things, and vice versa (concrete things become abstract things).[18] The same information is presented in different modalities.[19] For Lakoff and Turner (1989),[20] ontological metaphors tend to emphasize the physical and behavioral characteristics of humans, animals, plants, natural objects, and manmade objects. Examples of such metaphors are

"People are animals" (e.g., "Achilles is a lion"), "People are plants" (e.g., "She is a tender rose"), and "People are machines" (e.g., "My boss is a bulldozer"). Generally, ontological metaphors map the structure and visual features (e.g., type of being, color, shape, and texture) of a conceptual domain onto the structure and visual features of another domain. For instance, in many Islamist motifs, jihadists (and martyrs-to-be) are depicted as falcons. The "jihadist as falcon" image symbolizes bravery, swiftness, and ferocity in battle. It represents all the qualities that a Muslim holy warrior is said to personify, including his or her ultimate martyrdom.[21]

Figure 14.1 displays a portrait of Osama bin Laden surrounded by references to Al Qaeda and jihadism. These references pertain to terrorist attacks on the U.S. embassies in Kenya and Tanzania (in 1998), the USS *Cole* (in Yemen in 2000), and the World Trade Center (in New York City in 2001). In terms of structural metaphors, this drawing highlights certain characteristics to the detriment of others. In particular, the jihadist motif here accentuates Islamic victories against the United States and, at the same time, totally neglects Islamic defeats against the United States and the West (e.g., the loss of Kuwait in 1991 during the Persian Gulf War). From the standpoint of orientational metaphors, the picture of Osama bin Laden (along with his prestigious "Mujahadeen" nickname right below him) was appositely placed by jihadist propagandists in the middle of the drawing. Such a type of graphic tactic places U.S. targets on the margins of the drawing that, thereby, makes them look inferior and

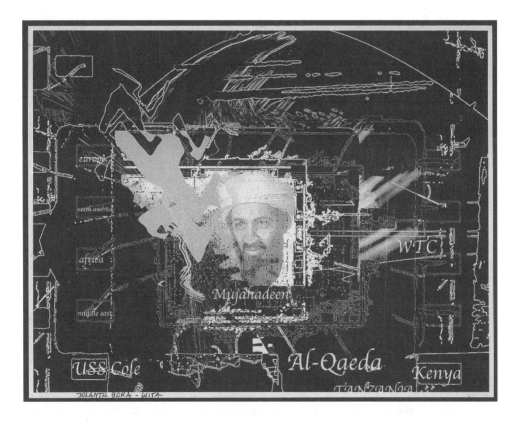

Figure 14.1.   The Black Standard of Jihad, called Raya ("There Is No God but Allah, and Muhammad Is His Messenger"). Combating Terrorism Center (2006). The Islamic Imagery Project: Visual Motifs in Jihadi Internet Propaganda. West Point, NY: Combating Terrorism Center.

drastically less powerful. In like fashion, the names of geographical regions (i.e., Europe, North America, Africa, and Middle East) are placed on the margins as well. This means that these regions are being conquered by Al Qaeda and jihadism. Lastly, in regard to ontological metaphors, the drawing is mostly black, a prime color in Islam that signifies Islam itself. The symbolic meaning of the color black is thoroughly explained in Case Study III. The next three sections are detailed, comprehensive case studies of visual motifs in Islamist terrorism.

CASE STUDY I: WATERFALLS

Charismatic leaders are known for using language brimming with verbal imagery, symbolic allusions, and metaphors.[22] Water, for example, is of great significance in Islam. It is regarded as a blessing from Allah that provides and supports life. The Arabic for water, *ma*, is mentioned sixty-three times in the Qur'an. As it is written, Allah's throne rests on water.[23] The life-giving aspect of water is revealed in Qur'an 16:65: "And Allah has sent down the water from the sky and therewith gives life to the earth after its death. Indeed, that is a sign for a people who listen [i.e., devout Muslims]."

Metaphorical Meanings of Waterfalls

In Islamist visual propaganda, a waterfall is often used as the focus of an image or in combination with other symbols (e.g., trees and lush greenery) that together denote a larger meaning. In this case, the larger meaning evokes notions of religious piousness, purity, the divine, and the Garden (i.e., Paradise). At the same time, it also hints at a more dynamic or active progress toward human transcendence—in which the evil and decadent earth will, one day, be wiped out. In this sense, waterfalls are related to the soul, its spiritual progress, and ultimately its ascendance to Paradise. This is clearly exemplified in the first words of the jihadist statement ("Supremacy and Purity").

Whether they are depicted through short falls or huge cascades, waterfalls symbolize both ideas of religious purity and Allah's guaranteed assistance and generosity to devout Muslims. The waterfall image can be interpreted through both an orientational metaphor and an ontological metaphor. Orientationally speaking, a waterfall comes from a high point (i.e., to see it, one has to look "up" or "above"), in the same way that Paradise is "up" or "above" (i.e., the place that pure, pious Muslims will enter one day). On the other hand, the hellish bottomless pit is "down" or "below," and it is reserved for infidels. Ontologically speaking, the waterfall symbolizes a celestial being of a spiritual nature, and, like a spirit, the water cascade is falling from the sky to help or save true, devout Muslims on earth. In other words, it is an Islamic miracle of some sort.[24]

Visually, a waterfall operates as a symbol of abundance (as in "plenty" of water). Plenty of things are awaiting jihadists in Paradise.[25] From this vantage point, the waterfall is compared to the afterlife, which constitutes an abundant energy source that will be perpetually accessible. In the Qur'an, the afterlife is recurrently symbolized as the Garden (a symbol of Paradise). The Arabic term for the Garden is *janna*, the quintessential garden.[26] In traditional Islam, the Prophet Muhammad received a revelation (by Allah) about the Garden of Paradise. Muhammad described the Garden as being supplied by waterfalls, rivers, and fountains: four rivers, water, shade, fruit, and pavilions in which the rewarded ones can rest.[27]

Dangers of Structural Metaphors

Structural metaphors direct our attention toward only one attribute of some abstract experience, highlighting that aspect and simultaneously toning down or hiding other attributes of it. This quality of metaphor is manipulated by Islamists to induce targeted audiences into looking at things in the particular light that Islamists wish. At the same time, this process makes it less probable that the targeted audiences will pay attention to other aspects of the ideas presented.[28] In a study conducted by Daphne Burdman (2003),[29] it was revealed that the Palestinian Authority (PA) launched a campaign to indoctrinate Palestinian children into a doctrine of self-sacrifice (martyrdom). Children are persuaded to engage in stoning and suicide bombings against the IDF (Israel Defense Forces), and told that, as soon as they die, they become martyrs. In September 2000, the PA Ministry of Education Curriculum Committee introduced its first textbooks put together by the PA itself.[30] The PA published additional books that blatantly direct teachers toward specific didactic methods. One of these textbooks features an Islamist motif of a waterfall, leading Palestinian pupils to believe that an afterlife with waterfalls and a plethora of wonders will greet them when they die. Because the PA-driven indoctrination of Palestinians begins at infancy, the latter will be much less aware of other facets of the ideas presented to them.

Origins in Medieval Islam

Already in the Middle Ages, in the desert areas of the Middle East, the valuable and basic component of water, as exploited in the ancient Persian gardens, was understood by Muslims to represent Paradise, the place of eternal ecstasy after death, as this garden met all the basic conditions of nomads and desert people—namely, shade, privacy, pavilions, perfumes, calming sounds, and, most importantly, water. Thus, the Qur'anic Garden is an extension of ancient Persian emphases. In the Qur'anic Paradise, waterfalls are everlasting and unfailing, and the rewarded ones recline upon soft couches.[31] In Qur'an 47:15, it is written,

> This is Paradise, which the righteous have been promised. There shall flow in it rivers of unpolluted water, and rivers of milk forever fresh; rivers of delectable wine and rivers of clearest honey. They shall eat therein of every fruit and receive forgiveness from Allah.

Because the jihadist mind captures reality, in many respects, in terms of imagery, it is not difficult for visual propagandists to exploit significant medieval Islamic symbols in order to recruit would-be martyrs ready to sacrifice their lives against infidels. To this point, a statement such as "On the Way of the Blessed Jihad" illustrates the power of the sacred waterfall image: Allah has sent spirits to protect you; eternal Paradise is high and above, and will soon open its doors for you. For this reason, what jihadists anticipate, upon dying, is this idyllic model of world happiness. It is a conceptual system that plays a central role in defining their everyday realities. As explained in Qur'an 9:111, "If you die fighting for Islam, you would die a martyr and the rewards in Paradise would be wonderful." Properly understood, then, the waterfall metaphor becomes a powerful vehicle for communicating a particular and unique kind of message that is intrinsically poetic. At the same time, the metaphor is an efficient means of control; its primary purpose is to create a dominant, shared meaning system about which little resistance is expected on the part of the recipients (e.g., jihadists or would-be martyrs).

CASE STUDY II: HANDS

The human body is an important cognitive channel for humans to interpret the abstract world. In Islamic culture and history, there is a good deal of imagery about hands. The symbol of the hand is deeply loaded with a religious-cultural specificity that necessitates contextual understanding of that specific body part. Perhaps the most significant use of the hand motif, culturally and religiously, is the one showing hands raised toward heaven in an act of prayer. Like in many religions, prayer in Islam requires particular hand gestures, and raising hands is one of its more identifiable signs.

The Hand Symbol in Muharram

The hand is a symbol that has great depth of meaning during the month of Muharram. During that month, the hand symbol honors the death of Abbas, whose hand was amputated when he was carrying water to the wounded baby of Hussein at the battle of Karbala. The tiny silver hand worn by small boys in the month of Muharram commemorates this event, and it serves to recognize the wearer's subordination to Abbas.[32] In Shia extremism, the severed hand of Abbas pays tribute to the entire Karbala event when Imam Hussein (the son of Ali) was martyred, in the year 680, along with his followers by the soldiers of the Umayyad caliph. Because the hand is related to Abbas, it works as a model of sacrifice and persistence in Muslim interpretation.[33] **Muharram** is the first month of the Islamic calendar and one of the four sacred months of the year. Because the Islamic calendar is different from the Gregorian calendar, Muharram varies every year (as it is part of the lunar calendar).[34]

Symbol of Power

Because in Islam the hand is so sacred, it has become a symbol of luck and protection from evil. The "Hand of Fatima" (also called *khamsa*) calls to mind Fatima Zahra, the daughter of the Prophet Muhammad, and is still used as an amulet throughout the Middle East today.[35] Hands are also associated with power and authority, and frequently evoke the Qur'anic narratives about the "hand of Moses" that performs miracles (i.e., Qur'an 20:22, 26:33, and 28:32). Since seventh-century Islam, the hand has been used to signify the tribal chief's ability to not only project power over non-Muslims or apostates but also protect his own belongings and territory.[36]

The symbol of the Salafi Front of Tunisia is made up of a hand lifted up heavenward and holding a Qur'an. It is a symbol of cosmic significance that connects Salafis closer to Allah, which makes them feel more powerful. The Qur'an considers the hand a form of association with Allah; the hand becomes an ontological metaphor for divine power.[37] More precisely, the hand takes on physical attributes of Allah-conferred power; indeed, as mentioned in Qur'an 36:83, "Glorious is he in whose hand is the dominion of all things." Qur'anic references to divine assistance and intervention testify to the jihadists' earnest belief that they are agents of Allah's will, carrying out Allah's work. The power of such Salafi ideology lies in its ability to create a selected and distorted interpretation of material reality.

The Salafi Front of Tunisia gained prominence during the Arab Spring in early 2011. This Islamic fundamentalist movement champions a restoration of Salafi rule and holy war.[38] The hand depicted in its logo is a left hand; the five left-hand fingers are an ontological metaphor for the members of the house of Muhammad (*Ahl al-Bait* in Arabic).[39] In early Islam, this left hand symbol personified the "five pure ones": Muhammad and four key followers. In layperson's terms, it refers to the five quintessential people and paradigmatic framers of Islam.[40]

It is worth mentioning that the symbol of the hand also lends itself to an orientational metaphor. The hand is lifted up toward Paradise because "up" is high and positive (as opposed to a hand that is down or pointed toward earth). In fact, very few Islamic symbols show the hand "down." The hand-up symbol is also a structural metaphor because it illustrates Salafis' total devotion to Allah and Qur'anic teachings by highlighting only one body part (to the detriment of other body parts). This differs from Christianity in the sense that most symbols of Christians looking heavenward tend to show their entire body (with their arms and faces looking up to God), not just one hand.

Clasped Hands: A Symbol of Unity

One of the jihadist hand symbols described by the Combating Terrorism Center is an Al Qaeda motif depicting clasped hands. The motif symbolizes unity among the various jihadist groups and the ummah overall. More precisely, Al Qaeda uses handshakes to represent unity between Al Qaeda and other Islamist organizations, forging a symbolic bond that meshes many offshoots of the jihadist movement together. Each of the arms has a slightly different color, indicating the aspiration to bring the missions of local jihad movements (often nation-based ones) under one single banner: the Sunni ummah. In this manner, the "clasped hands" motif can associate the concerns and activities of Al Qaeda with those of other Islamist groups (e.g., "Hand-in-Hand with the Mujahedin") and Muslim constituencies.[41]

In a similar vein, the "clasped hands" symbol is an ontological metaphor that represents the entire world itself. A concrete thing (i.e., clasped hands) becomes an abstract thing (i.e., the world). The symbol attempts to illustrate a greater, pan-Islamic unity between Muslims of all walks of life. Symbols of this nature are used to internationalize, or "pan-Islamicize," locally or nationally based Islamist conflicts. In a similar image, a hand holds the wrist of another, apparently pulling the latter to safety, or at least making sure that the jihadist will not fall. The text of the image states, "The Hand of the Powerful: delivering Iraq from the occupation." The text of a third image is the beginning of the profession of faith to Allah. Taken as a whole, all these images evoke the power of a unified ummah.[42]

CASE STUDY III: THE COLOR BLACK

Color is a compelling source of motivation and inspiration in Islam. One color in particular, black, comes out as a versatile symbol. To begin, black is used to symbolize devotion to Islam and absolute piousness in both the Sunni and Shia traditions. For instance, both the Taliban and the Islamic Republic of Iran stress the wearing of black turbans particularly, and black clothing overall, for Muslim students and clergy. In jihadist motifs, the color black tends to highlight the importance (or frequency) of jihad and arouses deep feelings about the perceived need to restore the caliphate.[43]

Black Standard of Jihad

In Figure 14.2, the **Black Standard** (also called **Black Banner**, **Banner of the Eagle**, **The Banner**, or simply **raya** in Arabic) represents three symbols: (1) the flag used by the Prophet Muhammad in Islamic tradition (also carried in combat by many of his supporters, including his nephew Ali ibn Abi Talib), (2) an eschatological symbol in Shia Islam (heralding the advent of the Mahdi), and (3) a symbol used in both past and present jihadism.[44] According to tradition, Muhammad said that the arrival of the Mahdi would be portended by the Black Standard.[45] Although the Prophet had multiple banners, his most important one was the larger black raya, which was purportedly made from Aisha's headcloth. Aisha was one of Muhammad's twelve wives. This larger flag was also known as **The Punishment**.[46]

After the death of Muhammad, the Umayyad Caliphate succeeded as the main leaders of Islam. The **Umayyad Caliphate** existed between 661 and 750 AD, and it was the second of the four main Islamic caliphates established after Muhammad died.[47] Although the Umayyads were the sovereign establishment of the Islamic world at the time, they were Sunnis and were considered by the Shi'ites as voracious, greedy, and religiously defiant rulers. For this reason, the leader of the Abbasids, Abu Muslim, led a revolution against the Umayyad Caliphate. The revolution had the objective to establish a superior Islamic ruling house that would uphold orthodox Islam at the heart of its regime. Since that event, black has been adopted as the color of the Abbasid Empire, because the Abbasids wanted to increase their Shia base. This is how the Black Standard has been used as a symbol of religious upheaval and jihad. In Shia belief, the flag also brings to mind expectations about the afterlife. In today's Islamist movement, it is simply used to symbolize both offensive jihad and the return of the caliphate.[48]

The statement on the Black Standard, as shown in Figure 14.2, is the **shahada**, the Muslim decree of faith or the Islamic profession to Allah ("There Is No God but Allah, and Muhammad Is His Messenger"). The historical Black Banner had no inscription on it. Only in the twentieth century did Islamist organizations start to inscribe the shahada on it. Today, Islamist organizations that use the flag include Al Qaeda, al-Shabaab (a Somali-based cell of Al Qaeda), the Islamic Courts Union (another Islamist group in Somalia), Hizbul Islam (a third Islamist group from Somalia), and the Islamic State of Iraq (an umbrella organization for a number of Iraqi insurgent groups established since October 2006).[49]

Ontological Metaphor for the Black Standard

As Islamic extremism grew stronger after the advent of the Muslim Brotherhood in the twentieth century, the black within the pan-Islamic colors was chosen to pay homage to the

Figure 14.2. Visual dialogue JG3VD2 / Jolanta Gora-Wita. Library of Congress, Prints & Photographs Division, Exit Art's "Reactions" Exhibition Collection [reproduction number, e.g., LC-USZ62-123456].

Black Standard of Muhammad. The flag itself is an ontological metaphor for the conquest of Dar al-Harb (the "House of War") by Dar al-Islam (the "House of Islam"). Dar al-Islam refers to the divinely perfect and respectable abode of true Muslims. In *The Black Banners*, Soufan (2011)[50] explains the title by remarking that quotes from various hadiths (concerning "Black Banners" of a "new army" transforming the world) have some type of prophetic resonance with many modern-day Islamists. One day, Islamists hope, the entire globe will be covered with Black Standards. In other words, the flag is an ontological metaphor for the ultimate objective of Islamists: the restoration of the worldwide caliphate. Consequently, offensive jihads will be waged all over the world. As Ortony (1993)[51] explains it, metaphors are an efficient way to influence adherents, promote change, and improve the ability to remember powerful images. It is no accident, then, that Osama bin Laden chose the color black for his Al Qaeda's flag. On the other hand, Afghanistan's national flag was originally black, but, today, it is only one third black. Afghanistan's motive is to show that the country should not be perceived as Islamist. In fact, it has collaborated with the International Security Assistance Force (ISAF) to fight Al Qaeda.[52]

Black: Color of the Intifada

During the Palestinian Intifada, particularly the First Intifada (1987–1993), black was a very important color. For example, black flags symbolized the Palestinians' refusal to be displaced from their sacred land. The population was advised to erect black flags on their roofs, along-side the Palestinian flag, as a symbol of their relentless resistance to the Israelis.[53] The creation of black smoke by burning tires is something to behold: the pillars of smoke coming from black tires were a widespread ontological metaphor for the Intifada itself. Tire burning had even preceded the method of throwing rocks and Molotov cocktails. As such, the burning tire was a metaphor for poverty and misery resisting a stronger and wealthier oppressor. The black smoke itself was a sign of declaration of war. Burning tires became a thorough and methodical procedure. Tires were burnt every single day, at specific times, a ritual that was observed across all towns and villages of the West Bank and the Gaza Strip.[54]

The Palestinians were persistently waging the tire-burning Intifada. In fact, according to IDF's estimations, between 150,000 and 250,000 tires were burned during the uprising. By incessantly burning tires, they demonstrated their commitment to the struggle and refusal to capitulate.[55] Palestinians were cheering up at the sight of the rising columns of black smoke. The smoke itself was a metaphor of time (i.e., smoke can last a long time). Black smoke served as reassurance that the combat was far from being a fleeting eruption. Many inversions and contrasts featured in the Palestinian uprising; examples were the flame and the color black of the smoke, or the earth and heaven connected by a black pillar ("sending a fax to Allah"). In terms of orientational metaphor, "down" was the painful reality of earth, whereas "up" was the rosy dream of heaven.[56]

On the whole, this "black smoke" anecdote serves to illustrate that, as an active tool of human cognition, the metaphor is an important method to shape reality or structure knowledge. At the end of the day, a group's knowledge is rooted in perceptual experience.[57] Through such metaphor-based and symbol-based perceptual experience, the Palestinian people enact judgments, evoke emotions, make decisions, and provide interpretations about the nature of reality. Another important conclusion is that knowledge of the universe is not objective and value neutral. It only has meaning within the perceptual and expressive activities of a cultural group's members.[58]

LOW CONTEXT VERSUS HIGH CONTEXT

Edward T. Hall (1976)[59] developed the model of high context and low context to describe how cultures view the world. **Context** refers to the situation, background, or environment associated with an event, phenomenon, or person.[60] For Hall (1959),[61] context is the "information that surrounds an event" (p. 6); in other words, the context in which information is produced is crucial to meaning. He noted that cultures tend to use a varying range of information-processing structures to provide context. When the context is based on codes, theories, and grammar, and when it is clear and unequivocal, the culture is said to be a **low-context** culture. Conversely, a culture in which messages are more ambiguous and in which less has to be said or written—because the meaning tends to reside within the environment (i.e., it depends more on the context)—is labeled a **high-context** culture. In low-context cultures, individuals attempt to describe the world in more objective terms; communication is more elaborate, specific, detailed, and clear-cut.[62] For example, a stop sign to notify motorists that they must stop before proceeding is low context: it is clear and understood in the same way by all qualified drivers.

High-context communication is also based, in large part, on nonverbal communication, and the time and situation in which the communication occurs. Hence, in high-context cultures, information does not tend to be fully delineated or expressed openly so the world can understand; it is more internalized within the culture in which the information is shared. In low-context communication, the sender communicates as if the listener knows little and must be told everything through explicit or well-understood messages. In high-context communication, the listener is already familiar with the context and does not need to receive much background information. What the listener must do is fill in the gaps based on past knowledge of the sender, setting, or other contextual signs.[63] No culture is exclusively low context or high context; rather, what we have are cultures that tend to lean toward a specific worldview. In addition, in every society, there are situations that are **countercultural**: even in high-context cultures, there are situations that are low context (and vice versa).[64]

Abstractive Communication versus Associative Communication

Another way to describe low-context and high-context communication is by comparing abstractive with associative communication. **Abstractive communication** is "factual inductive" communication in which explicit information is required. On the other hand, **associative communication** pertains to shared patterns and meanings in communication. In abstractive cultures, communication is direct and specific; in associative ones, it is indirect. For example, in associative cultures, communication between labor and management may use mottos, symbols, pictures, or colors; in abstractive ones, it may be very specific, such as a request for an $8.00 hourly wage raise.[65] Those who deal with all associations of an event may take note of many details of the environment. In contrast, those who pay attention to only part of the evidence are abstracting those elements that are important and applicable. Glenn (1981)[66] claims that in abstractive cultures, cause-and-effect relationships are essential, whereas in associative cultures, communicators process information by making associations among events that may not be rational or logical.

Information processing in abstractive cultures does not need to rely on context; therefore, explicit messages or factual information-processing approaches are the key mode of communication. In associative cultures, effective communication is contingent upon the context and can only be understood fully by those who share a large amount of shared meanings and similar thought patterns.[67] Symbols operate within a context. Terrorist symbols, aimed at a global audience, will be more understood by constituents and nonconstituents alike if they are low context and abstractive. National and ethnic symbols tend to be high context and associative—more readily and fully understood by individuals of that nation or ethnic group.[68] By extension, as we will see in the two case studies, the meaning of a sign or symbol is not fixed. Rather, it is subject to various interpretations according to context. This phenomenon is called **multi-actuality**.[69]

Logos Oriented versus Pathos Oriented

For Hall (1976), those who use a low-context communication style are "expected to communicate in ways that are consistent with their feelings" (p. 79), whereas a person from a high-context culture will establish the context and the setting and allow the message to develop without referring to the issue directly. In case of conflict, high-context cultures generally use indirect, nonconfrontational, and unclear language, falling back on the listener's or reader's ability to capture the meaning from the context. Low-context cultures tend to rely on a more direct, confrontational, and clear approach to guarantee that the listener gets the message exactly as it was sent. In the end, low-context cultures are more factual (**logos oriented**). What this means is that knowledge is more often transferrable. High-context cultures are more emotional (**pathos oriented**). What this means is that knowledge is situational and relational; more time is needed to encode and decode meaning from the specific set of information.[70]

Convergent Thinking versus Divergent Thinking

It should be clear by now that considerable differences exist between the thought patterns of high-context cultures and low-context cultures. **Thought patterns** are forms of reasoning and approaches to communication that vary from culture to culture.[71] Two opposing thought patterns are convergent thinking and divergent thinking. **Convergent thinking** focuses on synthesis and analytical problem solving to attain an unambiguously defined outcome (i.e., low context). **Divergent thinking** underlines a fluid thinking pattern. It is the ability to (1) move from one perspective to another, (2) connect diametrically opposed ideas in a meaningful way, and (3) bring a new idea to accomplishment (i.e., high context).[72] Low-context cultures tend to stress logic and rationality, based on the notion that an objective truth can always be reached thanks to linear methods of discovery. High-context cultures, on the other hand, think that truth will emerge through nonlinear discovery methods and without having to rely on rationality.[73] A thorough understanding of symbolism in terrorism requires one to be a **flexible communicator**, a communicator who is familiar with both convergent and divergent thinking. A flexible communicator is an individual who possesses a large body of information based on both factual and contextual modes.

CASE STUDY I: LIONS

Lions have been an important symbol for thousands of years and appear as a theme in cultures and religions across many civilizations. In various places, lions have been the subject of positive depictions as creatures that appear strong (i.e., the lion is strong, as opposed to the weak lamb or doe). Throughout history, countries such as England and Spain have used the heraldic symbol of the lion to refer to themselves as mighty states. The most consistent depiction serves to uphold the nation's image of royalty, strength, and courage. For instance, in the Bible, the lion was chosen as the sign of the tribe of David (the direct ancestor of Jesus Christ). To this point, the Lion of Judah is the symbol of the Jewish tribe of Judah in the Book of Genesis (Genesis 49:9). Judah was a tribe that was promised the land of Israel as a covenant with God. Likewise, the common motif of the "majestic and powerful" lion in China was introduced to the country in the first century AD. Even today, many Chinese believe that lions protect them from demons and ghosts. As a result, the Chinese New Year's "lion dance" is performed to cast away evil spirits.[74] Symbols of lions in Islamist visual motifs are both low context and high context. They do not contradict each other; rather, as we will see, high-context views complement low-context ones to fit the Islamists' agenda. To be more precise, some unique interpretations of lions have been designed by Islamist groups to better communicate messages of holy war to their constituents. Therefore, it is the task of scholars, experts, and practitioners to elucidate those high-context views.

Low-Context Islamist Views

The symbol of the lion in Islam shares many of the traits that are attributed to lions by most other cultures: the lion brings to mind qualities of strength, heroism, valor, stateliness, and chivalry. Because of these commonalties, the image of the lion in Islam seems direct and clear to most outside observers. It is low-context communication because the aforementioned traits (i.e., strength, heroism, valor, stateliness, and chivalry) tend to be the same across many cultures and can be understood fully by most observers (without having to examine the context first). It is abstractive communication because no specific pattern of thinking needs to be acquired in order to understand why these traits are associated with the image of the lion. And it does not constitute situational or relational knowledge based on a specific cultural context (i.e., it is not pathos oriented).

In the early Islamic days, the lion was associated with the followers of Muhammad and their heroic accomplishments in the fields of holy war. In Shia Islam, the lion motif emerged as a symbol of strength. Still today, during the month of Muharram (as mentioned in "Case Study II: Hands"), images of lions, or men dressed in lion costumes, are often witnessed during the commemorations of martyrs. One of these commemorations is called the Day of Ashura (i.e., the Ashura procession). The purpose is to honor all the martyrs killed on the battlefields from the seventh century to the present day.[75] Another image of the lion in Shia Islam is associated with imams. The symbol of the lion evolved into an image of the unquestionable leader. More precisely, it was used as an important means for punishing anyone refusing to give his or her allegiance to the imam or challenging the tradition of serving and protecting the imam.[76]

In line with these contentions, the lion has been used by Islamist scholars like Sayyid Qutb to allude to the spirit of warfare. The lion represents a form of honor for high-profile Islamist leaders and low-ranking jihadist militants alike. For example, when describing the late Abu Musab al-Zarqawi (a jihadist affiliated with Al Qaeda), Islamist propagandists used the lion symbol to portray him as a strong, heroic warrior, and as a Muslim striving to accomplish the righteous path of jihad. Likewise, Ibn al-Khattab (a Saudi-born Islamic terrorist and financier who worked with Chechen jihadists in the First and Second Chechen Wars)[77] was depicted as a brave jihadist leader and martyr willing to die for Allah. Thus, the lion symbol is broadly understood to be the spitting image of the king of all animals (i.e., a strong warrior) and the figurative use of the religious, personal, and battle-hardened characteristics of a single jihadist leader (i.e., a successful, heroic, and brave warrior).

High-Context Islamist Views

In some instances, Islamist symbols of lions have particular connotations that have been deeply internalized within Islamist culture, thereby making it difficult for outside observers to fully understand the meanings attributed to lion symbols. The reason is that some Islamist symbols are based on conventions that most readers would not understand well. Ideology is often conveyed in symbolic terms. Symbols represent an assortment of meanings that far transcend the inherent qualities of the symbol itself.[78] For example, in 1987, at the end of the Soviet war in Afghanistan, Osama bin Laden built a compound to train Arab Afghan fighters against Soviet forces. The compound was called al-Masada ("The Lion's Retreat"). According to Coll (2004),[79] the image of "The Lion's Retreat" symbolized the ability of a specific people to be cunning and establish a place anywhere, even in the midst of danger. However, it is unlikely that other cultures would associate lions with this situation. In Western culture, foxes would be used (i.e., as in the "fox's den").

One image[80] shows the key "Believers": Osama bin Laden, Abdullah Azzam, and Ibn al-Khattab. Abdullah Azzam was Osama bin Laden's professor at King Abdul Aziz University in Jeddah, Saudi Arabia. He was the main founder of Al Qaeda in 1988; he actually coined the name for it (Al Qaeda means "The Base"). In this figure, Osama bin Laden's photo is superimposed on a lion's face. Symbolically, this pictorial superimposition means two things: (1) Osama bin Laden was the head of the lion and (2) he was the head "lion," that is, the leader of the pride of lions. In the first case, bin Laden lived up to his name, "Lion of Islam" (in fact, Osama means "lion" in Arabic).[81]

This is clearly low context and an example of how the literal image of the lion can be understood by most people as a symbol of the supernatural power ascribed to the former Al Qaeda leader. Ayman al-Zawahiri, the new leader of Al Qaeda, even referred to Osama bin Laden as "the lion of Islam."[82] Conversely, in the second case, the lion refers to the global jihadist insurgency (i.e., a pride of lions). Here, the figure of the lion is that of an animal moving with its pack toward a particular objective. This metaphor is more of a high-context nature. To corroborate this idea, as reported by *The New York Times* (2011),[83] the day after bin Laden was killed, Al Qaeda sympathizers wrote the following on a blog: "The lions will remain lions and will continue moving in the footsteps of Osama."

CASE STUDY II: DOVES

Over the past several millennia, doves have appeared as symbols of harmony and purity in many belief systems, including Judaism, Christianity, and Paganism, as well as military and pacifist groups. For example, according to the biblical story of Genesis (8:11), a dove was sent by Noah after the flood in order to locate land; it returned to the ark with an olive leaf in its beak, telling Noah that there was land somewhere. Christians have used Noah's dove as a symbol of hope and peace. In many instances, Muslims have also used the dove as a symbol of hope and peace. Just like it was for the lion, the symbol of the dove in Islamist visual motifs is both low context and high context. Again, the two perspectives do not contradict each other; rather, they complement each other to fit the terrorist-jihadist agenda. As an isolated example, in the 1940s and 1950s, the image of the dove was used as a peace symbol in Soviet communist propaganda. However, during that time, the Soviet Union was responsible for the deaths (through mass killings and famine) of close to fifteen million people.[84] What peace means to Soviet communism is to be interpreted very differently through a Western lens. In this case study, the same framework of interpretation will be applied to the Islamist dove symbol.

Low-Context Islamist Views

There are four reasons why the symbol of the dove in Islam shares many attributes as those witnessed across other major cultures and religions. First, the dove is a universal symbol of purity; it is a living thing of the three-dimensional world that has been selected to represent a human concept of enormous quality: sacredness. From this perspective, the dove acts as a powerful symbol of the ummah (a pure and sacred Islamic cultural identity), in the same way that it symbolizes purity, gentleness, beauty, and devotion in a faith like Judaism. Second, at the international level, the dove is also a symbol of hope and peace that has resonated well across the vast majority of cultures and religions; it fits into a cognitive framework that allows for global optimism to be shared by many people. Third, the dove is a symbol of love. In many Islamic poems, the Muslim reader recognizes the dove as a symbol of love.[85]

Fourth, and more importantly, like many belief systems, Islam considers the dove a holy messenger from Paradise.[86] For example, Al-Masjid al-Nabawī (also called the Prophet's Mosque), a mosque built by the Prophet Muhammad in Medina, shows a white dove sent by Allah and carrying a letter.[87] Because the dove is perceived as being so close to God, it has come to represent worship of a deity. For example, in Christian symbolism, the dove is a symbol of the Holy Spirit, in reference to Matthew 3:16 and Luke 3:22, where the Holy Spirit is compared to a dove at the Baptism of Jesus (when the dove descended upon Jesus after he was baptized by his cousin John the Baptist). The symbolism of the Holy Ghost by a dove is a common notion in Judaism as well.[88] In Islam, the act of devoting oneself to Allah may get one to be likened to a dove. For instance, recounting the imagery of doves, Ingersoll (1923)[89] quoted an Algerian source for doves being called **imams** (leaders of prayer in Islamic mosques) because they "prostrate themselves by inclining their necks in devotions to the Creator" (p. 136).

High-Context Islamist Views

Most beliefs and dogmas would possess much less meaning without visual motifs. Visual motifs contain a variety of meanings that go well beyond the essential qualities of the symbol itself.[90] To begin, in Islamism, the very image of the dove as a symbol of "purity and sacredness" can be ambiguous when it is co-opted by Islamist groups as a sign of holy war. The association rests on the principle that jihad, in and of itself, is pure and sacred, and the white dove is the best symbol to exemplify what a true Muslim is supposed to do: to accomplish jihad, the supreme act of purity and sacredness that pleases Allah. As explained by Elias (2005),[91] more often than not, the dove symbolizes Qur'anic revelation, in the Islamic world, to fulfill the Muslim obligation to strive in the path of Allah: jihad.

In a similar fashion, although the dove may also symbolize hope, it is not hope in a Western sense. Rather, it is hope that can only be achieved through military conquest or victory. For instance, according to Kaufman (1991),[92] during the Intifada, doves were used to express hope of ceasefires, but it was the hope that hostilities would abate once the Palestinian people win against Israel. Faisal Husseini, widely mistaken as a peace activist by the West, was actually a Palestinian extremist and a relative of Haj Amin al-Husseini (the Grand Mufti of Jerusalem who was a friend of Adolf Hitler). Not surprisingly, he was considered a dove in the Muslim world, not in a "peace" sense but in a "hope" sense—hoping he would deliver the Palestinians from the evil State of Israel. Nevertheless, from 1982 to 1987, this nice "dove" was repeatedly placed under arrest by the Israelis on terrorism-related charges. He was imprisoned several times between 1987 and 1989, but remained active in the Intifada. In this context, the Islamist dove designates a pure person who has been chosen by Allah to wage or lead holy war.[93]

In many Islamist motifs of holy war, white doves are flying out of bomb blasts or other depictions of warfare. When used in this manner, the white dove symbolizes a martyr's soul rising to Paradise.[94] The symbol of the dove is transferred to the body of the dead hero. This is because the martyred body is a mediator: he or she is going to fly away, as expressed by the dove's "escaping" attributes, departing from the ground, finding its way into or out of the elements, and moving in or between different worlds.[95] One representation shows the white dove sitting in its nest and looking at U.S. fighter jets. The dove is in front of a spider's web that spans the entrance to a cave. This image brings to mind a well-known story in which the Prophet Muhammad, being chased by the Quraysh tribe, found refuge in a cave. Muhammad's position in the cave was hidden by that spider's web. Doves helped the Prophet distract his enemies outside the cave of Ghar al-Thawr in the great Hijra.[96] The **Hijra** refers to the escape of Muhammad and his followers from Mecca to Medina.[97] This "dove" anecdote stands in sharp contrast with the Matthew 10:16 verse, which instructs Christians to be as wise as serpents and as inoffensive as doves. In the Islamist case, the Muslim is as wise as a dove.

In addition, the dove is also a symbol of protection. It can represent an agent of Allah sent to protect the Iraqis involved in warfare. To boot, a spider's web, shaped as the map of Iraq, suggests that participating in jihad (against the U.S. occupiers of Iraq) will be blessed by Allah as it would be akin to following the path of the Prophet.[98] As a tool of ideological indoctrination, the dove is framed as a clear symbol of deliverance. However, from a Western perspective, "deliverance" in Islamism is only a half-truth because freedom can only come through jihad or martyrdom—which is sealed by Allah's complete approval and protection.

SUMMARY

Visual motifs are visual themes or patterns that represent certain subjects or categories of subjects. They help create symbolic cohesion by means of setting, background, color, intensity of light, images, and organization of text. Islamist visual motifs are a form of guerrilla communication. Guerrilla communication refers to political activism achieved through the manipulation of photos, cartoons, or words. In this chapter, the analysis of Islamist visual motifs was twofold: the first part was an analysis based on Conceptual Metaphor Theory (using the three categories of metaphors [structural, orientational, and ontological metaphors]). Structural metaphors (the first category) perform the function of highlighting the characteristics of one structured experience or activity to the detriment of other experiences or activities; certain aspects of a phenomenon receive special attention, whereas other ones tend to be ignored. Orientational metaphors pertain to our orientation in space, usually with respect to polar oppositions such as "up" versus "down," "central" versus "peripheral," and "front" versus "back." Up" is generally positive, and "down" is negative. Ontological metaphors consist of projecting entity characteristics onto areas of life that have a different status—whether physical or nonphysical. Thus, nonthings like ideas become things, and vice versa. For example, in one of the case studies, it was shown that waterfalls were used as structural, orientational, and ontological metaphors to symbolize ideas of religious purity and Allah's guaranteed assistance and generosity to devout Muslims. Ultimately, it is easier for propagandists to convince jihadists and martyrs-to-be that they will enter Paradise after fulfilling their task of killing infidels. The second part of this analysis consisted of examining Islamist motifs based on Edward T. Hall's distinction between low context and high context. When a culture's context is based on codes, theories, and grammar, and when it is clear and unequivocal, the culture is said to be a low-context culture. Conversely, a culture in which messages are more ambiguous and less has to be said or written—because the meaning tends to reside within the environment—is labeled a high-context culture. For example, in one of the case studies, the symbol of the lion in Islamist visual motifs shares many traits as those attributed by most other cultures (i.e., low context). At the same time, in some instances, Islamist symbols of lions have particular connotations that have been deeply internalized within Islamist culture, making it difficult for outside observers to fully understand the meanings attributed to lion symbols.

NOTES

1. Bearne, Eve (2003). Rethinking Literacy: Communication, Representation and Text. *Reading, 37*(3), 98–103.

2. Jones, Owen (1987). *The Grammar of Ornament*. Mineola, NY: Dover Publications.

3. Andre, Virginie (2012). "Neojihadism" and YouTube: Patani Militant Propaganda Dissemination and Radicalization. *Asian Security, 8*(1), 27–53.

4. Hall, Edward T. (1976). *Beyond Culture*. New York: Doubleday.

5. Berger, Warren (2001). *Advertising Today*. London: Phaidon Press.

6. Fighel, Jonathan (2007). Radical Islamic Internet Propaganda: Concepts, Idioms and Visual Motifs. In Boaz Ganor, Katharina Von Knop, & Carlos Duarte (Eds.), *Hypermedia Seduction for Terrorist Recruiting* (pp. 34–38). Amsterdam: IOS Press.

7. Hunter, Ryan, & Heinke, Daniel (2011). Radicalization of Islamist Terrorists in the Western World. *FBI Law Enforcement Bulletin, 80*(1), 24–31.

8. Combating Terrorism Center (2006). *The Islamic Imagery Project: Visual Motifs in Jihadi Internet Propaganda*. West Point, NY: Combating Terrorism Center.

9. Bronack, Stephen, Cheney, Amy, Riedl, Richard, & Tashner, John (2008). Designing Virtual Worlds to Facilitate Meaningful Communication: Issues, Considerations, and Lessons Learned. *Technical Communication, 55*(3), 261–269.

10. Ibáñez, Francisco José Ruiz de Mendoza, & Hernández, Lorena Pérez (2011). The Contemporary Theory of Metaphor: Myths, Developments and Challenges. *Metaphor and Symbol, 26*(3), 161–185.

11. Hogler, Raymond, Gross, Michael, Hartman, Jackie, & Cunliffe, Ann (2008). Meaning in Organizational Communication: Why Metaphor Is the Cake, Not the Icing. *Management Communication Quarterly, 21*(3), 393–412.

12. Gow, Gordon (2001). Spatial Metaphor in the Work of Marshall McLuhan. *Canadian Journal of Communication, 26*(4), 63–80.

13. Lakoff, George, & Johnson, Mark (1980). *Metaphors We Live By*. Chicago: University of Chicago Press.

14. Lakoff, George, & Johnson, Mark (1980). Conceptual Metaphor in Everyday Language. *The Journal of Philosophy, 77*(8), 453–486.

15. Deetz, Stanley, & Mumby, Dennis (1985). Metaphors, Information, and Power. In Brent Ruben (Ed.), *Information and Behavior* (pp. 369–386). Piscataway, NJ: Transaction Publishers.

16. Lakoff, George, & Johnson, Mark (1980). Conceptual Metaphor in Everyday Language. *The Journal of Philosophy, 77*(8), 453–486.

17. Deetz, Stanley, & Mumby, Dennis (1985). Metaphors, Information, and Power. In Brent Ruben (Ed.), *Information and Behavior* (pp. 369–386). Piscataway, NJ: Transaction Publishers.

18. Lakoff, George, & Johnson, Mark (1980). *Metaphors We Live By*. Chicago: University of Chicago Press.

19. Waterworth, John (1997). Creativity and Sensation: The Case for Synaesthetic Media. *Leonardo, 30*(4), 327–330.

20. Lakoff, George, & Turner, Mark (1989). *More than Cool Reason: A Field Guide to Poetic Metaphor*. Chicago: University of Chicago Press.

21. Renard, John (1994). *All the King's Falcons: Rumi on Prophets and Revelation*. Albany, NY: State University of New York Press.

22. Conger, Jay (1991). Inspiring Others: The Language of Leadership. *Academy of Management Executive, 5*(1), 31–45.

23. Faruqui, Naser (2001). Islam and Water Management: Overview and Principles. In Naser Faruqui, Asit Biswas, & Murad Bino (Eds.), *Water Management in Islam* (pp. 1–32). New York: United Nations University Press.

24. Ahmad, Mirza Tahid (2010). *An Elementary Study of Islam*. Tilford, UK: Islam International Publications.

25. Dickie, James (1985). The Mughal Garden: Gateway to Paradise. *Muqarnas, 3*, 128–137.

26. Brookes, John (1987). *Gardens of Paradise: The History and Design of the Great Islamic Gardens*. London: Weidenfeld and Nicolson.

27. Khansari, Mehdi (1998). *The Persian Garden: Echoes of Paradise*. Washington, DC: Mage.

28. McCagg, Peter (2003). Conceptual Metaphor and the Discourse of Philanthropy. *New Directions for Philanthropic Fundraising, 22*, 37–47.

29. Burdman, Daphne (2003). Education, Indoctrination, and Incitement: Palestinian Children on Their Way to Martyrdom. *Terrorism and Political Violence, 15*(1), 96–123.

30. Zimeray, F. (Member, European Parliament for France) (2001). Controversy about New Books Culminated in Amendment 177 to Prevent Funding of Antipeace Projects. Press release.

31. King, Ronald (1979). *The Quest for Paradise: A History of the World's Gardens*. New York: Mayflower.

32. Donaldson, Bess (1973). *The Wild Rue: A Study of Muhammadan Magic and Folklore in Iran*. New York: Arno Press.

33. Babaie, Sussan (2011). Voices of Authority: Locating the "Modern" in "Islamic" Arts. *Getty Research Journal, 3*, 133–149.

34. Ilyas, Mohammad (1994). Lunar Crescent Visibility Criterion and Islamic Calendar. *Quarterly Journal of the Royal Astronomical Society, 35*, 425–461.

35. Rogers, Amanda (2012). Warding off Terrorism and Revolution: Moroccan Religious Pluralism, National Identity and the Politics of Visual Culture. *The Journal of North African Studies, 17*(3), 455–474.

36. Lawrence, Bruce (1999). The Eastward Journey of Muslim Kingship: Islam in South and Southeast Asia. In John Esposito (Ed.), *The Oxford History of Islam* (pp. 395–432). New York: Oxford University Press.

37. Achrati, Ahmed (2003). Hand and Foot Symbolisms: From Rock Art to the Qur'an. *Arabica, 50*(4), 464–500.

38. Wright, Robin (2012, August 19). Don't Fear All Islamists, Fear Salafis. *The New York Times*, p. A19.

39. Achrati, Ahmed (2003). Hand and Foot Symbolisms: From Rock Art to the Qur'an. *Arabica, 50*(4), 464–500.

40. Schubel, Vernon (1991). The Muharram Majlis: The Role of a Ritual in the Preservation of Shi'a Identity. In Sharon Abu-Laban, Regula Qureshi, & Earle Waugh (Eds.), *Muslim Families in North America* (pp. 118–131). Edmonton: University of Alberta Press.

41. Combating Terrorism Center (2006). *The Islamic Imagery Project: Visual Motifs in Jihadi Internet Propaganda*. West Point, NY: Combating Terrorism Center; and Maréchaux, Maria, & Maréchaux, Pascal (1987). *Arabian Moons: Passages in Time through Yemen*. Dubai, UAE: Concept Media Pte.

42. Combating Terrorism Center (2006). *The Islamic Imagery Project: Visual Motifs in Jihadi Internet Propaganda*. West Point, NY: Combating Terrorism Center.

43. Combating Terrorism Center (2006). *The Islamic Imagery Project: Visual Motifs in Jihadi Internet Propaganda*. West Point, NY: Combating Terrorism Center.

44. Cook, David (2002). *Studies in Muslim Apocalyptic*. Greenwich, UK: Darwin Press; and Nicolle, David (1993). *Armies of the Muslim Conquest*. Oxford: Osprey Publishing.

45. Cook, David (2002). *Studies in Muslim Apocalyptic*. Greenwich, UK: Darwin Press.

46. Nicolle, David (1993). *Armies of the Muslim Conquest*. Oxford: Osprey Publishing.

47. Blankinship, Khalid Yahya (1994). *The End of the Jihad State, the Reign of Hisham Ibn 'Abd-al Malik and the Collapse of the Umayyads*. Albany: State University of New York Press.

48. Combating Terrorism Center (2006). *The Islamic Imagery Project: Visual Motifs in Jihadi Internet Propaganda*. West Point, NY: Combating Terrorism Center.

49. McCary, John (2009). The Anbar Awakening: An Alliance of Incentives. *The Washington Quarterly, 32*(1), 43–59; and Stevenson, Jonathan (2010). Jihad and Piracy in Somalia. *Survival: Global Politics and Strategy, 52*(1), 27–38.

50. Soufan, Ali (2011). *The Black Banners*. New York: W. W. Norton.

51. Ortony, Andrew (1993). *Metaphor and Thought* (2nd ed.). Cambridge: Cambridge University Press.

52. Rubin, Barnett (2007). Saving Afghanistan. *Foreign Affairs, 86*(1), 57–78.

53. Nachmani, Amikam (2001). The Palestinian Intifada 1987–1993: The Dynamics of Symbols and Symbolic Realities, the Role of Symbols, Rituals and Myths in National Struggles. *Civil Wars, 4*(1), 49–103.

54. Mach, Zdzislaw (1993). *Symbols, Conflict, and Identity: Essays in Political Anthropology*. Albany: State University of New York Press.

55. Mach, Zdzislaw (1993). *Symbols, Conflict, and Identity: Essays in Political Anthropology*. Albany: State University of New York Press.

56. Mosse, George (1975). *The Nationalization of the Masses. Political Symbolism and Mass Movements in Germany from the Napoleonic Wars through the Third Reich*. New York: Howard Fertig.

57. Deetz, Stanley, & Mumby, Dennis (1985). Metaphors, Information, and Power. In Brent Ruben (Ed.), *Information and Behavior* (pp. 369–386). Piscataway, NJ: Transaction Publishers.

58. Deetz, Stanley, & Mumby, Dennis (1985). Metaphors, Information, and Power. In Brent Ruben (Ed.), *Information and Behavior* (pp. 369–386). Piscataway, NJ: Transaction Publishers.

59. Hall, Edward T. (1976). *Beyond Culture*. New York: Doubleday.

60. Würtz, Elizabeth (2005). A Cross-Cultural Analysis of Websites from High-Context Cultures and Low-Context Cultures. *Journal of Computer-Mediated Communication, 11*(1), Article 13.

61. Hall, Edward T. (1959). *The Silent Language*. New York: Doubleday.

62. Gudykunst, William B., & Nishida, Tsukasa (1986). Attributional Confidence in Low- and High-Context Cultures. *Human Communication Research, 12*, 525–549.

63. Hall, Edward T., & Hall, Mildred Reed (1990). *Understanding Cultural Differences*. New York: Inter-Cultural Press.

64. Triandis, Harry (1995). *Individualism and Collectivism*. Boulder, CO: Westview Press.

65. Triandis, Harry C. (1982). Dimensions of Cultural Variation as Parameters of Organizational Theories. *International Studies of Management & Organization, 12*(4), 139–169.

66. Glenn, Edmund (1981). *Man and Mankind.* Norwood, NJ: Ablex.

67. Korac-Kakabadse, Nada, Kouzmin, Alexander, Korac-Kakabadse, Andrew, & Savery, Mawson (2001). Low- and High-Context Communication Patterns: Towards Mapping Cross-Cultural Encounters. *Cross Cultural Management: An International Journal, 8*(2), 3–24.

68. Gallois, Cindy (1997). *Communication and Culture: A Guide for Practice.* New York: John Wiley & Sons.

69. Watson, James, & Hill, Anne (2006). *Dictionary of Media and Communication Studies* (7th ed.). Don Mills, ON: Hodder Arnold.

70. Würtz, Elizabeth (2005). A Cross-Cultural Analysis of Websites from High-Context Cultures and Low-Context Cultures. *Journal of Computer-Mediated Communication, 11*(1), Article 13.

71. Würtz, Elizabeth (2005). A Cross-Cultural Analysis of Websites from High-Context Cultures and Low-Context Cultures. *Journal of Computer-Mediated Communication, 11*(1), Article 13.

72. Cropley, Arthur (2006). In Praise of Convergent Thinking. *Creativity Research Journal, 18*(3), 391–404.

73. Chen, Guo-Ming, & Starosta, William (1998). *Foundations of Intercultural Communication.* Boston: Allyn & Bacon.

74. Oliva, Judy (1995). *New Theatre Vistas: Modern Movements in International Literature.* New York: Routledge.

75. Suleman, Fahmida (2011). The Iconography of Ali as the Lion of God in Shi'I Art and Material Culture. In Pedram Khosronejad (Ed.), *The Art and Material Culture of Iranian Shi'ism: Iconography and Religious Devotion in Shi'i Islam* (pp. 215–232). New York: I. B. Tauris.

76. Sindawi, Khalid (2008). The Role of the Lion in Miracles Associated with Shi'ite Imams. *Der Islam, 84*(2), 356–390.

77. Combating Terrorism Center (2006). *The Islamic Imagery Project: Visual Motifs in Jihadi Internet Propaganda.* West Point, NY: Combating Terrorism Center.

78. Paden, John (1973). *Religion and Political Culture in Kano.* Berkeley: University of California Press.

79. Coll, Steve (2004). *Ghost Wars: The Secret History of the CIA, Afghanistan, and Bin Laden, from the Soviet Invasion to September 10, 2001.* New York: Penguin.

80. Retrieved July 7, 2014, from http://www.au.af.mil/au/awc/awcgate/usma/ctc_islamic_imagery_project.pdf; see p. 31.

81. Van Dyk, Jere (2012, August 24). *Al Qaeda Calls for bin Laden Book Author's Death.* CBS News. Retrieved July 7, 2014, from http://www.cbsnews.com/8300-503543_162-503543.html?contributor=10471441

82. Van Dyk, Jere (2012, August 24). *Al Qaeda Calls for bin Laden Book Author's Death.* CBS News. Retrieved July 7, 2014, from http://www.cbsnews.com/8300-503543_162-503543.html?contributor=10471441

83. Baker, Peter, Cooper, Helene, & Mazzetti, Mark (2011, May 1). Bin Laden Is Dead, Obama Says. *The New York Times*, p. A1.

84. Courtois, Stéphane (1999). *The Black Book of Communism: Crimes, Terror, Repression.* Cambridge, MA: Harvard University Press.

85. Kugle, Scott (2003). Pilgrim Clouds: The Polymorphous Sacred in Indo-Muslim Imagination. *Alif: Journal of Comparative Poetics, 23*, 155–190.

86. Jennings, Sue (2009). The Doves of Peace. *Nursing & Residential Care, 11*(6), 310–311.

87. Flaskerud, Ingvild (2011). The Votive Image in Iranian Shi'ism. In Pedram Khosronejad (Ed.), *The Art and Material Culture of Iranian Shi'ism: Iconography and Religious Devotion in Shi'i Islam* (pp. 161–179). New York: I. B. Tauris.

88. Schechter, Solomon (2010). *Studies in Judaism: Second Series* (Vol. 1). Charleston, SC: Nabu Press.

89. Ingersoll, Ernest (1923). *Birds in Legend, Fable, and Folklore.* London: Longmans.

90. Paden, John (1973). *Religion and Political Culture in Kano.* Berkeley: University of California Press.

91. Elias, Jamal (2005). Truck Decoration and Religious Identity: Material Culture and Social Function in Pakistan. *Material Religion: The Journal of Objects, Art and Belief, 1*(1), 48–71.

92. Kaufman, Edy (1991). Israeli Perceptions of the Palestinians' "Limited Violence" in the Intifada. *Terrorism and Political Violence, 3*(4), 1–38.

93. Cohen, Hillel (2013). Palestinian Armed Struggle, Israel's Peace Camp, and the Unique Case of Fatah Jerusalem. *Israel Studies, 18*(1), 101–123; and Karsh, Efraim (2005). Arafat Lives. *Commentary, 119*(1), 33–40.

94. Marzolph, Ulrich (2003). The Martyr's Way to Paradise: Shiite Mural Art in the Urban Context. In Regina Bendix & John Bendix (Eds.), *Sleepers, Moles, and Martyrs: Secret Identifications, Societal Integration, and the Differing Meanings of Freedom* (pp. 87–97). Copenhagen: Museum Tusculanum Press.

95. Bombardier, Alice (2013) Iranian Revolutionary Painting on Canvas: Iconographic Study on the Martyred Body. *Iranian Studies, 46*, 10–21.

96. Donner, Fred (2010). *Muhammad and the Believers.* Cambridge, MA: Harvard University Press.

97. Shaikh, Fazlur Rehman (2001). *Chronology of Prophetic Events.* London: Ta-Ha Publishers.

98. Combating Terrorism Center (2006). *The Islamic Imagery Project: Visual Motifs in Jihadi Internet Propaganda.* West Point, NY: Combating Terrorism Center.

Chapter Fifteen

Semiotic Analysis of Terrorism

DEFINITION OF SEMIOTICS

Semiotics is the study of signs, as well as their processes and systems. In the words of Sebeok (1991),[1] semiotics is "the exchange of any message and the system of signs that underlie them" (p. 60), and allows us to understand and formulate the signs' meanings. Sometimes referred to as **sign theory**, semiotics was introduced by Ferdinand de Saussure (1916),[2] a Swiss linguist and semiotician. Semiotics comes from *semiotikon*, a Greek word that means "sign." Semiotikon encompasses the study of signs and their interpretation.[3] A **sign** is a thing that stands for another thing; it is designed to represent something else. Messages contain signs, which are transmitted through sign systems. These sign systems are called "codes." Meaning can only happen or emerge insofar as the message receiver understands the code.[4] From this vantage point, semiotics concentrates on the interpretation of sign functions and the receiver's comprehension of meaning.[5]

The overarching objective of semiotics is to study **semiosis** (the creation and comprehension of signs) as it emerges in both human and nonhuman spheres. The sphere of semiosis in which sign processes function is called the **semiosphere**. The semiosphere is our social world of communication: our symbols, images, thoughts, emotions, hopes, fears, interpersonal relationships, conflicts, and so forth. Without the semiosphere, human communication could not operate or have much meaning.[6] Because humans are actors in the semiosphere, they become **semiotic animals**, creatures or beings who are capable of using signs and symbols to reflect on human communication, and are therefore capable of being entirely mindful, or acting in full awareness, of the culture in which they operate.[7] In other words, the semiosphere regulates and enhances human communication.[8]

When the study of human semiotics is located within specific cultural contexts, it falls under the category of **cultural semiotics**.[9] Cultural semiotics goes beyond the traditional verbal mode of expression and covers extralinguistic modes such as nonverbal communication, pictures, and images.[10] It is a branch of the field of semiotics that examines human signifying practices in particular cultural circumstances; it also attempts to interpret meaning making as a cultural practice. Semiotics, as first defined by Ferdinand de Saussure (1916),[11] is "the science of the life of signs in society" (p. 2). Cultural semiotics adds to Saussure's originating insights by investigating how the "codes" of both language and nonverbal communication are produced by cultural processes. Thus, cultural semiotics analyzes the social dimensions of meaning, as well as the power of human methods of signification and interpretation in shaping human behavior and society. Cultural semiotics emphasizes cultural meaning-making practices of all kinds, whether visual, verbal, or acoustic in nature.[12] These different processes of meaning making, or channels (e.g., speech, writing, and pictures), are referred to as **semiotic modes**. Semiotic modes consist of visual, verbal, written, gestural, and musical channels of communication. They also include various combinations of several of these modes.[13] Lastly, of equal relevance in the semiosphere is the role of mass communications. More precisely, there is a **semiotic law of media**: that is, not only do the media evolve, but the sign systems of culture change as well. Therefore, investigating the implications of this law is a chief goal of cultural semiotics.[14]

SAUSSUREAN SEMIOTICS

Ferdinand de Saussure (1916)[15] was one of the framers of the modern study of language. He laid out the theory that signs possess two elements: a signifier and a signified. The **signifier** is the visible, or material, element of a sign, whereas the **signified** is the absent element. For example, in a written manuscript, the letters of the word on a page are the signifiers; the meanings that reside beneath the written letters are the signifieds. The sign itself is what connects the signifier with the signified. Accordingly, in a written manuscript, a word is a sign that has both a physical presence on the surface of the page (signifier) and meanings inside the text and within the connotations and cultural backgrounds surrounding the word (signifieds). As another example, let us look at a national flag: the signifier is the flag itself, which individuals can see and feel. The signified is what the flag stands for. If we take the example of the ex-Soviet communist flag, with a hammer and a sickle, we know that it denotes the Soviet Union and connotes communism, Lenin, Stalin, the Red Army, and so forth.[16] The relationship between the signifier and the signified is also known as signification. **Signification** refers to the action of signs creating these fundamental relationships between signifieds and signifiers that are the basic building blocks of meaning.[17]

"Terrorist": Signifier and Signified

It is clear, by now, that each sign possesses both a signifier and a signified. The word "terrorist" is a sign that is made up of the following: a signifier (the word "terrorist") and a signified (a person or organization committing acts of terror against targets such as innocent civilians).[18] By extension, the signified "terrorist" is generally regarded as a common denominator for any "person who launches attacks on premeditated and/or unintended targets" on governments, such as the government of the United States, Russia, Colombia, Sri Lanka, or the like. However, it is also important to mention that there is no signifier that is totally meaningless or signified that is completely formless. The same signifier could represent a different signified (and, therefore, become a different sign). To this point, the signified "terrorists" (and the violent deeds they perpetrate) can be described differently across the world: to Western civilizations, terrorists are the archenemy, the evil ones, and the threats to global peace. Whereas some terrorist actions are signifieds for Islamic fundamentalism, other actions, such as the use of predator drones in the Middle East, are signifieds for terrorism as well. The signified aspect of a word is often accompanied by broader political, legal, and cultural nuances.[19]

Indeed, as discussed in chapter 2, one person's terrorist can be another person's freedom fighter. What the West thinks is evil may be revered in other civilizations. Given these circumstances, the term **empty signifier** refers to a signifier whose referent is ambiguous and can vary easily, and whose meaning differs extensively based on interpretation.[20] In the case of the Global War on Terror (GWOT), the signifier "terrorism" appears everywhere. However, the signified, the actual wrongdoers and what they do, are perceived quite differently depending on the observer. Because the designation of the signified is determined by the speaker, the meaning of "terrorism" is subjective and fluid. The signified switches drastically according to context and time; the only aspect that remains stable is the signifier "terrorism."[21] Terrorism's meaning is not completely open; it is constantly embedded within dehumanizing, terrifying, and cruel images, myths, and stories.[22] Nor does the meaning of terrorism remain permanent through pure and objective definitions—even the most scholarly definitions.[23] Rather, its meaning develops within cultural and communicative contexts; the "what" and "who" of terrorism are determined by the play of discourse and subject to the effect of context and sender "expressions."[24]

Denotation versus Connotation: Description

The signifier tends to denote, and the signified tends to connote. **Denotation** is an example of first-level analysis: what the audience can read or see on a page or image. Denotation has to do with something literal and has no purpose of being symbolic. **Connotation** is an example of second-level analysis: what the denotation represents. It is typically related to symbolism; the connotation of a specific text or image tends to represent something further. A more profound, symbolic meaning is generally encoded within that text or image. Denotation, on the other hand, is the literal meaning of a signifier.[25] To transmit a message successfully, both the sender and the receiver must use the same code. The denotative meaning of a signifier aims at communicating the objective content (be it semantic or visual) of the represented thing. Thus, in the case of a word (e.g., "book"), the intention is to merely describe the physical object. Any additional meanings or inferences will be connotative meanings. A connotation is a cultural or emotional association that some word or image carries. This association is subjective and commonly understood, and it constitutes an addition to the literal meaning of a word or image.[26]

Eco (1976)[27] defines denotation as having a "cultural unit or semantic property" (p. 86), something that corresponds to its referent. On the other hand, connotation does not automatically correspond to its referent. Rather, it uses the denotative sign, but it is not necessarily consistent with the culturally recognized attribute of the possible referent. For this reason, connotation is said to take the denotative sign to the second level of signification (i.e., second-level analysis). That is, the denotative, agreed-upon meaning of a sign can be given a unique and specific meaning—something that adds to or even embellishes the meaning. From this perspective, connotation is a denotative sign that not only maintains its symbolic character, but also brings an additional and higher level of interpretation.[28]

Denotation versus Connotation: 9/11 Attacks

Peirce (1958)[29] uses the term "denotation" to express the "object of a sign" (p. 2). The object of a sign is true no matter what anyone or any group thinks. For example, the 9/11 attacks were predominantly attacks against the "World Trade Center (WTC)," which denotes a series of buildings—permanent structures in which people worked—that were ultimately caused to collapse. At the denotative level, the Twin Towers are just towers; they are not to be taken as symbols. Denotation, then, operates as a descriptive indicator of the actual event of September 11, 2001; no opinion or interpretation is offered. In contrast, connotations refer to the meanings implied as a result of something; they are interpreted based on a specific context or cultural understanding. The Twin Towers represented particular, unique qualities of the sign—the immense power of global trade that was crushed to the ground. Depending on the cultural perspective, the connotative aspect of the WTC can be regarded as a symbol of multiple values.[30] For instance, in the words of Osama bin Laden, the Twin Towers were "legitimate targets" that supported "the evil U.S. economic power."[31] In a similar vein, a U.S. flag was raised by firefighters at the WTC site immediately after the attacks occurred. It was shipped to Afghanistan to be hoisted high at a temporary prison detaining Taliban prisoners. Whereas the flag denoted a piece of red-white-blue cloth, it connoted the tragedy of 9/11 (and the names of the victims were written on it); it was a symbol that represented and validated the retaliation. Original ownership of the flag was also claimed by Shirley and Spiro, two yacht owners, who claimed that the flag was stolen from their boat moored in Manhattan.[32]

PEIRCEAN SEMIOTICS

Sometimes known as "the father of pragmatism," Charles Sanders Peirce was a U.S. philosopher, linguist, semiotician, logician, mathematician, and scientist. Unlike Saussure's semiotic model, Peirce's (1931)[33] semiotic framework consists of a three-part model of signification: (1) the **representamen** (i.e., the sign itself; what something is), (2) the **object** (i.e., the "referent"; what the sign refers to or symbolizes), and (3) the **interpretant** (i.e., the audience's interpretation or the effect in the mind of the interpreter). This framework is referred to as Peirce's "representamen-object-interpretant" model (see Figure 15.1). Peirce's model is like a triadic relationship or a three-way interaction.

Figure 15.1 shows a triadic relationship in which all three parts of the framework are important in the meaning-making process between the sender and receiver of a message. If any of three parts is missing or is not taken into consideration in any study or examination, then it cannot be a true Peircean perspective. What is perceived as reality is necessitated by the representamen-object-interpretant relationship. For Peirce (1931),[34] meaning is a triadic inter-relationship of these three categories. Terrorism succeeds, in large part, thanks to media effects of arousing fear. To be considered "terrorism," acts of terror necessitate representation.

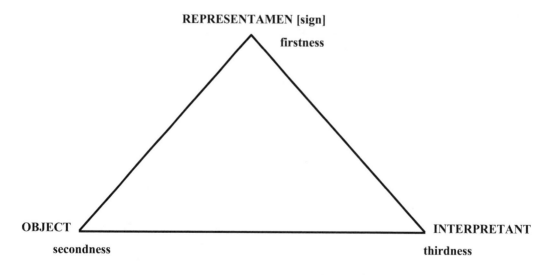

Figure 15.1. Peirce's Representamen-Object-Interpretant Framework

Hence, to explain this, a semiotic examination of this very representation is needed. Just like it was for Saussurean semiotics, the semiotics of Charles Sanders Peirce also offers a sound method of sign analysis.

Representamen

Sometimes called a **sign-vehicle**, the representamen is the sign—that is, "something that is." It is the objective description of what something is. It exists outside consciousness and in a universe manifested in the phenomena of life mediated by signs.[35] For Peirce (1958),[36] a sign is anything—from pictures, words, signals, microscopes, or legislative representatives— which stands for something else. So, the representamen is "something that represents." Taken as a whole, representamen means **representation**, the use of a sign that stands for and takes the place of something else. Through representation, individuals can structure the world and reality by naming its elements. Signs are organized in order to produce semantic constructions and express relations. A representation is a form of recording where the sensory information about an object is described in a medium.[37] Because the representamen stands for a given object, it is akin to Saussure's "signifier."[38]

Object

The representamen symbolizes its object. To be a representamen, it must represent something else: an object. According to Peirce (1931),[39] an object is something from which a person can derive meaning. This aspect corresponds to Saussure's signified, whereas the representamen corresponds to Saussure's signifier. The object is the meaning or concept—what the sign refers to (i.e., the referent). The representamen does not offer acquaintance with the object; instead, it functions only to represent it. For instance, a piece of vermillion paper that acts as a sample (= representamen) of the actual paint inside a container (= object) merely shows the shade of vermillion; it is implied that people are already familiar with all of the paint's characteristics (e.g., its contents, purpose, etc.). Likewise, as arbitrary signs, symbols like words regulate the semantic connection between the sign and its object.[40]

Interpretant

The interpretant refers to the meaning of the concept when it is decoded by the audience-receiver. It is the resulting idea created by the sign and, at the same time, the effect in the mind of the interpreter as created by the sign. In a nutshell, it is the interpretation or meaning that the sign carries for the receiver. The representamen eventually produces a response (i.e., what is to be interpreted) based on the relationship it has with the object.[41] In Peircean terms, it is the interpretant that produces the meaning for a sign. **Interpretance** is the practice, often within a community or culture, to identify relevant sensible parameters in its context or environment and use them to generate meaning.[42] Interpretance has much in common with cultural semiotics, in which the meaning of language or nonverbal communication is shaped by cultural processes. The very interpretation of reality "essentially involves the notion of a community, without definite limits, and capable of an increase in knowledge" (Peirce, 1958, p. 406).[43]

The fully expressed meaning of a sign lies within **habits of interpretation**. Such habits are evaluated based on the interpretants themselves (i.e., the historical embodiment of their society or culture). In most cases, the typical interpretant is influenced by his or her experience and knowledge. As meaning depends on one's experience and knowledge, as well as context in general, the interpretant has the potential to create multiple interpretations of meaning.[44] In particular, the media (e.g., movies, television, etc.) have a profound impact on interpretants' judgments of an event like a terrorist attack. Nevertheless, for the message receiver, perception is interpreted as immediate and real—even when mediated solely through movies and television. The authority and validity of the media are reinforced through conventional signs, or symbols that possess meanings built up from habits of interpretation. The images of media organizations often favor a particular point of view that symbolically represents the world. This is often how the meaning of a symbol is determined by its interpretant.[45]

Finally, the representamen-object-interpretant framework was slightly revisited by Cohen, Adoni, and Bantz (1990)[46] when they provided a model to describe the omnipresence of media in our society. As such, based on their model, we live in three realms of reality (not just one): (1) the **real objective world** (i.e., what occurs "out there," which is analogous to the representamen), (2) the **symbolic world** (i.e., how the world is portrayed in the media, akin to the object), and (3) the **subjective world** (i.e., the world as audiences view it in their minds; as seen by the interpretants).

CASE STUDY OF PEIRCEAN SEMIOTICS: 9/11

Terrorism is symbolic language. It is a semiotic gesture that acts as a signal, message, symbol, and media representation. The images of the planes crashing into the Twin Towers are anchored into our memories. The goal of terrorism is to send a meaningful signal; one particular signal has the purpose to frighten and coerce others. Accordingly, terrorism is, above all, a communicative process between the perpetrators and their audiences.[47] This case study of the September 11, 2001, terrorist attacks, based on Peirce's representamen-object-interpretant framework, illustrates that the nature of terrorism is inherently semiotic: it is rooted in the symbolic representation of violence or, even better, the expression of violent symbolism against the symbolic.

Representamen

Like Saussure's signifier, the representamen is just what it is: the destruction of the Twin Towers by airliners, which obliterated about twelve million square feet of Class A office space and cost $16 billion in damage,[48] and which took the lives of close to 3,000 people. Whereas the Pentagon is still there and has been repaired, the Twin Towers were totally destroyed. The representamen is also the image—played for three days and without interruption—of a burning 110-story building (i.e., the South Tower of the World Trade Center) after the second hijacked airplane was repeatedly shown plunging into it. For most audiences across the world, it was the first time they were exposed to footage of an aircraft flying into the World Trade Center. They became aware of this thanks to images they saw on television. The type of representamen, in this case, is a sign that constitutes a categorical and incontestable image: a passenger plane hitting a skyscraper.

Object

The object comes into play when the sign represents a deliberate act of terror. More precisely, the object is reflected in the idea that the image (of the plane crashing into the building) symbolizes an extremely violent terrorist act; it is a defilement of human conscience that goes beyond comprehension. Put differently, in this object phase, viewers put the two together: a hijacked aircraft + crashing into a building = an extremely violent terrorist act. U.S. terrorism statutes stipulate that bombing constitutes terrorism if the targets are extensions of U.S. interests or authority.[49] Notwithstanding politics or worldview, the vast majority of people agreed that the images of 9/11 denoted violence and destruction. Without television, no object (in regard to 9/11) would have emerged. The reason is that television sets were the main media that allowed us to see what happened. In the words of Lanigan (1997),[50] "The world is spatially located and enframed in the TV set in front of which we sit and watch and listen" (p. 388). So, for most people, the object emerged when they became aware by viewing the image on television.

As a result, many institutions and publishers worldwide have used images of the attack on the Twin Towers to symbolize "terrorism." The processing of images is natural or spontaneous in the sense that mass-mediated images correspond to an analogical method of communication. Often, visual recognition of things or events does not need prior acquaintance with various representational styles or media. Cognitive access to images seems the same for most people, irrespective of socioeconomic status. So, viewers tend to enact the same psychological processes when viewing images. On September 11, 2001, the images of the ill-fated airliners crashing into the Twin Towers were processed in relatively the same manner by all people who saw them. The ability of people to understand media images, process information, and, thereby, make deductions (when using information and communication technologies) is called **cognitive access**.[51]

Interpretant

The interpretant is the resulting impact in the mind of the interpreter. Ideas are not directly, instinctively known or experienced; their meanings are acquired by a process of inference. The thoughts one has (interpretant) stem from Peirce's triadic relationship: an interpretation of the thought as a sign of an object.[52] The 9/11 terrorist attack was interpreted by most as a deliberate and premeditated act of terror—an act that the terrorists perpetrated for political, ideological, and religious purposes and to terrorize the West. In Harris's (2004)[53] words, 9/11 was "a symbolic drama, a great ritual demonstrating the Power of Allah" (p. 15). In the interpretant phase, viewers use their minds and create interpersonal narratives and media discourses. Unlike the object, the interpretant adds the qualification that the 9/11 attack was intentional, calculatedly chosen, and committed by evil anti-West haters.[54]

Indeed, in the interpreters' mind, the Twin Towers were deliberately obliterated because they symbolized power (i.e., economic, political, and cultural power). The WTC symbolized American success, sovereignty, capitalism, individualism, globalization, liberalization, modernity, and architectural innovation. Another important interpretant is that these symbols of power were not immune; they were vulnerable (exemplifying the weakness of governmental power), and similar structures could be targeted in the future.[55] As Kappeler and Potter (2005)[56] argue, interpretants are conceptual blueprints that enable viewers to interpret reality and wrap their thoughts and beliefs around that reality. On that fateful day, sentimental landmarks were targeted for their symbolic value, much less for their potential impact on the economy or daily business routines. What matters is the interpretant, the viewers' emotional reactions. In semiotic terms, the symbolic nature of terrorism is magnified by the power of televised media (i.e., the aftermath of the 9/11 terrorist attacks).

For Baudrillard (2005),[57] 9/11 was a terrorist attack because it symbolized the suddenly violent desecration of the "tough guy" image of the United States as a nation. If a few terrorists had detonated bombs with no other impact than their own deaths and a modicum of collateral damage, 9/11 would not have carried the same level of significance. If the WTC had not collapsed, the event would not have been repeatedly watched by three billion people.

Baudrillard (2010)[58] comments on the symbolic meaning of the Twin Towers: after the towers were smashed to pieces, they symbolized the decline of some of the aforesaid attributes that had made the United States so unique (i.e., its success, sovereignty, capitalism, individualism, etc.). The WTC does not embody a competitive system anymore, but a countable system where competition has vanished in favor of correlation. The attack on the Twin Towers was a symbolic move, even if the WTC collapse may not have been the chief aim of the actors involved. In the words of Baudrillard (2003),[59]

> Neither politically nor economically did the abolition of the Twin Towers put the global system in check. Something else is at issue here: the stunning impact of the attack, the insolence of its success and, as a result, the loss of credibility, the collapse of image. (p. 82)

Through the symbolic collapse of the Twin Towers, an act of extreme violence became a terrorist act. The interpretant here is that, through the gargantuan physical damage and loss of human life, and through the temporary disruption of financial and social routines, the power, success, and future of the United States (symbolized by the Twin Towers) were perceived as threatened. One of the signifieds for the Twin Towers was the word "fragile." It is the shared and cultural experience of 9/11 that transformed the WTC into a memorable subject of cultural semiotics; until that fateful day, the topic of the "fragility of America" (as a result of the towers' collapse) would not have entered most human conversations. Today, however, say the words "World Trade Center" or "Twin Towers" to anyone, and their minds will instantly recall everything that went along with the terrorist attacks on those buildings (e.g., passenger airplanes crashing, people jumping off buildings, a giant fireball, the WTC collapse, as well as Al Qaeda, Osama bin Laden, Afghanistan, Iraq, the USA Patriot Act, and so forth). In addition, the use of the words "September 11" or "9/11" to symbolize all that happened in New York City and Washington, DC, has become a sign or a code word that encapsulates the indescribable chaos and confusion of that tragedy.[60]

Mass-mediated images of the September 11, 2001, terrorist attacks were repeated time and time again to become anchored into our collective consciousness. Although repetition does not change the sign's relation to its object, it has an effect on our interpretation of that sign-object relationship. For example, repetition of televised images can increase our fears, cause us to take unprecedented decisions, and even alter the entire order of a nation's priorities.[61] In the aftermath of 9/11, the existing terrorism laws were considered inadequate or lacking; for this reason, the USA Patriot Act sailed through Congress and was passed into law on October 26, 2001. In essence, the **USA Patriot Act** significantly reduces restrictions in the capacity of law enforcement agencies to collect intelligence within the United States. It gave formal definition and justification to the GWOT. The act was the interpretant, the argument that legitimized the invasions of Afghanistan and Iraq. New U.S. terrorism laws became interpretants that also became blueprints in many parts of the world. Attacks on the WTC and the Pentagon led to the creation of new meanings of terrorism and the establishment of a new world order against terrorism. Of course, it also led to higher reciprocation from existing and new Islamist organizations.[62]

THE ICON-INDEX-SYMBOL TRIAD

A similar model is the icon-index-symbol triad, another product of Peirce's (1931)[63] scholarship. These three are essential characteristics of signs: signs that represent iconically, those that represent indexically, and those that represent symbolically. Iconic sign relations are based on resemblance; essentially, they are images. Indexical sign relations define their objects based on actual connections. For example, smoke is an index of fire. Symbolic sign relations link objects through meaning. In brief, this triad underscores the different ways the sign refers to its object: the icon by a property of its own, the index by a connection to its object, and the symbol by an agreed-upon rule for its interpretant. For instance, the famous triangular road sign showing two schoolchildren walking with their bags is (1) an icon (describing, by way of similarity, these children), (2) an index (the sign being erected as a result of the proximity of a school), and (3) a symbol (referring to schoolchildren at large).[64]

Icon

Also called a **likeness** or **semblance**, an **icon** refers to its object by a process of similarity (e.g., an image, photo, map, diagram, graph, etc.). In other words, an icon resembles or mirrors its object; it describes (facets of) the object to which it refers. Anything, be it an individual, an event, or a law, is an icon of anything, inasmuch as it resembles that thing and is used as a sign of it.[65] The simple image of the plane diving into the South Tower is an icon: an image of the jetliner smashing into the building. In addition, an icon is not subject to a code that people have to learn or teach; it develops merely out of a need to describe something objectively. Icons point to intelligible figurative characteristics of what they refer to. Thus, people can establish iconic communication irrespective of cultural or historical contexts and of previously established social or conventional conditions. Iconic communication can be easily shared and understood across most cultures, because the minds of people are designed to instantly comprehend images and figurative expressions.[66]

Index

An **index** is a sign that determines its object based on an actual connection, regardless of interpretation. Two examples are smoke as the sign of fire and the pointing finger as the sign for the object to which the finger is pointed. An index is a representation that refers to its object because it is based on a dynamical or spatial connection both with the object and with the senses or memory of the individual for whom it acts as a sign. Nevertheless, an index is not a representation that refers to its object due to any similarity or analogy that the sign has with that object or because it is connected to general characters that the object has.[67] Indices (plural of index) lay the basis for identifying the objects described in time and space (through causes, pointing arrows, etc.). The index has to do with **causality**, the relationship between cause and effect. Indices are natural signs that people interpret on the basis of causal phenomena in the universe. These signs are manifestations of both natural and nonnatural occurrences.[68] For example, a footprint in the mud is an index because it indicates that a foot made it.[69] Likewise, on 9/11, when the first aircraft crashed into the North Tower at 8:46 a.m., most witnesses determined that it was a sign of the pilot's appalling error or a gross mechanical glitch. However, when the second plane plunged into the South Tower at 9:03 a.m., it was clear to all that it was a sign of a well-coordinated terrorist attack. Due to the major role of signs in our daily lives, the human brain has developed a remarkable cause-and-effect ability to put things together.[70]

Symbol

A **symbol** is a sign that denotes its object merely because it will be interpreted to do so. It is a sign that is made a sign primarily for the reason that it is interpreted as such in a given society or culture, through repetition (i.e., habits of interpretation) or conventional rules, and without paying attention to the motives that initially governed its selection.[71] A symbol consists of a conventional or agreed-upon rule, norm, or practice. So it very much derives from conventional knowledge and enables to generalize simple and complex objects or events. An example would be the habit that we have developed about interpreting the two schoolchildren in the triangular road sign not as two particular individuals, but as young, precious beings to whom all motorists need to pay attention when driving.[72] In view of the fact that symbols are based on learnable codes, they are often arbitrary; their power is social and connected to a particular society or culture that distinguishes the individuals they semiotically connect.[73]

CASE STUDY OF ICON-INDEX-SYMBOL: MUNICH MASSACRE

On September 5, 1972, during the Summer Olympic Games in Munich, West Germany, the **Munich massacre** was an attack committed by Black September (a Palestinian terrorist group) on eleven members of the Israeli Olympic team. All Israeli athletes and coaches who were held hostage were killed on the next day, along with a German police officer. Immediately after the hostage crisis began, the Palestinian terrorists demanded the liberation of more than 200 prisoners held in Israeli prisons, and the release of Andreas Baader and Ulrike Meinhof, the founders and leaders of the Red Army Faction (i.e., Baader-Meinhof), who were held in German prisons. Five of the eight Palestinian terrorists were killed by German police officers during their failed rescue attempt. The Munich massacre unfolded before an international audience of almost 800 million viewers.[74]

Icon

An icon is a sign that is connected to the thing for which it stands by some resemblance and likeness. Finding a cause-and-effect relationship between a sign and the thing it represents is not the purpose of icons.[75] For example, one of the most famous icons of the Munich massacre—arguably, the most recognizable and iconic image of the tragedy—was the photo of a hostage taker standing on the balcony of the Israeli athletes' building at the Munich Olympic Village. The Palestinian terrorist had a **balaclava**, a type of headgear that covers the whole head, showing only the eyes and/or mouth.[76] Another icon was the footage of tight-tracksuit-clad members of Black September carrying AK-47s and grenades. A third icon was the image of Kehat Shorr and Andre Spitzer, two Israeli hostages, talking to German agents during the hostage crisis. A fourth icon was the televised vision of the site (i.e., a nearby airport) where the hostages were taken.[77]

Index

An index is a sign that relates to the thing for which it stands because there is a cause-and-effect relationship between the sign and the object that it represents.[78] In brief, it is a descriptive sign conveyed from a sender to a receiver. In the Munich massacre, the strongest index was the hostage crisis in which eleven Israeli athletes and coaches, and their eventual slaughter, were involved. To outside observers, the cause-and-effect relationship was that of a hostage-taking incident and subsequent killing, giving obvious signals to the world that the Munich tragedy was a terrorist attack. The cause-and-effect relationship also manifested itself to the world clearly when the State of Israel immediately identified the incident as a terrorist attack. Israel's official policy in the early 1970s was to never negotiate with terrorists in any situation. According to the Israeli government, hostage negotiation would open the door to future hostage crises. Similarly, on September 6, 1972, during the second day of the attack, at

4:30 p.m., an antiterrorist squad of German police was sent off to the Munich Olympic Village. Dressed in Olympic sweatsuits and equipped with submachine guns, their plan was to move into the heart of the hostage crisis from the ventilation shafts and exterminate the terrorists.[79] The presence of an antiterrorist squad was an index of an occurrence of terrorism somewhere. Lastly, the footage that showed one of the kidnappers looking out from the balcony door while one of the police agents stood on the roof (at a short distance from him) also indicated a hostage-taking situation.[80]

Symbol

A symbol denotes an arbitrary or agreed-upon connection between an object (or event) and what it stands for. Such symbolic connection is usually developed by individuals within a specific societal or cultural system.[81] The strongest symbol of the Munich massacre was the message that Black September was fighting Israel and what it symbolized. To some extent, Black September was also fighting the West, as the group requested (among other things) the release of Andreas Baader and Ulrike Meinhof, the two notorious German terrorists who epitomized anti-Western and anticapitalist hatred. The Munich massacre was also a symbol of Black September's depravity: by slaughtering Israelis in front of an audience of almost 800 million people, the group went disproportionately beyond the mere infringement of conventional standards of international conduct. To this point, King Hussein of Jordan—the only leader of a Muslim nation who publicly condemned the Munich massacre—called it a "savage crime against civilization perpetrated by sick minds."[82] Terrorism discourse bestowed symbolic meaning to the tragedy.

In line with these assertions, the Munich massacre symbolized a unique opportunity for Palestinians to expose the world to the predicament of their fellow brothers and sisters living in Israeli-occupied territories. The hostage-taking incident is a classic example of success in regard to the ability of terrorists to attract media attention. It made terrorism look like a cost-effective method of communication, and a vehicle of communication for exerting an easy form of intimidation.[83] As one of the Black September leaders expressed,

> We recognized that sport is the modern religion of the Western world. We knew that the people in England and America would switch their television sets from any program about the plight of the Palestinians if there was a sporting event on another channel. So we decided to use their Olympics, the most sacred ceremony of this religion, to make the world pay attention to us. (p. 15)[84]

The media-oriented Munich massacre led to similar incidents in the following years, such as the hostage crisis at the headquarters of the Organization of Petroleum Exporting Countries (OPEC), in which six employees were held at gunpoint by Carlos the Jackal and his men (in December 1975). The most widely publicized hostage crisis occurred in November 1979, when Iranian activists stormed the U.S. embassy in Tehran. The tragedy lasted for 444 days.[85] What the Munich massacre illustrates is that most people around the world were able to deduce that the fateful event was a grand terrorist strategy to achieve global power by causing fear and terror in the civilian population through exemplary murders among them. It symbolized terrorism as a mighty weapon of influence. Through fatal bodily harm on eleven Israeli athletes and coaches, the event was able to influence the collective psyche of humanity.[86]

SUMMARY

Semiotics is the study of signs, as well as their processes and systems. A sign is a thing that stands for another thing; it is designed to represent something else. The overarching objective of semiotics is to study semiosis, the creation and comprehension of signs. When the study of human semiotics is located within specific cultural contexts, it falls under the category of cultural semiotics. Cultural semiotics goes beyond the traditional verbal mode of expression and covers extralinguistic modes such as nonverbal communication, pictures, and images. In a similar fashion, Ferdinand de Saussure (1916) was one of the framers of the modern study of language. He laid out the theory that signs possess two elements: a signifier and a signified. The signifier is the visible, or material, element of a sign, whereas the signified is the absent element. Nevertheless, one person's terrorist can be another person's freedom fighter: the same signifier could represent a different signified (and, therefore, become a different sign). Along with signifier and signified, denotation is an example of first-level analysis: what the audience can read or see on a page or image. Denotation has to do with something literal and has no purpose of being symbolic. Connotation is an example of second-level analysis: what the denotation represents. It is typically related to symbolism. Another semiotic model, Peirce's (1931) semiotic framework, consists of a three-part model of signification: (1) the representamen (i.e., the sign itself; what something is), (2) the object (i.e., the "referent"; what the sign refers to or symbolizes), and (3) the interpretant (i.e., the audience's interpretation or the effect in the mind of the interpreter). For example, in the case study of the 9/11 terrorist attacks, the representamen was the destruction of the Twin Towers by hijacked airliners. The object was what the sign represented: a deliberate act of terror. The interpretant was the resulting impact in the mind of the audience, based on cultural and historical contexts: most people worldwide agreed that it was a barbaric act determined to undermine important U.S. and Western values. A similar model is the icon-index-symbol triad, another product of Peirce's scholarship. An icon refers to its object by a process of similarity (e.g., an image, photo, map, diagram, or graph). The simple image of the plane diving into the Twin Towers is an icon. An index is a sign that determines its object based on an actual connection, regardless of interpretation. Two examples are smoke as the sign of fire and the pointing finger as the sign for the object to which the finger is pointed. A symbol is a sign that is interpreted as such in a given society or culture, through repetition (i.e., habits of interpretation) or conventional rules. In the case study of the Munich massacre, it was found that many images of the tragedy served as simple icons (e.g., the hostage taker standing on the balcony). In terms of index, the cause-and-effect relationship was that of a hostage-taking incident and subsequent killing of innocents, giving obvious signals to the world that the Munich tragedy was a terrorist attack. In terms of symbol, the Munich massacre sent the message that Black September was fighting Israel and the West.

NOTES

1. Sebeok, Thomas (1991). *A Sign Is Just a Sign*. Bloomington: Indiana University Press.
2. Saussure, Ferdinand, de (1916). *Cours de linguistique générale*. Paris: Payot.
3. Langer, Susanne (1953). *Introduction to Symbolic Logic*. New York: Dover.
4. Nöth, Winfried (1990). *Handbook of Semiotics*. Bloomington: Indiana University Press.
5. Peirce, Charles Sanders (1931). *Collected Papers*. Cambridge, MA: Harvard University Press.
6. Hoffmeyer, Jesper (1996). *Signs of Meaning in the Universe*. Bloomington: Indiana University Press.
7. Deely, John (2005). *The Semiotic Animal: A Postmodern Definition of Human Being to Supersede the Modern Definition as "Res Cogitans."* Sofia: New Bulgarian University.
8. Lotman, Yuri (2000). *Universe of the Mind: A Semiotic Theory of Culture*. New York: I. B. Tauris & Co.

9. Danesi, Marcel (2010). Semiotics of Media and Culture. In Paul Cobley (Ed.), *The Routledge Companion to Semiotics* (pp. 135–149). New York: Routledge.

10. Semetsky, Inna (2006). The Language of Signs: Semiosis and the Memories of the Future. *Sophia, 45*(1), 95–116.

11. Saussure, Ferdinand, de (1916). *Cours de linguistique générale*. Paris: Payot.

12. Thibault, Paul (1991). *Social Semiotics as Praxis: Text, Social Meaning Making, and Nabokov's Ada*. Minneapolis: University of Minnesota Press.

13. Kress, Gunther, & van Leeuwen, Theo (2001). *Multimodal Discourse: The Modes and Media of Contemporary Communication*. London: Arnold.

14. Danesi, Marcel (2010). Semiotics of Media and Culture. In Paul Cobley (Ed.), *The Routledge Companion to Semiotics* (pp. 135–149). New York: Routledge.

15. Saussure, Ferdinand, de (1916). *Cours de linguistique générale*. Paris: Payot.

16. Matusitz, Jonathan (2007). Vexillology, or How Flags Speak. *International Journal of Applied Semiotics, 5*(1), 199–211.

17. Bonham, Matthew, Heradstveit, Daniel, Nakano, Michiko, & Sergeev, Victor (2007). *How We Talk about the "War on Terrorism": Comparative Research on Japan, Russia, and the United States*. Oslo: Norwegian Institute of International Affairs.

18. Bonham, Matthew, Heradstveit, Daniel, Nakano, Michiko, & Sergeev, Victor (2007). *How We Talk about the "War on Terrorism": Comparative Research on Japan, Russia, and the United States*. Oslo: Norwegian Institute of International Affairs.

19. Matusitz, Jonathan (2012). *Terrorism & Communication: A Critical Introduction*. Thousand Oaks, CA: Sage.

20. Laclau, Ernest (2007). *Emancipation(s)*. London: Verso.

21. Bonham, Matthew, Heradstveit, Daniel, Nakano, Michiko, & Sergeev, Victor (2007). *How We Talk about the "War on Terrorism": Comparative Research on Japan, Russia, and the United States*. Oslo: Norwegian Institute of International Affairs.

22. Steuter, Erin, & Wills, Deborah (2008). Infestation and Eradication: Political Cartoons and Exterminationist Rhetoric in the War on Terror. *Global Media Journal: Mediterranean Edition, 3*(1), 11–23.

23. Tuman, Joseph (2003). *Communicating Terror: The Rhetorical Dimensions of Terrorism*. Thousand Oaks, CA: Sage.

24. Goffman, Erving (1959). *The Presentation of Self in Everyday Life*. New York: Doubleday.

25. Chandler, Daniel (2001). *Semiotics: The Basics*. London: Routledge.

26. Fiske, John (1982). *Introduction to Communication*. London: Routledge.

27. Eco, Umberto (1976). *A Theory of Semiotics*. Bloomington: Indiana University Press.

28. Gaines, Elliot (2001). The Semiotic Analysis of Media Myth: A Proposal for an Applied Methodology. *The American Journal of Semiotics, 17*(2), 1–16.

29. Peirce, Charles Sanders (1958). *The Collected Papers of Charles Sanders Peirce*. Cambridge, MA: Harvard University Press.

30. Gaines, Elliot (2002). The Semiotics of Media Images from Independence Day & September 11th 2001. *The American Journal of Semiotics, 17*(3), 117–131.

31. Bamber, David (2001, November 11). Bin Laden: Yes, I Did It. *The Telegraph*, p. A1.

32. Chen, David (2002, March 3). For History or Tax Break, Claiming a Sept. 11 Icon. *The New York Times*, p. 35.

33. Peirce, Charles Sanders (1931). *Collected Papers*. Cambridge, MA: Harvard University Press.

34. Peirce, Charles Sanders (1931). *Collected Papers*. Cambridge, MA: Harvard University Press.

35. Deely, John (2010). Realism and Epistemology. In Paul Cobley (Ed.), *The Routledge Companion to Semiotics* (pp. 74–88). New York: Routledge.

36. Peirce, Charles Sanders (1958). *The Collected Papers of Charles Sanders Peirce*. Cambridge, MA: Harvard University Press.

37. Hall, Stuart (1997). *Cultural Representations and Signifying Practice*. London: Open University Press.

38. Silverman, Kaja (1983). *The Subject of Semiotics*. New York: Oxford University Press.

39. Peirce, Charles Sanders (1931). *Collected Papers*. Cambridge, MA: Harvard University Press.

40. Gaines, Elliot (2002). The Semiotics of Media Images from Independence Day & September 11th 2001. *The American Journal of Semiotics, 17*(3), 117–131.

41. Hoopes, James (1991). *Peirce on Signs*. Chapel Hill: University of North Carolina Press; and Short, T. L. (2009). *Peirce's Theory of Signs*. Cambridge: Cambridge University Press.

42. Hoffmeyer, Jesper (2010). Semiotics of Nature. In Paul Cobley (Ed.), *The Routledge Companion to Semiotics* (pp. 29–42). New York: Routledge.

43. Peirce, Charles Sanders (1958). *The Collected Papers of Charles Sanders Peirce*. Cambridge, MA: Harvard University Press.

44. San Juan, E. (2007). Signs, Meanings, Interpretation: C.S. Peirce's Critique of Deconstruction and Post-Structuralism. *Kritika Kultura, 8*, 57–79.

45. Gaines, Elliot (2002). The Semiotics of Media Images from Independence Day & September 11th 2001. *The American Journal of Semiotics, 17*(3), 117–131.

46. Cohen, Akiba, Adoni, Hanna, & Bantz, Charles (1990). *Social Conflict and Television News*. London: Sage.

47. Tuman, Joseph (2003). *Communicating Terror: The Rhetorical Dimensions of Terrorism*. Thousand Oaks, CA: Sage.

48. International Monetary Fund. (2001, December 18). World Economic Outlook: The Global Economy after September 11. Press release.

49. Skoll, Geoffrey (2007). Meanings of Terrorism. *International Journal for the Semiotics of Law, 20*, 107–127.

50. Lanigan, Richard (1997). Television: The Semiotic Phenomenology of Communication and the Image. In Winfried Nöth (Ed.), *Semiotics of the Media: State of the Art, Projects, and Perspectives* (pp. 381–391). New York: Mouton de Gruyter.

51. Newhagen, John, & Bucy, Erik (2003). Routes to Media Access. In Erik Bucy & John Newhagen (Eds.), *Media Access: Social and Psychological Dimensions of New Technology Use* (pp. 3–23). New York: Routledge.

52. San Juan, E. (2007). Signs, Meanings, Interpretation: C.S. Peirce's Critique of Deconstruction and Post-Structuralism. *Kritika Kultura, 8*, 57–79.

53. Harris, Lee (2004). *Civilization and Its Enemies: The Next Stage in History*. New York: Simon & Schuster.

54. Mesnard y Mendez, Pierre (2002). Access to an Identification of "Terrorism": Words and Actions. *Rethinking Marxism, 14*(2), 109–121.

55. Miller, Claude, Matusitz, Jonathan, O'Hair, Dan, & Eckstein, Jacqueline (2008). The Role of Communication and the Media in Terrorism. In Dan O'Hair, Robert Heath, Kevin Ayotte, & Gerald R. Ledlow (Eds.), *Terrorism: Communication and Rhetorical Perspectives* (pp. 43–66). Cresskill, NJ: Hampton Press.

56. Kappeler, Victor, & Potter, Gary (2005). *The Mythology of Crime and Criminal Justice* (4th ed.). Long Grove, IL: Waveland Press.

57. Baudrillard, Jean (2005). *The Intelligence of Evil or the Lucidity Pact*. New York: Berg.

58. Baudrillard, Jean (2010). *The Agony of Power*. Los Angeles: Semiotext(e).

59. Baudrillard, Jean (2003). *The Spirit of Terrorism and Other Essays*. New York: Verso.

60. Stamelman, Richard (2003). September 11: Between Memory and History. In Judith Greenberg (Ed.), *Trauma at Home: After 9/11* (pp. 11–20). Winnipeg, MB: Bison Books.

61. Gaines, Elliot (2002). The Semiotics of Media Images from Independence Day & September 11th 2001. *The American Journal of Semiotics, 17*(3), 117–131.

62. Skoll, Geoffrey (2007). Meanings of Terrorism. *International Journal for the Semiotics of Law, 20*, 107–127.

63. Peirce, Charles Sanders (1931). *Collected Papers*. Cambridge, MA: Harvard University Press.

64. Bundgaard, Peer, & Stjernfelt, Frederik (2010). Logic and Cognition. In Paul Cobley (Ed.), *The Routledge Companion to Semiotics* (pp. 57–73). New York: Routledge.

65. Peirce, Charles Sanders (1931). *Collected Papers*. Cambridge, MA: Harvard University Press.

66. Lotman, Yuri (2000). *Universe of the Mind: A Semiotic Theory of Culture*. New York: I. B. Tauris & Co.

67. Burks, Arthur (1949). Icon, Index, and Symbol. *Philosophy and Phenomenological Research, 9*(4), 673–689.

68. Bax, Marcel, van Heusden, Barend, & Wildgen, Wolfgang (2004). *Semiotic Evolution and the Dynamics of Culture*. Berne, Switzerland: Peter Lang.

69. Bundgaard, Peer, & Stjernfelt, Frederik (2010). Logic and Cognition. In Paul Cobley (Ed.), *The Routledge Companion to Semiotics* (pp. 57–73). New York: Routledge.

70. Hulswit, Menno (2002). *From Cause to Causation: A Peircean Perspective*. New York: Springer.

71. Burks, Arthur (1949). Icon, Index, and Symbol. *Philosophy and Phenomenological Research, 9*(4), 673–689.

72. Bundgaard, Peer, & Stjernfelt, Frederik (2010). Logic and Cognition. In Paul Cobley (Ed.), *The Routledge Companion to Semiotics* (pp. 57–73). New York: Routledge.

73. Lotman, Yuri (2000). *Universe of the Mind: A Semiotic Theory of Culture*. New York: I. B. Tauris & Co.

74. Klein, Aaron (2007). *Striking Back: The 1972 Munich Olympics Massacre and Israel's Deadly Response*. New York: Random House.

75. Park, Keith (1997). How Do Objects Become Objects of Reference? *British Journal of Special Education, 24*(3), 108–114.

76. Bar-Zohar, Michael Bar, & Haber, Eitan (2005). *Massacre in Munich: The Manhunt for the Killers behind the 1972 Olympics Massacre*. Guilford, CT: Lyons Press.

77. Reeve, Simon (2000). *One Day in September*. New York: Arcade Publishing.

78. Park, Keith (1997). How Do Objects Become Objects of Reference? *British Journal of Special Education, 24*(3), 108–114.

79. Large, David Clay (2012). *Munich 1972: Tragedy, Terror, and Triumph at the Olympic Games*. Lanham, MD: Rowman & Littlefield.

80. Reeve, Simon (2000). *One Day in September*. New York: Arcade Publishing.

81. Bates, Elizabeth (1976). *Language and Context: The Acquisition of Pragmatics*. London: Academic Press.

82. Cooley, John (1973). *Green March Black September: The Story of the Palestinian Arabs*. London: Frank Cass & Co.

83. Schmid, Alex P., & de Graaf, Janny (1982). *Violence as Communication: Insurgent Terrorism and the Western News Media*. Beverly Hills, CA: Sage.

84. Dobson, Christopher, & Paine, Ronald (1977). *The Carlos Complex: A Pattern of Violence*. London: Hodder and Stoughton.

85. Follain, John (1988). *Jackal: The Complete Story of the Legendary Terrorist Carlos the Jackal*. New York: Arcade Publishing; and Daugherty, William (2001). *In the Shadow of the Ayatollah: A CIA Hostage in Iran*. Annapolis, MD: U.S. Naval Institute Press.

86. Mesnard y Mendez, Pierre (2002). Access to an Identification of "Terrorism": Words and Actions. *Rethinking Marxism, 14*(2), 109–121.

Chapter Sixteen

Symbolic Terrorism in the Global Village

GLOBAL VILLAGE

Developed by Marshall McLuhan (1962),[1] a Canadian philosopher and media scholar, the **Global Village** describes the electronic interconnected world. Today, it is a metaphor for the internet in general. The internet globalizes communication by allowing users throughout the world to connect with each other. Electronic communication on the internet is called **computer-mediated communication** (**CMC**). As early as 1968, McLuhan already made us aware that, thanks to the Global Village, every terrorist group of the future will have a sophisticated—and hence skilled—terrorist fringe. McLuhan predicted that highly developed electronic media would diffuse terrorist propaganda around the world.[2] The Global Village theory also posits that media are extensions of people, which corroborates Peirce's contention that signs are extensions of sensory and cognitive processes (see chapter 15). In essence, signs are tools; they represent things that extend some sensory, bodily, or intellectual capacity. In the same way that an axe extends the power of a person's hand to cut wood and the wheel extends the power of the human foot to travel greater distances, media extend the ability of individuals to communicate with each other better—across the entire world—than they would through the voice or hands.[3]

New Media

The concept of **new media** refers to any technology or digital device that is interactive, networkable, dense, and generally easily usable. Other aspects of new media include user feedback, creative participation, and real-time creation of original, unregulated content. Examples of new media are the internet, websites, computer multimedia, video games, CDs, and DVDs.[4] In the context of terrorism, we will focus exclusively on the internet and websites. The internet is occasionally called "cyberspace." **Cyberspace** denotes the "virtual world" or the World Wide Web. The term "cyberspace" was mentioned for the first time in Gibson's (1984)[5] book entitled *Neuromancer*. Cyberspace combines textual interactions and virtual worlds for optimal global communication among human beings.

The internet allows for the establishment of smart communities. A **smart community** refers to people's ability to develop networked intelligence thanks to the internet, just a few mouse clicks away. The internet abrogates geometry; time and space do not matter much.[6] A similar term is the **Internet of Things** (**IoT**). Because the principal communication form on the internet is from human to human, the IoT is a mental picture in which the internet extends into our daily lives through a wireless network of distinct objects and symbols.[7] The IoT is essentially an arena that resembles the Wild West two centuries ago. The internet is an immense, mostly uncharted territory that has no clear borders. In that territory, all existing technologies can play a role, and ad hoc solutions are generally the norm. Control is limited.[8]

Blogosphere

A **blog** is a discussion website where entries are designed in diary style, and they are controlled and administered by its sole author (i.e., a blogger). Entries are posted in a reverse chronological order. Blogs can be linked to other blogs and refer to them in their posts, and bloggers (and other readers) can upload comments on each other's blogs.[9] Thanks to the freedom and ease of posts in blogs, this medium represents an ideal propaganda platform for terrorist organizations to advocate their ideologies and an operation platform through which they can plan attacks.[10] The **blogosphere** is the entire sphere of blogged discourse or social web.[11] The blogosphere is a massive network of all blogs and their interconnections.[12] In the blogosphere, blogs exist together as a collection of linked communities or as a social network in which daily bloggers can post their opinions. After the term was officially adopted in 2002, it has been mentioned in multiple media outlets and sometimes is even used to refer to the internet. The concept of the blogosphere brings to mind Habermas's (1989) public sphere.[13] As described in chapter 6, the public sphere alludes to the social "geography" of public communication—the domain of reason, argument, and discourse where public opinion appears. With respect to new media and the internet, the public sphere empowers mass media audiences that used to be passive by giving them the means to play a part in the global domain.

Convergence Theory

Convergence theory refers to the incorporation of technologies with cultural forms and evolutionary propensities.[14] The theory postulates that new media can reach much greater audiences. Introduced to the world in 1991, the internet is the logical result of this convergence model: all of the power of traditional media—which multimedia conglomerates were trying to influence or control—is now accessible via a global network. The multimedia industry that guaranteed the combination of all media into a cohesive, interactive experience now has a tremendously powerful tool to deliver this experience into households, schools, and businesses across the world.[15] As a result, the internet represents (1) a move from medium-specific content toward content that travels across numerous channels, (2) the growing interdependence of communication systems, and (3) various ways of accessing content.[16] In addition, advances in technology that unites people may diminish cultural diversity and increase value similarity. **Value similarity** among internet users enables clear communication about what normative behaviors and cognitive responses are expected of people. Therefore, Convergence Theory stresses the concern that new technology can cause people worldwide to speak, think, and behave in more similar ways.[17] It is no surprise, then, that the internet can bring terrorists closer together and reduce diversity among them.

NEW MEDIA–ORIENTED TERRORISM

New media–oriented terrorism is terrorism that has assumed digital, internet-based, and CMC forms thanks to the Global Village.[18] The internet has become a crucial tool for global terrorism. It can smooth the progress of global terrorism in several ways. It can provide the basis for organization, instructions, control, and communication among dispersed groups without much hierarchy or infrastructure. It allows smart communities of terrorists to emerge: it is a vehicle for intelligence gathering, giving access to a wide range of material on possible targets, from maps to architect drawings of high-rise buildings. One of the internet's most valuable usages is for propaganda, to communicate messages, pictures, and concepts that motivate would-be or current terrorists. Terrorists use websites, email, and chatrooms for fundraising by seeking donations from terrorist sympathizers and engaging in other illegal activities.[19] In early 2008, the number of international terrorist websites was reported to be about 7,000.[20] By June 2013, there were over 8,000 Islamic terrorist websites alone.[21]

Cyberspace: The Safest Communication Channel

Of all public communication channels used by terrorist groups, cyberspace is the safest for five major reasons. First, the unparalleled anonymity offered by the technology has allowed countless internet users to participate in terrorist subcultures without jeopardizing their own life or reputation by any means; cyberspace has reinforced extremism in terms of getting hold of larger audiences worldwide in an immediate and anonymous manner.[22] Hence, the internet is perfect for terrorists-as-communicators; it allows for asynchronous communication among activists, and between activists and sympathizers. It grants instant synchronicity and efficacy by safely communicating through encryption or password-protected means.[23] Second, as a universal system of interconnected networks, the internet is decentralized; it is usually not subjected to strict control or restriction; in many countries, there is little censorship; and it allows access to any user who needs it. The structure of present-day terrorist groups is making CMC more meaningful and useful for them.[24]

Third, any terrorist organization can use **Open Source Intelligence (OSI)** without being captured. Analogous to a smart community, OSI operates on the principle that, through the internet, any type of information can be easily accessed, used, or manipulated for any purpose.[25] Fourth, cyberspace enables terrorists to engage in linking. Very similar to the blogosphere, **linking** is the act of referring users from one website to another. Various extremist groups—extreme right, extreme left, radical Islam, anarchists, and Holocaust deniers—have built a linking system (among them) on the internet. Hamas websites often link to Holocaust deniers' websites (and vice versa). Extreme-right websites tend to link to various extreme Palestinian websites (e.g., by posting images of dead children or body parts, while nobody can find out where the images come from).[26] Fifth, cyberspace allows terrorists to launch online terrorism universities, which are virtual platforms where terrorists can learn to "construct weapons ranging from simple IEDs to nuclear, biological, and chemical weapons" (Weimann, 2006, p. 127).[27]

Symbolism on Terrorist Websites

Symbols on a typical terrorist website's homepage include weapons or other signs indicating the use of force. Hezbollah posts a symbol of a knife with dripping blood on one of its key websites, the Shining Path and the IRA show masked fighters flaunting weapons, the Kahane Lives site displays a raised fist, and the websites of the MRTA in Peru and the National Liberation Army in Colombia both display a rifle held aloft. Some of these symbols were designed before the advent of the internet; cyberspace has just made things more visible. The flags, emblems, or logos of terrorist organizations often appear on the sites' homepages. Parenthetically, some sites display the colors of the terrorist flags. The terrorist sites not only display text, but also rich graphic and visual elements. Indeed, since 2002, many terrorist sites have included other symbolic elements such as songs, speeches, and video clips. These are more frequent on non-English sites. Some of these websites even give visitors the option of downloading the terrorist flags, emblems, or logos. Although many sites do not display the full violent nature of the terrorist organizations (some of them even stress their purportedly peace-loving nature), this pacifist stance is not shown in their flags, emblems, or logos. [28]

Terrorist websites use multiple metaphors and symbols of victimization and empowerment to disseminate their message. These displays are able to arouse the emotions of sympathizers and potential sympathizers. In the jihadist vision represented on these websites, the West (particularly the United States) oppresses the ummah, and imagery is used to portray innocent Muslims as wounded or killed, homes as destroyed, and so on. As the websites express it clearly, the only response to these "barbarities" is terrorism. For this reason, there are images of AK-47s, knives, U.S. casualties, and the 9/11 terrorist attacks. Terrorists position themselves as the chosen defenders of pure Islam and the Arab cause. The symbolism is of the ummah that has been hijacked by the infidels (led by the United States), who only holy warriors can resist and overcome. The typical splash page for a terrorist website displays, in the upper-right corner, an F-15 or F-16 in the midst of an attack, and an Islamist leader (e.g., Osama bin Laden) holding an AK-47 and looking self-assuredly upward in response. [29]

Overall, symbolism on terrorist websites shows that an important channel that terrorist organizations use to convey their message is visual communication. Visual communication functions as a vehicle for moving individuals toward a desired behavior. In the context of terrorism, it plays a pivotal role in accomplishing a mission. An example that demonstrates the importance of visual communication in affecting behavior is a road sign (like a stop sign). The road sign not only informs the motorist what he or she should anticipate down the road, but also tells him or her how to behave in the given situation. [30]

E-JIHAD

E-jihad is the practice of using the internet to instruct jihadist recruits and current fighters on how to wage jihad. It does so by essentially spreading messages of jihadist violence. [31] E-jihad reflects the reality that the global jihadist movement has adapted to technological modernity, finding novel ways to keep the movement moving forward. In doing so, jihadist websites have created a virtual global community (see the "Jihadisphere" subsection). Numerous analysts agree that these websites are increasingly proliferating. In addition to offering Islamist guidelines and operational training, they also communicate a wide assortment of deeply emotional and powerful visual messages to prospective jihadist recruits and current fighters. E-jihad is intense in both content and form, affecting anyone exposed to it. [32] As recognized by Cetina (2005), [33] "The information transmitted between Al Qaeda participants is not only cognitive or symbolic in nature, but has strong sensory and motivating components" (p. 223).

Jihadisphere

A synonym for e-jihad is jihadisphere. **Jihadisphere** denotes an online community of warriors and supporters united by their common devotion to a global jihadist ideology. It is a virtual community in which users can share their thoughts and ideas without much trouble; therefore, it becomes an important vehicle for jihadist proselytization and radicalization. [34] In the mid-2000s, most jihadist websites were published in Arabic alone and, consequently, were not accessible to a large percentage of internet users. [35] Today, however, most jihadist websites are also publicized in English (in addition to the Arabic language and other languages). [36] Another term akin to both e-jihad and jihadisphere is neojihadism. **Neojihadism**, too, denotes the jihadist public sphere, which has become a favored sphere for both jihadist and Islamic fundamentalist propaganda and radicalization.[37] Neojihadism is defined as a universal religious, political, and terrorist movement, like "a subculture, a counterculture and an ideology that seeks to establish states governed by laws according to the dictates of selectively literal interpretations of the Qur'an and the traditions of the Prophet Muhammad, through enacting violence" (Lentini, 2008, p. 181).[38]

E-Jihadist Videos

The three-dimensional world of underground, face-to-face contacts is sometimes replaced with websites, chatrooms, and blogs loaded with thousands of videos from battlefield clips, as well as videos of Muslim massacres and suffering in Bosnia, Chechnya, and Iraq. Since 9/11, jihadists have been very successful in posting such videos online in order to amplify or broadcast their message. The beheading videos are an example of a broader, state-of-the-art new media campaign that grows on a daily basis. In the early 2000s, e-jihadist videos consisted of "last will and testament" footage of martyrs, recording their motivations and hallowing them as heroes. The videos were uploaded after the mission was over to boost credit and recruit more suicide volunteers.[39]

Within this discussion of e-jihadist videos is the exploitation of the internet to broadcast the performance of hostage executions in Iraq. One of the first victims of these executions was twenty-six-year-old Nick Berg. In this 2004 performance, the immediacy of vision was exposed on the internet by jihadists in a type of ritual. The video depicted five hooded jihadists standing behind Berg, who was sitting, wearing an orange jumpsuit (similar to the one worn at Guantánamo Bay), with his arms tied behind his back. After a statement was read aloud condemning abuses of Iraqis by U.S. troops at the Abu Ghraib prison, one of the men took out a knife and decapitated Nick Berg. Berg's head was sawed off and held aloft. The brutal method of Berg's beheading became the blueprint for future e-jihadist beheadings. Indeed, on September 21 and 22, 2004, U.S. hostages Eugene Armstrong and Jack Hensley were decapitated in the same manner, supposedly by al-Zarqawi's group. Another beheading video showed footage of the surveillance and actual abduction of the victim, followed by his imprisonment, interrogation, and eventual murder. This e-jihadist video became a "how-to" or documentary film.[40]

One could easily deduce that, through such ritualized forms of killing, the performative feature of e-jihadist videos turns the internet into a platform that can reestablish existential autonomy to jihadists.[41] When looking at the sacrificial aspects of these videos, the depth of both sacred and profane discourse in the statements, and the way the hostages' heads are severed and used, it is evident that these sacrificial rites are similar to those in other religions and throughout history.[42] E-jihadist videos are undoubtedly catching the attention of audiences worldwide. For example, in May 2004, "Nick Berg" was the second most popular search on Google after "American Idol."[43] The exposure to such "spectacle killings" is a clear objective of e-jihadists because they are well aware that, by June 2012, the world had already close to 2.5 billion internet users.[44]

E-Jihadist Imagery

E-jihadist imagery is efficient because it works like a magical type of panoptic power: it has the ability to both impress and terrify viewers.[45] For instance, jihadists are creating and spreading photos and songs to motivate anti-U.S. holy warriors. Posters or collages of photos extoll the virtues of Al Qaeda operations and incite anti-U.S. violence. The images are generally implanted within bulletin boards or stockpiled in digital archives, allowing them to be replicated and diffused quickly on the internet. The songs, called **anashids**, vary extensively in content and origin but usually consist of "sing-song tone" chants in conjunction with military sound effects. Anashids promote suicide operations by evoking early Islamic conquests or the pure stature of Islamic culture. Like photos, short audio segments are inserted (in threads) in bulletin boards, whereas high-quality ones constitute the audio background of multimedia productions like proselytizing and beheading videos.[46]

In terms of linguistic symbolism, a particularly large number of jihadist websites and blogs use Islamic motifs as their website addresses. In the aftermath of the September 11, 2001, attacks, many websites with the word "jihad" in them modified their names or addresses. Instead, "innocent" Islamic names were used in different variations as their new addresses to avoid being taken down, hacked, or cracked by local or federal authorities. Figures of speech and key words are also used to "trap" supporters and potential recruits because such linguistic symbolism provides the necessary seduction through online **dawa** (i.e., Islamic call, propagation, and proselytizing). As one can see, e-jihadist marketing techniques are comparable to those used by commercial businesses.[47]

THREE STAGES OF E-JIHAD INDOCTRINATION

E-jihad can successfully attract new jihadist recruits and indoctrinate them when it follows a three-step online radicalization process. The three stages were laid out in detail by Fighel (2007),[48] in his book chapter entitled "Radical Islamic Internet Propaganda: Concepts, Idioms and Visual Motifs." In the first stage of e-jihad indoctrination, well-known and conventional Muslim idioms and key words ("buzz" words) are employed to subtly indoctrinate potential recruits. They appear on website addresses, and they link to information hubs where original Islamist texts, speeches, claims of responsibility, video clips, and recordings are uploaded. Although some idioms and key words appear to be legitimate and inoffensive, they can carry a subtle message and double meaning based on the interpretation of radical Islamic viewpoints. An adequate scholarly and expert understanding of Islamic culture and religion can help explain how particularly explicit idioms and key words are used to communicate a hidden agenda.[49]

When entering a website for the first time, the first thirty seconds are the most important for the viewer to decide whether the site is worthwhile. To captivate the viewer, those idioms and key words are fashioned as visual motifs (in addition to the name of the website address) in order to send a positive signal about the site's content. The Islamic phrases listed below exemplify how website addresses can be used for messaging, columns, scholarly dialogue, claims of responsibility for violent assaults, and warnings of future attacks. These Islamic phrases include *Al-Walaa wal-baraa* (i.e., absolute allegiance to the ummah and total rejection of non-Muslims), *Alneda* (i.e., "The Call," referring to the calling for the true and genuine believers to become true Muslims), *Bilad al-Haramain* (i.e., "The Land of the Two Shrines," referring to Mecca and Medina), *dawa* (i.e., proselytizing), *Janna* (i.e., "Garden," alluding to Paradise), and *Ribat/Ard al-Ribat* (i.e., "The Land of the Frontier Post"). All these websites are exploited as recognized and legitimate Islamic symbols and as a platform for fashioning a radicalized interpretation by Islamists.[50]

The second stage of e-jihad indoctrination involves a rapid visual screening process in which the eyes examine additional jihadist motifs on the first or main page of the site. Some of the central elements are jihadist visual motifs and calligraphy shapes that can easily charm and bewitch users, leading them to believe that this is finally the website that they were looking for. To enhance the captivating process, some sites play audio recordings of Islamist songs or Qur'anic verses as viewers read the content.[51] More sophisticated visual motifs are cleverly designed to accomplish the usual goals of jihadist propagandists. For example, they create jihadist mental concepts or frame reality for their audiences. Using Islamic symbols and images can easily bring back emotional or historical collective memories, thus creating a subconscious emotional response. It is almost like subliminal communication; these motifs produce feelings of profound beliefs or suppressed, obscure concepts within the target audience as a way to convey ideas.[52]

The third stage of e-jihad indoctrination consists of validating jihadist websites as "authentic" Muslim websites (e.g., by using the Hijra-based lunar calendar and dates). The "authentic" Muslim blogs and websites avoid posting dates of the Gregorian calendar, as it is identified with Western civilization. Judiciously selected Islamic scriptures, words, and motifs, including imagery, provide interactive ways for jihad aficionados to be increasingly involved with the global movement. The notion of **resonance**, the phenomenon whereby a message fits an audience's existing perceptions,[53] is the likely result of this dialectical process. The motifs used in most jihadist websites are rooted in mainstream Sunni Muslim tradition and history, as well as cultural references of the ummah in general. A specific timeline describing the successful spread of Islam from the seventh to tenth centuries tends to emerge within these motifs. These motifs, idioms, and calligraphy mirror the aspiration to portray the nature of pure, "authentic" Islam by radical schools of thought. Mullahs (Islamic scholars) interpret this as a logical improvement of traditional Muslim theology.[54]

One can also notice the "authentication" technique through the exploitation of the sword as a symbol for the diffusion of Islam and its association with "Din Muhammad Bil-Saif"—that is, the spread of Muhammad's religion by the sword (i.e., jihad). Another element identified in most jihadist and radical Muslim websites is the specific shape of the Arabic scripts used. Most Arabic scripts seen on these websites are shaped in ancient design methods; they become ingenious symbols for the return to Salafism and pure Islam (and, by the same token, a rejection of modernity). Banners are also designed in old Arabic calligraphy and style as opposed to modern regular Arabic fonts. The main commonality of all these Arabic scripts can be traced back to Islam's Golden Age, an age that radical Islam in general and Al Qaeda in particular want to see again in order to restore both Islam's magnificence and the caliphate.[55]

YOUTUBE EFFECT

YouTube is a free video-sharing website that was created in February 2005. By January 2012, the site was already serving four billion views a day.[56] Coined by Naím (2007),[57] the **YouTube effect** is "the phenomenon whereby video clips, often produced by individuals acting on their own, are rapidly transmitted throughout the world thanks to video-sharing Web sites such as YouTube, Google Video, and others" (p. 104). Any user can log on to YouTube at any time and any place worldwide. The user can upload and download videos to share information (e.g., his or her "side of the truth") with a local community, his or her diaspora, or even the rest of the world.[58] YouTube, then, is pluricentrist; it allows users to express their views by uploading videos in various languages and, hence, reach out to millions of people. Once disseminated on YouTube, a video clip can be copied and saved in other locations, like websites, desktops, or memory sticks, and can then be reposted online with very few restrictions.[59]

YouTube offers a new platform for propaganda diffusion and radicalization, with the luxury of little control or censorship. With YouTube, there is a high guarantee of immediate visibility and diffusion; even short videos can be sufficiently long for effective exposure.[60] YouTube is truly a safe vehicle for the diffusion of extremist ideas. As opposed to traditional media channels like books, newspapers, or DVDs, the video-sharing website is much more able to reach millions of people. For terrorist organizations and their backers, the platform also gives them a chance to not only publicize their cause but also develop their legitimacy and credibility outside their immediate sphere of influence. This, in turn, may contribute to the radicalization of people within remote regions, especially youths, and attract outside support toward particular struggles (as illustrated by the comments posted by YouTube viewers). The YouTube effect provides an additional dimension to three-dimensional conflicts. Moving from the physical domain into the virtual one, terrorism has become a new battlefield in which a war of emotions and ideas is pursued, giving rise to unprecedented opportunities for propaganda and radicalization.[61]

Through the YouTube effect, and in parallel with globalization, the internet, the advent of top-notch communication technologies, and rapid territorial mobility, a certain number of e-jihad warriors have brought their neojihadist terror to the virtual world.[62] Many e-jihad warriors belong to the **Millennial Generation** (or **Millennials**), a generation greatly influenced by high-tech telecommunications like mobile phones, the internet, and computer networks. Social networking sites like Facebook and YouTube are now the main sources of information for the Millennials. It should come as no surprise that mobile phones are used by terrorist youths to explode bombs or record beheadings of Thai Buddhists so they can post such videos on YouTube.[63] In his examination of visual motifs in jihadist YouTube videos, Weisburd (2009)[64] found that the high degree of violence in jihadist videos impacts teenagers who, in turn, are more likely to use extreme violence (in comparison with their peers who are not exposed to such jihadist videos). This finding is also shared by Ilardi (2009),[65] who contends that internet-based propagandist material gives potential jihadists valid reasons and motives to take extreme actions. They do so by applying what they learn (in the virtual world) to the real world.

VIRTUAL CALIPHATE

The **virtual caliphate** refers to the idea of a global Islamic state diffused through the internet. Already in the 1990s, Osama bin Laden realized that the internet was a great opportunity for international terrorists to not only keep in contact with one another but also develop a grand plan to take over the world. The virtual caliphate consists of thousands of interconnected computers, chatrooms, and servers held together for a common goal. Numerous e-jihadists rely on cutting-edge technology to plan terrorist attacks and share templates for the caliphate. Al Qaeda has likely managed to design a virtual version of its former base in Afghanistan. Likewise, U.S. jihadists have launched a magazine titled *Islamic Revival* and made it available for download. The magazine is devoted to the restoration of the caliphate and the overturn of democratic governments (and their constitutions). *Islamic Revival* laments the fact that the caliphate's rebirth does not preoccupy the average Muslim's mind.[66]

On January 1, 2007, an important headway was made when one of Al Qaeda's internet public relations front, the Global Islamic Media Front (GIMF), developed an encryption program called Mujahideen Secrets. The Mujahideen Secrets program represented a milestone in the virtual caliphate's evolution; it allows methods like terrorist attack plots, weapons assembly, and recruitment to happen in a virtual environment that is even more unobstructed. Radical clerics also spread the message (to followers) about Mujahideen Secrets, insisting that they get the program and use it to continue the holy struggle. The overall mission remains identical: to convert all Muslims and non-Muslims alike to radical Islam. To this point, Al Qaeda has asked followers to enter the Western blogosphere so they can present the truth credibly through visual or oral claims.[67]

Case Study I: Inspire

Inspire is a good illustration of the virtual caliphate. ***Inspire*** is an English-language online magazine published by Al Qaeda and aimed at British and U.S. readers. The first issue appeared in July 2010. The principal objective of *Inspire* is to diffuse Islamist propaganda to the West so that the caliphate will be ultimately restored. The magazine seems like an effective way for Al Qaeda to exploit the internet in order to reach audiences outside the Middle East. The magazine is also an ideological instrument to target the United States and other Western governments, with the purpose of stimulating homegrown terrorism. *Inspire* is almost like an Al Qaeda brand; it can enhance awareness, increase the number of recruits, generate funds, and even raise terror.[68] The magazine offers instructions such as how to "Make a Bomb in the Kitchen of Your Mom" and communiqués from past and current leaders like Osama bin Laden. Various articles call for terrorist attacks on U.S. soil, recommending that readers open fire at a Washington, DC, restaurant or drive a pickup truck to "mow down" people on the street.[69]

According to U.S. authorities, Samir Khan, a U.S. blogger who migrated to Yemen and joined forces with Al Qaeda, was a key author for the magazine. The October 2010 issue includes one of his articles; it is entitled "I Am Proud to Be a Traitor to America."[70] In September 2011, he was killed in a drone strike in Yemen, along with Anwar al-Awlaki.[71] **Anwar al-Awlaki** was a U.S.-born Yemeni imam. Involved in the coordination of terrorist attacks for Al Qaeda and notorious for posting videos of his anti-Western sermons, he was considered the "bin Laden of the Internet."[72] According to U.S. government officials, al-Awlaki used *Inspire* to issue death threats against various individuals. In addition, the two **Tsarnaev brothers**, responsible for the Boston Marathon bombings in 2013, said they were inspired by al-Awlaki.[73]

In terms of symbolism, on the upper-left corner of the main page, *Inspire* features the logo of the al-Malahim media foundation, Al Qaeda's media branch. The main image on the front cover depicts an armed jihadist bowing (to Allah) in front of what looks like a map or a globe. In addition, its title comes from a verse in the Qur'an, "Inspire the believers to fight" (Qur'an 8:65). The effects of that verse have been deeply felt. Indeed, *Inspire* has called for attacks on athletic and iconic events in the United States. The April 15, 2013, terrorist attack at the Boston Marathon symbolized both, and it was perpetrated on Patriot's Day (a state holiday in Massachusetts). Most *Inspire* articles describe the expectations of jihad. The arguments presented cite the complications of faceoffs with U.S. forces and the problems of traveling overseas to wage jihad. Therefore, the solution for true, devout Muslims is individual, obligatory jihad to attack the enemy, especially when the Islamic nation is strategically frail.[74]

Case Study II: Jihad Cosmo

Another good illustration of the virtual caliphate is *Jihad Cosmo*. **Jihad Cosmo** is Al Qaeda's women's magazine—written in Arabic—that combines beauty and fashion guidelines with advice on suicide bombings.[75] According to the issue's editorial, the purpose of the magazine is to educate women and include them in the war against infidels and those who oppose the reestablishment of the caliphate. Complete interviews with martyrs' wives are transcribed; these interviews commend their husbands' decisions to sacrifice their lives in suicide missions. Umm Muhanad, a female interviewee, even praised her husband for his bravery after his suicide attack in Afghanistan.[76] *Jihad Cosmo* reads much like undistinguished women's magazines with a jihadist twist: how to meet one's future mujahedin husband, how to raise one's children for jihad, and beauty tips for the modern jihadist lady. In regard to the latter, additional advice includes staying indoors to maintain a clear complexion and going out of the house only when strictly necessary. The magazine places particular emphasis on the perks of martyrdom: how to attain full security and happiness by sacrificing one's life for the cause.[77]

In terms of symbolism, *Jihad Cosmo*'s Arabic name is Al-Shamikha, the alternative to *Cosmopolitan* magazine. Al-Shamikha means "The Majestic Woman."[78] The lustrous magazine's front cover features the barrel of a submachine gun next to the image of a veiled woman.[79] The imagery on the main page suggests that female jihadists have been called to wage defensive jihad rather than offensive jihad (although a certain number of women have been suicide bombers). As described in chapter 9, defensive jihad means retribution for injustices, usually in a Muslim country that has been occupied by infidels. Defensive jihad is reserved for Muslims who have been called to rise in defense of families, justice, and the ummah. Thus, it is a communally binding Islamic principle that symbolizes the necessity of armed resistance in the face of perceived aggression.[80] By extension, by publishing an online jihadist magazine catering to female audiences, Al Qaeda is clearly trying to accomplish its dream of the caliphate. As a reminder, female readers are urged to raise children to be mujahedin ready for holy war.

SIKH SEPARATISTS' WEBSITES

In the context of terrorism in India, Sikh separatists have created a very large number of websites that symbolize the Sikh's religious, cultural, and political views. Many useful websites have to do with Sikh issues, particularly political websites and those emphasizing the violation of human rights in the Punjab province. Most Sikh websites seek to promote their ideal sovereign state of Khalistan, meaning "Land of the Pure" (see chapter 8).[81] Sikh separatists' websites emerged immediately after the large Sikh movement in Punjab was overpowered by Indian authorities in 1994. Unlike the three-dimensional situation in Punjab, the dream of an independent Khalistan in cyberspace has been well articulated—although its character is gradually shifting.[82] A concrete example of a website symbolizing the demand for Khalistan is the website of the Council of Khalistan (CoK; http://www.khalistan.net). The CoK organization has been the most successful within the Sikh diaspora and those championing the Khalistan movement. It was founded by Dr. Aulakh Singh in Washington, DC, in 1987. The objective was to campaign for an independent Khalistan. Today's website representation of the CoK is mostly text oriented.[83] Most content is devoted to news about CoK activities (and the documentation of such activities) on its main page; there is also a page with contact information.[84]

Symbolically speaking, the graphic illustration of the earlier version of the CoK website used the long-established Sikh colors of saffron, blue, and white; it also portrayed the scene of the Golden Temple in Amritsar with the Sikh symbol of the Khanda (see chapter 8 for more information).[85] Unlike its previous version, the current version of the CoK website includes other symbols, such the hawk (Khalistan's national bird). Nevertheless, it still includes traditional Sikh colors, like saffron. A similar evolution in the symbolism of these websites can be seen on other Sikh websites, too. It illustrates the change in the Sikh method to advocate its goals. An example is the website of the Dal Khalsa organization (http://www.dalkhalsa.com). In contrast to its earlier version, the current website's main features are sporadic news about

Sikh political and religious issues, some of which come directly from scanned articles from traditional media coverage. Like the CoK website, the hawk is represented as well (but, here, it is done twice). The homepage also contains links to archives, the Sikh constitution of Dal Khalsa, and the "Directory of Martyrs" of 1984. The particular orientation toward the Sikh martyrs and the fact that the constitution of Dal Khalsa does not even include the name "Khalistan" supports the claim that the Sikh separatists' strategy has evolved. [86]

EXTREME-RIGHT GROUPS IN CYBERSPACE

In Europe, hundreds of websites created and administered by extreme-right groups like neo-Nazi and skinhead organizations have been found. European institutions have increasingly shown their concerns about this rising phenomenon. In Italy alone, over 150 extreme-right websites awash with Nazi and Fascist propaganda have been identified. In Spain, approximately ninety extreme-right groups have their own websites. [87] Research indicates that extreme-right groups exploit the internet for several reasons. For example, based on research by Glaser, Dixit, and Green (2002), [88] the internet is used for diffusing propaganda and stimulating violence. In this regard, the traditional tools for propagating ideological "meetings of the minds" are enhanced through the internet. In addition, when looking at U.S. extreme-right organizations, Zhou, Reid, Qin, Chen, and Lai (2005) discovered that such organizations use the internet to expedite recruitment, reach a global audience, and develop relationships with other groups.

Research on revolutionary movements stresses the overall ability of the internet to spawn collective identities. Part of the reason is that the internet can affect the enablement of exchange of resources and information. It can also foster solidarity and share objectives. By extension, research on violent radicalization indicates that isolated individuals can develop a common identity thanks to extreme-right websites, persuading themselves that they are not alone (i.e., that they instead belong to a community, even if it is a "virtual" one). As revolutionary movement scholars have also stressed, the internet can play a large role in facilitating the process of mobilization by decreasing the cost of communication between many individuals and alleviating the difficulties of coordinating transnational or global demonstrations. [89]

In regard to Italian extreme-right organizations in particular, data indicate that they rely heavily on their websites for an important aspect of ideological propaganda, namely, the collection and diffusion of information: texts (i.e., excerpts or even entire texts can be downloaded) of masterworks of the extreme-right literature (e.g., "The Protocols of the Elders of Zion"), works by Fascist or neo-Fascist scholars (e.g., Julius Evola), and information on a variety of current and past social and political issues. Examples of the latter are documents on bioethics, abortion, the Freemasons, and the Italian Social Republic (also known as the Salò Republic). The Salò Republic was the puppet regime established by Mussolini in 1943 after a ceasefire was signed between Italy and the Anglo-American forces. Other documents pertain to philosophy, religion, and spirituality (e.g., books on or by Carl Jung, Confucius, the Buddha, etc.); biographies (e.g., of Mussolini and Hitler); accounts on the Nazi or Fascist period; and political declarations of extreme-right organizations. [90]

KAMIKAZE CYBERPUNK

Kamikaze cyberpunk has the objective of appropriating past suicide or terrorist incidents (along with symbols and artifacts related to these incidents) and reliving them in a new but different way. More particularly, kamikaze cyberpunk involves recycling old suicidal or terroristic behaviors and expressing them through wall murals or on the internet in order to answer a specific (global) call or create a new movement. "Recycling" here also involves recycling of technology, weapons, and objects. The purpose is to change their functional nature for suicidal or terroristic purposes. Just as it was for the punk movement in the 1970s and 1980s, terrorists use and modify the products and technologies made by the establishment itself. In cultural studies, kamikaze cyberpunk is an example of bricolage (see chapter 5). In *The Savage Mind*, Lévi-Strauss (1966)[91] employed the term "bricolage" to denote patterns of mythological thinking. It is the process of constructing a new social identity by appropriating objects and symbols from other heritages and cultures. Bricolage is reflected in the appropriation of key elements in Islam as a tool for supporting war against the establishment. The use of technology for raising awareness, endorsing a project, or recruiting volunteers for a cause is handled by bricoleurs. The savage mind exploits rituals by reshaping old symbols and reusing cultural artifacts.[92]

Internet images illustrate how graphic communication can be used as a vehicle of suppression, operation, and even liberation. Such images can be used to symbolize social and political issues. They function as social commentaries and embody the dominant ideologies to preserve the status quo.[93] The introduction of the internet has symbolized the ubiquity of overloaded signs and symbols that can be used as terrorist weapons. Any private internet user can be a bricoleur. When it becomes an army of bricoleurs, technologies, aesthetic codes, and advertising tactics can be used against the enemy itself. What the terrorist and cyberpunk share in common is the perception of an inflexible establishment, namely, the Western establishment. For this reason, appropriation and bricolage are good methods with which to communicate their agendas.[94] One graffiti artist appropriated elements of the Nike logo (and tagline—i.e., "Just Do It") and meshed these elements with images of the planes crashing into the Twin Towers.[95] In brief, the graffiti artist—whose "art" was uploaded online by multiple terrorist groups—is making a powerful ideological statement: the "Just Do It" tagline sends the message that smashing jetliners into high-rise buildings becomes second nature, in the same way that Japanese kamikaze pilots directed their planes on U.S. aircraft carriers during World War II. Hence, kamikaze cyberpunk here illustrates that kamikaze martyrdom should be the duty of every jihadist against the West.

The specific technique of kamikaze cyberpunk is called subvertising. A combination of "subversion" and "advertising," **subvertising** consists of transforming the marketing message of a brand into a vehicle for a different message.[96] Aware of the immense recognition received by well-known international brands, terrorist groups have resorted to bricolage so as to reach out to larger audiences for propaganda purposes. In this case study, the Nike symbol is subverted into a terrorist slogan. The objective, of course, is to advertise global jihadist ideology. By hijacking famous brands and turning them into propaganda vehicles, terrorist movements are able to benefit from the massive popularity of, and the millions of dollars poured into, brand recognition. Subversion can be very powerful and, in this particular case, radical. Terrorists took a U.S. brand and turned it against its own country of origin. One of the central purposes of subvertising is to capture the attention of the viewer by juxtaposing easily recognizable images in order to create shocking and disturbingly frank realities.[97]

SUMMARY

The Global Village describes the electronic interconnected world. Today, it is a metaphor for the internet in general. The internet is occasionally called "cyberspace." Cyberspace denotes the "virtual world" or the World Wide Web. In addition, the internet allows for the establishment of smart communities. A "smart community" refers to people's ability to develop networked intelligence thanks to the internet, just a few mouse clicks away. A similar term is the Internet of Things (IoT). A particular form of smart community, the blog represents an ideal propaganda platform for terrorist organizations to advocate their ideologies and an operation platform for planning attacks. The blogosphere is a massive network of all blogs and their interconnections. New media–oriented terrorism is terrorism that has assumed digital, internet-based, and CMC forms thanks to the Global Village. As we have seen, of all public communication channels used by terrorist groups, cyberspace is the safest for five major reasons. A specific form of new media–oriented terrorism is e-jihad. E-jihad is the practice of using the internet to instruct jihadist recruits and current fighters on how to wage jihad. A synonym for e-jihad is jihadisphere, an online community of warriors and supporters united by their common devotion to a global jihadist ideology. Another synonym is neojihadism, which, too, denotes the jihadist public sphere. E-jihad can successfully attract new jihadist recruits and indoctrinate them when it follows a three-step online radicalization process. In the first stage of e-jihad indoctrination, well-known and conventional Muslim idioms and key words ("buzz" words) are employed to subtly indoctrinate potential recruits. The second stage involves a rapid visual-screening process in which the eyes examine additional jihadist motifs on the first or main page of the site. Some of the central elements are jihadist visual motifs and calligraphy shapes that can easily charm and bewitch users. The third stage consists of validating jihadist websites as "authentic" Muslim websites (e.g., by using the Hijra-based lunar calendar and dates). The YouTube effect is the phenomenon whereby video clips can be rapidly diffused throughout the world. YouTube, then, has become a new platform for propaganda diffusion and radicalization, with the luxury of little control or censorship. The virtual caliphate refers to the idea of a global Islamic state diffused through the internet. Two examples of this are the Al Qaeda magazines called *Inspire* and *Jihad Cosmo*. The first one is an English language online magazine aimed at British and U.S. readers. The second one is a women's magazine written in Arabic. Outside the world of Islamism, the internet has been extensively used by terrorist groups as well. For example, in the context of terrorism in India, Sikh separatists have created a very large number of websites that symbolize the Sikh's religious, cultural, and political views. As such, the websites of the Council of Khalistan (CoK) and the Dal Khalsa organization cater to the Sikh diaspora to advocate the sovereign state of Khalistan. Likewise, hundreds of websites created and administered by extreme-right groups like neo-Nazi and skinhead organizations have been found, particularly in European countries like Italy and Spain. Finally, kamikaze cyberpunk has the objective of appropriating past suicide or terrorist incidents (along with symbols and artifacts related to these incidents) and reliving them in a new but different way. In the case study, terrorists took a U.S. brand (Nike) and turned it against its own country of origin. Namely, the "Just Do It" tagline sends the message that smashing jetliners into high-rise buildings is good, and it illustrates the belief that kamikaze martyrdom should be the duty of every jihadist against the West.

NOTES

1. McLuhan, Marshall (1962). *The Gutenberg Galaxy: The Making of Typographic Man*. Toronto: University of Toronto Press.
2. McLuhan, Marshall, & Fiore, Quentin (1968). *War and Peace in the Global Village*. Corte Madera, CA: Gingko Press.
3. Danesi, Marcel (2010). Semiotics of Media and Culture. In Paul Cobley (Ed.), *The Routledge Companion to Semiotics* (pp. 135–149). New York: Routledge.
4. Levinson, Paul (2012). *New New Media*. London: Pearson.
5. Gibson, William (1984). *Neuromancer*. New York: Ace.

6. Ning, Huansheng (2013). *Unit and Ubiquitous Internet of Things*. New York: CRC Press.

7. Dey, Anind (2001). Understanding and Using Context. *Personal and Ubiquitous Computing Journal, 5*(1), 4–7.

8. Zorzi, Michele, Gluhak, Alexander, Lange, Sebastian, & Bassi, Alessandro (2010). From Today's INTRAnet of Things to a Future INTERnet of Things: A Wireless- and Mobility-Related View. *Wireless Communications, IEEE, 17*(6), 44–51.

9. Barlow, Aaron (2007). *The Rise of the Blogosphere*. Westport, CT: Praeger.

10. Yang, Christopher, & Ng, Tobun (2007). Terrorism and Crime Related Weblog Social Network: Link, Content Analysis and Information Visualization. *Intelligence and Security Informatics, 7*, 55–58.

11. Biamino, Giulia (2012). A Semantic Model for Socially Aware Objects. *Advances in Internet of Things, 2*, 47–55.

12. Nasr, Amir Ahmad (2013). *My Isl@m: How Fundamentalism Stole My Mind—and Doubt Freed My Soul*. New York: St. Martin's Press.

13. Habermas, Jürgen (1989). *Structural Transformation of the Public Sphere*. Cambridge, MA: MIT Press.

14. Negroponte, Nicholas (1995). *Being Digital*. New York: Alfred A. Knopf.

15. Hilf, Bill (1998). Media Lullabies: The Reinvention of the World Wide Web. *First Monday, 3*(4), 10–21.

16. Jenkins, Henry (2006). *Convergence Culture*. New York: New York University Press.

17. Fisher, Cynthia, & Gitelson, Richard (1983). A Meta-Analysis of the Correlates of Role Conflict and Ambiguity. *Journal of Applied Psychology, 68*, 320–333.

18. Martin, Gus (2010). *Understanding Terrorism: Challenges, Perspectives, and Issues*. Thousand Oaks, CA: Sage.

19. Lewis, James (2005). The Internet and Terrorism. *Proceedings of the Annual Meeting, 99*, 112–115.

20. Hoffman, Bruce (2007). Countering Terrorist Use of the Web as a Weapon. *CTC Sentinel, 1*(1), 4–6.

21. Al Shahri, Mansour (2013, June 4). 8,000 Terror Websites in Kingdom Crosshairs. *Arab News*, p. A1.

22. Torres Soriano, Manuel (2012). The Vulnerabilities of Online Terrorism. *Studies in Conflict & Terrorism, 35*(4), 263–277.

23. Biamino, Giulia (2012). A Semantic Model for Socially Aware Objects. *Advances in Internet of Things, 2*, 47–55.

24. Matusitz, Jonathan (2012). *Terrorism & Communication: A Critical Introduction*. Thousand Oaks, CA: Sage.

25. Hacohen, Eli (2010). Digital Hate: Terror, Anti-Semitism and Racism on the Internet. In Hans-Liudger Dienel, Yair Sharan, Christian Rapp, & Niv Ahituv (Eds.), *Terrorism and the Internet: Threats—Target Groups—Deradicalisation Strategies* (pp. 3–6). Landsdale, PA: IOS Press.

26. Hacohen, Eli (2010). Digital Hate: Terror, Anti-Semitism and Racism on the Internet. In Hans-Liudger Dienel, Yair Sharan, Christian Rapp, & Niv Ahituv (Eds.), *Terrorism and the Internet: Threats—Target Groups—Deradicalisation Strategies* (pp. 3–6). Landsdale, PA: IOS Press.

27. Weimann, Gabriel (2006). *Terror on the Internet: The New Arena, the New Challenges*. Washington, DC: U.S. Institute of Peace.

28. Tsfati, Yariv, & Weimann, Gabriel (2002). www.terrorism.com: Terror on the Internet. *Studies in Conflict & Terrorism, 25*(5), 317–332.

29. Lewis, James (2005). The Internet and Terrorism. *Proceedings of the Annual Meeting, 99*, 112–115.

30. Tattarini, Mirko (2007). Kamikaze Cyberpunk: Threats and Alternatives in the Age of Viral Power. In Boaz Ganor, Katharina Von Knop, & Carlos Duarte (Eds.), *Hypermedia Seduction for Terrorist Recruiting* (pp. 188–198). Amsterdam: NATO Science for Peace and Security Series.

31. Blunt, Gary (2003). *Blunt, Islam in the Digital Age: E-Jihad, Online Fatwas and Cyber Islamic Environments*. London: Pluto Press.

32. Ranstorp, Magnus (2007). The Virtual Sanctuary of Al-Qaeda and Terrorism in an Age of Globalisation. In Johan Eriksson & Giampiero Giacomello (Eds.), *International Relations and Security in the Digital Age* (pp. 31–56). London: Routledge.

33. Cetina, Karin Knorr (2005). Complex Global Microstructures: The New Terrorist Societies. *Theory, Culture & Society, 22*(5), 223–224.

34. Ducol, Benjamin (2012). Uncovering the French-Speaking Jihadisphere: An Exploratory Analysis. *Media, War & Conflict, 5*(1) 51–70.

35. Awan, Akil (2007) Radicalization on the Internet? The Virtual Propagation of Jihadist Media and Its Effects. *RUSI Journal, 152*(3), 76–81.

36. Ducol, Benjamin (2012). Uncovering the French-Speaking Jihadisphere: An Exploratory Analysis. *Media, War & Conflict, 5*(1) 51–70.

37. Andre, Virgine (2012). "Neojihadism" and YouTube: Patani Militant Propaganda Dissemination and Radicalization. *Asian Security, 8*(1), 27–53

38. Lentini, Pete (2008). *Antipodal Terrorists?* In Richard Devetak & Christopher Hughes (Eds.), *The Globalisation of Political Violence: Globalisation's Shadow* (pp. 181–202). London: Routledge.

39. Foreign Broadcast Information Service (2004, March 3). *Terrorism: Computer Art Productions Encourage Anti-US Mujahidin*. Rosslyn, VA: Foreign Broadcast Information Service.

40. Saniotis, Arthur (2005). Re-Enchanting Terrorism: Jihadists as "Liminal Beings." *Studies in Conflict & Terrorism, 28*, 533–545.

41. Shahzad, Syed Saleem (2003, May 15). The New Face of Terror Unveiled. *Asia Times Online*.

42. Saniotis, Arthur (2005). Re-Enchanting Terrorism: Jihadists as "Liminal Beings." *Studies in Conflict & Terrorism, 28*, 533–545.

43. Moeller, Susan (2009). *Packaging Terrorism: Co-Opting the News for Politics and Profit*. New York: Wiley-Blackwell.

44. Internet World Stats (2012, June 30). *Internet Usage Statistics*. Retrieved June 9, 2013, from http://www.internetworldstats.com/stats.htm

45. Saniotis, Arthur (2005). Re-Enchanting Terrorism: Jihadists as "Liminal Beings." *Studies in Conflict & Terrorism, 28*, 533–545.

46. Foreign Broadcast Information Service (2004, December 21). *Terrorism: Militants Use Music to Spread Ideology, Encourage Violence*. Rosslyn, VA: Foreign Broadcast Information Service.

47. Fighel, Jonathan (2007). Radical Islamic Internet Propaganda: Concepts, Idioms and Visual Motifs. In Boaz Ganor, Katharina Von Knop, & Carlos A. M. Duarte (Eds.), *Hypermedia Seduction for Terrorist Recruiting* (pp. 34–38). Amsterdam: IOS Press.

48. Fighel, Jonathan (2007). Radical Islamic Internet Propaganda: Concepts, Idioms and Visual Motifs. In Boaz Ganor, Katharina Von Knop, & Carlos A. M. Duarte (Eds.), *Hypermedia Seduction for Terrorist Recruiting* (pp. 34–38). Amsterdam: IOS Press.

49. Rogan, Hanna (2007). Abu Reuter and the E-Jihad Virtual Battlefronts from Iraq to the Horn of Africa. *Georgetown Journal of International Affairs, 8*(2), 89–96.

50. Fighel, Jonathan (2007). Radical Islamic Internet Propaganda: Concepts, Idioms and Visual Motifs. In Boaz Ganor, Katharina Von Knop, & Carlos A. M. Duarte (Eds.), *Hypermedia Seduction for Terrorist Recruiting* (pp. 34–38). Amsterdam: IOS Press.

51. Mishra, Smeeta, & Semaan, Gaby (2010). Islam in Cyberspace: South Asian Muslims in America Log In. *Journal of Broadcasting & Electronic Media, 54*(1), 87–101.

52. Fighel, Jonathan (2007). Radical Islamic Internet Propaganda: Concepts, Idioms and Visual Motifs. In Boaz Ganor, Katharina Von Knop, & Carlos A. M. Duarte (Eds.), *Hypermedia Seduction for Terrorist Recruiting* (pp. 34–38). Amsterdam: IOS Press.

53. Ettema, James S. (2005). Crafting Cultural Resonance: Imaginative Power in Everyday Journalism. *Journalism, 6*(2), 131–152.

54. Fighel, Jonathan (2007). Radical Islamic Internet Propaganda: Concepts, Idioms and Visual Motifs. In Boaz Ganor, Katharina Von Knop, & Carlos A. M. Duarte (Eds.), *Hypermedia Seduction for Terrorist Recruiting* (pp. 34–38). Amsterdam: IOS Press.

55. Fighel, Jonathan (2007). Radical Islamic Internet Propaganda: Concepts, Idioms and Visual Motifs. In Boaz Ganor, Katharina Von Knop, & Carlos A. M. Duarte (Eds.), *Hypermedia Seduction for Terrorist Recruiting* (pp. 34–38). Amsterdam: IOS Press.

56. Oreskovic, Alexei (January 23, 2012). YouTube Hits 4 Billion Daily Video Views. Retrieved June 8, 2013, from http://www.reuters.com/article/2012/01/23/us-google-youtube-idUSTRE80M0TS20120123

57. Naím, Moises (2007). The YouTube Effect: How the Technology of Teenagers Became a Force for Political and Economic Change. *Foreign Policy, 158*, 103–104.

58. Andre, Virgine (2012). "Neojihadism" and YouTube: Patani Militant Propaganda Dissemination and Radicalization. *Asian Security, 8*(1), 27–53.

59. Karpf, David (2010). Macaca Moments Reconsidered: Election Panopticon or Netroots Mobilization. *Journal of Information Technology & Politics, 7*(2), 143–162.

60. Cayari, Christopher (2011). The YouTube Effect: How YouTube Has Provided New Ways to Consume, Create, and Share Music. *International Journal of Education & the Arts, 12*(6), 1–30.

61. Andre, Virgine (2012). "Neojihadism" and YouTube: Patani Militant Propaganda Dissemination and Radicalization. *Asian Security, 8*(1), 27–53.

62. Bahr, Nan, & Pendergast, Donna (2007). *The Millennial Adolescent*. Victoria: Australian Council for Educational Research Press.

63. Winograd, Morley, & Hais, Michael (2008). *Millennial Makeover: MySpace, YouTube, and the Future of American Politics*. New Brunswick, NJ: Rutgers University Press.

64. Weisburd, Aaron (2009). Comparison of Visual Motifs in Jihadi and Cholo Videos on YouTube. *Studies in Conflict and Terrorism, 32*, 1066–1074.

65. Ilardi, Gaetano (2009). Home-Grown Terrorism and Radicalization Activities: More Than Meets the Eye. *Australian Police Journal, 7*, 110–119.

66. Lappin, Yaakov (2010). *Virtual Caliphate: Exposing the Islamist State on the Internet*. Dulles, VA: Potomac Books.

67. Lappin, Yaakov (2010). *Virtual Caliphate: Exposing the Islamist State on the Internet*. Dulles, VA: Potomac Books.

68. Merriam, Lisa (2011, October 6). *The Al Qaeda Brand Died Last Week*. Forbes.com. Retrieved July 10, 2014, from http://www.forbes.com/sites/realspin/2011/10/06/the-al-qaeda-brand-died-last-week/

69. Freedman, Daniel (2011, September 26). *Al-Qaeda's Dumbest Terrorists*. Forbes.com. Retrieved July 10, 2014, from http://www.dfreedman.org/10420/al-qaeda-dumbest-terrorists

70. Goodman, J. David (2011, September 30). American Who Waged "Media Jihad" Is Said to Be Killed in Awlaki Strike. *The New York Times*, p. C2.

71. Mahan, Sue, & Griset, Pamela (2012). *Terrorism in Perspective* (3rd ed.). Thousand Oaks, CA: Sage.

72. Madhani, Aamer (2010, August 24). Cleric al-Awlaki Dubbed "bin Laden of the Internet." *USA Today*, p. A1.

73. Coker, Margaret (2013, May 6). Cleric Cited by Tsarnaev Lives On-Online. *The Wall Street Journal*, p. A7.

74. Al-Suri, Abu Mus Ab (2010). The Jihadi Experience: The Open Fronts and the Individual Initiative. *Inspire, 1*, p. 20.

75. *The Week* (2011, March 11). "Jihad Cosmo": An Al Qaeda Women's Magazine. Retrieved June 9, 2013, from http://theweek.com/article/index/213158/jihad-cosmo-an-al-qaeda-womens-magazine

76. *Daily Mail* (2011, March 13). Glossy "Jihad Cosmo" Combines Beauty Tips with Suicide Bombing Advice. *Daily Mail*, p. A1.

77. Winter, Bronwyn (2011). Ruin: What Happens When You Keep on Buying the Same Old Line? *WSQ: Women's Studies Quarterly, 39*(3), 270–274.

78. Cavendish, Julius (2011, March 14) Al-Qa'ida Glossy Advises Women to Cover Up and Marry a Martyr. *The Independent*, p. A1.

79. *The Week* (2011, March 11). "Jihad Cosmo": An Al Qaeda Women's Magazine. Retrieved June 9, 2013, from http://theweek.com/article/index/213158/jihad-cosmo-an-al-qaeda-womens-magazine

80. Blanchard, Christopher (2011). *Al Qaeda: Statements and Evolving Ideology*. Washington, DC: Congressional Research Service.

81. Mitra, Subrata (2012). Sub-National Movements, Cultural Flow, the Modern State, and the Malleability of Political Space: From Rational Choice to Transcultural Perspective and Back Again. *Transcultural Studies, 2*, 8–47.

82. Sokol, Dominika (2007). The Sikh Diaspora in Cyberspace: The Representation of Khalistan on the World Wide Web and Its Legal Context. *Masaryk University Journal of Law and Technology, 1*(2), 10–21.

83. Gunawardena, Sue (2000). Constructing Cybernationalism: Sikh Solidarity via the Internet. *International Journal of Punjab Studies, 7*(2), 263–322.

84. Sokol, Dominika (2007). The Sikh Diaspora in Cyberspace: The Representation of Khalistan on the World Wide Web and Its Legal Context. *Masaryk University Journal of Law and Technology, 1*(2), 10–21.

85. Gunawardena, Sue (2000). Constructing Cybernationalism: Sikh Solidarity via the Internet. *International Journal of Punjab Studies, 7*(2), 263–322.

86. Sokol, Dominika (2007). The Sikh Diaspora in Cyberspace: The Representation of Khalistan on the World Wide Web and Its Legal Context. *Masaryk University Journal of Law and Technology, 1*(2), 10–21.

87. Caiani, Manuela, & Parenti, Linda (2009). The Dark Side of the Web: Italian Right Wing Extremist Groups and the Internet. *South European Society and Politics, 14*(3), 273–294; and Caiani, Manuela, & Parenti, Linda (2011). The Spanish Extreme Right and the Internet. *Análise Social, 46*(201), 719–740.

88. Glaser, Jack, Dixit, Jay, & Green, Donald (2002). Studying Hate Crime with the Internet: What Makes Racists Advocate Racial Violence? *Journal of Social Issues, 58*(1), 177–193.

89. Caiani, Manuela, & Parenti, Linda (2009). The Dark Side of the Web: Italian Right Wing Extremist Groups and the Internet. *South European Society and Politics, 14*(3), 273–294.

90. Caiani, Manuela, & Parenti, Linda (2009). The Dark Side of the Web: Italian Right Wing Extremist Groups and the Internet. *South European Society and Politics, 14*(3), 273–294; and Caiani, Manuela, & Parenti, Linda (2011). The Spanish Extreme Right and the Internet. *Análise Social, 46*(201), 719–740.

91. Lévi-Strauss, Claude (1966). *The Savage Mind*. Chicago: University of Chicago Press.

92. Tattarini, Mirko (2007). Kamikaze Cyberpunk: Threats and Alternatives in the Age of Viral Power. In Boaz Ganor, Katharina Von Knop, & Carlos Duarte (Eds.), *Hypermedia Seduction for Terrorist Recruiting* (pp. 188–198). Amsterdam: NATO Science for Peace and Security Series.

93. Sajid, Muhammad Akbar (2012). Semiotic Representations of America in Pakistani Media: A Critical Discourse Analysis of the Pakistani Newspaper's Semiotic Discourses. *International Journal of Research in Linguistics & Lexicography, 1*(2), 14–22.

94. Tattarini, Mirko (2007). Kamikaze Cyberpunk: Threats and Alternatives in the Age of Viral Power. In Boaz Ganor, Katharina Von Knop, & Carlos Duarte (Eds.), *Hypermedia Seduction for Terrorist Recruiting* (pp. 188–198). Amsterdam: NATO Science for Peace and Security Series.

95. Retrieved July 10, 2014, from http://www.myconfinedspace.com/2006/09/11/just-do-it/

96. Cortese, Anthony (2007). *Provocateur: Images of Women and Minorities in Advertising*. Lanham, MD: Rowman & Littlefield.

97. Bearder, Pete (2012). Word on the Street: Subvertising and Rewriting the Urban Visual Landscape with Street Art. In Liam Murphy Bell & Gavin Goodwin (Eds.), *Writing Urban Space* (pp. 6–14). New Alresford, UK: Zero Books.

Index

abjection, and war rape, 218–219
abortion, 156
abstractive communication, versus associative communication, 267
Abu Ghraib, 27
acting out, 189
activity segregation, 121
aerial-borne suicide, 185
affirmation, in symbolic DNA of terrorism, 93
agitation effect, 23–24
AK-47, and terrorist violence, 209–210
Alawites, 245
Allah, 128, 144, 194–195; marry for, 196
Allahu Akbar ("Allah is greater"), 215
altruism, 190
altruistic suicide, 190
amplification effect, 48
anashids, 298
animal: communication, 5–6; semiotic, 277; symbolic, 6
anomic suicide, 189
anomie, 189
anthroposemiosis: communication and, 4–5; overview, 4; symbolic culture and, 5; zoosemiosis versus, 5–6
antiabortion violence, 156
antiglobalization: grobalization, 59–60; Lexus and olive tree, 60–61; overview, 59
anti-multiculturalism, 61
anti-Western fashion, case study, 248
AOG. *See* Army of God
apostates, 175
appropriation of symbols: case studies, 245–247; overview, 244; symbolic manipulation, 244; symbolic transformation, 244–245
April 19, 1993, 37
Al-Aqsa Martyrs' Brigade, 31

Arab Convention for the Suppression of Terrorism, 20
Arabic language: as linguistic symbolism in terrorism, 29; of Qur'an, 26, 29
Arab-Israeli War, 81
Arafat, Yasser, 19–20, 120
Armageddon, 142–143
Army of God (AOG), 156
artifactual media, 4
Asahara, Shoko, 77, 142–144
Ashura procession, 100
Asian iconoclasm, 50
Assassins, 186
assaulted millennial groups, 141
associational catalyst, 197
associative communication, versus abstractive communication, 267
asymmetric warfare, 52
Atta, Mohamed, 145
attrition warfare, 160
audience, impact on, 47–48
Augustinian paradigm, 180
Aum Shinrikyo, 30, 77
Aum Shinrikyo, VNRM case study: Armageddon, 142–143; first reality and second reality, 143–144; overview, 142; poa, altruistic killing, 143
authenticity, of brands, 241, 243
avoidance rituals, 76
al-Awlaki, Anwar, 301
Azzam, Abdullah, 178

Baader-Meinhof, 60
Babri Mosque, 150
Bangladesh Liberation War, 80–81
al-Banna, Hasan, 177
barrack buster, 209
Basque ethnonationalism, 115–116

Glossary

Abject: object that elicits disgust (chapter 11).

Abjection: pollution or contamination (chapter 11).

Abstractive communication: "factual inductive" communication in which explicit information is required (chapter 14).

Abu Ghraib: U.S. detainment and interrogation facility in Iraq (chapter 2).

Acting out: a defense mechanism whereby one communicates emotional conflict and feelings through actions rather than words (chapter 10).

Activity segregation: situation in which clashing groups not only live in different areas but also avoid any interaction with each other (chapter 6).

Aerial-borne suicide: suicide terrorism using gliders, mini-helicopters, and airplanes (chapter 10).

Affirmation: the third part of the symbolic DNA of terrorism; it refers to the affirmation of a new identity through an essential myth associated with the group's origin or a utopian myth about the idyllic life that the group will relish in the future (chapter 5).

Agitation effect: the idea that terrorism is a vehicle of armed propaganda to communicate the presence of an emerging opposition, increase popular consciousness, and explain the terms of the struggle (chapter 2).

AK-47: developed in the Soviet Union in the late 1940s, it is a selective-fire, gas-operated assault weapon (chapter 11).

Alawites: a Shia Muslim minority group in Syria (chapter 13).

Allahu Akbar: an Arabic phrase meaning "Allah is greater" or "Allah is [the] greatest" (chapter 11).

Altruism: the principle that promotes the survival chances of others to the detriment of one's own (chapter 10).

Altruistic suicide: a type of suicide whereby a person is significantly integrated into a group so that he or she believes that no sacrifice is too great (chapter 10).

Amazon feminism: a worldview that opposes the idea that certain characteristics or interests are fundamentally masculine (chapter 11).

Amplification effect: the fear that grants terrorism the supreme power of multiplication effect (chapter 3).

Anashids: "sing-song tone" chants in conjunction with military sound effects and used extensively in jihadist imagery (chapter 16).

Anomic suicide: a type of suicide whereby the victim is incapable to cope with a crisis in a rational way and chooses suicide in order to solve the problem (chapter 10).

Anomie: a condition stemming from the lack of norms and moral guidelines in society. Anomic individuals generally feel alienated, disconnected, and powerless (chapter 10).

Anthroposemiosis: the study of human communication. It uses all the sensory means of communication (e.g., visual and tactile) as well as purely verbal means (chapter 1).

Antiabortion violence: a form of pro-life terrorism based on an expression of moral indignation of abortion (chapter 8).

Apostate: someone who leaves his or her religion (chapter 9).

Appropriation: a practice whereby a group borrows symbolic elements from other groups to create something new (chapter 13).

Al-Aqsa Martyrs' Brigade: Palestinian suicide squad created in reference to the martyrs who died in combat when defending the Al-Aqsa Mosque in East Jerusalem (chapter 2).

Army of God (AOG): a Christian terrorist organization focused on antiabortion, particularly against abortion clinics in the United States (chapter 8).

Artifact: "something made" with a particular cultural function in mind (chapter 11).

Artifactual media: visual symbols, pictures, paintings, sculptures, books, letters, and so on (chapter 1).

Asahara, Shoko: Aum Shinrikyo's Supreme Leader (chapter 4).

Ashura procession: in Shia activism, it is a procession that commemorates the day Imam Hussein ibn Ali (Muhammad's successor, according to the Shi'ites), died in battle (chapter 5).

Assassins: a terrorist cult in modern Iran and Syria (chapter 10).

Assaulted millennial group: a group considered by society as dangerous and placed under surveillance by law enforcement organizations (chapter 7).

Associational catalyst: a set of constant reminders about the greatness of being elevated as a martyr (chapter 10).

Associative communication: shared patterns and meanings in communication (chapter 14).

Asymmetric warfare: the use of extreme but sporadic violence by a weaker group against a stronger power (chapter 3; chapter 10).

Atta, Mohamed: one of the 9/11 ringleaders (chapter 7).

Attrition warfare: a strategy of warfare to wear down the enemy (chapter 8).

Audience: a group of individuals involved in an event, either passively or actively (chapter 3).

Augustinian paradigm: a concept describing how religious fanatics long for the purity and eternal peace of godly places (chapter 9).

Aum Shinrikyo: a Japanese dead cult or a millennial sect (chapter 7).

Authenticity: the objective of a brand to provide efforts to draw a wider audience. Successful brands walk the talk: they say what they do and do what they say (chapter 13).

Avoidance ritual: ritual that causes group members to stay away from an individual and apply rules regarding privacy and separateness (chapter 4).

al-Awlaki, Anwar: a U.S.-born Yemeni imam. Involved in the coordination of terrorist attacks for Al Qaeda and notorious for posting videos of his anti-Western sermons, he was considered the "bin Laden of the Internet" (chapter 16).

Azzam, Abdullah: a Palestinian living in Saudi Arabia and Osama bin Laden's professor of Islamic jurisprudence in Jeddah (chapter 9).

Baader-Meinhof: a German Marxist terrorist group in the 1960s and 1970s (chapter 3).

Babri Mosque: in Hindu tradition, it is a mosque that was erected on the site of a Hindu temple demolished by the Moguls (chapter 8).

Balaclava: a type of headgear that covers the whole head, showing only parts of the face (chapter 15).

al-Banna, Hasan: an Egyptian scholar who founded the Muslim Brotherhood in 1928 (chapter 9).

Banner of the Eagle: *see* **Black Standard** (chapter 14).

Banner, The: see **Black Standard** (chapter 14).

Barrack buster: the IRA's favorite homemade mortar (chapter 11).

Basques: an ethnic group inhabiting regions bordering Spain and France (chapter 6).

Battle of the Bogside: battle that took place in Derry, Northern Ireland, in August 1969, between the local Nationalist residents of the Bogside and the Royal Ulster Constabulary (RUC) (chapter 6).

Battle of Vienna: a major battle between the Holy Roman Empire and the Ottoman Empire in Vienna. The latter lost the battle on September 11, 1683, and had to retreat the following day (chapter 2).

Battle of Zenta: a major battle between the Holy League and the Ottoman Empire in Zenta (today located in Serbia). The Ottomans were defeated on September 11, 1697 (chapter 2).

Beam, Louis: a former KKK member who has developed a model for leaderless resistance among whites (chapter 8).

Beer Hall Putsch: an unsuccessful attempt by Hitler and the Nazis at seizing power in Munich (chapter 5).

Beheading video: a video created by Islamist groups showing a Muslim beheading an individual who is kneeling and making his or her last plea (chapter 11).

Biopolitics: the idea that the body of the terrorist becomes a destructive weapon (chapter 10).

Black Banner: see **Black Standard** (chapter 14).

Black Standard: an Islamic symbol that represents three things: (1) the flag used by the Prophet Muhammad in Islamic tradition (also carried in combat by many of his supporters, including his nephew Ali ibn Abi Talib), (2) an eschatological symbol in Shia Islam (heralding the advent of the Mahdi), and (3) a symbol used in both past and present jihadism (chapter 14).

Black Tigers: the Tamil Tigers suicide attack squad (chapter 8).

Black Widows: Islamist female suicide bombers in Chechnya, willing to be martyrs in the name of Allah (chapter 12).

Bleeding text: in jihadist imagery, it is text dripping with blood (chapter 11).

Blog: a discussion website where entries are designed in diary style, controlled and administered by its sole author (i.e., a blogger) (chapter 16).

Blogosphere: the entire sphere of blogged discourse or social web (chapter 16).

Blood feud: a long-running conflict between social groups of people. It is akin to vengeance (chapter 4; chapter 12).

Blood sacrifice: sacrifice of one's life for a nation; it means death for a fatherland or motherland, or even a party or movement (chapter 10).

Bloody hands: image connected to an item or a gesture: for example, a bloody hand carrying a sword, pointing, or represented as a raised fist (chapter 11).

Bloody martyr: image of the martyr's blood; associated with Islam's vital force and warlike qualities (chapter 11).

Bloody Sunday: a tragedy that occurred in Derry, Northern Ireland, in which thirteen Catholic civilians were killed by British paratroopers (chapter 2).

Bloody sword: the image of blood dripping from a sword, which has profound Salafi connotations (chapter 11).

Blowback theory: theory positing that the global hegemony of empires and the additional global military presence of the United States have prompted resistance in the form of terrorism and attacks on symbolic targets like the Twin Towers in New York City (chapter 3).

Body politic: a metaphor explaining how a nation is to be viewed as a corporate entity, being compared to a human body (chapter 12).

Brand: a symbol that differentiates one product or service from another (chapter 13).

Brand awareness: the degree to which a brand is recognized by the general audience and associated with a specific product (chapter 13).

Brand management: a communication function that consists of examining and planning how a brand should be positioned in the world, to what type of audience the brand should be targeted, and how the ideal reputation of the brand should be preserved (chapter 13).

Breivik, Anders Behring: a Norwegian terrorist who committed two successive terrorist acts on the Norwegian government, civilians, and a training camp for youths in southern Norway (around the Oslo area) on July 22, 2011. A total of seventy-seven individuals died, and another 151 were wounded (chapter 3).

Bricolage: the method of creating a new social identity by adopting or "stealing" symbols and artifacts from various customs and cultures (chapter 5; chapter 16).

Burqa: an outer garment covering the entire body (chapter 12).

Calendar of events: Hezbollah's calendar of events, including symbolic dates (e.g., religious memorial dates) that are exploited to create a culture of resistance and recruit new members into the terrorist group (chapter 5).

Caliph: the person establishing man's role as representative of Allah on earth and, hence, a successor of the Prophet Muhammad (chapter 9).

Caliphate: a one-world Muslim government, like a grand Islamic state, led by a supreme religious and political leader called the "caliph" (chapter 9).

Caliphate of Cordoba: a medieval Muslim state that spanned most of the territory of Spain (chapter 9).

Canalization: the idea that ritualistic behavior builds a canal, guiding psychic energy to stream from its regular randomness toward a mythic goal (chapter 4).

Capital punishment: punishment by death; in ancient times, it usually meant that the offender had his or her head cut off (chapter 11).

Carlos the Jackal: a Venezuelan-born Palestinian terrorist who became a media celebrity as the world's most glamorous terrorist (rather than a dangerous killer) (chapter 13).

Cartographic propaganda: the creation of maps for propagandistic intent; it is a conscious attempt to advance an ideological vision of geographical expansionism through false claims (chapter 6).

Causality: the relationship between cause and effect (chapter 15).

Celebrity terrorism: the act of committing such a devastating terrorist attack that the target audience and government will commemorate or observe the day upon which the attack was perpetrated (chapter 2).

Christian Identity: a nineteenth-century philosophy positing that white Christians are the real Israelites (chapter 8).

Christian Identity Movement: an extremist Christian movement that combines poisonous antigovernment politics with an apocalyptic, end-of-the-world vision (chapter 8).

Christian terrorism: terrorist attacks committed by groups or individuals who appeal to Christian motives or goals for their actions (chapter 8).

Christoslavism: an ideology postulating that Slavs are intrinsically Christian (chapter 8).

Circassians: a Muslim ethnic group defeated and forced out of the Sochi area by the Russian Empire (chapter 3).

Citizenship: mainstream people who are representative of an enemy state (chapter 3).

Clash of Civilizations: theory postulating that cultural and religious differences between global civilizations (generally Islam and the West) are a major source of terrorism today (chapter 3).

Clausewitzian terror: terrorism used as a strategic weapon to wreak psychologically debilitating effects on mainstream citizens (chapter 3).

Co-construction of reality: the idea that all parties involved in a given culture agree on what reality is (i.e., consensus reality) (chapter 1).

Cognitive access: the ability of people to understand media images, process information, and, thereby, make deductions (when using information and communication technologies) (chapter 15).

Collective memory: the belief that remembering is a social habit in the sense that people disclose to others the memories they have about important moments or people in their lives (chapter 1).

Collective sacrifice: controlled violence that is culturally or socially driven (chapter 4).

Combating Terrorism Center: an academic institution at the U.S. Military Academy (USMA), in West Point, New York, specializing in terrorism and counterterrorism studies (chapter 14).

Communication: an exchange or sharing of meanings represented by signs (chapter 1).

Comprador ruling elites: Third World leaders considered to have been put in power by the West (in spite of their incompetence and their corrupt, bloody past) (chapter 3).

Computer-mediated communication (CMC): electronic communication on the internet (chapter 16).

Concept: mental representation of the universe in which people live (chapter 1).

Conceptual Metaphor Theory: framework that describes the world (and how we function in it) through three categories of metaphors: structural, orientational, and ontological metaphors (chapter 14).

Condensing symbol: a symbol that strikes deep into the unconscious and projects its emotional quality to forms of behavior or situations that are far removed from the initial or intended meaning of the symbol (chapter 8).

Conflict tourism: the popularity that past (and even current) conflict sites enjoy in regard to tourism and travel (chapter 6).

Connotation: an example of second-level analysis; what the denotation represents (chapter 15).

Connotative meaning: the expressive or particular uses of a symbol (chapter 1).

Construction: the first phase of the social construction of culture (chapter 4).

Contamination: pollution or infection. Contamination requires that something is made impure in terms of its definition and usage (chapter 6).

Context: the situation, background, or environment associated with an event, phenomenon, or person (chapter 14).

Contextualism: a view holding that truth only has meaning when it is situated within a definite context (chapter 4).

Contrast symbol: technique that consists of categorizing reality by contrasting the good traits of one group with the evil traits of the enemy group (chapter 7).

Convergence Theory: theory postulating that new media can reach much greater audiences (chapter 16).

Convergent thinking: thought pattern that focuses on synthesis and analytical problem solving to attain an unambiguously defined outcome (chapter 14).

Convictional social identity: identity based on conviction and belief, which means that they operate on the principle of volition and choice (chapter 4).

Cosmic-level warfare: view that one has to fight spirits at the vertical level (chapter 7).

Cosmic war: spiritual struggle that symbolizes the fight between good and bad, and between truth and evil (chapter 10).

Countercultural: even in high-context cultures, there are situations that are low context (and vice versa) (chapter 14).

Credendum: a doctrine to be believed by the public; it is often expressed through the symbolism and language of struggles or political movements (chapter 6).

Credibility: the objective of a brand to engender faith and loyalty among viewers (chapter 13).

Credibility-enhancing display (CRED): practice whereby a physical symbol is displayed when it is used to generate profound levels of commitment to a movement or when the objective is to foster solidarity and in-group effort (chapter 1).

Cross burning: the KKK's practice of burning crosses on hillsides or close to the homes of people who they wish to intimidate (chapter 11).

Cult: a system of ritual practices (chapter 4).

Cultic milieu: the type of mind linked to a cult's observance of unconventional, or rejected, knowledge (chapter 4).

Cult of death: a glorification of death as part of a major plan to promote a movement and change the world (chapter 5).

Cultural adaptation: the "melting pot" theory and the opposite of multiculturalism (chapter 3).

Cultural cannibalism: the intentional elimination of symbolic landscapes that represent a culture (chapter 3).

Cultural epidemiology: when culture is viewed in terms of the ideas that are broadly disseminated throughout a population (chapter 4).

Cultural feminism: a traditional view of gender roles that theorizes femininity as nonviolent mostly due to women's role as actual and/or potential mothers (chapter 12).

Cultural frames: interpretive devices that people use to make sense of the raw data of experience (chapter 4).

Cultural group: a group of people with a shared system of symbols and ideas (chapter 4).

Cultural hegemony: the domination of one cultural worldview over another in a specific society (chapter 2).

Cultural knowledge: networks of causally interconnected ideas—ideas for which there is some point of agreement among members of a group (chapter 4).

Cultural Marxism: left-wing domination of a culture through multiculturalism (chapter 3).

Cultural metaphor: an image seen to represent a culture (chapter 13).

Cultural model: external representation of a culture created by the main agents of that culture (chapter 4).

Cultural Revolution: a social-political movement (1966–1976) bent on enforcing communism in China by eradicating capitalist, traditional, and cultural elements from Chinese society (chapter 13).

Cultural semiotics: branch of semiotics that goes beyond the traditional verbal mode of expression and covers extralinguistic modes such as nonverbal communication, pictures, and images (chapter 15).

Cultural terrorism: the physical damage of cultural sites or artifacts (that belong to the enemy) or, sometimes, the physical displacement of the enemy's cultural activities (chapter 3).

Culture: the social construction and historical transmission of patterns of symbols, denotations, connotations, ideologies, values, beliefs, norms, traditions, and artifacts from generation to generation (chapter 4).

Culture of death: the purposeful devaluation of human life leading to murder and/or self-murder (chapter 10).

Cyberspace: the "virtual world" of the internet, or the World Wide Web (chapter 16).

Dar al-Harb: the abode of infidels and immoral societies in the world (chapter 7).

Dar al-Islam: the divinely perfect and honorable abode of true Muslims (i.e., the area of the world ruled by Islam) (chapter 7).

David and Goliath metaphor: when enemies come from two different tribes and their beliefs are diametrically opposed, and when the "sizes" of two conflicting parties are diametrically opposed as well (chapter 3).

Dawa: Islamic call, propagation, and proselytizing (chapter 16).

Death cult language: a type of discourse focusing on the glorification of death (chapter 10).

Defensive jihad: jihad decreed by Muslim religious scholars and lawmakers; that is, a widespread mobilization for the ummah under threat, whenever sacred lands and values are under attack from infidels (chapter 9).

Defensive weapon: lighter weapon and weapon with a limited range and damage (e.g., handguns, etc.) (chapter 11).

Dehumanization: a method by which an in-group underscores the "inferiority" of an out-group by expressing intensely derogatory statements (chapter 7).

Demographic group: group based on nationality, educational status, and so on (chapter 4).

Demonstration effect: the creation of an exaggerated impression of the strength of a terrorist group and the weakness of a government (chapter 2).

Demonstrative terrorism: type of terrorism performed for publicity reasons (chapter 2).

Denied: the first part of the symbolic DNA of terrorism; it refers to the sense that the terrorists' identity and existence have been denied and risk being shattered by some group (chapter 5).

Denotation: an example of first-level analysis; what the audience can read or see on a page or image (chapter 15).

Denotative meaning: the direct or instrumental uses of a symbol (chapter 1).

Depluralization: process whereby new members get sequestered within isolated environments (chapter 4).

Desecration: the defilement of things holy and the act of robbing things of their sacred character (chapter 3).

Desired identity: the idealized image that the leaders have of the terrorist organization and what it should become under their leadership (chapter 13).

Dialectical sensitivity: people's ability to serve as transnational communicators, understand cultural differences among communities, and know how to reach out to global audiences socially, ideologically, and culturally (chapter 2).

Differentiation: the objective of a brand to differentiate itself from other brands and position itself as a better option for the audience (chapter 13).

Dispensing of existence: the philosophy that enemies have no legitimate claims to anything, not even any rights to life (chapter 7).

Divergent thinking: thought pattern that underlines a fluid thinking pattern. It is the ability to (1) move from one perspective to another, (2) connect diametrically opposed ideas in a meaningful way, and (3) bring a new idea to accomplishment (chapter 14).

Doctrine over existence: the practice whereby new members must renounce values, beliefs, attitudes, or behaviors that deviate from the terrorist group's values and expectations (chapter 4).

Domestic politics model: model that foresees nuclear weapons as political tools to advance narrow-minded domestic and bureaucratic interests (chapter 11).

Dominionism: when Christian extremism adheres to the belief that the world should be governed through a theocratic Christian dictatorship (chapter 8).

Dress code: a set of written or unwritten rules about clothing. It is a visual sign of difference and belonging (chapter 13).

Earth Liberation Front (ELF): an extremist environmental advocacy group that traces its origin to Brighton, England, with the creation of Earth First! (chapter 5).

Easter Rising: an armed insurrection mounted by Irish Republicans in 1916 to end British rule in Ireland (chapter 8).

Ecotage: sabotage committed for ecoterrorist purposes (chapter 5).

Ecoterrorism: acts of violence or sabotage perpetrated in favor of ecological or environmental causes, against individuals or their property (chapter 5).

Egoism: an excessive or extravagant sense of self-importance (chapter 10).

Egoistic suicide: a type of suicide based on an individual's desire to reap the rewards of a better life in another world (chapter 10).

E-jihad: the practice of using the internet to instruct jihadist recruits and current fighters on how to wage jihad (chapter 16).

Elves: members of the Earth Liberation Front (ELF) (chapter 5).

Emotive narrative: text, music, and/or soppy/emotional segments included in a video (chapter 10).

Empty signifier: a signifier whose referent is ambiguous and can vary easily, and whose meaning differs extensively based on interpretation (chapter 15).

Encumbered self: a person who has an attachment and an obligation to individuals and groups that, in part, constitute his or her identity (chapter 4).

Enemification: the portrayal of out-groups as enemies—usually a permanent label (chapter 7).

ETA: considered a terrorist organization by the United States and many European countries, it is the main organization of the Basque ethnonationalist movement (chapter 6).

Eternal return: in myth theory, it refers to the source of what is "new" to be discovered in the past (in order to be in line with a group's collective identity) (chapter 5).

Ethnic nationalism: see **Ethnonationalism** (chapter 6).

Ethnic victimization: the safety of a group being jeopardized by violence and conflict (chapter 6).

Ethnie: a population with a myth of common ancestry, common historical memories, many elements of a shared culture, a strong connection to a homeland, and strong social cohesion among many of its members (chapter 6).

Ethnonationalism: a category of nationalism characterized by the desire of an ethnic group to have absolute authority over its own territory and its own political and cultural affairs (chapter 6).

Ethnosymbolism: a philosophy that stresses the importance of symbols, values, and traditions in the creation and preservation of a modern nation-state (chapter 8).

Eucharist: the act of Christ's sacrifice (chapter 8).

Evilification: the practice of demonizing other groups and systematically pigeonholing them as outcasts (chapter 7).

Exaptation: using adaptation for specific purposes other than those for which they were initially created (chapter 7).

Exclusivism: the practice of being exclusive vis-à-vis all other groups (chapter 7).

Exemplary dualism: an apocalyptic theme in which sociopolitical or socioreligious forces are viewed as absolute contrast categories (chapter 7).

Expiation: the act of making atonement in order to please a deity (chapter 4).

External adaptation and survival: the manner in which the organization is able to "familiarize itself" by living up to its constantly changing external environment (chapter 4).

Extrinsic faith: process of using religion for ulterior motives, as a means to an end, and/or as a religion to be used rather than lived and experienced (chapter 7).

Face: an alleged feeling of favorable social self-worth that an individual or a cultural group wants others to have of them (chapter 4).

Facework: specific verbal and nonverbal strategies that help preserve and repair face loss (chapter 4).

Fantasy theme: the fundamental unit of analysis in symbolic convergence theory. A fantasy theme can be just a word, a phrase, a sentence, or even a large paragraph (chapter 5).

Fantasy type: a standard script using a prominent, spectacular template to explain new events (chapter 5).

FARC: see **Revolutionary Armed Forces of Colombia** (chapter 13).

Far enemy: infidel, non-Muslim civilizations and the irreligious regimes they have imposed on Muslims (chapter 9).

Fatalism: an extremely regulated existence (chapter 10).

Fatalistic suicide: a type of suicide caused by disproportionate social regulation that fundamentally restricts an individual's freedom on a daily basis (chapter 10).

Fatwa: Islamic decree (chapter 9).

Fawkes, Guy: leader in the Gunpowder Plot, a terrorist attack against the Protestant Parliament in England with a planned assassination of the Protestant King James (chapter 2).

Fear fashion: see **Terrorist chic** (chapter 13).

Fedayeen: several different, primarily Arab groups throughout history committed to suicide missions (chapter 2).

Fedayeen Saddam: terrorist organization led by the Ba'athist government of Saddam Hussein (chapter 2).

Fictive kin: a situation in which people who do not know each other personally cultivate emotional ties on the basis of social identification, particularly in times of crisis or suffering (chapter 6).

First reality: reality in the three-dimensional world; the one we experience in everyday life (chapter 7).

Fitna: internal divisions in Islam (chapter 9).

Five Ks: the five symbols in Sikhism: kirpan (a dagger), kara (an iron bracelet), kesh (unshorn hair), kacch (breeches), and kangha (a small comb in the hair) (chapter 8).

Flexible communicator: a communicator who is familiar with both convergent and divergent thinking. A flexible communicator is an individual who possesses a large body of information based on both factual and contextual modes (chapter 14).

Fragile millennial group: group that experiences long-lasting internal stressors and self-perceived threats from external forces (emanating from mainstream society) (chapter 7).

Freedom Birds: female Tamil Tigers fighting for the Tamils' liberation struggle (chapter 12).

Free-wheeling fundamentalism: concept that denotes extremism based on selectively used biblical verses or a reinterpretation of certain verses to create an alternate version of a particular religion (chapter 8).

Gender: a collection of physical, mental, and behavioral characteristics that make masculinity different from femininity (chapter 12).

Gender communal terrorism: mass terrorism committed against another gender (chapter 11).

Gender role reversal: a phenomenon whereby females break established boundaries and, thereby, jeopardize the order and stability of a culture (chapter 12).

Geo-body: the idea that the newly shaped image of a nation's territory will be clearly recognizable by anybody belonging to the group (chapter 6).

Geographic symbolism: see **Map symbolization** (chapter 6).

Geopolitical code: a practice whereby ethnonationalist groups offer an alternative map to achieve their long-term agenda (chapter 6).

Gesture: any observable bodily action communicating thought or feeling or that has significance in symbolic action (chapter 1).

Ghazwah: a nickname for the raid led by Muhammad in 627 against pagans and Jews (chapter 9).

Ghutrah: see **Keffiyeh** (chapter 13).

Girl militancy: the ultimate transgression of traditional femininity, which, through political violence, evokes a more extreme form of feminism that calls for the end of patriarchal oppression (chapter 12).

Globalization: interconnections between individuals through the removal or reduction of space and time barriers. It also implies a freer flow of technology, capital, products, and services, as well as cultures, ideas, and laws, across the world (chapter 3).

Global Village: the electronic interconnected world; today, it is a metaphor for the internet in general (chapter 16).

Golden Age of Assassination: the practice of assassination and bombing by individualized rebellions against authorities and private property in the nineteenth and early twentieth centuries (chapter 2).

Golden Temple in Amritsar: Sikhism's holiest shrine and the spiritual center for the Amritdhari Sikhs (chapter 8).

Goldstein, Baruch: an American-born Zionist who killed twenty-nine Muslims at the Ibrahim Mosque in 1994 (chapter 8).

Graffiti: "minor media" that often present signs or images that are hastily written, brief, and fragmentary (chapter 6).

Grammar of terrorism: a set of linguistic rules and definitions as to what constitutes terrorism and the victims thereof (chapter 2).

Greater jihad: the struggle that someone has within him- or herself to fulfill what is right (chapter 7).

Great Siege of Malta: a battle that took place between Western Christian combatants and the Ottoman Empire, after the latter invaded the island of Malta. The Ottoman Empire lost the battle on September 11, 1565 (chapter 2).

Grey Wolves: a Turkish ultranationalist and neo-fascist youth organization (chapter 1).

Grobalization: the imperialistic ambitions and needs of MNCs, or even entire countries, to plant themselves into various areas of the world to allow their power, influence, and revenues to grow even more (chapter 3).

Ground-level warfare: the view that warfare is waged against demonization on earth (chapter 7).

Group delirium: collective dreams that electrify individuals in a movement's cause or religion (chapter 5).

Guantánamo Bay: a detainment and interrogation facility at a U.S. Naval Base in Cuba (chapter 2).

Guerrilla communication: political activism achieved through the manipulation of photos, cartoons, or words. It is an attempt to create subversive outcomes through interventions in the process of communication (chapter 14).

Guillotine: a standard device for decapitation invented during the French Revolution (chapter 2).

Guilt by association: a form of symbolic linkage whereby terrorists connect individuals to the larger entities that they want to target (chapter 3).

Gurdwara: the physical space in which the Sikh congregation assembles in the presence of its most important holy scriptures (chapter 8).

Gynocentric feminism: see **Cultural feminism** (chapter 12).

Habits of interpretation: in sign theory, these are habits evaluated based on the interpretants themselves (i.e., the historical embodiment of their society or culture) (chapter 15).

Hadith: a collection of sayings by Muhammad. His sayings are acts of approval or disapproval ascribed to Muhammad (chapter 9).

Hamas: the Islamic Resistance Movement created in the Palestinian territories in the late 1980s (chapter 9).

Hard target: armed target like a battle tank or a well-defended structure (chapter 3).

Hate couture: see **Terrorist chic** (chapter 13).

Heavenly Garden: eternal life in Paradise (chapter 10).

Heaven's Gate: a religious doomsday cult based in San Diego that committed mass suicide in 1997 (chapter 4).

Hereditarian social identity: identity founded in natural (i.e., determined) orders that do not depend on conviction or belief (chapter 4).

Hermeneutics: the science and art of trying to understand and interpret the meaning of universal or personal languages, texts, and symbols (chapter 1).

Hezbollah: a Shia terrorist organization founded in Lebanon in 1982 (chapter 5).

High context: when messages are more ambiguous and in which less has to be said or written—because the meaning tends to reside within the environment (i.e., it depends more on the context) (chapter 14).

Hijra: the escape of Muhammad and his followers from Mecca to Medina (chapter 14).

Hindutva: "Hinduness"; it is the idea that all Indians belong to the Hindu nation and need to be unified in a single community (chapter 8).

Hindutva terrorism: a militant movement advocating Hindu nationalism (chapter 5).

Holy Communion: see **Eucharist** (chapter 8).

Home territories: zones or areas in which entrance is restricted to members, such as temples, sacred sites, or even an entire holy land (chapter 6).

Homosocial reproduction: the process whereby descriptive characteristics of societal power structures are perpetuated across several generations (chapter 12).

Honor: the righteousness and purity of a code; it serves to define status, respect, and reputation for the person, family, and community (chapter 4).

Honor killing: the murder of a relative or even an entire group of people based on the perpetrators' belief that the victim has caused dishonor to the family or culture (chapter 4).

Human-borne suicide: suicide bodysuit (chapter 10).

Humiliation by proxy: sentiments of indignation and moral shocks resulting from the witnessing of injustices against distant "brothers" and "sisters" (chapter 2).

Hunger protest: see **Hunger strike** (chapter 10).

Hunger strike: a form of pressure in which individuals fast as an act of political protest or to induce feelings of guilt in others, generally with the hope of achieving a goal (e.g., policy change) (chapter 10).

Hybrid culture: culture that develops naturally over time as groups come together on a shared process of interacting (chapter 4).

Hypermovement: a movement to which an organization is symbiotically connected. It is subject to obedience to rules and widespread institutionalization over time (chapter 4).

Icon: a sign that refers to its object by a process of similarity (e.g., an image, photo, map, diagram, etc.) (chapter 15).

Iconoclasm: an attack upon a sacred symbol (chapter 3).

Iconography: a method to look at the classification, description, and interpretation of visible symbols (chapter 1).

Idea: any substance of the mind, including perceptions of how things are or how they should be (chapter 4).

Ideal identity: see **Desired identity** (chapter 13).

Identicide: a strategy of warfare that intentionally annihilates a group's identity (chapter 11).

Ideology: belief system or worldview that frames the human mind and influences social and political conditions (chapter 2; chapter 4).

Idioculture: a system of shared knowledge, principles, feelings, and behaviors. For group members, such a system functions as a frame of reference and source of interaction (chapter 2).

Idris, Wafa: the very first female Palestinian suicide bomber (chapter 12).

Ijtihad: an interpretation of the Qur'an that allows Muslims to revisit Islamic history and use it to validate their theological understandings of the Qur'an (chapter 9).

Ikhwan: Islamic religious guerrillas comprising the principal military body of the Arabian ruler Ibn Saud. In the 1910s and 1920s, the Ikhwan were composed of Bedouin tribes and irregular tribesmen. Today, the Ikhwan is the name for the Muslim Brotherhood in Arabic (chapter 9).

Imagespeak: term that describes how individuals produce forms of shared symbolic language to assign contextual symbolism to an object (something that can be seen) (chapter 13).

Imagined community: a community that is not (and cannot be) based on everyday face-to-face interactions between its members (chapter 6).

Imam: leader of prayer in an Islamic mosque (chapter 14).

Improvised explosive device (IED): a homemade bomb mainly deployed in terrorist attacks (chapter 11).

Index: a sign that determines its object based on an actual connection, regardless of interpretation (chapter 15).

Influence operations: actions taken with the main goal of influencing the actions, behavior, attitudes, or opinions of others (chapter 10).

Information: the most basic unit of communication; it can be a simple symbol or a complex message (chapter 1).

Injustice frame: mental structure that identifies an aggressor (e.g., a state) who has committed an injustice against the activist group and its constituents (chapter 2).

Inscape: term suggesting that the homeland is transformed as a sacred reason for living up to the fight, something to be engaged visually day in and day out (chapter 6).

Inspire: an English language online magazine published by Al Qaeda and aimed at British and U.S. readers (chapter 16).

Institutionalization: the ideology or political philosophy that promotes a country's or culture's policies (chapter 3).

Institutional memory: a collective set of facts or experiences held by a group of people (chapter 2).

Instrumentality: the useful and task-fulfilling property of a symbol (in addition to its symbolic value) (chapter 1).

Instrumental rationality: rationality based on a firm cost-benefit calculus in regard to goals; it requires the rejection or modification of goals if the costs of achieving them are too high (chapter 10).

Interactional territories: zones or areas in which people meet informally for the social outlet (e.g., lounges and local gyms) (chapter 6).

Internal integration: the formation and upholding of effective relationships among the members of an organization (chapter 4).

Internalization: the third phase of the social construction of culture (chapter 4).

Internet of Things (IoT): a mental picture in which the internet extends into our daily lives through a wireless network of distinct objects and symbols (chapter 16).

Interpretance: the practice, often within a community or culture, to identify relevant sensible parameters in its context or environment and use them to generate meaning (chapter 15).

Interpretant: the audience's interpretation or the effect in the mind of the interpreter (chapter 15).

Interpretation: process that involves the construction of meaning out of contextual cues (chapter 1).

Intifada: the Palestinian uprising that occurred between 1987 and 1993 (chapter 6).

Intrinsic faith: a principal motive in life, an end in itself, a religion to be deeply lived and experienced from within (chapter 7).

Invasion: type of territorial encroachment whereby people, with no right to entrance or use, cross the boundaries anyway (chapter 6).

Iranian Revolution: in 1979, it was a revolution that imposed an Islamic Republic in Iran under the Grand Ayatollah Khomeini (chapter 9).

Irish hunger strike: a 1981 event during which Irish Republican prisoners in Northern Ireland became hunger strikers (chapter 10).

Irredenta: a territory that is culturally or historically linked to one nation but is controlled by a foreign government (chapter 6).

Istishhad: the Arabic word for martyrdom, a martyr's death, or heroic death (chapter 10).

Islamic revival: a revival of the Muslim religion, across the Muslim world, that made a significant comeback at the end of the 1970s (chapter 9).

Islamic Revolutionary Guards Corps (IRGC): Iran's well-trained military wing established to protect the country's Islamic system (chapter 5).

Islamikaze: the new brand of Islamic suicide terrorists (chapter 10).

Islamist chic: the practice of appropriating politically loaded Islamist symbols and give them a new meaning—often a personal meaning (chapter 13).

Islamization: the process whereby a country or culture converts to Islam (chapter 9).

Jackal, Carlos the: see **Carlos the Jackal** (chapter 13).

Jacobins: rebels led by Robespierre during the Reign of Terror at the end of the French Revolution (chapter 2).

Jahanam: "Hell" in Arabic (chapter 10).

Jahiliyyah: a state in which individuals are astray from spirituality and divine guidance and are at variance with the teachings of the Qur'an (chapter 9).

Janna: see **Heavenly Garden** (chapter 10).

Jihad: struggle in the way of Allah (chapter 9).

Jihad by the hand: a type of jihad whereby Islamists choose to do "what is right" by resisting injustice and wrongs through action (chapter 9).

Jihad by the sword: violent armed fighting in the way of Allah (holy war) and the most common method by Salafi Muslims (chapter 9).

Jihad by the tongue: a type of jihad concerned with propagation (speaking the truth and diffusing the word of Islam with one's tongue) (chapter 9).

Jihad Cosmo: Al Qaeda's women's magazine—written in Arabic—that combines beauty and fashion guidelines with advice on suicide bombings (chapter 16).

Jihadism: a system of propagating offensive jihad, waging it in conquest, and using it to advance Islam (chapter 9).

Jihadisphere: an online community of warriors and supporters united by their common devotion to a global jihadist ideology (chapter 16).

Jihadist chic: see **Islamist chic** (chapter 13).

Jihadist globalism: modern-day jihadist violence as a reaction to Western forms of modernization (chapter 9).

Jihad of the heart: "inner struggle" jihad that consists of fighting the evil that has penetrated the self (chapter 9).

Jihad vs. McWorld: model illustrating the fight between jihad and "McWorld" (i.e., the economic and political processes of multinational corporations [MNCs]) (chapter 3).

Jinn: genies; spirits who occupy an unseen world in dimensions unconceivable or unsuitable to the universe of human beings (chapter 7).

Judicial category: category of decapitation best illustrated by the present-day method of public execution in Saudi Arabia: decapitation by sword (chapter 11).

July 7, 2005, London bombings: terrorist incident in which four homegrown Al Qaeda suicide bombers detonated bombs aboard London Underground trains and a double-decker bus (chapter 3).

Junk terrorism: the idea that religious violence can be the result of the hijacking of a religion (chapter 7).

Just war: a type of war that has been legitimized in moral or religious terms (chapter 7).

Kalash: see **AK-47** (chapter 11).

Kalashnikov: see **AK-47** (chapter 11).

Kalashnikov culture: the attitudes and behavior that are characteristic of a particular belligerent cultural group, one that stresses the importance of resolving political disputes through assault rifles (chapter 11).

Kali: the Hindu goddess of terror, destruction, empowerment, and sexuality (chapter 8).

Kamikaze cyberpunk: method consisting of appropriating past suicide or terrorist incidents (along with symbols and artifacts related to these incidents) and reliving them in a new but different way (chapter 16).

Karbala: the absolute willingness to submit to the will of Allah, to the point of dying for him (chapter 10).

Kasab, Ajmal: the only terrorist survivor of the 2008 Mumbai terrorist attacks (later, he was hanged) (chapter 4).

Keffiyeh: an old-fashioned Arab headdress made from a square scarf and often worn by Arab men (chapter 13).

Key to Paradise: literally, it refers to a button on a grenade that is the detonation and, therefore, the key to Paradise. Metaphorically, it is the ultimate objective of the shahid: to enjoy the highest place in Paradise (chapter 10).

Khalistan: the Sikhs' dream to establish an autonomous, sovereign Sikh state (chapter 8).

Khalsa: a symbol implying that the Sikhs are committed to the achievement of divine power and justice (chapter 8).

Khanda: a Sikh symbol that denotes a domesticized type of violence (chapter 8).

al-Khattab, Ibn: a Saudi-born Islamic terrorist and financier working with Chechen jihadists in the First and Second Chechen Wars (chapter 14).

Khomeini, Ruhollah: the Grand Ayatollah who became the First Supreme Leader of Iran during the 1979 Islamic Revolution (chapter 5).

Kinder, Küche, Kirche: a German catchphrase meaning "children, kitchen, church" (chapter 12).

Kirpan: a ceremonial sword that represents the Sikh's duty to resist oppression (chapter 8).

KKK: see **Ku Klux Klan** (chapter 11).

Klan: see **Ku Klux Klan** (chapter 11).

Kneecapping: firing a shot in the back of the knee joint, thereby making the victim unable to walk adequately again (chapter 3).

Korean People's Army (**KPA**): the largest military organization in the world (with about 9,500,000 active, reserve, and paramilitary personnel, as of 2013) (chapter 11).

Kufiya: see **Keffiyeh** (chapter 13).

Ku Klux Klan: an extremist white supremacist group active in the United States (chapter 11).

Kulturmensch: a "cultural being" who takes a position in his or her value sphere; the cultural being makes decisions based on cultural values and lives off them as well (chapter 4).

Kurdistan: a geocultural region spanning southeastern Turkey, northeastern Iraq, and parts of Syria and Iran (chapter 10).

Kurdistan Workers' Party: a secular terrorist organization responsible for perpetrating numerous acts of terrorism against Turkey (chapter 10).

Laager culture: a metaphor for an ethnonationalist minority that considers itself under siege. In military history, a laager was a mobile fortification that was vulnerable to attacks (chapter 6).

Landscape of identity: the notion that identity is territory bound (chapter 6).

Lashkar-e-Taiba: a Pakistan-based terrorist group (chapter 4).

Last night: in Islam, it is a list of verses extolling the virtues and heroic deeds of the Prophet Muhammad. Overall, it is an interpretation of warfare allowing Muslims to determine who is a "true" or "false" Muslim (chapter 7).

Law of the Pursuer: a traditional Jewish law whereby an individual must be killed by any bystander after being warned to stop an action or decision (chapter 8).

Leaderless resistance: a strategy whereby one person (or a very small, highly cohesive unit) mounts acts of antigovernment terrorism independent of any command structure or support network (chapter 8).

Lebenswelt: the world of shared human experience that produces symbolic systems, organizational cultures, cults, rituals, and religions (chapter 4).

Leopold, Aldo: a U.S. writer, scientist, ecologist, forester, and ecologist. He was a major inspiration for the Earth Liberation Front (ELF) (chapter 5).

Lesser jihad: the external, physical effort to defend Islam (including terrorism) when the ummah is under threat (chapter 7).

Lexus: the epitome of what is modern, technological, and global (chapter 3).

Liberation Tigers of Tamil Eelam (**LTTE**): see **Tamil Tigers** (chapter 8).

Likeness: see **Sign** (chapter 15).

Liquid life: rampant individualism (as a result of unfettered capitalism) and a rapid destabilization of social bonds (chapter 3).

Liquid modernity: theory positing that late modernity and postmodern consumerism lead to ambiguity and increasing uncertainty within individual souls in society (chapter 3).

Linking: the act of referring users from one website to another (chapter 16).

Logo: a graphic symbol that portrays the true values of an organization; it also includes typography, color, and slogan (chapter 13).

Logo-map: a map on which an ethnonationalist group incorporates celebrated cultural icons, changes the name of the cities, adds new things, or subtracts existing things (chapter 6).

Logos oriented: factual (chapter 14).

Lord's Resistance Army: a new religious movement and terrorist cult in northern Uganda and South Sudan (chapter 4).

Low context: when the context is based on codes, theories, grammar, and when it is clear and unequivocal (chapter 14).

Madrid train bombings: terrorist incident in which four trains were blown up by an Al Qaeda–inspired group in Madrid on March 11, 2004 (chapter 2).

Mahdi: the prophesied savior of Islam who will rule for up to nineteen years before the Day of Judgment (chapter 9).

Mahdism: the belief that humanity will end upon the return of the Muslim messiah and the establishment of the subsequent pure Islamic state (chapter 9).

Manhaj: the symbol of absolute Islamic truth (chapter 9).

Manipulation: a form of social influence that can change individuals' perception of reality by distorting reality or deceiving (chapter 13).

Männerpresse: a metaphor describing the obsession of the German male-controlled media with the female body (chapter 12).

Map symbolization: the selection of symbols, for propagandistic purposes, in order to inform the map reader what is relevant and what is not (chapter 6).

Marine-borne suicide: suicide terrorism using watercraft and scuba divers (chapter 10).

Martyrdom: heroic death, usually in battle, that is sanctified by a deity or Supreme Being (chapter 10).

Martyrdom video: a video recording, mostly from Islamist activists, championing the participation in a suicide attack and extolling the virtues of dying as a hero in holy war (chapter 10).

Martyropathy: a synonym for "culture of death" (chapter 10).

Mass: a symbolic act in which people participate in the Eucharist (chapter 8).

Mass-mediated terrorism: the process whereby the media broadcast terrorist acts on a regular basis (chapter 3).

Mass rape: see **Gender communal terrorism** (chapter 11).

Matam: a public congregation in which Shia Muslims assemble for sacred purposes (chapter 5).

McVeigh, Timothy: the convicted perpetrator of the Alfred P. Murrah Federal Building in Oklahoma City (chapter 2).

Meaning: shared mental representation of a connection among things or events (chapter 1).

Meaning frameworks: the social boundaries that surround definitions or interpretations in a culture (chapter 1).

Meaning making: human activity that consists of assigning meaning to the experience of life (chapter 1).

Mechanical media: telephone, radio, television, computer, video, satellite, and so on (chapter 1).

Meinhof, Ulrike Marie: cofounder and co-leader of Baader-Meinhof (or the Red Army Faction) (chapter 12).

Meme hacking: appropriating another group's symbol (usually a flag, brand, or logo) and using it against that very group (chapter 1).

Mens rea: "guilty mind"; the willingness to kill along with the willingness to die (chapter 10).

Metaphor: vehicle or process of communication that allows understanding of one thing in terms of another or as a concept of communication that makes sense of one concept by mentioning another, often unrelated concept (chapter 14).

Metonym: a figure of speech consisting of a thing or concept that is not called by its own name; rather, it is called by the name of something closely related to that thing or concept (chapter 6).

Militant chic: see **Terrorist chic** (chapter 13).

Millennial Generation: a generation greatly influenced by high-tech telecommunications like mobile phones, the internet, and computer networks (chapter 16).

Millennial group: group claiming that the existing world and its leaders are corrupt, unfair, or otherwise wrong. Therefore, these people need to be killed and replaced (chapter 7).

Millennials: see **Millennial Generation** (chapter 16).

Millenarian group: see **Millennial group** (chapter 7).

Monkey wrenching: extreme actions taken by ecoterrorists (chapter 5).

Moral shock: situation that creates public outrage and, consequently, smoothes the progress of recruitment to movements involved in the issue (chapter 2).

Moscow theater hostage crisis: a hostage-taking incident that happened in October 2002; all forty Chechen terrorists were killed, and 130 hostages died from the toxic substance used by the Russians (chapter 12).

Mossad: the Israeli national intelligence agency (chapter 3).

Muharram: the first month of the Islamic calendar and one of the four sacred months of the year (chapter 14).

Mujahedin: a "person doing jihad" who achieves honor through warrior initiations, endurance rituals, and cruelty in combat. The objective is to fulfill the will of Allah (chapter 4).

Mullah: Muslim scholar (chapter 7).

Multi-actuality: the idea that the meaning of a sign or symbol is not fixed. Rather, it is subject to various interpretations according to context (chapter 14).

Multiculturalism: the existence of multiple cultures in a community or country. The term denotes both cultural diversity (i.e., as related to the demographic composition of a particular community, institution, city, or nation) and the ideology or political philosophy that promotes such diversity (chapter 3).

Multiplier effect: in the context of terrorist chic, terrorist objects and/or symbols become culture as a commodity, and they are exported to nonterrorist cultures (chapter 13).

Multivocality: the capacity of symbols to communicate different meanings to different groups (chapter 1).

Mumbai terrorist attacks: terrorist attacks perpetrated by a Pakistan-based group in November 2008. Approximately 165 people died, and over 300 others were wounded (chapter 4).

Munich massacre: an attack committed by Black September (a Palestinian terrorist group) on eleven members of the Israeli Olympic team (chapter 15).

Muslim Brotherhood: one of the largest and most influential Islamic movements in the world (chapter 9).

Myth: a system that both symbolizes ideology and provides a sacred story that directs our faith and shapes our conduct (chapter 5).

Myth entrepreneurship: the art of excelling at devising myths to maintain the social order (chapter 5).

Mythomoteur: a myth that bestows a group its sense of purpose. It gives shape and direction to a movement's or group's cause (chapter 5).

Myth resurrection: the notion that symbols can and frequently do articulate, embellish, simplify, or resurrect myths. Old symbols can be made to come back because symbols tend to be plastic and malleable (chapter 5).

Name-giving code: name that has a shared meaning for people within a specific culture (chapter 2).

Nasrallah, Hassan: the current Hezbollah leader (chapter 13).

National Razor: nickname for the guillotine during the French Revolution (chapter 2).

National Socialism: see **Nazism** (chapter 5).

Natural media: voice (speech, language), the face (expressions), and the body (gesture, posture) (chapter 1).

Nazi chic: the use of Nazi-themed images, styles, and paraphernalia in popular culture and fashion (chapter 13).

Nazism: the ideology of the Nazi Party in Germany. A major Nazi theme is the domination of society by human beings considered as racially superior, while cleansing society of people declared inferior (in terms of health, intelligence, etc.) and deemed to pose a risk to national survival (chapter 5).

Near enemy: apostate Muslims, apostate governments, and their warped systems of thought (chapter 9).

Negation: the second part of the symbolic DNA of terrorism; it refers to a complete negation of the identity of individuals who pose the threat (chapter 5).

Negative cult: a system that represents the core of the group's sanctions as well as its legal institutions. It is symbolized by a structure of restrictions and cultural taboos (chapter 4).

Neglected Duty, The: a written manifesto bringing forth the idea that many Muslims worldwide have abandoned the practice of jihad (chapter 9).

Neojihadism: a subculture, a counterculture, and an ideology that seeks to establish states governed by laws according to the dictates of selectively literal interpretations of the Qur'an and the traditions of the Prophet Muhammad, through enacting violence (chapter 16).

New Age ideology: a syncretic mix of beliefs and attitudes, including Eastern religious thoughts, occult traditions, unconventional "healing techniques," and "consciousness-raising" maneuvers (chapter 7).

New media: any technology or digital device that is interactive, networkable, dense, and generally easily usable. Other aspects of new media include user feedback, creative participation, and real-time creation of original, unregulated content (chapter 16).

New media–oriented terrorism: terrorism that has assumed digital, internet-based, and CMC forms thanks to the Global Village (chapter 16).

Nonphysical symbols: symbols that can be linguistic, behavioral, sociocultural, or ideological (chapter 1).

Nonverbal communication: the means of sending and receiving wordless messages (chapter 1).

Norms model: model under which decisions about nuclear weapons are based on weapons acquisition (or restraint in weapons development) (chapter 11).

Nuclear grandeur: the philosophy that nations attempt to build or acquire nuclear weapons to represent or enhance their overall prestige (chapter 11).

Nuclear weapon: an explosive device of which the destructive force comes from nuclear reactions (chapter 11).

Object: the "referent"; what the sign refers to or symbolizes (chapter 15).

Objectivation: the second phase of the social construction of culture (chapter 4).

Occidentosis: see **Westoxification** (chapter 3).

Offensive jihad: giving a religious cover to the violent expansion of the Islamic world, to conquest, and to the invasion of unbelievers' territories (chapter 9).

Offensive weapon: weapon that poses a greater threat to a country's stability (and even the whole world's stability) because it necessitates a coordinated response from potential targets (chapter 11).

Olive tree: the epitome of what is traditional and parochial (chapter 3).

Omar, Mullah Mohammed: the spiritual leader of the Taliban and considered an international terrorist by the U.S. Department of State (chapter 13).

Onomastics: the study of proper names in general as well as the origins of names (chapter 2).

Onomatology: see **Onomastics** (chapter 2).

Ontological metaphor: metaphor that helps propagandists interpret life by using common objects and substances that are frequently personified. Such a metaphor consists of projecting entity characteristics onto areas of life that have a different status—whether physical or nonphysical (chapter 14).

Open Source Intelligence (OSI): method operating on the principle that, through the internet, any type of information can be easily accessed, used, or manipulated for any purpose (chapter 16).

Organizational culture: culture that reflects the shared and learned values, beliefs, and attitudes of an organization's members (chapter 4).

Orientational metaphor: metaphor that pertains to our orientation in space, usually with respect to polar oppositions such as "up" versus "down," "central" versus "peripheral," and "front" versus "back." Up" is generally positive, and "down" is negative (chapter 14).

Orienting system: a general outlook on the world that includes beliefs, feelings, habits, and relationships from religious, personality, and social spheres (chapter 4).

Othering: the labeling and degrading of groups other than one's own (chapter 7).

Ottoman Empire: a Muslim empire that occupied much of southeastern Europe, western Asia, the Caucasus, North Africa, and the Horn of Africa. The empire lasted from the thirteenth to the early twentieth centuries (chapter 2).

Palestinian Liberation Organization (PLO): an organization of which the purpose is to establish an independent State of Palestine. It is considered a terrorist organization by the United States and Israel (chapter 12).

Pan-Germanicism: the ultimate agenda of the Third Reich, it was an ideology that promoted the unity of the Germanic and Aryan peoples worldwide (chapter 5).

Pansurgency: a global movement seeking to instigate revolutions in order to rout Western civilization and substitute it with a new world order (chapter 9).

Particular symbols: symbols that consist of objects, ideas, or events used within specific groups (chapter 1).

Pathological narcissistic terrorism: terrorism committed as a way to preserve the honor and virtues of one's group (chapter 10).

Pathos oriented: emotional (chapter 14).

Patriarchal terrorism: the meticulous use of violence by men in a serious attempt to control women (chapter 11).

Payback: see **Revenge** (chapter 12).

Perceived identity: the public opinion about the terrorist organization; that is, the set of attributes that are viewed as representative of the terrorist organization (in the eyes of the public) (chapter 13).

Performative violence: a particular means of communication through which terrorists attempt to produce social transformations by performing symbolic acts of violence (chapter 2).

Permanent campaign: a process of continuing transformation. The objective is to maintain legitimacy and credibility (chapter 13).

Personification: the transmission of human traits to nonhuman beings (chapter 5).

Persuasion: a type of influence whereby the sender wants to make the receiver accept or change a belief, attitude, or action through rational or symbolic processes (chapter 3).

Persuasive cartography: a method whereby a group diffuses its doctrine by altering a map (chapter 6).

Philosophy of the bomb: the idea that bombing enemies is the best method for agitation effects and the creation of social change (chapter 2).

Phineas Priesthood: a radical Christian Identity movement comprising white supremacists, antiabortionists, and environmental and animal rights activists (chapter 8).

Phineas Priests: see **Phineas Priesthood** (chapter 8).

PKK: see **Kurdistan Workers' Party** (chapter 10).

Place: an area with definite boundaries, with which a particular group identifies, and where a series of events happen (chapter 6).

Pleasure principle: a principle that has two key objectives: the seeking of pleasure and the avoidance of pain (chapter 10).

Pneumopathology: spiritual insanity, unlike psychopathology (which denotes a psychological disorder). In layperson's terms, pneumopathology is a practice whereby a leader creates an environment of "spiritual sickness" in order to deform reality itself (chapter 4).

Poa: a Tibetan meditative method to give good karma in the cycle of reincarnation (chapter 7).

Poeisis: ritual that brings forth a new existence by transforming a current one (chapter 4).

Polysemic: said of a symbol, sign, or message that prompts multiple readings (chapter 6).

Positive cult: a system of norms that impose the rules for group-based, normative behavior. It is a system of rites that rally group members closer to the sacred (chapter 4).

Postmodern terrorists: terrorists who possess (or want to possess) WMDs to wreak massive havoc (chapter 11).

Predatory martyrdom: phenomenon whereby a suicide terrorist kills him- or herself as part of a jihad against enemies, but does it alone and all by him- or herself (chapter 10).

Presentational category: category reduced from a symbol to a sign (chapter 11).

Presentational ritual: ritual that incorporates acknowledgments, invitations, compliments, and similar services for each new recruit (chapter 4).

Prestige symbol: an object or artifact that reinforces the group's belief in its power and influence (chapter 11).

Primordial symbols: symbols that carry great psychological significance and can be seen in one form or another across all cultures (chapter 1).

Principle of Abrogation: a tenet in the Qur'an to resolve the contradictions between Meccan and Medinan verses. According to that principle, in regard to any controversial topic (e.g., killing, treatment of infidels, or ethics), the later (Medinan) verse abrogates (i.e., has precedence over) the earlier (Meccan) verse (chapter 9).

Projected identity: the appearance (i.e., signs and indications) that the terrorist organization conveys to the public—both consciously and unconsciously—through communication and symbols (chapter 13).

Projective identification: psychological defense mechanism whereby the self-image of in-group terrorists becomes, in part, psychologically dependent on the out-group scapegoat (chapter 7).

Propaganda: public communication aimed at a group of people and created to influence attitudes and behavior in times of crisis (chapter 5).

Propaganda by the Deed: radical method whereby terrorism became a tool of communication to stir up the populace and cause a revolution (chapter 2).

Provocation effect: method whereby terrorism is used to provoke a nation into overreacting and taking excessive countermeasures (chapter 2).

Pseudospeciation: the propensity to pigeonhole people based on race, ethnicity, class, doctrine, religion, sexual orientation, and so on, and to classify them into stigmatized categories (chapter 7).

Psychoanalytic transference: a process in which deep emotions are transferred from one object to another. It can also be a redirection of feelings from one person to another (chapter 7).

Public character of terrorism: the notion that terrorism is a conspicuously public endeavor targeting the psychological and emotional state of the audience who witnesses the disaster (chapter 3).

Public communication: a purposive effort to inform or affect the behaviors of large audiences within a specific time using a coordinated set of communication activities (chapter 13).

Public identity: identity of an organization that comprises certain characteristics that its members see as central, distinctive, and enduring (chapter 13).

Public relations: practice that consists of controlling the dissemination of information to the public; the goal is to uphold a particular point of view about the organization (chapter 13).

Public sphere: a domain in which public opinion can be formed (chapter 6; chapter 16).

Public territories: zones or areas where any citizen can go (e.g., a national forest) (chapter 6).

Punishment, The: see **Black Standard** (chapter 14).

Punitive rape: a type of rape used to punish in order to produce silence and control (chapter 11).

Al Qaeda: an international jihadist network created in 1988 that targets dispersed, symbolic people and permanent structures in its holy war on Western adversaries (chapter 9).

Al Qaedaism: the symbol of a "jihad brand" that offers a political and a religious basis on which Muslims can revitalize the long-established Islamist doctrine (chapter 9).

Al-Quds: what Arab speakers call Jerusalem (chapter 6).

Al-Quds Force: the "Jerusalem Force"; a special terrorist unit of the Islamic Revolutionary Guards Corps (IRGC) (chapter 6).

Qur'an: the predominant religious text of Islam, which Muslims believe is the verbatim word of Allah given to the Prophet Muhammad (chapter 9).

Qutb, Sayyid: an Islamist intellectual and key player in the Muslim Brotherhood (chapter 9).

Qutbism: synonym for modern jihadism (chapter 9).

Radical chic: see **Terrorist chic** (chapter 13).

Ram: one of the incarnations of Vishnu and a key figure in the Hindus' fusion of nationalism and religion (chapter 8).

Ram Rajya: the rule of Ram or the perfect rule of the Golden Age of Ram (chapter 8).

RAND Corporation: a nonprofit global policy institution based in Santa Monica, California. Since the 1970s, it has been a frontrunner in terrorism and counterterrorism studies (chapter 3).

Rape of Nanking: during the Second Sino-Japanese War, it was an event in which roughly 20,000 to 80,000 Chinese women and girls were raped by Japanese troops (chapter 11).

Raya: see **Black Standard** (chapter 14).

Red Army Faction (RAF): see **Baader-Meinhof** (chapter 3).

Red Brigades: a Marxist-Leninist terrorist group based in Italy, particularly active in the 1970s and 1980s (chapter 3).

Redemption: the act of saving oneself (and others) from sin that could bring about eternal damnation (chapter 10).

Reductionism: the practice of understanding an object or occurrence at one level of examination by reducing it to more fundamental processes (chapter 1).

Reign of Terror: during the French Revolution, it was a movement of widespread violence committed by the French state (chapter 2).

Rejectionism: position that describes a long-established attitude or policy of rejection toward some group (chapter 6).

Religious development: the child's growth within a well-defined community with shared narratives, traditions, teachings, rituals, and symbols that bring individuals closer to the sacred and improve their relationship to the community (chapter 7).

Religious exclusivism: philosophy according to which one religion is true and all others are wrong (chapter 7).

Religious fundamentalism: the belief that religious doctrines or texts contain the fundamental, straightforward, intrinsic, absolute truth about humanity and deity (chapter 7).

Renovation: the fourth phase of the social construction of culture (chapter 4).

Replacement of relationships: the practice of disowning membership of one's former groups or friendship circles, even including one's own family (chapter 4).

Replacement symbol: a weapon that acts as a game changer; something that can alter the outcome of the conflict (chapter 11).

Representamen: the sign itself; what something is (chapter 15).

Representation: the use of a sign that stands for and takes the place of something else (chapter 15).

Resonance: the phenomenon whereby a message fits an audience's existing perceptions (chapter 16).

Retaliation: see **Revenge** (chapter 12).

Retribution: see **Revenge** (chapter 12).

Revenge: a destructive action against an individual or group in response to a grievance, whether real or imaginary (chapter 12).

Revolutionary Armed Forces of Colombia: a Colombian Marxist-Leninist terrorist group clashing with the Colombian government since the 1960s (chapter 13).

Revolutionary millennial group: group that embraces a theology of violence, believing that only the violent overthrow and total annihilation of society can bring spiritual salvation (chapter 7).

Rhetoric: discourse in which source encoders (i.e., message senders) aim at informing, persuading, or motivating particular message receivers in specific situations (chapter 5).

Rhetorical trope: a figure of style, an analogy, a myth, or a metaphor. Rhetorical tropes are essential for any meaningful act of persuasion (chapter 5).

Riaño, Idoia López: see the **Tigress** (chapter 12).

Rite of purity: a form of ritual that emphasizes the cleanliness (i.e., virtue, innocence) of the group (or the cause) in contrast with that of the evil (i.e., unclean) enemy or outside world (chapter 4).

Ritual: a symbolic act that is formal or recurrent in a tradition (chapter 4).

Ritual as communication: a sacred ritual in which people come together in fellowship and a great speech or communicative event takes place (chapter 4).

Ritualistic murder: any violent act characterized by a sequence of repeated physical, sexual, and/or psychological assaults, along with a methodical use of symbols, ceremonies, and/or machinations. The necessity to repeat such acts can be cultural, sexual, economic, psychological, and/or religious (chapter 11).

Ritual terrorism: terrorism committed against people as a human sacrifice to a deity (chapter 4).

Robespierre, Maximilien: leader of the Jacobins during the Reign of Terror (chapter 2).

Role: the total of all behavioral expectations of a social system toward the role owner (chapter 4).

Role embracement: a process whereby one immerses oneself in a role and allows it to shape how one thinks, feels, acts, and communicates with others (chapter 4).

Role making: when a person interprets a role in terms of what he or she does with that role (chapter 4).

Role taking: when a member acts in line with the expectations set by the terrorist group (chapter 4).

Routinization: when a positive cult becomes an authenticated custom or a custom centered on a long-established and bureaucratic charismatic leadership (chapter 4).

Sabra and Shatila massacre: in 1982, it was the slaughter of close to 3,500 Palestinian and Lebanese Shia civilians by a Lebanese Christian militant group in the Palestinian refugee camps of Beirut (chapter 13).

Sacral nationalism: a type of nationalism in which ethnic or cultural groups use religious imagery and symbolism to advance their political agenda (chapter 6).

Sacred space theology: the worldview that land that was lost centuries ago (e.g., as a result of conquest) must be restored (chapter 7).

Sacrifice: selfless noble deeds (chapter 10).

Sacrificial category: category of decapitation best illustrated by beheading videos (chapter 11).

Sacrificial myth: a system of beliefs incorporating a complex set of symbols and rituals to magnify the suicide attackers' potential to cause harm and attract more recruits in the process (chapter 10).

Saffron terror: terrorism spurred by Hindu extremist nationalism. The term comes from the association of the color saffron with Hindu nationalism (chapter 8).

Saga: a description or chronicle of the achievements of a key individual, group, society, organization, or even country (chapter 5).

Salaf: the earliest Muslims who were considered the role models of Islamic practice (chapter 9).

Salafi jihadism: self-claiming Salafi groups that have cultivated an interest in jihad since the mid-1990s (chapter 9).

Salafi movement: see **Salafism** (chapter 9).

Salafism: an Islamic movement adhering to a literalist, strict, and ultraconservative approach to Islam (chapter 9).

Salafist movement: see **Salafism** (chapter 9).

Sands, Bobby: the first IRA volunteer to become a martyr as a result of the 1981 Irish hunger strike (chapter 10).

Sapir-Whorf hypothesis: theory postulating that language shapes people's thoughts and frames the nature of social life (chapter 2).

Sasachacuy: an ancient pre-Hispanic word that means "difficult times" (chapter 13).

Scene: the setting, social context, or environment in which the symbolic interaction occurs (chapter 4).

Schema: a mental structure of predetermined ideas, a framework that represents some characteristics of the world, or a prearranged pattern of thought or behavior (chapter 1).

Second party: the direct target of the message (chapter 3).

Second reality: the outcome of an initial and intentional act of the imagination (chapter 7).

Secret knowledge: a collection of secrets successively unveiled to inner initiates who have stood the test of trustworthiness (chapter 4).

Security model: model according to which nations develop nuclear weapons to improve national security against foreign hazards (nuclear threats in particular) (chapter 11).

Self-deindividuation: the practice of eliminating a new member's individual identity, both externally and internally (chapter 4).

Semantics: the study of meaning (chapter 1).

Semblance: see **Sign** (chapter 15).

Semiosis: the creation and comprehension of signs (chapter 15).

Semiosphere: the sphere of semiosis in which sign processes function (chapter 15).

Semiotic animals: creatures or beings capable of using signs and symbols to reflect on human communication (chapter 15).

Semiotic law of media: theory according to which both the media and the sign systems of culture evolve (chapter 15).

Semiotic modes: processes of meaning making that consist of visual, verbal, written, gestural, and musical channels of communication (chapter 15).

Semiotics: the study of signs, as well as their processes and systems (chapter 15).

Sendero Luminoso: see **Shining Path** (chapter 11).

Sentiment pool: a community that reaches common agreement on a specific event or situation and, ultimately, what course of action should be taken to redress the injustice that the group has endured (chapter 2).

Separatist terrorism: terrorism motivated by ethnonationalism (chapter 6).

September 11, 1565: the day upon which the Great Siege of Malta ended; the Ottoman Empire lost a major battle against a coalition of Western Christian combatants (chapter 2).

September 11, 1683: the day upon which the Battle of Vienna took place after the Austrian capital had been invaded by the Ottoman Empire for two months; the worst defeat for Islam (chapter 2).

Sexual-based terrorism: see **Gender communal terrorism** (chapter 11).

Sexual terrorism: see **Gender communal terrorism** (chapter 11).

Shahada: the Muslim decree of faith or the Islamic profession to Allah ("There Is No God but Allah, and Muhammad Is His Messenger") (chapter 14).

Shahid: "martyr" in Arabic (chapter 10).

Shahidka: see **Black Widows** (chapter 12).

Shame culture: culture in which people feel easily humiliated and are ready to strike back against what they perceive as insults (chapter 4).

Sharia: Islamic law derived from the Qur'an and the hadiths (chapter 9).

Shi'ites: Muslims who tend to be more ecstatic (i.e., exhilarated, beatific, and frenzied) in religious practice and have expectations that a messiah will bring justice on earth (chapter 9).

Shillelagh: an Irish fighting stick, club, or cudgel, usually made from a sturdy knotty stick with a big knob at the top (chapter 11).

Shining Path: a Peruvian terrorist organization seeking to replace bourgeois democracy with Maoism (i.e., hoping to impose communist rule through a pure proletariat) (chapter 11).

Sica: a small dagger used by the Zealots-Sicarii to kill targets (chapter 8).

Sicarii: a splinter terrorist group of the Zealots (chapter 8).

Sign: a representation of an object that suggests a link between itself and its object (chapter 1; chapter 15).

Significance quest: the idea that various "sacred carriers," such as blood feud, are being exploited as defense mechanisms in the ongoing fight against infidels (chapter 4).

Signification: the action of signs that create fundamental relationships between signifieds and signifiers and that are the basic building blocks of meaning (chapter 15).

Signified: the absent element of a sign (chapter 15).

Signifier: the visible, or material, element of a sign (chapter 15).

Sign theory: see **Semiotics** (chapter 15).

Sign vehicle: the representamen as the sign; "something that is" (chapter 15).

Sikhism: a monotheistic religion mostly practiced in northern India (chapter 8).

Single-issue terrorism: a category of terrorism that seeks to resolve specific issues in order to change attitudes about these issues (e.g., pro-life, animal, and antinuclear movements) (chapter 8).

Sinn Féin: an Irish Republican party traditionally associated with the Provisional IRA (chapter 2).

Smart bomb: in suicide terrorism, it is the notion that he or she can choose where and when the detonation of their body will be (chapter 10).

Smart community: people's ability to develop networked intelligence thanks to the internet (chapter 16).

Smile of joy: a symbol for the suicide jihadist's indoctrination into believing that he or she will now be rewarded by Allah with eternal life in the Heavenly Garden. This is why the suicide killer expresses his or her cheery attitude before the final act (chapter 10).

Social code: code that bestows the terrorist group the symbolic resources for making statements about itself and for controlling interpersonal activities among members (chapter 13).

Social construction of reality: model according to which cultures construct a reality around concepts, determining many aspects of their world through the meanings they assign to the construct (chapter 1).

Social glue: a system of social solidarity that makes all individuals who follow it coalesce into a single moral community (chapter 7).

Social group: people interacting with one another (chapter 4).

Social identity: the characteristics shared by individuals in small or large groups (chapter 6).

Socialization: a process through which we construct a social self and a feeling of attachment to social systems (chapter 4).

Socially constructed emotions: symbolic emotions experienced by individuals as a result of their membership of a specific group (usually vis-à-vis another group) (chapter 1).

Social marginalization: the process of becoming or feeling marginal in society (chapter 3).

Social objects: objects created as human beings engage in social acts. They depend upon social interaction and interpretation (chapter 4; chapter 11).

Sociological sticky stuff: the glue that holds a religious group or culture together (chapter 7).

Soft target: unarmed target that can be easily destroyed (e.g., an assembly of people) (chapter 3).

Soft weapons: concepts or ideas that are easily marshaled for propaganda purposes—as in the support and sanction of war and terrorism (chapter 1).

Soldier of Allah (SoA): see **Mujahedin** (chapter 4).

Speech act theory: theory positing that speakers employ language to achieve intended actions, and, in this manner, hearers deduce or interpret intended meaning from what was expressed by speakers (chapter 5).

Spin: a method of offering an interpretation of an event to sway public opinion in favor or against a particular group or person (chapter 5).

Spirituality: the search for and connection with that which one takes to be a holy or sacred transcendent being (a God or a higher power) (chapter 7).

Splitting: psychological defense mechanism whereby the enemy is seen as totally different, morally weak, and worthy of extermination (chapter 7).

Standpoint feminism: theory postulating that women's experiences of the world fundamentally differ from men's; therefore, they are in a better position to observe and evaluate this system (chapter 12).

Status symbol: a type of societal recognition that can be material and/or social. It is a visible symbol of one's social position and a perceived indicator of one's social status (chapter 10).

Strategic desirability: in the context of female terrorism, it denotes the idea that the woman can symbolize the dangerous gentle sex, especially in consideration of the gendered behavioral norms and women's second-class status in the cultures where terrorist attacks occur (chapter 12).

Strategic signaling: method whereby terrorists communicate (to their audience) their intention and determination (chapter 10).

Strategy: in the context of terrorism, it is the art and science of developing and using the political, economic, social-psychological, and military powers of the state (chapter 11).

Structural metaphor: metaphor that performs the function of highlighting the characteristics of one structured experience or activity to the detriment of other experiences or activities (chapter 14).

Subvertising: transforming the marketing message of a brand into a vehicle for a different message (chapter 16).

Suicide terrorism: an attack upon a target, in which a terrorist intends to kill others and/or create significant damage, while being aware that he or she will die in the process (chapter 10).

Sunnah: the normative way of life practiced and preached by Muhammad (chapter 9).

Sunnis: Muslims who typically follow the orthodox version of Islam, called the Sunnah (chapter 9).

Supernatural forces: phenomena that are not subject to the laws of nature or that are said to exist above and beyond nature (chapter 7).

Superterrorism: terrorism using WMDs (chapter 11).

Sura: chapter in the Qur'an (chapter 9).

Symbol: token, mark, sign, emblem, or watchword that stands for something else. A symbol is a mental structure, or some type of knowledge representation (chapter 1; chapter 15).

Symbolic animal: the idea that the human being is capable of engaging in symbolic communication, human thought, affect, and action (chapter 1).

Symbolic convergence theory (SCT): theory positing that sharing group fantasies produces symbolic convergence. Examples of fantasies are jokes, stories, metaphors, and human interpretations of events (chapter 5).

Symbolic cue: a brief or condensed signal like a symbol, sign, or word that represents a fantasy theme (chapter 5).

Symbolic culture: culture based on meaning or information shared through symbolic communication (chapter 1).

Symbolic DNA of terrorism: model postulating that even the most dangerous terrorist groups, particularly those determined to kill innocent targets massively, use a mythic or symbolic scheme rooted in religion or an ideological or mythic scheme resembling religion (chapter 5).

Symbolic footprint: practice that consists of establishing an interaction with and even claiming a territory in one way or another (chapter 11).

Symbolic frame alignment: a phenomenon whereby the actions of a group resonate with the symbols and beliefs of the society in which those actions are taken (chapter 2).

Symbolic framing: mental structure centered on symbolism and its interpretation within a historical or cultural context (chapter 1).

Symbolic interactionism: theory postulating that human beings are able to communicate through shared meanings (e.g., symbols, words, visuals, signs, roles, etc.) (chapter 4).

Symbolic interpretivism: an approach based on the premise that meaning is a product of a culture's socially constructed reality (chapter 1).

Symbolic manipulation: a technique whereby a group appropriates preexisting symbols and adjusts them to promote a movement, cause, or doctrine (chapter 13).

Symbolic meaning: open-ended meaning not based on a literal, direct cause-and-effect relationship. Rather, it depends on how meaning is constituted by the sender, on the environment in which it is produced, and on how the receiver interprets the meaning (chapter 1).

Symbolic power: power to construct reality through symbolism (chapter 2).

Symbolic self-completion theory: theory according to which individuals who experience status anxiety may engage in self-symbolization. They do so by attempting to gain some type of status symbol in order to bolster their identity or compensate for their own inadequacies (chapter 10).

Symbolic totemism: a symbol of group belonging and sentiment (chapter 6).

Symbolic transformation: the technique of modifying one's own group's existing symbols to clarify relationship messages (chapter 13).

Symbolic transformation of experience: process whereby the mind categorizes reality by creating symbols to better process information. This information is stored in people's minds for later "recognition" of their constructed world (chapter 1).

Symbolic trinity: a three-part framework that consists of symbolism, rhetoric, and myth (chapter 5).

Symbolism: the language of symbols or the practice of representing things by symbols; the creation of meaning through the use of symbols (chapter 1).

Sympathetic magic: a rudimentary tradition of magical thinking whereby one can hurt, humiliate, or murder another simply by destroying a cultural symbol of the victim (chapter 3).

Taliban: an Islamist movement active in Afghanistan since 1979 (chapter 11).

Tamil Tigers: a terrorist organization that wants the Tamil people to be totally independent from the Sinhalese-led government in Sri Lanka (chapter 8).

Temple Mount: the holiest site in Judaism (chapter 6).

Terra sancta: hallowed territory that symbolizes the lifelong, holy goal to recapture the homeland from the violators, invaders, or contaminators (chapter 6).

Territorial encroachment: encroachment that can be of three forms (violation, invasion, or contamination) (chapter 6).

Territorial marker: any symbol used by people to identify their territory (mostly walls) (chapter 6).

Territorial purification: when two groups hate each other so much that they would push each other into the sea (chapter 6).

Territory: possession and/or control of land (chapter 6).

Terror: rooted in the Latin *terrere*, it roughly means "practicing the trembling" or "causing the frightening" (chapter 2).

Terror glorification: institutionalized practice of incitement whereby terrorists are systematically turned into role models (chapter 2).

Terrorism: the use of violence to create fear (i.e., terror or psychic fear) for political, religious, or ideological reasons. The terror is deliberately directed toward noncombatant targets (i.e., civilians or symbols), and an important purpose is to gain the highest amount of publicity for a group, cause, or person (chapter 2).

Terrorist chic: the appropriation of objects and/or symbols of terrorist groups or individuals; these objects and/or symbols are used in popular culture or fashion. Terrorist chic is the belief that terrorism is cool (chapter 13).

Terrorist mural: any piece of artwork (mostly graffiti) or writing created on a wall, ceiling, or large permanent structure by a terrorist group or people supporting the cause of a militant group (chapter 6).

Terrorist self: self that is constantly constructed through symbolic interaction with like-minded others in their terrorist cultural group (chapter 4).

Terrorist socialization: an ongoing, interactive process through which people develop terrorist social identities and learn the ways of thinking, feeling, and acting through symbolic interaction in the terrorist culture (chapter 4).

Theosophy: a complex belief system mixing Eastern religions, reincarnation, and the belief in man's ability to become godlike (chapter 7).

Thinking mode: type of mental model or cognitive system that helps a particular cultural group to categorize things (chapter 4).

Third party: the target beyond the direct target of the message (chapter 3).

Thought pattern: form of reasoning and approach to communication that varies from culture to culture (chapter 14).

Three Ks: see **Kinder, Küche, Kirche** (chapter 12).

Thuggee: see **Thugs** (chapter 8).

Thugs: Hindu assassins who traveled in groups throughout India for several centuries (chapter 8).

Tigress, The: a very active female terrorist for ETA called Idoia López Riaño (chapter 12).

Totalism: an absolute strategy of mind control (chapter 7).

Trance: a whole different emotional state (chapter 7).

Transnational injustice community: network of individuals ideologically linked through similar identities and perceptions of shared injustice (chapter 2).

Transnational injustice symbol: an event or situation exploited by politicians or terrorist leaders as an excuse to avenge perceived injustices before geographically, socially, and culturally scattered audiences (chapter 2).

Transnational Islam: a feeling of a growing universalistic Muslim identity (chapter 9).

Tribalism: a group's collective identity characterized by blood ties, common ancestry, steadfast loyalty, solidarity, conformity, and often an "us-versus-them" philosophy (chapter 4).

Trophy category: category of decapitation. The trophy head is an intricate, irrepressible, and long-established icon of death, motif of war, sign of the fighter, and symbol of life (chapter 11).

True culture: the communicative power of humans that makes human communication unique among species (chapter 1).

Truth claim: concept according to which even fundamental teachings of a religion can be interpreted in multiple ways (chapter 7).

Tsarnaev brothers: the two brothers responsible for the Boston Marathon bombings in 2013 (chapter 16).

Twelfth Imam: in Shia Islam, it refers to Muhammad al-Mahdi, the last imam who disappeared a long time ago and who will return from occultation (chapter 9).

Twelver Shia Islam: the largest branch of Shia Islam that believes in twelve divinely chosen leaders, known as the Twelve Imams (chapter 9).

Umayyad Caliphate: Islamic empire that existed between 661 and 750 AD, and was the second of the four main Islamic caliphates established after Muhammad died (chapter 14).

Umbrella effect: concept that denotes how people worldwide can feel increasingly connected through a transnational term (chapter 2).

Ummah: the international community of all faithful Muslims (chapter 2).

Umwelt: concept suggesting that human beings live in a world that is constructed out of their own symbols (chapter 4).

Uncertainty avoidance: the degree of intolerance for risk or uncertain situations in a given culture (chapter 10).

Unencumbered self: a person whose identity makes no fundamental reference to other people or groups (chapter 4).

UNESCO: United Nations Educational, Scientific, and Cultural Organization (chapter 3).

United States Patriot Act: an Act of Congress that significantly reduces restrictions in the capacity of law enforcement agencies to collect intelligence within the United States (chapter 15).

Universal symbols: symbols shared by groups of people worldwide (chapter 1).

Value bases: important moral resources for ethnic identities and nation-states (chapter 3).

Value rationality: a type of decision making based on a conscious ethical, religious, or other belief, regardless of its chances of success (chapter 10).

Values: the standards that people use to define worth, importance, or correctness (chapter 4).

Value similarity: thanks to the internet, people worldwide speak, think, and behave in similar ways (chapter 16).

Value sphere: a system of values dominated by its own inherent laws (chapter 4).

Vehicle-borne suicide: suicide terrorism using trucks, cars, and motorcycles (chapter 10).

Vengeance: see **Revenge** (chapter 12).

Verse of the Sword: violent verse in the Qur'an (9:5) that has been the main catalyst for both ancient and modern jihad (chapter 9).

Violation: unjustified use of territory (chapter 6).

Violent eschatology: the doctrine that the earth must be cleansed before the second coming of a messiah (chapter 9).

Violent new religious movement (VNRM): religious-based terrorist group that strongly believes in creating a radical transformation of society that the terrorists themselves have been called to bring (chapter 7).

Violent true believer (VTB): a person devoted to an ideology or belief system championing massacre and suicide as a logical means of advancing their cause (chapter 3).

Virago: a beautiful woman who oozes commendable and heroic qualities (chapter 12).

Virtual caliphate: the idea of a global Islamic state diffused through the internet (chapter 16).

Visual motif: a visual theme or pattern that represents a certain subject or category of subject (chapter 14).

Vocabulary of motives: a set of words or phrases created to provide "legitimate" explanations for particular actions (chapter 2).

Wahhabism: an ultraconservative branch of Islam advocated by fundamentalists in Saudi Arabia (chapter 9).

War in Darfur: a campaign of ethnic cleansing perpetrated by Sudanese Muslim militias against Darfur's non-Arabs (chapter 11).

War of Ideas: a paradigm explaining that major differences of ideals between the West and the Muslim world tend to clash (chapter 3).

War rape: see **Gender communal terrorism** (chapter 11).

Weapon of mass destruction (WMD): a weapon that can kill and bring significant harm to a large number of humans (and other life forms) and/or cause great damage to permanent structures (chapter 11).

Weapon of mass persuasion: any method to influence the mind and behavior of a targeted population (chapter 10).

Weapon of war: light or small arm initially designed and procured for use by armed forces (chapter 11).

Weapons combination: the practice of joining weapons in different combinations. An example of this is the symbolic motif in Islamist terrorism that combines premodern and modern weapons (chapter 11).

Westoxification: symbol for anti-Western sentiment and militancy against Western influences (chapter 3).

West-struck-ness: see **Westoxification** (chapter 3).

World Jerusalem Day: a ceremony promulgated by Khomeini to achieve the Sunnis' and Shi'ites' mutual goal of conquering Israel and delivering Jerusalem (chapter 5).

World Monuments Fund (WMF): a private, global, and nonprofit institution committed to the preservation of cultural heritage sites worldwide (chapter 3).

Worldview: a formal or informal schema of beliefs that frames our perception of the universe (chapter 4).

Yellow tiger: a culturally important creature that represents heroism, militancy, and nationalism within the Tamil Tigers (chapter 8).

YouTube effect: the phenomenon whereby video clips, often produced by individuals acting on their own, are rapidly transmitted throughout the world thanks to video-sharing websites such as YouTube and Google Video (chapter 16).

al-Zarqawi, Abu Musab: former leader of Al Qaeda in Iraq (AQI) (chapter 9).

al-Zawahiri, Ayman: the new Al Qaeda leader since the death of Osama bin Laden (chapter 2).

Zealots: a historical Jewish terrorist group involved in violent acts against the Romans and their "collaborators" (chapter 8).

Zoosemiosis: animal communication (chapter 1).